Police Dog Tactics

SANDY BRYSON

DETSELIG ENTERPRISES LTD.

Calgary, Alberta Canada

©2000 Sandy Bryson
Cataloging Information in Publication

Bryson, Sandy
Police Dog Tactics

Includes bibliographical references and index
ISBN 1-55059-197-5

1. Police Dogs I. Title
HV8025.B79 2000 363.2'32 C99-911256-2

All photography by the author unless otherwise noted.

Legal content: Canine case law is embryonic. Case material presented here articulates clear judicial reasoning that is available to assist police dog handlers on the street. Officers can access current federal and state law through on-line computer services. This book is not a substitute for legal advice by a competent attorney.

Information contained herein was obtained from sources believed to be authentic and reliable. The author, advisors, and publisher make no guarantee of results and accept no liability whatsoever for any physical injuries or other harm to person or property resulting from the application or adoption of any of the procedures, tactics, legal principles, or other considerations presented or implied in this book.

Detselig Enterprises, Ltd.
210-1220 Kensington Rd. N.W.
Calgary, Alberta T2N 3P5
Telephone: (403) 283-6947
e-mail: temeron@telusplanet.net
www.temerondetselig.com

We acknowledge the financial support of the Government of Canada through the Book Publishing Industry Development Program (BPIDP) for our publishing activities

Printed in Canada
ISBN 1-55059-197-5
SAN 115-0324

Book layout and cover design by David M. Daly, dalydesign

Maria da Silva and K-9 Luka, Amador County Sheriff's Department.

For the children.

And still the debate is focused too much on how to support the police, not enough on how to support the children— children who die far more frequently than the police, children who have no training in survival, no bulletproof vests, no 'backup.' Where do children go for training in survival and in making peace?

— *fist stick knife gun:*
a personal history of
violence in America
Geoffrey Canada

Corning Police Department

CONTENTS

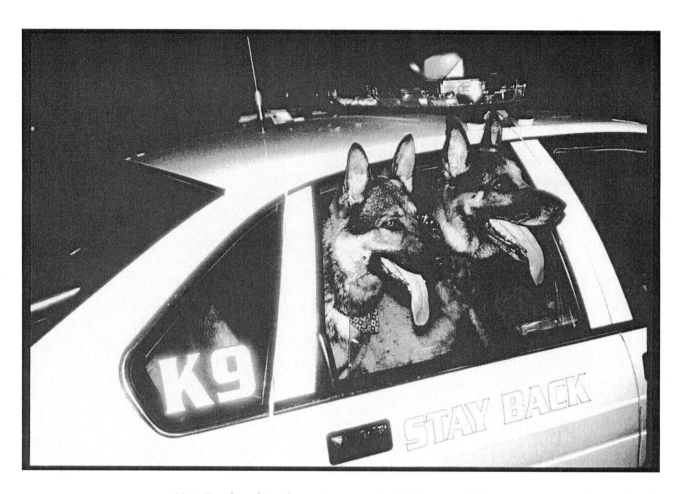

K-9s Daark and Reicher—Deputy John Muldown and Daark received the Bronze Star for Heroic Duty, Butte County Sheriff's Department, California.

Acknowledgements

For this Second Edition of *Police Dog Tactics*, I want to thank all the police and rescue professionals who appear in the book as well as the others who have contributed their time and invaluable information. Special thanks for the ongoing support of Retired Sheriff Larry Kuhl, Sheriff Skip Veatch of Alpine County, Sheriff Hal Barker of El Dorado County, K-9 trainers Bill Schroeder and Jim Barnes, Detective DeAnna Stevens of West Sacramento Police Department, California Deputy Attorney Randy Saavedra, and Dr. Robert Gorrindo of Carson Valley Veterinary Hospital.

Electronic communications from thousands of U.S. and international law enforcement officers and administrators have confirmed the concepts that *Police Dog Tactics* presents. Thanks for Internet and production support to Chesa Keane of TAO Consultants, fine artist and illustrator Joanne Mehl, and David Daly of Daly Design.

Front Cover: Deputy Brian Blair, K-9 Luka, Amador County Sheriff's Department, and Officer Officer Tod A. Sockman, West Sacramento Police Department. —Photo by Lesly Fleck.

Back Cover: Illustration by Joanne Mehl. Detective DeAnna Stevens, K-9 Reicher, West Sacramento Police Department; kirkwood Ski Patroller Brent SMith, Avalance Dog Sequoia. —Photos by Sandy Bryson.

From *fist, stick, knife, gun: A Personal History of Violence in America* by Geoffrey Canada. Copyright ©1995 by Beacon Press, Boston MA. Reprinted with permission of the publisher.

From the map supplement of National Geographic's *Living with California's Faults* by Rick Gore. Copyright © 1995 by National Geographic Society, Washington, DC. Reprinted with permission of the publisher.

From *Police K-9 Team Study: The Friendly Force* by Sandy Bryson, Lynette Hart, Ruth Zasloff and Sarah L. Christiansen. Copyright © 1995 by University of California. Reprinted with permission of the publisher.

From *Collison Course* by Ralph Nadar and Wesley J. Smith. Copyright © 1995 by Ralph Nadar. Reprinted with permission of the publisher.

From *The Wolf: The Ecology and Behavior of an Endangered Species* by L. David Mech. Copyright © 1986 by Bantam Doubleday Dell Publishing. Reprinted with permission of the publisher.

Brandy detects cocaine, K-9 Deputy Kim Edner, Mariposa County Sheriff's Department, CA

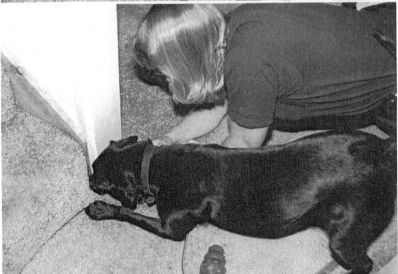

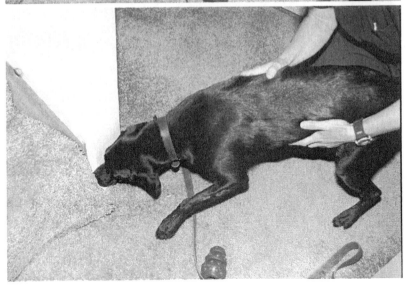

PREFACE

Communities need police K-9 more than ever in the 21st Century. We are living through a technological revolution in crime that outpaces our ability to keep current in intelligence or to keep up on the street. Gangs, drugs, advanced communications, rapid air and ground mobility across both state and international borders—it is impossible to field enough police officers. At the most basic level offenders know when there is no police dog on duty in their neighborhood. That is when they run. That is when they go to ground with the officer. That is when they challenge officers with weapons.

The Friendly Force—the police dog—protects handlers and cover officers. Most officer murders occur at night. Officers are attacked suddenly, often before they realize the suspect is present or observing them. Fifty percent are ambushes. Where officers are weak, the dog is strong. At night the K-9 sees clearly. His senses alert him to the armed suspect nobody realizes is there. In dangerous searches, foot pursuits, assaults, and fights, the dog gives officers the edge, apprehending suspects quickly and safely.

As a detector, the dog is still unsurpassed because he is able to multiplex trained odors in unusual situations and new environments.

In this edition of we present the following updates:

— Electronic resources to research the latest case law, keep accurate records, and prepare for court.

— New tactics photos, K-9 officers sharing their biggest challenges, and officer safety techniques.

— Bright line Supreme Court ruling on K-9 use of force. The federal case *Vera Cruz v. City of Escondido* is extremely important for K-9 units throughout the United States. The case required the court to decide whether force capable of inflicting serious—but not fatal—injuries qualifies as lethal force under *Garner*. Beyond the impact of the decision is the responsibility it bestows upon all police dog handlers and the remarkable luck that this incident, which could have happened to any agency, happened to professionals who displayed conduct becoming an officer. Detective DeAnna Stevens, who conducts the interview with Escondido Officer Eric Distel, was the first K-9 handler for West Sacramento Police Department and has extensive street experience with two police dogs.

— Summary of *Watkins v. City of Oakland* reminds K-9 officers of critical issues at the moment of arrest.

— Important new case cites for narcotics detection and arson investigation.

— New resources for drug information and international travel medicine.

CHAPTER 1

The police dog is a tactical tool. Unlike hardware, however, the police dog is alive. He has a brain.

The Friendly Force

"He was like having another deputy around.
Every deputy knew if Justice was on the scene,
the suspect would be arrested."

—Lieutenant Richard White and K-9 Deputy Fred Johnson,
Fresno County Sheriff's Department, California

The police dog is a tactical tool. Unlike hardware, however, the police dog is alive. He has a brain. On the street, canine intelligence gives the officer a tactical advantage but also a major technical challenge. Performing with a K-9 is an order of magnitude more complex than working without the dog. This is true whether the dog is a specialist search dog or used exclusively for patrol or crosstrained. The teamwork must be there—the timing, the technique, and the strong drive.

The live K-9 is a 24-hour-a-day responsibility for the police officer. The degree to which the police dog is an asset instead of a liability is the degree to which the handler and dog have the desire to work together effectively as a team. The police agency shares the responsibility for its police dog teams. How teams are selected, trained, tasked, and used on the street will ultimately determine the success or failure of that department's K-9 unit.

The mechanisms of training, deploying, and daily living with a police dog are not well understood by much of the public and by part of law enforcement itself. It is easy to count the number of incidents where a dog has been misused. It is not easy to count the number of times a dog's actions have averted the injury or killing of an officer or a citizen, indeed the injuring or killing of a suspect. Deterrent effect is difficult to measure. Dogs are not considered a police imperative, like a gun or a baton.

Taking a look at handler-dog team interaction may be instructive in an immediately applied sense for better management (selection, training, and deployment) and in the long term for overall policing effectiveness. Police dog careers are relatively (lamentably) short. Given limited budgets, the increase of violent crime, and the rising percentages of high-risk calls officers face each year, agencies must work diligently to increase the efficiency and effectiveness of their operations. We need to examine and perfect the use of the tools we have available. Police dogs are a special tool because of their live personalities, their interaction with the officers and with the civilians in the community.

In some ways, the dog makes the officer's job and home life more rewarding, in some ways more difficult. Regardless, the presence of this intelligent animal complicates the officer's life and work. K-9 team reliability depends on two elements, the dog's behavior and the handler's ability to *read* (understand) that behavior. When performing a search, for example, the dog's *alert* is behavior that signals *detection* (perception with recognition) to the handler.

The well trained police dog gives the K-9 officer the tactical edge, the lead over his street opponent, and the lead over officers in specific situations trying to do the same

UC Davis K-9 study of 103 departments in California. Many officers reported that a significant percentage of calls involve a high safety risk. The mean percentage of high risk calls where the officer judged the K-9 to be important in apprehending the offender was 81.9% (n = 265 patrol officers). The responding officers (n = 249) reported a mean total of 6.32 apprehensions with contact, that is arrests where the dog physically contacted the suspect. For those officers who rated 99 - 100% of their calls as high risk, the mean total increased to 7.97 apprehensions with contact. For those officers who rated 10% or fewer of their calls as high risk, the mean total dropped to 3.9.

Asked if the K-9 had ever saved the officer's life in the line of duty, 38.1% said Yes, 54.8% said No. Of those who answered Yes, over half elaborated, noting the dog alerted to suspects hiding or sneaking up behind the officer, assisted in fights and took down violent subjects. One K-9 died, and one received stab wounds. Of those who answered No, over half said the situation (life/death) had not yet arisen, many said the K-9 had saved them from injury, not necessarily death, and some said it was unknown what a suspect might have done absent the dog.
—*Proceedings of the Western Society of Criminology Conference held February 24-27, 1994.*

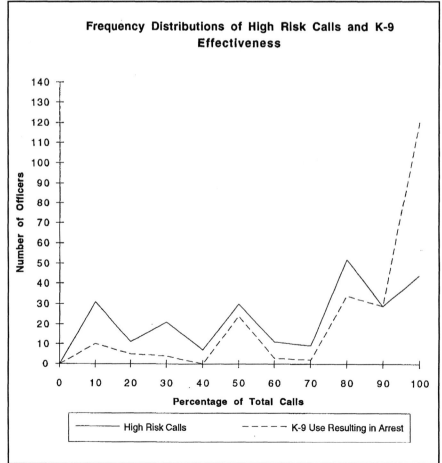

Figure 1

Police Canine Programs
Selected Large Cities - January 1994
Number of Dogs by Type and Selected Program Data

City	Patrol Only	Patrol/Narc	Patrol/Bomb	Patrol Total	Narc Only	Bomb Only	Search & Rescue	Total Dogs	Uniformed Patrol Officers	Ratio Patrol Officers To Dogs	Full Time Trainers	Take Home Vehicles	Sergeants Assigned Dogs
New York	14	0	0	14	9	9	3	35	20,067	1,433	5	NO	1
Los Angeles	16	0	0	16	6	3	0	25	6,500	406	1	YES	0
Chicago	17 (1)	28	0	45 (1)	6	6	0	57	10,200	227	2	YES	0
Houston	21	0	0	21	10	4	0	35	1,983	94	2	YES	2
Philadelphia	4	15	11	30	0	0	0	30	6,000	200	3	NO	0
San Diego	31	6	8	45	2	0	0	47	875	19	0	YES	5
Dallas	4	2	4	10	2	0	0	12	1,430	143	1	YES	0
Detroit	19	0	0	19	2	6	1	28	4,000	210	1	NO (2)	0
Phoenix	11	1	1	13	2	0	0	15	1,050	81	0	YES	0
San Antonio	6	0	0	6	1	0	0	7	950	158	0	YES	1
Baltimore	5	32	32	37 (3)	0	0	0	37	1,850	50	3	NO	0
Washington, D.C.	44	6	0	50	6	5	0	61	4,200	84	3	NO	1
St. Louis	9	2	1	12	0	0	0	12	800	66	1	YES	2

NOTES: 1. All dogs are currently assigned to Transit System work. No dogs in car patrol work. 2. Take home vehicles assigned to on-duty call-out teams only. 3. All patrol dogs are cross-trained for explosive and narcotics detection. Five dogs failed cross-training program.

SGT. JACK DOHERTY, SAN DIEGO POLICE DEPARTMENT

job without a dog. Dr. Lawrence J. Myers, Institute for Biological Detection Systems at Auburn University, has written that trained police dogs are currently a leading detection and deterrent system for law enforcement.

In a 1992 study of police K-9 teams conducted by the University of California, Davis, of 103 police and sheriff's departments in California, the officers reported that a significant percentage of calls involve a high safety risk *(Figure 1)*.

Dogs not under control do not protect officers properly, forcing them instead to take actions that jeopardize their safety every time they deploy their canines. The dog needs to be of high quality. So does the handler, who is, first of all, a cop. Like the controlled use of his hands, the officer has to control his dog.

Basic police canine tactics are universal. Canine deployment varies from department to department, depending upon the size of the agency and the environment in which the officers work. Crime is also universal, but resources vary from agency to agency. A rural Wyoming officer has to wait 45 minutes for backup. A Florida city officer has two cover units, three perimeter units, and an airborne tactical unit on-scene in three minutes. All gradations of money, manpower, lifestyle, and environment lie between.

When studying police dog tactics, officers must take these differences into account. What works in a valley city may not be possible in the mountains. What an officer can do safely in one area may put his life in jeopardy in another. The differences occasionally become a source of misplaced rivalry. Shared experiences typically build a brotherhood.

In the 1960s the U.S. had 3.3 police officers for every violent crime reported. In 1993 there were 3.47 violent crimes reported for every officer.

Adam Walinsky, "The Crisis of Public Order," *The Atlantic Monthly*, July 1995

The Internet has changed the way research is done. Case law updates are now available on commercial and government Web sites. Handlers may consult attorneys who track K-9 case law or obtain full text cases online without having to deal with issues of delay, reliability, expense, or applicability. U.S. Supreme Court and federal circuit court opinions are available electronically immediately upon publication. State courts also publish quickly online.

Large city district attorneys and state attorney general's offices typically subscribe to legal source sites such as:
— Lexis-Nexis.com
— WestLaw.com

The officer may arrange periodic access or regular updates, perhaps every six months, by the government attorney.

Other options are free sites where officers may input case names, cites, or do key word searches, and review the latest pertinent decisions from the courts. You can obtain the full text of all bright line rulings that will evolve into black letter law. Most judges are competent writers (some are brilliant), and the full case is often more instructive than an attorney's brief. The other advantage of full text printouts—each decision shepherds previous, familiar decisions, so that handlers retain, for example *Graham v. Connor*, by seeing it cited again and again in context.

Web addresses change frequently, but here are law sites and search engines currently running:
— findlaw.com
— vcilp.org
— law.cornell.edu
— ljextra.com
— usscplus.com
— lawrunner.com

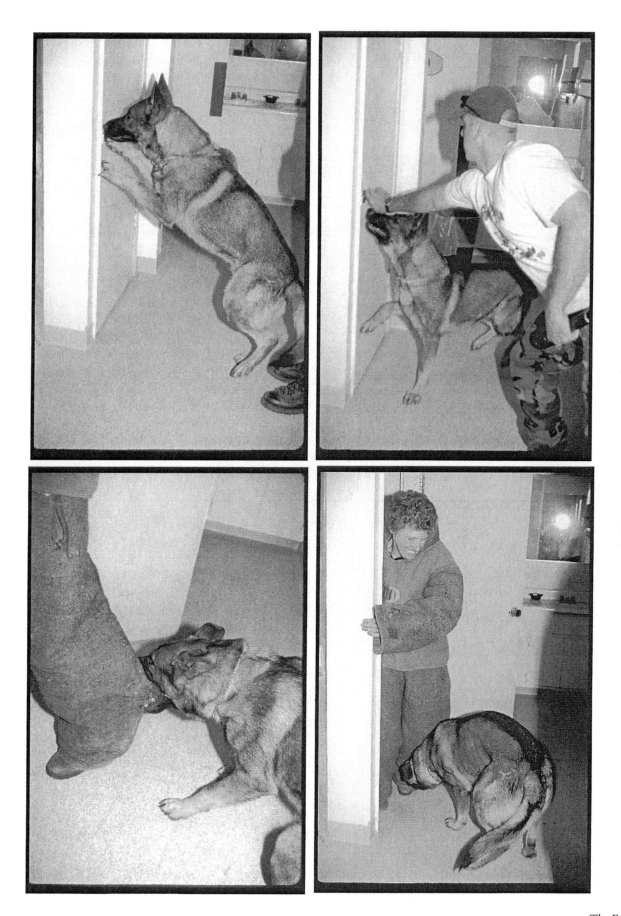

PHOTOS BY LESLY FLECK

Medical Aspects of Police Canine Bites
by Charles J. Rennie, III, M.D., FACEP*

The medical aspect of police canine bites has quickly become, over the past several years, a club that plaintiffs have attempted to wield against canine units. The primary contentions have been that police canines uniformly cause severe injuries, much more so than non-police canines, and that this represents an inappropriate use of potentially lethal force. To date, plaintiffs' attorneys have had a dismal track record in proving this. No police canine case in which I have been involved has resulted in a finding for plaintiffs or the awarding of monetary damages to the plaintiffs for the bite.

The number of dogs in the United States is unknown, since county licensing captures only a small portion of the total number. 1968 estimates, however, were something over 25 million. Dog bite statistics are equally difficult to come by. The incidence in major urban areas appears to range between 300 and 700 per 100,000 population, with rural areas varying from the 271 per 100,000 of rural Ohio to the 2059 of West Texas. Dog bites generally account for 80% to 90% of mammalian bites in any U.S. series on the subject (human bites account for 4% to 20%). Police canine bites account for a small fraction of this total. Deaths from bites range from approximately 50,000 annual deaths from snake bites worldwide to 1000 annual deaths from crocodile bites in Africa to approximately 18-20 deaths annually in the United States from dog bites. In contrast to this, I have personally seen no deaths caused by police canines, have read of no police canine-caused deaths in the medical literature, and heard of no police canine-caused deaths in any of the extensive mortality and morbidity conferences I have attended over a span of some 17 years. I have heard of only one police canine-related death in the police literature (*Robinette v. Barnes*, 854 F.2d 909 (6th Cir. 1988)).

Dog bites were formerly not sutured. Most bites are now sutured in most medical centers (puncture wounds are usually left open). Infection rates are difficult to assess, but have ranged in past series from 6-13% (excluding puncture wounds). This data is somewhat questionable, because many of these series were compiled before current oral and intramuscular antibiotics were on the market. Exactly which dog bites should receive antibiotics is still a matter of some controversy. There is no evidence in the literature that police canine bites become infected more frequently than non-police canine bites.

The plaintiffs' counsels have usually used two articles in an attempt to bolster their claims that police canine bites are severe. One is a series out of Los Angeles County-USC Medical Center that looks at 486 patients admitted to the jail ward with the primary diagnosis of dog bite. The study is severely flawed. The methodology excludes trivial dog bites where suspects are cleared at outside hospitals and released for booking and includes patients with more severe injuries transported to LAC-USC. It also excludes potentially critical non-police canine bites, which is the population that the study is using for comparison. Even though the study concentrates on more severe injuries, only 3 out of the 486 patients required an operation, and at least 2 of those could have been done under local anesthesia. This hardly proves the contention that police canines inflict severe, life-threatening injuries!

The second article examines, microscopically, the area immediately underneath the skin and immediately adjacent to the penetrated area of a police canine bite and compares it to a similar area adjacent to a gunshot wound. Plaintiffs' counsel has used this in an attempt to equate dog bites and gunshot wounds. The ridiculousness of this should be apparent to even those of marginal intelligence.

In spite of their inability to prove their contentions, plaintiffs are persisting in their lawsuits against police canine units. A number of steps can be taken to further reduce the impact of such lawsuits, however.

First, on-site observation of how a suspect uses the bitten body part is extremely important. These observations should be carried into the hospital and can make a great deal of difference in a case. I once consulted on a case where a suspect sustained minor wounds to both ankles, requiring minimal suturing. From the way the suspect limped into court using a tripod cane (with the jury viewing the performance), one might have assumed major injury to

*Department of Emergency Medicine, Los Alamitos Medical Center, California

limb, if not life. Fortunately, there were excellent notes in the medical chart from both physician and nurse that the patient was walking with no difficulty whatsoever while in the hospital. Similar notes from a law enforcement officer would be equally effective in a case such as this.

Other observations can also be important. One case I was involved in concerned a suspect who evidenced abnormal behavior and appeared to be brandishing a firearm. When stopped in his car, he failed to follow commands and repeatedly lowered his arms below door jamb levels; this ultimately led to his being bitten by a police canine. His excuse was that he was hearing impaired as a consequence of a prior antibiotic complication. This might have been true and might have prevailed in a subsequent lawsuit, except that an alert officer noted in his report that the patient was able to follow the physician's commands in the Emergency Department even when the suspect was out of sight-line of the physician and could not have been lip-reading. An alert observation saved the day. I cannot stress enough the importance of an alert peace officer recording his or her observations after the bite. Law enforcement officers enjoy paperwork no more than physicians do, yet a small amount of additional paperwork can sometimes save massive headaches later on.

Prompt first-aid for the suspects after the bite occurs, and prompt paramedic involvement and transport if needed are important both to minimize any adverse effects of the injury and to maintain an environment that does not appear pejorative or malicious.

Law enforcement personnel should relate the circumstances of the bite to the Emergency Medicine physicians and nurses treating the patient. Emergency medical personnel make, or should make, an attempt to be unbiased, but if the sole account of the incident is that of the patient, the medical record can work against law enforcement. Patients in police custody represent one of the few instances where the history of the problem can, and should, be taken from someone else in addition to the patient. Omissions and/or distortions by the suspect/patient can lead to less than optimum care, and the suspect's comments will almost uniformly lead to pejorative notes in the chart such as "beaten by police and attacked by dog." Such notes are inflammatory and can adversely influence a jury, but they can be significantly mitigated by the inclusion of an objective account from the officer. "Suspect apprehended by police canine while resisting arrest after committing carjacking at gunpoint" reads much better than "leg ripped open by police dog."

An effort should be made to communicate to the Emergency Medicine personnel the likelihood of a lawsuit and the importance of precise, accurate, complete, and objective charting (we shouldn't need reminding of this, but we're human). A "four cm serrated laceration" can be the same thing as a "bloody, jagged, gaping, torn area of tissue," yet I guarantee that the latter is going to get the suspect a lot more mileage. Precise measurements are also critical; what is presented as a gaping canyon of a laceration on an enlarged photograph shown to a jury can be properly deflated by a chart that notes that it was only a 2 cm wound.

If pictures are going to be taken, at least some must be taken *after the wounds have been treated.* The jagged, gaping laceration that was just described, containing a quart of gravel and enough grass to reseed your lawn, is not the wound that the suspect is going to live with. The latter is reflected much more by the appearance of the wound after treatment. Few items are as difficult to explain to a jury in these cases as the bloody picture taken by law enforcement before any treatment is rendered. I may realize that the net result after treatment is a linear scar that will be barely noticeable and entail no functional deficit, but this can be very difficult to communicate to a jury swayed by the "before" pictures. Additionally, the Emergency Department should remove any bloody drapes and gauze from the vicinity; the pictures should be as completely neutral as possible.

After treatment, observations should be made again regarding how the suspect uses the affected body part, for the same reasons as outlined above.

Reports should be as concise as possible when dealing with mechanisms of injury. Do not say the suspect "slammed into the ground" or "was hurled to the ground" unless that is exactly what is meant. Enormous problems can be caused by the use of such loose language, and the impact on a jury can be substantial.

In summary, police canine bites are a small fraction of the total dog bites in the United States. Suspects bitten by police canines have not fared well in the legal system when litigating against law enforcement agencies. On the other hand, one or a small handful of victories by plaintiffs could put police canine units out of business across the country. It is critical that law enforcement personnel apply the extra effort and take the often-simple steps that will hopefully ensure continued success against groundless lawsuits.

Officer Charles Husted
SACRAMENTO PD

I've been an officer with Sacramento Police Department for 10 years. I've been a K-9 handler almost four years with Pele, my first dog. We are still learning, but we're to a point now where he and I are partners. I can tell you what he's going to do most of the time. He can read me as well. We are definitely a team. He can tell by my body actions and my voice what's going on in my head.

His awareness is apparent during patrol. If I'm dealing with a guy, and the contact starts going negative, I'm going to start reacting a certain way. Instantly, Pele barks. He'll sit there and stare at me, but once I start touching the guy like I'm going to arrest him or search him, he'll lean out the window and start barking. Obviously, that in itself is a deterrent. Sometimes you think that the guy's going to run, but if he sees the dog he won't.

I have asked people, "Why didn't you take off running?"

They say, "You had the dog, and I didn't want to get bit."

They make the right decision.

We had an armed robbery of a convenience store. The description had gone out on Nicholaus Edwards, 28, of Sacramento, also sought as a parolee at large.

I was in the area on patrol and spotted a guy on a bicycle that matched the description. When I made contact, the guy didn't start fighting instantly, but he wanted to leave on his bike. I tried to detain him. He didn't become aggressive right away; he just wanted to get out of there.

At first I was not convinced that this was the suspect. When he started to resist, I started thinking maybe this was the guy.

The whole time, as I am trying to control the suspect, the dog is leaning out of the car barking. I start to get the suspect under control. Then I have to call for help, and he gets the advantage on me. He pulls a gun out of his waistband, we begin to struggle over the gun, and I get hit in the face.

Once that happens, I forget I even have a dog. Pele's barking at the top of his voice, but I forget he is there. I am thinking about saving my life.

A couple of months before this incident, I'd gone to a police K-9 tactics class. They talked about getting behind your engine block in a gun battle. That's what I tried to do.

At first I was not convinced that this was the suspect. When he started to resist, I started thinking maybe this was the guy.

I didn't make it; I got shot first. Even after the shooting, I still did not remember that I was a K-9 handler. I used the tactics from my training as a police officer.

In retrospect I am really thankful that the dog did as he is taught to do. We train him to stay in the car until he is called, whether I'm getting shot at, beat up, he's supposed to stay in the car. He did. The window was down. He could have gotten out at any point, but he stayed in the car.

Afterwards, when I went back into my car, the whole front seat and window were slobbery. He got from the back seat into the front. But he had enough control to stay in the car. If he had gotten out of the car prior to me calling him, I would have had two things to worry about—getting shot at and what's my dog doing?

I'm by myself shooting it out with this guy. He gets off five or six rounds. One goes through my shoulder. The impact transformed me from "I'm about to die" fear to "how dare he try and take me from my family" anger. I wasn't about to let this guy get away.

He runs.

As soon as he runs, the big K-9 lightbulb goes on. Hey, my dog can catch that guy!

The scary thing was he didn't just turn his back and run down the street as fast as he could. He is running sideways, still shooting back at me.

"Pele, get him!"

We do this all the time at training. He jumps out of the car, runs down the street and gets the guy. This time, his spring is wound so tight, when I finally say the magic word, he flies about ten feet and hits the ground running, barking the whole way.

Seeing the dog coming, the suspect decides to shoot at the dog instead of me, the officer shooting 9mm's at him.

Pele jumps up and bites the guy's gun arm. The gun goes flying. The guy falls down on his back. As I'm running up, he tries to crawl away, so Pele reattaches to his leg.

I'm holding him at gunpoint. I don't know if he's got other guns. He's yelling, not about me shooting him, but about the dog, "Get this dog off me! Get this dog off me!"

I tell him I'm not calling the dog off until other officers arrive.

That 30 seconds seemed like an eternity, standing over the guy, realizing he just shot me. I'm alive but don't know how injured, knowing the adrenaline is handling all that.

Once the officers got there, I called Pele off. He let go and came back to a heel. I figured he was hot, heeled him back to the car, and he jumped inside. I poured him some water. Then I realized, wait a second, I got shot. I have to go to the hospital.

Another handler came and took the car and my K-9, who is friendly with the cops.

Pele had 50 or 60 arrests prior to this. As an officer, I'm actively looking for felonies because the dog is a tool that not many officers have. I want to use him as much as possible to apprehend felons fleeing from us. That previous experience helped him get through the shooting successfully. He stayed in the car until he was told, he called off the bite and came back to a heel, he heeled back to the car and I gave him "good boy!" When it was over, it was over.

It is important for handlers to get their dogs as much experience as they can. We have no lack of felonies in our city. Rural officers have to seek out more training than I do. The officer has 25 or 30 years on the department. The dog has only five or six years, depending on injuries.

I read wanted posters, get to know people in the area I work. Before work I'll run people for warrants, and I know these people by face. If I see someone I know has a felony warrant and he flees, then I am within department policy to send my dog. It is incumbent upon K-9 officers to be proactive. Otherwise, they wait for other officers to stir up stuff and set perimeters. Even in my city, that doesn't happen often. You have to do it yourself, if you want your dog to get experience.

Pele does narcotics. He's ball crazy. His biggest issue with narcotics is that when he gets frustrated, he bites at stuff.

The dog's sense of smell is astounding. I had just worked an overtime shift. My dog was in the car waiting to go home. About a mile and a half away a shooting call goes out. Officer-involved shooting. Officer down. Say no more, I'm there.

The officer shot was a good friend of mine. He was in serious condition. We had a perimeter but no idea where the shooter was.

Ironically, I went to school with the suspect, Joseph Bernal Rosales. I had played baseball with him. I knew his family.

We had four K-9s searching. Another agency responded with their dogs. We had a huge perimeter, helicopters. We were going to find this guy if it took all night. Our game plan was to search outside areas. Plan B was to go door-to-door. In a housing project, there aren't a lot of places to hide outside.

A few minutes into the search my dog's tail and ears go up. It was dark. He has a problem with cats, but his demeanor indicated human interest. I thought, maybe this guy's on the roof. I tell my guys, hey, he's on to something. Watch your back.

Pele goes by one side of this house, lifts his head near a window, then all of a sudden runs around the corner out of my view. I didn't know if the guy was standing around the corner or what. I get around the corner, hear him barking, and see him jumping up on a front door, scratching and barking.

I'm amazed. How could he do this? The windows are closed. Watching my dog, I'm thinking there must be 50 cats inside. It was everything you see in training on box searches. The dog was saying, "The guy is in this house!" You have to trust your dog. Basic training says do not second-guess your dog.

So I trusted the dog, called him back from the door, radioed we might have something, and knocked on the door. No response. Knocked again. No response.

Finally a man answers the door. As the door opens, I see the shadow of a person go from the front room toward the back of this house.

"Are you here by yourself?" I ask.

He says it's him and his mother and points to an elderly lady lying in a bed.

"Anybody else?" I just saw a shadow

"Oh, nobody else's in the house."

"OK, well why don't you come outside." We bring him out.

I'm thinking, great, he's in the house, he just shot an officer, and he's obviously armed. Maybe this is a SWAT deployment. Let's get the lady out first and go from there.

My dog's really jacked up. We're trying to get the elderly woman out of the house. We're waiting for the SWAT team to get over there. I'm doing the bluff at the door. The dog's barking.

"I know you're in the house. I'm going to send the dog in to get you." Bark bark bark.

About two minutes of that and a guy comes out of a back bedroom into the light.

It's him. I went to school with the guy and know him on sight. He's pretending to be intoxicated, like he's been there drinking all night, stumbling out. We take him into custody. It's done.

I watch everybody doing their jobs and think, my dog just found this guy. If we didn't have police dogs, would he have gotten found? Who knows? We had a scared parolee who had just shot a cop. He knew that, if caught, he was going to go back to prison for the rest of his life. He had to be pumping fear scent.

It goes back to experience. We have foot pursuits, and I try to teach officers not to run in front of us because I don't want the dog biting an officer. After a car chase or something like that, it's hard to get especially younger officers or other agencies to hold back just a few seconds until we pass by. Pele's to a point where he discriminates, even on a foot pursuit. I've sent him through crowds of officers, and he'll weave through

My dog's really jacked up. We're trying to get the elderly woman out of the house. We're waiting for the SWAT team to get over there. I'm doing the bluff at the door. The dog's barking.

them and take out the guy we're chasing.

That's hard to train. It's almost impossible to re-create. A bunch of guys running in bite suits, the dog will key on them anyway. My dog has had many searches where he goes past citizens. It's not about just going out and biting people. You have to have actual search experience. Finding the bad guy is what they're for.

If you have a perimeter, and the dog bites whatever is in that perimeter, you're going to lose your program. It's not a search and destroy mission. The officer has to direct and verbally control his dog. The dog has to respect you as his handler. Not just his friend, but also as his handler. That doesn't mean you should have to beat him up or choke him out. It's a level of respect that he has for you. When you call him back, if he's not in the scent cone, he should come right back.

I've had times where I didn't realize he was in the scent cone. When he would delay returning, I'd get frustrated, start raising my voice. Then I'd realize he was working the scent.

We were searching for two burglary suspects. I'd checked probably half a dozen yards, hopped a fence to the next street over, and started checking yards again. It was summer and hot. To give the dog a break, I downed him in a front yard.

The lieutenant pulls up to talk about the search. Pele's eight feet away on a down stay, and my back's toward him. We talk about 30 seconds and the lieutenant says, "Where's your dog going?"

Thinking "cat," I spin around. A few yards away Pele's disappearing into a bush.

A guy starts screaming. The dog knew the suspect was there and couldn't wait. He got the job done. We joked about me being just a chauffeur for the dog.

We had an auto theft. I got behind the stolen car. The driver was a known felon. Sometimes passengers are just fleeing witnesses. That policy changes if it's a fresh crime and the passengers have knowledge. In this case I had two felons but only one police dog.

We usually train to go after the driver. I figure the dog will key on the driver. I can tell he is looking for a place to stop or crash and take off running. He goes down a dead-end street. I'm thinking, OK, any time now.

He slams on his brakes, the doors open, passenger runs to the right, driver to the left. I get out, send the dog, and he apprehends the driver. Meanwhile, I capture the passenger. I call Pele off the driver and into a down stay beside him. The dog lies there barking at him. He won't run. Next I handcuff him.

Afterward the sergeant says, "Wow, how'd you do that?" I knew Pele would do what he's supposed to do. I might as well do something myself.

When I was new to the unit, I sent Pele after an auto thief and he took him down right away. The guy's screaming, "Get the dog off me."

Being a kind person and not wanting to inflict undue damage, I call the dog back to a heel. He outs as he is supposed to and comes running back to me, still 30 yards away.

As soon as the dog lets go, the bad guy jumps up. He gets over a chain link fence with razor wire and boogies into a field.

I'm thinking, Oh no!

I'm not going to send my dog over razor wire, so I grab the bottom of the fence and Pele wriggles underneath, disappearing into the darkness. Frantic, I locate a pole, climb it, and jump over the razor wire into the muddy field.

Officers on the far street radio, "Call your dog, he's got the guy." Before the suspect climbed the fence again, Pele caught him and was not letting go. I wasn't about to call him off again until I got there.

The suspect said, "Hey, I almost made it."

I said, "Yeah."

I'll never do that again. I trained the down. Luckily, my dog doesn't do cheap shots. As long as the suspect doesn't get aggressive, he won't bite him again. Bad guys are afraid of police dogs. That fear is a valuable deterrent.

Last week I had a parolee in his forties, in and out of prison all his life, 6' 2" 200-plus pounds, basically a bad character that had run from parole officers. We had a perimeter. Five minutes into the search the dog found him in some bushes about five or six houses away. This guy's supposed to be armed and dangerous, so I had a SWAT officer with me. I'm right with the dog as he finds the guy, takes hold of his arm, and I'm pointing my gun at him, telling him to get his hands up so I can see them.

The bite lasted two to three seconds at most. He said, "OK, OK, OK" and got his arms up, so I called Pele out. SWAT took him into custody. We get out to the car and looked at the guy's injuries. His forearm had compression marks, slight scratches, but no punctures. The skin was red where the dog had bitten and squeezed.

An older officer standing there said, "What's wrong with your dog?"

At first I thought he was kidding. Looking at his face, I saw he was serious.

"What do you mean?" I asked.

"Your dog just left scratches on him."

"I'm not out to hurt people," I said.

He looked at me like I was crazy. Here was a worst-of-the-worst criminal. He thought my dog should send this guy to the hospital.

I told him, "Wait a second. This guy felt that bite. His arm hurts, I guarantee you. It'll be bruised tomorrow. He's going to remember this bite. I'm thankful he doesn't have to go to the hospital—less headache for me. The dog did his job, and it hurt enough that he surrendered."

We are out here for specific purposes. Our task is to find people and take them into custody. How that custody-taking goes will determine the injury. Pele has sent only three or four people to the hospital, because the suspects have fought with the dog resulting in greater injury.

The dog is a certain level of force. He does what you tell him. We are fortunate to have the ruling that dogs are less than lethal force. We have to be responsible. Because if that ruling changes, what's the point in having dogs? We have guns. The dog is an asset to finding crooks, saving officers' lives, preventing injury to citizens, as well as to suspects.

Back to my shooting—my dog probably saved Edwards' life. I was not going to let him get away. Most likely I would have caught up to him, or he would have shot it out with other cops, and may have died. I wouldn't feel good about that. Handlers who get dogs because of how fast they are, how hard they hit, and how much damage they do should be ashamed. They should re-evaluate if they want to be dog handlers, or in fact police officers. Departments that have those kinds of handlers and deployment issues are going to lose their programs to lawsuits.

When I first got into canine, I was so excited. The first year I went to every single K-9 trial in California. I would leave on a Friday to get there early to practice. It was very competitive.

That destroyed a lot of things at home with my family. All of a sudden this police dog took priority over the rest of our life. You forget about your spouse. You forget about your kids. You cannot let that happen. I know that now. I might go to one dog trial a year, but I bring the family. It's fun. I don't take it as seriously anymore. In the hierarchy of what's important to you, your police dog should not be above your family. It's fun to compete, but keep it in perspective. A great trial dog does not necessarily make a great police dog. Does your dog perform on the street?

Our department has administrators with K-9 experience, which really helps the unit. Handlers have promoted to sergeants, lieutenants, and captains. I get asked, when are you going to take the sergeant's test? I'm not interested in going down that road until this dog serves his life as a police dog. I owe that to him. Until he gets injured or too old, I'm going to let him work, because that's what he loves to do. K-9 gets in your blood. It's a lot of work and time, but it's so rewarding. Right now I have the best job in my department.

Deputy Brian Blair
Amador County Sheriff's Department, California

I got a typical trespass call, which usually ends in a warning to leave the property. When I got there, everybody was standing around armed near a car hidden in manzanita bushes. Our narcotics unit had information there was probably a grow involving at least three people.

I took Luka out of the patrol car wearing his regular working collar. The property owner had heard partying down the hill. Hiking down, we started seeing equipment associated with a marijuana grow—25 black plastic pots, bags of fertilizer, potting soil—about a quarter mile from the vehicle. The dog immediately started pulling hard into the brush, tracking on deer trails.

As the brush thickened, I ended up crawling on my hands and knees. Shoving through the manzanita was rough, and I kept asking myself, do I believe the dog? How far do I go with this?

Suddenly Luka stopped and cocked his head. Looking ahead, I saw three men working their way toward us. They didn't see me. I downed the dog and waited.

When they were about twenty feet away, one of the men said, "Yeah, I'm sure we came in this way."

Before they walked right into me, in a low voice, I said, "Sheriff's department. You move, the dog bites you." They froze.

Directing the men into a clearing, I had them kneel and started cuffing. When the sergeant arrived, we took them into custody, along with their green dope. They led us to three grow sites that nobody would have found without a dog. A consent search of their houses netted scales, packaging, and more dope. They were supplying the whole juvenile community with their dope.

One night I got a "man with a gun" call to cabins on Carson Drive where I'd been dispatched earlier to a party. Everybody was drunk as usual. Big bonfire. Seventy-five year old father said, "My son (42-years old) just came home, walked through the house, grabbed his gun, and headed out. Said he was going to go kill somebody."

We drove up Carson Drive but saw nobody.

My backup unit came on the air, "We've got the guy across from Carson Drive on the highway headed toward the cabins." When they tried to contact him, he ran off into the brush (ditching the gun), came back out and gave up, denying everything.

Dispatch ran him, and he came back a felon. As I took my dog out of the patrol car to search for the weapon, I had to stop two deputies from heading out into the brush ahead of us. Luka tracked to a greasewood bush where he alerted and circled the bush. I saw the gun stuck a foot up from the base of the bush. I pulled the dog back, gave him his toy, and sent the deputies to retrieve the gun.

They couldn't see it. I had to go back and point out exactly where it was stuck in the bush…with the hammer cocked back!

Luckiest guy in the world. Can you imagine what would have happened if that guy had dumped the gun, with the deputies following him, and it had discharged in the bush?

I do this because I enjoy it. You have to enjoy the training. You cannot be totally compensated for all the extra, hard work it takes to be a top quality team. When the dog performs well, it reflects on the whole agency and everybody shares the satisfaction. On many calls the dog has gone way beyond my expectation, as far as finding things, doing things we haven't even trained.

We were called to recover a gun used in a shooting. A young girl had been shot. I was astonished when the dog found the disassembled weapon. He found the grips first, then a hash pipe, then the pistol buried under about six inches of gravel. We were told to go down to the campsite where the shooting had taken place to look for the shell casing. Of course the question is, "Where do you start?" You have a large area. You're looking for blood spots…next the dog's standing there with a huge bong (dope pipe) in his mouth. The dog recovers evidence you're not even looking for. He did find the shell casing.

Multi-agency operations require adequate planning, particularly where SWAT and K-9 will be acting together. Based on weeks of surveillance, several agencies in our area planned a raid on a large marijuana grow. Nobody knew how large the grow actually was. Two 10-man SWAT teams were briefed to take out two grow sites, which turned out to be four grow sites. They estimated 3000 plants. It turned out there were more than 10,000 plants, worth over $24,000,000. They called for two K-9 teams but could have used ten.

The growers were Mexican nationals believed to be armed, with regular trafficking routes through the rugged terrain, and they were living like Viet Cong guerillas. It was blistering hot in the daytime.

At the briefing we were shown a map and told, "From your drop-off point, go down this hill a couple hundred yards, cross the creek, and we'll be directly up the hill."

The SWAT teams moved into position in advance. Barking would of course have blown their cover. It took them over three hours to get in place.

Meanwhile we had to wait at our drop-off point. I looked at the bad photocopy of the topographic map and walked down to some railroad tracks, comparing the distance to where we were going. The thousand feet of elevation change did not look good.

Finally we were deployed. As we were hiking into the canyon, the raid went down. We didn't know what was happening. Radio transmissions indicated that the suspects ran everywhere. SWAT called, "Send the dogs in now!"

We weren't even close to being in position. We could see the helicopter circling above a ridge. The "little creek" on the map was actually a river. The water was up to our waists when we crossed. The other handler headed in his designated direction toward the other SWAT team.

Across the river we hit a scent trail. My dog immediately found a shoe, then a hat, then other fresh evidence indicating people came through. There was no well-defined trail. The grow was about a mile from our start point, but the last half mile up the mountainside was so steep I was hanging onto branches. The dog couldn't even sit. He was covered with burrs. The heat was intense.

Across the river we hit a scent trail. My dog immediately found a shoe, then a hat, then other fresh evidence indicating people came through.…the last half mile up the mountainside was so steep I was hanging onto branches. The dog couldn't even sit. He was covered with burrs. The heat was intense.

Finally, I got into a huge, dense marijuana grow concealed under oak canopy. I radioed, "Where are you?" Ten yards away, officers could hear me but we couldn't see each other. They said two guys got away…in the direction I'd just come up. I realized they'd made it to the river before we even started up the trail.

Planning is one thing. When it starts going bad, nobody knows. What if one of us had fallen into the river? The helicopters should have been used to drop the dog teams into the scene, when and where we were needed, not 30 minutes later, after the bad guys got away.

In an adjacent county a man pointed a revolver at a tow truck driver. California Highway Patrol broadcast the plate and complete description of the driver and the vehicle, including a yellow kayak tied on top. The vehicle check showed the suspect lived in our town of Pioneer.

About 10 pm, CHP spotted the suspect westbound on Highway 88 and trailed him behind a semi truck. At Dew Drop, as he turned onto Shake Ridge Road, I pulled in behind him with CHP at my back. We lit him up. At 10 mph he failed to yield, but as soon as we cleared the single lane road section, he escalated to 65 mph, crossing both lanes on the winding road, deadly for anybody coming the other way. My patrol unit is the worst-handling sport utility vehicle made. He was setting me up for a sharp left-hand turn off Cedar Road to his house.

When he turned up the driveway, the dust was so thick I didn't know if we were on a road or going crosscountry. All I could see were taillights. Behind me, CHP lost sight of my overheads in the dust.

Near the end of the pursuit, there was a stump about a foot and a half high that I didn't see. The suspect went around it. I nailed it. Backing off, I saw the driveway again.

Meanwhile the suspect's vehicle had disappeared behind a storage shed, where he bailed. First we searched a trailer on the property. At the suspect's vehicle, my dog started tracking along a fence leading toward the parents' house. He tracked across the deck of the house then down a ravine. He was pulling against his collar, digging in, so I knew he had a fresh track.

At the bottom of the ravine he stopped, head up. The scent was obviously pooling. The suspect had to be nearby. Shoving his head down, he dragged me into the manzanita.

I saw a green T-shirt. The guy was lying down. I yelled, "Let me see your hands."

He didn't move. I remembered the neighbor saying, "Hey, this guy's got all sorts of guns."

I sent the dog.

Luka grabbed the suspect's right elbow. He yelled, "OK, I give up!" As soon as I saw his hands, I called the dog off and took him into custody. He was burly, 5'11", 230 pounds and I could barely get his arms behind his back

No sooner did I get him handcuffed than he said to me, "Nice dog!"

Officer Dave Kain

Corning Police Department, California

As soon as the jury saw the dog tear into the methamphetamine, no matter what happened during the rest of the trial, they would automatically find him guilty.

Günnar has been activated since February 1997. He is certified in patrol and has assisted me finding fleeing suspects and making many arrests. He is also certified in narcotics detection. We have breached $3 million in seizures so far in the greater Corning, Highway 5 corridor, including assists in Glenn County. The majority of incidents involve seasoned CHP (California Highway Patrol) officers making the determination that there may be drugs in a vehicle, and we confirm that for them.

At this time in our area, marijuana and methamphetamine are the most prevalent illegal drugs. When I first got Günnar, as soon as he hit the street we did a probation search and located a broken down methamphetamine lab in an apartment closet.

Recently I had a search with the task force in a big junkyard. It was a long search, and Günnar was just about licked. We hadn't found anything. As I was sending him back to the car, he did a spontaneous alert on a fifth wheel—started walking by it then, bang, did a 180, ran back to the door and alerted on it. The task force searched the trailer and found residue, scales, and baggies, but not much dope. For the experience, we searched around the rest of the trailer. Where the fifth wheel goes over the bed of the truck, Günnar alerted on the wall area. Subsequent search revealed a false compartment in the wall of the trailer exactly where he alerted. The compartment contained over 2.5 ounces of methamphetamine.

In court the gentleman represented himself and subpoenaed my dog. When it came time for Günnar to come to court, the defense requested that we do a detection demonstration in front of the jury to show whether or not the dog could locate the drugs. The judge refused to allow the dog into court because he felt it was too prejudicial against the defendant. As soon as the jury saw the dog tear into the methamphetamine, no matter what happened during the rest of the trial, they would automatically find him guilty, The defendant ended up pleading to the original offense so that he didn't have to continue the trial. He went to state prison.

The local judges respect the use of the dog. We have written search warrants solely on the K-9, and the judge has issued the warrant based on the use of the K-9.

During department K-9 training in an equipment yard, the trainer hid dope in a trencher (ditch digger). While searching the area, Günnar repeatedly alerted to a blue haul trailer 50 feet away, feverishly pawing and chewing on it. I was surprised because the trailer was not part of the exercise. I pulled him off. We kept working and he quickly found the drugs in the trencher. As soon as he found the training drugs, though, he totally set that aside, dragged me right back to the trailer and alerted to it.

To confirm my suspicions, I put Günnar away and asked another handler to search with his dog. He had the same alert on the back portion of the trailer. Later, talking to their MET team (marijuana eradication team), we learned that they had just used the trailer in an operation where they found 1200 marijuana plants. They had made several trips transporting the marijuana. The dogs were detecting plant residue in the trailer.

Most of our finds are on vehicles, including bicycles. I had stopped a bicycle. The driver refused to give consent. He had a small fanny pack. Since the bicycle follows the same rules of the road as cars, I deployed the dog to search the exterior. He alerted on the fanny pack. We opened it up to find a small amount of marijuana and a pipe inside.

Working a dog not only involves you putting faith in the dog, but you also have to convince everybody else. Many officers do not believe what the dogs can do.

In the early morning hours I got called to a search in Glenn County. Highway patrol had a rental car with a couple of suspicious individuals who refused to consent to a search and would not provide any information. The officers allowed me to ask for a consent search, but again the subjects refused, saying they didn't want me to use my dog to search their car.

One officer put the subjects in the back of his patrol car and taped their conversation while I did an exterior search of their car. The dog alerted on the trunk. We opened the trunk. Günnar jumped in and started chewing on the spare tire. It was flat and had obviously been recently removed. I told the officers I thought narcotics were concealed in the spare tire. They relieved me to go back to Corning, and I cleared the scene. They released the individuals without searching the spare tire.

Then they listened to the tape. Apparently the suspects had said, "The dog's found it. We're done for!" When they relocated the vehicle in Red Bluff and stopped it, they found three kilos of cocaine concealed in the spare tire.

Largest single seizure—22 pounds of cocaine concealed in the door panels on both sides of a CHP car stop in Glenn County. Initially, the officer had found the trip switch for the door panels, and the dog confirmed that it was dope. Popular concealment locations—meth in magnetic key holders behind the dash and money inside air filters.

A truck driver CHP stopped was a methadone user from Canada who had been driving only 3-4 weeks. He piqued the CHP officer's interest when he referred to the reefer as a "thing-a-ma-bobber." He was running a mixed load of boxes of toys and fresh spinach from Southern California to Canada but was carrying only a quarter capacity, hardly enough to pay the fuel bill. My dog alerted across the back of the rig. We put him inside, and he alerted high. We hand searched but could find nothing and concluded they had already made a delivery.

Günnar jumped in and started chewing on the spare tire.

Officer Ken Hedrick
Officer Ron Ortiz

Hayward Police Department, California

Officer Hedrick:
In Hayward, California, K-9 backs up any call.
When we get new people in the unit, we teach them: "Don't wait to get called. If you think they may need you, go." Because if you wait until they ask, it could be way too late.
New handlers are apprehensive about using the dog; you have to almost push them off the pier. After you get over that initial fear of using the dog, it becomes no big deal. Like new cops, the first time you make an arrest for drunk in public, you think it's the biggest arrest you've ever made. Next time it's not so bad. Then you do a burglary, a rape, a homicide.
Once you realize the dog is an extension of you, your main concern is the thing at the end of his face called the nose. I want the dog to take me to where the crook is. I want to make up the options—give up, come out, surrender, go peacefully. You want to fight, then it's going to be me and the dog. That's why we teach new handlers, "It's not the bite, it's the nose."

Officer Hedrick, K-9 Aerro

If I go through my entire K-9 career without a bite, so what? As long as he takes me to the crook, intimidates him as necessary, assists me arresting him.

We had a cat burglary in progress two blocks away. I truck down there, cruise the area, look down the street and see the guy moving near the house. Two houses away, he spots me. He's on a dead run like somebody lit a firecracker under him. He darts over to another house and disappears behind it.

I start the dog tracking. Dog goes over the fence. I go over the fence. We search the back yard. Dog's on the back fence running back and forth. Peeking over, I see the guy hiding in a bush just on the other side of the fence from the dog. So I call the dog to me, and we flip over the fence.

I had put this out on the air. All of a sudden two cops walk into the area. I have to down the dog, move the cops back, and now the dog's having trouble pinpointing the guy in the bushes (scent's going through the fence). Finally he dives in and bites the guy, who fights, we roll around on the ground and I get him hooked up. Cops come in, take him out, put him in a car, when it dawns on somebody, "Hey, we never patted this guy down." Get him out of the car, find a loaded .32 in his waistband.

Finally he dives in and bites the guy, who fights, we roll around on the ground and I get him hooked up.

Later we talked to him and asked, "Why didn't you use the gun?"

He said, "I didn't think about it. When that dog was biting me, all I could think about was I had to get the dog off me. It took all my concentration to think about that."

I am of the philosophy Get It Done. The majority of your searches as a K-9 handler, you're on point. You need to learn to clear areas, always leaving yourself a safe zone. If it goes crazy, you can get back to your safe zone. If you confront the suspect, always bring the suspect back to your safe zone. There could be dual or multiple suspects. Order him back, prone him out, wait until your cover officers get there, hook him up, get him out, go back in, search, and clear as you go along.

I keep my cover officers behind cover, direct the dog to search out ahead, move up to secure the area, search the next area—be it a field or building. That's the way I was taught in the service and have always found that to be the best way. I don't want my cover in my pocket watching the dog, not watching high, not watching my back. It happens that you're concentrating on the dog, you think you have two cover officers behind you, you glance back and you've only got one. Now it's, where'd the other guy go?

One night with my old dog Asco, we're training in a warehouse, teaching the dogs to search the big aisles where the forklifts go, penetrating the stacks of pallets. My dog's running these aisles, searching, when the brakes come on, we see his fanny go up, and he skids to a halt with this bloody scream. He comes howling back to me with this cobweb on his face.

Officer Ortiz:

We had a burglary at a large complex up in the hills. The call was at least 30 minutes old. Officers were collecting evidence. I drove up with the dog and decided to get him out and walk around the scene. Right away he alerts, starts dragging me up the hill with the wind. I'm not sure, but trusting my dog, I've been with him for a long time, I'm going to go with him. He takes me up the hill.

The sergeant sees the dog dragging me up there and says, "What's going on?"

I go, "You might want to go up ahead and check because he's definitely en route someplace."

The sergeant drove up about a quarter mile and found one of the suspects coming out of the woods. The victims positively identified him. There were two suspects, so I said there was a good possibility they split up someplace, let me cast the dog out and see what he does.

After a couple minutes, the dog headed back downhill in a direction away from the crime scene. He takes me into a carport area, up a set of steps, into the creek, a quarter mile down the creek bed, back up to condominiums, into the middle of the complex, to the back of a condo under the bedroom window, stops, takes a deep breath, and wags his tail.

I'm on the radio, "Sarge, I need you to get over here. I think we've got something."

He says, "Never mind. The second suspect's been identified. We're en route now to his condo. I don't know what you have, but stand by."

I stood there for a couple minutes knowing my dog had something in that room.

A bunch of cars pulled up and it's the investigating officer with the first suspect who walks him directly to the first condo, where I'm standing. He says, "This is where he lives." The window where my dog was alerting was the second suspect's room.

When you learn about scent discrimination, you understand what the dog was doing.

The FBI was here to do a search warrant on an auto theft suspect. They wanted him really bad. They went to a house high in the hills. He went out the back window, down into a creek, and disappeared. They're calling for the dog. It's been over 45 minutes. I get called at home. I go out and meet with them at a fence where he was last seen going into a field. I asked how far they'd gone. They said, "Well, we did go down there and look around a little bit, but he's so long gone."

I take my dog on a long line. We'd been working on tracking quite a bit. We move into area and his head goes down on track. He goes down into the creek, along the creek bed, crosses, and heads up the embankment toward eucalyptus trees. I've got two cover officers with me. The dog's evidently got something, but we can't see any tracks.

We move into a grassy field, look in the direction he's headed. There are two footprints.

The dog works his way up the hill another quarter mile. We see an old ranch barn almost ready to collapse. Way back underneath, the guy's lying there looking at me. The dog's all excited. We're all pumped up, get on the radio, "Uh, the suspect's in custody." The FBI's saying, 'We cannot believe it!"

A six-hour search starts at 2 o'clock in the morning. Basically, it was a home invasion. One of our officers picks it up. As he pulls in behind the vehicle, they slide open the rear windows on the vehicle and open fire on his car. The pursuit ends down the freeway when the suspects crash. Five suspects leave the vehicle on foot.

Luckily, the officer standing by sees the suspects go and says, "They went into this (residential) area." The officer, who was very experienced, knew that unincorporated area. They set up a perimeter quickly, call in five dogs and the helicopter unit. They call me from home.

San Leandro is the first unit on the scene, I am second. The sergeant asks me, "What do you want?"

"I want every dog we have."

Five suspects to search in a six-block radius. The San Leandro dog, Ken's dog Asco, my dog Zaro, and two others. I have one side of the street, Ken the other. We put another K-9 unit down near the cemetery to check the end of the perimeter and began a methodical yard-by-yard search through the neighborhood, using three-man tactical teams with the helicopter to light some of the areas as we move.

Hedrick:

The first find was mine, and it wasn't even a suspect. The first house I go to, send the dog around into the back yard, and Asco has the prettiest alert you'd want to see. Prancing like a show horse. Hitting the fence, back and forth. We're peeking around but don't see a suspect. We go out, send the dog along the fence toward some tall trees. Asco goes over, dives in a bush, and we hear, "Aaarrrraaarrraaarrr!"

"Come on out with your hands up!"

"Aaarrrraaarrraaarrr!"

"Aus, hier!" he comes back.

We listen. Nothing. Send him back in, same thing.

"Wait a minute. Time out. This isn't a person. It's an article."

We go over and see a loaded Browning 9mm, one of the guns the suspects had used.

The first house I go to, send the dog around into the back yard, and Asco has the prettiest alert you'd want to see. Prancing like a show horse.

Officer Ortiz, K-9 Kavik

Ortiz:

We'd started to work into the wind. Coming back, we found a suspect that had actually been missed by a dog from another agency. It was just one of those things where the wind was swirling. We found a suspect hiding in the front compartment of an old abandoned truck, probably the same suspect who dumped the gun Kenny found.

So—this is awesome—we've got one in custody. Now we're moving. Even at that point, with the gun and one in custody, we've got a sergeant saying, "Call it." We're upset, saying, wait a minute. We know they're in here. We know they're armed. Let's go.

We start working up the street. In a backyard Zaro alerts at a basement entrance. Before I can say anything, this guy's yelling, "I'm comin' out. I give up! I give up." We take him into custody.

We've deployed so the dogs won't be alerting on each other and to minimize crossfire potential. We're moving methodically in the same direction. Zaro alerts again to an apartment complex and literally drags me toward it. I'm trying to slow him down, but he takes me to a garbage can. I open up the lid and find three pieces of body armor, three guns, ski masks.

Now Zaro alerts big-time on the fence line, but toward the opposite side of the fence where Kenny's working. Two yards down I'm talking quietly on the radio to Kenny, "Ken, he's alerting to your side." Ken's dog Asco is hot.

I come around the corner to a long driveway leading to a four-car garage. Asco runs over and starts chewing on the roll-up garage door. I check the side door, which is locked. We surround the place and contact the owner.

"Anybody supposed to be living in your garage?"

"No, it's unlocked."

"It's locked now."

"No, it's always unlocked!"

Oh great. They're in there. Pull the dog back.

"Come out, OK? You've got the choice. Or we're going to kick the door and send Fido."

"OK, we're comin' out!"

We ended up with all the suspects, except one female. Another agency detained her, got her information, then for some reason with all the things going on, decided to let her go. We picked up all four of the main players. Total search time, about three hours.

Officer Straw, K-9 Wyatt

Officer Dan Straw
Redding Police Department

This spring we had K-9 training at the Redding Airport with Corning Police. We were doing a training search of an airplane in the main hangar. Dope was planted on the plane. We did that search. I rewarded my dog. Wyatt has been on the street for almost three years and has had over 800 finds. Almost immediately, he dropped the ball, ran over to another plane, and did a spontaneous alert to its belly.

The aircraft was a six-seat twin engine contracted to NASA, on loan in northern California for detecting fire hot spots with infrared. The dog searched the belly of the aircraft intently then jumped into the passenger compartment and alerted in the middle of the cargo deck. Mechanics pulled the service records of the airplane and found out it was an asset forfeiture plane seized back in 1984, running cocaine from Mexico to the States. The aircraft had reportedly been "clean" ever since.

Six months ago I was called to search a rural location near Richfield. There were two trailers on the property. I searched the trailers with my dog and got 5-6 oz. of methamphetamine and .5 oz. of heroin. Our information was this guy was a pound dealer, so we expected much more. After searching, I gave my dog a 20-minute rest while I walked the property. In the pasture I noticed a barn with several locks on the door—odd to see a locked barn. We cut off the locks and searched the barn.

Wyatt searched the main part of the barn, which had gross masking odors, including human feces and a truck leaking oil and gasoline. There was a stack of hay bales 14 feet high. The floor was dirt. Initially the dog climbed up the bales and indicated narcotic scent was stovepiping to the top. Then he climbed back down and alerted aggressively at the base of the hay bales. We removed the hay to the pasture then started digging. The soil was soft and unconsolidated. We uncovered 5 white plastic paint buckets that contained 9 pounds of methamphetamine, 8-9 pounds of marijuana, and a half pound of heroin.

Here in the "crank capital," I do not risk using the dog near fresh meth labs or hazardous chemicals. Working with the task force, Wyatt alerted outside a motel room door. They wrote paper behind his alert and discovered a meth lab inside the room. One of our Corning patrolmen made a traffic stop. The driver denied consent and had obviously been around the block a couple times, so the officer called for Wyatt to do a free air sniff outside the car. He alerted to the trunk. We wrote paper on that car and got a bathtub lab out of the trunk—red phosphorus and other chemicals, glassware, and a portable ice chest.

Recently, one of our officers stopped a car and called me over. He had a couple Hispanic guys who spoke very little English and two white girls in the car. I searched the car and got an alert on the right rear passenger seat where one of the females had been sitting. The dog aggressively dug and tugged at the fabric on the seat. The driver was adamant: "You're not going to find nothing. You're wasting your time. I don't do drugs."

We ended up arresting the female. During the booking search at the jail they found about 2.5 oz. of methamphetamine she was carrying in her body cavity.

The task force trusts Wyatt. He has saved them so much search time that now they go where he alerts and examine those areas. If he doesn't alert in an area, they pack it in. We have gotten so much dope because of the dog. Without him, I would have had to let many vehicles drive off. The dog is a great tool to develop probable cause, and it will hold up in court. If you are good, the dopers develop their own "work" schedule around the K-9 officer's shift to avoid the dog.

We ended up arresting the female. During the booking search at the jail they found about 2.5 oz. of methamphetamine she was carrying in her body cavity.

All of a sudden there are a million places that could hide a person. Somebody's life is depending on you.

Marilyn Muse

Assistant Resource Officer, U.S. Forest Service

As a ranger in Yosemite National Park, I had become a member of YOSAR (Yosemite Search and Rescue) and a backcountry ranger at Tuolumne Meadows during the winter. We lived in Tuolumne six months of the year snowed-in at 8500 feet. During the winter of 1982-83, the biggest winter on record, we were up there seven months because the road was closed. We patrolled the greater Tuolumne Meadows area up to Tioga Pass, at 10,000 feet the highest road pass in the Sierra. We had no mechanized transport. Travel was totally on foot or skis. We lived 25 miles from Yosemite Valley and 15 miles west of Lee Vining.

In Tuolumne, my partner and I were fully responsible for all aspects of SAR, from taking the initial report to coming up with a search strategy. We ordered all resources that were needed, went out and, hopefully, found the lost people then managed their rescue and evacuation. The remoteness added to the incredibly helpless feeling you get when you go out searching for people. You realize that the person may be unresponsive and down, and you are relying upon your eyes, your ears, and your effectiveness in moving around in the terrain. All of a sudden there are a million places that could hide a person. Somebody's life is depending on you.

I saw the dog teams that were called into the Park and was impressed by their effectiveness. I saw that combining my work as a ranger with training a search dog would be combining two loves.

After going to conferences and checking into dogs, I waited a full year to get my first puppy for SAR training, realizing the large commitment involved. I was open to breed type, although my first dog as a kid was a German shepherd. Because I wanted the dog to be at least six months old before I returned to Tuolumne for that tour of duty, it was critical to get a young pup by June. I needed to show the Park Service that the dog had potential in order to take one back up with me. Dogs are not normally permitted in the Yosemite backcountry. And the dog had to be physically able to travel over the snow.

Before having a working dog, all I had ever asked of my canines was that they love me unconditionally and don't poop in the house. Selecting a dog with the right physical and mental attributes was essential, so I sought help with that as well as with the initial training.

German shepherd Sage passed her first mission-ready test with WOOF Search Dog Unit at 11 months when we came out of Tuolumne in the spring. We then went to Alaska. My first assignment was Wrangell-St. Elias National Park—big time backcountry. We were allowed to take Sage with us. One of my first searches up there was a drowning.

Our helicopter pilot had asked if I knew about the search going on in another part of the Park. Several days into the search, it was a recovery operation. I did not claim water search certification but had begun training for subsurface victims in both snow and water. The search location was a deep, cold lake, and there were a number of witnesses. The family had watched the young man turn the boat over. At that time the Alaska State Troopers had jurisdiction. They had been diving and dragging, diving and dragging, but located nobody.

The lake was medium-sized, comparable to Tenaya Lake in Yosemite. Lake currents were not strong enough to move a submerged body. I worked Sage from the boat and the shore. One of the highest pressures was that the father went out with me. He offered to row me around in the boat. We went out after midnight to four in the morning. Nobody except the father believed a dog could do this kind of work. Canine water search today is the capability that authorities give the least credence.

On the Alaskan lake I did have a documented find, confirmed by the District Ranger Dave Panebaker. The divers had become exhausted and cold. Visibility in the water was low. The divers were tired and unwilling to return to the water. Motorized watercraft were being operated in the area, which I knew was not optimal for scenting. After everyone went to bed I was basically on my own, and the dad said, "I'll row you around if you're willing to go out." Late June at that latitude we had twilight all night and didn't have to use flashlights. The air had cleared significantly. Search conditions were ideal. Performing swimming alerts into the cold water from both the boat and the shore, Sage narrowed the location of the body to a 50-foot radius, enabling the divers to make the recovery.

I have seen the transition in our culture from straightforward lost person searches to early suspicion of criminal involvement in missing person incidents. Of course we always had what we called the "bastard searches," where the guy turned up in a bar or the kid showed up at home. However, when a search is limited to only one day, then turned over to detectives to begin a criminal investigation, the opportunity to complete the search and find the person alive may be lost.

A recent search for two young girls illustrates how we may be guilty of preconceived ideas about where missing people go, resulting in strategies that are not flexible enough to cover likely areas. Due to the age of the girls, how they were dressed, the scenario in which they got lost going to and from the car, administrators concluded they surely would not be farther than a two-mile radius. When they showed up healthy but lost six miles away, everyone was surprised. In fact they had not searched some logical travel routes out of the immediate area. Conversely, we may go out too far too quickly for the tall, strong, equipped skier or hiker and neglect closer options.

Strategically, we need to think "outside of the logical."

Certainly dog training, like rescue training in general, has improved in recent years. The Internet has created greater information exchange worldwide. Big agencies take SAR training very seriously, but there is room for improvement in smaller agencies with, say, a sergeant in charge of search operations who receives insufficient equipment or training support. To their credit, most agencies are now responding much sooner to missing person reports, not waiting the 24 hours or two days to see if the person walks out. Agencies typically recognize the critical window of opportunity to rescue disaster victims, avalanche victims, and victims of water accidents, hypothermia, or other emergencies. Initiating searches sooner and providing air support, both in transport and search, has paid off for all of us on the ground.

Like police K-9 handlers, rescue dog handlers are finding that although the right dog really can do it all, finding the time and funds to meet the professional standard in all categories limits the team. Many K-9 officers have discovered that, although their dogs certainly have the drive and control to do urban disaster, they do not have the time to do their patrol work plus disaster training, certification, and response. Training procedures are another issue. We have also raised our expectations and standards for the different types of search work. Pointing to disaster search, dog teams are now integrated into FEMA and international task forces.

Res. Deputy Bill Schroeder
K-9 Trainer

Working the streets of a major city, San Leandro, my police dog Score saved my life many times. One night we were called near downtown Oakland to search a warehouse. On entry Score alerted, spun around, and nailed a guy hiding right beside the door. He was big, and he was holding a pipewrench ready to break my head.

Statistically, over 80 percent of the police service dog's work is searching, whether that be area search, building search, evidence search, or in the case of multi-trained dogs, drug search. Yet, the typical training session revolves around bite work, with little emphasis placed on search. This is probably due to the fact that it takes more time to set up a search problem and then work through the problem. However, officers and trainers must be willing to spend the time to set up realistic search scenarios, scenarios that stress officer safety tactics and stretch the time limits of both the handler and the dog.

Many officers and trainers, again due to time, limit the length of their searches. With searches in training lasting 3 to 5 minutes, it is no wonder that both the officer and the dog are not working up to speed after a 30 minute search. Both are practically useless after a 2- to 3-hour search.

It is very important to vary the lengths of the searches.

It is also extremely important to practice officer safety tactics when performing a training search. Not that all training searches should employ officer safety tactics, as problem solving for the dog should be an important aspect of that training. However, the handler should be capable of directing a cover officer or officers and still maintain complete control over the dog while performing the search.

Too often, search training consists of a handler entering the search area, alerting the dog, sending the dog, and then wandering through the search area waiting for the dog to alert or make an apprehension. Little thought is given to the handler's visibility or the safety of the handler, should that be a real search for an armed suspect.

Remember—you will perform in the field as you have trained!

If you work training searches with only the handler and dog in the area, then the introduction of a cover officer, in a real situation, will divert the attention of both the handler and the dog. Use a cover officer, or officers, if you would normally use one on a real search. The handler and cover officer will both benefit from the training.

If you work for an agency that does not have the personnel to provide cover on searches, work out training scenarios that have you thinking safety as you search. Train your dog to work under those conditions, so that the dog does not have to be continuously sent out to search while you look for cover or concealment in a search area.

Remember, you and your dog are a team. If you send your dog to apprehend a suspect, then you had better be prepared to back up your dog in any manner necessary. Nothing disturbs me more than to see a dog biting a suspect, the suspect fighting back, and the handler standing by not assisting the dog in any way. Get in there and help your dog. With the dog biting, get in there and restrain the suspect. Then call off your dog. But, practice this in training. Know what your dog will do when you jump in on the fight. Train-train-train. Let your dog know he is not supposed to bite you when you come in to assist. I think you will like the results of teamwork.

*Remember—
you will perform
in the field as you
have trained!*

Ret. Deputy Jim Barnes
K-9 Trainer

If you say, like I do, I want the officer to be an experienced officer, done with his jail time and on the road at least 2-3 years before he goes into K-9, somewhere along the line you run into the experienced officer who, almost as a survival thing, has learned to mask his emotions. You're not supposed to get angry with people because they spit on you. You're not supposed to get angry with people because they beat their kids. You don't show emotion. When they get the dog and go into training, it's hard for a lot of peace officers to all of a sudden show the emotion and enthusiasm that's necessary in praising the dog, to let the dog know he's doing right. The dog is like a 7-year-old child. You've got to show him the emotion, whoop and holler, get down and get dirty with him when he's good. If you're not willing to do that, the dog either becomes confused or takes infinitely longer to learn what you are trying to teach him because he doesn't know what's right. The best K-9 officer gets right down and plays with his dog.

There's a contradiction here between the young officer who hasn't evolved into the emotionless, straightline individual some people evolve into as a defense mechanism and the inexperienced officer who may become overly dependent on his dog. The officer has to be able to function just as well without the dog as with him. If you take an officer who has been on the street for a year and he's still unsure of himself, put him in as a K-9 officer, he's liable to become overly dependent on his dog instead of on his own skills and training.

I try to draw a mental picture for peace officers—the scales of justice. I tell them you have to dispense praise equal to correction. The scales tip back and forth all the time, but they should always end up in balance. If you've got too much enforcement all the time, you've got a cowering dog who's going to do this because he's afraid to make a mistake. If you use too much praise, the dog will never be under control. He'll just be running around like a wild man. You have to keep both in balance. If you don't do either one, then nothing will ever happen.

Early in the obedience training, I will take an officer's novice dog, and go plodding around the field using exaggerated monotone praise. Invariably the dog will virtually go to sleep in about 3 minutes. I'll be plodding along in the same fashion, no enthusiasm, no desire to do it. He's just there because he has a leash on him. Then I'll turn right around and do the same exact thing, walking quickly, crisply, "Oh all right! I said Fus!" Instantly, the dog will come to life, perk up and start reacting.

If the officer still doesn't do it correctly, I will shoot him on video. I will tell him what he is doing, tell him to take the dog and do the same routine again all on video. I want you to take this home and look at it. I want you to think about this every time you work your dog. Enthusiasm on one hand, crisp commands on the other hand. *Videocameras are one of the greatest training aids ever provided.* For search, for protection, when the officer sees his performance on screen, he can't argue with the facts.

Video is also a good way to educate administrators about K-9. To have a K-9 unit, you have to have somebody inside the department at an upper level of management who is knowledgeable about police dogs and who either covertly or overtly supports the dog unit.

"Man with a gun." "Man with a knife." These are no-win situations. Think of the *whole* tactical situation. Don't just send the dog on a suicide mission then stand back and watch what happens. Have a *plan*. Use the dog tactically to *activate* that plan. Come up behind the man on foot. Ram him with a car. Do *something* else, beyond just "send the dog."

The chances of a dog alone disarming a man are not good. At some point an officer has to move in and take charge of the man. Maybe the man will be dead by then—shot by the handler or by cover officers, or by his own gun. Maybe he will give up. Or maybe he will combat the dog and arresting officers. Regardless, use the dog to improve your tactical position, to protect the public and fellow officers, and to take the guy out of action more safely.

You may lose the dog. Don't be in a hurry to do that. But be ready to do that if you have to. Some officers are very attached to their dogs. Some have dumped hundreds of hours into training, probably thousands of hours into service with their dogs. Some officers are not very attached to their dogs. Some have only had a few weeks of training and have not been on the street very long. Some handlers are basically afraid of their dogs. For complex reasons, certain handlers will more readily send their dog into a hazardous situation than others. Some dog handlers feel immune from harm. They have no plan of action.

The best, most mature handler may actually use his dog more readily than the less experienced, or less able handler. The best handler has long ago come to terms with "what if" where public or officer safety is at stake and where he has to bring the situation to an immediate end. But he does so with a plan he can articulate as having the best chance of saving human lives in the face of deadly force.

Use the dog with a plan. Don't let the dog *be* the plan. The dog is not infallible. The dog is not hard to defeat. A barehanded man can defeat the dog. A man with a gun is even more dangerous.

With a mental patient, you have lost every element of psychological advantage the K-9 presents with a mentally stable person. You have to assume it is extremely likely he will fire on the dog rather than throwing the gun down.

The plan might be I'll call out to him 3 times in rhythm. On the 4th beat, I'll send the dog. If he distracts in any way, drive into him. If he points in anybody's direction, take him out. Go. "Drop the gun or I'll send the dog!" "Drop the gun or I'll send the dog!" "Drop the gun or I'll send the dog!" Send the dog. Use this opportunity to improve your tactical position.

The dog was staring out in the brush. I thought, "I wonder why he's looking out in the brush. Should I go out in the brush?"

But this is only if you *have* to do something. Does this individual pose an immediate threat to anybody? Can you wait him out? Can you set up a perimeter, stay behind cover, talk to him, watch for that one overt movement, that unguarded moment? What does your department allow you to use as a decoy, a distraction to resolve the situation—to force the suspect's hand—besides K-9? Would gas be effective? How about a flash-bang grenade? How about a lot of flash-bang grenades? Why do you want to send the dog? What do you expect to accomplish?

You have about 1 millisecond to decide this.

You have hours to write about it later. That's why we value the cop who can paint a word picture to the court. Judge and jury need to be able to see and feel the situation as it happened to the officer. Put everything down—facial expressions, furtive movements. "I sent the dog hoping he would divert the suspect's attention. The dog ran from me straight toward the suspect. When the suspect swung the gun down and fired on the dog, I feared for my own safety." The ability of the officer to articulate the dynamics of a critical incident is invaluable.

Don't put the dog in harm's way needlessly.

Deputy Terry Fleck
El Dorado County Sheriff's Department,
South Lake Tahoe, California

I think there's a compromise between being overzealous—sending dogs on suicide missions that are clearly SWAT calls—versus being too conservative for fear of injuring your partner, friend, dog. We have to orient ourselves to using the dog as a tactical tool.

One night the watch commander was our K-9 sergeant who had just gone to K-9 officer survival school. We had a subject drunk with a handgun inside a house. The call was domestic violence. The female fled the residence. He's the only one inside, drunk with a gun. This particular watch commander made the decision to use the dog as a tactical tool to clear that house and to take the suspect into custody had it become necessary. That's becoming a logical trend, because it's not a SWAT call on the one side. But we need to use the dog as a tactical tool to prevent injury or death to an officer.

You can get into this big time. The urban officer isn't going to operate like the rural officer, and the rural guy's not going to operate like the urban cop. No doubt about it, small communities do things differently from downtown Los Angeles. Certainly tactics may vary, but officer safety is always first. The point is not what we do here versus what you guys do there. This is the point—combining safe tactics with use of the dog as a tactical tool to promote officer and public safety.

I had an armed robbery, kidnap, fleeing in a vehicle, vehicle overturned, suspect fled on foot and did what they typically do—he went to ground about 200 yards away. He hid out under a tree in a snow-well. When I arrived, I could see the officers' scuff marks going right past the tree in the hardpack. The suspect was hiding under there with the handgun watching them the whole time. They passed within arm's reach of him. The dog found the suspect and took him into custody within 60 seconds. Those are the ones that make our program: "Had it not been for the dog..."

Armed encounters: City cops are more likely to get into armed encounter situations than we are. Still we need to train for armed encounters, and we need to train with live fire so the dog doesn't become a liability. *"How you train is how you perform."* We used to isolate dog training from officer safety training. Not any more, you can't.

Impact weapon: Often overlooked by K-9 handlers. It's an excellent tactical tool just as your dog is a tactical tool. You may need 2 tools. Or one tool may be more advantageous than the other.

Maintenance training: "We're gonna go do tracks. We're gonna go lay out evidence. We're gonna do obedience. We're gonna go do drugs," isolated from reality. We need to create realistic scenario training, street calls where you roll right into them, do your search, do your track, do your evidence search. More in the context of in-progress calls. Robbery in progress, burglary in progress... Tough to do. Typically, SWAT trains probably second to the amount of training K-9 teams do. Do we just, "Three articles out. Find 'em. Good boy. Get back in the car." Or, "Track starts here. Harness up. Find 'em. Good boy. Get back in the car." Certainly advanced K-9 handler schools throughout the country are creating realistic scenarios based on actual incidents that have occurred.

Unlike mass production weapons, dogs are not alike in temperament or trainability. If you know the dog's aggression level is very high, I think you are going to have to be more conservative in deploying the dog and in controlling your suspect. You want to minimize damage in order to minimize your liability exposure. I hope the days are over where "the bigger the badder the dog, the badder you are in the biz." If the K-9 can't find the guy, it doesn't make any difference how aggressive the dog is. I think the searching skills of the dog are his most important capability. The aggression level of the dog must be sufficient but is not the ultimate test of the dog's skills.

I was very conservative in using my first German shepherd Dirk. I had to emphasize calloffs in maintenance training. My current police dog Blazer is a completely different temperament. I was looking for a softer dog because Tahoe has more SAR and hasty search type work.

This particular dog is almost like a human officer in that the more pressure you apply to him, the more he responds back. If you're passive and compliant you pretty much get a passive and compliant bite. Yet if you take this dog on, his aggression level increases.

To train K-9 cover officers in El Dorado, a medium-sized department, we provide a departmental class through our yearly advanced officer training. We go through the dog unit's capabilities, officers' function either as first reponder to that incident or as a cover officer, showing them what we'd like them to do ideally. Think dog if they can.

On an actual search, I tell my cover officer before we start what I want him to do. I caution him of the mistake backup officers typically make, "You're going to want to watch the dog. Watch from my shoulders on up. Watch my flanks. I'll watch the dog. I guarantee your safety as far as the dog is concerned."

My cover can be anywhere he wants to be between 90-270 degrees. Parallel to me or behind me. Just so he doesn't get out in front. Before K-9 was integrated into department procedure, officers failing to set up a perimeter or searching out ahead of the dog was a problem. Now they don't make that mistake.

The primary tactic is to build a strong framework to support the program before the dog teams go out on the street.

Communication is key—among K-9, patrol, and investigations officers.
— Detective DeAnna Stevens and K-9 Reicher

CHAPTER 2

Building The Police Dog Program

"I know to an absolute certainty these dogs are valuable tools.

They are less than lethal tools.

They find felony suspects.

But most important, they save policemen's lives."

—Lt. Edward Baker,
Los Angeles County Sheriff's Department, California.

United States police dogs began service in 1907, when patrol dog teams went on the street for South Orange Police Department, New Jersey, and New York City Police Department. Professor Samuel G. Chapman's book, *Police Dogs in North America* tracks the rise and fall of police canine programs up to the recent past. To their credit, these initial U.S. canine teams, frequently operating by trial and error, gained valuable experience that has produced high quality police dog teams, trainers, and technology. Besides exchanging information with Canada, Great Britain, Germany, France, and other nations that use police dogs, U.S. teams have developed effective ways to implement K-9 in this country where edged weapons and ballistic weapons are common on the street. The 1980s and 90s changed police dog programs as well as other areas of law enforcement. Federal civil rights actions, use of force cases, drug trafficking, economic feasibility—many issues affect police dog units.

Today, law enforcement has the tactical tools necessary to build effective police dog programs. *The primary tactic is to build a strong framework to support the program before the dog teams go out on the street.* Just as departments cannot arm police officers without adequate administrative, training, and operations procedures, so these departments need to build rather than backfill their K-9 programs. Administrative support, sound management policies, adequate training, documentation, and, most important, reliable performance—these essential factors determine if the K-9 program will serve as an asset or a liability to the department.

"You have to start from the top and address how you interact with superiors who do not have any technical background about dogs. If you cannot win over the support and understanding of people in key policy-making positions and decision-making positions, then you have problems, and your program is going to have problems. You can have the best training in the world, the animals and the most dedicated people, but minus these other components,

I believe you are going to have problems. There are also key governmental officials outside the department who also need some training and insight to make the program successful. The foundation you lay in that regard is important—county supervisors, city managers, district attorney, and city counsel."

—Sgt. Charlie Walters,
Orange County Sheriff's Department, California

"It is no secret that groups such as the Police Misconduct Referral Service are targeting police practices such as the use of police dogs for litigation. To this end, such groups are organizing comprehensive computer banks on agencies and even individual officers which they openly share with others engaging in litigation against law enforcement.

"Accordingly, it would seem incumbent upon those of us in law enforcement to become equally organized in our response to such efforts by these so-called watchdog groups. In addition to reviewing and, where appropriate, modifying your existing K-9 policies, it is highly recommended that trainers, administrators, K-9 associations and defense attorneys adopt a uniform standard consistent with these current legal standards. Otherwise, a valuable law enforcement tool could be seriously restricted if an unacceptable standard is forced upon us by those whose interests may be contrary to effective police work."

—Bruce D. Praet, Attorney,
Santa Ana, California

The philosophy of "If you don't put it in writing, it can't be held against you." fails when confronted by 42 U.S.C., §1983, the statutory basis for federal law suits, which requires proof that a specific policy or custom of the government caused the injury. Unwritten policies, if encouraged or allowed by a police agency to the extent that they become "customary" or show "deliberate indifference" regarding "patterns and practices" may serve as the basis of a Section 1983 action. While the existence of a police dog policy will not prevent the department from being sued, it may enable a successful defense in civil or criminal cases.

Law enforcement officers must consult their legal advisor. Some police procedures ruled permissible under Federal constitutional law are of questionable legality under State law or are not permitted at all. Conversely, some State law is more restrictive than Federal law. A determination of whether police dog team conduct amounts to excessive use of force or unreasonable search must take into account all of the circumstances surrounding the incident in each individual case. The courts are looking to the situation leading to the use of the police dog. There is no substitute for the actual authority or the advice of competent legal counsel. Note: Any change in department policy should first comply with the meet and confer process even though it may otherwise be consistent with the law.

Many States have laws similar to California *Penal Code* § 600:

(a)   felony to inflict serious injury on police dog; misdemeanor for non-serious injury

(b)   misdemeanor to interfere with or obstruct police dog

(c & d) penalty enhancements for related serious injuries to dog or another

(e)   mandatory restitution for veterinary bills, animal replacement and salary of handler for down time.

Officer Eric Distel of the Escondido Police Department provided the following account of his arrest of Robert L. Vera Cruz to Detective DeAnna Stevens (ital) of West Sacramento Police Department. At the time of the June 1998 interview, Distel had served Escondido Police for ten years as an officer, seven as a K-9 handler. His first K-9 partner of four years was Artus. His second K-9, Andy, attended the interview. Both German shepherds are family dogs that the Distels' two children enjoy and that assist in presentations to local schools.

Ninth Circuit Judge Alex Kozinski's opinion, which follows Officer Distel's account, crystallizes essential K-9 use of force concepts.

OFFICER ERIC DISTEL:

It was New Year's Day, 1992, about 10:30 at night. We had a radio call that there was an enraged, drunken male trying to break into a closed business. The employees who were closing the Del Taco phoned us and said there was a guy outside trying to scratch the windows, threatening to kill us, please get here. We were en route. Officers got there, and he was gone.

Officers spoke to the employees. They said he threatened to go get a weapon, specifically a gun, and come back and kill them. The officers left the scene. The employees continued to clean up.

Twenty minutes later I was parked up the street doing reports and the call came out again. I was close. I pulled into the parking lot of the business. I pulled up on the west side of the building and was able to look down the north wall. I saw that the back door was open. I saw Vera Cruz reaching into the building pulling out hoses and buckets. He was enraged, just crazy, and throwing them out into the driveway.

I was thinking, OK, I have a burglary in progress. He has made good on his threats. At this point he's actually in the building, and he's clearing a path to get to the employees. I look over. There's a light right above the door, and I saw one of those big Rambo-type survival knives strapped to his hip.

I get out of the car, grab the dog and yell to him, "Hey, I want to talk to you."

He looks at me and starts walking away.

I yell, "Stop, or I'll send the dog!"

I am thinking, he is armed, he is attempting to kill these people inside, he's obviously very violent and hostile, and he just committed a burglary. As soon as I told him to stop or I'd send the dog, he started running.

"Stop, or I'll send the dog!" He kept going.

I cut the dog loose. It was a very short chase. He took him down on the sidewalk.

This was my first dog and my first bite, the first real apprehension outside of a training scenario.

When you pulled around the back, you saw that you had a felony in progress. Had you already made the decision, if it goes bad, I'm utilizing the dog?

Keeping in mind the nature of the call, it would obviously depend upon the suspect's actions. As soon as he started running, and I saw the open back door and the knife, he punched his own ticket. The decision was already made as to what I would have to do. If I hadn't seen the door, the knife, he probably would not have been deployed. I would have just had a drunken guy running away.

You did have corroborating information that this guy wasn't there to just grab a taco and a soda. He was there earlier making threats. You already had information he was possibly armed with a gun as well.

He said he was going to go get a gun and come back.

So he comes out of the business and you do your announcement, stop or I'm going to send the dog, and he basically ignores you.

He starts running.

So he takes off and you deploy the dog. What else was going on? What were your thoughts?

As soon as he started running, I cut Artus loose. First time handler on your first bite, I remember thinking, I can't believe this guy's doing this. Because so many times before that, you know, you yell at people running, or you give your announcements—I give up, I surrender—and here's this guy who is that stupid to think that he could outrun a dog. He lost.

The dog took him down and he pitched forward on the sidewalk. The first thing I did, while the dog was on the bite, was I ripped the knife sheath off his belt and threw it aside.

While the dog was on the bite and I was disarming him, he kept pulling vigorously, and I told him, "Quit fighting the dog."

After I disarmed him I called the dog off right away, figuring we were just going to stay there waiting for cover. I had called for cover. Everything would be OK.

Well, after I called the dog off, the guy got up and started walking away! I walked behind him with the dog on lead. At that point, I did not perceive him as being a threat any more. I had him contained. I could hear the sirens in the distance. They were coming to help. So I just walked behind him until the first guys got there.

When they showed up, a couple officers took their sticks out and walked backwards up the street in front of him, while I walked behind him. We were trying to corral him from going any further or attacking us. I think what looked good for us later in court was the restraint used after the bite.

January 1st, I assume it's chilly in Escondido. What was this guy wearing?

A black leather jacket

You did not know if he was still armed, right?

Actually, I did not. I just ripped the knife right off his belt.

You made a conscious decision based on his demeanor not to use the dog again once he got up and walked off?

Yes. My cover officers showed a tremendous amount of restraint. They walked backwards with their batons at the ready, and I followed with the dog. Finally, at a telephone pole, he went down to his knees and we handcuffed him. The only actual use of force was when the dog bit him.

What type injuries did he sustain from the dog bite?

He sustained a laceration in the bicep/tricep area of his arm. That was not immediately apparent because he had the black leather jacket on. It was dark. His jacket was not terribly damaged. He said it hurt, but his clothes were not torn apart.

He was transported to the hospital and medically evaluated. Is that your policy?

Yes, for any K-9 contact. He was transported to the hospital by another officer with a back seat in his unit.

Can you tell some of the things you experienced incident to this situation?

Initially, one of the things that caused me stress was the district attorney's decision not to prosecute him for the resisting arrest, the drunk in public, the attempted burglary. It worried me. I had this bite, and our DA was not going to file on it. We would not get a conviction on it. He was just some poor drunk who got bitten. That ended up playing a large role in the federal trial.

Did your family suffer any consequences reference this incident?

To be honest, I was kind of a pill. My wife did not like it a whole lot. You want to lose about 10 pounds? Get sued.

What did you do to prepare to testify?

I went over the report, and I visualized myself being asked certain questions—very hard questions—and answering them. If I did not know the answers…you don't embellish or fabricate. If you don't know, you just say you don't know. Even though it is not good to have three years elapse between the time of the incident and the actual lawsuit, the time allowed me to mentally prepare to testify.

What was testifying like?

That was a little stressful. You do not want to take it personally. As a police officer, you protect and defend the Constitutional right to litigate. On the other hand, you do take it personally. They are accusing you of being a racist, of using excessive force with malice. You try to come across being calm and sincere, and be yourself. But they are going after your retirement, your kids' college, your house. I was a little nervous.

So there was a lot at stake there for you also. Describe your K-9 training in a nutshell.

Our K-9 unit has weekly training, four hours. Once a month we have an eight-hour training session. We have yearly certification that follows POST guidelines. We try to not just meet but go above those guidelines.

Reference POST guidelines, part of the evaluation is a hands-off callout. Do you practice this?

Constantly. Even though sometimes tactically you might not always want to out your dog verbally, just the repetition of doing it, having that level of control of your dog, is important. I have called Andy out at 300 feet. He drops, I call him back. If your dog will out verbally from 300 feet away—and Andy's a hard biter, not a soft show dog—then he will come off anywhere. I don't have to hit him with a flashlight.   I don't have to flank him.

How many dogs are in your agency?

Five. We are supposed to have six, but our staffing is a little low.

What other important things should handlers know?

Probably one of the least comfortable things about his case was the fact that it was my first bite. I have always been a good report writer, but this was my first bite report. I don't remember how many pages it was, but it was written in pencil. I tried to get as much stuff in there that, at that particular level of expertise, I thought was relevant.

Compared to the reports I am doing now, I should have done that one in crayon. It was so primitive. It lacked a lot of detail that I should have had in there. It was uncomfortable for me when I was testifying. At the point of testifying in the lawsuit, I had been a handler for four years, and I was kicking myself. Why did I forget to put that in there? Why did I phrase it like that? You just do not learn by that unless you have actually been through it.

It is very important to articulate the facts, even something we don't think is important or pertinent, but it is.

That is one of the things we try to do with all of the handlers we have gotten since then. We have brain-picking sessions where it is, hey, read my bite report and tell me about it. We will go over it and say, "Think about the way you stated this. Ask yourself this question. Answer that question." I developed a 25-point checklist, and I have them go through and outline in detail everything they should be addressing in court. A 10-second incident now is 10 pages single-spaced with aerial photographs and measurements.

Have you been sued since then?

One subsequent lawsuit that did not worry me that much. It was an armed robbery in a jewelry store. The guys were in a stolen car. They tried carjacking two people in the parking lot. It was a circus. Officers arrived, and they fired shots at the officers then ran and hid in some brush. My dog Artus found one of the guys. He started running, so Artus took him down. He could not find an attorney to represent him; he was in prison. So he tried doing the lawsuit himself. After he was deposed, he decided it would be wise not to pursue a lawsuit.

During a high stress incident the officer can experience a two-thirds loss of neurological activity, including tunnel vision, auditory blocking, and loss of fine motor coordination. The presence of the dog adds stress because he is one more responsibility for the officer. This additional stress has a positive effect if the dog and handler operate as a team.

OPINION BY: ALEX KOZINSKI, Circuit Judge (*Vera Cruz v. City of Escondido*, 139 F.3d 659 (9th Cir.1997))

We hold that deadly force under *Tennessee v. Garner*, 471 U.S. 1 (1985), means force reasonably likely to kill.

I

1992 did not start well for Robert Vera Cruz. After drinking more than two six-packs of beer on New Year's Day, he headed over to the local Del Taco restaurant. The Del Taco employees were cleaning up after closing and refused to serve Vera Cruz, who then challenged them to a fight. When the challenge was declined, Vera Cruz angrily hit the restaurant window and went home.

Just after returning home, Vera Cruz's thirst also returned and so he set out for the liquor store, which happened to be next door to the Del Taco. Before leaving, Vera Cruz strapped a knife to his hip—to protect himself from the Del Taco employees, he explained.

Responding to a call from said employees, Escondido Police Officer Eric Distel and his K-9 companion were the first to arrive at the scene. Distel spotted Vera Cruz in a doorway at the rear of the Del Taco throwing objects out of the building. When the officer identified himself, Vera Cruz began walking away.

Distel then warned Vera Cruz to stop or he would release the dog; Vera Cruz started running. After giving another warning, Distel released the dog, who bit Vera Cruz on the right arm, bringing him to the ground. After disarming Vera Cruz, Distel ordered the dog to release his bite, and the dog immediately complied. Vera Cruz sustained a large laceration and several puncture wounds on his upper right arm; he required surgery and eight days of hospitalization.

Vera Cruz sued the City of Escondido, its chief of police and several police officers, including Distel, under 42 U.S.C. § 1983, claiming he was the subject of an unreasonable seizure [*3] in violation of the Fourth Amendment. The jury found by way of a special verdict that the officer had not used excessive force. Vera Cruz moved for a new trial, arguing that the district court erred in refusing to instruct the jury on the deadly force rule of Garner. The Court there announced that police may only used deadly force "where the officer has probable cause to believe that the suspect poses a threat of serious physical harm, either to the officer or to others [.]" 471 U.S. at 11. The district court denied the motion, holding that "the evidence presented in this case would not permit a reasonable jury to find that the force applied against the plaintiff was deadly force." Appellant makes various claims; we consider here only the deadly force instruction. n1

n1 We address appellant's other claims in an unpublished disposition

II

While the Supreme Court in *Garner* established a special rule concerning deadly force, it did not explain what it meant by that phrase. n2 In fact, what the phrase means [*4] is far from obvious. Given the frailty of the human body, and the wide variety of conditions under which the police must operate, almost any use of force is potentially deadly: A suspect may slip, fall and sustain a lethal head injury, even though the police used only moderate force; a small cut, if left untreated, might become infected and cause death. Yet we do not read *Garner* as covering all uses of force that might result in death, no matter how remote the possibility. The question is, how likely must death be in order to consider the force deadly?

n2 This omission most likely is attributable to the fact there was no doubt in Garner that deadly force had been used because the police had shot and killed the fleeing suspect. Justice O'Connor in dissent expressed concern that the majority's sweeping language "unnecessarily implies that the Fourth Amendment constrains the use of any police practice that is potentially lethal, no matter how remote the risk." *Id.* at 31 (O'Connor, J., dissenting) (emphasis added).

[*5]

Vera Cruz urges us to adopt the Model Penal Code's definition of deadly force. According to the MPC, deadly force means "force that the actor uses with the purpose of causing or that he knows to create a substantial risk of causing death or serious bodily injury." Model penal Code § 3.11(2) (1962) (emphasis added). Vera Cruz argues that he was entitled to a deadly force instruction because he presented evidence that police dogs can cause serious bodily injury.

Although we have mentioned the "significant risk of death or serious bodily injury" formulation in three other dogbite cases, we have done so only in dicta. In fact, two of the cases simply refer to the fact that one of our colleagues relied on the MPC in his lonely effort to define deadly force in *Chew v. Gates,* 27 F.3d 1432, 1453 & n.4 (9th Cir. 1994) (Norris. J., concurring and dissenting). See *Quintanilla v. City of Downey,* 84 F.3d 353, 357 (9th Cir. 1996), ("Deadly force has been described as 'force that creates a substantial risk of causing death or serious bodily harm.'" (emphasis added)) cert. denied, 117 S. Ct. 972 (1997); *Fikes v. Cleghorn,* 47 F.3d 1011, 1014 (9th Cir. 1995) (deadly [*6] force "might be defined as force that creates a substantial risk of causing death or serious bodily harm (emphasis added)). The plaintiffs in those cases failed to present any proof that the dogs in question (or police dogs in general) were capable of causing more than "superficial bites" which did not "require serious medical attention." *Quintanilla,* 84 F.3d at 358. Thus, the earlier cases had no occasion to decide whether force likely to result in serious injury (but not death) amounted to deadly force.

Our case squarely presents this question. Vera Cruz himself required surgery and eight days of hospitalization. At trial, four witnesses testified that such injuries are not unusual; police dogs can—and often do--cause serious harm. One witness testified that he knew of cases where dogs had bitten a person on the face, bitten part of a person's nose off, bitten people in the genitals, and bitten a woman's breasts. At the same time, Vera Cruz presented no evidence that dogbites are likely to result in death. See p. 2927 and n.3 infra. This case, thus, requires us to decide whether force capable of inflicting serious--but not fatal--injuries qualifies as lethal force under *Garner.*

We now reject the MPC definition as inapposite to the Fourth Amendment context. The MPC definition and Garner's deadly force rule serve entirely different purposes: The MPC is designed to govern criminal liability; Garner's deadly force rule sets the boundaries of reasonable police conduct under the Fourth Amendment. We decline to put police doing their jobs in the same category as criminals doing theirs. Because criminal activities serve no legitimate purpose, there is no reason to spare criminals from even remote consequences of their actions: deterrence, by forcing criminals to assume responsibility for all the harm they cause by their anti-social conduct, is the very essence of criminal law. Law enforcement personnel, by contrast, serve important purposes; the risk of personal liability, if taken beyond its proper scope, may make police timid and deter activities necessary for our protection. Criminals, moreover, can largely control the circumstances of their crimes, and can thus

regard to their underlying intent or motivation." *Graham v. Connor*, 490 U.S. 396, 397 (1989) (emphasis added). Moreover, the MPC formulation, containing the disjunctive "or," would turn the deadly force rule into a "serious bodily injury" rule, rendering Garner's distinction between ordinary force and deadly force a virtual nullity. This is plainly not what the Supreme Court had in mind in Garner.

Other circuits do seem to have adopted the MPC's definition of deadly force, though none of those cases presented a record like ours. Two of the circuits--the Tenth in *Ryder v. City of Topeka*, 814 F.2d 1412, 1416 n.11 (10th Cir. 1987), and the Eleventh in *Pruitt v. City of Montgomery*, 771 F.2d 1475, 1479 n.10 (11th Cir. 1985)—dropped footnotes approving the MPC's definition in dicta. It's not apparent why they did so, since both cases involved shootings, which are clearly deadly force after Garner. See n.2 supra. And the Eighth Circuit in *Mattis v. Schnarr*, 547 F.2d 1007, 1009 n.2 (8th Cir.,1976) vacated as moot sub nom. *Ashcroft v. Mattis*, 431 U.S. 171 (1977), a pre-*Garner* case, also included the obligatory MPC footnote, but the issue of what constitutes deadly force was not even posed; the issue, rather, was whether deadly force could be used to stop a fleeing felon who himself had not used deadly force.

The most relevant out-of-circuit case is *Robinette v. Barnes*, 854 F.2d 909 (6th Cir. 1988), where the suspect was actually killed by a freakish dog bite. The court there did rely extensively on the MPC's definition, but it focused on the "substantial risk of causing death" prong of the definition, concluding that deadly force was not used because there was no showing that the unusual circumstances which resulted in the suspect's death were foreseeable. *Id.* at 912. Robinette did not consider the "substantial risk of causing . . .serious bodily injury " prong of the MPC's definition. Indeed, other language in Robinette suggests that the Sixth Circuit might follow our ruling if presented with an argument like that raised by *Vera Cruz*: "[T]he mere recognition that a law enforcement tool is dangerous does not suffice as proof that the tool is an instrument of deadly force." *Id.* at 913.

In short, the out-of-circuit cases, like our own earlier cases, are not very helpful because they did not confront the question presented here. Those courts seem to have seized the MPC's definition for want of anything better, but did not consider—had no reason to consider—how it would apply on a record like ours.

minimize the risk that force will be necessary; law enforcement [*7] personnel must take the situation as they find it.

The MPC's definition of deadly force is also at loggerheads with Fourth Amendment case law. A central consideration under the MPC's definition—the subjective intent of the actor—is an impermissible consideration in the Fourth Amendment context: While it makes perfect sense for criminal law purposes to consider whether "the actor uses [the force] with the purpose of causing or that he knows to create a substantial risk of causing death or serious bodily injury," the question in police brutality cases is "whether the officers' actions are 'objectively reasonable' in light of the facts and circumstances confronting them, without

As we read *Garner*, deadly force is that force which is reasonably likely to [*8] cause death. While there are few enough clues in *Garner*, our interpretation does find support in the Court's reasoning there. First, *Garner* noted that use of deadly force actually frustrates the interest of the criminal justice system because it's a "self-defeating way of apprehending a suspect... . If successful, it guarantees that [the criminal justice] mechanism will not be set in motion." 471 U.S. at 10. Second, the court concluded that any law enforcement benefits, such as discouraging escape attempts, don't outweigh a nonviolent suspect's fundamental interest in his own life. *Id.* at 10-11. Both of these considerations hinge on the assumption that the use of deadly force threatens a suspect's life. Were this assumption relaxed—say, by positing that deadly force need only cause serious bodily injury—these concerns would be implicated to a far lesser degree and the Court may well have struck the balance differently.

Vera Cruz presented no evidence that properly trained police dogs are reasonably capable of causing death. See *Don Burton, Inc. v. Aetna Life and Casualty Co.*, 575 F.2d 702, 706 (9th Cir. 1978) ("[A] litigant is entitled to have the jury charged [*9] concerning his theory of the case if there is any direct or circumstantial evidence to support it."). In fact, *Vera Cruz* presented no evidence at trial that police dogs can kill under any circumstances. n3

n3 At oral argument before us, plaintiff's counsel stated:

Number one there was testimony as to a number of deaths from police dog attacks. It came from Mr. Bogardus and Dr. Meade. There haven't been many; two or three was their testimony. Secondly, we have the testimony of the capacity of the dog to cause death.

After searching the record, we can find no such reference either to a number of deaths caused by police dogs or to their capacity to kill. Mr. Bogardus did testify about two incidents in which police officers were allegedly killed by suspects after releasing their dogs. R.T. vol. 3, at 409, June 22, 1995.

Nevertheless, we will assume that a properly trained police dog could kill a suspect under highly unusual circumstances. The prospect of such an aberration doesn't convert otherwise [*10] nondeadly force into deadly force. *Robinette v. Barnes*, 854 F.2d 909 (6th Cir. 1988) — the only reported case where a police dog actually killed a suspect — illustrates our point. In Robinette, the suspect bled to death after a police dog bit him on the neck. Apparently, the dog was trained to bite whatever part of the anatomy was nearest if an arm was unavailable and

the suspect had hidden under a car so that only his neck was exposed. *Id.* at 912. The *Robinette* court held that the use of the dog did not amount to deadly force because the outcome was "an extreme aberration [.]" *Id.* at 912. In judging whether force is deadly, we do not consider the result in a particular case — be it that the suspect was killed or injured — but whether the force used had a reasonable probability of causing death. Were the rule otherwise, all uses of force would be subject to *Garner's* deadly force requirements because almost any use of force could cause death under peculiar enough circumstances. To be entitled to a deadly force instruction, a plaintiff must present evidence that the force used, in the circumstances under which it was used, posed more than a remote possibility [*11] of death. n4 Because Vera Cruz presented no such evidence, the district court did not err in refusing to give a deadly force instruction.

n4 Whether a particular use of force is reasonably likely to cause death is a function of two factors: (1) the degree of force and (2) the accuracy with which it is directed at a vulnerable part of the human anatomy. The greater the force, the less accurately it need be directed to cause death. Thus, a bullet has such killing capacity that it will be deemed lethal if deliberately discharge in the general direction of the victim. But a bullet shot in the air as a warning will not be deemed deadly even if it accidentally hits a tree branch which falls and kills the suspect below.

AFFIRMED.

Summary: Watkins v. City of Oakland, 145 F.3d 1087 (9th Cir. 1998)

The question of whether a police canine was left on the bite for an unreasonable period of time is for the jury to decide.

In this case, Officer Chew and his canine, "Nero," responded to a silent alarm at a commercial warehouse. Four other officers also responded and they established a perimeter outside the warehouse after seeing a person running inside the building. There was no evidence as to whether the person was armed. Officer Chew gave two loud announcements: "This is the Oakland Police Department canine unit. Give yourself up or I'll release my dog who is going to find you and he is going to bite you." Plaintiff did not surrender to the police and claimed that he did not hear the announcements.

Officer Chew released Nero, a 72 pound German shepherd, to search. Nero ran out of sight of officer Chew, located Plaintiff who was hiding in a car, and bit him. Upon arriving at the scene, Officer Chew did not call Nero off of Plaintiff; instead, he ordered Plaintiff to show his hands. Plaintiff, who was recoiling from the dog's bite, failed to comply. Officer Chew then pulled Plaintiff out of the car onto the ground. Nero continued to bite until Plaintiff complied with Officer Chew's orders to show his hands. Officer Chew and another officer stated that ten to fifteen seconds elapsed between the time Officer Chew ordered Plaintiff to show his hands and the time Plaintiff complied with that order. Nero continued to bite Plaintiff throughout that period.

Officer Chew justified his delay in calling off Nero because plaintiff, while resisting the dog, failed to show his hands to prove that he was unarmed. Plaintiff explained that he did not show his hands because he was resisting the dog and recoiling from the pain of the dog's attack. Plaintiff further claimed that Officer Chew continued to allow Nero to bite him even though he was obviously helpless and surrounded by police officers with their guns drawn. Plaintiff was subsequently handcuffed, arrested and ultimately charged with burglary.

Plaintiff sustained multiple lacerations and punctures on his left foot and a jagged tearing of the skin exposing the tendons. X-rays taken at the hospital revealed fractures of the second and third metatarsals. Plaintiff underwent two skin graft surgeries and a year and a half after the incident, still suffered mobility problems and complained of pain.

Plaintiff filed a Section 1983 action against officer Chew, the Chief of Police, and the City claiming a violation of the Fourth Amendment prohibition on the use of excessive force in effecting the arrest. Specifically, Plaintiff contended that the duration and extent of force applied in effecting the arrest after the officers caught up with Nero amounted to an unconstitutional application of force.

The Defendants filed a motion for summary judgment based on qualified immunity. The district court denied the motion finding that Plaintiff had raised a genuine issue of material fact as to whether the force used against Plaintiff, including allowing Nero to continue biting him until he showed his hands, was reasonable under the circumstances.

The Court of Appeals affirmed the denial of summary judgment. The appellate court held that the law was clearly established "that excessive duration of the bite and improper encouragement of a continuation of the attack by officers could constitute excessive force and would be a constitutional violation." Since Plaintiff raised a genuine issue of material fact as to whether the actions of Officer Chew in allowing his dog to maintain the bite on Plaintiff were reasonable, the appellate court agreed with the district court that the jury must decide that issue.

POLICY ISSUES

The existence of a written policy is necessary to show that the use of the police dog as an instrument of force and as an instrument of search complies with general department policy, statutory requirements, and judicial rulings regarding the use of force and methods of investigation. The individual officer, line supervisor, and administrators incur liability for the actions of the police dog.

Policy should mirror case law. No written policy covers every situation. The courts have established a three-part test which should be applied to any situation where the use of a police dog is considered. First, the seriousness of the offense must be evaluated. Since some misdemeanors, such as brandishing a firearm, might warrant the use of a dog more than some felonies, such as a white-collar fraud, it is recommended that department policy call for an evaluation of the suspected offense, but not restrict it to felonies.

Keeping accurate records is a basic building block of police dog training.

The second factor which must be considered is the potential risk of harm to officers or others. Not only should this be part of the criteria in the department's policy, but handlers must articulate this and other factors in their reports (suspect fled prior to a justifiable check for weapons). The third factor is whether the suspect was actively resisting or attempting to evade arrest by flight. Although not all three factors must necessarily be met, it is suggested that flight from officers, without more, is not sufficient to warrant the use of a dog (the fleeing "suspect" could be innocent of any crime, or could even be a victim).

Avoid *shall* and escalation clauses in the policy. How can policy dictate beforehand which tool the patrol officer will use in any particular situation? In *Scott v. Henrich,* 39 F.3d 912 (9th Cir. 1994), Montana law enforcement officers were called to an apartment by a report of a suspect who had fired a gun and acted crazy. Banging on the door and identifying themselves, the officers saw, as the door opened, John Scott standing in the doorway pointing a long gun at them. The officers shot him. In the ensuing wrongful death case the court held that in determining reasonableness, whether the officer had less intrusive alternatives is irrelevant. Do not impose liability if none exists by law.

MODEL K-9 POLICY

FIELD SERVICES DIVISION
OPERATIONS ORDER ___

EFFECTIVE: _____

SUBJECT: GUIDELINES FOR THE USE OF POLICE SERVICE DOGS

PURPOSE: The purpose of this policy is to provide the _____ _____
Department with an internal set of guidelines for the use of police service dogs. This policy is not intended to provide the standard of care for any civil or other external proceeding and the determination of compliance with this policy is expressly reserved to internal proceedings within the _____ Department.

The decision to use a police service dog in accordance with this policy shall be deemed an act of discretion and shall be reviewed in light of information reasonably available to the officer(s) at the time the decision is made. The ultimate disposition of any related criminal proceeding shall have no bearing on determining the reasonableness of any such decision.

POLICE SERVICE DOG PROGRAM

I. POLICY

A. The police service dog program mission is to provide a reliable patrol dog capability through the employment of trained officer-dog teams to aid in law enforcement. The primary task of the canine team is search and apprehension of criminals. A police service dog may be used to apprehend an individual if the canine handler reasonably believes that the individual has either committed or is about to commit any offense and if any of the following conditions exist:

1. There is a reasonable belief that the individual poses an immediate threat of violence or serious harm to the public, any officer, or him/herself.

2. The individual is physically resisting arrest and the use of a police service dog appears necessary to overcome such resistance.

3. The individual(s) is believed to be concealed in an area where entry by other than the canine would pose a threat to the safety of officers or the public.

4. It is recognized that situations may arise which do not fall within the provisions set forth in this policy. In any such case, a standard of reasonableness shall be used to review the decision to use a police service dog in view of the totality of the circumstances.

NOTE: Absent the presence of one or more of the above conditions, mere flight from pursuing officer(s) shall not serve as good cause for a canine apprehension.

B. Prior to the use of a police service dog to search for or apprehend any individual, the canine handler or supervisor at the scene shall carefully consider all pertinent information reasonably available at the time. This information shall include, but is not limited to:

1. The individual's age or an estimate thereof,

2. The nature of the suspected offense involved,

3. Any potential danger to any other police officers who may attempt to intervene or assist with the apprehension,

4. Any potential danger to the public which may result from the release of a police service dog.

C. Unless it would otherwise increase the risk of injury or escape, a verbal warning followed by a reasonable period of compliance shall precede the release of any police service dog.

D. A department supervisor shall be notified as soon as practicable following any police service dog apprehension.

E. Prior to going off duty, the canine handler shall complete all necessary reports associated with the use of a police service dog in an apprehension.

NARCOTIC DETECTOR DOG PROGRAM

I. POLICY

A. The Canine Detection Program mission is to provide a practical and credible statewide drug detection capability through the employment of trained officer-dog teams to aid in the investigation, apprehension, and prosecution of persons engaged in illegal drug activities. The primary task of the canine team is to locate drugs (controlled substances, narcotics).

B. The drug detector dog may be used to:
1. Search vehicles, buildings, parcels, areas or other items deemed necessary;
2. Obtain a search warrant by using the dog in support of probable cause;
3. Assist in the search for narcotics during a search warrant service;
4. Assist in drug education programs for the Department.

C. The drug detector dog will not be used to search a person for drugs. If a drug dog alert causes the officer to believe that a person may be in possession of drugs, the officer in charge of the investigation will determine how to proceed. Personal possessions may be searched by the dog only if removed from the person.

D. The decision to use the dog rests solely with the dog's handler. The handler is responsible for the deployment of the dog as a method of investigation.

E. The drug detector dog team may be available for use by other law enforcement agencies. Requests by other agencies must be approved by the canine supervisor and will be considered on a case by case basis.

F. Training of the drug detector dog will be conducted by the Department designated trainer using actual controlled substances as training aids. The controlled substances will be secured at each Department designated facility, and all personnel will adhere to established procedures for access, accountability, and use.

G. The drug detector dog handler will keep a log of all training and searches performed by the canine. It is important to use the dog team as frequently as possible in order to build expertise and credibility.

TYPICAL ELEMENTS OF K-9 PROGRAM PROCEDURES

Procedures delineating the tactical use of the police dog must be in compliance with overall department policy and must be revised periodically to meet the changing dynamics of the street as well as judicially mandated requirements. The K-9 unit generally supports all divisions within the department. Each department will set up its K-9 command based on the size of the agency and tasks assigned to the dog teams. Elements each department must consider include:
- Central command or parallel structures within substations/precincts?
- Organized under the patrol section or a special enforcement bureau?
- Commanding officer(s) of the police dog unit?
- Selection, rank, and responsibilities of the dog unit supervisor?
- Will that supervisor himself normally be a K-9 handler?
- Does the department encourage members to assist in dog training, and are all members assisting the police dog unit by acting as suspects/offenders or as assistants for detector dog teams considered to be acting within the scope of their departmental duties and employment for purposes of employee benefits and protections?

K-9 commander duties typically include:
- Supervise K-9 operations
Note: When a dog is injured (trauma or narcotic ingestion), the supervisor can assist dispatch in notifying the veterinarian, advising the mechanism of injury, vital signs, physical assessment, method of transport, and requesting care instructions. The high level of risk to human lives prohibits rushing the canine, Code 3, to definitive care.
- Liaison with the trainer
- Knowledge of dog training and operations
- Maintain policy and procedures
- Coordinate handler and dog selection
- Budget proposals
- Equipment maintenance
- Training sites and personnel
- Supervise K-9 records and prepare statistical reports
- Coordinate intra- and interagency training
- Coordinate incident review procedures
- Coordinate police K-9 trial participation.
- Coordinate public education/demonstrations

K-9 equipment includes:
- Dog team equipment (collars, leads, feed, groom, kennel, transport)
- Veterinary service (emergency medical supplies, drug antidotes)
- Training equipment (protective equipment, all training aids)
- Drug dog teams (drugs, acquisition, storage, accountability procedures)

San Francisco International Airport Police Bomb Dog Unit with Air Force One.

- Agility course (climbs, tunnels, jumps, mobile and stationary obstacles)
- K-9 vehicles (identification, interior modifications, K-9 exit system)
- K-9 officer uniforms

THE K-9 OFFICER

What we are dealing with in law enforcement is a situation that does not even exist in a wartime environment. We have placed people in urban warfare-type situations for *20 years* with no relief. K-9 officers in particular are on the front lines. Typically, a city K-9 officer will have three calls waiting when he goes on shift, then dispatch keeps updating the call. He is responding to a burglary when he gets diverted to go to an armed robbery. Before he clears that call, he is called to a suspect shooting at such-and-such location. By the time you finish your shift things may have slowed down, but there are the reports. There is court the next day. No wonder some officers have to *shut down* in order to survive.

We have not had a chance to study these officers—how they got there or what kind of people they were when they started. We have no idea if the people who started resembled the people who are out there now, 10 to 20 years later. What we may in fact be doing is pushing human beings beyond the limits they are equipped to handle, physically and psychologically. We see people getting sick due to stress and retiring early due to stress.

When you talk about a police officer who is using his dog for a forty hour week then adding 30-40 hours overtime on top of that... Maybe there should be federal regulations on the number of hours a police officer can work. Pilots are regulated. Engineers on trains and other forms of transportation employees are regulated. But they do not monitor police officer time.

—Bill Schroeder, K-9 Trainer

Like big city jurisdictions, small rural agencies try to maintain adequate police coverage with reduced budgets. Despite mutual aid response, however, the K-9 officer in a typical town or rural community often finds himself responding to high risk calls without backup or waiting a long time for cover. Working alone as well as working overtime challenges rural K-9 officers.

Selecting the right officer to be a police dog handler is just as important, if not a higher priority, than selecting the dog. The candidate must be a competent police officer first, a K-9 handler second. Most departments require potential handlers to be off probation and to have patrol experience. Obligating handlers to a minimum number of years in the dog unit helps insure the agency will recover its investment. The K-9 officer must have maturity, initiative, health and fitness, affection, and enthusiasm for the working dog, and a lifestyle suited to handling a police dog. He needs strong verbal and written communication skills. He should be prepared to work night shifts, weekends, and emergency callouts. The time demanded by police dog service prevents most handlers from serving in other special units.

K-9 officer duties include:
• Effective use of the police dog
• Canine health and safety
• K-9 vehicle and equipment maintenance
• K-9 skills advancement by training
• K-9 reports
• Public relations, education and demonstrations

Some departments require the officer to complete duty in other units, such as the jail division, before applying to serve in the K-9 unit. In most departments the K-9 applicant must, as a minimum, have completed his probationary period (typically one year) as a newly hired officer. Service as a police dog handler is a highly desired position in most medium to large departments. The selection process is frequently competitive. Some departments rotate officers through special units, such as motors, investigations, SWAT, or K-9. Some permit the handler to work in the dog section as long as his dog remains in service. Other departments allow their handlers to obtain replacement dogs as necessary and to remain in K-9 for a specified period of time, or for as long as they meet the standards. Handlers working for small departments tend to have more influence on K-9 policy and procedure in general, service guidelines in particular.

Departments that make a practice of rotating officers through K-9 are usually the same departments with time limits for service in other specialized areas, such as narcotics. In his book *Undercover Operations Survival in Narcotics Investigations*, Tony Alvarez, Los Angeles Police Department, uncovers the faulty reasoning displayed by this practice:

"Rotating officers in and out of the specialized assignment is more of a politically expedient statement than a cure to avert future corruptive practices.

"We in law enforcement recruit our people from the society at large. To my knowledge there is no way that the process will expose all of the bad apples applying to be police officers. Management has to prepare themselves in order to expose and stop these bad apples which end up embarrassing and corrupting other officers. If management places the right policies and safeguards in place, along with the proper audits, these occurences would be minimal.

"Certainly, rotating officers will not stop corruption from taking place. As a matter of fact, if the officers going into a narcotics assignment are aware of the short duration, they will not be as dedicated as they should be towards the job and the section for which they will work."

The illogic of across-the-board time limits for K-9 handlers is underscored by the success of units which encourage their police dog teams to stay with the program. One department had "officers of the year" emerge for several years from their K-9 unit. Like any special assignment, performing expertly as a police dog handler does not happen overnight. Not even in two or three years. Experienced handlers verify it takes a couple of years just to get up to speed with a new canine partner. Performing reliable search or detection work is formidable, demanding far more energy, ingenuity, and initiative than many officers realize when they begin.

When a large department opened several K-9 positions for highway interdiction, a bright, motivated officer who was working a major drug pipeline applied to be a handler. He was chosen and sent to a large private vendor that imported foreign trained dogs. After a short introductory period with the vendor, he and his new dog started working the highway. The dog was brilliant. They immediately began making narcotic arrests. However, life with a dog required major adjustments for the officer, who called up a nearby K-9 handler one night to ask how to make the dog stop barking so he could sleep.

Cut loose without any provision for regular training, the officer got creative and amassed an impressive record of dope and money seizures. On the way he developed love and respect for the canine. Nine months later the officer was moved to another position, and the dog changed to a different handler.

Here was a team doing outstanding work, with a handler who, mostly through his own initiative, had developed a strong working relationship with his animal. The department's reaction was to reassign the officer. In a system like this, where is the motivation to perform high calibre work on the street?

Many officers view the police dog as an assist in the corporate-style agility course of agency promotions. K-9 becomes an elite unit with goals unrelated to employing the dog's special powers. Staff officers typically make more money than line officers. Competition gets fierce at the upper levels of the management pyramid. What many agencies fail to consider and incorporate into their planning is that most of the exciting, original work to be done in law enforcement happens on the street. We need highly intelligent, inquisitive minds there. This is especially true in K-9, where the full potential of the police dog has yet to be realized.

Term limits mitigate against K-9 in another very important way. Knowing the assignment cannot be permanent, the typical handler will not invest the effort necessary to understand the dog's perception. Reading the dog is literally everything. Extensive police academies teach officers to pay attention to their own perception, their fellow officers' perceptions, suspects' perceptions. Every level of the agency recognizes it takes time in service, a significant amount of time, to grow skillful reading ourselves, our partners, and the bad guys. Perception is the essence of police work. Tactics is the game of perception.

Debra Freeman's Smokey

K-9 introduces another player in that game. Four legs and a tail, certainly, but a player with a will that must be understood and controlled by the handler. The dog cannot be allowed to make decisions or act on his own. But his value lies in his heightened level of perception, frequently far superior to individuals on either side of the crime line.

THE POLICE DOG

Police dogs, like police officers, *are individuals*. The successful service dog program recognizes the importance of selecting the right officer, the right dog, and developing the relationship between the two as a team.

A classic study of dog behavior by John L. Fuller and John Paul Scott was undertaken to increase knowledge about the effect of genetics on the behavior of human beings. The scientists chose the dog for their study, "because it shows one of the basic hereditary characteristics of human behavior: a high degree of individual variability." Michael Fox and Randall Lockwood have explained how such diversity benefits the wolf pack. In a social unit characterized by hierarchy, cooperation, and division of labor, a range of temperaments is necessary. Only one wolf can be the alpha. As a rule only one female at a time can bear young. Society requires the timid as well as the aggressive, the deliberate as well as the impulsive, followers as well as leaders. Variety of temperament is another of the traits that qualify the dog for pethood. The unique relationship between dogs and people is enhanced by the fact that a dog can be found to match almost every human personality.

C.O. Whitman, as quoted by Konrad Lorenz in *Man Meets Dog*, said that the decline of instinctive behavior is: "the open door through which the great teacher, Experience, can enter and bring about all the wonders of the intellect." "When the dog is fully mature," Seeing Eye's trainer Doug Roberts said, "a special sort of bonding occurs where the dog feels like it is part of the person. You don't get that in many human-dog associations. You can get really close attachment between the pet owner and his pet...but the twenty-four-hour-a-day *I'll take care of you* association, that's a bit different."

Michael Fox wrote in *The Soul of the Wolf*: "Man has made the dog in his own image." Man is the God of the dog universe. Bill Koehler says that dogs have knowledge of right and wrong, but of course it is man who defines the terms and metes out the appropriate reward or punishment. Koehler says, "Come, sit, down, stay—that's not really dog training. What you're trying to do is get the dog to be responsible for his own actions, so that when he has to avoid a dog fight, stay out of trouble, or remain on a sit-stay or a down-stay on a blanket with six other dogs and you're a quarter of a mile away, he knows that if he moves, God is gonna strike him dead on the spot, or you're gonna come flying through the air and make a correction."

Besides their voices—barking, growling, whining—dogs use their bodies to express a wide range of feeling, including fear, dominance, aggression, submission, affection, and playfulness, through various body positions combined with eye, ear, mouth, and tail signals. For this reason, when "reading" a dog, it's important to evaluate the whole dog, not just its ears or its tail. A wagging tail, for example, is not always friendly. An upright, stiffly wagging tail combined with a direct stare and a snarl is a strong aggressive statement meaning watch out! Loose, free tail wagging indicates a general friendliness or excitement on search.

Body position can either be expansive, contracted, or neutral. Expansive body position means the dog literally expands its body and its movements. It may raise its hackles, hold its tail erect, arch its neck, and prick its ears. Expansive, outgoing displays are generally either aggressive, confident, or playful. Contracted displays, on the other hand, express either fear, defensive aggression, or submission. In these cases, a dog makes itself smaller by flattening its ears, drawing its head in, tucking its tail between its legs and lowering its body in an attempt to take up less space and become as inconspicuous as possible. Some dogs, like people, will assume as part of their character either a contracted or expanded demeanor, so it is possible with some degree of accuracy to evaluate the personality, as well as the emotional state and intent, of an individual dog by the way it carries its body, head, and tail.

The head is particularly important. A dog that is barking and snarling out of fear will show clearly fearful body language: a crouching body tilted back, away from the object of aggression; ears back, tail down with rear body muscles tensed and pulling back, lips pulled back revealing the teeth. This dog would probably rather escape than attack. On the other hand, a barking dog showing expanded, dominant body language—tail up, ears pricked, neck arched—is announcing its offensive, rather than defensive, attitude.

People sometimes think a dog that barks and shows a lot of teeth is a good candidate for a police dog. Generally this is not the case. Neither is the dog that tries to dominate every encounter, including his relationship with people. The extemely defensive or prey-driven or hyperactive dog will be detrimental to law enforcement. The dog that shows displacement, refusing to confront challenging or threatening situations, will not do police work. The dog that is a reject from someplace else, the dog that has not been allowed to interact with people, that has been constantly kenneled, the dog that has schizophrenic tendencies may actually develop schizophrenia and will be a liability to law enforcement.

L. David Mech writes in *The Wolf*:

"A pattern of behavior involves the entire animal. Usually there is a rearrangement of the posture and position of most parts of the body, and there may also be whimpering, growling, or other sounds. Perhaps certain changes in body odor also occur, but little is known about this. To a human being the most obvious aspect of behavior is the visual.

In 1950, Scott described the visible aspects of fifty common behavior patterns in dogs and discovered that most of these patterns had also been reported in wolves. All but one of those that had not been observed in wolves have since been witnessed by researchers at the Chicago Zoological Park (Ginsburg, 1965).

"Different behavior patterns result from various combinations of the wolf's basic motor capacities which are similar to those of the dog. Scott (1950) described these motor capacities as follows: 'The dog is capable of moving the neck and trunk in the limited way characteristic of most mammals.

The police dog is sound, stable, and friendly with family members, including the children. A strong social drive with the desire to play is essential. Do not leave small children alone with any large dog.

Response to stress: positive v. negative.

Responsiveness to the handler balances high drive.

The legs are chiefly capable of flexion and extension in the sagittal plane, and the front legs are capable of a limited amount of adduction...The ears may be held erect or depressed. The tail may be moved down or up and may be wagged from side to side. The facial muscles are capable of considerable movement during emotional expression, although not so much as in man.'

"Schenkel (1947; 1968) studied most of the wolf's social behavior patterns in detail, and the following discussion is based on this work. It deals mainly with behavior termed 'agonistic,' that is, having to do with social competition. Schenkel recognized three levels of expression in wolves, although he felt that it is *impossible to define accurate limits to them* (italics added). One level involves the peripheral structure of the body such as the face and scent organs. A second level involves 'nondirected' behavioral changes, for example erection of hair, changes in breathing rate, and reactions of the pupils. The third level of expression includes social behavior that is clearly directed toward another wolf (or by the police dog toward another dog or human being), and that may involve reaction, social exploration, and social impression all at the same time. Examples are threat, bluff attack, and invitations to play. Although these levels are discussed separately, in expressing each psychological state in the wolf (or the dog) they actually react together."

European trainers have for many years identified multiple character traits and drives describing dog behavior relevant to basic needs, protection, and search. Police dog trainers have refined these definitions for K-9 officers evaluating canine fitness for police service. Any trait in the extreme or any drive in excess is undesirable. For example, bravery to its absolute degree (fearlessness) is not found in normal individuals, for it would negate completely some responses necessary to self-preservation. Similarly, a dog with extreme prey drive that goes into a focused "feeding frenzy" when biting during an apprehension will not call off reliably.

Equally important, the lack of a trait or drive may disqualify a dog for police work. For example, a dog lacking aggression may make a good pet but not a police dog. A dog lacking search drive will have limited capacity as a police patrol dog. And a dog lacking trainability should not be a working dog.

Drives may interfere with each other or mask deficiencies. For example, a dog lacking aggression may show displacement, substituting an excessive activity drive for lack of other drives needed for police work. The dog with an extreme drive to gain rank will repeatedly challenge the authority of his handler.

Other drives not identified here, hunger and reproduction to name two, may interfere with or enhance these working drives. Like his wolf ancestors, the dog is basically a pack animal. The handler and his family are his ordered pack. The K-9 handler and his family must maintain ascendancy, that is controlling influence, over the police dog.

Dogs are opportunists. As Mech points out in *The Wolf*, the lines distinguishing the details of character and drive are impossible to define precisely. It is well known certain handlers

The stopping power of canine contact.
Butte County Assistant Sheriff Jim Nylander and K-9 Enz.

CHARACTER TRAITS

POSITIVE:
- Sound temperament: the dog's attitude toward life
- Courage/Bravery/Hardness: positive response to stress (genetic)
- Confidence: positive response to stress (conditioned)
- Normal sensory threshold: lowest level stimulus eliciting a response

NEGATIVE:
- Softness/Shyness: negative response to stress
- Sharpness: excessively aggressive response to stimuli

DRIVES IMPORTANT TO A POLICE DOG

AGGRESSION:
- **Fight**: attack perceived adversary
- **Defense**: stand ground, fight if attacked
- **Prey**: kill prey
- **Rank**: achieve higher status in the pack
- **Protection**: defend the pack
- **Guard**: defend territory
- **Survival**: defend self

SEARCH:
- **Hunt**: pursue object out of sight
- **Track**: work ground scent
- **Air Scent**: work windborne scent
- **Retrieve**: bring object back to the pack
- **Homing**: return to territory or the pack

SOCIABILITY:
- **Play**: achieve physical contact with the pack
- **Pack**: achieve emotional contact with the pack
- **Activity**: move and act (running the fence, digging chewing, turning circles...)
- **Trainability**: obey the pack leader (handler)

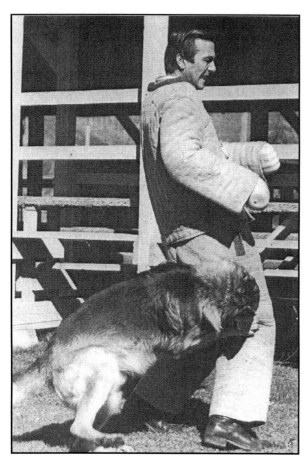

can compensate for or reinforce certain drives. The courageous, friendly dog with strong drive who enjoys expansive behavior shaped and controlled by training makes the best police dog. Regardless of sex or breed, every dog must be evaluated and selected for use based on individual merit. Ultimately, the dog and handler must be evaluated as a team.

"Look at that dog. You'd say he's not a day over four. He has the classic lines, a hard dog with an extremely high drive level. He's interested in searching, and he's very street smart. You watch that dog. When the car slows down, he's scanning, he's real tuned in on searching. Most people who've been bitten and whom we've arrested tell me afterward, boy, that's a nice dog. That is a really well trained dog."

— K-9 Sergeant

The long-term effect of stress or overtime on police dogs has yet to be studied extensively. Stress affects other types of working dogs, such as guide dogs and herding dogs. Logically for K-9s, as for police officers, an increase in the level and frequency of job related stress will decrease the dog's service life. The high burnout rate (two years) of some city police dogs supports this theory. But many variables, not the least being the dog's innate character and the handler himself, affect the dog's ability to perform police work.

Clearly the dog's reliability depends on his handler's ability to read and control him. The handler should recognize fatigue or stress related behavior in his dog and take appropriate action as he would for any medical dysfunction.

A strong aggressive drive is important, not only for making arrests but also to maintain the energy and endurance necessary for day-to-day patrol. Pursuing and apprehending an offender calls upon the dog's search and aggression drives. Fight and protect instincts are important if the offender tries to defeat the dog or attacks the officer.

As shown in Figure 2, most police dogs behave positively in the presence of others. The typical K-9 is reported to be friendly, affectionate, relaxed and playful with the officer's spouse, partner and children, and the majority react the same way toward other people in general. Fewer than half reportedly react in a protective or potentially aggressive manner to people at the officer's home.

"K-9s are excellent, positive community relations." They are "social with children and the public, a requirement for service dogs." Other attributes include friendly, tolerant, approachable, and stable.

Handlers indicated that fellow officers' reactions to the K-9 are largely positive: 82.2% like the dog, are friendly or play with the dog. Other officers respect the K-9 for its value as a tool and as a result of successful arrests. Only 10.4% are reported as afraid or showing apprehension toward the K-9. Fewer (8.7%) do not like the program.

Officers have a remarkably extensive and close relationship with their K-9s, even though they may not spend a decade with a single dog. The handler is fully responsible for managing all of the dog's activities. At home, over ninety percent of the officers said the police dog is treated as a loved family pet. They typically pet the dog, talk to the dog, and over half brush their dogs daily. Many dogs sleep inside the home or in kennel runs. The mean time spent playing with the dog was 5.7 hours per week. Many indicated "a lot" or "daily" play. Play and exercise are known stress release activities for canines. —UC Davis "Police K-9 Study," proceedings of the Western Society of Criminology Conference, February 24-27, 1994.

COMPARISON: MAN v. DOG

HEARING
> MAN: 20 to 20,000 cycles per second
> DOG: 20 to 35,000-70,000 cycles per second

The police dog hears much better than his handler.

SEEING: The dog has muted color to color-blind sight. The dog has better aptitude than man for identifying moving objects, even in low light conditions. Dogs have a wider scope of vision due to eye placement on the dog's head.

TOUCHING: *Nosing, licking, and pawing* gives the dog important tactile information about the source material.

SCENTING: The police dog has about 200 million olfactory receptors in his nose, 20 times the number in man's. *Scent or odor: Airborne molecules that activate the sense of smell upon contact with the individual's nasal receptors.* The brain perceives scents when the dog inhales through the nose or mouth. Odor molecules reach the mucus-coated olfactory epithelium, where nerve cells extend from the outside environment directly into the brain. Unlike other neurons, these constantly replicate. Scent molecules bind to receptors on hairlike cilia, and the neurons fire messages directly to the brain's olfactory center, for example the scent of a particular offender, his track, a drug, or other odor the dog is detecting. Laboratory tests have demonstrated a mouse can discriminate genetic differences among its potential mates by smell alone. It is a considerable step from the recognition of genetic individuality among rodents to the identification and tracking of individual human subjects by dogs. However, the relatedness of the mammals, a class of vertebrates that evolved less than 100 million years ago, leads us to think that what applies to the mouse and the rat will apply at least to other mammalian species with an adequate sense of smell, such as the canine.

Figure 2

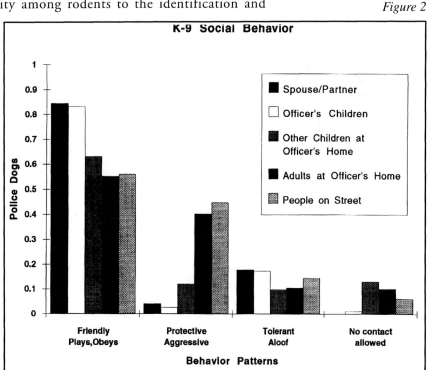

Every human body is a scent signature. Because no one can interview a dog, experts theorize how a dog determines a person's direction of travel or discriminates for one person's track. All types of odors diffuse from us and mark us as individuals: shoe materials, clothing, perfume, and particularly sweat, carrying such chemical messages as epinephrine, the primary component of fear scent. Also, human bodies constantly shed microscopic flakes of dead skin and gases, leaving a trail of decomposing, odorous particles. Dogs tend to follow the freshest human scent, particularly scent held in vegetation crushed underfoot. Most police dogs air scent or trail with their heads up scanning the air. Some are trained to track, detailing the ground picture to find the man.

Researchers have conducted specialized, limited data studies to determine how different interfering chemicals affect canine scenting. Extensive work remains to be done in this field in order to predict how capable the dog will be in a variety of circumstances. Each dog and search area varies significantly. Variables include:

DOG AND HANDLER
> Training
>
> Experience
>
> Performance

SEARCH AREA
> Type—open area, building, vehicle
>
> Temperature and Humidity
>
> Distractions

TIME
> Recovery time, important if the dog is exposed to volatile chemicals then allowed to air, or breathe uncontaminated air
>
> Exposure time, important if the dog has to search through interfering scent
>
> Time of the incident, important if the dog has to track
>
> Length of time the source has been in place
>
> Time of day or night

SCENT
> Vaporization
>
> Diffusion

Trainers differentiate between chemical reactions that occur in the nasal passages to inhibit scenting and masking scents that the dog may ignore naturally or learns to work through by training. Fever and certain drugs damage the dog's scenting capability. A dog with an elevated body temperature induced by working in hot conditions may look like he is sniffing while he actually smells little or nothing. Certain compounds have their own strong, characteristic odors—coffee, garlic, cooking fish, dirty sox, for example. These scents probably do not attack the dog's nasal receptors. He can probably ignore these scents or learn to detect the presence of certain odors despite the masking scents. Dogs have demonstrated their ability to work through tear gas and smoke, but it is unknown what percentage reduction in scenting acuity, if any, may occur.

Certain compounds may cause dysosmia, for example, some cleaning agents, deodorizers, alcohol based perfumes, paint fumes, petrochemicals such as gasoline. Carpet cleaners are notorious, possibly because dogs sniff the floor more frequently than other places. The combinatorial effect with nasal membranes is unknown, as well as the longevity of the effect.

Auto exhaust inhibits canine scenting ability. Beyond the mechanical blockage of the olfactory receptors by vehicle emissions, there is evidence the gases actually disable receptor cells by chemical reaction. We know that sniffing enough exhaust fumes long enough will kill a man or a dog. This has implications for the police dog riding to the scene or sitting in a patrol vehicle at the scene waiting to be deployed.

The receptor cells in the dog's nose replace themselves under normal healthy conditions. We believe that airing the police dog's nose after exposure to certain chemicals will help his scenting ability.

POISON CONTROL CENTERS

Sniffing and contacting chemicals endangers police dogs. *Alerting the local veterinarian should be the K-9 handler's first line of defense against the negative effects, potential or actual, of any specific chemical.* With several hundred thousand potentially toxic substances on the market, it is impossible to remain knowledgeable of their toxicities. Poison control centers located throughout the United States and Canada have been organized to aid physicians, veterinarians, and others in health-related fields with information on poisons and the treatment of poisoning. All available information on the toxic ingredients in thousands of medicines, insecticides, pesticides, and other registered commercial products as well as controlled substances has been placed confidentially by the government in these poison control centers. As new products are marketed or illegal drugs appear, information regarding the toxic ingredients is forwarded to the centers.

NATIONAL ANIMAL POISON CONTROL CENTER (NAPCC)

1-900-680-0000
(Caller pays on phone bill.)
1-888-4-ANI-HELP
1-888-4-264-4357
(Credit card)

POLICE DOG SELECTION
AND ACQUISITION

The department trainer should evaluate all candidate dogs, both untrained and pretrained dogs, for service potential. Criteria include:

- **Age:** Mature, usually 18 months to 4 years
- **Breed:** Working dog with adequate size to assist arrests; deterrent image for psychological impact; physically capable of performing the required search tasks
- **Sex:** Intact male or spayed bitch
- **Health and physical fitness:** X-rays and medical evaluation by the department veterinarian
- **Character and drive for police work:** Aggression for patrol tasks; search drive for detection tasks; sociability for public relations tasks and off-duty life

The importance of selecting a police dog with sound temperament and balanced drive cannot be overemphasized. Unsound dogs are being sold to some police agencies. The liability certain agencies and individual officers are incurring as a result of bad practices in the industry has a negative affect on all agencies with K-9 units. The police dog should not have to be kenneled outside the handler's home at all times off duty because he is a liability to the officer or the officer's family. It is irresponsible for any department to allow a dog on the street that is unsafe or out of control.

During a familiarization period, the trainer should assist the officer to determine if he can bond and work effectively with a particular dog. Other considerations:

- Who is responsible for locating candidate police dogs?
- Who pays for the purchase of the dog?
- Who retains legal ownership of the dog?
- Who pays for food, medical care, and other dog expenses?
- After the officer's commitment to the unit is complete, will he have the option of purchasing the dog from the department?
- Will department owned dogs be used for breeding?
- Will any special provisions/requirements be made for retired police dogs in order to mitigate liability?

RECORDS

Departments should place *commendations for restraint in the use of force* in the K-9 officer's personnel file. Keep the K-9 records in the officer's personnel file to give them peace officer protection. Dog training records should stay with the department in the handler's file, not with the trainer, in case the trainer leaves. Keep all records on the history of each dog. Lawsuits often occur *years* after the incident.

Documented training and evaluation of the police dog team is essential to your department. You may never be sued, but you must be ready. Document all training, training problems and the corrective action taken to solve those problems. Be honest, as a jury *will not believe* that a dog or handler has *never* had a problem in a training exercise or on the street. Show what was done to correct the problem and *that it was corrected.*

Maintaining separate report forms for specialized tasks makes it easier to prepare court testimony for crosstrained dogs (e.g. narcotics tracking). Creating separate computer files for specialized K-9 tasks simplifies statistical analysis.

If a dog bite occurs, the K-9 officer should report to the supervisor for the investigation. *Have a single supervisor approve all reports related to the same incident to avoid discrepancies.* For example, the time of the dog apprehending the suspect v. the time of the handcuffing as reported in the handler's report and other reports and logs. Officers involved in the incident should not describe the dog's action in their reports but should refer to the K-9 officer's report. *The K-9 officer describes the incident, showing how his actions reflect department K-9 policy regarding (1) the seriousness of the offense, (2) the potential risk of harm to officers or others, (3) the suspect actively resisting or attempting to evade arrest by flight, or (4) a situation where the decision to use the police dog is reasonable in view of the totality of the circumstances.* If the dog contacts the suspect or anyone else during the apprehension, describe the action taken to obtain medical treatment for the subject(s), and refer to the physician's report. The K-9 officer's report should not attempt to describe the wounds in words or sketches. Shoot photographs of any injuries at the medical facility under the doctor's supervision after the wounds are cleaned before bandaging. Maintain photographs with the incident file.

Document officer and dog injuries in your police report. If a suit occurs, the department should cross-complain against the person suing you. When suit potential exists, get witnesses. Hostile witnesses are important. Get their statements on tape and marry them to those statements. The police notebook isn't enough. The plaintiff's attorney will do their own tape.

The department should attempt to settle by civil process *immediately* for misbites on innocent civilians. Do it that day if possible. The situation is similar to the "stray bullet from a policeman's gun." Take care of medical bills. Settle with the victim in order to better serve him and to cut your losses.

■ The National Conference on Criminal Justice Standards and Goals, when referring to firearms training stated, "The shooting course should simulate *real* conditions." Make your K-9 maintenance training simulate *real* conditions, not just a repetition of basic exercises. Recreate actual situations encountered on the street.

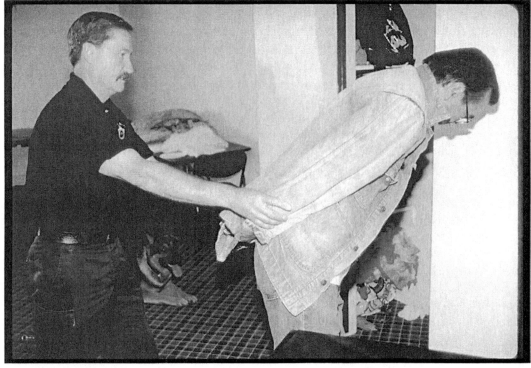

KATS 2000
K-9 Activity Tracking System

KATS2000 is a dynamic record keeping system designed for law enforcement, search and rescue, and related K9 operations. Initially designed by officers in need of a record keeping system for their own agency, the system has now become a reliable database manager for K9 operations.

Developed by Eden & Ney Associates, KATS is Year 2000 compliant, Windows NT, '95 and '98 compatible. Featuring hands free setup, you type the word "setup" to install in minutes.

KATS provides easy navigation throughout the system with an online help system. The manual is built into the database and available at the keyboard—no need to carry a manual. An extended reporting system lets the user select over 20 reports.

KATS also features spell checking when integrated with Microsoft Office or Word packages. Direct Internet connectivity from within KATS links to online resources.

An extensive case law database for administrators and a database for tracking training activities are included in KATS v2.0. A resource index maintains fast-access to information on decoys/agitators, property references, training sites, veterinarians, etc.

The system tracks medical expenses, equipment cost, maintenance and upkeep expenses throughout the year and provides reports ready for submission at budget time. A snippet feature allows you to customize text.

The system tracks patrol, narcotics, explosives, arson, and SAR profiles without requiring the purchase of separate modules, and updates are available at the Web sites:

K9tactics.com & policek9.com

Eden & Ney Associates Inc.
12894-63A Ave.
Surrey, BC Canada
V3X 1S5
TEL 604-507-2962
FAX 604-501-6139

MODEL SETTLEMENT AGREEMENT

WHEREAS, on or about _____, 199__, _____ (hereafter "_____") was temporarily detained by officers of the _____ Department:

AND WHEREAS, _____ received personal injuries arising out of and related to this detention and contact with officers and police dog(s) of the _____ Department:

AND WHEREAS, the City of _____ (hereafter "City"), Officers _____(hereafter "Officers") and _____, without any admission of liability, desire to settle all claims and potential claims which might arise between them and arising out of the above-described incident;

IT IS THEREFORE AGREED TO AND BY THE PARTIES RECITED HEREIN THAT:

1. City agrees to make a total payment in the sum of _____ dollars (_____) upon the notarized execution of this Settlement Agreement by _____.

2. _____ acknowledges that the City and officers have fully informed him of his right to seek legal counsel prior to signing this Settlement Agreement and that he signs this agreement voluntarily with a full understanding and waiver of the right to counsel and each and every term of this Settlement Agreement.

3. _____, for his part and in consideration of the payment referenced in Paragraphs 1 and 2 above, discharges City, Officers and any of their past and present agents, officers, servants, and employees, and each of them and each and every agent, employee, and representative thereof, from any and all actions, causes of action, obligations, costs, attorneys fees, damages, losses, claims, liabilities and demands of whatever character, including but not limited to, the generality of the foregoing releases and any and all causes of action or claims of whatever character including but not limited to, intentional torts, negligence and constitutional claims, and all matters alleged and which could or would have been alleged and all other counter-claims and cross-claims and all other pleadings which were filed or which could have been filed in said action.

4. _____ does hereby expressly agree that this release extends to all claims of every nature and kind whatsoever, known or unknown, suspected or unsuspected, on his parts against City and each and every agent, officer, employee, servant and representative thereof and advisedly waives all rights granted to him under Section 1542 of the California Civil Code, *[for example]* which Section reads as follows:
"A general release does not extend to claims which creditor does not know or suspect to exist in his favor, at the time of executing the release, which if known by him must have materially affected a settlement with the debtor."

5. _____ does understand and hereby expressly agrees that this general and special release shall inure to the benefit of the successors in interest of City and each and every agent, officer, employee, and representative thereof and shall be binding upon _____ and each of his successors in interest, agents and representatives.

6. It is further understood and agreed to by all parties to this Settlement Agreement that this settlement is a good faith compromise of a disputed claim, and that the payments referenced herein are not to be construed as an admission of liability on the part of any party hereto.

7. This Settlement Agreement constitutes the entire agreement between the parties hereto, and the terms of this agreement are contractual and not a mere recital.

8. The undersigned each states that he or she has carefully read the foregoing Settlement agreement and knows the contents thereof and signed the same of his or her own free acts and will.

9. All parties and their counsel agree to cooperate in the preparation and excution of all documents called for by the terms of this Settlement Agreement.

10. It is further expressly agreed to and by the parties to this Settlement Agreement that the rights, obligations and liability established by the terms and conditions of this Settlement Agreement will not become effective and binding on any party hereto until such time as all parties have executed this agreement as called for herein.

11. It is further understood that this Settlement Agreement is without prejudice to the rights of any party hereto to pursue any remedy he or she may have against any party who is not expressly referenced in this agreement.

CITY OF _____

By: _____ Dated:_____

By: _____ Dated:_____

_____, Attorneys for

City of _____ and Officers

By: _____ Dated:_____

STATE OF _____ COUNTY OF_____

On this _____ day of_____, 20___, before me, the undersigned, notary public in and for the State of _____, personally appeared _____ known to me to be the person whose name is subscribed to the within Settlement Agreement, and acknowledged to me that he executed the same.

Witness my hand and official seal.

NOTARY PUBLIC

REVIEW

For critical incidents involving K-9, possibly including a shooting, review procedures should copy department procedures for shootings. Immediately after the incident, the handler or other officers should not give any statements, such as the number of rounds fired, description of bites by the dog, what the dog did or did not do. Death or severe injury to a police dog can cause critical incident stress disorder (CISD) in the handler similar to losing a human partner: anger, denial, flashbacks, nightmares, headaches, or other pain. Affected officers should be given administrative leave for counseling.

TRAINER SELECTION AND DUTIES

The K-9 trainer must have the professional capability to train police officers and dogs, including a working knowledge of police canine behavior and reinforcement training. Whether an outside contractor or an officer inside the department, he or she must have experience as a police officer and experience handling a police dog on the street. The trainer should be able to take a qualified candidate, place a high-potential "green" or untrained dog with him, and train a working police dog team. The trainer also needs the intelligence and observational powers to troubleshoot problems arising during training and on the street.

The department decides how to allocate initial and maintenance training responsibilities and what authority the trainer will have regarding the K-9 program—selecting officers, selecting dogs, standards, testing, and performance evaluations.

INITIAL TRAINING

The initial academy for each police dog team provides training according to Performance Standards that should as a minimum comply with State P.O.S.T. standards:

- **Police dog science: Canine physiology and behavior; scent theory; reinforcement training**
- **Legal issues: Federal and State court rulings; legislation**
- **Department police dog policy**
- **Canine care and emergency veterinary medicine**
- **Control and directability**
  - Obedience-agility off lead to assure the dog will perform specific tasks for the officer in response to voice or hand commands, including:
  - Heeling at normal, fast and slow pace, turning at heel in any direction, and sitting at heel automatically
  - Sitting, lying down, standing, staying, or recalling at a distance or in motion
  - Negotiating obstacles with confidence, including jumping, climbing up and down, penetrating structures, and traversing elevated, unsteady, or unusual structures

- **Protection and Apprehension**
  Training the officer to direct and control the dog in situations including:
  - Protecting officers from assaults
  - Controlling fights
  - Pursuing and apprehending felony offenders
  - Deterring violence during arrest procedures

- **Search strategy and tactics**
  - Tracking, air scenting, K-9 officer safety and survival

- **Area search**
  - Police dog team search and controlled aggression to locate, apprehend, and

arrest hidden/resisting offenders in outside areas
- **Building search**
    - Police dog team search and controlled aggression to locate, apprehend, and arrest hidden/resisting offenders inside small or large structures

Standards could include collateral or special enforcement skills such as:
- **Evidence search**

    Finding articles, including weapons or other property hidden in outside areas or structures, and chemicals, such as blood, semen, or accelerants
- **Drug search**

    Finding drugs such as marijuana, hashish, cocaine, for heroin hidden in buildings, vehicles, packages, or outside areas.
- **Search and rescue**

    Nonaggressive search to find missing persons/disaster victims
- **Bomb search**

    Finding explosive materials hidden in buildings, vehicles, aircraft, packages, or outside areas

"If it pants like a dog and barks like a dog, it must *be* a dog" is a tactical error that has actually saved a few officers' lives on high risk vehicle stops and building searches. Departments, however, should not make the same error selecting their K-9 training programs. International as well as domestic studies have shown that prior trial or sport

Typical canine bite wounds.

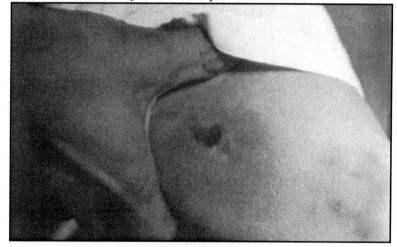

training does *not* qualify a dog for police work. In fact dogs programmed for set routines can conceal serious faults that only surface when they are confronted with realistic scenarios, surprise situations, of the type police dogs confront daily on the street.

Nor does the dog's prior training with a different handler reduce the amount of initial training time the K-9 officer must spend with the dog to bond with him and perform reliable street work. Two to four weeks is generally not enough initial training time to complete either basic patrol dog training or specialized detection training. "Reading" a dog takes time and experience. The business of importing or selling dogs should not preclude responsible training for high caliber performance on the street.

Testing allows qualified evaluators to determine if K-9 teams meet the performance standards for street duty. Testing should be coordinated with the department trainer and revised as necessary according to department policy. Tests should include academic exercises as well as street simulations/scenarios to evaluate police dog team proficiency. Field

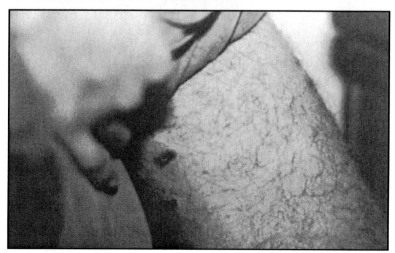

Officer Bob Triplet and K-9 Keno in the dead of winter, Spring Creek Correctional Center, Seward Alaska.

tests should be conducted in realistic work environments for that team (e.g. night, rain, snow, etc.).

MAINTENANCE TRAINING

K-9 team maintenance training is typically conducted weekly or bi-monthly under the supervision of the department trainer. Time allocated for the supervised training should as a minimum comply with State P.O.S.T. requirements. Objectives include:

• Remediation for street problems
• Advanced street scenarios
• Training exercises with other agencies and task forces
• Public programs
• Biannual evaluations by qualified police dog trainers who are outside the department and who will make the objective determination of whether each team meets the performance standard

THE IMPORTANCE OF COMMUNITY RELATIONS

A surprising number of people—people who make up a jury—would rather be beaten, knifed, or shot than bitten by a police dog. They *think* they would. On TV people get shot, beat up. That type of violence has become familiar to our society. The big bad wolf is still a fairy tale. People fear being "eaten, mauled, chewed" by "ravaging, uncontrolled beasts." Some adults who were threatened or actually bitten by a dog during childhood are terrified of dogs. No matter how many times you repeat, "A dog bite is just a dog bite. People don't die of dog bites," television calls it unleashed evil. Prime time.

"The use of police dogs is out of control."
"...90 lb chainsaws..."
"They are targeting minorities..."
"You deserve to get bit—whether you give up or not—you get bit."

Some allegations of excessive force by K-9 officers are true. Such teams do not belong on the street. Education is necessary to combat damage to police dog units, training the public about police dogs and training dog units to maintain a high professional standard.

What is the ratio of hours the K-9 team spends doing public relations tasks versus enforcement? Several cities with active K-9 units have dog teams *assigned* to community relations. They make presentations to their schools, civic organizations, and public events on a rotation basis.

The police dog unit's public image is critically important. It pays to get public support because the public will keep the K-9 unit alive. People want and deserve to see dogs that are under control, dogs they perceive as approachable family dogs.

Many people, both inside and outside law enforcement, do not know how well trained police dogs work, what they can and cannot do, and therefore do not support their presence in the community.

The K-9 can be a valuable tool to bridge the gap between "them" and "us." The police dog program should become part of the department's long-term strategy and organizational philosophy. What officers are and what we do is part of our long-standing values, traditions, and culture.

The American culture places high value on the human-animal relationship, particularly the man-dog partnership. The lifesaving capability of canines is established in tradition. People recognize human quality in an officer who can relate to a canine and who depends on that canine. They perceive that the officer with a dog is able to relate to them and their problems. And perception is reality.

Police dog teams can assist *community policing* by providing closer ties between the police and citizens, moving the officer from a position of anonymity in the patrol car to direct engagement on the street, making operations more visible to the public, and actively seeking citizen input and support to prevent crime.

Kids love to collect K-9 baseball cards. The same scene repeats itself at K-9 trials: An 8-year-old kid runs up to a cop, "Hey officer, d'ya have a card of your dog?" If his department doesn't do baseball cards, the cop scuffs his boot in the dirt and looks away, "No, sorry." Funny how a little kid with a dirty ball cap can dropkick a man.

The kid runs over to the next K-9 car, "Hey officer..." This time he gets a card. He examines it, making sure the police dog sticking his head out of the car matches the picture on the card.

"This is Blazer, huh?" flipping the card over to read the dog's resume. "How many burglars' he caught?"

"As of last night, eight," the cop grins, leaning against the car, forgetting for the moment how much his back hurts.

"Cool."

Videoproductions, news videos, and brochures provide excellent public education tools for the entire agency as well as the K-9 unit.

"Many departments lose the value of the dog for public relations. We are the greatest public relations unit in the Chicago Police Department. Bar none. This has saved our unit in big budget areas. Suddenly, they're looking around saying, 'Well, where can we cut our budget? How can we save money?' And somebody will say, 'Let's get some of the K-9 budget.' On a number of occasions, it has been proclaimed: 'Money can be cut from other units, but there is nothing in the department that can equal the public relations of a K-9.'

"The K-9 unit does 400 to 500 public relations assignments per year. The police department is always looking for good relations with the people. The police officer can go out and stand there and talk and hand out material, but nothing makes the impression the dog makes. You can take a picture of John Q. Public standing next to a K-9. A little girl with her arms around a K-9. Over 30 years the department strived to keep that image because we need the public support. If you lose public support for your program, no matter what you've done on the street, you're vulnerable."

—Sgt. Kenneth Burger,
K-9 Trainer Retired,
Chicago Police Department.

Greg Liddicoat, Nevada State Fire Marshall, and Mills.

DOG HANDLER READINESS

Judy L. Salviolo, R.N., C.E.N., M.I.C.N.

Peace officers are trained to shoot or not shoot, to interview witnesses, victims, and suspects, as well as to read life threatening situations. Handlers are trained to work their dogs. On the street the officer may be ready psychologically and intellectually. But is he *ready* to meet the complete physical demands of the job? What does physical readiness mean for the police dog handler?

It is important to understand why handlers in particular need to be physically ready. Each person has his own personal standard of health and fitness. That level may or may not be appropriate for the rigors of police dog handling. The officer may be able to physically handle his regular duties without injury to himself. He may be overweight, have slightly high blood pressure, his yearly medical physical with laboratory blood tests showing elevated cholesterol. Occasionally he works out, especially during dog training. This policeman feels he is in good enough physical condition to perform his job safely.

Beyond the unpredictable nature of police work, the job of K-9 handler forces such officers to deal with high risk, high stress situations more frequently and often longer than regular patrol officers. The minimum standard of physical fitness is probably not an acceptable or safe level when put into the perspective of long foot pursuits, complex building searches, tedious evidence searches, and other specialty tasks performed in most K-9 units by relatively few dog teams. Police dog handler duties will include searching for bad guys in rainy or icy conditions, usually at night, searching for lost children or invalids when lives are in jeopardy, searching for weapons, searching through debris, and continuing to work long after other officers have been relieved.

All these situations demand handler and dog fitness, being agile in the worst situations, hit the deck, duck, side-step, sprint, jump, spin, lift, maintain balance, traverse difficult terrain for miles, as well as working many hours under stressful conditions. *Readiness* equals a body able to perform the activity requested of it with minimal risk. In order to achieve and maintain his own state of readiness, the K-9 officer has to consider nutrition, regular physical examinations by a physician, exercise adequate for physical fitness, and miscellaneous health issues.

NUTRITION

Academic health science stresses the *four food groups* and *three meals a day*, often not possible given the unusual demands of police work. What then becomes extremely important are the types of foods consumed and adequate fluid and caloric intake:
1. Eat foods low in salt and fat
2. Limit caffeine use
3. Limit or eliminate refined sugar in food products
4. Eat modest food portions, be aware of overeating and only eat when hungry
5. Large volume fluid intake, preferably water and fruit juices
6. *Emergency Food Pack* in patrol car

Salt and fat warnings are well publicized. Officers need to remember there are great amounts of fat in fried foods, snack foods, chips of all sorts, and doughnuts. Lean red meat eaten only two times a week, vegetables, fish, or chicken at other times, helps to control fat and cholesterol intake. Butter and oil/margarine products used in small amounts also helps to decrease fat intake. Naturally occuring sodium makes it unnecessary, and inadvisable, to add salt to any food. Salty foods can elevate blood pressure. Sodas hide high sodium content. Limiting or not using fast foods or sodas pays dividends.

Caffeine...hey, I need my coffee to get through the shift! For most healthy people, caffeine in moderate amounts is O.K. Drinking more than two or three cups of regular coffee or tea is too much caffeine. Caffeine is present in chocolate and many sodas. The key to safe caffeine use is moderation. Depending on the doctor's advice, your medical history or physical symptoms may bar you from using any caffeine.

Most highly processed foods contain sugar. The theory of sugar giving a quick energy rush has some truth. The rest of the truth is after the *rush* comes the *dump*. This is a feeling of lower energy than before eating. Obviously, the low energy feeling conflicts with peak performance.

So what does an officer eat on patrol? Fruit, fresh, dried or canned, sliced vegetables, cold leftover beef or chicken, thermos of soup, sandwiches, nuts, popcorn, bagels, and dairy products such as low fat cheese, yogurt, cottage cheese and milk. Preparation time and effort is generally minimal. Nutritional value is high. Regulating your intake of all foods to match your exercise rate or caloric burn rate keeps your body lean and strong.

Fluid intake is critical to the working police dog handler. Adequate hydration can forestall many ills and discomforts. Problems such as constipation, headaches, low energy, hemorrhoids, altitude sickness, urinary tract infections, and even in some cases kidney stones can be prevented by drinking a minimum of two quarts of fluid per shift. The best liquid to drink is water, lots of it. Gatorade, juices or other electrolyte drinks are beneficial during work and stressful assignments. Some fruits can also add liquid to the total intake. Alcohol, obviously not consumed on the job, dehydrates the body. Drink adequate water the day after using alcohol. Staying hydrated takes conscious effort. Ways to achieve two quarts of liquid each day include: drink a glass of water after every void and upon rising each morning; keep a half gallon bottle of water/juice in the patrol car and drink it every day; consider drinking liquid each time you water your dog. An easy indicator of too little fluid intake is the urine color: bright yellow or dark amber colored urine means too little fluid in the system. *The clearer the urine, the better.*

Good nutrition is imperative to a healthy and *ready* body. Each police dog handler is the only person who controls what he eats, how much he eats, and what he drinks. Nutrition is the responsibility of each handler and is a major component of physical readiness.

The *Emergency Food Pack* will benefit the dog team responding to a request for assistance searching a criminal or lost person during the night, in a rural or backcountry setting. The pack contents will vary according to individual preference. The idea is to have portions of dried fruits, nuts, meat sticks, juices in boxes, water, and dog food assembled in a belt pack, rotated periodically for freshness, and always kept in the patrol vehicle. On extended assignments food becomes important to performance. Having an "Emergency Food Pack" ready gives the team a higher level of readiness.

REGULAR PHYSICAL EXAMINATION

Being responsible for diet and exercise addresses the outward functioning and appearance of the body which the handler is able to monitor. Regular physical examination by a physician increases the police officer's awareness of his body's internal functions. Through routine exams, several health problems can be diagnosed and treated early. Due to the nature of police work, officers can suffer from high blood pressure precipitated by stress. If a good dietary pattern has not been established, high cholesterol levels and high glucose levels may be detected before adverse complications occur. If a regular exercise schedule has not been established for an individual officer, it may be wise to get an examination prior to undertaking a rigorous workout regime. This is especially important if the person suffers from high blood pressure or elevated cholesterol, because the physician may alter the individual's workout plans in order to correct the problems first.

Physical examination:

1. Blood pressure checked monthly if within normal limits—140/88 or lower. If it is over 140/90, check blood pressure 3 times in one week. If all 3 readings are elevated, consult a physician.

2. Choose a physician who is familiar with sports medicine and who treats disorders with diet and exercise and medicine if necessary. Ask several friends about their physicians and then make a choice after speaking with the doctor.

3. Yearly physical if over 40 years of age. Yearly if routine laboratory results are above the suggested upper limits.

4. Routine physical examination every 2 to 3 years if under forty and no known medical problems.

5. Yearly laboratory tests for blood chemistry. These tests are available at health fairs for reasonable fees. The blood chemistry test gives a printout of cholesterol levels, glucose, liver function, triglycerides, electrolytes, and many other parameters. If levels are above the normal ranges given on the printout, contact your physician.

6. In-depth studies: X-rays, EKG, and lung function tests only as requested by the physician.

EXERCISE AND FITNESS

Physical readiness is directly related to aerobic exercise, moving the body. Limberness and strength can be achieved by stretching exercises and weight training—anaerobic exercise. Combinations of both aerobic and anaerobic exercise regimes result in optimum physical fitness. A police dog handler will increase his endurance and reduce the potential for physical injury by adhering to an exercise schedule. By joining a commercial health club or by working under a departmental trainer, the officer should set up a training schedule to meet his individual goals. Using a trainer and working out consistently helps insure training will ultimately lead to physical fitness. Many departments invest in aerobic exercise equipment, weight machines, and sets of free weights. Choices for aerobic exercise machines include the stair climbing and cross country ski machines. Cross country skiing works out both the upper and lower body aerobically. Weight machines enable many strength exercises targeting single or multiple muscle groups on one piece of equipment.

One drawback to a totally indoor fitness program is the possible lack of consistent fitness workouts for the police dog. The K-9 partner must also be in top physical condition. While some dogs bounce around inside the unit the entire shift, most K-9's do not get enough exercise riding for hours in a patrol car. Exercise programs involving the dog include running (if the officer has strong, stable knees), fast walking (as good as running except less damage to hip, knee and ankle joints), crosscountry skiing (dogs may not be allowed on set tracks), roller blading (where the dog will not be a hazard), and swimming. Integrate outside and inside workouts, say three days inside and four days outside, to cover physical training for the dog. In the end the handler is responsible for his own and his dog's fitness.

Back care deserves special attention. Back injuries are common in police work. Daily specific back exercises with the constant awareness of body position prevent most back injuries. When taking a dog on the sleeve or holding the agitated dog on lead, the handler should absorb the shock loading through his legs, keeping the knees bent in a stance with one foot ahead of the other. Limiting the number of hits will decrease the chance of injury or back strain.

Exercises to strengthen the back strengthen the abdominal muscles which provide back support. Fifteen minutes a day of bent-knee situps and leg lifts while lying flat on the back are the best back strengthening exercises. These are also good after a back injury to help relieve the pain of the healing strain. Awareness of the potential for back injury and faithful daily back exercises is the best method for keeping a back strong and pain free.

Keys to physical training:

1. Warm up prior to any workout with controlled stretching exercises to help prevent muscle injury. After completing the workout, repeat stretching exercises to minimize sore, stiff muscles.

2. Beginning level of fitness: Do aerobic workouts 3 times a week for a duration of 20-30 minutes each. Maintain the heart rate near maximum for 20 minutes. Exercise physiologists gauge exercise intensity by VO_2 max (measure of your body's ability to take in oxygen, transport it through the bloodstream, and convert it to energy at the cellular level). Outside laboratories, intensity is usually expressed as a percentage of maximum heart rate. Maximum heart rate = 220 - age in years.

MAXIMUM HEART RATE TABLE

AGE -	20	25	30	35	40	45	50	55	60
MRH -	200	195	190	185	180	175	170	165	160

The standard predictive equation for the target heart rate to achieve the desired level of training:
MAXIMUM HEART RATE X PERCENT EFFORT = TARGET HEART RATE

For example, a 30-year-old cop wanting to train at 90 percent effort, multiplies 190 by 0.90 for a target rate of 171 beats per minute (stop briefly during training to check your pulse, counting the beats for 10 seconds and multiplying by 6, or use a heart-rate monitor).

More accurate is the *heart-rate reserve method*, which incorporates the resting heart rate of each individual (determine in the morning before you get out of bed):

(220 - AGE - RESTING HEART RATE) X PERCENT EFFORT + RESTING HEART RATE = TARGET HEART RATE

For example, the target heart rate for that same 30-year-old cop, who has a resting heart rate of 60, would be 177 beats per minute. He needs to reach the target rate to achieve aerobic effect.

3. Higher level of fitness—Aerobic workouts 3-5 sessions per week for a minimum of 30 minutes each session at MHR. Weight training 3 times per week in addition to the aerobic workouts.

Weight training regimes are best designed by a qualified coach. Weight workouts are geared to strengthen specific muscle groups. The type of weight machine or free weights used for each individual muscle group determine how to conduct the exercises and the number of repetitions. Weight lifting tears down muscle so it can "rebuild" after the workout. There will be little gain if weights are lifted daily, unless on alternating days the upper body is exercised in exchange for a lower body workout the other days. Some people prefer to do a complete weight lifting workout every other day.

4. Reaching for the highest level of fitness—Six to seven days each week of aerobic training, increasing the workout duration according to the individual's capacity and desire. Usually, 30-60 minutes per workout is the minimum at this level. The officer integrates weight training into the fitness schedule to maximize strength and endurance.

Departments often want specific tests to measure each person's physical fitness level. Fitness is difficult to quantify because it involves more than just motion, endurance, strength, and flexibility. It is more a lifestyle than a test given at a particular time. Some departments prefer to give time and incentives to officers who consistently maintain a level of fitness training. Physical fitness significantly affects officer survival.

IMPORTANT HEALTH ISSUES

Smoking. Media and medical centers widely distribute information highlighting the dangers of smoking and second hand smoke. Smoking directly affects police dog team performance. Endurance decreases no matter how hard the officer trains. Overall health risks increase. Blood pressure rises, often the heart rate too. The smoker's probable life span decreases as the risk of heart disease, lung disease, cancer, and stroke rises dramatically.

The dog is a victim if his handler smokes at home or in the patrol car. Dogs are susceptible to various cancers triggered by environmental hazards, such as smoke, chemicals, and toxic fumes. If the officer cannot or does not want to stop smoking, reduced exposure will benefit the dog and his scenting capability.

Dog bite wounds. Cleanse initially by flooding with clean water. Scrub with a betadine solution, rinse and use a sterile dressing over the wound. If the skin is broken or there is severe swelling, seek medical attention. The attending physician will fill out a workmen's compensation report. Dog bites can become infected. Depending on the severity of the bite, antibiotics may be prescribed starting with an initial dose at the medical facility. Bites on the hand with crushed bones or severed tendons put the police officer at special risk. Get immediate care. Report every dog bite.

Human bite wounds. Bites from people are extremely prone to infection. Get immediate medical attention. AIDS and hepatitis pose real threats. Stay alert to avoid being bitten by suspects. If a suspect has a bleeding wound, a bloody nose, or you are responding to the scene of an accident, wear latex nonsterile gloves. Carry disposable gloves in a uniform pocket.

AIDS and most other human diseases are not zoonotic, that is they are not communicable from lower animals to man under natural conditions. However, in the course of apprehending and arresting a suspect, if the K-9 contacts the suspect, good practice dictates wearing gloves to clean blood or other secretions off the dog, letting the dog drink clean fresh water, and avoiding direct contact with the dog's saliva or any wounds he may have sustained.

Chemical exposure. Drugs such as cocaine, caustic chemicals, explosives, and other hazardous substances found in methamphetamine labs, vehicles, or buildings undergoing search can be absorbed through the skin or breaks in the skin and through the respiratory system. Grabbing a package of drugs away from the alerting police dog jeopardizes the unprotected handler. Exercise care when handling these chemicals. Wear disposable nonsterile gloves when exposure is likely on a K-9 search. Use caution and wear appropriate gear when entering high risk areas. Establish a plan and maintain clear communications linkage to emergency medical services for every police dog call.

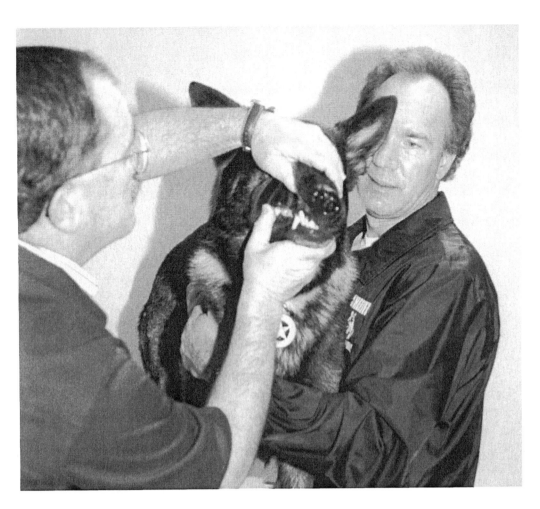

K-9 CARE
by Robert Gorrindo, D.V.M.

The scene is an urban disaster. Your dog is searching 3 collapsed structures. At one point he penetrates a black hole into a basement. When he comes out, he lies down briefly. You take the dog over to the patrol vehicle, put the dog inside, and go back to be a spotter for another K-9 team. When you come back an hour later, your dog is dead. His spleen ruptured from the blow of a fall.

If you had examined your dog when he came out of the rubble, if you had palpated his sternal area, would you have felt the lack of uniformity, the swelling, the asymmetry? Could anyone have saved him?

DAILY EXAM

Undoubtedly, the single most important part of caring for a dog is learning what is *normal*. Normal is health. Good health is a must for performance. One need not be a dog owner/breeder or go to veterinary school to appreciate when something is different, something has changed. Since dogs have a right side and a left side, with few exceptions they have two of most body parts. If something looks unusual, check the dog's other side. If both sides look bad, then probably both need help. Your veterinarian (not to mention your dog) likes to treat new problems rather than long-standing problems. Be assured that from a care/maintenance point of view, knowing what is normal is critical.

How does one learn normal? The only way to learn what is normal for your dog is to dedicate a part of every day to *hands on* inspection. Mouths must be opened, joints must be felt, and ears need to be smelled. There are no shortcuts. However, with practice, familiarity will make this a quick, effective, and very productive part of your day.

Attitude is the first test. How does he greet you the first time you see him in the morning? Is he at his normal level of activity? Does he jump to greet you? Remember that normal for a 7-year-old dog may be abnormal for a 1-year-old. In addition to watching for attitude, behavior, and enthusiasm changes, watch to see how he gets up. Was he smooth and quick, or did he show a reluctance which indicates pain or discomfort? After you greet him, turn him loose to warm up. Watch for movement problems. Does exercise cause coughing or difficult breathing? Start your exam after he has settled down.

Start with the head. First are his eyes. Look for clear eyes, no discharge, no redness. Make sure both eyes are equal in size. Eyes that squint or tear abnormally need attention. Both of these signs indicate pain. Any change in the clearness of the cornea needs to be evaluated. Gray, pink, or black color changes on the corneas are the first signs of pannus. This is a serious condition which will eventually cause blindness if left unattended.

Now rub your hands over the top of his head, base of the ears, and sides of the face. Look for skin and coat changes, scabs on the lips, and signs of trauma. Curl up both upper lips and look at the gums and the outside surface of the teeth. Make sure you recognize normal gum color, a valuable tool to assess your dog's condition after trauma. Blood loss and shock will cause either pale gums or slowed capillary refill time. Capillary refill time is how long it takes for an area on the gums to return to its normal color after it has been blanched by digital pressure. Normal capillary refill time is 1 to 2 seconds.

Open the mouth and look at the roof of the mouth, tongue, and inside surface of the teeth. Smell the mouth. Bad teeth stink.

The next stink is from bad ears. Any abnormal odor is of concern. Many ear infections develop below the part of the ear canal you can see. Ear canal diameters are very small for the last half of their length, and without an otoscope it is not possible to evaluate them. Your clues for ear problems are odor, pain, redness, head tilt, itching, and shaking. There is no excuse for chronic ear disease as your presenting complaint when you visit your veterinarian.

The nose is next. Clear (like water) discharge in equal amounts from both nostrils is normal. *Any* discharge from only one of the two nostrils or any discharge that is not clear is abnormal. Remember both nostrils must be the same. One more quick look at the throat (feel for lumps) and neck, and you can go on to the trunk.

Run your hand along the topline in both directions. It is easier to see and feel changes in skin and coat condition this way. Many small tumors and cysts are difficult to identify if you are not careful. Rub your hand along the ribs and flank in the same manner. Crank up the tail. Look at his bun. You do not need to touch it, just look at it. German shepherd owners need to identify fistulas (draining tracts from colon to skin) early, not after it is too late to treat. Now drop his tail and put your hands in the flanks. Is there any pain or distention (this could be a bloat and torsion)? Deep chest dog owners must know at a glance if their dog is distended in the flank.

As the exam ends, palpate all the joints, toes included, of both front and hind legs. At some point during the day, identify his stool to compare it with his normal stool, and if possible watch to see that he urinates freely.

This most fundamental part of your dog's day should last about two minutes total.

ROUTINE CARE

Your daily physical exam tells you how effective you are as a groomer. Skin and coat needs vary dramatically between individual dogs. Needs also vary geographically.

Undoubtedly, the single most important part of caring for a dog is learning what is normal.

Skin that is either too dry or too wet is unhealthy. People living in high humidity regions try to dry the skin while desert people use conditioners with their shampoo to try to trap moisture in the skin.

This is very generic advice. Brush and bathe routinely. Be aware of cyclic shedding changes. Since each geographic area is different, each dog needs to be evaluated and treated individually. Changes in the coat or skin other than mild flakiness or routine shedding may indicate previously unsuspected disease. Nutritional deficiencies (zinc), hormone problems (hypothyroidism), and allergies (food, contact, or inhaled) are examples of diseases which may show themselves as skin disease.

Anyone wanting to see a violent confrontation need only place 10 veterinarians, breeders, or dog trainers in one room and say "what's the best way to feed a dog." Such a variety of opinions indicates there is no single correct answer. Keep it as simple as possible. There are several high quality dog foods available. Each has minor differences. Some have specific applications. For the most part, the top few dog foods are close in quality. Dogs that are traveling or frequently confined might do better with low residue dog foods. Dry dog food fed once or twice each day, a multiple vitamin given daily, and fresh water are adequate. One rule all of us can live with: feed a dog food he likes to eat, a food that does not cause vomiting or diarrhea, and a food that allows him to perform at his maximum activity level. Nothing else counts. Dogs with specific growth, disease, or aging problems need individual attention and may have specific dietary requirements that your veterinarian will evaluate. Make his feeding schedule predictable, and do not overfeed.

The following nutritional situations need attention. Bloat and torsion is a disease of the stomach of deep chested dogs. Dogs are presented for evaluation with a history of changing from normal to dying in a few hours time. The stomach fills with gas after a meal, begins to turn and while turning it closes the escape route for the gas (small intestine and esophagus). The twisting stomach may or may not take with it the spleen. The resulting circulation failure results in severe shock and potential rupture of the stomach wall. Death is usually from shock and cardiovascular changes. Some people believe the type of dog food is responsible (no trend has been seen at our hospital). Most people agree the typical presentation is a dog that ate and drank water and then exercised. There is evidence that dogs can be born with structural defects which render them susceptible to a bloat and torsion episode. Advice for prevention of bloat and torsion includes: (1) Feed dogs twice daily after soaking food in warm water for 20 minutes; and (2) do not buy puppies or dogs whose ancestry has had bloat and torsion.

The second nutritional situation is chronic loose stools. There is no reason for their existence. With rare exception, changes in type of food, feeding schedules, parasite control, or diagnosis and treatment of underlying disease will allow for normal bowel function.

The final note on nutrition applies to growing dogs. A well done trial showed that when comparing 2-year-old dogs raised *overfed* with dogs which resembled *junkyard* dogs (lean), the overfed dogs were more likely to have shoulder, elbow, hip, or stifle joint problems. The lesson to be learned is puppies raised as lean dogs have less chance of severe lameness problems as adults.

Let's not forget bones. Dogs love them, and it is fun to feed them. The safe way to feed bones is to give only large (knuckle) bones. Take them away as soon as they have been whittled down to a size the dog can break and ingest. These 1 to 2 inch diameter bones are the type that cause obstructions. Working dogs have a particular interest besides intestinal obstructions. They can't afford to own fractured canines or molars. Therefore, if for no other reason, help save their big biters by not feeding bones.

Preventive medicine is next. Before we address routine veterinary care, we need to talk about veterinary medicine. If you consider the time invested in these working dogs, they quickly become very valuable. When choosing your veterinarian, keep these factors in mind. Choose a veterinarian who has a strong interest in your *type of dog* and the *kind of work* you do. This is especially important for police agencies. Emergency situations may take all your choices away. However, for your routine, predictable medicine and surgery, choose a veterinarian who has the same interest you do. Also, choose a doctor who is aware of the specialty practices that are available. Specialty practices (surgery, neurology, dermatology, internal medicine, radiology, oncology, etc.) have given the dog handler choices which not only add to the quality of life but also save lives and return dogs to normal function. A doctor unwilling to get a second opinion or refer a case is a truly scary person.

Most hospitals have their own vaccination program. Regardless which program you use, the important part is to find the doctor you are comfortable with and stick with his plan. People split hairs over vaccine types, kinds, and quality. If you have a good doctor, he will be using good vaccine. Routine programs should include a minimum of distemper, hepatitis, parainfluenza, parvo, and corona virus. Kennel cough is indicated in some situations. Thorough examinations, physicals, and routine labwork should be done concurrently with yearly vaccinations.

The geographic distribution of Lyme's disease is changing rapidly. The efficacy of the vaccine is improving. The disease is spread by the bite of a tick. Your doctor will explain more as further studies are conducted.

Rabies also falls into the realm of geographic diseases, but the potential for human disease recategorizes it. Rabies virus vaccination programs are consistent with local laws.

Besides yearly vaccines, your dog needs routine fecal exams. An increasingly common intestinal parasite is giardia. Unlike hookworms, whipworms, and roundworms, which are easy to find on fecal exams, giardia is difficult to find. Any dog that feels well, is active, but has a fetid and/or slimy diarrhea is a giardia candidate.

Heartworm prevention has evolved to an extremely safe, inexpensive and easy (give a pill once a month) task. Even though it is a seasonal risk (mosquito vector availability), and some geographic areas are free of the disease, preventive measures are important to protect your valuable investment. All dogs that travel need heartworm prevention medication.

External parasites include fleas, ticks, and lice. Fleas commonly cause severe allergic skin disease. Ticks can bother ears, skin, or transmit disease (Lymes). Lice cause severe itching and less frequently blood loss anemias. Check with your doctor for the program that works best in your area.

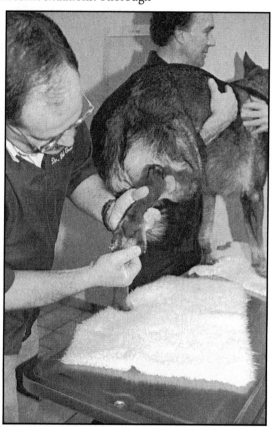

Hit a vein, save the dog's life.

Conditioning is vital. Dogs need the stamina to work enthusiastically all day long, all night long, or in bad weather. Some dogs must work at altitude. Strength and endurance must be developed through a normal exercise and diet program. Out of shape dogs are just as common as out of shape people. Both jeopardize high risk situations.

MEDICAL CONSIDERATIONS

Preventive medicine begins with routine physical exams, vaccinations, and fecal exams. Nutritional needs are monitored carefully. Housing is dry and clean. Exercise cannot be forgotten. Overweight dogs with poor muscle tone keep orthopedic surgeons busy. Not only are they frequently injured, but they don't heal well. Good preventive medicine is an ongoing activity.

Trauma or emergency situations rarely affect only one body system. Chest trauma may result in either blood loss (shock) or lung (ventilation) problems. Sources of this type of trauma range from cars and baseball bats to knives and bullets. The two immediate concerns with chest trauma are to stabilize ventilation and provide for rapid intravenous (IV) administration of drugs, fluids, or blood. If you are not prepared or qualified to do this, go somewhere for help. The first choice is a veterinarian, but human hospitals can also be very helpful.

Many dogs have an intact mediastinum. The mediastinum is a shelf dividing the right and left sides of the chest. Theoretically, a dog with an intact mediastinum can breathe adequately if only one side of the chest is perforated. However, if there is any chance one or both sides of the chest have lost their integrity (vacuum), then you must assume the dog now needs positive pressure ventilation until the chest is stabilized. Immediate intervention is the only hope for these dogs. Oxygen masks may be tried, but their value depends on how much air is entering the lungs. Passing an endotracheal tube into an unanesthetized dog in air hunger is not easy. The dog usually needs to be sedated or anesthetized so it can then be intubated and given positive pressure ventilation. CPR in the field without proper instrumentation will rarely be effective.

Establishing an open vein to push fluids or IV drugs is a task that should be attempted. This procedure is not particularly difficult. With initial instruction and regular practice, it should be available as an option. Catheters and electrolyte replacement fluids belong in the first aid kit. Shock can be helped with IV fluids and IV corticosteroids. Valium can be given to sedate convulsing animals exposed to excitatory drugs, and specific narcotic antagonists also save lives. Cardiovascular or pulmonary insults, whether trauma, blood loss, shock or ventilation problems, are extremely dangerous. An attempt should be made to provide O_2, improve ventilation, give fluids and IV drugs as needed. The best situation—other than avoiding the trauma—is to keep close contact with people skilled in these lifesaving procedures.

Nervous system trauma is the most frustrating because of the fragility of nervous tissue. The brain and spinal cord are well protected from injury in normal situations. Bony barriers prevent damage in all but the most severe trauma. Damage done to the brain (usually swelling secondary to the brain bouncing off the inside wall of the skull) or spinal cord (ruptured disc, fractured vertebrae) requires immediate evaluation and treatment. Unless the nervous tissue trauma is affecting respiratory or cardiovascular function, chest trauma should be dealt with first. Proper restraint may help prevent additional damage to the injury site.

If evaluation of damage and definitive care will be delayed more than 1 hour, anti-inflammatory drug administration may be helpful.

Accidental exposure to controlled drugs may have severe nervous system effects.

The doses are starting points. Give drug to effect if the initial dose is not adequate. IV is best—cephalic vein or jugular vein. Second choice is tongue or heart (you have nothing to lose).

Exposure	Signs	Therapy - mg/kg
Opiates	Depression, stupor	Naloxone .05 IV, IM Nalorphane 1.0 IV
Cocaine, stimulants	Hyperexcitability	Diazepam 0.5 IV

Musculoskeletal diseases include growth and lameness problems you have identified on your daily physical exam. Fractures usually are from trauma. Unless there is an open fracture or severe blood loss, they are not particularly dangerous. Dogs accommodate for the pain by not using the leg. Robert Jones bandage or a metasplint stabilizes the fracture until surgery.

Lacerations present 2 problems. Blood loss is most important. Common sense, pressure, and occasionally a tourniquet will control bleeding. If help is more than 2 hours away, a clean dressing and oral antibiotics are helpful to minimize infection.

Gastrointestinal (GI) diseases other than dilatation and torsion usually are not acute emergencies. Foreign bodies certainly are emergencies. But since the signs of obstruction are very similar to other GI diseases, it is usually 1 to 2 days before these dogs are seen and diagnosed. In most cases, this time lag does not seem to change the prognosis. Acute bloody vomiting or diarrhea is an exception and must be dealt with immediately.

The urinary system is rarely a problem site. Inability to urinate from stone obstruction at the os penis can be life threatening. Female dogs frequently pass small stones through their relatively large urethra. Male dogs have a bone in their penis which effectively reduces the diameter of the urethra so that most stones do not pass. Male dogs lifting their leg, straining and unable to pass urine or just dribbling urine are obstructed until proven otherwise. If the obstruction continues untreated, secondary kidney failure and a ruptured bladder are potential sequelae. Note that prostate disease and bladder infections give the same signs.

The common urogenital disease of the intact female dog is a pyometra. Any female dog not feeling well 3—6 weeks after her last heat is suspect. A pyometra is a uterus full of pus. These dogs may or may not have a discharge.

Dogs that are dry and well fed can maintain normal body temperature. If they become wet, particularly if it is windy, they may easily develop hypothermia. Fresh water should always be available, either in the patrol vehicle or field tactical vest. Well conditioned animals deal with exercise stress well and are less likely to develop hyperthermia than their out of shape counterparts.

Finally, consider the hearing loss produced by loud noise—gunfire. We are all aware of the damage loud noise inflicts on the human ear. Pilots have IC's and jet engines, heavy machine operators have both low and high frequency effects, police officers have range training as well as street incidents. We also consider a dog's hearing to rank high, along with his senses of smell and vision, in affecting his performance. Put yourself in your dog's shoes when exposing him to unnecessary gunfire noise.

Inability to urinate from stone obstruction at the os penis can be life threatening.

FIRST AID KIT

First aid kits are the equivalent of a spare tire for your squad car—a necessity. This kit contains the things to help you and your dog in an emergency or when you are too far from trained medical help. The well stocked kit will take care of a minor problem at midnight so you do not have to pay an emergency fee at a veterinary hospital.

Your kit should contain a reference book dealing with common emergencies and poisonings. These books will help you decide if you have a critical situation. We are all aware of common poisons such as antifreeze and insecticides. But a search can expose your dog to so many possibilities that it is impossible for the handler to know about every single plant, chemical, drug, etc.

Robert Jones splints require bandage scissors, roll cotton, gauze, porous and elastic tape. A metasplint is handy. Telfa pads and antibiotic ointment are for dressings. Have an antibiotic plus steroid ear ointment and an antibiotic opthalmic ointment. Don't believe those tales about hot and cold noses. Get a thermometer, and remember normal temperature is 101.5°F ± 1°. Procedure gloves and betadyne keep your dog and you clean. If you want to evacuate his stomach, give him apomorphine or ipecac. If he has diarrhea, lomotil works well. Initially, amoxicillin is adequate as an antibiotic for wounds or respiratory diseases. Prednisone tablets are great for hot skin or hot joints until you can get full treatment. Have 18 and 20 ga IV catheters, IV sets and lactated ringer solution available. These are for trauma as well as dehydration from vomiting and diarrhea. Dexamethazone treats shock and snake bites. You will need syringes and needles for the dexamethazone plus the valium and either naloxone or nalorphine.

Your friendly veterinarian will not only supply you with these items, but is also capable of training you in the necessary techniques. In emergency situations, call the doctor to get help treating your dog until transportation or more highly trained help arrives. The kit is valuable only if the handler has learned how to use it.

One final thought—GENETICS

An alarming situation is developing. Genetics counts. Not only is genetics important to secure all the good characteristics, but it seems genetics counts equally for (not) selecting bad characteristics. We have known you could dramatically change the odds on good versus bad hips in a puppy by picking the right parents. Now it seems that was the tip of the iceberg. There are published accounts of genetic control in the German shepherd in the development of behavior problems, cataracts, epilepsy, hip dysplasia, pancreatic insufficiency and elbow dysplasia. Good sense would encourage us to learn about the dam and sire's health history before we choose a puppy or young dog. These are considerations for imported as well as domestically bred dogs.

These techniques are the end result of many enjoyable experiences with great dogs and even greater people—what has worked for me in this hospital. However, there are many ways to skin a cat, and I suggest you and your department develop a good working relationship with your veterinarian.

GENETICS AND ORTHOPEDICS
by Robert Richardson, D.V.M.

There is not a week in my life that I don't do complicated surgery, provide medical palliation, or perform euthanasia on a patient with an avoidable orthopedic problem. Avoidable for you, only in the context of not selecting such an individual as your police dog or service companion. Orthopedic problems have penetrated the genetics of breeds so thoroughly that even unaffected parents can produce disabled pups. You must do some careful homework. As a team, you and your K-9 will be expected to be human and superhuman. Your K-9's soundness and your sensible approach to his lifestyle will give you the ultimate reward.

Your bonding will happen early. In a new relationship it soon becomes difficult to separate your heart from your head. Some wonderful dogs will be afflicted with disabling orthopedic conditions. Take an objective approach with your new partner until you have proven his complete soundness. Be as thorough as possible in selection. Ask questions about all conditions known to you or your department. Except for degenerative disorders of the spine, most of the listed conditions can be diagnosed before 6 or 7 months. This discussion presents the most common disqualifying conditions. As noted, certain breeds have high predilections for certain disorders.

Hip dysplasia: Significant and commonly encountered affliction of most breeds of dog, even the corgi, Lhasa apso, schnauzer, etc. The term simply means defective development of the acetabulum (socket) and femoral head. These individuals may *bunny hop*, show pain on rising, or simply be awkward. A hard, enthusiastic, young police dog candidate may not immediately show the pain or dysfunction he is experiencing. It is possible to detect loose and ill fitting components at relatively early ages. X-rays are useful as early as 5 or 6 months and should be performed on all potential police dogs before they begin training. Anesthesia is often necessary to provide comprehensive examination, including well positioned X-rays. Six months is the earliest I feel comfortable evaluating elbows for dysplasia. If your dog is under anesthesia at 6 months for hip films, consider doing elbows too. If you want surgical correction of these problems, discovery at this age is very beneficial to the outcome.

Overnutrition: It has been well documented that overfeeding the large breed pup predisposes to orthopedic diseases. I recommend the ribs on your pup be easily palpable from 4 to 12 months, and maybe beyond. Take note, *high protein* foods do not necessarily mean *high quality* protein. The claim high protein could even apply to foods made of purely nonessential amino acids, the protein building blocks. Balance of the appropriate amino acids and reasonable overall levels of nitrogen will lead to the best nourishment. Ask your veterinarian for recommendations. Overweight, bulked-up adults are at risk with respect to their ligamentous structures. Police dogs are athletes. The fat you put on them may actually impair performance and, worse, lead to injury. Rupturing the anterior cruciate ligament is especially common in the *buffed* dogs. *Macho* or *macha* dogs don't bite any harder or run any faster or climb any better. Slim and trim is your best goal for K-9 performance, health and longevity. Try restraining a skinny adult coyote some day, or better yet a 15 pound gibbon ape.

Elbow dysplasia: This term denotes a group of disorders which develop due to growth asynchrony of the radius and ulna. These bones are parallel and must grow synchronously to be normal. The resulting joint pathology can be attributed to an incongruity of the articulating surfaces of the radius and ulna as they meet the humerus. It is believed this incongruity leads to vulnerability of the anconeal process, medial coronoid process, and the humeral condylar surface which faces the medial coronoid process. The terms for these pathologies are: ununited anconeal process (UAP), fragmented coronoid process (FCP), and osteochondrosis dessicans (OCD) usually of the distal-medial humerus. Repair of these items is usually advisable and has little risk with fair to good chances of benefit. The joint incongruity is another issue and may be responsible for continued lameness, as it is probably impossible to correct. Elbow X-rays are increasingly requested by breeders and should be performed at 1 year along with Orthopedic Foundation for Animals (OFA) preliminary hips, and earlier if ever lame. If your veterinarian recommends anesthesia for positioning, I suggest you comply. As in hips, positioning is essential to accurate interpretation. X-ray diagnosis of this complex of problems can be difficult because of the very subtle changes in early clinical expression, usually at 5 months. In time, the changes (arthritis) become easier to see on the X-rays, consequently more difficult to help with surgery.

Conformation: It would not be a bad idea for officers selecting any dog for service to observe and take notes at dog shows, paying particular attention to the best *movers*. Look at the angle of the knee and tarsus. Note how the judge checks bite, controllable temperament, and many other attributes. Pay attention to the term angulation, usually applied to the rear limb. Overangulation can be just as deleterious as *too straight*. In the rottweiler, a lack of angulation will predispose to patellar luxation and can be associated with OCD in the hock joint. If there is too much angle in the carpus, as in some German shepherds, dogs coming off elevated surfaces can have a leverage disadvantage. Keep in mind the best show dogs may not be good working dogs. However, watching and asking questions can give you insight about all dogs and maybe help you make a better selection.

Hereditary is a difficult term. The difference between the rottweiler, German shepherd, goldfish, or Boston terrier is heredity. Breed predisposition is more pertinent. Selection of the best individual within the desired breed is your main task. Hip dysplasia has gained notoriety as a hereditary disorder by sheer numbers of careful lineage studies. Other problems such as OCD, FCP, UAP, and transitional segmentation of the spine are very likely hereditary but lack numerical validation.

Panostitis, AKA *pano, panosteitis, growing pains*: Though primarily a disease of the adolescent large breed dogs, I have diagnosed it in a 6-year-old German shepherd *Zoll* dog in Germany. The worst case I can remember was in a 25 pound basset hound pup. It can shift from leg to leg and persist for several months. It often presents with such pain, one considers fracture as a differential diganosis. It can recur, though it usually does not. Treatment consists of analgesics, occasionally steroids, rest and patience. Some cases are serious enough, with high fever, to suggest the possible need of antibiotics. Diagnosis is usually made by discovery of very sensitive midshaft long bones. X-rays are very helpful. In my experience, the German shepherd is the most commonly afflicted breed. There are no known sequelae.

Shoulder: OCD and biceps tenosynovitis are the most common afflictions of the shoulder. OCD manifests as a painful shoulder, maybe both shoulders, at about 5 to 8 months. X-rays confirm this condition. On X-rays, flattening of the humeral head represents the bed from which a cartilage flap has lifted. Surgery to remove this flap is highly successful, and "normal" function can usually be expected. I do not personally agree with exercise or rest alone (masterful neglect) to help shoulder or any joint OCD. Without an operation, a relatively common later life syndrome of biceps tenosynovitis results from the loosened cartilage flap disintegration and sequestration of pieces in the biceps tendon sheath. Surgery can remedy this too, but the condition is a little more uncomfortable for the patient than OCD alone. I have seen several cases of torn biceps tendon in rottweilers. This injury can occur when the *flexed* biceps muscle (just like your biceps) is suddenly taken in the downward direction by great force. I believe, but cannot prove, this occurs in the rottweiler because they have a relatively bulky muscle pattern compared to some of their tendons. If they don't make a jump, by hanging up a wrist they can easily put several times their body weight on this ligament, which is never bigger than a slender pencil.

OCD of the tarsus is seen in the Labrador, golden retriever, rottweiler, chow, but rarely in the German shepherd. It can be debilitating and should be considered in any lame dog with very straight hocks.

The carpus (wrist) is rarely a problem in the young dog unless there is some obvious deformity. In the older dog it may be associated with hyperextension injuries sustained when landing full force on just one front foot (examples are frequent jumping out of patrol car windows onto pavement, jumping from high walls). Carpi with too much angle are at some disadvantage here, suggesting the higher frequency of these injuries in German shepherds with sloping pasterns. The *high rise* syndrome, landing full force on the front feet from a 10 foot jump, can happen to any breed.

Degenerative myelopathy: The progressive deterioration of conduction fibers in the spinal cord. There is no discomfort. The first sign may be a *swaggard gait* (ataxia) in the rear legs. The dog may not know where his foot is in space and demonstrates slowed replacement of the foot when knuckled over (decreased conscious proprioception). It can go from barely detectable to paralysis in months. While seen most often in the aging German shepherd, the disease can affect other breeds. There is no cure, though steroids aften slow the disease progression. In my experience, intervertebral disks, spinal malformations and instabilities, tumors and meningitis are more common, and a diagnosis of degenerative myelopathy is usually correct after ruling out these other disorders. Do not be too hasty accepting degenerative myelopathy as a diagnosis upon physical examination, as you may be overlooking a curable disease.

Stenotic canal: A malformed, small or tight spinal neural canal. Seen in the Doberman, rottweiler neck and the German shepherd lumbosacral area, it is not usually a problem in and of itself, but it can be associated with wobbler or cauda equina syndrome in later years. Sometimes these areas pinch nerves early in age due to loose linkage of spine to sacrum (in the pelvis). Surgical removal of the restricting bone, and or stabilization of the loose link, can be beneficial if clinical signs develop. In a small number of cases, this condition is probably something that will occur even with your closest scrutiny and attempts at avoidance.

Transitional segments: When our spines develop, nature needs to decide at points of transition just what kind of vertebra to build—cervical, thoracic, lumbar, sacral. Sometimes there is confusion. The most pertinent level is at the lumbosacral (LS) junction. The last (7th) lumbar vertebra may act like a sacrum. Or the first sacral segment may take on characteristics of the last lumbar. Instability or stenosis may be associated. Normal wear and tear of the disk (narrowing with age and associated bulge into the neural canal) may eventually lead to compression of the cauda equina nerves and a syndrome often called cauda equina syndrome involving nerves to the tail, bladder, bowel, and leg (sciatic nerve). Cauda equina means horse's tail—the descriptive term for what the bundle of nerves looks like at the lumbosacral junction. Occasionally the OFA readers will report transitional vertebra on the standard protocol hip X-rays. If this is the case for the police dog, have a *lateral* pelvic X-ray taken *coning down* on the LS junction. If there is any question, and if the dog is clinical, further consultation would be advised.

Cauda equina syndrome (CES): Clinical signs include a weak tail. The officer should know his dog's normal tail set in order to monitor any changes. Owners have gone back to family albums to recall the normal tail set. A pendulous tail may be the first and only sign you see in cauda equina syndrome. The Rott and Dobie don't have a tail for this observation, but the anal sphincter is more apparent. If the anal sphincter is weak, it may gape open, and the dog may be fecally incontinent or pass gas or feces when barking (not nice in a squad car in the winter). Rear limb ataxia, pain on rising, knuckling over on toes and worn toenails, carrying the leg so far forward the knee touches the ribs (sciatica), and a rocked croup are a few of the other signs of CES. Special X-ray studies are often needed to diagnose this condition. The bowel and bladder diameters are often good indicators of pelvic nerve function. Too large is a good indication of pelvic nerve pressure at the LS junction.

Treatment of CES is often surgical. The purpose is to relieve pressure (decompress). Most of my cases are German shepherds, but many other breeds are seen as well.

Acute disk rupture: This can happen to any breed of dog. The disk is a 2-part cushion between the vertebrae. The outer case of fibrous tissue, the annulus fibrosis, contains the gelatinous core, the nucleus pulposis. Normal wear and tear of the annulus will allow nuclear expulsion, and/or annular bulging. The result of such an event may run the spectrum of minor pain to paralysis. The medical and surgical urgency of disk rupture relates to stopping the process of rupture, if possible, and restoring lost circulation to the spinal cord. The cord is a tubular brain. If it dies, it won't come back. The signs may be similar to a stomach ache in some early cases, with abdominal splinting, and reluctance to jump. In advanced cases the signs may include severe neurologic impairment and paralysis. When medicating the pain-only patient, be careful not to take away all pain in haste to return the dog to active service. This scenario can result in irreversible paralysis. I have seen a great number of dogs lost because of this *medical practice*. Besides, if your dog is always medicated, when will you know he's better?

If I had to choose a pup, I would probably choose a couple of alternative individuals of breeds applicable to the intended service. I would select from breeders who can boast a proven litter. Then I would meet the mature offspring and of course the dam and sire. I would ask the breeder to read the list of problems below and to state if they have ever been diagnosed in their line. The dam, sire and several of the offspring would have been OFA certified including elbows. I would have the puppy or dog examined from tooth to tail. I would spend time on obedience with this animal and watch for gait abnormalities. I may show the puppy or dog to gain the opinions and validation of experts. I would keep my emotional distance until I was certain about my dog's soundness. I wouldn't hesitate to investigate any lameness. I would be prepared, and half expecting, to start all over again with another dog. I would look forward to bonding and serving with my perfect choice.

The list is not long, but it is important to distance yourself from these disorders:

Ask if the breeder has certified the dam and sire with OFA. Ask about both elbow and hip dysplasia, cauda equina, transitional segments, disk ruptures, degenerative myelopathy, OCD of any joint including shoulders, knees, tarsus.

Don't ask your veterinarian to be your geneticist. There are ethics involved in the doctor-patient-client relationship that will likely serve to keep most doctors' opinions to themselves.

When medicating the pain-only patient, be careful not to take away all pain in haste to return the dog to active service.

Officer Casey Bokavich, K-9 Dax and
Sgt. John Hawkins, Redding Police
Department, California.

CHAPTER 3

STREET PATROL

"The dog is a tactical tool.

Make him part of the plan.

But do not let the dog *be* the plan."
—Deputy Jim Barnes, K-9 Trainer
El Dorado County Sheriff's Department, California

Depending on the incident, the K-9 team may be contact or cover.

Competency in basic police dog operations is the prerequisite for tactical training and deployment. The team must have reliable performance capability in obedience, agility, search, protection, and apprehension. For patrol work, the dog must have balanced drives and a strong affinity for his handler. The handler must be a competent, experienced police officer who has maturity, initiative, and who has developed a close working relationship with his dog.

Essential performance standards are not recognized by the law enforcement agency that purchases either an imported or domestic pretrained dog, places him with an officer for a few weeks of training exercises, then puts the officer and dog out on the street.

Bonding, developing the human-animal relationship necessary for police service, takes time. It takes the dog and handler living and working together. Sometimes the officer and the dog develop a successful working relationship. Sometimes they do not. To work reliably with the dog, an intelligent individual, the officer, even if he is an experienced handler, must go through a program of consistent, comprehensive training with his canine partner. A professional training program is essential whether the dog is pretrained or "green," with little or no previous training.

The department will not save money by failing to provide high quality initial and maintenance training. The department is liable. The error may play out in court or in settlement decisions that cost the department far more than the training, decisions that jeopardize police dog teams everywhere. The error may cost the department a potentially good handler, a good dog, both the handler and the dog, or the entire police dog unit.

What is the handler doing?
The dog does not determine who to apprehend; the handler does.
All I am concerned with when defending a case is that the use of force was
appropriate under the circumstances presented to the officer.
—Eugene Ramirez, Attorney, Los Angeles, California

Justifiable Use of Force: What a reasonable person would determine to be that level of force necessary to effect the arrest. These are the instructions given to the jury deciding if an officer has used reasonable force to achieve a lawful purpose on the street.

Available to the patrol officer are verbal skills, empty-hand controls, chemical agents, impact weapons, and firearms. The K-9 officer incorporates another dynamic tool, the trained dog, into the system. On the street, each incident has so many variables that it is not possible to predetermine what tool the officer should or will use. The K-9 officer must evaluate each situation, integrating dog handling with other skills, combining tactics to produce a positive effect.

Sometimes the least force is most effective. An offender is walking down the street. The K-9 unit rolls up, "Stop here. I need to talk to you. Don't run or I'll send the dog." Verbal tactics combined with K-9 presence. The suspect stops. Officers handcuff and search the offender while the dog sits quietly panting in the back of the patrol car. Sometimes the dynamics of the situation calls for the immediate use of force. A shooter confronts an exposed officer or people in the area. The officer may fire his weapon and send the dog at the same time. Or, faced with a high risk situation, the officer may decide not to deploy the dog.

Under the Fourth Amendment, police may use only such force as is objectively reasonable under the circumstances. All determinations of unreasonable force "must embody allowance for the fact that police officers are often forced to make split-second judgments—in circumstances that are tense, uncertain, and rapidly evolving—about the amount of force that is necessary in a particular situation." *Graham v. Connor.*[9]

"Requiring officers to find and choose the least intrusive alternative would require them to exercise superhuman judgment. In the heat of battle with lives potentially in the balance, an officer would not be able to rely on training and common sense to decide what would best accomplish his mission. Instead, he would need to ascertain the least intrusive alternative (an inherently subjective determination) and choose that option and that option only. Imposing such a requirement would inevitably induce tentativeness by officers, and thus deter police from protecting the public and themselves. It would also entangle the courts in endless second-guessing of police decisions made under stress and subject to the exigencies of

What if the offender uses your dog as cover? Will you shoot?

9. *Graham v. Connor*, 490 U.S. 386, 397 (1989)

the moment.

"Officers thus need not avail themselves of the least intrusive means of responding to an exigent situation; they need only act within that range of conduct we identify as reasonable." Scott v. Henrich.[10]

POLICE DOG CONTROL

"There is a common thread which runs through all the training conducted by the K-9 Unit and a skill which the handler must possess before he can work the field with his dog. This mandatory skill is control of the dog. Because the K-9 Unit is deployed in a densely populated, urban environment, the handler must have control over his police dog. To allow K-9 teams to be deployed without such control would invite possible injuries to innocent persons and would create an unacceptable liability for the City. The handlers must develop control over the dogs in a number of ways. K-9 searches are conducted off-leash. Therefore, the handler must be able to control his dog without the use of physical restraint devices. The handlers learn to control their dogs by voice commands and by hand signals."
　　　—Captain Dick Bonneau, Los Angeles Police Department, California

How many people do you arrest who stand still and comply? Can you control your dog if the suspect dances or screams, puts up an arm to ward off the dog and stares at him, takes a martial arts stance, runs back in fear while giving up, or rolls off a fence and gives up as the dog detains him?

There are times an officer needs the K-9 to apprehend an armed, motionless offender. There are times the officer needs to keep the K-9 from biting a physically active offender.

10. *Scott v. Henrich,* 39 F.3d 912 (9th Cir. 1994).

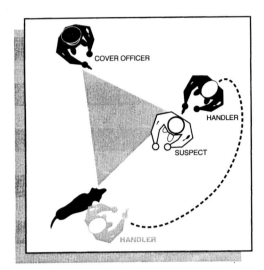

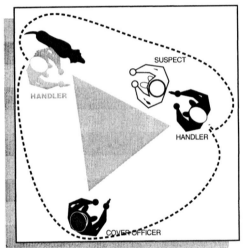

Command control is essential. What has been misidentified as a "tactical out," where the officer must physically pull the dog off a passive suspect, is in fact a bad street tactic. A dog does not know the *aus* until the suspect can stand still, fall down, or flee, and the dog will call out. A dog does not know the apprehension until the suspect can fight, flee, or hide, and the dog will make the apprehension. The trained police dog performs apprehensions and calloffs in response to his handler's verbal commands.

Pay attention to what happens in training. One department did not. The dog was hot and cold in training, not dependable on the bitework, a good searcher but tending to back off under pressure. Sometimes the dog would spin, leap, and act like a clown at inappropriate times, his display of avoidance behavior.

One night they were chasing a stolen vehicle across a parking lot. In full view the suspect jumped out of the car and ran. Sent in pursuit, the K-9 ran after the suspect, followed by the handler and a cover officer. Midway across the parking lot, the dog broke off the pursuit, ran back to the approaching officers, and spun circles in front of them. Although the handler repeatedly commanded him forward, the dog danced alongside, blocking and tripping him.

Across the lot the suspect disappeared through a wood fence into an apartment. Looking over the fence, the cover officer saw a smashed window with curtains moving inside. The dog refused to enter the yard. Disgusted, the handler snapped a lead on his dog and took him back to the patrol car. Meanwhile, the cover officer called for the suspect to come out. When the handler returned, his cover officer was arresting the suspect.

Back in the parking lot, however, their lieutenant drove onto the scene just as the dog got out of the patrol car window and fled toward the freeway, behavior clearly showing he did not want to be a police dog.

In another city during the Christmas season, the police chief told his K-9 sergeant to have their dogs patrol the busy shopping malls. "Let the good guys know we're out here, and send a signal to the bad guys that we're out here too." This directive caused concern: "My dog will be looking for the bad guy. What about all the kids running around?" Sadly, the dogs had little street experience with normal, friendly people. They worked evenings or nights to answer high risk calls. Highly defensive, they perceived most situations as threats. How many police dogs are part of proactive community policing programs?

CONTACT-COVER

At the scene of an arrest, the K-9 officer may be the *contact* or primary officer, or he may be the *cover* or backup officer. The K-9 team must be capable of performing effectively as contact or cover, depending on the incident. If there is a high probability the offender will fight the arresting officer, for example, the handler may conduct all the business of the encounter as the contact officer to reduce the potential for injury, both to officers and to the offender himself. If there is a high probability of an escape attempt, particularly with multiple offenders, the K-9 team acting as cover gives full attention to the suspects through a position of surveillance and control.

Events change. Primary and cover officers' roles change. What starts out with the contact officer calling the K-9 unit for backup may end up with the K-9 officer taking over the contact position at the scene, while the officer who made the initial contact moves to the cover position.

The shaded triangle represents the *Area of Responsibility* covered by the backup officer and the K-9 team. Officers must stay clear of this triangle while the offender is being controlled, handcuffed, and searched. The officer handcuffs the offender standing, kneeling, or prone, depending on the level of threat. Good handcuffing tactics using the police dog as cover combine verbal skills with physical alternatives and control. Keep the dog in your peripheral vision. You must be able to disengage or escalate as needed. If you cannot perform the tactic reflexively, then it will not work.

When handcuffing, have the suspect put his hands together behind his back, move in quickly with a control hold, use the dog as a distraction (tell him you are getting the wallet out of his pocket), get the cuffs on.

Give compliance commands to suspects while making K-9 assisted arrests. One officer remarked, "I don't say anything to suspects. They never comply anyway." What is this officer's liability? While it is true many offenders struggle with the dog, the handler has the responsibility of telling the suspect what he wants him to do. Be authoritative but calm with the suspect. Use the necessary additional control methods at the same time. The objective is to bring the situation under control. The handler who fails to give verbal commands fails to use one of the safest, most effective tools available to him.

Yelling or screaming at the suspect typically escalates the situation. Clear commands get compliance. Shouting incites the dog and causes general chaos. Suspects take advantage of confusion at a scene. Remember, it is hard for the dog to understand commands through a wall of sound.

Arresting officers are at risk during the calloff. Most

Combative suspect. The K-9 covers the arresting officer. Facing the suspect, the police dog is a strong deterrent. If the suspect fights, the officer may push him toward the dog to assist. If he knocks the officer to the ground, the dog will take protective action in response to verbal commands.

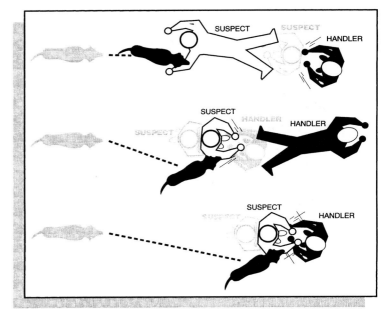

During the arrest, if the offender fights, the handler shoves him forward or backward, steps back, and draws his baton to assist the K-9.

Standing, kneeling, or prone arrest. Keep the dog in your vision close enough to respond if needed but at a distance that ensures control. You control whether the offender can or cannot see the dog.

The cover officer stays out of the arrest triangle and moves as necessary to keep the handler out of his line of fire.

K-9 officers spend a few seconds distracted by calling the dog off. At that moment the suspect draws a weapon and fires. *Focus on the offender* while commanding the dog to the watch position. Do not look away. In milliseconds the offender may shoot or throw a knife. If the suspect is armed, *maintain cover* until he complies and you move forward to arrest him.

> Most officers are not used to working with a police dog. You know your ability. But that gentleman down the street, that other officer, his ability may not be as strong as yours. *You have to back up your dog.* Understanding your dog's strong and weak points is critical. Train yourself to compensate for that, recognize it working the streets, make your adjustments. Suppose your dog's a just-adequate open area searcher and you get a bad guy running into the woods. You have to compensate for your dog. Suppose your dog is not strong enough to take a particular person down. You have to get in there and do it. *The team concept is extremely important.* Stemming from ignorance, a lot of departments expect too much of their K-9s.
>
> —K-9 Officer

Depending on the dog, 8-feet, 10-feet, 12-feet, whatever you're comfortable doing. The backup officer is going to be offside, the dog in front, both focusing on the suspect. Now the suspect's only route of escape is straight back. I come up and apply a twist lock. O.K., I'm behind him. He knows I'm here already. Now I tell him to place his hand on the back of his head. 'If you fight, my dog comes, I got you.' Now I come up underneath his arm, rotate it underneath, place his hand in the small of his back, and I have him in a standing modified handcuffing position. If he does *anything*, all I've got to do is *step back* and *push*. Here comes the dog. I'm out of it. My backup officer is over there. The only thing now is the dog and the bad guy. If he's struggling with the dog, I draw my baton. Anything happening now is in front of me. Both my backup officer and I are completely out of the scene. It's strictly now between the K-9 and the bad guy until I choose to re-engage.

Another example: You shove him away, the bad guy reaches into his pants and pulls out a weapon. If the shooting starts, I'm out of the way. If the backup officer has to shoot, I'm not in the line of fire. If he goes down with the dog, decides to fight the dog, here I am, out comes the baton.

The handler doesn't *have* to push away. The handler can hold him. Now we can control a difficult subject from the front and the back. It's an optional thing. The handler always has control. Which way you hold onto the suspect, how the dog comes in, call him away, call him off—you've still got control. The backup officer assists only if he is needed. If he's not needed, he backs off completely. He lets the K-9 and the handler handle the situation. This takes training and discipline for the cover officer. If the backup officer comes to assist without being requested, you've got nothing but mass confusion. The handler doesn't know. The K-9 doesn't know.

Use the dog as a psychological tool. The dog is a diversion when you're taking someone into custody. I pull up, position the car, I get out of the car, and when I move behind the suspect I pop the door. I want the suspect to see the dog. I tell him, 'Look, if you fight, you've got 1 of 2 choices—either you fight me or you fight the dog.' So who's going to make the decision? That guy right there, and you've already got control.

What if the K-9 unit is the second unit there, and before that the primary unit is already out talking to the suspect? You've got a K-9 handler and K-9 out of position. What do you do there? When the dog team arrives, the non-K-9 officer relinquishes his primary position. He moves into a cover position, and the K-9 officer takes over the primary position. All he does is back up because the K-9 might be used. Already, you've not only defused the situation, but you've got everybody in exactly the position you want. The handler should be schooled in handcuffing both sides, right or left, and using the dog both ways.

The handler should be the officer giving instructions at the scene. He directs the dog, the suspects, any other personnel there, including the supervisor if he's there. He says you have to have these deputies here, Sally and Joe here, not over there. It is the handler's responsibility. The K-9 officer is under so much liability for the general public, for the officers, for the suspects, for everyone involved, it is an absolute. He is the technician, the expert.

—K-9 Officer

OFFICER PROTECTION

The offender who fights a K-9 officer has to deal with a *team*, the handler and the dog. Protection is discretionary. The officer may command the dog to stay at a distance while he controls the offender. He may have to fight the offender and call for the dog to assist. He may disengage in order for the dog to assist controlling the offender.

If the suspect attacks another officer, that officer decides: fight or feed. If he fights, *do not deploy* the police dog. If he feeds, disengages, pushes the suspect away, and moves back, deploy the dog. The suspect then has to deal with you, your dog, your baton, control holds, handcuffs, and other techniques. The other officer's job is to cover you, while you and your K-9 control the suspect. If you need assistance, tell the cover officer. After the suspect complies and you have recalled the dog, you may direct the cover officer to handcuff the suspect. *Disengaging requires specialized training with the K-9 team* because officers are generally trained to engage a combative suspect.

Control the head and you control the dog. After the suspect is handcuffed and searched, walk behind him to the vehicle, keeping the dog on lead and alert. Except for emergencies—the

Handcuff and frisk under the watchful eyes of the K-9. The offender's wide stance gives the handler control and time to react.

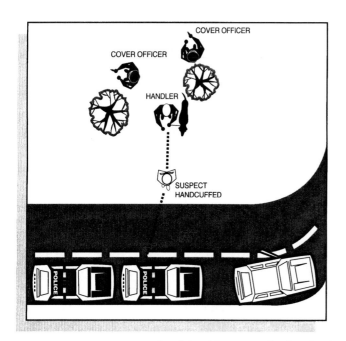

offender breaks or slips a cuff or produces a gun—the officer is not justified using his K-9 to apprehend a handcuffed offender. The lead becomes a safety factor if anybody trips or falls during the walk to the vehicle. Maintain a safe distance, usually 5 or 6 feet. Use a slip lead for short transports, a 6-foot lead for longer distances over rough ground.

Security guards at a shopping mall called the police when they arrested a shoplifter but failed to search him adequately. Handcuffed, the offender had pulled a gun out of his waistband, fired at them repeatedly, and fled. The call went out for a K-9. Responding within minutes, the dog team started to search in the direction of flight. The dog immediately picked up a track leading across a field to farm silos. The dog alerted at an outside door. Upon entry, the officer did not direct his dog or keep him in sight. The situation got worse when he heard the dog barking in another part of the building. Advancing toward the sound, the handler turned a corner and saw the suspect standing motionless, dry-firing his empty pistol at the dog. The dog sat barking in front of him.

Taking the suspect into custody. Handcuff and search the suspect before escorting him to the police unit. Walk with the dog on a slip lead in case the offender trips and falls. Cover officers stay alert in case he tries to escape or other suspects appear at the scene.

GUNFIRE

Controlled response during gunfire is a critically important tactic for the police dog. He should not attack automatically on gunfire. The dog responds during gunfire to the commands given by the K-9 officer, who may be returning fire and taking cover. The dog should be capable of working off lead during a shooting to maximize the handler's accuracy with his weapon. This requires training, including training with live fire. Familiarize the dog with various positions, different types of weapons, and the handler's quick movements during a shooting. Give him experience confronting gunfire during pursuits and apprehensions.

Officer experience deploying the dog during a shooting is essential. The handler develops confidence commanding the K-9 in a high stress circumstance. He knows what to do, and he knows what to expect from the dog. In a real shootout, if the dog changes his behavior, the handler has a better chance of reading the situation, which may save a life.

Be aware of the potential effect of gunfire on the dog's ears. The percussion can damage the dog's eardrums. Dogs have different responses to weapons discharge depending on their aggression drive and tolerance for pain.

Armed offender in a public area. A police dog may be deployed through a crowd, in a shopping mall, parking lot, or on a sidewalk, where the officer cannot fire his weapon. Focus the dog on the fugitive. Maintain visual contact and verbal control of the K-9. If people or vehicles get in the way, or if the suspect runs around the corner of a building, down the dog or call him to heel until you can deploy him safely.

MAN WITH A GUN

A man holding a gun is standing out in an open area of the city. The gun is held low, the barrel pointing toward the ground twenty yards away. Officers shout at the man to put the gun down. He does not respond. SWAT sets up a perimeter behind cover. Repeatedly they call through a car mike, Drop the gun. Still no response. A K-9 team is on scene. The handler deploys the dog. The dog runs forward to make the apprehension.

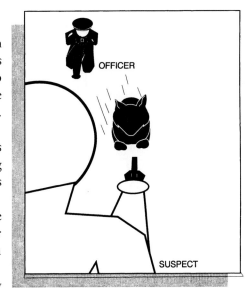

Without lifting the barrel of the gun, the man shoots the dog. SWAT does not return fire. When this happens, the handler loses it, gives a blood-curdling yell, runs out and tackles the guy. Instantly, the other SWAT team members follow. They disarm him.

The handler remembers nothing after seeing the man in the field. He doesn't remember his dog getting shot. He doesn't remember yelling or rushing out. The next thing he remembers is sitting in a patrol car with his dead dog in his lap.

In a combat situation, what do you do? Every K-9 officer needs training in the decision making process and weapons skills needed for tactical responses to lethal confrontations. Principles of movement:

- Use the dog as a distraction.
- Use the dog to assist apprehending the suspect.
- Do not sacrifice the dog to a higher level of force if it is not necessary, but do not hesitate to use the dog if it is necessary.
- Simultaneous to shooting and sending the dog, maintain cover or a low profile.
- When advancing on the suspect, use safe and effective tactics to control the dog and the suspect.
- Once the suspect is incapacitated, remove the weapon, handcuff, summon medical care: *follow department policy.* Despite injury to the dog, perform your duty as a police officer until you are relieved or the situation ends.

No cover. Fire, send the dog as a diversion, and make yourself as small as possible. The oncoming dog presents a small, fast-moving target.

A subject is holding a gun but not aiming it. If you tell the subject, "Drop the gun!" "Drop the gun!" "Drop the gun!"...at what point do you say, "That's enough"?

What is the immediate threat to you, to others, to the subject himself? Is there a safe option for distracting or disarming the subject? Can you execute a tactical retreat and regroup? Can you contain the subject and wait him out? Can you use chemical agents effectively? Can you deploy special weapons teams? *If you deploy the dog, what else are you going to do? Do not just send the dog and hope for the best. Develop a plan.*

MAN WITH A KNIFE

Principles of movement are the same. The reactionary gap is a factor. Facing off a knife-wielding attacker at close range, the K-9 officer is fully justified in the use of deadly force, no less the use of his dog. If he has no safe alternative, he must act decisively.

A K-9 officer arrived at the scene of a suspicious person call. As the handler left his cruiser, the suspect stepped out from hiding and began firing at the officer. The officer returned fire and took cover at his car, meanwhile deciding if and when to send his dog. As the handler was reloading, the suspect advanced aggressively toward him.

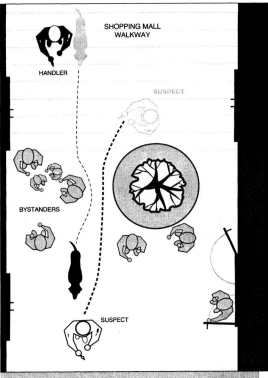

Not hesitating, the officer sent the dog as a tactical diversion, quickly reloaded, returned fire, and stopped the offender 10 feet from the door of the patrol car.

In this case the dog's purpose is to contact the offender and immediately inflict pain in order to prevent him from shooting the officers or citizens, or possibly himself. If the dog does not assist taking the offender under control, the risk of the K-9 being shot increases and the police lose a major tactical advantage.

The K-9 team is just that, a team. The suspect must deal with the search and apprehension capability of the dog. Simultaneously, he must deal with the handler's control techniques. If the suspect gives up prior to the apprehension, the handler recalls the dog. *The police dog is one law enforcement tool that can be recalled after deployment. A bullet cannot. The dog is one law enforcement tool that, if taken away from you by a suspect, will not be used against you.*

During a foot pursuit, the officer sent his dog after a fleeing suspect. The suspect passed a jogger running the same way. The suspect then rounded a corner while still being pursued by the police dog. At that point, the officer did not allow the dog to turn the corner too, since the dog would have been out of his control. He recalled the dog. If the dog is about to leave the handler's sight, he should be recalled or commanded to lie down, depending on the circumstances. In this situation the dog did not attempt to confront the innocent person. The

What are your options? What would a reasonable, objective officer do in this situation? If the offender drops the gun, arrest him. If he struggles with the dog, hold your position. If there is a diversion or other option, use it. If he swings the gun toward you, fire.

K-9 should not be sent after any suspect if the officer believes innocent persons may be mistaken as the suspect.

County sheriff's deputies were assisting the city police during student riots at a large university. Officers were attempting to clear an intersection of rioters but were pelted with rocks and bottles thrown by the rioters. A K-9 officer saw one subject throw large rocks and bottles filled with gasoline at them. Pursuing the subject and others westbound across railroad tracks and through apartment complexes, they came into the rear loading dock of a supermarket. The police dog was on lead.

The suspect in the rock throwing had taken a position in front of the crowd. The handler focused his dog on the subject by yelling at him to stop where he was or he would release the dog. The subject yelled back at the K-9 officer, then began to run through a group of rioters. The handler released his dog to run through the crowd after the suspect.

The police dog grabbed the suspect by the left lower leg, causing him to trip and fall to the ground. The suspect was taken into custody. The pursuit was approximately 100 yards. The suspect sustained no puncture wounds, but had visible teeth scrapes on his leg. He was booked for assaulting a peace officer.

Maintain cover and control the dog. Note the black ice. Gunfire can damage dogs' ears.

LOS ANGELES COUNTY SHERIFF'S DEPARTMENT

Master protection. Exiting the car door has less impact
on the dog's joints than jumping out of a window.
Do not bring the dog out the driver's side into traffic.

Options:
• 1) Place the K-9 team at close range. Before releasing the dog, focus him on the suspect beyond the cover officers. Or move up directly behind the lead officer.
• 2) Give separation for 2 K-9s at a scene. If a K-9 is in pursuit and the suspect changes direction, do not send a second dog.
• 3) Do not send the dog to dodge oncoming traffic.
• 4) In open terrain deploy from the K-9 unit.

HIGH RISK VEHICLE STOPS

When the handler makes an *investigative stop* of a pedestrian or a *traffic stop*, the police dog acts as a deterrent. For example, the officer observes a vehicle with a burned out tail light. Conducting a vehicle stop on the violator's car, he parks to the rear, offset to afford him a corridor of safety. The officer makes a safe approach and contacts the driver. Record check reveals a suspended license, no warrant. Citing and releasing the driver, and advising him not to drive, the officer writes the citation and talks on the radio near the patrol car. If available, he records the stop on a video camera mounted inside his patrol car. The police dog should be alert but should not be a distraction to the officer performing routine duties.

Typically, at the scene a window in the K-9 vehicle will already be down so the handler can deploy the dog from a short distance in an emergency. Some departments equip their K-9 vehicles with remote control devices that open a door or window for the dog to exit. Electronic openers can fail to operate when needed. Or they can operate accidentally. The electronic control unit is one more piece of equipment the officer has to carry, maintain and use safely. Each department has to weigh the tradeoffs in reliability versus technology for the type calls its K-9 officers handle.

An officer observed a vehicle make an illegal U-turn. As he initiated the stop, his dog started barking and bouncing from side to side in the rear of the police cruiser. Record check came back with a $50,000 warrant for the driver for conspiracy. As the officer arrested the driver, the K-9 jumped out of the window. For a few seconds the officer turned away from the suspect. At that moment, the driver pulled out a loaded revolver, fired 3 rounds at the officer, ran to his car, and drove away. Hit in the chest and shoulder by 2 rounds, the officer was able to radio for help before he collapsed. The handler who cannot control his dog jeopardizes everyone at the scene, including himself.

Officers used different techniques on vehicle stops. Practice making vehicle stops with local units so that you know how to assist them and they know how to work with

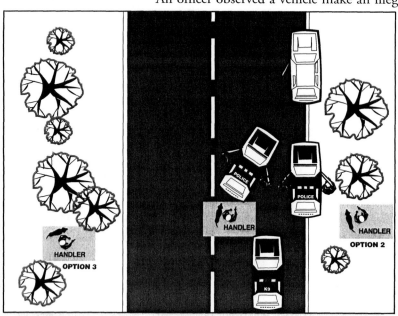

your K-9 unit. If you cover highway patrol stops, for example, set up training exercises to simulate what will happen if the other agency is the primary unit or if you are the primary unit.

One agency made a hot stop and got the dog out to clear the suspect vehicle. Without the handler's knowledge, a backup officer got into the passenger side of the K-9 car. When the dog finished clearing the vehicle, the handler sent him back into the patrol car, where the dog immediately bit the backup officer.

To cover a hot stop, when you know there is a high threat level, place the K-9 team where the dog can see an escape route, such as the passenger's door. Other potential escape routes, such as the driver's side, may be out of the team's control. If a suspect runs that way, either let him go or move behind the other units to focus the dog before sending him.

Watch the traffic. On a felony stop, all traffic should be stopped. If it is not, *think* before sending the dog after a suspect escaping across the highway. One handler used poor judgment, and his dog paid the ultimate price. The suspect got away. The car that hit the K-9 collided with a patrol unit. Where traffic is a hazard, cross the highway with the dog before sending him in pursuit. If the suspect weaves back across traffic again, stop or recall the dog before he enters the roadway. Citizen and suspect safety are critical factors. Suppose the dog takes the suspect down in front of oncoming vehicles. How big is the wreck and who caused it?

Historically, the barking dog has stopped occupants thinking about running. Two sheriff's units stopped a stolen vehicle with 4 occupants on a dark country road. Realizing their backup was an hour away, the second deputy barked into his external mike the entire time he wasn't busy hooking up an offender. "We thought we'd have ourselves a couple o' cop cars," one of the men said in booking. "It all happened so fast, I didn't see there weren't no real dog til it was over."

Suspects fleeing a stolen vehicle "suckered" the K-9 into pursuit around the corner of a building, the handler running behind. As soon as he turned the corner, the dog was shot. With the cover officer in pursuit, the second suspect doubled back on the K-9 officer and shot him from the rear.

Remember: "Cover Saves Cops." This is just as true for the K-9 officer as for any patrol officer. The dog may act as a diversion. He may capture an offender. But he does not afford his handler much greater personal protection from firearms than other officers. As the lead team, the police dog team is frequently at greatest risk.

Metro police stopped a vehicle in what turned out to be the middle of a Mexican-Iranian gang war. Occupants bailed out of the vehicle. A K-9 team pursued the driver five blocks to a garage where gang members were living. As the dog team approached the structure, they were met by shots fired through the walls.

The police dog fell. The street light exploded. As the handler frantically reloaded in the semi-dark, another armed suspect burst out of the garage. That suspect went down when the handler shot him just as a helicopter with five SWAT officers appeared on scene.

On vehicle stops, designating the K-9 as a cover team uses the police dog to best advantage. Some departments and some situations, however, dictate the K-9 unit be the primary unit. The K-9 officer is now in charge of the scene. Where the roadway permits, position the dog car just to the left and behind the suspect vehicle. The second or cover unit sits alongside. Officers use their doors for cover. Depending on the vehicles and the lighting, angling the units may provide better protection. The K-9 officer commands the suspect(s) to exit their vehicle one at a time. He directs each suspect to back up toward his location or between the cars to a cover officer who handcuffs, searches him, and secures him for transport.

Advocates of this technique feel the K-9 officer should be in the key position in order to have the best view of each exiting suspect and to react quickly if he runs or if he decides to fight the arresting officer. The drawback to this technique—if a suspect tries to escape or gets violent,

High risk stop, the handler as lead officer. Position the police cars for safety and suspect visibility. If a suspect runs and the dog deploys, another officer must take the lead.

or if the shooting starts and the scene breaks up—the K-9 officer has to choose between responding the dog or continuing to direct the operation. He cannot do both.

Before sending the K-9 to clear a vehicle, the handler has to focus his dog on the right vehicle, not on any officers or other people. A vehicle door must be open for the dog to enter. He should not be jumped through a window. If all doors are closed, the dog may still be used to check around the exterior of the vehicle for the scent of a person hiding inside. The K-9 officer and all other officers on scene stay behind cover until the handler indicates the vehicle is safe to approach. If the dog has entered the vehicle and appears

to be biting an occupant, the handler decides whether to approach the vehicle or stay behind cover and call the dog out.

If he moves forward behind the dog, the handler places one hand on the trunk lid in case an occupant tries to open it. After making a safe approach, the officer positions himself to afford some cover as the dog enters the car. Control the suspect(s) before risking exposure.

This is a high risk procedure that should not be attempted if there is another option, such as waiting for more backup, firing an aerosol grenade or ferret rounds into the vehicle. An armed offender inside the vehicle has the advantage over the dog. Any incident involving high powered weapons or an extemely high risk

Search for concealed suspects. The dog sniffs the exterior or enters an open door. Emergency use only. Requires frequent, realistic training. Be prepared to respond if the dog alerts. Be cautious if he does not alert.

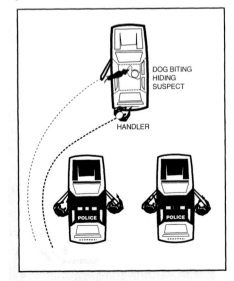

DOG BITING HIDING SUSPECT

HANDLER

POLICE   POLICE

vehicle may only be a suicide mission for the K-9, and subsequently for the handler. Keep your priorities straight. Regardless whether the plate reports clear or stolen, *any vehicle may be high risk*. The threat potential from a new sedan with a driver in a business suit may be as high as a dirty van with tinted windows.

By throwing a rock at the rear window a K-9 officer startled the occupant of a stolen vehicle into discharging a weapon. That simple act surprised the man, who revealed his position. At the same time, the act probably saved the dog's life. In jail the offender claimed, "If the cops had sent that dog in, I would'a blown him away."

A dog checking a vehicle is no guarantee it is clear. Officer safety is just as important on the approach after the dog exits as if there had been no dog. Wait to make the final approach until the K-9 has returned to the handler and he signals to go ahead.

Late at night, responding to a possible driver under the influence, the K-9 unit catches up to the vehicle as it bobs and weaves through a residential neighborhood. The car is moving erratically at 10-12 miles per hour. Thinking DUI, the officer flips on his lights and siren. For a while the car fails to yield. Then it stops. All in one motion, the officer stops, calls for the driver's hands on the steering wheel over the PA, opens the window for the dog, exits and moves toward the front of his patrol car. Out of the vehicle steps a broad-shouldered white male, 6 feet 4 inches, 230 pounds.

Ambush. The handler decides: hold the dog back and peek around the corner, wait for the suspect to make a move, or send the dog.

"Stop! Turn around and place your hands on top of your head."

No response. The subject walks toward the officer, jamming his hands into his pockets. More commands.

No response.

Here he comes.

Officer safety ends any more conversation. Out comes the baton. Out comes the K-9 at 92 miles an hour.

Seeing the dog running toward him, the subject drops to his knees with "C'mon doggy!"

This is the first clue the officer has. In milliseconds he asks, "What's wrong with this picture?" answers the question, and calls the dog out in time for the K-9 to close his mouth before slamming into the grinning man. The man hugs the dog and pets him.

Some miracle prevented him from getting bitten. Some miracle and an alert officer. Trying to drive his mom's car, the 35-year-old subject had the mental capacity of a 3-year-old.

Stolen vehicle. Felony car stop. They get everybody out, bring them back one at a time to arrest them, and have the last suspect leave the driver's door open. The handler can see a shadow figure with a head visible in the back seat. The officers call for the figure to come out. No response. They question the suspects, who say nobody is left inside. The K-9 officer sends the dog to search the car. The dog runs forward and jumps in. The dog growls. The car rocks. Headlights show him biting and wrestling a figure in the back seat. Approaching the car, the handler sees the K-9 attacking...a 4-foot tall teddy bear.

APPREHENDING ARMED SUSPECTS

Walking down the street, two armed robbery suspects are stopped and challenged by a canine officer. One suspect turns and runs. The officer has to decide instantaneously whether to send his police dog to stop the fleeing suspect. He sends the dog and seeks cover. The other suspect takes cover, draws and shoots. As the officer is fired upon by the second suspect, he maintains cover and returns fire. The handler then calls his K-9 back to help deal with the higher threat level. The second suspect is shot and falls, but the handler does not approach him without backup. Any dog that cannot be called off from a distance may present the handler with a problem in such a difficult situation.

A K-9 officer was dispatched to a corporate business complex to assist controlling a burglary suspect found by perimeter officers hiding next to a building. The suspect refused to submit to arrest. Cover officers asked the handler to use the dog to remove the suspect from concealment in the bushes near the wall of the building. From cover on the radio unit, the K-9 officer called to the suspect, giving him the opportunity to come out. When he did not comply, the handler sent the dog to detain the suspect. As the dog penetrated the bushes, the handler saw what he thought was a pistol in the suspect's hand stab briefly toward the sky. The handler informed the cover officers he had seen a weapon. Then the suspect, still concealed although the bushes were shaking, began firing. The officers returned gunfire. First out of the bushes came the rear end of the dog, tugging and pulling. Next came the empty-handed suspect in the firm grip of the police dog. Fortunately, the dog had not been hit in the firefight. Calling the dog off the suspect into his watch position, the handler advanced to arrest the man, who had by this time positioned himself face-down in the grass, hands behind his back, ready to be cuffed. The suspect had been shot in the leg. Knives and cash were recovered from his person. The empty pistol was found on the ground near the wall.

FIGHTS

As a peace officer, you are charged with the responsibility of keeping order. You have to deal with each incident on a case-by-case basis. After the incident is over, you will have to justify using your dog or not using your dog just as you would the use of other weapons. If neither combatant is using deadly force, your first action might be to call from behind cover: "Police officer with a dog. Get your hands up and face the sound of my voice." You may have them face the dog if they can see him. Or your patrol car, particularly if the dog is visible inside.

I was pulling up to cover this officer on a subject stop. We were out on somebody who was supposed to have a gun in the area. This really big guy, about 6 feet 4 inches, weighing about 300 pounds and muscular, decides to fight the officer. When I get stopped and get out, he takes off running.

So there are 2 officers chasing him and he's running down the street. I hit the button for the dog and send him. He runs past both officers, nabs the guy in the rear end, holds on, and the guy stops, 'OK, OK, get your dog!'

The reserve officer in pursuit with the lead officer grabs the guy's arm and tries to get him in a wrist lock before I have time to call the dog off. He struggles with the suspect, accidentally kicks the dog, and I'm yelling *Aus*—all this happens in about 3 seconds. Well the dog comes off the first bite, gets the kick from the reserve officer and locks onto him. I can't prove this, but I believe the dog thought he had a second guy to deal with right there in his face. I immediately called *Aus* a second time, and the dog came right off.

The officer was all right, but I ragged on him the rest of the night about shoving in there before I called the dog out. He was apologizing to me. He likes my dog, wants to be a K-9 officer someday. I felt bad because it's a matter of training. The department doesn't even give the regulars training with the K-9 unit. Everything the other officers learn about what to do around a K-9 comes from whatever happens on duty.

—K-9 Officer DeAnna Stevens

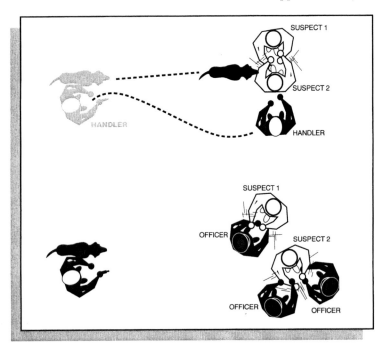

Fight in progress. Do not rush the dog into combat. After one bite, they might unite against their common enemy, the dog. From cover look and listen—fists, sticks, knives, or guns? Are their friends waiting in the dark? Barking may end the fight. If you decide to break up a fistfight, team up with the dog, use an impact weapon and take one person down at a time. Or wait for backup. Don't send a dog to a gunfight.

The dog and I entered a steak club to do a routine bar check in the town of Frisbee. As we entered the club, a fight was in progress. In order to handle the situation, I arrested the two intoxicated fighters and ordered others to go home due to their intoxicated condition. After a while, I had the two combatants inside my patrol unit and had cautioned several other drunks to find means other than driving to get home.

Then another problem arose when one large and very intoxicated patron decided that he was not going to leave, and in fact was going back inside regardless of all the good advice I was giving him. Now, you have to keep in mind that my dog was new to all this; he had never trained at night, had never been in a bar and had never seen a drunk person before, much less a whole bar full of drunks.

The dog was positioned at my side, taking all of this in, when I decided that the large drunken individual would have to be arrested. I told the drunk that he was under arrest and started to handcuff him. He unexpectedly attacked me, knocking me temporarily unconscious. The K-9, without having to have a command, jumped on the attacker and began to do battle with a mad man four times his size. As I began to regain consciousness, I could see the dog fighting with a large drunk who was attempting to get to me either to continue the attack on me or to avail himself of my weapons and use them against me.

In the few moments it took me to regain full control of my thoughts and faculties, I could see my K-9 fighting with the attacker while keeping himself between me and the attacker. I got to my feet and called the dog off and again tried to handcuff the suspect. But, you guessed it, the battle was on again.

The suspect apparently learned a lesson from the dog and, during his renewed attack, bit my hand, biting down on one finger all the way to the bone. He was attempting to bite my finger off. My dog, still somewhat dazed from his first real battle and smarting from the beating and eye gouging he received from this giant madman who apparently felt no pain, noticed that I was now in deep trouble. The attacker was beating my head while trying to bite my finger off.

The dog leaped over me and again engaged the attacker, biting him hard enough to cause him to release his bite from my hand. For the second time, in a very brief period of time, I was stunned and fell to the ground unable to assist the dog in his heated battle with an attacker, who was showing no sign of weakening or ceasing his attack. Fortunately, I was able to call for help on my hand-held radio. The dog had managed to get a good bite, and this time was not going to let go regardless of the severity of the beating and kicking he was receiving all the time keeping himself between me, still on the ground, and the suspect, who was still trying to get to me while fighting with the dog.

I was unable to assist with the suspect, and by now, the rest of the patrons in the bar decided it was time to leave. I was trying to get up and trying to keep the remaining patrons from leaving, as I would surely need some witnesses after this was over. The suspect finally began to realize that the dog was not going to release his grip and began to stop fighting. The dog held his grip firmly until the backup deputies arrived, at which time he released the suspect to the other deputies and ran over to me and licked my face as if to say, 'It's OK now.'

—Deputy Fred Johnson by Lieutenant Richard White

You arrive on-scene with two big males fighting and no backup. If the police dog team has to handle the fight alone without backup, the dog should be sent to distract one combatant while the officer controls the other. If the offenders run, the officer has to decide if he has reason to give chase. If so, he targets *one at a time*. His dog and he act as a team to take one into custody. After securing that offender, or turning him over to a cover unit, the team may pursue the second offender. The K-9 officer and his dog should *never separate to give chase*. Suppose your dog takes a man to the ground while you run a few more blocks to apprehend the other suspect. You have lost, actually you have given up, the ability to control or cover your dog.

When other officers are first on the scene, the K-9 team should act as a cover unit in case one of the offenders runs. *Sending a police dog into a fight where officers are engaged will probably get the officers bitten.*

One night in a western city, an officer is dispatched to a call of five men reportedly fighting in the street. The K-9 officer on duty responds as cover. When she arrives at the scene, the handler sees three men moving around in front of the other officer's patrol car. The patrol car is empty. She does not know what is going on. Exiting the patrol vehicle, the K-9 officer glances around to find the other policeman while keeping the three subjects in view. Movement in a side alley catches her attention. Looking down the alley, the handler sees the other officer chasing a fourth subject while a fifth runs immediately behind them.

Radioing for more backup, the K-9 officer orders the three subjects near the car to lie down on the pavement. Ignoring the officer, the three men take off down the alley after the others. Running behind them, the handler shouts at them to stop. When they keep running, she hits the car door release and draws her baton. The dog reaches her and runs at heel.

Farther down the alley, with no warning, the lead suspect spins around to challenge the pursuing primary officer. It is an open-hand challenge. The officer has no baton, no chemical weapons, and no cover. Without breaking stride, he brings up his fist and brings down suspect number one. Placing a boot on the back of the prone suspect, the officer draws his pistol and orders the oncoming four to the ground. Running toward the scene, the handler knows she is on a rescue mission. She hopes the dog will even the odds. She hopes even more for the arrival of backup.

The suspects refuse to go down. They start taunting the lead officer in unintelligible English. They have produced no weapons. They know their rights. This officer, this cowboy, cannot shoot them. They can take the officer out, "rescue" their buddy, and the officer will not shoot them.

They forgot the handler, who puts the dog down, comes up silently behind one suspect, buckles his knees, and prones him beside the dog. Seeing this, hearing the distant sirens, two more lie down. The handler's suspect thrashes around kicking. The dog is barking. The lead officer is trying to handcuff the now-squirming suspect under his boot. The last standing suspect kneels 10 feet away from the K-9 and spreads his arms. Calling softly to the police dog, "Good boy! Come here!" he inches gradually toward the canine. Harassed from

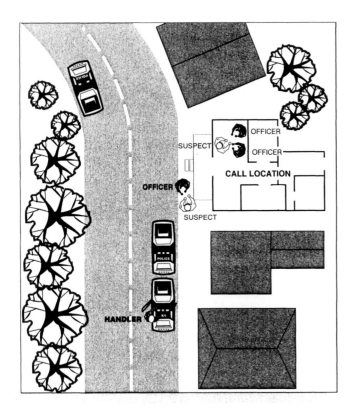

both sides, the dog stays down, but barely, barking first in one direction then the other. The handler struggles to restrain the prone suspect, command the dog, and order the other suspect down.

Bad as this incident was, it could have been much worse. Tactical errors by the primary officer were compounded by a police officers' association meeting at shift change that night admonishing everybody to "Keep your batons holstered. The media is after us on those two lawsuits last week." Chemical agents were not issued by the department. The K-9 officer had serious doubts about using the dog. Those doubts colored both officers' discretion and damaged their ability to regain control of the situation.

DOMESTIC DISPUTE

A husband and wife were arguing. The husband apparently had a gun to the wife's head. The man had many guns inside the house. Finally, the wife dialed 911 wanting help on the scene. The officer responded with his supervisor and the K-9.

Taking over the telephone from his wife, the man sounds intoxicated. He is told to come outside. Some time elapses. Finally, he comes out. Right away the officers tell him to put his hands out where they can see them. Now supposedly he is armed. He digs his hands into his pants pockets, clenching them into fists, so the officers don't know what he has. He is coming down the front walk directly toward the officers at a fast pace. The hands are still bulging in his front pockets. He does not acknowledge the orders to remove his hands from his pockets, to put them on top of his head. Now the officers are announcing the police dog will be sent to bite him if he does not comply. He is coming ever closer to the units and to the officers staged there.

The handler sends the dog. The dog bites through the pants pocket against the suspect's symmetrical fist, which looks like a ball. Everybody moves in, but they're still having a problem getting his hands out. He's been drinking. Ultimately, he is taken into custody for felony assault. He had assaulted the wife.

Even beyond appearing to have a gun in his hand, the probability was high that without the dog's presence he would have gotten shot. The dog's action protected the officers taking the man into custody. Normally, the K-9 would not be used on individuals involved in a family dispute. But this was a case of extremely high liability, a high danger point for the suspect. The degree of force was appropriate.

My K-9, two other deputies and I were dispatched to a particularly volatile call at an apartment complex south of the city. We were looking for a suspect who had savagely beaten his wife with a baseball bat after breaking into her home, then told her he was going to kill a deputy when they arrived.

As the deputies fanned out to search the area, the dog alerted me not to go near a large garbage bin. I called to the other deputies when the suspect jumped out of the bin with a bat in a combative stance. The suspect swung the bat with great force, narrowly missing the officers. I could not release the dog, as he could be killed by the bat. We attempted to reason with the suspect to no avail. Repeated requests to drop the bat fell on deaf ears. The suspect kept yelling that we would

Domestic dispute. K-9 team covers the perimeter in case a subject fights or flees. Bringing the dog into the scene may escalate the violence.

have to kill him and kept threatening to kill the deputies and repeatedly swung the bat at us.

After a while, we had maneuvered the suspect into an open wet grassy area away from the apartment complex. During this entire episode, we had the suspect surrounded, but due to the wet grass, could not get adequate footing to grab him from a blind side without subjecting the deputies to undue risk. After a period of time, the suspect tried to attack one of the officers. At that time I sent the dog, and he bolted toward the suspect during a moment of distraction. He hit the suspect hard, knocking him down. Then the dog got the bat away, allowing us to capture and handcuff the suspect without having to seriously injure or kill him. The 6 p.m. news treated the viewing public to a story about how the K-9 saved the suspect from his worst enemy, himself.

—K-9 Officer

The K-9 officer who at first assesses the risk of deploying his dog as too high does not give up but stays alert for an opportunity. *He* makes the decision to send the dog.

VEHICLE PURSUIT

Police were searching for a robbery suspect who had fled in a car chase and slipped into a wooded area. In a few minutes a K-9 found one suspect crouched in the limbs of a tree. The dog jumped against the tree trunk barking. The handler called the dog back to allow the suspect to climb down. Returning, the dog excitedly circled his handler, who was standing beside another officer. Leaping up, the dog bit the officer in the face, lacerating his ear and cheek.

Thirty minutes later, checking out another suspect sighting, dog and handler were back in their patrol car. As the car stopped, the K-9 targeted a man running under a helicopter hovering across a vacant lot. Bolting out the window as his handler called futilely after him, the dog grabbed the man beneath the chopper. He was the tow truck driver the police had called to remove one of the vehicles.

Both men received lawsuit settlements from the city.

What was the handler doing? High stress, fast moving street situations may cause the K-9 to act unexpectedly. Teams new to the street or experienced teams not paying attention will have problems unless the handler anticipates what the dog might do and maintains control.

At the end of a high speed chase through suburban streets, the suspect vehicle jumped a sidewalk and headed out across a dirt field, throwing dust and clods of dirt. Pursuit vehicles jumped the curb in the same place. Each officer's head hit the ceiling. The dog's did too. When the suspect vehicle slammed to a stop, the officers had seatbelts. The dog did not. The K-9 flew over the console headfirst into the dash. The handler briefly checked the dog, who shook himself then barked to get out.

Jumping out of the patrol unit, the handler sent his dog in pursuit of the running driver. Resolutely, the dog tried. He made it about 50 feet. There he staggered, paddled sideways a few yards, and finally sat down shaking his big head and staring

Fleeing vehicle crash. A high speed pursuit ends when the suspect vehicle crashes and the occupants bail out. Officers take the driver into custody and set up a perimeter. The helicopter on scene gives the arriving K-9 unit a direction of travel. Soon after he exits the patrol car, the police dog picks up the fugitive's hot track and captures him in a wooded area less than a quarter mile away.

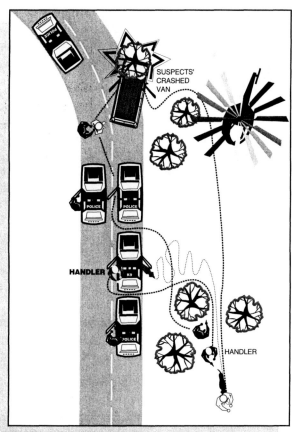

vacantly into the car lights. Realizing what had happened, the handler picked up his 90 pound partner, lay him in the back seat of a patrol car, and climbed in to hold the dog during the fast ride to the hospital. The dog had a concussion and eventually recovered.

Dog's skulls are incredibly hard. But impact damages their brains, like ours. Vehicle pursuits often end in crashes. Police dogs are vulnerable to highway accidents. High speed turns, bumps, and unexpected stops put the dog at higher risk than the officer. While the K-9 officer typically wants to be the lead vehicle in order to focus the dog on the fugitive, he may sacrifice the dog in the process. Restraint is usually a better tactic in pursuits involving the K-9 unit. The best tactics implement strategy that *anticipates* what suspects will do. For example, once a chase begins, divert the K-9 unit to a pickup point for a helicopter. Deploy the dog as soon as the suspect abandons the vehicle or wherever a containment perimeter has been established.

Deputies from a small rural county joined a chase that had begun two counties and 40 miles south where the driver and passenger of the van had robbed a bank. Rolling in pursuit were two K-9 units, eight police cruisers, and four highway patrol units. Beyond an intersection, deputies had set up a roadblock. When the suspects *hit* the roadblock the device flattened all four tires. That did not deter them, however, from driving on the rims at speeds over 80 miles per hour. Finally, in a remarkable display of stupidity at the state line, the van driver crashed through a fence, bounced 400 yards across a cow pasture, and shot into a willow lined ditch.

Hot on his wheels were all the cop cars. They too made the turn and plowed through the manure, fanning out at random as the vehicle pursuit ended. The K-9 units were closest. Two suspects. Two police dogs. The suspects had disappeared into the ditch. The problem ahead—focusing the K-9s on separate tasks—blinded the handlers to the problem overtaking them from behind—18 officers, all with guns drawn, racing toward the ditch. Media cameras were not far behind. A highway patrolman ran past a handler shouting "Get 'em! Get 'em!" The K-9 lit up. Seeing the dog's look, the patrolman froze. By now uniformed figures were swarming the ditch. The handlers loaded the dogs back into their units.

Officer safety determines field tactics. The police dog does not provide a shield or confer any special powers on the handler or the cover officers. When men of zeal obstruct a K-9 operation, if those men are wearing badges, get the dog out of the way.

As the second unit on a stolen vehicle stop, the K-9 team arrives just as the driver makes a critical decision—footbells. Jumping out to give chase, the handler hits the door release and vaguely hears an officer behind her say, "Carl, let the dog get him."

The overzealous officer keeps running, oblivious that he is blocking the dog's view of the fleeing suspect. Expecting the dog to pass her, the handler glances back just in time to see the dog nail the officer in the leg. She calls the dog out. Without breaking stride, the dog executes a perfect callout and redirect.

The police dog starts gaining on the suspect. Over his shoulder, the bad guy gets that oh shit look. He scales a brick retaining wall. The officers have him at gunpoint, calling for him to get his hands out where they can see them. Instead he throws his legs over, preparing to jump down the other side. Woofing, the dog finds his way around the wall. He grabs the suspect by the foot. Humpty-dumpty. Instantly calling the dog back out into view, the handler and cover officers complete a tactical approach and arrest.

Highway patrol chases an armed suspect for 15 miles over a mountain pass. At the bottom of a steep grade the suspect bails out of the car. Darkness and two feet of snow do not stop him. Arriving at the scene, the K-9 unit finds tracks jamming through stands of white pine and alder, heading toward the creek. The tracks sink knee deep into the wet snow. Only minutes behind, the handler feels he can overtake the suspect.

At the creek's edge, flashing his light down into the icy water, the officer realizes the suspect has forded the stream. He and his dog do the same. The police dog picks up the track on the other side. Running parallel to the creek for several hundred feet, the track turns left again across the water. Officer and dog follow. Three times, the offender re-crosses the stream, each time through deeper water. On two of the crossings he evidently runs *in* the stream for a distance before climbing out.

After the fourth crossing where the suspect tripped and fell forward, hand prints go as deep as the footprints. Several places the shoe prints point in opposite directions. They thrash through bushes.

The dog is intense. The tracks lead east into a stand of brush and fir. Branches break ahead of them. Calling his dog to heel, the handler takes cover behind a thick fir on the edge of the stand.

Using his scariest voice, he calls into the dark, "Bad guy, we have you surrounded." He cues the K-9 to bark.

"Bad guy, you are cold...you are tired...you will *freeze to death* out here. My dog knows where you are. Give up. Come forward to the sound of my voice."

Out of a small tree, "I can't get down."

In the officer's light the suspect is hugging a fir tree, his butt hanging out five feet above the snow. The tree is shaking. "Don't let the dog bite me."

"Bad guy, drop out of there. Keep your hands in the air where I can see 'em."

The tree is shaking hard. "Do it now or I release the dog." He sights along the gun barrel, the dog in his side vision.

As the suspect lets go and crashes into the brush, snow cascades from several trees, causing a whiteout. The dog goes ballistic. It takes all the handler's concentration to command his dog while straining to see those hands.

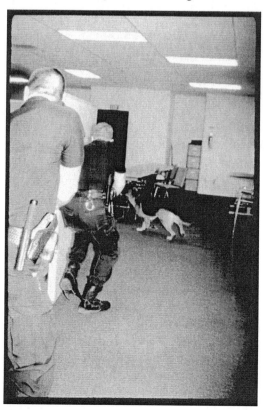

COVER OFFICER TACTICS

■ K-9 deployed—Take your lead from the handler. Do not get in front of the handler or dog. Watch the handler's back, not the dog.

■ K-9 apprehension—Do not approach the suspect. Do not shout or distract the dog. If the suspect fights you, push him away.

■ K-9 incident report—Do not describe what the dog team did in your report. Refer to the K-9 officer's report.

■ K-9 officer injured—Have a transport plan for the dog.

SWAT team insertion. Rapid deployment with K-9 onto rooftops, roadways, or other strategic areas. Note low profile of dog in head-on view. Officers and dog are prepared to deploy in seconds.

K-9 AND SWAT

The SWAT (Special Weapons and Tactics) crisis entry was conceived in Los Angeles as a silent, high-safety search and secure operation. Rapid deployment has evolved into a lightning-fast, high-risk, objective-oriented operation with a diversion on entry. Explosive entry techniques for tactical teams, breaching barricaded facilities with demolitions to effect a rescue with speed and surprise, enables officers to surprise occupants and act before they can react. A typical house can be taken in 6 seconds. Officers are totally occupied with high-stress decision-making. Offenders are imitating this type entry to immobilize occupants and burglarize innocent citizens in minutes, using high-powered weapons, before the victims can dial 911.

Combining SWAT-type teams with K-9 teams requires careful planning and tactical training. First, departments considering using elements of these units together have to decide if a K-9 is actually needed. Most SWAT situations do not require a dog, or the dog would be a hindrance or hazard if deployed. Second, there is a high probability of the dog getting killed if used on entry. Third, many hours of training are required getting the dog accustomed to SWAT officers, with hoods, masks, and unusual movements, and achieving the control necessary with a dog tough enough to perform reliably when exposed to SWAT situations. Generally, only the largest urban departments with high demand for special enforcement units can justify tasking police dogs in a primary SWAT role.

A SWAT team was inside a house. A K-9 team was searching outside the house. The dog alerted underneath the building's crawlspace. Peeking with a mirror, the handler saw the rear end of his dog disappear. The animal hoisted himself up through an apparent hole in the floor. Yelling to his cover officer to stay there, the handler ran around into the house. Inside he found his dog sitting at heel beside one of the SWAT team members. Three subjects were proned on the floor under arrest. Casually approaching the officer, the handler asked in a low voice, "Did the dog bite anybody?" "No," came the reply. "He got in and was about to bite when you yelled something and he came over and sat."

For SWAT to deploy with K-9, the handler must understand scent diffusion and how the dog reacts in different environments. In addition to obeying voice commands, the dog can work by hand signals alone. The handler has to read the dog's alerts accurately, including brief behavior changes, or indications, just as he would the patrol dog on a building search. Precise coordination, K-9 direction and control are even more critical to prevent the accidental biting of SWAT officers.

Like patrol dogs, the dog on a SWAT mission must be controlled during gunfire. The handler either directs the dog to apprehend or else detains the dog, depending on circumstances, while officers are firing. The dog goes after a suspect *only when the handler sends him.* This prevents needless injury to the dog and also protects the friendly forces from the dog.

Police dogs are used in SWAT applications for two primary purposes:

1. **Outer perimeter control:** The dog team is placed on the outer perimeter near any potential escape routes. If the suspect flees past the inner perimeter to the outer perimeter, the dog is an alternative to deadly force.

2. **Building search:** After the SWAT team clears a building, the dog re-searches it. This double check system often finds suspects.

Two armed suspects were holding hostages in a school. The SWAT team did not know where the suspects were inside the building, so they called the SWAT/K-9. After the building was *cleared without using the dog,* one suspect was still missing. When deployed, the dog had no trouble scenting him behind a wall. Even with the dog alerting in front of them, SWAT officers had difficulty finding him.

Shots fired call—position unknown. Because of incorrect location information given to dispatch, a K-9 officer was directed to a sniper's kill zone thinking he was going to conduct an area search for a hidden suspect. The officer advised he was at the location, left the patrol car and entered the field. A sniper then fired from the second story of a nearby hotel. The officer took cover, called for backup, and returned fire while controlling the dog in a down stay. Hands up, the sniper fled the hotel. Racing in pursuit, the K-9 hit the sniper from behind and brought him down in the hotel parking lot. Cautiously, the K-9 officer advanced, called off the dog, and arrested the suspect.

"Generally, we wouldn't use the SWAT team on area search. If you had a serious enough felony, known armed suspects and a good perimeter, yes. Usually, SWAT searches a building or structure rather than a city block.

"There have been some times when we deployed a team in thick brush. A warehouse in

SWAT entry. Crisis entry with explosive diversion. Highly trained SWAT team makes entry and secures the interior of the structure in seconds. This extremely effective tactic uses surprise and speed to control occupants and weapons. Large police agencies train rigorously to use K-9 in tactical operations. If your department cannot maintain a full time tactical unit with K-9, keep the dog outside or at the perimeter to capture fugitives.

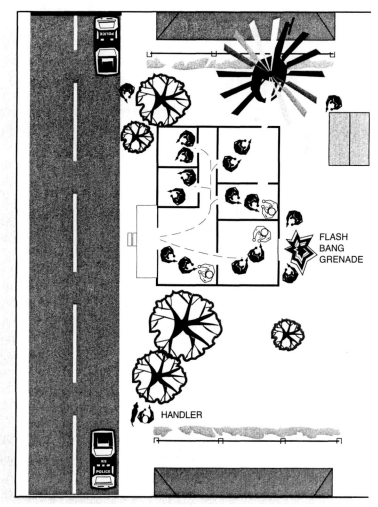

FLASH BANG GRENADE

HANDLER

Downey was robbed. We had literally just finished a barricaded incident here in East Los Angeles at 5:30 in the morning. I was calling to say, "This is over." They said, "Did you hear what's happening in Downey?" I said, "I've got a dozen SWAT guys here suited up ready to go. We can be there in 15 minutes. Can you use us?" There were eight suspects armed with AK-47s, mini 14s, two-way radios from the suspects who were inside to three suspects who were outside as lookouts in a van. They had a scanner. Very sophisticated. Five days earlier, they had stiffed in a 211 call to the place to see what the response would be.

"They went in through the roof of this place during the early morning hours. Five suspects waited inside with three in the van outside. When the first group of employees arrived, they took them all down then hit the safe.

"Somebody got on the phone and dialed 911. The first two Downey units got there and were both ambushed from behind. One officer got hit four times in the back—.223 rounds—and survived. The other was hit in the leg. There were 60 rounds fired in front of the store. The five suspects inside fled to the back and literally John Wayne'd it out the back door, firing their .223s at the lock and hasp. Blew the lock off the door. Otherwise they would have all been contained. We had nine hostages and five heavily armed suspects inside. Fortunately, they got out.

"The back of this warehouse butts up to a freeway. The freeway embankment is all covered with very very thick brush. The building was contained about 6 a.m., just before sunrise. We elected to deploy three K-9 search teams, which included the dog, handler, and three SWAT backup deputies. They each had an area of responsibility. We actually shut down the freeway. When they started the search, it was 8 a.m. on a Tuesday morning following Columbus Day. The Santa Ana Freeway is a major north-south thoroughfare. What we actually ended up shutting down was that freeway, two north-south interchanges, and north and south off-ramps. It was a major decision, but it had to be done.

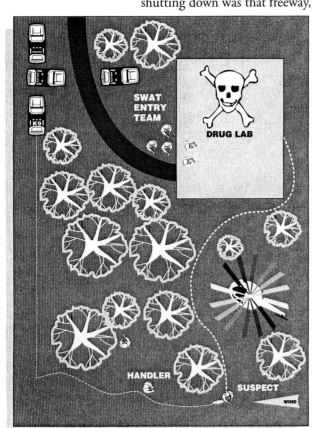

Drug lab. Night operation to take out a drug lab. As officers enter the building, a suspect escapes. Helicopter infrared sees the suspect and advises the K-9 team. Vehicle tracks, man tracks, and warm body contact areas are visible to the infrared camera until they cool to the background temperature.

"Within a couple minutes they found a mask, bulletproof vest, and an AK-47. We weren't dealing with amateurs. We couldn't allow the freeway traffic to continue. If we encountered another suspect and got in a firefight, everybody on the freeway's endangered. So we shut down the freeway. Then they continued to search, K-9 on point with three SWAT deputies behind and to either side. The minute they found that bulletproof vest and AK-47, all the rules changed. The dogs were not actually going into the brush. It was thick. They were going around the perimeter. The handler and backup deputies maintained their distance. It took about an hour, maybe a little longer to clear a half mile. About 25 yards of open area, the remainder thick brush.

"We had air support with a FLIR camera even before we deployed the dogs. Infrared wasn't seeing anything at that time. It became critical when these K-9 teams started to approach one another. When they got visual, one team would hold, the other would search. They'd go to a certain point, the other team would work. They ended up finding three bulletproof vests, three weapons (the 2 AK's...these had double banana clips on them), and about $50,000 in cash stashed back there.

"We then dealt with the building, and we used about 16 deputies inside to clear the building with three more dogs.

The inside was all set up like a warehouse with long aisles. Two SWAT deputies started at one end, two at the other end, start with the dog, letting the dog work down a corridor. The SWAT team would follow. Start with the next, maybe a different dog, hold. There was constant leapfrogging for SWAT.

"While we were searching the building, one suspect came out of the bushes about 300 yards beyond our perimeter. It was stupid. If he'd stayed there, he would have escaped. But he came out and walked right into one of the patrol deputies.

"They finished the building about 1330. Before we left there, I said, 'We've got to search this freeway again. The freeway's got to be shut down. We've got to bring in three fresh dogs, three fresh handlers and search it again.' In the area where we were searching, there were rabbits, skunks, heavy brush. I recognize these dogs are not perfect or infallible. What I told the guys the second time was, *'You've got to get the dogs as deep into the brush as you can.'* And I told the SWAT guys, 'You've gotta go into the brush. You can't walk the perimeters. You've gotta go out there and kick, prod, and look.'

"We searched it again. We didn't find any other evidence and no sign of other suspects. I sure felt better when we packed up our bags to leave after searching the area again.

"Our SWAT teams are full time. Twenty-five percent of their time is training in SWAT, the other 75 percent of the time, they are together as a unit. I don't know whether you can find a group of people more disciplined than these. You put four patrol deputies in a situation like that with Berettas that will go 15 or 16 rounds. If one round was fired, they'd all fire. Our people train constantly. They get two hours a day to work out—the first two hours of a 10 hour shift. Their firearms training is based on two shots to the body, two shots to the body, two shots to the head. We know that issue of fire contagion is just not going to occur. *We do 100 to 120 SWAT activations a year.* Most departments are much smaller. They don't have the luxury of, whap, you pull in all those people, the helicopter, and real quickly, establish a perimeter, have the containment, and have the number of people you need to do the search."

"The McDonald's hostage-taking incident involved 20 hostages. There is actually a videotape showing the team leaping the counter and taking the guy down. I convinced the

■

We do 100 to 120 SWAT activations a year. Most departments are much smaller. They don't have the luxury of, whap, you pull in all those people, the helicopter, and real quickly, establish a perimeter, have the containment, and have the number of people you need to do the search.

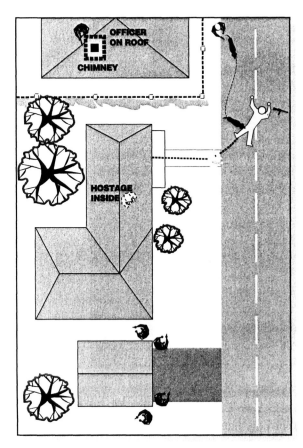

OFFICER
ON ROOF

CHIMNEY

HOSTAGE
INSIDE

Hostage/barricade incident. K-9 apprehends an offender testing the containment, trying to escape. If he surrenders, takes a hostage or points the gun, do not send the dog.

operations commander, 'Look, these guys are trained to do what they say they're going to do.' Fortunately, there was a TV camera across the street that had been set up and left there. You can actually see them make their entry. When he saw that he says, 'I can't believe it.' In two seconds they went from that counter and had cleared the entire front area. They knew they had an armed suspect. If you sent patrol deputies in there, everybody would go to the crook. Six of these guys never looked at the suspect. They had zones of responsibility, 'You're supposed to go there, cover the hostages, and look for another crook.' Although they knew there was an armed guy standing 15 ft away, they never looked at him.

"A handler responded to a request for a K-9 search and was briefing the people on what he was going to do. The field sergeant said, 'No, you're going to take this group (four or five new deputies).'

"The handler said, 'No, this is my search. You've got trainees here new to patrol. I'm not going to take them with me. I'll take these two deputies.'

"This handler was not known for tact and diplomacy. He's like the police dog—he barks quite loudly. You have to bark louder. In this case, he was right. That speaks to the issue of having a K-9 supervisor there who can be the liaison between your handler, the field people or the field sergeant. He's comfortable and knowledgeable about tactics. Supervisor-to-supervisor he can say, 'No, it's appropriate for this guy to conduct the search with experienced people, not trainees. I understand you need to get your people trained, but we can do that in a training environment. It's not appropriate where we're looking for a 211 suspect.'

"There was obvious conflict. Neither officer was going to bend. Tactfully he didn't handle it as well as he should have. But tactically, he was telling the guy what is correct. It would be the same thing with taking a SWAT team out. You're not going to let a field sergeant dictate how a SWAT team works. The dog is a specialized piece of equipment, and the handler has trained extensively for K-9 operations. Someone who is not familiar with their ability, their tactics, their limitations shouldn't be telling them how to conduct the search.

"During the Olympics, we had a barricaded robbery suspect way up in Antelope Valley, driving time two hours. They put us all on one of our big Sikorsky helos—the entire team, all 12 people—flew us out there in the middle of the night. We get there, this guy had pulled a robbery and is barricaded inside his own house.

"We developed a plan to deploy the team. As was my custom, the handler was with my entry team. We staged at a point on the corner of a house next to the suspect's house discussing tactical plans. We had to wait because we had a street light behind us and were concerned about it. It was two o'clock in the morning, and we were concerned about backlighting.

"I was trying to tell the team commander, 'I need to shoot out that street light before we can move, because we're going to be illuminated.' He didn't want to do it. Finally, I persuaded him to meet me and take a look at this street light. He said, 'OK, go ahead shoot it out.' So we shot out the street light.

"Well all this took about an hour. We're still staged at the corner of this house in the bushes, looking at the suspect's house, going over plans. All this time, Dave's dog is trying to get up, acting very antsy. I said, 'Dave, what's wrong with this dog?' He says, 'The wind is blowing this way, he's picking up the scent of the suspect. The guy's in the house, he wants to go.'

"I said, 'Well, kick him in the butt or something, but keep him quiet.'

"We did our phone calls and PA's. We finally gassed the place. And after having been in that location for two hours, we made entry. We cleared the whole place using the dog. No suspect.

"So we come out. Dave takes the dog off leash with, 'Let's take a break.' The dog heads right for that bush and takes the guy down. For two hours that guy was 18 inches from us, heard everything we said. He was armed. It could have been a disaster. A good find. They flew us back. I have a photo on my desk—one of the plastic mannequins they use for training tied to a pole, covered in bushes, flashing road lights and arrows pointing to the guy, 'Follow the yellow brick road to the suspect.' The dog found him.

"At the time, the deputy had about 18 months as a K-9 handler. He had seen a suspicious vehicle blacked out at a convenience store. "I know this suspect matches the description I heard about at briefing and the car matches, but I can't put two-and-two together, and I can't quite recall what it is." He started to follow the car. He ran the plate. The car failed to yield. He requested a unit backup. There was a mini-pursuit of just a few blocks. Other units took the lead in the pursuit. A male suspect was inside with a female passenger.

"Apparently the suspect told the female to leave and run to a house. Just as the car came to a stop in front of the house, the young lady went inside. The suspect exited the car and ran to the rear yard, deputies believed to a garage. Not knowing what they had, they requested the dog to search the back. By the time he arrived, the handler realized this was an armed robbery suspect that he had heard about in briefing.

"The handler, a sergeant, and one other deputy had the garage contained. The handler made the standard K-9 announcement in English and Spanish, giving the suspect the opportunity to respond. No acknowledgement to that. As he approached the garage, the only way to enter was to lift up the garage door. He did that and the dog went in. A shot was fired. The dog retreated to the handler's side. The sergeant and the handler returned fire, unaware the dog had been hit. They opened the garage door again and saw the suspect standing with a gun in his hand pointing it in their direction. They fired again, fatally wounding the suspect.

After the incident was over the handler saw the dog was bleeding and took him to the vet. The dog had surgery then spent a month recovering before returning to service.

"After the initial exchange of gunfire, where the dog was hit, the deputy and sergeant returned fire, then immediately closed the garage door. The question from a tactical standpoint is, 'Why go in a second time?' At that point you really have a barricaded suspect. You Monday-morning-quarterback it. There was an issue of timing. When you get involved in a shooting, things either go real fast or they go real slow and you're not thinking as clearly as you might otherwise be doing. They elected to reopen the door, perhaps under the belief the suspect had been hit and was down. What would have been best would be to back off, contain it, and call for a SWAT team.

Gang surveillance. Rival gangs outnumber and outgun the police. In these highly charged situations, dogs are most effectively used to enhance officer safety, perform perimeter patrol, or search for narcotics.

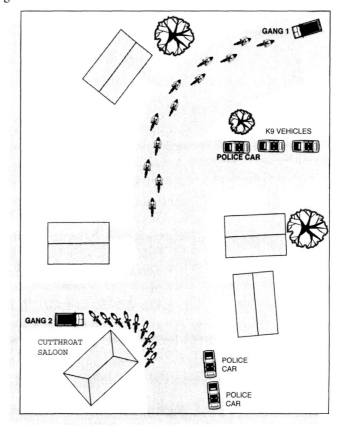

"A team was called by one of our less experienced handlers. I talked to the watch commander before I authorized the use of a SWAT team, 'That's in the gray area. It's a wobbler. It could call for the use of a team, but I understand under the circumstance why you'd be reluctant to do that.' I discussed it with the handler. His thinking was, 'Yeah, I could send the dog in there. My concern is, if I'm going to encounter an armed suspect in his own house, where he's familiar with the territory, and we know there are multiple weapons inside, for my backup I'd rather have a SWAT team than two patrol deputies. I'd be more comfortable in that circumstance having a team.' So that's what we did, we sent the team.

"An officer was sent to a city where they had a possibly barricaded suspect, believed to be mentally deranged, wouldn't come out of the house, and they thought he was armed with a knife. That wouldn't necessarily qualify for a SWAT team. They made their announcement and went in—two patrol deputies led by the K-9 team. Shortly after they entered the location, they smelled natural gas. There was the statement, "I smell gas." They suddenly realized what was going on. Either the guy was trying to commit suicide or blow up the house.

"They said, 'Let's back out,' at which point the suspect, who was concealed high in the residence came out from hiding with a cigarette lighter in one hand and a propane torch in the other and proceeded to light the torch. Everybody was running ass over teakettle backwards, this huge ball of flame following right on their heels. They all got out, including the dog. The officers and dog were not injured. The suspect was on fire when he came out of the place. The house burned to the ground.

"There were not sufficient circumstances to warrant handling it any other way. They didn't detect the gas odor inside until they got inside."

—K-9 Administrator

K-9 AND CHEMICAL AGENTS

Most police dogs are minimally affected by synthetic agents (Chloroacetaphenone (CN) and Orthochlorobenzalmalononitrile (CS)) used as less than lethal force weapons against aggressors. Lacking well developed tear ducts, or lacrimatory glands, and covered by the natural protection of fur, dogs typically "work through" CS and CN effectively. However, residue from these gases may affect anybody who handles the dog's fur.

Oleoresin Capsicum (OC), Natural Oil of Pepper, has been used successfully by animal control officers because the inflammatory agent adversely affects most animals, including dogs. Producing an intense burning sensation, OC causes mucous membranes to swell, immediate eye closing, uncontrollable coughing, gagging, and gasping for air. In humans these physiological effects typically produce an instantly compliant subject who has lost coordination, vision, and upper body motor control, thereby precluding any further aggressive behavior. While effective with many people who are violent due to alcohol, drugs or who are emotionally disturbed, all effects appear to be temporary and usually disappear completely within 45 minutes.

Tests with police dogs indicate that the effects of OC depend on several factors:
• The amount contacting the dog's mucous membranes if he "takes a hit" of the agent
• The delivery system, if it is "wet" (a liquid stream) versus a vapor (gas) as well as the footprint (distribution)
• The dog's aggression drives, if he can block the effects of OC while biting the suspect.

Recovery time also depends on the dog. The ability to pay attention to basic commands usually returns within 30 minutes. The ability to scent and therefore to search reliably remains highly variable. Test the dog's response in training.

Use common sense. Don't rely on the police dog for a reasonable period of time after he contacts OC, especially if he is symptomatic: rolling on the ground, pawing at his eyes and nose, coughing or gagging, staggering. If possible, talk quietly to him, protect him from harm, and rinse off his face and muzzle with cool fresh water.

OC is biodegradable and does not require any special decontamination. Normal ventilation removes the spray from the environment within 45 minutes. If you are planning to bring a K-9 in after you get the situation controlled, the dog will be viable in the area soon after. Generally, after an incident where OC has been used, there will be sufficient time, while people are being handcuffed, taken out, put in the car, for residual material to dissipate, even after the use of a grenade. Fifteen to 30 minutes later, the police dog will probably have no difficulty in the area.

Depending on the delivery system, the police dog may be used to assist controlling a violent and aggressive suspect at the same time you are spraying him with an aerosol weapon. Once the assailant becomes incapacitated, call the dog off and monitor the suspect.

INJURY TO THE POLICE DOG

As a peace officer, are you ready to face the possibility of having to use lethal force? As a K-9 officer, are you ready to deal with the possibility of an offender *killing your dog?* If a suspect threatens your dog, he is threatening you by extension. A knife-wielding attacker who stabs your dog is going to stick you next. If you have to use deady force, have you considered that when you shoot, you may also kill your dog?

Have you thought about how you will respond if your dog is shot? If you and your dog are shot at the same time? Even if you are mentally conditioned not to give up, the added stress of an injured K-9 partner will make it harder to *keep your priorities straight.* The dog may be screaming in pain. Yet trying to aid the dog, even to call him back to you or to command him to down, may jeopardize your position or that of your cover officers. The dog may be bleeding profusely while trying to continue fighting an assailant. You have to keep fighting the armed adversary or multiple adversaries until the scene is brought under control. You, the human end of the K-9 team, must continue to fight to *survive.*

A man in a red ball cap, white bermuda shorts and a white sweatshirt enters a gun shop in Scott's Valley, California. Stealing a pistol, he runs across the street, loads the gun and starts waving it at people, firing at random. Somebody calls the police. Pulling a woman out of her car, the man steals the car. Leading a high-speed chase to Santa Cruz, he turns off the freeway into a gas station behind the government center, police cars right behind him.

"Stay back! He's on the gas station side!" Police order people out of their cars, trying to get them out of the way.

"Lookout! He's comin' your way. He's comin' out!"

"The guy looked pretty pumped," a local man tells the TV cameras, "but he acted all casual about it. He got out and started filling his gas tank like he was going to drive off or something. It was pretty crazy."

Police know the gunman. He has had more than a dozen contacts with officers in the past nine years. One officer disarmed him before. He is the son of a prominent citizen.

The police dog is barking. The gunman pumps gas with his right hand, holding the pistol casually in his left. Officers order him to drop the gun. He fills the tank, replaces the hose, screws on the cap.

The K-9 officer deploys the dog...who targets somebody beyond the pumps. The offender is the only person at the scene not yelling or jumping around. He is totally cool. Almost grinning.

The officer recalls his dog to redirect him. As the dog returns to the handler, the gunman casually walks between the officers and the rear of the car toward the driver's door.

"Put that gun down!" No response. The officer resends the dog.

The dog runs toward the gunman. Raising the gun in both hands, the man fires in the direction of the police and hits the dog. Yelping in pain, the K-9 hits the man, biting his leg. Police return fire. Nine bullets find their target. The man falls. The handler calls the dog out.

Releasing his hold, the K-9 comes back to the officer. For a long moment the gunman lies prone on the pavement, officers yelling for compliance from behind cover while the K-9 limps among them. Then they move forward to handcuff the body. The gunman dies. The police dog goes to the hospital.

In two weeks the K-9 is back on the street. He is a lucky dog. The gunman's bullet passed through his shoulder, traveled the length of his body missing all his vital organs, and exited his rear leg muscle. Several hundred feet away from the scene of the shooting, the county courtroom has bullet holes in the walls from the gunfire.

After the incident, the handler is concerned whether his dog will work reliably on the street. With the trainer, officers reconstruct a similar scenario using gunfire. The handler deploys the K-9. The dog does not hesitate to apprehend the actor.

Critical Incident Stress Debriefing (CISD) should be conducted after any incident faced by emergency service personnel causing them to experience an unusually strong emotional reaction that has the potential to interfere with their ability to function at the scene or later. CISD is designed to decrease the time necessary for normal people having normal reactions to abnormal events to recover and prevent long-term or permanent psychological or physical damage. Police service falls into this category, particularly after a shooting, including trauma to the police dog. Stress that would tend to break any normal officer is compounded by a K-9 injury. Most administrators and patrol officers understand this and will support counseling the handler.

A defense lawyer clearly did not understand the special effects of K-9-related stress. During a deposition, the attorney grilled the handler over and over for details of events immediately following the dog's death. How many officers took the offender into custody, where was the number on the house he ran from, which car did they place him in, the color of his shoes, the dog's final position on the pavement, location of entry and exit wounds, that sort of thing. Apparently, he had no concept of the auditory and visual "blocking" that officers often experience under high stress. Finally noticing the effect recalling the incident was having on the officer, the attorney commented, "What's the matter with you? This happened a year ago. Anyway, we're only talking about a dog here."

K-9 officer, "Do you have any kids?"

Lawyer, "Yeah, why?"

K-9 officer, "That dog was my kid."

This behavior is normal for K-9 officers. In fact a solid emotional investment in the dog—*the bond*—is essential to high calibre performance in law enforcement. The same type officer cares about his wife or her husband, his or her children, his or her partners on the street. Experiencing a loss, grieving, and recognizing that grief signals a healthy officer. Family, respected friends inside and outside the department, including the department trainer and K-9 supervisor, and sometimes another dog to train can all help the recovery process.

One handler stated his feelings to the veterinarian as his patrol dog was losing the battle with degenerative myopathy: "This is tearing my guts out."

Certain lawyers have attempted to use the K-9 officer's bond with his dog as a weapon against him in court. In one case an aggressor who was trying to kill the officer killed the police dog. Then he killed himself. Later, individuals brought a wrongful death suit against the department and the officer, blaming the dog for inciting the suicide. In fact, the officer was shown to have displayed remarkable courage and command control of the scene during and after the incident.

Despite returning to the street with a second dog, a handler still felt the effects of the first getting killed in the line of duty: "I got confused. My first police dog was always out with me. Then I went through the period without a dog where I had to do everything on my own. Now I have the new dog, but I sometimes forget to use him. Like the other night on a domestic call. We knew the guy was in the house. We're standing around waiting for a key. I noticed a large window, took the screen off and went in. As soon as I got inside, the hair stood up on my neck. All I could think was, 'Jeez, how stupid. My dog's out in the car.'"

Administration as well as fellow patrol officers should recognize the early warning signs and symptoms of *Post-Traumatic Stress Disorder (PTSD)*. The pathogenic core of PTSD may be biological or psychological or both. Once it is diagnosed, peer counseling and support may be needed. Professional therapy may be needed. Officers who cooperate in the recovery process can have a critical, positive effect on the individual's career in law enforcement.

Beyond the mental preparation all police officers should maintain, the K-9 officer needs additional awareness. To the list of direct, positive concepts needed to focus weapons skills and relieve stress, the K-9 officer must add:

- I will read my dog's alerts.
- I can cover my dog
- I can control my dog
- I can use my dog in the ways necessary to save my life or the life of someone else.

Crisis Rehearsal is an important technique for K-9 officers as well as regular patrol officers. You should spend time constructing mental scenarios about what could happen on the street with your K-9, then going over in your mind what both of you could do. Officers who pre-think emergencies in this way, who do active mental exercises, are far better prepared than those who only react to unrehearsed situations.

Deputy Terry Fleck and K-9
Tracker, El Dorado County Sheriff's
Department, California

*"Small departments do not have special immunity
from gangs, drugs, weapons offenses or other violent
crimes. When police dogs find concealed suspects,
they often save officers' lives and the lives
of the suspects themselves."*

CHAPTER 4

HIGH-RISK SEARCHES —FINDING OFFENDERS

"Read and reinforce the dog.

You cannot *force* the dog to search."

—Sandy Bryson

The Los Angeles Police Department Metro K-9 Division started in 1980 with pilot K-9 teams. Within months, the program was so successful K-9s were made a permanent part of the Department, and the number of teams increased to 15 K-9s. Compared to other cities with police dog units, the LAPD unit is relatively new. Yet these teams do over 2000 searches per year, a third of them resulting in arrests. *More than thirty percent of the offenders taken into custody are armed at the time they are arrested.*

Washington, D.C., Metropolitan Police has 61 police dog teams, currently the nation's largest K-9 unit: 50 patrol dogs, 5 bomb specialists, 6 narcotic specialists.

The City of San Diego's high rate of shootings in the early 1990s involving suspects armed with *baseball bats, edged weapons, and other non-traditional weapons* prompted strong community support for their 50-plus police dog teams as an alternative force.

Other departments, large and small, report similar dangerous-offender statistics. Small departments do not have special immunity from gangs, drugs, weapons offenses, or other violent crimes. When police dogs find concealed suspects, they often save officers' lives and the lives of the suspects themselves.

Police were inside a large city warehouse searching for a felony suspect. The K-9 team had covered three delivery bays when the dog lifted his head and alerted to an office door along the back wall.

Looking cautiously through a window, the handler and cover officer could see the metal desk, filing cabinets, and storage shelves. The top of the desk was in disarray. Quietly opening the door, the handler admitted the dog, commanding him to apprehend the suspect. He promptly ran around a cabinet behind the desk and seized the arm of the suspect hiding underneath.

Calling the dog back to her location, the handler told the suspect to show his hands and come out or she would send the dog back in again.

Briefly they saw a hand and the back of the suspect's head, then he withdrew again under the desk.

After calling another warning and getting no response, the handler deployed the dog. The K-9 ran in and grasped the suspect's shoulder.

The police dog may be used to capture suspects who are armed, or believed to be armed, or actively resisting arrest when less than lethal forms of apprehension are appropriate. If necessary, the dog may be used in the emergency of a lethal confrontation.

In most agencies, searches for known juvenile offenders are limited to those instances where the severity of the crime, the subject's age and propensity for violence, whether or not the subject is believed to be armed, or other critical factors would reasonably justify the use of a K-9 search.

The deterrent value of the police dog is significant. Suspects frequently surrender, knowing they will be apprehended by the dog if found. This realization often eliminates a search.

On command the police dog should aggressively seek out the suspect(s). Upon locating suspect scent, the dog should work it until he locates and apprehends the suspect or is called off. Responsibility for the dog's action rests with the handler. Passive, quiet suspects are no less dangerous than active, verbally abusive suspects. The handler controls the dog and may decide to search in a nonaggressive mode if he knows the person is compliant and unarmed.

Years ago, relatively few suspects were armed with guns or knives. This is of course not true today. Many combative suspects have to be physically restrained by the handler when the dog locates them. In the confusion of suspect and officer movement during apprehension, the dog must be trained to obey commands from the handler rather than making independent decisions. The K-9 training program must stress handler command and control methods. During a search, the dog operates under the direction and control of the officer, who is trained to remain close enough to the dog to call or signal the dog out and away from an offender. The K-9 apprehends on command and also protects the handler from close quarters assault.

In many situations, canines can enhance officer safety and aid in the capture of criminals who might otherwise escape. However, it is also critical that each officer and supervisor have a clear understanding of department policy. Officers must be able to make informed decisions so they can do their job without jeopardizing their career, or needlessly becoming the subject of civil liability or criminal prosecution.

Night is the most dangerous time to search for suspects. Dog scenting capability is most favored at night, but all other factors of K-9 team deployment are least favored in darkness, when officers depend on artificial lighting or existing light enhancement, and when the suspect can lie concealed by darkness, watching and listening for police officers and the dog. The suspect receives a clear picture of the officers' location. The officers typically have no idea where the suspect lies in waiting.

After a parolee convicted of murder was apprehended for petty theft at a shopping mall, he got away from security guards and ran off into the night. The responding police K-9 began checking the forest across the street, where the guards said the man had disappeared. The handler deployed his dog into the wind while he and his backup moved from tree to tree. A few minutes later, the dog alerted in the officers' lights, dived into a gully, and seized the suspect, who was lying in wait to shoot the officers. The dog's direct action caused the man to drop the gun. The handler called off his dog, and a cover officer made the arrest.

The detector dog sometimes solves hidden problems. The K-9 unit responded to a location with an open front door and security bars bent back. Making entry, the dog team began searching the first floor. The dog went to the back of the house and made a high alert, then he started up the stairs to the second floor. The handler saw two suspects sitting at the top of the steps.

Stopping the dog, he told the suspects to sit still and get their hands up. One of the suspects complied, but the second jumped up and ran. The cover officer took the first suspect. The handler sent the dog after the second. The K-9 ran down the hallway and bit the man on the left shoulder. He immediately raised his hands. The handler called the dog out. Both suspects were taken into custody.

The K-9 team completed searching the upstairs. As the team went back downstairs to exit, the dog again alerted high. Investigating the ceiling area above the bathroom, the handler observed a trap door. In the crawl space above he located a third suspect concealed behind boxes. Ordering him down, the officer took him into custody.

> We've gone up and done searches where they said, 'Definitely not. They're not here. We searched the place. Nobody's here.' After hearing that one night, I went into a junkyard with the dog and found three guys. Basically, we can damn near guarantee going in the dog will find the crooks. Ninety-nine percent of the time. The few suspects we've missed have all been handler error. We've gone back and analyzed everything. I missed a suspect. We went back and analyzed it. Sure enough, it was my fault. I missed a spot.
>
> —K-9 Officer

What does scent do? Why is scenting a valuable search technique? What are the best tactics in typical situations employing the police dog? What is the role of the cover officer in a canine search? To understand these and other important factors determining police K-9 tactics, officers need to know basic details about scent.

THE SCENT CONTINUUM

Distinguished writer David Quammen gives us a clear idea of the extraordinarily complex subject of *scent diffusion:* "A *hole*, in the sense that a river-runner uses the word, is essentially a whirlpool laid on its side, with its axis of rotation perpendicular to the main current. It's a cylinder of water and froth that recirculates constantly, in position, like one of those giant spinning brushes at an automatic car wash. For a rough approximation of how it feels to drop into one, you could take a pass through the car wash on your bicycle. Some kayakers know the same sort of feature under other terms: *sousehole, reversal, hydraulic.* Reversal is especially apt because, stuck in the maw of a hole, you'll feel like you've suffered one.

"How do these river holes function? According to a renowned authority named William Nealy, 'Hydraulics are caused by water passing over an obstacle and creating a recirculating upstream flow below.' The velocity of the water dropping over the obstacle, Nealy explains, is far greater than the water velocity below the hole, which creates an excess of piled water with nowhere to go. Gravity pulls some of the piled water back upstream—because upstream in this special case, from the pile to the hole, represents a natural downhill slide—and that water rolls under, down through the hole again, further driving the cycle. 'Hydraulics,' Nealy adds, 'come in an infinite variety and are a source of amusement and/or fear for boaters.'

"Fluid dynamics is one of the most complex branches of physics. Why? Just between you and me, it's because liquids and gases can move everywhichway. Water, to take our present case in point, is a straightforward substance so long as it sits in a beaker, flat as old beer, being measured or weighed or boiled or frozen or otherwise defined by its physical parameters. But as soon as you pour the beaker, as soon as the stuff starts to flow, the physics of water becomes unspeakably complicated. Magnify the beaker into a reservoir (or, preferably, a snow-covered mountain range), then release all that water as a tumbling river: Presto splasho, the complications are virtually infinite. And this near-infinite complexity is in light merely of classical fluid dynamics—let alone the coy wobbles and winks that chaos theory has recently added.

"Follow the subject of fluid dynamics into its technical literature, and you come quickly to

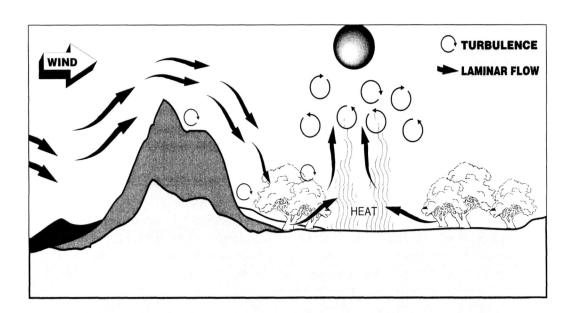

Scent vaporizes then fuses like gas or smoke. Solar energy changes to heat, driving the wind in smooth laminar flow (flat open space, night, low clouds) that assists the scenting dog, or turbulence (steep terrain, natural or manmade windbreaks, midday, clear, high temperatures) that makes detection more difficult.

such concepts as turbulence, laminar flow, viscosity, Reynolds number, boundary layer shear stress, Benard cells, and vorticity. Get a loose grip on those few ideas and then it's time to bail out, take my word, because within another page or three you're bound to encounter some nosebleed-inducing equations. It's all very erudite, but I won't pause to explain even the bit that I comprehend, which is minuscule, since it can't help a man out of a hole.

"The fluid dynamicists wouldn't say 'hole.' They'd say 'vortex.' Vorticity is a powerful, far-reaching, generalized notion within the study of turbulent fluids. Vortices occur in various manifestations. A whirlpool is one type of vortex. An eddy is also a vortex, though flatter and less energized. Hurricanes and little prairie-wind twisters are vortical."

Breezes around the outside edges of buildings, smoke curling around a wall inside a building, fresh wind hitting a ridgetop and changing from laminar to turbulent flow—all exhibit vorticity. Aerodynamics and hydrology are of course branches of fluid dynamics, the former dealing with moving air, the latter with water.

Air and water transport scent. Scent rides thermal currents like a sailplane and may chimney straight up. Wind hitting a building deflects into complex rolls and patterns. Any obstacle, large or small, that interrupts the laminar flow of wind or water will cause some type of turbulence.

In a closed or contained volume of air or water, scent will *load* or *pool*, meaning intensify, for some time after the source enters the space because the rate of vaporization of scent into the confined space exceeds the rate of scent diffusing or escaping outside the boundary. This happens when a suspect hides in the still air of a ravine under a canopy of trees. The dog enters the ravine and goes crazy, appearing to scent the suspect everywhere.

This happens also when a few kilograms of narcotics in a cardboard box are placed in the cab of a truck. In the case of live subjects or large quantities of dope, the rate of vaporization may be very high. In the case of a live subject who dies, there may be two peaks—the first when the body is hottest, the second when the body decays. Or the rate of vaporization may change in response to differential heating, for example the cycle of cold night versus hot day.

The police K-9 officer studies the practical applications of thermodynamics and the physics of flow in order to deploy his dog most effectively. Knowing the basic principles of fluid flow is essential for the K-9 officer or backup officers to predict where the dog will possibly locate scent or detect the source. While a dog on alert will sometimes bite the water in a lake or puddle or stream, indicating he is *tasting* the scent, as a practical matter we refer to scent or odor as *airborne molecules that activate the sense of smell upon contact with the individual's nasal receptors.* The continuum of scent traveling from the source to the canine nose is governed by the *rate of vaporization and diffusion,* determining whether the dog can detect the source.

If something *breaks* the scent continuum, that is it becomes *discontinuous,* the dog may or may not be able to find it again. There are many ways this can happen. One of the most common situations is the K-9 team searching into a downslope wind at night. If they are in the lee of the hill with the wind surging over the top, turbulence creates a giant curl like a surfer's pipeline that hits the lee slope vertically, rolls under slightly, then washes downhill.

Here comes the police dog. Entering the downhill scent wash, he alerts uphill. But when he moves under the curl of the wave, inside the pipeline, he loses the scent. It may be 50- or 100 feet or more above his nose. If he searches downhill, he may recover the scent, but each time he tries to follow it uphill (dogs don't fly), it is gone. This effect commonly occurs when the subject is high on the hillside, on top of a building or outcropping, at the top of the hill, or even part way down the other side, depending on the terrain and weather. Some dogs will stand up on two legs *reaching* for the scent. The handler who reads what his dog is doing can give search teams valuable information even if he does not make the find.

Turbulence created by buildings can actually help the dog make a detection. A security guard looking for a burglar had twice flashed his light into the L-corner of a storefront. The guard thought nobody could hide in the few cacti planted there. Enter the police dog. As soon as he cleared the corner on the sidewalk, the K-9 lifted his nose and headed straight into the L. Turbulence on the lee side of the building had flushed the suspect's scent out to the sidewalk. The dog's performance amazed the security guard and the suspect equally.

There may not be enough scent to trigger any response by the dog. The handler has to incorporate scent diffusion into his search tactics. Scent can be sucked out of building vents, windows, or chimneys by the venturi effect of outside winds. Air conditioning systems can force scent outside so there is little or no detectable odor inside at canine head level. Warm air rising in obedience to the basic laws of thermodynamics may carry scent in a laminar flow pattern straight up to a ceiling or roof. Convection currents driven by differential heating can cause turbulence, elevating the scent beyond reach of the dog's nose or driving it down walls or into different rooms where the dog cannot pinpoint the source.

Five deputies failed to find a suspect here.

Every human body has a scent signature unique to that person, like his fingerprints. Woods Hole marine biologist Jelle Atema says, "We're just leaky bags of amino acids." The sweat glands produce perspiration as the body's temperature rises, also in response to emotional stimuli such as stress or fear. The eccrine sweat glands—located all over the body, but concentrated in the armpits, soles, and palms—react primarily to heat stimuli and emotional stress, and regulate the body's temperature. Apocrine sweat glands respond to emotional stimuli and are located mostly in the armpits, groin, and around the navel. Factors such as age, race, sex, size, physical and psychological conditioning affect the amount a person sweats. Additional factors, such as

food, clothing, and lifestyle, cumulatively affect the air or ground scent picture presented to the searching dog.

When the dog sniffs the air or ground for a person, he perceives components of all these factors. We do not know exactly which information is important to the dog, what he files in memory, what he discards, what he perhaps cannot detect.

AIR SCENTING v. TRACKING

We do know the police dog must be trained to work the scent to source, whether by following a track or by casting into a scent cone. In general terms, as the dog gets closer to the source, the scent intensifies. Reliable detection does not come naturally. It is learned behavior. Although the act of tracking or air scenting is typically instinctive behavior to canines, reliability comes through training and experience:

> There were coyote tracks and fresh droppings everywhere, but he kept his nose right on the man's tracks.
>
> —Tracking

> As soon as the dog went through the door, I knew there was somebody in that room. He was casting and sniffing and whining, rising on his hind legs and lifting his tail.
>
> —Air scenting

> She alerted on a broken sack of dog food in the debris. I thought, oh great, the dog finds food. Then she started pawing through the kibble. That was strange. We shoveled the food away with her scratching at the floorboards underneath. There were two bodies under that floor.
>
> —Air scenting

> You know the ugly smell of tar heroin. I guess they thought they could fool us by putting hamburger meat in front of a bag of peanut shells loaded with tar heroin. They didn't fool the dog.
>
> —Air scenting

In addition to targeting the source through masking scents or distractions, the K-9 must train to *recover lost scent* and to *trace it to the source*, instead of chasing scent or losing it in turbulence.

Two officers roll dark into a baseball field at night. A sedan parked in the middle of the field holds an armed offender. The sedan's windows are open. The officers plan to use the dog in a surprise apprehension. At the instant the dog leaps through the window, the officers will light up and ram the sedan with their push bar, order the driver out, and hook him. Simple.

The handler sends the dog out into the dark. Barely visible, the dog runs over to the vehicle, lifts his head and tail as if alerting, then runs to the right, away from the vehicle. The K-9 officer sees his young, inexperienced patrol dog run toward the dugout, circle under the dugout roof in the wake of the eddying scent, and start barking.

Getting a clue, the offender takes off.

What started out as bad game strategy ended up as a home run for the bad guy. Consider what would have happened if the dog had the experience to focus on the vehicle as a primary search target. When the dog sniffed the driver's scent, he should have turned toward the vehicle, tracing it to the source instead of chasing it into the dugout. Had these cowboy tactics actually been carried out, the dog and the officers could all have been injured.

Another incident occurred in a forest on the Canadian border. Fleeing a murder, the suspect vacated a stolen pickup, engine running, near an overgrown dirt road and disapeared into the woods and flat swampland. He had been raised in the territory. The officers pursuing him had not.

The level terrain contained no landmarks and no possibility of establishing a perimeter to contain the subspect. Little wind penetrated the dense stands of beech and pine. Air search was infeasible. in the light rain, slippery logs covered by long grass competed with mud bogs to trap the searchers. Dogs and handlers were equally at risk. After the first broken-ankle-twisted-knee, safety tactics were modified in a hurry.

The call went out for tracking dogs. Neither of the department's two patrol dogs was trained to track, and the handlers advised there was nothing they could do. When dispatch reported that the nearest tracking K-9 was a couple of hours away, the sergeant decided to secure, anticipating that the man would hide for a day or so and show up somewhere eventually.

Eventually he did, taking two more lives.

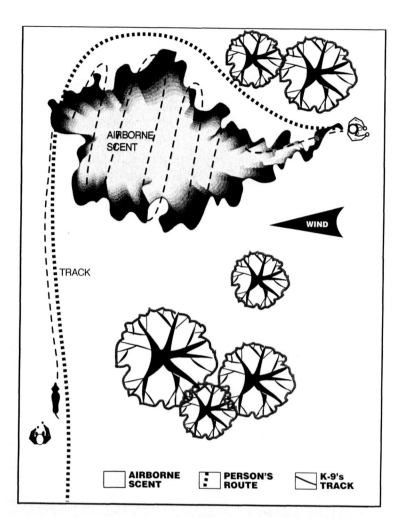

What more could have been done? In this incident, where the officers were not equipped for backcountry search and where there had been no tactical training for this type situation, probably no more could have been done.

If the training and support had been in place, however, both K-9 functions, tracking and air scenting, could have been used. Once they identified the stolen vehicle, officers could have maintained surveillance without contaminating the truck or the area.

A police dog with tracking capability could have deployed in the vicinity of the truck, even several hours later. The air scenting K-9s could have searched a couple of key intersections then maintained surveillance. One of the air scenting dogs could have performed a search of the area surrounding the scene of departure in case the suspect had doubled back when the cops left.

Meanwhile, local residents should have been consulted about potential hideouts in the area (sheds, mines, logging camps) and plainclothes officers assigned to patrol the area in unmarked units. A dog team with both tracking and air scenting capability would have been valuable waiting in the immediate area to respond to a sighting. A helicopter could have inserted a K-9 team in the event of a sighting.

Officers who work with police dog teams need to understand the differences between tracking and air scenting and how to use both capabilities.

Tracking v. air scenting. Tracking, *the dog detects scent on or near the ground and traces the path the person walked or ran.*

Air scenting, *the dog detects scent diffusing from the person or object then brackets the scent cone toward the source. The police dog will typically leave a track to sniff a strong scent cone from the offender.*

Tracking or air scenting, the dog searches under command control. Handler and backup officer(s) move from cover to cover. In most circumstances except heavy traffic, the dog works off lead, prepared to apprehend the offender.

Tracking—The dog sniffs the actual route the subject took, discriminating for his track scent from point A, where the dog first detects the subject's track, to point B, where he either finds the subject or stops tracking. If the dog stops tracking briefly to investigate (the suspect hid behind a rock or crossed a stream), he resumes nearby at point B with no significant interruption and tracks to C. The K-9 officer describes the track from A to C in his report.

Detectable scent diffuses from a track for hours, more or less, depending on circumstances. Track or trail scent is negatively affected by solar radiation, high temperature, wind, hard smooth surfaces, desiccation (drying), heavy rain, snow, or ice. Track scent is positively affected by cool temperature, humidity, dew or light rain, vegetation, low wind, low incident radiation, or darkness. Fresh crosstracks may distract an inexperienced dog.

Weather tends to disintegrate track. Wind acts not only to blow scent away, removing gases and particles that identify the track to the dog, but also to aerate, dry out, and reduce bacterial activity. While low to moderate wind conditions are an asset for air scent search, the less wind the better is the rule for tracking.

High humidity favors tracking, and humid conditions combined with moderate temperatures encourage discrimination in the tracking dog for a significant time after the track is laid. Light rain freshens track scent; however, pouring rain or heavy snow breaks up the track. Solar radiation *burns out* a track. Direct sunlight kills bacteria and also generates locally high temperatures that dry out and destroy scent-producing reactions. The best tracking conditions usually occur in the night, early morning or evening, on north-facing slopes, or across low, damp grasses.

The dog that is capable of tactical tracking will track or trail off lead. The officer controls the dog verbally while the team moves from cover to cover. If the dog locates a suspect, there is no lead or harness that the suspect might seize or that might interfere with the arrest procedure.

A track performed by Seattle Police Officer D. A. Kitts and his partner, police dog Casey, was typical of this department's capability. At 0237 hours Officer Kitts and Casey responded to a home on 92nd on a burglary that had just occurred. A homeowner flushed three white male burglars out of his house. When the officer arrived, the homeowner showed him the last place he saw the suspects.

Kitts took Casey to that location and told him to *seek*. The dog tracked into the backyard of the neighboring house on the east side. The track went around the house and into the front yard. Casey then jumped the fence into another location on 92nd and tracked through the yard out to 25th Avenue Northeast. Casey turned northbound on 25th Avenue Northeast and tracked to Northeast 94th where he turned westbound. The track went down to 23rd Avenue Northeast, and Casey turned southbound.

Casey tracked southbound into an apartment complex, through the complex and out to northeast 92nd. The dog turned westbound on Northeast 92nd and tracked across Ravenna Avenue Northeast and then across Lake City Way Northeast. The track went southbound along the Lincoln Tow lot in the 9100 block of Lake City Way Northeast. Casey then turned westbound and tracked along the south side of a location on Lake City Way Northeast. The track continued westbound into a location on 20th Avenue Northeast and came back out to the street.

Casey then turned southbound on 20th Avenue Northeast. At that point the handler spotted two white males ahead. Casey was tracking right to them. The K-9 officer ordered them to stop, which they did. They were sweating and had obviously been running. The handler could hear someone breaking through the brush to the west. Another patrol unit arrived and took the two men into custody.

Meanwhile, Casey started to track westbound into a location on 20th Avenue Northeast. The handler followed Casey through the yard. Casey tracked through the brush between the yards. At a location on Northeast 90th, Casey began circling a Toyota pickup located in a carport at the rear of the house. Looking into the truck, the officer saw a white male attempting to hide. He ordered the suspect to show his hands, and he complied. A patrol unit arrived to take the man into custody. The suspect was sweating and had obviously been running.

All three suspects were booked into jail for investigation of burglary. Casey did not make contact with any of the suspects.

Air scenting—The dog sniffs the air in a directed pattern through a designated area inside or outside, discriminating for the scent(s) he is commanded to search. In his report, the K-9 officer describes the area the dog has searched and his probable coverage.

Scent diffuses from a body (alive or dead) or an object for days, weeks, or longer, depending on circumstances. Detectability depends on the *rate of vaporization* of the target scent and concealment, wind velocity and turbulence, collectively called *diffusion*. The air scenting police dog is frequently able to clear buildings or areas more rapidly and safely with higher accuracy than officers alone.

Typically, police dogs are trained to discriminate for one or more of the following:

- General human scent   • An individual, based on prescenting
- Evidence   • Narcotics   • Explosives   • Accelerants

In the course of searching for a human subject, the dog trained to track and air scent may perform either or both functions, depending on circumstances. The dog that is trained to perform only tracking or only air scenting cannot be considered reliable in both functions.

At the scene where a person is buried in debris or submerged in water, only air scent is available. Tracks leading up to the scene where the person is concealed (muddy tracks through the window of a building, ski tracks leading into an avalanche) may provide helpful information.

At the scene where a person walks through an area then climbs into a vehicle and drives away, only track scent is available, and the track scent ends at the point of departure in the vehicle.

Dogs detect evidence, narcotics, explosives, or other chemicals by air scenting.

The temperature zones the dog is experiencing down at nose level can vary considerably from the air temperature up at the handler's face. You are walking around with your head up 5- to 6 feet in the air. You feel the air temperature to be 85 degrees. Yet the temperature at grass level may be 72 degrees—quite a difference. You do not realize the dog is searching a different temperature zone.

Moving from that 12- to 18-inch-high grass onto short grass where the surface temperature hits the low 90s, you are walking around still feeling 85, while the dog's scent picture changed from 72 to the low 90s. Then he moves over to an asphalt driveway where he

■

Cold weather tracking requires specialized training. Dogs typically track more reliably through soft snow than on hardpack, ice, or water-covered ice.

runs into 110 to 115 degrees. In a matter of seconds, the K-9 has encountered a drastic temperature change, which affects the scent as well as his scenting ability dramatically.

In snow the K-9 needs experience tracking through crosscountry skier tracks, hikers, snowshoers, and people playing (lying down and rolling) in the snow. Where many people are wearing the same rubber boots as the subject, the dog has to follow the subject's scent, not rubber boots. With snow cover there is no crushed vegetation for the dog to follow.

—Sgt. Kenneth Burger, Retired,Chicago Police Department

It is necessary to note that some handlers claim their dogs can track or trail a suspect who is driving a vehicle or a victim who is being kidnapped inside a vehicle. Cases reportedly document dogs either following on foot or *drop-trailing*, that is getting out of a patrol vehicle periodically to sniff and to confirm a direction of travel. Allegedly a combination of air scenting and tracking enables the dog to do this over a distance of many miles, several days after the event occurs.

If a dog is indeed capable of such a remarkable performance, the handler would be well advised to perform a substantial number of training scenarios to show the *reliability* of the evidence he will give the court in a future case.

SCENT DISCRIMINATION AND CONTAMINATION

Discrimination as it applies to scenting means *selecting for* certain target scents and *screening out* other scents. The dog is scent discriminating when he is tracking because he is reading a particular *scent picture* and continuing to select for that set of target scents as he moves along. Certain elements of that scent picture can change (like a photo slightly out of focus), but the dog is still able to recognize the scent picture. The person creates the track or trail scent by leaving gas molecules and small particles behind in his path and by crushing or otherwise disturbing material en route.

A suspect flees from officers across a grass lawn. Fence-hopping across several other yards with grass, he tries to fool the pursuing police dog by running across the street, down an alley, and across more front lawns. The scent of vegetation and crushed bacteria together with the scent of the suspect himself make up the initial scent picture the dog sniffs. But when the suspect cuts across the street the "green" components of the scent picture change to asphalt and whatever unfortunate bacteria live on the street. Despite such distractions, the experienced tracking dog continues to perceive the suspect in the same way the human nose perceives garlic whether it appears in a Caesar salad or spaghetti.

In order for a dog to track, in addition to the *existence* of detectable track scent, the dog must understand *this is it!* This is the scent picture we want you to follow or to search for.

Through training, the dog learns *prescenting*. If the handler points out a track for him to sniff or presents an item for him to sniff, he does a take on that scent—memorizes it—and searches for more. If the handler shows the dog the track, the dog sniffs that place on the ground and proceeds to follow the scent picture. If the handler prescents the dog by letting him sniff a scent article, or item bearing the target scent, he proceeds to sniff the air and the ground, searching for matching scent.

Frequently, the police dog has to learn as the situation develops what scent he is after. He is lucky if the driver bails out of the vehicle, for instance, and he can sniff the car seat before starting to search. Or the handler can take a *scent print* (gauze pad impression) of the seat. If there is a known point of entry on a burglary, the dog can sniff the ground or the window sill at that point. Or a weapon previously held by the suspect.

But the K-9 team may have no more information than, "It was a short guy with brown hair and lighted tennis shoes. He ran through that vacant lot over there a few minutes ago."

Typically, the responding K-9 team will request a perimeter, air support, and will start clearing the lot accompanied by a cover officer. The handler directs the dog to cast in an air scent pattern.

If the dog *hits* a track, sniffing the ground intently, the handler has to decide whether to let him continue. The officers are lucky if they can visually confirm that the shoe print in the dirt matches information about the brand of tennis shoe.

The handler can usually tell from the dog's reaction if the track is *hot* or fresh. Police dogs normally alert to the *fear scent* or epinephrine many fugitives discharge while evading arrest. Without prescenting the dog or obtaining supporting evidence, if the dog keys on a fresh track, he may be scenting the suspect or a neighborhood kid who just ran through.

It is important to point out that if the dog has not been prescented, or told to find a person he knows, and therefore does not have enough information to discriminate for a *particular person*, the task of searching for a *human* subject represents a basic level of discrimination. You are not looking for a horse, or a cat, or a puppy. It has to be a person.

Through training, the dog learns what scents are common to people. He learns to recognize generic human scent. During a building search, if the police dog detects general human scent coming out of a closet, even though he has never sniffed the suspect before, he will alert to the closet door.

Relatively few police dogs in the U.S. perform reliable tracking. Very few K-9s can work a track over 12 hours old. Fewer still are trained to identify a suspect or object in a lineup by scent discrimination.

Dogs vary widely in the ability to find evidence. Drug detector dogs, bomb dogs, and accelerant or arson dogs discriminate for the discrete scents they have learned to identify through training.

Contamination, as applied to scent, refers to any physical or chemical process imposed on the scent continuum that *changes* the scent picture beyond canine recognition.

Late one evening in a national park, a ranger patrolling the mountain highway sees an individual duck furtively behind a tree as he drives by. This stretch of road has no campgrounds or trail crossings, it is dark, and the person's reaction is atypical.

Curious, he turns around. Locating the area, he pulls off the road and exits his unit. Scuff marks down the bank on one side trail dirt across the road. Investigating, he heads across the road toward a large fallen log.

Three shots fired from behind the log hit him, two in his body armor, one a flesh wound through his leg.

The ranger returns fire, emptying his pistol into the log, gets back to his unit and radios for help.

That night and the next few days over 180 officers converge on the area. Their tracks efface whatever scent intelligence might have informed a police dog.

A couple of days later, the park brings in two K-9 teams to sniff along the highway. The offender remains at large.

Scent decay refers to the natural aging process of a scent source, either a track or a subject/object. Sources with biological components, including most tracks and dead human bodies, *change odor* as they age in addition to the scent merely dissipating or disappearing. Biodegradation breaks the source down into simpler products, each stage of the decay process giving off its own complex of scents. By contrast the rate of vaporization from chemical compounds like cocaine or heroin may provide detectable scent for years.

ADMISSIBILITY OF DOG TRACKING EVIDENCE

"John and Amy Cox returned to their home in Burlingame at about 11:15 p.m. Their parents were out of town. When they arrived, they noticed that a door which had been unlocked when they left and which could only be locked from the inside was locked. When they got into the house, they noticed that the front door handles or knobs had been removed. Amy screamed, and they heard a large crash from their parents' bedroom. They heard someone running down the hall and loudly pulling at the dead-bolted door which opened onto the backyard. They ran to a neighbor's and called the police.

Keep your "rolling resume" updated for court affidavits.

"Officer Gyselbrecht of the Burlingame Police Department arrived at approximately 11:39 p.m. with a police tracking dog, Sarge. The officer walked several steps inside the front door and commanded the dog to "track." Sarge ran down the hallway and into the bedroom. From there, the dog ran through the opened and damaged back door, across the backyard, and into an adjacent game reserve.

"After about 35 minutes and over an area of about seven-tenths of a mile, Sarge ran into some high bushes and began to growl and bite. Inside the bushes was found the defendant, out of breath, and perspiring. The bottoms of his trouser legs were wet, and there were leaves on his jacket, and mud and grass stains on his shoes.

"Later that night, a penlight was found approximately 75 feet north of the burglarized residence. Although the surrounding area was wet, the penlight was dry. The next day, a pair of pliers was recovered hidden at the base of a bush, about five houses north of the residence. Tests of metal fragments found on the teeth of the pliers and of the spacing of the teeth were compared with marks on the door knobs and yielded results which were consistent with the theory that the pliers were used in the burglary.

"In his own defense the defendant claimed that he had helped a woman start her car, and she invited him for a ride. As they were driving south on the freeway close to the area burglarized he made unflattering remarks about her car, and she told him to get out. He was walking on the freeway when the dog came along and attacked him. He ran into the bushes to escape from the dog.

"The defendant was convicted by a jury of burglary. He appealed. The questions on appeal were: (1) whether dog tracking evidence may be properly admitted; (2) whether evidence of dog tracking is sufficient to support a conviction; and (3) what kind of instruction about such evidence should the jury be given.

"The Court of Appeal ruled that evidence of dog tracking is properly admitted if it is supported by a sufficient foundation; that evidence of dog tracking must be corroborated by other independent evidence to support a conviction; and finally, that the jury should be instructed that dog tracking evidence should be treated as any other evidence with its weight left to the trier of fact.

"What must be shown as a condition precedent to the admissibility of dog tracking evidence is:

1. The dog's handler was qualified by training and experience to use the dog.
2. The dog was adequately trained in tracking humans.
3. The dog has, in actual cases, been found by experience to be reliable in tracking humans.
4. The dog was placed on track where circumstances indicated that guilty party to have been.
5. The trail had not become so stale or contaminated as to be beyond the dog's competency to follow."

People v. Malgren (1983) 139 Cal.App.3d 234.

Model K-9 Team Performance Record

AGENCY: _____

OFFICER _____ ID NO. _____

DOG _____ BREED _____ SEX:M F   AGE _____

1. I have been a police officer for _____ years. During this time, I have had the following training and experience:

_____
_____
_____
_____

__ Resume attached

2. I have been a K-9 officer for_____ years. During this time, I have had the following training and experience:

_____
_____
_____
_____

__ Resume attached

3. I have worked with the dog named above for _____ years.

During this time, we have had the following training and experience:

_____
_____
_____

__ Resume attached

K-9 TRAINING/TESTING REPORTS   _____ Attached   _____ Available
K-9 INCIDENT REPORTS   _____ Attached   _____ Available

4. My dog has successfully tracked suspects_____ times. Unsuccessful tracking events include:

    __ See attached report(s) __ Explanation below

_____
_____
_____
_____

At issue is the *reliability* of dog tracking evidence. The trial judge will want to know what training the dog and handler have received in tracking suspects and how often the K-9 has successfully tracked suspects in the past. If the K-9 is of a particular breed that is suited for tracking, this should also be brought to the attention of the trial judge.

The handler should be able to testify exactly when and where the K-9 picked up the scent. The officer or witness who can place the suspect at the location where the K-9 picked up the scent will have to testify. It would be helpful to the case if the witness can testify that this area remained undisturbed until the K-9 arrived.

The Ninth Circuit Court has emphasized that the tracking dog's reliability is established by his training and performance. If it is the first time the dog is actually being tested by tracking rather than training, the circumstances attending this "first performance" warrant closer scrutiny, requiring the track not be stale or contaminated, and circumstances indicate the track was made by the accused to protect against mistaken identity.

Some states do not recognize the tracking ability of the dog. If the K-9 team does a track and comes upon the subject, the find is of no value unless, during the investigation, independent evidence places the subject at the crime scene. These states require the jury be instructed it must find separate evidence linking the defendant to the crime independent of the evidence provided by the tracking dog. These courts have stated it is impossible to cross-examine a dog, and therefore the dog's "testimony" cannot be challenged. To corroborate the dog's track, it must be shown that the dog was put on the trail at some place and time where the evidence shows that the guilty party had been and had made the trail.

The court in *People v. Centolella*, 305 N.Y.S.2d 460 (1969), responded to this view by noting that such evidence falls into the category of opinion evidence rather than hearsay: "The animals are not witnesses against a defendant any more than a microscope or a spectrograph. (These) are not subject to cross-examination any more than the animal. It is the handler who is the witness and he is merely asked to testify to what the animal actually did, not his opinion as to the guilt or innocence of a person. A person is no more placed in jeopardy by the action of an animal than he is by a breath analyzer or a blood test."

Most states subscribe to this view, also expressed in *People v. Gonzales*, 218 Cal.App.3d 403 (1990), that the corroborating evidence need not be evidence which independently links the defendant to the crime. It is sufficient if the evidence merely supports the accuracy of the dog tracking. That the man tracked in *Malgren* was the man found was corroborated by the fact that the bottoms of his pants and his shoes were wet and the dog had tracked through a wet, muddy area where a person walking or running would have gotten his pants and shoes wet. By contrast in *Gonzales*, evidence linking the suspect to the footprints was not presented. The court did not know whether the shoes the suspect was wearing when apprehended were dirty or consistent with the prints made. Had such evidence been presented, the appeals court would presumably not have reversed the lower court conviction. Officers should note such details in order to provide corroboration.

COMMUNICATIONS

Efficient communications are required for search operations. Intra- and interagency radio systems must include *tactical frequencies* for emergency traffic among ground units, including fire and rescue, ground-to-air links, and mutual aid involving city, county, state, and federal officers.

A 22-year-old *youth* authority ward did the freedom shuffle away from a minimum security work camp one night. As commonly practiced at such facilities, the ward's issued clothing was blue jeans with a blue work shirt over a white T-shirt, helping him look right at home in the rural community. He was a white male with brown hair, brown eyes, and medium height.

About the only thing in the department's favor was the ward's weight, over 240 pounds. That fact and an alert citizen who, over his morning cup of coffee, saw the ward shuffling up the highway in funny black canvas shoes.

Instantly, half a dozen marked corrections vans were dashing around town. The ward's prosperous dimensions did not prevent him from hiding. For two days, despite numerous sightings, he managed to elude capture. A reporting party called in, the sighting was confirmed, everybody ran over there, and ... nothing.

The second morning a house was burglarized. Missing were food and a .45 semiautomatic pistol.

Finally, it occurred to somebody to request a police dog. A deputy responded with his K-9. At the location, a 70-year-old gentleman reported seeing the man walking up the street about ten minutes earlier. The street led up a long hill with no residences. On the left was open hillside. On the right was a ravine filled with manzanita, alder, and poison oak.

Starting at the bottom, the handler released his dog to search the ravine. There was a strong upslope breeze.

Seconds later a corrections van crested the hill, sliding to a stop about halfway down. Apparently the driver saw something, because he exited the van yelling, "Come out of there, we know you're down there," plunged into the ravine, seized something behind a bush at the bottom, yanking and pulling.

At this point the police dog had not reached the scent cone. Neither the dog nor the handler could see the ward. But the K-9 had seen this exercise many times in training. He knew who the bad guy was—the guy making all the noise.

Ignoring the handler's *Aus*, the dog bit the corrections officer. Now the noise got really loud.

Fortunately, the ward did what wards do best—he lay motionless in the brush. The handler called the K-9 out, and both officers took the man into custody.

In this case corrections and the sheriff's department had no common radio frequency. Corrections claimed their officer was not aware there was a police dog in the ravine. He did, however, see the patrol unit and deputy. His actions were unsafe, both for himself and for the deputy. Some corrections officers become so accustomed to a "hands-on" style with wards that they are careless. The handler learned a special lesson in K-9 control from this exercise. The incident illustrates the all-important human *communications* that must occur between officers of different agencies as well as within the agency.

K-9 SEARCH TACTICS

K-9 Tactics—Felony Suspect Search, p. 156 charts the police dog operation. Ideally the incident that starts with an escape or illegal entry progresses:

    1. CONTAINMENT   2. INTELLIGENCE   3. DEPLOYMENT   4. ARREST

Search operations are subject to many variables beyond the department's control. The following highlights typical K-9 search procedures. The remainder of the chapter details the basic tactics illustrated by actual search operations.

1. CONTAINMENT

If a K-9 officer is in foot pursuit, or to start a K-9 search pursuant to an escape or a hiding felony suspect, establish communications, air surveillance and containment. Coordinate the operation on a common tactical frequency. Request a helicopter immediately, if available. Set a perimeter to contain the suspect, if possible. Request search teams: canine unit and cover officers.

Typically, the search area expands exponentially with time. Rapid response minimizes the size of the search area and the length of the suspect's track. Large departments have substantially greater resources in manpower and equipment than small or medium-sized agencies. Departments with

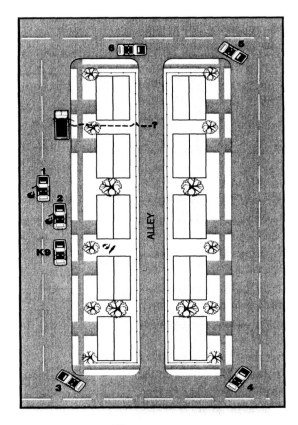

limited manpower may rely on allied agencies to assist establishing a perimeter before the suspects get away.

2. INTELLIGENCE

Give the K-9 officer all available intelligence: type crime, time of occurrence, suspect description, building layout or area map, start location, location of other units. Brief all units, including the helicopter, prior to deployment.

Patrol officers contact homes or businesses in the area to advise people of the incident. Tell them a police dog will be searching the area. Direct them to stay inside or to vacate the building, depending on the circumstances, and to keep pets contained, especially dogs. Fugitives commonly hide in garages, barns, outbuildings, vehicles, under houses and decks.

Offenders frequently hide close to command centers or highways. During briefings or field transport, the handler watches his dog in case he detects a person concealed nearby. The handler may interrupt a procedure if he observes unusual sniffing or alerting behavior. Depending on the situation, he may direct other officers to take cover, to maintain their position while he and the dog search, or he may request other officers to check out the area in question.

3. DEPLOYMENT

Rapid response to set perimeter requires manpower. Search systematically. Secure areas behind search teams. If the area is not contained, search systematically, place resources strategically, and be prepared to change tactics in response to a confirmed sighting.

The cover officer, or officers—handler discretion—is trained to cover the K-9 officer, not watch the dog. Department handlers or SWAT members are preferred cover officers. Recruited for backup at the scene of an escape, an inexperienced patrolman must be briefed by the handler as to his responsibilities and how to operate around the police dog. Outside, backup officers typically carry a long gun or shotgun, depending upon the type of terrain. The cover officer works close behind or parallel to the handler, never in front, and protects himself using officer safety tactics. If the K-9 officer has no backup, and if the arrival of cover will be extended, the handler must decide: a) to continue in pursuit; b) to take up a surveillance position; c) to discontinue and redeploy at a later time.

The K-9 officer leads the search team and directs his dog. The dog searches off-lead, requiring the handler to maintain control of the dog by voice command. The dog is aggressive or nonaggressive in response to his handler's commands. Cover officers take direction from the handler. Typically when the handler stops, the cover officer stops, and if the dog approaches a cover officer, he stands still. The search team is responsible for taking the suspect into custody if located by the police dog.

If an uncontaminated scent guide (clothing, bedding, vehicle upholstery or equipment only the subject has touched) is available, advise the handler or pick it up with a scent-sterile instrument (stick, baton, pliers), place in an unsealed paper bag and transport to the scene. The handler may prescent his dog on an item the subject has contacted recently (dog sniffs the car seat of the suspect vehicle), or he may use a sterile material to absorb scent (blood stain, handle of a weapon). Few police dogs are trained to identify a suspect in a lineup. However, the verified scent guide can assist detection.

The helicopter is a high profile but highly efficient method of transporting search teams. Insertions/extractions may expose officers to the hidden suspect. If armed, he may take this opportunity to shoot or flee. Officer safety tactics will dictate how the K-9 search team deploys in these situations. The police dog must have flight experience. The handler and cover officers should be aware if the dog will be protective of the aircraft once inside (muzzle if necessary). It is the handler's responsibility to secure the canine on-lead in and about the aircraft, to follow proper loading/off-loading procedures, to keep his dog away from the instruments and from interfering with the pilot and crew.

Dog teams typically require 3- to 4-times the water other officers need. Except for resupply of water, the police dog team should arrive equipped to work in the field a full shift. The handler should be carrying enough personal gear to extend that shift if necessary, particularly if the duty becomes a tactical surveillance operation.

Dogs have extremely limited capability in hot weather (temperatures over 90° Fahrenheit) or warm weather in direct sunlight. Dogs do not see in total darkness, but they do see well at night—comparable to night vision glasses. The dog's eyes need time to adjust if he enters a dark area from a lighted area, for example pursuing a suspect into a building. The dog's nose needs time to adjust if he enters a scent-contaminated area (garage, paint shop, drug lab). Carbon monoxide and other toxic gases can disable or kill the dog as well as the officers.

Vehicle emissions are a typical hazard. Park the K-9 unit well upwind of other running vehicles at the command center. After exiting a fumy environment, the dog may appear to be sniffing normally but is actually anosmic (dysfunctional sense of smell). Air out his nose and conduct a brief test (search for an item) to ensure he is detecting scent.

BUILDING SEARCH. For burglaries, forced entry, or pursuit to a building, the handler may request additional officers. After the dog searches the perimeter, officers seal off escape routes. Whenever possible, determine the building layout.

Depending on department policy, before releasing a dog for the purpose of locating a suspect concealed in a building, the handler or other officer may call a warning to the effect that a police dog will be released if the person does not make himself visible and come forward. If possible, make the announcement over the public address system of a patrol car. Making the announcement at the point of search team entry is a high risk procedure. No announcement need be made if doing so jeopardizes officer safety. Inside the building, the search team uses standard tactics to perform a systematic patterned search of the interior, detailing room by room and floor by floor, posting officers to prevent suspects from evading or escaping.

BARRICADED SUBJECTS, armed terrorists or saboteurs typically require negotiators, tactical entry, rapid assault, chemical agents, or other special tactics, not a police dog. The very *sound* of a K-9 barking may break the dynamic balance needed for negotiations in a barricade incident.

Only a few, highly specialized SWAT teams in major metropolitan areas are qualified to utilize K-9 on rapid deployment or emergency entry. Confusion, gunfire or hostages typically render the patrol dog useless or dangerous in these situations. Do not put the police dog in harm's way needlessly.

The police dog is valuable on the perimeter during engagement. After special tactics brings the scene under control, it is standard procedure in many departments to clear buildings with K-9 teams to locate anyone hidden inside.

AREA SEARCH. If the dog is trained to track, deploy the K-9 team on any known fugitive track or line of travel. Preserve the location of an identified offender track. Do not contaminate the ground scent with people or vehicles. Very few police dogs are able to work a track over 12 hours old.

If the dog is trained to air scent, deploy the K-9 team to search any likely areas or to check out any reported suspect sightings. The team uses standard tactics to perform a systematic patterned search within defined boundaries. The handler must be prepared to describe what areas he has searched and to estimate a probability of detection (POD).

Suspects sometimes move back into areas that were previously searched. Dog teams can recover these areas or search low probability areas to increase public safety.

4. ARREST

The apprehension phase is frequently the most dangerous part of the entire search operation. The K-9 officer has already advised his cover officer(s) in advance how his dog reacts to gunfire, what his tactics will be in the event of an alert or ambush, and the search team has agreed upon the arrest tactics.

If the suspect runs, do not run in front of the dog and give chase unless requested to do so by the handler. After the suspect is apprehended, if the handler and dog are struggling with a suspect, do not intervene until the handler requests assistance or is clearly endangered. If any officer is in foot pursuit and finds a service dog approaching, stop immediately and stand motionless.

If the dog gets injured, the handler should perform the emergency procedures necessary and advise if he needs assistance, keeping in mind the safety of those assisting. The dog is the K-9 officer's partner, so the team will be under considerable stress. If the handler is injured and unable to command his dog, an officer who knows the dog should take control of the K-9, put him on lead, and transport him to his vehicle or his home. In an emergency, contact animal control for assistance. Unless a person's life is at stake, every effort should be made to control the K-9 rather than destroy this valuable animal.

Most police departments require that everyone bitten, no matter how slight the injury, receive medical treatment. Dog bites often break the skin with the attendant possibility of infection. Every suspect who is bitten or claims to have been bitten by a police dog must be taken to a medical facility and examined by a physician. Take photographs of wounds according to department procedure. *Refer to the physician's report for all information about the injury.*

Although not involved in the primary search mission, the police dog team may search for weapons, drugs, contraband, stolen items, cash, or other evidence. Initiate evidence searching as soon as possible after the offender is in custody to prevent contamination or scent loss.

The handler has the exclusive responsibility of describing the dog's performance in his report. Cover officers or others should reference the handler's report to describe the dog's actions. Schedule a search team debriefing as soon as possible after the incident. This often neglected procedure is a valuable problem solving and team building tool.

BUILDING SEARCH—THE DETAILS

In a city warehouse incident, the first officers on scene didn't wait. They searched the building themselves and found nothing. When the K-9 unit arrived, the handler decided to search the building as a practice exercise. He made the announcement. No response. They entered the building, the K-9 searching out ahead of them. Turning a corner into a hallway, the dog located a hiding suspect. He knifed the dog, but the officers took him into custody. The officers' comment: "Man, we screwed up. That could have been one of us." Though severely injured, the police dog lived and recovered to go back on the street.

Establish the command post well away from the areas where the suspect is believed to be hiding. Gather intelligence for incoming units. Request a police dog unit ASAP. Some supervisors want officers to wait until they arrive in order to assess the situation. As soon the supervisor arrives and determines that K-9 will be needed, request the dog team. Officers at the scene set the perimeter away from the building, providing better officer safety and preventing officer scent from diffusing into the building. If at all possible, keep everyone out of the building to give the dog team, or multiple dog teams, the advantage of initial entry whereby the suspect scent will be the strongest human scent inside.

Maintaining the perimeter to prevent escape is a key to capture. Perimeter officers do not leave the scene to answer other calls or wander around in the vicinity, either inside a building or on the perimeter of an area. Limiting radio traffic to emergency transmissions is important strategy affecting K-9 search tactics. The scent or noise of a moving officer can distract the K-9, who is working to find one or more offenders. This applies to building searches and also to the perimeters of areas. If suspects know the dog is coming, they will wrap a jacket or other protection around an arm to ward off the dog, change their location to make it more difficult for the dog, or pick up a blunt or sharp object to use as a weapon against the K-9 or the officer.

When the police dog team arrives, the primary unit briefs the responding K-9 unit and advises the position of all units on scene. At that time, the dog team or the lead dog team takes charge of the search operation. The K-9 officer is responsible for calling the shots if his department policy states: "The decision to apply a service dog to a specific police function will remain with the dog handler concerned."

COVER TACTICS

Familiarize the dog with his backup. Have the officer pet the K-9. Although this procedure probably means nothing to the dog, the cover officer will benefit from the initial contact. In training the dog learns that officers will be following the handler and under normal circumstances will discriminate between the search team officers and suspects.

An officer who is afraid of dogs may request another task. Do not criticize this decision. People terrorized by dogs, especially as children, often retain irrational fear as adults. The same officer may show great courage in a combat situation. Do not compound the mission stress for this officer or the search team.

The search team develops a plan to conduct the search. Normally, each K-9 team will use a cover or backup officer who will be equipped with a shotgun, rifle, or other designated weapon.

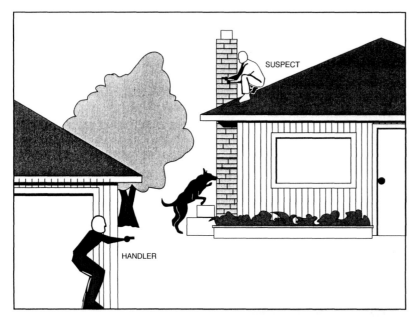

SUSPECT

HANDLER

The cover officer works to the rear or parallel to the handler, but never in front. If the dog approaches him, he must follow the handler's prior instructions—generally, he is to remain motionless until the dog goes by.

The cover officer's function is to protect the handler and himself. He should stay close to the K-9 handler's back. He is responsible for watching elevated locations where offenders may be hiding as well as scanning locations to the rear. The K-9 officer will be watching the dog and scanning the area ahead and to both sides of the team. During a search, every time an officer speaks he gives away his position. Maintaining the advantage of position is critically important. When the two officers work as a team behind the dog, they can work silently and can communicate by gestures or contact.

Before entering a building, conduct an outside perimeter search to clear the roof, if possible, and the surrounding property. The suspect may be watching from inside. Use cover, move quickly, randomly, and direct the dog to search systematically.

Moving as a unit distracts the dog less than having multiple officers moving separately through different parts of a room, or different rooms. If the handler is widely separated from his backup, it may be difficult or impossible to communicate a change in tactics. A change in the dog's behavior—something less than a full alert—may be more difficult to read if the handler and cover officer are separated.

If a suspect is hiding high, the suspect's scent may rise, then drop down. Many times it will drop down in a corner, along a wall or against some feature of the terrain. The dog will alert up. The cover officer may pinpoint the suspect before the dog does. Sometimes the building's air conditioning system will blow the suspect's scent out an exterior vent, making it difficult or impossible for the dog to detect him without actually reaching him.

The handler will work the dog! The backup officer must blind himself to the dog and concentrate on covering, searching, and officer safety. Typically, the dog will clear a room or area ahead of the handler. The backup officer will cover him looking high, also protecting and covering to the rear. Once that room or area is clear, the dog team and backup officer will move to the next area. If enough personnel are available, officers should secure rooms and floors as they are searched so the suspect cannot ambush the K-9 team. There is rarely enough manpower to adequately secure outside areas behind search teams unless perimeter units change positions.

Officer safety determines the best tactics. Teams may enter the basement first, clearing each floor systematically. Or a helicopter may stage teams on the roof. Rooftop entries are usually a SWAT entry. Beware the dog jumping off.

As a supervisor I've been in situations involving the search of large residences where there was nobody in the array of people on the scene qualified to go in with the handler and dog. The handler has to watch the dog. If you go in as backup and you don't know the dog, and you aren't familiar with how they work and what they're doing, you're probably just going to be afraid. I went in, if for no other reason than I'm comfortable with the dog. I'm not going to be looking at the dog.

We teach this in our basic police academy, in the regional academy we have in the sheriff's department. We go through the use of police dogs with all the officers. We show them how the dogs work and how to work with the K-9 teams.

—K-9 Lieutenant

A compelling reason to move as a closely coordinated unit is the cover officer's exposure to the dog. The dog usually ignores the cover officer. His ability to discriminate may break down in a firefight at close range. Gunfire inside can destroy orientation. If the handler and cover officer are out of contact, the dog may take on the cover officer.

Announcing the presence and intent of a police dog team before starting a search is a matter of department policy and handler discretion. Before releasing a dog for the purpose of locating a suspect concealed in a building, the designated officer or the handler may call a warning to the effect that a police dog will be released to search if the person does not make himself visible and come forward. Where available, use the public-address system from a patrol car or helicopter to broadcast the warning. If warning is given the suspect that he will be bitten if he does not surrender, and in fact he does not comply, the police dog team will make the apprehension as they have been trained, and that action will be defensible in court.

The officer may decide not to make an announcement if there is reason to believe that the suspect is armed or that officer safety or public safety would be jeopardized. Announcements are generally not advised before starting open area searches for felony fugitives. The suspect has made clear his intent. Calling out to him from a hovering helicopter or patrol vehicle may cause him to give up. But the K-9 officer calling out, thereby revealing his position, may enhance the suspect's existing tactical advantage. The bottom line, as in all dog deployment, is do what is safe and practical.

ENTRY

Sending the dog in by himself is a dead-end tactic. For all spaces except closets, alcoves, or small rooms, you have to make entry. You have no other way of knowing what the dog has or has not searched. In the event the dog alerts or locates the suspect, you have to enter to take him into custody anyway.

Once found by the dog, he is likely to be more aggressive toward the dog if the officers are not present to back up the K-9. If he knifes or strikes the dog, you may hear nothing.

You are responsible for directing and controlling the dog. You have to be there to do this.

Typically the K-9 search team crosses doorways using the diagonal (handler and backup move to a targeted location inside) or the wrap-around (handler and backup "roll in" on opposite sides of the doorway). The method chosen depends on the type door, the availability of cover, and the threat.

It is the handler's discretion whether to cast the dog ahead, in case the suspect is lying in wait, or to enter with the K-9. One night an Oakland police officer was glad he chose to hesitate a few seconds before entering a warehouse. The thug had a pipe wrench poised to crack the officer's head and was caught swinging it instead at the dog.

Practice on a regular basis having the dog locate suspects lurking just inside your point of entry. On an outside search, this might be behind the first tree or bush. Excited police dogs that explode into the building or search area often fail to search effectively at first.

Be ready for the startled suspect himself to blast out of the building, the dog in hot pursuit. Some offenders decide the cops are the lesser of two evils.

Follow department entry procedures. Announcing the K-9 sometimes brings people out. It also puts the suspect on notice. Outside or in large buildings, do not compromise officer safety by revealing your position.

K-9 ANNOUNCEMENT

This is the Police Department
/Sheriff's Department
/Department of Corrections.
Come out with your hands up.
Do it now!
If you do not come out,
a police dog will bite you.

Este es el Departamento de Policia
/Departamento del Sheriff
/Departamento de Correciones.
Salgan para fuera con sus manos arriba.
Aganlo ya!
Si no salen el perro policia los mordera.

SEARCH

Do not focus on the dog applies to the handler as well as the cover officer. *"Watch your dog!"* the typical warning by the K-9 trainer means *read your dog.* It does not mean disregard anything else that is happening. Focusing on the dog can get the handler and the cover officer killed.

The area of responsibility and areas of threat require keeping the dog in your peripheral vision and deploying the dog as an extension of *your own senses and awareness.* This takes experience and is the hallmark of a responsible handler.

The dog has to adjust to the handler's behavior—bending, peeking around corners, kneeling, moving fast then standing still, whispering, gesturing—probably not your normal behavior.

Fear of slick floors interferes with building search. Clip the dog's nails to increase traction and reduce noise. The dog that is confident on all types of flooring, metal grates, and balconies walks on his pads with a normal stride and concentrates on detection.

Many officers neglect to carry water on searches. Supplies stored in the patrol vehicle are useless to the K-9 team on an extended tactical operation. You cannot predict when it will be over. Faucets are not dependable. Toilet water is unsafe. Outside connectors may be unsafe also. Hydrate the dog as frequently as he needs it. Plastic bottles with center plungers come in all sizes and shapes and let the handler water his dog quietly behind cover in the dark.

Despite his duties as a handler, the K-9 officer should spend part of his training searching without his dog to maintain his awareness of the threat potential. He also needs to fulfill the cover officer role occasionally. Handlers often forget their cover as they command the dog. The search team—handler, cover and the dog—should function as a unit.

GUN HANDLING

Hold the pistol in a one- or two-hand hold pointed downward. The "belt tuck" position provides good stability and accommodates the "third-eye concept" to gain rapid target acquisition where your eyes see. The cover officer with a long gun also maintains a secure two-handed grip with the barrel pointed downward. Besides finding the adversary, the K-9 search team has the additional problem of not shooting the dog accidentally. During an exchange of gunfire, a police dog was shot in the foot from behind by his own handler.

It seems obvious that the cover officer must be strong enough to carry a long gun plus his regular weapons the distance of the search. A deputy found out that after several hours and seven hot sweaty miles of backcountry behind a

K-9 handler, he had to take refuge in his air conditioned patrol unit. City police officers tend to think of area searching in terms of a vacant lot or a park: small, square, and flat. Given a choice, the suspect will head for better cover. If he has been working out for six months or more in a prison yard, he will have better endurance than the typical patrol officer.

All search team officers must have flashlights, even in daylight. Many times the dog will search a dark location. The search team must follow. Every handler should carry two high powered flashlights and a smaller backup light on his person during night searches, one emergency light during daylight hours. Do not shine your flashlight on the dog. Shine it on the Problem Areas where the suspect may be hiding.

The police dog presence does not change the Reactionary Gap, the 21-foot rule for an offender with an edged weapon. The suspect who is prepared to cut you probably has no fear of the dog and no doubt in his mind that he can take you both out. The handler confronted by a knife-wielding suspect at 14 feet has no safe alternative but to shoot and send the dog. The diversionary tactic may save the handler's life and that of his canine.

The suspect is listening. *Use a low voice or hand signals.* The handler who constantly recalls his dog gives their position away over and over again. K-9 panting is unavoidable. The distinctive sound of clicking toenails may be reduced by regular trimming.

Do not fire the dog up or down a stairway like an unguided missile. You may be sending him on a suicide mission. An option is to have the dog sit, climb the stairs, then call the dog. Or climb the stairs with the dog at a free heel. Practice climbing and descending stairways by having the dog pause, stand or sit on landings and on the steps themselves. Practice climbing backwards pointing a gun, clearing the stairway with the dog at your side. If the dog is used to bolting up and down the stairs in the police station or at home, he may take the fastest route and bail off the side of the stairs.

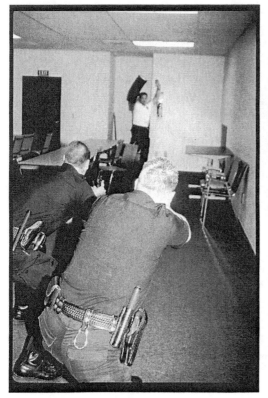

From cover call the dog out, call the suspect out, direct him to a location for arrest, then redirect the dog to search the area.

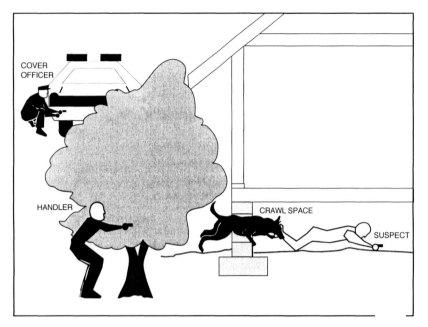

COVER OFFICER

HANDLER

CRAWL SPACE

SUSPECT

Shut elevators down or block the doors open. You do not want the suspect changing floors to backdoor you. You also cannot risk getting trapped or shot in elevators.

As a search team entered the lobby of a city office building, the K-9 ran over to the elevators and disappeared in one. The handler tried to pry the doors open but was too late. The animal's barking echoed through the elevator shaft. His joy ride ended on the fifth floor where the handler found him after sprinting up the stairwell.

Do not permit the dog to run down hallways or disappear around corners. If the dog moves rapidly along the hall past unchecked areas and alerts to a door, the handler must decide whether to follow or to call the dog back to

If the dog alerts, consider gas, water, or other tactics to clear voids. Confined with a suspect kicking, striking, blocking, stabbing, or shooting him, the dog will have difficulty performing a recall.

sniff the intervening doors. If the dog tracked along the hall, the handler may decide to make the entry the dog has selected.

The best tactic is to search each room systematically.

During a building search, the K-9 team was working down a hallway when a suspect appeared out of a room pointing a gun. The handler fired, at the same time sending the dog.

The officer should not hesitate to fire at the suspect who is a direct and immediate threat to his life.

Do not disregard a full-blown alert to a window. Has the yard outside been searched? An experienced police dog may lift his head to sniff fresh air coming through a window or vent, but he will generally move on quickly.

Proof the dog off typical search distractions—cats, citizens, cover officers shooting nearby, sirens, helicopters. Do not wait for distractions on actual search operations. Set up training scenarios. Which do you think will be more exciting to the dog at first exposure—a cat leaping away from a dumpster or an armed offender crouching inside the dumpster?

THE ALERT

The typical *air scent alert profile* is a high nose and tail carriage with the dog sniffing back and forth, bracketing the scent cone as he closes in on the suspect. A high scent cone or a barrier will cause jumping, climbing, and barking.

The typical *tracking profile* is the dog sniffing the ground, sometimes to the feet or body of a suspect before realizing he is at source and making the apprehension. Sound or movement by the suspect will also cause an alert. The handler will tell the search team when the K-9 alerts.

The importance of thinking scent diffusion was clearly demonstrated by a suspect concealed inside a caged shed in an equipment yard. The front wall of the shed was solid wood 4 feet high with open metal caging to the roof. A sliding wooden door in the center of the wall was closed and appeared padlocked. By reaching through the cage, the suspect had made the padlock appear secure.

Searching the yard, the police dog alerted toward the shed roof. Glancing inside, the handler could see no one. Backing off, he scanned the shed roof. He called for cover. Low-crawling with his dog along the front of the cage, the handler discovered the open lock, but the dog was never able to scent the suspect near the wall, only away from the wall high in the air.

After taking the suspect, who had been lying immediately behind the cage wall, into custody, officers used cold smoke to investigate the pattern of scent diffusion. Placed near the floor behind the cage wall, the smoke curled inward, rose to the ceiling, and diffused outward beyond the eves. After clearing the roof, the smoke fell toward the pavement where the dog had alerted.

APPREHENSION

When the dog alerts, hold your position. Do not illuminate the dog as he works the scent cone. Do not call out, "Bad guy, we know you're there!" and rush in behind the dog.

First, until the dog goes to source, turbulence is a factor. Second, bad guys expect the handler to rush in behind the dog.

Where might the suspect be? Where might other suspects be? If you know there are multiple suspects, your option might be to stay behind cover, order the suspect(s) out, and let the dog complete the apprehension until everyone shows or the suspect comes back to your location.

The dog may pass by one suspect in the course of detecting the other. While targeting the strongest scent, the dog may give only a brief indication that he detects a second scent. If the handler observes that indication, he may prevent an ambush or decide to redirect the dog to the second suspect.

Sometimes detecting multiple suspects will put the dog in conflict. He may go from one location to the other, frustrated because he cannot access either suspect. In such cases the handler may have to call the dog back to his side and request backup officers to search the elevated or concealed locations the dog cannot reach. At that point the K-9 team becomes the cover team in case a suspect attempts to escape.

Expect to find another suspect after the dog finds the first. Do not let down your guard during the arrest.

ARREST

During suspect contact, the dog is under the handler's control. Most police dogs are trained to attack on command. If the suspect resists, attempts to flee, or attacks the handler or other person, the dog will normally be deployed to assist performing the apprehension and arrest.   Wherever is located, search team officers must pay close attention to the handler's commands. He will inform them when they can take control of their suspect. All felony suspects should be treated as if they are armed. Approach the suspect only when the handler states he has control of the dog. At this point, the search team officers control the suspect while the handler controls the dog.

If the dog and the suspect, or the handler and suspect are involved in an altercation, do not approach until the handler has physically controlled the dog.

If the handler is injured, request another K-9 officer to the scene. Most dogs will react normally to calm behavior and allow the officer to lead them away. If the handler is injured and the dog is protecting him, request further measures be taken by other K-9 officers. Techniques to call off the protective dog should be worked out in training before the team goes on the street. These techniques should be practiced on a regular basis within the K-9 unit.

A handler sent her patrol dog into a building after a suspect. The dog got knifed in the neck. When he came out, she could not see the knife wound and sent him back in again. He bit the suspect, then collapsed.

Get suspect number 1 out of the area or building before searching for number 2. This may be a good time to water or relieve your dog behind cover. It may also be the time suspect number 2 sees his chance to change locations or escape, so maintain surveillance.

The canine is not a reliable detector of furtive movement. Pulling a trigger requires very little movement. There are many ways that suspects move while being taken into custody. *Officers* have difficulty detecting furtive movement. The dog should never be expected to make this distinction.

SWAT team approaches the building and makes entry as a unit with the dog in the lead. It is counterintuitive that a weak signal, if the right frequency, will have significant effect. In tactical situations, with the properly trained K-9, a low unit profile with low volume commands and hand signals is highly effective.

Weigh the risks of lifting the K-9 into an attic. Is the dog likely to fall through the ceiling or ducting? Is the handler going to follow the dog up there? Is gas an option? Is waiting an option? If feasible, the dog may be the best option.

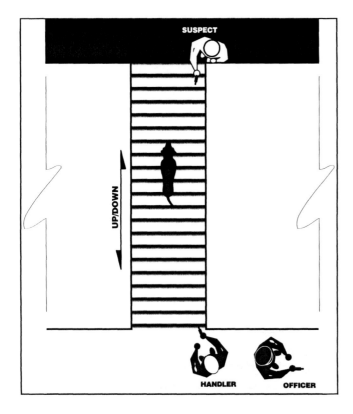

SUSPECT

UP/DOWN

HANDLER   OFFICER

*Practice clearing
stairways. Beware
of sending the dog
on a suicide mission.
Suspects know that
where the dog goes,
officers are sure
to follow.*

A K-9 officer was going off shift before daybreak. The unfenced police lot was located in the highest crime district of the city. After a night of many arrests, the tired handler had put her dog in the patrol car and was talking to an unarmed plain clothes officer who suddenly stared in alarm, "He's got a knife!"

Glancing at a man coming out of the dark, the handler said, "Nahh, it's his keys."

Blinking back fatigue, she realized he had a knife in each hand. Drawing down on the man, she shouted, "Drop the knives, drop the knives."

Now he was close.

He dropped the knives onto the pavement.

As the handler holstered to move in, the man bent over and tried to pick up one of the knives.

The handler kicked both knives across the lot, and the plain clothes officer recovered them. The man was drunk.

Later the handler said, "I was in shock. This really brought it home to me. Here I am an experienced officer, I've worked three police dogs for this department in eight years, I've made hundreds of arrests, and *I* had trouble seeing the weapons, seeing what was going on. How could this decision be left to a dog?"

Look for the hands. Don't be in such a hurry to call the dog off that you fail to get the offender under control.

Police service dogs don't need to exercise human judgment. The trainer and handler condition the dog to recognize a stimulus, a situation, and to respond. At any time the dog makes an error, such as when a drunk falls against the handler and the dog thinks it's a handler attack, the handler commands the dog not to bite the person.

It is the handler's decision whether his dog bites someone or not, never the dog's.

A person standing passively, arms outstretched, with a gun pointing at the handler, is not going to knock the handler down until he fires a shot, and then it's too late.

—Sgt. Louis C. Castle
Culver City Police Department

Reading canine behavior changes can save the officer's life.

"In December we were called out from home (one of the hazards of being a K-9 handler) to assist the city on a silent burglar alarm with suspects inside the building. When we arrived on the scene, we gave the usual announcements for those inside to give up and come out.

"As usual, those inside chose to ignore my invitation. The K-9, my cover officer and I entered the building, a large supermarket. Within 3 minutes, the dog led us to the rear of the store where a small storage area was located. The canine was giving me the signal that the suspect was 'hiding high,' which meant I had to climb up in the rafters again. This is one part of the job I always hate—it's hot, dirty, dark and very easy to get hurt in the confined space.

"Police officers quickly found a ladder, and the dog and I climbed the ladder to a small crawl space above the walk-in coolers. The area was not large enough to stand up in, so I was crawling around in the attic. As I reached a vent, I started to stand up when the dog ran by, almost knocking me down and pushing me aside. At first I was upset because I could not see anything. Just then the dog ran into a small space immediately to my left, and I heard the suspect yell out. He was removed from the attic and arrested. Considered to be armed and dangerous, the suspect was wanted by state parole. The search took a total of 7 minutes."

—K-9 Officer

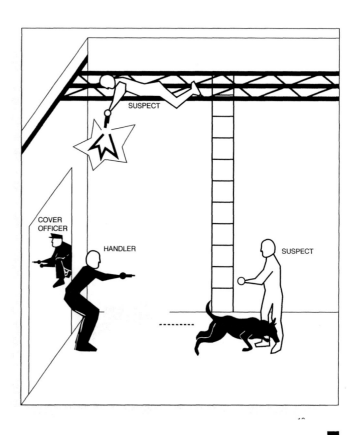

In a city where gangs actively sell drugs on the street, compete for business, and commit crimes against each other, a vehicle had just been taken in an armed robbery. The suspect was using a .380 auto to ply his trade. Officers went into a vehicle pursuit. Shortly after, when the two suspects bailed, they set up a perimeter, called for air support, and called for the K-9.

The handler started his search where one suspect was last seen mid-block. The search led around the block to a small house where the dog alerted and entered the crawl space beneath the building. Locating the suspect, the dog was met with a kick to the head. He reacted quickly and bit the leg.

Next to the building, the dog picked up a shirt belonging to the second suspect and continued to alert along the wall. The handler observed grease on the side of the building where someone had climbed up. The air unit flew over and saw the suspect on the roof. He was taken into custody without incident. Afterward, both suspects cooperated with officers searching for the weapon.

Penetrating crawl spaces to apprehend suspects is dangerous. A suspect on parole for burglary was exceptionally strong and obviously spent his prison time lifting weights. Responding to a call that the suspect was firing a 12-gauge shotgun, officers recovered the weapon, but the suspect was still at large, shirtless, in his underwear.

A K-9 alerted to a crawl space sectioned by drywall and plumbing pipes. When the dog went in, the suspect, hiding up in the piping, fell onto the dog, grabbed him with both hands, and began to swing him side-to-side. The handler had to crawl in to arrest him.

Getting him prone and handcuffed was difficult despite the dog's assistance. As they came out, a crowd of locals applauded and began cheering loudly. The suspect was a local thug who liked to terrorize the neighborhood.

Sending the dog into tight spaces requires training targeted at reinforcing the calloff. The dog is at a disadvantage in these situations, which he perceives, and will typically extract himself and the suspect.

A suspect discovered hiding under a house refused to come out. Commanded to enter, the K-9 seized his leg and started dragging him out. Instead of complying, the suspect braced his legs against both sides of the entry hole. Meeting such resistance, the dog pulled harder. The handler had to give repeated commands before the dog would call off.

Do not depend on your backup to watch high areas of concealment at all times. Keep the dog in your peripheral vision, but focus on places a person could hide.

Police dogs employed in high crime areas where they are involved in fights, pursuits, felony searches, weapons fire on a regular basis need time on a regular basis to relax, relieve stress, act like dogs, and interact with normal, friendly people. Part of those normal, friendly encounters should be on duty among people in the community and fellow officers.

Condition a high-drive, athletic dog to make an arrest every time he gets out of the patrol car, and you have a formula for serious behavioral problems.

Small, undermanned departments and isolated state troopers have similar problems. Cover is distant or non-existent, and helicopters are a luxury.

How can a department conduct realistic training and problem-solving if there are not enough officers to cover the street? If the average response is 15 minutes, how do you get containment when the suspect clears the fence and is gone in 2 minutes? If the handler is constantly on the defensive because he typically operates alone, how does his attitude affect his dog?

When the fight is on, the police dog often suffers painful abuse before the team can get the suspect under control.

The suspect was a follow-home type bandit. The hot prowl turned into an armed robbery when the owner confronted the suspects. One suspect wearing a bandanna over his face stuck a gun in the owner's face. Surprised by a rapid entry team, the suspects bailed out the rear of the house. Police set up a perimeter. Searching the backyard, the K-9 poked his nose into a bush along the hedge row. A suspect struck the dog hard across the side of his head and tried to bull his way past. He began punching the dog in the head. Defending himself, the dog bit both arms. It took two officers to handcuff the suspect.

After a vehicle and foot pursuit, police throw up a quick perimeter and request K-9. The air ship is seconds away. The K-9 handler arrives backed by another handler on his search team. The dog follows the suspect's path to an alley. Three houses down, he doubles back on scent to the rear of a house. He alerts on a shed. Suddenly the suspect bolts out from the shed. Officers call for him to stop. Instead he runs onto a junk pile. When the handler sends his dog, the offender grabs the dog by the neck pulling him through the pile and fighting him. Twisting, the dog grips the man's inner thigh. Finally the suspect complies.

The police dog running into a dark room from a lighted area will probably be unable to see a motionless suspect. There is a brief but finite adjustment time. Dogs are not able to see in total darkness. The K-9 eye has light-gathering capability similar to a night scope or night goggles. Police dogs have run into suspects before scenting or seeing them. In some cases this has cost the dog's life. Think about this before you blindly fire a dog into a dark room.

We train in big, wide-open buildings high up, because these incidents produce the greatest problem. With a suspect hiding

Cover the K-9 team on a systematic search, securing areas behind them. Ventilation systems may create turbulence or force the suspect's scent outside. Check diffusion at doors, windows, heaters and vents. Tracking capability pays off where the dog alerts to a door despite scent diffusing inward. Scent may diffuse down blank walls. Note areas the dog cannot search adequately.

down low, the scent concentrates within 3 or 4 feet of the floor. The scent is readily available. The dog can easily identify the source. But once you start jacking that guy up 10 to 15 feet off the floor, the scent balloons out. The dog may pick up the scent, but he has more difficulty identifying the source because the scent carries vast distances. The longer the subject is in position, the greater the scent volume expansion.

In one case, the dog unit searched through the building. The paper man was sitting outside doing the paper, and suddenly a subject fell to the pavement. It was a kid. He broke his arm. He fell out the window right in front of the officer doing the report.

He said, 'The dog found me 3 or 4 times. He came up, barked, the handler couldn't find me, took the dog away, and the dog came back, stood there and barked.'

He was up 25 feet off the floor in a window well. It was dark and not readily accessible. The handler would have had to climb up onto a railroad car. A ramp led into this big warehouse to carry railroad cars where they offloaded furniture and other cargo. The handler had failed to climb up on top of the railroad car to make the find. The dog did everything he could.

If the dog does something with such a dramatic attitude change that you're thinking, 'I wonder if anybody's here?' That isn't the time to look, it's the time to search.

The subject's concealment may allow a minimal amount of human scent available to the dog. If out of the whole building, this whole space, the dog made an attitude change in one specific area, don't just look around and say, 'I didn't see anything.'

Why, in this entire building, did this dog make such an attitude change?

Many of these large, multi-story buildings in which we work have air shafts, or shafts to allow carrying additional electrical or water lines all the way up to the 15th or 20th floor. These can be very large. A person can actually climb up inside them. It's like being inside a chimney, so there may not be enough scent to trigger a full response.

The handler has got to read the dog.
—Sgt. Kenneth Burger, Retired, Chicago Police Department

SURVEILLANCE

Teach the dog to lie low, to be quiet, to watch. Police K-9s are effective when assigned to surveillance operations. If the dog is not an uncontrollable barker, his superior detection and apprehension capabilities are valuable on a stakeout.

After three rapes at a park entrance station, headquarters placed a female law enforcement ranger posing as the ticket agent in the entrance kiosk and spotted a K-9 team in the forest nearby. It was a long three weeks sitting in the woods watching cars go through the entrance, waking the dog when he snored too loudly, trying to stay warm and not fall asleep. The only excitement was a bear walking through one night. The dog's nose started twitching even before he woke up to alert and tell the bear to get out. The bear left. The handler felt reassured he might notice a rapist.

The night before the park had decided to abandon the whole operation, fall was in the air. A few minutes after 1 o'clock a large man in his mid-thirties came walking up the road fast.

It was not unusual for people to have car trouble along the highway driving to this altitude. This was not your typical stranded motorist, though. This guy was looking everywhere and striding straight to the kiosk. His hands were jammed into his jacket pockets. This was a man with a mission

Tactical communications should not interfere with hearing. In the dark, listen to determine if the dog is working. Is he sniffing or mouth breathing? Quietly padding on a patterned search? Stopped, waiting, indicating? Stomping, leaping, whining, barking, trying to get to the suspect?

Beware of backlighting the suspect and confusing the dog. Backlight the dog and confuse the suspect (opposite page).

The reliable dog will alert and stay at the scent source without assistance from the handler. Detection itself reinforces the police dog.

and he didn't waste any time getting to the point.

Reaching the kiosk, he twisted the knob and flung open the door. The ranger had heard the footsteps but did not expect the rapid entry. She bent over to get her gun out of the drawer, but he was on her.

He never heard the dog, he told the court later. That was his complaint—the handler didn't make an announcement. Without warning he felt himself being dragged backwards rather painfully by the gluteus maximus and cast unceremoniously, pants down, on the pavement.

BARRICADED SUSPECTS

Authorities sometimes forget to establish the command post upwind of the barricade. This is important so this nerve center for the on-scene decision makers does not lie in the diffusion pattern for chemical agents that may be used. Similarly the K-9 units should not be located in either the kill zone or downwind of diffusing chemical agents. The K-9 staging area should be well away from any utility trucks, ambulances, fire trucks, armored personnel carriers or other support vehicles. Media crews should not be permitted access to police dog teams while they are part of the barricade incident, even if outside the inner perimeter.

When working a barricaded suspect case, K-9 teams are typically deployed on the perimeter in case a subject escapes without taking a hostage. The K-9 vehicle needs a clear area so the dog can exit without interference or the officer can drive away if called to another location. Do not expose the dog to the exhaust of other vehicles idling near the canine car. The air conditioning system may not eliminate fumes that will disable the dog's scenting.

The police dog team has to be capable of operating on the same radio frequency as the incident command.

During a barricade incident one Midwest department directed two police dog teams to deploy on opposite sides of the outer perimeter. Evading by crawling under a deck and hedge rows, the offender ran between two houses past the K-9 car.

The team saw the fatigue-clad runner on his way to freedom but thought he was an officer. SWAT was talking on a separate frequency. Not until dispatch contacted command were they able to determine the offender had escaped.

MINES AND CAVES

When the police dog team got the call, a deputy had chased the driver of a stolen car into an undeveloped brushy area in California's gold country. As he stood waiting for the arrival of the K-9, the deputy smelled cigarette smoke. There was an old abandoned mine part way up the hill.

On arrival, the K-9 team climbed to the mine entrance. The dog immediately "went nuts." Nose down, they entered the long, horizontal shaft. Crossing puddles of mucky water, the dog did not pause. The cool moist air was an ideal scent reservoir. Several times they came to side tunnels. Without stopping, the dog's nose vacuumed the tunnel, making each decision to turn or go straight.

Suddenly the dog slammed into the offender, who had plastered himself against the rock wall, apparently hoping the dog team would pass him by in the dark.

Searching mines or tunnel systems is extremely dangerous. The canary dying or miners' lamps going out were used for years to indicate insufficient oxygen to support human life. Toxic gases or lack of oxygen can kill search teams in seconds. Tunnel collapse, falls into pits or off cliffs, entrapment, drowning, getting lost, and large furbearing animals are a few other hazards. Standing at the entrance, not knowing the type of mine, the layout of the tunnels, or other critical factors, you cannot evaluate the hazard properly. Without a professional who has firsthand knowledge of the subterranean system and appropriate caving or rescue equipment, it is not advisable for the K-9 team to enter holes in the ground.

AREA SEARCH—THE DETAILS

The county put out the call, "We have a stolen vehicle. The driver and passenger bailed. We need a dog unit down here Code 3. And a helicopter."

I go, "Set up a perimeter."

It's not like they were going anywhere. It's raining like you wouldn't believe. A major storm downpour on a Saturday night. I'm driving down there, and they're telling me, "Kick it up."

I'm all, "Excuse me, I'm on the river road." It curves along the levee west of the river. I have my lights on, and I'm driving...not exactly slow.

Meanwhile they're calling for all helicopters. None of the helicopters are up because of the weather.

I turn into the driveway blacked out.

They tell me, "Come all the way down to the patrol cars."

So I do. I stop my car. I don't even have a raincoat. I throw on my baseball cap, get out and say, "What's going on?"

The deputy says, "This is it, the car."

Of course they have the car all lit up in their spotlights.

They say, "We think he ran through the vineyards."

They already searched and caught the passenger. They found him hiding in an abandoned car, and took him out at gunpoint.

OK, fine. They're going, "Yeah the driver, we think he's in the vineyard." They go, "We already searched this area...and we searched around the house...and we searched this building...and it's locked.."

So I get the dog out of the car. There's a house, a barn, silos, abandoned vehicles, and a vineyard. They have a kind of half-assed perimeter set up. I'm standing in the group of patrol cars. I make an announcement from behind my unit then let the dog go. I tell this deputy, "Stay right on my elbow." I want him with me to know where he is.

He says, "No problem."

I direct the dog toward the vineyards. He's running out. He flips around, starts running back into this brush right beside us, and they say, *"We already searched that area."*

Needless to say, that's where the guy is. The dog's trying to control the guy. The guy is fighting him. I'm telling him, "Show me your hands."

The guy's screaming and not showing his hands. He's flailing around hitting the dog.

I go across, it's only a few yards, but this is the vineyard-from-hell. There are foxholes out there. I'm trying to be careful, trying to watch the suspect, and down I go into a big foxhole.

I get up. I'm all muddy and soaked to the bone. As I get up, I see this other deputy coming from the other side. He falls in a foxhole. Here we are, on our heads. The dog's still on the guy. The guy's still fighting.

I call the dog off, arrest the guy, and they're telling me, "We think there's one more out here."

My dog goes under this other abandoned car out there, an old truck. He's trying to get underneath, but there are no tires or wheels. It's set down on the ground. I'm thinking the guy's under there, and I'm telling him, "Good boy, get him out." Cause I *know* he's in there. My dog's just entirely too keyed on this thing. He jumps into the bed of the truck and starts digging, jumps back out, tries to get underneath.

This deputy looks underneath and says, "No one's down here, but the grass is flattened down."

I say, "Someone's here." I am thinking maybe he wrapped his body around the drive shaft or something.

It was the weirdest thing, because I know someone had been there. It had been about 40 minutes, and the scent must have still been hot under there. The rain was probably wiping out the scent in the field. We finished the search, and as the storm let up, they brought a helo over with infrared. Nobody found a third man. I think there were only two. The passenger probably spent some time under that truck where my dog alerted before he crawled under the car where they found him.

The driver my dog got was hiding in the bushes about 10 feet from one of the patrol cars. If he had been armed, we could have all been dead.

—Officer DeAnna Stevens

In the East a police dog found an offender hiding in a tree. The dog leaped up, biting his gun arm. Still the offender managed to get a round off at the officer.

The track was more than 6 hours old in the heart of Chicago, the middle of summer, hard pavement contaminated by pedestrians and litter. At the time the handler did not feel the dog would be able to complete the track. A bread truck driver had been killed around 5 in the morning. His body was found about 9 o'clock. The district crime lab showed up, and they went through the whole scene. Newsmen were out and all of a sudden the chief at the scene said, "Let's get the dogs here."

It's 6 hours after the incident, and the handler gets there and says, "Gee whiz! I don't know if my dog can do this." He's presented a hat that supposedly did not belong to the truck driver, so they assumed it belonged to an offender. Everybody had handled the hat, turned it inside out, and the crime lab has gone over it. They even dusted the bread truck for prints. Now he is asked to do a track from the crime scene.

The dog takes the hat, shakes it violently, and throws it up in the air. The handler feels a little embarrassed by that. The dog circles the van, comes out of the van, and takes off down the street. He is followed by the chief, his driver, police officers, and the news media. It's like a parade going down the street. The handler thinks, "You look like you're tracking. I gotta go with you. I don't know what you're doing."

All hard surface—going down alleys, through some gangways, coming out another street, going back down, crossing over another street, and finally stopping at the curb. The chief asks the handler, "What happened? How come he stopped?" The handler says, "I can only assume the guy must have gotten in a car here." And the chief says, "Well, that's very good."

About that time, some woman leaning out the window says, "What's going on?" She is overlooking the walk. They say, "Ah, nothing. We're doing an investigation." She relates how she saw two suspicious men standing at the curb. The officers say, "That's very nice." "They got in the car and they left," she says. They go, "Okay, thank you, lady." She says, "Do you want the license number of the car?"

The chief sends his driver up to get the license number. He traces it. It is in a high-rise apartment building.

The guy in the apartment says, "Yeah, I was coming home from work this morning.

I saw two friends who live downstairs and I stopped and picked them up." So the police go downstairs, they knock on the door, two guys open the door, they both throw up their hands and say, "We didn't mean to kill him."

Now the chief takes the two men back to the crime scene. He wants them to retrace their escape route. The handler's thinking, "Why don't you leave well enough alone? We caught the guys!" They took the exact route that the dog had indicated. This was very impressive. The chief gave a commendation to the handler and his dog. Had it not been for them, this guy would never have been found, notwithstanding the lady leaning out the window. The handler worries about setting a precedent: 'They're going to think we can do this all the time, any time.'

Building search dominates large city K-9 activity. There is much less need for tracking capability. Incidents requiring tracking usually involve hard surfaces—pavement, dirt lots, icy or hot asphalt, steel catwalks, wood planking—where there is no crushed vegetation scent and little irregularity in the surface to hold track scent. Dogs expected to track in cities have to train on the type ground where suspects typically run, not just a grassy park. Streets, sidewalks, and fences take priority.

—Sgt. Kenneth Burger

If there is a point last seen, for example a verified sighting, or a footprint, or an article carried by the suspect, the patrol dog trained to track may be prescented at that point and commanded to track.

If there is no point last seen or identifiable track or article bearing the suspect's scent, the dog will be commanded to search for any human scent in the area. Depending on access and prevailing wind, the K-9 team typically starts on the downwind edge of the search area, traversing into the wind to give the dog the advantage of detecting the suspect's scent cone at a distance. Once in the cone, the dog attempts to locate the source.

A long vehicle chase across a large rural county ended with the suspect bailing out of the car into a field. Called out to track the suspect, the police dog began working at the last seen point. He tracked through the field, past ten blocks with homes, and up to the door of the house where the registered owner of the vehicle *lived*. The handler did not know this until officers knocked, and the suspect himself opened the door.

Along a major highway an incident occurred involving a middle-aged white male and a 13-year-old juvenile. The K-9 team was called to the location where officers had found a vehicle parked beside the roadway. Five hundred feet west of the vehicle, the officer spotted an adult male walking out of the field. Contacting him, the officer found the man to be extremely nervous. Asked if there were other people in the field, he was evasive.

The officer deployed the police dog to search the field for other subjects. Since no crime had been established, the handler started his dog on a nonaggressive search from the subject's vehicle. The dog worked a zigzag search pattern across the field.

The wind changed direction several times, and the dog was redirected. Several hundred yards south of the officers, the K-9 alerted up a hillside and led the handler to a male juvenile lying flat on a blanket concealed by bushes. The dog walked up to the boy, nudged him with his nose, then came back to the handler, as he had been trained to do for nonaggressive search.

Officers later learned that the juvenile had been sexually molested by the offender. The offender had threatened the teenager, telling him to "stay put" while he handled the police.

Some agencies crosstrain police dogs for nonaggressive or rescue searching in addition to aggressive or felony search. Because of the time and money involved in the additional training and operations, most patrol K-9s are not crosstrained for rescue. Large cities have the budgets and the logistical capability of administering separate, specialized K-9 units for patrol, SWAT, narcotics, and rescue.

> When we advise them what the criteria are for K-9 search, here in this department you must be searching for a felony suspect. Anything less than a felony, we cannot routinely deploy a dog.
>
> The only misdemeanor we'll search for is a man with a gun. We'll ask for a little bit more than just, 'I saw five guys standing on the corner. One of them reached in his waistband. I thought I saw a gun, and they all took off running.' Now we're searching for one out of five. What happens if we search and find the other four?
>
> But if the guy gives us a description, yes, he was wearing black shoes, blue Levi's, red T-shirt, had short, cropped hair, and we definitely saw a gun, yeah, we'll go out and do that search. Whether we find the gun or not, that's very nice to know, but definitely not criteria, whether we find it or not. If the officer saw the gun, we'll search for that suspect.
>
> A lot of times you're searching for felony narcotics suspects. Most of the time, a guy takes off, you got him for sales, he's gotta be holdin'. When we find this guy, unless he's very desperate, he's not gonna have the dope with him anymore. So if the dog finds this guy, what are you gonna book him for? He's no longer got dope.
>
> When you tell me you want a search for a felony suspect, and he's gonna be booked for felony, I'll do the search. But as it goes a lot of times, they go in for booking, it's not there.
>
> —K-9 Officer

Two officers stop a large adult male for narcotics violation. They recover a pipe. He has warrants for felony assault.

They are in the process of cuffing him when he goes off on them. He begins striking the officers with his free arm, handcuffs attached. The suspect also tries to take the officers' guns. Hit several times with batons, he manages to get away and run northbound.

Police establish a perimeter and request K-9 units. Two dog teams split the area, one taking the street northbound.

At the first residence, the dog shows interest and sniffs eastbound into the backyard. As the K-9 team enters the yard the dog indicates toward a gate to an adjoining yard. As the handler and dog clear the gate, the handler looks left in time see the suspect rise up out of dead underbrush and take a swing with his handcuffed right arm.

The handler recoils, so he misses. The dog moves in to protect the handler and bites the suspect's left arm. The man begins hitting the dog with the cuffs. The handler yells for him to stop. He complies momentarily, so the handler outs the dog.

As the dog moves away, the suspect lunges out, hits the dog over the head, and delivers a tremendous kick to his chest. Despite the impact, the dog bites the suspect's leg and holds on as the man rolls on him kicking and punching.

Assisting the dog, the handler repeatedly calls for the suspect to stop fighting. Finally he complies. Outing the dog, the search team takes him into custody.

Urban searching presents the challenge of a *high level of confusion* for all the units involved, including the K-9. High density populations with transients or gangsters appearing unexpectedly anywhere at any hour increases the stress. In these situations *the handler keeping his head clear and thinking* will be important to bringing the operation to a successful conclusion.

> The suspect crashed the car midblock, jumped out, and ran to the right behind a house. An officer starts chasing him.
>
> The guy comes back out the next house over, runs across the street, and they see him jumping fences heading in that direction.
>
> So I come in, start searching. Nothing. I turn the corner, come on down the block and start hitting houses. When I'm at the fifth house, the dog's starting to get scent, going back in the other direction.
>
> Just as the dog starts hitting scent, the airship says he's gotta leave, they've got a pursuit going. He takes off.
>
> Three houses over the guy pops out. We see him. He sees us. He takes off running, jumps a fence, the dog can't see him, takes off running again, we lose him.
>
> Everything points that he has now entered back into the initial search area. There are no alleys, by the way.
>
> So instead of rushing over, I say, 'Let's be systematic about it. We have only 8 houses here. Let's finish these then go back across the block.'
>
> The airship has now come back. We hit 1,2, when I get to the third house, the dog runs around back. There is no suspect, but there are two garages. I check them. I open up the first garage, nothing.
>
> As soon as I open up the second garage, the dog is on a full-blown alert. He goes into the garage. I look in, and sure enough, there's Dudley in the back seat hiding, doors locked.
>
> I call the dog back, officers deploy, they order him out, and he is taken into custody.
>
> —LAPD K-9 Officer

Bad guys are prepared to *fight your dog* as well as you when a police dog finds them. Athletic offenders have a *high degree of mobility*, sometimes despite repeated encounters with police dog teams attempting to arrest them. In the following case, fast *communications* between dog teams finally convinced the suspect to cooperate with the cops because they showed up everywhere he ran. Nobody, not even the offender, was seriously injured.

> A white male burglary suspect wearing a tan jacket and gray pants is last seen running northbound from Jeffrey Ave.
>
> Two dog teams work parallel northbound from Kennedy on Clinton and Dole. The search progresses into the backyard of a residence. At this time one of the dogs alerts strongly along the east wall of the backyard.
>
> The handler advises the second team of the dog's alert from his side of the perimeter. The second team

If you see the weapon, retrieve it or call attention to it. From cover recall the dog and command the offender out of the tree.

When you encounter atypical offenders, check your field position.

responds to the rear yard of the residence where the dog begins to alert on an abandoned vehicle. The dog goes to the wheelwell (the vehicle has no wheels) and sticks his head under the vehicle.

The suspect screams and scrambles around under the car to get away. Crawling out from under the car, he runs toward the back wall of the yard.

The K-9 team chases him to the wall, the handler calling for him to stop.

Ignoring the officer, the suspect climbs the wall.

The handler sends the dog, who bites him on the right thigh. Trying to pull away from the dog, the suspect kicks him, breaks away, climbs the fence and runs westbound. The K-9 handler advises the first team the suspect is running toward them.

The first search team is in front of the residence. When they get this information, they respond back to the rear yard. The handler releases the dog to search for the suspect.

The dog runs immediately to the rear of the yard where he and the handler observe the suspect emerging from under a bench and running southbound. The handler calls for him to stop. He does not stop.

The handler sends his dog to intercept, which the dog performs by biting the suspect's right shoulder and knocking him forward. Striking his head against a brick barbecue, the suspect becomes extremely violent and commences punching and pulling at the dog's head and jaws. Kicking hard, he breaks from the dog and runs southbound once more.

Calling for him to stop, the handler resends the dog, who knocks the suspect to the ground, where the offender resumes fighting violently. Trying to assist the dog and control the suspect's arms, the officer keeps ordering him to stop moving.

At last becoming exhausted, the suspect stops and states, "OK, I quit, call the dog."

The canine is a 65- to 95-pound animal frequently fighting a powerful, determined individual over 200 pounds. Once the dog makes contact, he has only two primary assets—jaws and agility. These are substantial reasons to keep the dog lean and well-muscled, and to practice fight situations to prepare for using other weapons, from empty-hand controls to deadly force depending on the circumstances, to assist the dog.

Doing time for felony wife beating, a suspect had escaped from an honor ranch and was reported en route to the area to seek revenge on his wife. Observed near the residence, the suspect was last seen running from police into the house. K-9 was requested.

Upon arrival, the sergeant advised the handler that an officer had searched the first floor but not the second. He added there was a chance the suspect had made it to the rear yard where there were several hiding spots.

Sent to clear the yard, the dog immediately alerted to scent coming from an open storage shed. The dog followed his nose into the shed, pushed his head into a pile of clothes and debris, and pulled out the suspect. The suspect grabbed the dog's head and twisted it.

The dog yelped in pain but broke free and bit the suspect's leg. Grabbing the dog's head again, the suspect tried to twist it. But the handler had moved in to assist the dog, at the same time ordering the suspect to stop fighting.

He complied, the handler outed the dog, and the suspect was taken into custody.

Anytime a K-9 must be assisted over a fence or a wall, the suspect may be waiting to dispatch every climber one-by-one. Chain link fences are notorious for injuring dogs' legs. Throw a jacket or blanket over the top. Many handlers carry small steel bolt cutters. It is better to kick out a board fence and settle with the owner than to get shot going over.

California Highway Patrol stopped two male subjects for a taillight on a 2-lane mountain highway. As the officer walked up to the vehicle, the driver pulled a gun, shot him through the neck and drove away, leaving him unconscious on the roadway.

The two fugitives were escapees from a Midwestern prison. Deputies found the vehicle and the passenger within hours. The driver fled on foot.

He surfaced only once. He broke into an elderly couple's house, tied them to chairs at gunpoint while he ate, then took their cash.

The couple almost succeeded talking the offender into "hiding" in the trunk of their car while they "drove him to freedom." In the end he didn't buy it. Walking south out of their cabin, he disappeared into a deep canyon that parallels the highway for 45 miles before ending in the high Sierra.

For three days the CHP helicopter, hundreds of officers, and dozens of K-9 teams searched for the suspect. Three different times, one of the police dogs tracked the suspect for several miles, losing it each time on logging roads in the July heat. Each time officers found the prints they were headed up-county.

This offender knew about dogs. He had run from them a good part of his adult life. He knew, as his tracks showed, about running through a stream to conceal his scent. He knew about lying under bushes next to the command post where officers were milling about and he could hear all the radio traffic. Dogs would jump out of a police van excited to work and run right by him.

Early on the fourth morning a trucker rolling eastbound passed a suspicious hitchhiker matching the description put out to all commercial rigs. Seeing a person stepping out of the forest there was stranger than seeing a mountain lion. The trucker called on his CB, changing forever the suspect's criminal career.

His radio call jump-started a tired search. First on scene, the police dog immediately picked up a fresh track from the area of the sighting near the pavement. Working off lead, the dog moved quickly, sniffing the ground, rocks and low shrubs.   Covering the handler were two officers with rifles. They moved rapidly behind the dog, about 50 yards off the highway. Meanwhile, another police dog worked the north side of the highway and two searched west.

Abruptly the first dog quit tracking. His head lifted toward the highway, nostrils twitching. The handler watched. Nobody was supposed to be on the highway. Highway Patrol was holding traffic down the road. The helicopter was airborne but circling off-pattern to avoid creating turbulence.

Tail high, head up, the K-9 cast toward the highway. In a second he zeroed toward a bush 10 yards off the road. The handler saw a patch of blue, dived behind a bush, called the dog off, and yelled at the guy to come out.

Saying, "Hold the dog" and drawing a pistol, one of the backup officers rushed the bush, straddled the guy and jammed the pistol into his ear.

The offender's gun was never found. No one knew he was unarmed until they took him into custody. Not the cover officer who jumped astride him. Not the handler. The dog would have been vulnerable making the apprehension, but the officers were even more vulnerable. The bushes provided concealment but not cover. Deploying the dog to make the initial contact would have increased the safety of the arresting officers by acting as a diversion.

Diversionary tactics can get the dog killed. In a middle class neighborhood a man was reported firing a shotgun. An officer saw a man carrying a gun jump the wall of a residence into the yard.

Surrounding the area to search the yards, officers were assisted by a sheriff's helicopter and two police dog teams.

One of the K-9 teams approached the bushes next to a house where the gunman was hidden. The suspect opened fire, killing the dog.

Falling to the ground, the handler returned fire, as did several nearby officers. The officers, all uninjured, took the wounded man into custody. They credit their lives to the dog.

Officers cruise through a west coast airport at midnight. They check the tower and everything is Code 4. They come back at 1 o'clock and a car is parked in the mud beside the tower. The plate returns stolen out of Maine.

The arriving K-9 sniffs a Coke can dropped beside the car and heads north, flagging his tail, nose down.

The night is black without stars. The deputy is thinking, "It's just a property crime. If I put him on his rescue search, I can at least hold back. We'll do an aggressive search if we need to."

Crossing snow patches, the dog searches into a wooded section west of the runway. At a barbed wire fence, the dog turns and backtracks. Later, footprints will show that the person retraced his steps.

The K-9 trots at full speed. Running, the handler loses sight of the dog. He hears a "pop" ahead, like a branch snapping. Crouching down, the officer hears the dog returning, doing his rescue alert. As backup arrives, he gives the dog a "Show me" and hauls off again.

The deputy goes from tree to tree.

At the top of the hill, the dog is standing in the dark staring back at him. He is at the feet of a man in a sleeping bag. A pack, food and other things lie beside him.

Downing the dog and lighting up the top of the bag, the deputy sees the side of a head. He yells at the body, which doesn't move or respond.

Officers cover him while the deputy approaches the figure. Now he sees a hand and a gun. He knocks the .22 pistol away and handcuffs what turns out to be a dying man. AWOL from the military, doing burglaries across the country, he evidently ate his gun just as the dog came in the first time.

A crook who knew about my K-9 and me came to town one night thinking we were off duty. This particular crook had a string of outstanding warrants but felt that he would have no problem evading the deputies. The deputies put a plan together to arrest the crook, but he ran into a vineyard with the deputies in hot pursuit. After a while, he managed to evade the deputies, who put out a call for the dog.

On arrival, I sent the dog into the field. As he ran out on search, the deputies were yelling that he was going the wrong way. Within two minutes the dog caught up to the fleeing suspect, knocking him to the ground. The dog had located him at the end of a 20-acre vineyard.

This crook was really happy to see me, stating that he thought his world had come to an end when he felt two large hairy arms grab him from behind as he was running away. He said he would never have run had he known the dog and I were on duty.

—K-9 Deputy

■

Responding to a civil call, a Calaveras County deputy arrested Lance Ray Egbert on a $10,000 drug warrant. While the deputy interviewed others at the scene, another local criminal, Michael Edward Girard, commandeered the patrol car with Egbert handcuffed in the back seat. After a pursuit through the Sierra foothills, the men abandoned the car on a dirt road. Police quickly found driver Girard walking the road.

K-9s from neighboring Amador County were called in to search for Egbert, whose criminal history dates back to childhood ranging from burglary to escape. The first dog team on scene tracked almost an hour, until the handler discovered his dog was tracking a deputy who passed that way earlier.

Second on scene, Amador Deputy Brian Blair was briefing when his K-9 Duff alerted to a brush-choked ravine near the patrol cars. "I guess we know where he is," said Blair. They followed the dog as he tracked 20 yards into the brush, caught a crosswind, and air scented Egbert, who yelled his surrender. The find took less than two minutes. Still handcuffed, Egbert was waiting it out until the agencies gave up and left.

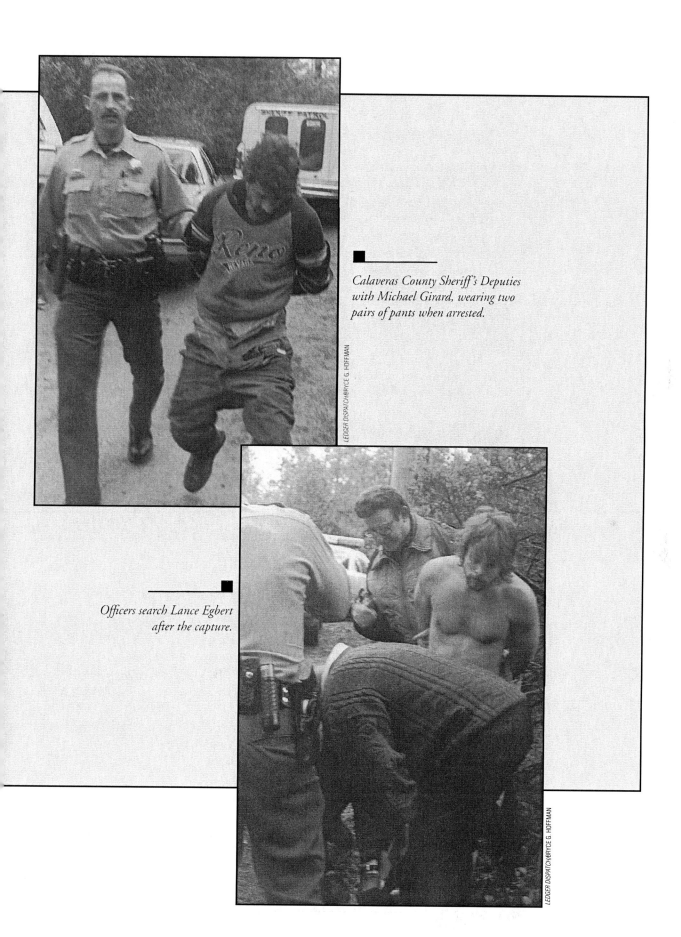

Calaveras County Sheriff's Deputies
with Michael Girard, wearing two
pairs of pants when arrested.

Officers search Lance Egbert
after the capture.

Deputies were in pursuit of a speeder who blew two stop signs then turned into a large mobile home park. Three suspects were in the car.

Stopping along the back street, two male suspects bailed out and split over the rear fence, leaving a female in the vehicle along with a large quantity of narcotics.

Calling for the county K-9 and more officers, the deputies set up a partial perimeter along the foothills. Behind the park lay immense acreage of greasewood, manzanita, and thick dead brush running hundreds of yards uphill into dense scrub oak. Rattlesnake country. Less than ideal tracking terrain. At over 100° F, temperatures were far from ideal.

Ten minutes later, the K-9 officer started his dog where witnesses had seen the two suspects climb the fence. The dog started tracking on lead. Soon the handler discovered he could not hold the lead and crash through the brush. He released the K-9.

The dog's head came up. He alerted toward a large oak log 15 yards away.

The next few seconds the handler remembers in snapshots. Many times he has analyzed seeing his K-9 on final approach, a wedge of green ball cap showing over the edge of the log, the dog airborne, jumping where the cap had been, the shout, "No, get your dog! You've got the wrong guy!"

The handler called, "Show me your hands. Show me both your hands!"

It was the right guy. It was also the dog's first apprehension. When the handler shouted, the dog responded as if called off. He went into a down-watch. The cover officer took the suspect into custody.

The deputy gave his black German shepherd a water break. The next phase was a 10-acre gully of brush and scrub oak with homes on three sides leading to thousands of undeveloped acres.

After beating the brush for another half hour they terminated because of the heat.

Heat is a limiting factor for K-9 operations, particularly where there are no available backup units. "On a hot day, we call in three dog teams. We'll run a dog for a maximum of 20 minutes out there."

One night the only K-9 unit in an undermanned industrial city got flagged down by state police. Seven police cruisers from the capital city across the river, including two police dog units, were in pursuit of a late model sedan driven by two suspects.

The suspect vehicle led the troop of cop cars at high speed across the bridge and through the industrial section of the sister city. Turning every 5-6 blocks, the crooks kept the lead and ran the chase in a circle. A couple of times they made a fast U-turn, waving at the pursuing officers.

Parked on a side street watching the lights go back and forth, the K-9 handler decided Jackie Gleason would be proud. Renaming the department Far Side PD, she thought briefly they should interview Gary Larson to become the new chief.

Not far from her position things came to a crashing halt when the suspects hit the brakes, jumped out, and ran. A K-9 unit rear-ended the suspect vehicle, triggering the domino effect. A couple of angry cops tackled the passenger, but the driver disappeared between the houses across the street.

Getting out of the patrol car to deploy her K-9, the handler saw the other city dogs already out. Asking a handler if he wanted backup, she got OK.

They started a yard search. Instead of working in parallel, the two teams searched around one house, crossed the street, and skipped a yard, leaving gaps in their search area.

Trying to cover them from behind, the handler was wondering if these guys had ever heard of a *systematic search* when something rustled in a yard behind a 6-foot board fence. The dog team ahead had passed the fence and was already crossing the street.

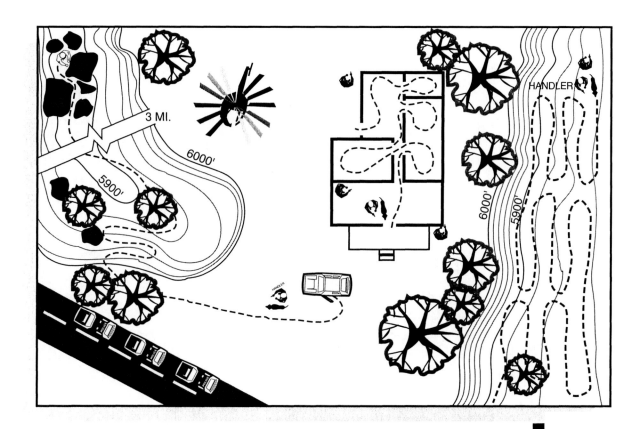

Quickly the handler vaulted over the fence. Crouched in a tomato patch lay the second suspect. She radioed one in custody.

How many calls for service on or near water does your agency receive during a normal year? Coastal agencies typically have a boat patrol, shoreline mileage, a port authority, extensive rivers or streams, boaters drowning in heavy spring runoff, or drug trafficking via waterways. While most dog teams spend only a small percentage of their time working around water, the ability to operate confidently in that environment gives your dog the edge.

An inmate escaped from a large prison complex. Police dogs tracked the fugitive over four miles. Where a freeway spanned a large river, the dog air scented the suspect in bushes on the other side.

Swimming across, followed by her handler, the dog located the inmate, who quickly surrendered.

Back at the institution, the offender told a corrections officer he was sure he was safe once he swam the river. So sure in fact he did not bother watching the river. He knew officers are "lazy and don't like getting their uniforms wet." He planned to sleep until dark then catch a ride on the freeway.

A dog is easily defeated in water. The reality of pursuit is, if you have a suspect swimming, you probably have that suspect. Water is as foreign to him as to the K-9. However, the police dog should be confident working in and about water.

Uncontained search areas expand rapidly. Agencies may request one K-9 team when two or more are needed. Assign air scenting K-9s to separate areas. Advise all field units of tracking teams' changing positions. Hold teams in reserve to investigate suspect sightings. Relieve teams regularly.

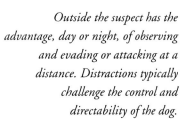

Outside the suspect has the advantage, day or night, of observing and evading or attacking at a distance. Distractions typically challenge the control and directability of the dog.

How well equipped and fit is the team? Water, flashlights, maps? How long are they prepared to search?

If the suspect fights when found, bring him under control as quickly as possible.

If 2 or more suspects are involved, you are at risk until everyone is in custody.

HELICOPTERS & DOGS—A TEAM

You watch the little white figures on the TV screen. You can see the faint cloudy outline of bushes and trees. Heat escaping under the eaves of the roof outline a building. The white square on the upper left of your screen is the engine compartment of a darkened patrol car approaching the building.

It is night. You are looking at heat images of events going on beneath the helicopter. The deep, muted red of the cockpit glows on the dusky face and hands of the pilot holding the aircraft in a steady orbit. Responding to a call from dispatch, the CHP (California Highway Patrol) helicopter has flown over a crack lab where one suspect broke through the net of agents and deputies and escaped into the night.

"H-20's in position," radios the pilot in the left seat to a deputy somewhere off-screen on the ground. Down on the extreme lower right of the picture tube he points a gloved index finger to a white elongated figure prone under what look like bushes. "We've got a hot spot about 50 yards off the southwest corner of the house. Toward Blue Canyon Road. Maybe you could send the dog over."

"H-20, K-9. We're on the way." Looking at the now stationary car in the upper left, you see 2 satellite figures divide off the main cell. One has 2 legs, the other with 4 legs is clearly a dog. As you watch, the team moves down screen around the building, close to it, skirting trees and bushes.

Then something extraordinary happens. As the dog team passes across the middle of the screen, you see the figure on the lower right grow brighter! Is the "heat on" for this guy?

Passing 100 yards or more beyond the figure that is hidden beneath the fainter but visible pattern of heavy brush, the K-9 team obviously cannot see the heat source the way the helicopter's infrared camera can.

Just as the observer is about to advise the handler below, the dog figure breaks a hard right and runs directly toward the now intensely glowing figure. "Alright, he's on it!" coaches the observer instead.

The handler follows as the dog breaks into a run. In another freak of FLIR-vision (Forward Looking Infrared), the subject's shape changes from a weenie into a bright object of light—the subject stood up. The view from the helicopter at altitude is vertical. The object glows so bright you can imagine the sweat pouring down the guy's face as he hears the dog coming.

The 2 figures become one oscillating piece of light. The handler figure moves in, merging with the main source of heat. Seconds after the capture, as other figures arrive, the dog, handler, and offender, who is now under control and under arrest, separate.

The handler's voice comes over the helicopter radio, "We got him, H-20. Thanks for the help. You put us right on target."

New K-9 teams have to learn how to perform law enforcement operations with helicopters. On interagency operations, the pilot and handler may not know each other. If the ship stays airborne throughout the operation, the two officers might never see each other. In an emergency, each officer will be relying on the presumed capability or critical judgment of the other.

Combining the dog team with the helicopter has proved effective for both arrests and rescues.

The development of high-resolution, commercially available infrared and high-powered search lights mounted on helicopters extends this valuable search capability. FLIR Systems Inc., Portland, Oregon, pioneered this technology.

The helicopter-dog tool, taken as an entity, has major advantages over fielding multiple officers on many types of searches. Where half the tool is limited, the other half can often step in and take over. Speed and maneuverability are helicopter strong points. Disadvantages are expense, weather, limited night capability, and the inherent risk of rotary wing operations. The major advantages are the eyes in the sky, immobilizing and detecting fugitives, rapid insertions and extractions.

Where the helicopter is weak, the dog team is strong. The dog's nose and eyes work effectively during the cool darkness. The dog team can usually search in weather that grounds aircraft and can often check out terrain where the helicopter cannot land. If the K-9 team locates the suspect, the dog can assist making the arrest.

Law enforcement missions appropriate for helicopter-dog operations:

Suspect searches	Patrol
S.W.A.T.	Surveillance
Narcotics interdiction	Remote area response
Airborne pursuit management	Investigation teams
Infrared imagery	Radio relay
Inter-agency airborne	Aerial command
communications interface	Major incident pre-planning
Disaster search and rescue	Photo flights
Damage assessment	K-9 transport
Area search and rescue	

A law enforcement helicopter should respond immediately:

• All prison or jail escapes to contain the area, identify potential escape routes, sight movement, help police dog teams capture fugitives and return them to custody

• One or more people fleeing the scene—car stop, arson, burglary, drug operation, terrorist operation—to contain and apprehend as above

• Victims of crime or unknown missing person (especially children) cases to protect the scene if suspect still at large, contain and air search the surrounding area, locate victims, direct medical responders.

Could a helicopter have helped prevent this situation?

SECURE THE LANDING ZONE

Dog handlers are frequently responsible for selecting and preparing a place for the helicopter to land. The landing zone is a hot spot. Even experienced officers have to remind themselves to stay alert around a running helicopter. A highway patrolman who had flown thousands of hours as an observer for the department got out of the ship one day and inexplicably walked uphill into the rotor blade.

Whenever possible, use predetermined landing sites familiar to the pilot. The safe landing zone (LZ) allows the helicopter to approach and depart at angles less than 15 degrees. Steep entry stresses the aircraft and puts the pilot and crew at risk. For tight helispots, provide a clear departure route. Although 60 by 60 feet is adequate for typical patrol helicopters, expand the size of the landing area to 100 by 100 feet for large military ships. Do not select slopes greater than 8 degrees to prevent a rotor blade striking the ground or slippage when the helicopter lands. If the ground is soft, planks or poles secured on the ground perpendicular to the skid gear can prevent sinking into snow or mud. Aircraft landing in snow or sand may create a whiteout that disorients the pilot or damages the engines. Ultimately, landing and departure are at the pilot's discretion, but pilots learn which officers they can trust to prepare a safe landing zone.

Helipad preparation and landing procedures:
1. Identify obstacles, avoid power lines, avalanche areas, water, ice, sand
2. Prepare a minimum 60- by 60-foot helipad (expand to 100 by 100 feet)
3. Helipad is firm, level (< 8 degrees), clear of obstacles or loose materials
4. Secure skid supports on soft ground or snow
5. Secure contrasting markers on snow pads
6. Secure police K-9s, incident command, fires away from LZs
7. Set smoke flare or other wind indicators downwind of the LZ
8. Aim night lights across the LZ, do not blind the pilot
9. Use tac frequency to give pilot helipad coordinates, elevation, weather
10. Watch the aircraft as it is landing or taking off in case you have to get out of the way
11. Do not approach the aircraft until waved forward by the pilot or crew
12. Crouch and walk (don't run) a straight-in approach to the front or side, never the rear, watching the crew at all times

Know your own territory. Learn the terrain, obstacles, quick flight routes, helispots, heliports, distances to fuel sources, typical winds and other features in your jurisdiction. Set up training scenarios deploying the K-9 unit with your departmental or regional helicopter.

Load calculations: Know the weight of your dog, yourself, and all weapons and tactical gear, separately as well as totaled. If in doubt, overestimate weight.

Practice static loading helicopters. Secure the dog on a strong 6-foot lead attached to the active ring of a choke collar or a wide collar cinched tight so the dog cannot back out of it. On approach and exit, control the dog at heel. After a little experience loading, most dogs are eager to get inside the aircraft to escape the rotors and will pull hard. Wait for the OK-to-approach wave from the pilot or crew. Follow his directions. Stay toward the front in view of the pilot, duck, and walk, don't run.

A K-9 training sequence at an airport or other landing zone:
1. Static loading, unloading at an airport
2. Hot loading, unloading the stationary helicopter
3. Hot loading, short flight, unloading

Dogs rarely get airsick. Carry a plastic garbage sack in flight to catch emissions from either end of the canine. Dogs typically do not spend enough time in aircraft during their short lives to affect their hearing.

Each aircraft has different specifications: hard points, hover altitudes, load limits, safety equipment, door configuration, and operating procedures. If the pilot and K-9 team go up without a crew, the handler will be responsible for securing the doors, cargo and equipment checks, and other duties.

Boarding an aircraft where the deck is 4 feet or higher or the steps are bolted to the strut, the dog may injure himself by taking a flying leap. Loading this type helicopter gets harder in deep snow. Lift the dog at least high enough for the animal to reach up, as he will instinctively, and grab with his front legs. When the dog's front paws grip the deck, push his rear up. Maintain lead control. *The control hold on entry prevents the dog from climbing onto the instruments.*

After the dog loads, guides his head toward you into a sit or down, maintaining the control hold. Climbing into the aircraft, move to a seat and place the dog on the floor nearby or under your legs. Wrapping the lead around a boot leaves your hands free to secure gear, buckle the seat belt, and adjust the head set. Hold the lead or secure the dog during flight.

Inside the aircraft the police dog might react defensively. Keep close lead control. The dog with high aggression drives should fly muzzled. Flight noise and crowding stresses dogs. The muzzle should permit openmouthed breathing and be easy to put on or remove during flight.

In or about aircraft if a crewman approaches to yell into your ear over the engine noise, be aware more than one canine has misinterpreted that movement toward the handler as a master protection scenario. Rotor wash excites the dog, who is already on guard. A helmeted crewman grabbing your shoulder might cause the K-9 to react protectively. Anticipate the approach, catch the officer's eye, point to the dog and snap your hand like gator jaws. He will get the idea.

Unless the pilot announces a change ("get out the right door this time"), unloading the aircraft reverses the loading procedure. Secure the lead while preparing to exit. After the doors are opened or the crew chief signals go, exit before the dog. Restrain the dog from freestyle jumping. Break his fall. To off-load heavy or unwieldy equipment, move away from the ship, secure the dog, and return for the gear. Drop heavy equipment near the helicopter for retrieval after the ship flies away.

K-9 TEAM INSERTION

Helicopter transport saves time and may afford surprise. *The pilot makes the decision—land, short haul, rappel. Each method has its own limitations and advantages.* Each requires practice and clear communications (hot mike) between the pilot and the dog teams.

A key notion is that of total jeopardy, choosing the transport technique that presents the least risk to the greatest number of people. Pilots must, as a minimum, meet FAA and agency experience and proficiency requirements. Ideally, pilot qualifications will include 5- to 10-thousand hours of total flight time (as much as possible in typical terrain), extensive experience in the landing or longline techniques used, and the ability to work effectively as a member of the team. Depending on area elevations, temperatures, light limitations, and mission requirements, the systems and techniques will vary from helicopter to helicopter.

1. Land, 1-Skid, Toe-in or No-Skid

The 1-skid is arguably the most frequently used technique where a helicopter cannot fully land. The advantage is it requires no special equipment, just a lot of pilot skill.

The pilot holds a skid or wheel touching, for example, a rooftop where load limits, slope, or ventilation units prevent landing. He can insert or evacuate teams from the top of a rock in a boulder field. It's risky but it's fast. The toe-in or low hover requires more caution and agility of the officers and a plan for transferring the K-9. In flight, the teams ride inside, or the officers ride the struts to accelerate deployment.

The pilot makes the decision— land, short haul, rappel. Each method has its own limitations and advantages.

The helicopter and descent teams are vulnerable en rappel.

LOS ANGELES COUNTY SHERIFF'S DEPARTMENT

Expedite by inserting multiple teams as rapidly as the aircraft will permit.

Be prepared to unhook and restrain the dog on the ground.

LOS ANGELES COUNTY SHERIFF'S DEPARTMENT

Once on the ground,
teams act as cover until
the ship is released.

LOS ANGELES COUNTY SHERIFF'S DEPARTMENT

Immediate deployment
takes advantage of the
helicopter as a distraction.
If you cannot deploy
immediately, move
to cover.

LOS ANGELES COUNTY SHERIFF'S DEPARTMENT

2. Insertion/Shorthaul

Pioneered by the Europeans and Parks Canada to transport dog teams and rescue litters to sites in the Alps and Rockies, the shorthaul has been used frequently and successfully by the National Park Service to rescue climbers off the walls of Yosemite, the peaks and couloirs of the Tetons and other parks. The insertion, an officer delivery system, is in essence a shorthaul in reverse.

Suspended beneath the helicopter harnessed to a longline system, the officer and dog can be ferried as easily as a rescuer and litter. Hover time over the delivery site is much less than rappeling, which most pilots believe enhances mission safety, but must be weighed against exposure during flight.

The moderate training requirements include redundant anchor and harness systems for the officer and dog.

3. Rappel

Rappel evolutions may be conducted with either one or multiple rappelers, based on specific site factors and helicopter load calculations. Wind over 30 knots is usually a limiting factor.

Details of rappeling from a given aircraft depend on its size and configuration, and the techniques require extensive initial and refresher training to execute safely. Aborting a heli-rappel evolution is much more difficult once personnel are en rappel. The pilot must contend with ropes that are on the ground, and the rappelers must manage their brake systems.

On the positive side, deployment via heli-rappel tends to be logistically simpler because a staging helispot near the target area is not needed. The canine harness must be secure, lightweight, part of the handler's field gear, and easy to put on. The canine descends on the rappeler's belay system or is lowered separately.

In case of communications failure during any maneuver, use prearranged hand signals for fouled lines, height above the ground, all clear, weapons fire, and so on.

Emergency procedures saved one officer who took an unexpected flight when the cargo hook he had detached from a sling load caught inside the shoulder of his flight suit as the helicopter took off. Neither the pilot, who radioed lift-off, nor the officer, who was bent over the load, knew that the receiver in the officer's helmet had failed.

The officer was the first to know this when he became airborne. Resisting the urge to reach up and grab the cable, which could have dislodged the hook and left him hanging by his arms, the officer clamped his hands hard onto his shoulder and said prayers to the gods who oversee the manufacture of military flight suits.

He knew it was useless to wave his arms, pound his helmet, or give any of the traditional distress signals. The pilot either would or would not eventually notice him, and his greatest problem was dislodgment of the hook.

The pilot did eventually see him in the helicopter nose mirror at an altitude of about 500 feet. The officer knew this because he instantly became weightless as they went into a rapid descent.

The flight suit, which was old and had holes but not one broken stitch in the shoulder, survived.

All techniques require the appropriate personal protective equipment and regular in-service training. For information on training curricula, standards, time requirements, and operations plans contact:

California Highway Patrol
Valley Division, Air Operations Unit
2390 Lindbergh Street
Auburn, California 95603

Grand Teton National Park
P.O. Drawer 170
Moose, Wyoming 83012

Los Angeles County Sheriff's Department
4700 Ramona Blvd.
Monterey Park, California 91754-2169

Office of Aircraft Services
U.S. Department of the Interior
Boise, Idaho 83637

AREA OF OPERATIONS

The Area of Operations (AO) as applied to law enforcement searches is the most general term defining a total area in which we expect an arrest to take place. The individual officer might not be able to see it all or even influence it all, but it is all involved.

The *zone of influence* refers to the area around each officer or suspect where he can have an impact on the operation, presumably with his weapon. The zone of influence will be different if you have, say, a high calibre rifle than if you simply have your sidearm. Cognizance affects the size of the zone. Whoever falls inside the zone will be detected. Whoever falls outside will be missed. Where zones intersect, whoever has the tactical advantage has a higher probability of controlling the situation.

Visibility, a self-defining term, will be different at night if you have night goggles or if you do not. The zone of influence implies surveillance capability, the ability to discern and discriminate a target.

The helicopter's zone of influence is primarily visual, including infrared or other surveillance technology, but he has the great advantage of perspective and mobility.

The police dog's superior scenting, hearing and vision enhances and extends the handler's zone of influence. Tactical errors (light yourself up, light up the dog, give the dog loud voice commands) reduce the handler's zone of influence while potentially expanding the suspect's. Failure to use critical information (K-9 behavior change) is a tactical error typical of complex situations.

Orchestrating the helicopter in the air with the officers and dogs on the ground itself becomes an issue the military calls C³I, Command, Control, Communications, and Information (pronounced "C cubed I"):

> *That totality of arrangement between our ability to get information and how we coordinate it throughout the system that is operating, then command and control it.*

USAF Colonel Charles J. Yoos, II, PhD, says that the Air Force, the Army, indeed all the branches of the military tend to face C³I problems whereby they have acquired the capability to gather more data and create more information than the operators can actually use. The C³I problem becomes one of *what are we going to do with all this?*

> Y'know the first thing I'd do would be to turn off the mike from my guy in the back seat, cause he didn't have anything to say that I wanted to hear. We've got all these signals coming up from all kinds of systems which tell us what the Sam's are doing, are they fired, and are we being painted with radar … That far exceeded my capability to even understand what was going on, so I just simply shut most of that off.
>
> —General Robin Olds
> Vietnam War Ace

That was a C³I solution that people would be generally unhappy about but understand was necessary.

A parallel C³I problem for law enforcement is a felony escape where multiple law enforcement agencies, helicopters, patrol units, and radio frequencies are involved. Tactical frequencies set aside for such operations disappear on busy nights when various special details are conducting operations. Clear broadcast frequencies become nonexistent due to continuous dialogue between field units and dispatchers. Much of the radio traffic may be irrelevant to the K-9 officer's mission, but some information is relevant, perhaps critical. The high rate of incoming signals starts jamming the officer's ability to reason and respond, called sensory overload.

It might be imagined that the officer's relationship with the dog in that situation is vitiated by the dog knowing that there is only one voice to hear, his master's voice. Not so, because if the noise level gets too high, the dog's cognition becomes overloaded, he gets confused.

A typical example is multiple movement. Everybody wants to chase the bad guy on foot. Nobody waits for the dog. If released he will bite everybody. We have identified a C³I problem. Now we have the terminology to describe the problem. We have no solution, but we know the terminology.

Law enforcement could do worse than to look at the military command and control solutions. Historically, the military has solved these types of problems pretty well. But there are the stories out of Desert Storm, Iraq, about all the soldiers who chipped in a few bucks apiece and went commercial and bought a GPS receiver so they could know where the hell they were. New technologies are causing the military to rethink the total C³I solution.

INFRARED

When infrared first became available, we found it was not fail-safe. We would have a certain search strategy—run both dogs in parallel yards, or maybe run a dog through the alleyway first, see if he finds anything, save us a lot of time.

In the early stages, when the ship came on scene, we'd get directed to a lot of different things. We'd be starting at the end of the block like we usually do, and they'd say, "About five houses down I got a hot spot."

So we would break away from where we're searching to head down there. We'd find water heaters, dogs, ...

I was directed on a search, "Four houses south of your position there is a pickup truck covered with a tarp."

I got down there, let the dog out of the car. He goes around the truck, gives me no alert whatsoever. I tell the airship, "The dog has cleared that pickup truck. He's got no scent."

He says, "Guys, he's gotta be there."

I go OK, send him again. No scent, no alert, no nothin'. We deploy on the truck. We go up, pull the tarp back.

Well, the owner was a gardener. He had freshly cut grass in the back of that pickup truck emitting the heat the camera was picking up.

—K-9 Officer

The minimum resolvable temperature difference (MRTD) of commercial FLIR technology has an order of magnitude of .10°C, depending upon the instrument, the selection of a wide or narrow field of view, and ambient conditions. The thermal imager senses temperature differences between the target and the background. If the contrast is not high enough, the target will not be visible. Infrared energy typically penetrates smoke, dust, smog, and blowing sand. Rain, snow or thick fog degrades the image.

High magnification gives a remote range for covert observation. The aircraft need not be directly over the target, therefore a subject has no sure way of knowing if he has been detected.

The ship can *clear* broad areas and identify targets for the K-9 to check. The aircraft typically uses the wide field of view to search for hot spots then brackets the target and switches to the narrow field of view for further investigation. System modules typically include a tracker unit that can lock onto a target.

Thermal energy also reflects. Smooth surfaces that absorb heat (rooftop, pavement) transmit detectable heat images after the body that was lying there has moved away. The heat signature lies like a shadow, gradually disappearing as the surface cools. An offender's fresh track in the snow, grass or sand may give off heat images briefly. Realizing how temporary these images are, the ship typically calls for a K-9 to work the track or to sniff the area where the body was lying and attempt to locate a track.

Most departments have a video recorder in the aircraft, or the capability of downlinking data, to create a permanent record as evidence. The same disk or tape may be re-recorded many times. Only significant incidents need be transferred to a master. Such recordings are excellent training tools for the K-9 officer and the other officers that work with the helicopter.

Operational altitudes range from 0 to 2500 feet. If the helicopter is directing the search team into a subject, he may maintain a 400- to 700-foot altitude. If the turbulence created by the aircraft interferes with the scenting dog, the ship may ascend or orbit offside.

The typical surveillance package includes a multi-million candlepower searchlight for detection, distraction, or to assist in apprehensions and rescues.

Where helicopter crews use night vision goggles (NVGs) in backcountry or other low-light areas, the ground-based K-9 tactics are similar to operations involving infrared. A major difference is the restricted range of airborne detection. The search light can be used simultaneously to light intensification equipment but not to view the same area.

Flying a patrol beat, FLIR is used proactively to detect problems a ground unit would have no way of seeing. An experienced FLIR operator can look at the monitor and identify a Ford, Chevrolet, or Dodge pickup. Based on his mental library and by comparing the target with other similar objects he is viewing in the same time frame, the operator can often estimate how long a vehicle has been parked by looking at the heat off the engine block, tail pipes, and recently applied disc brakes. Many burglaries have been interrupted this way. Air units locate covert operations (drug lab, chop-shop) in isolated areas. Anticipating the arrival of ground units, the airship can identify access routes and the shape of structures (doors, windows, ventilation units), hazards that may be camouflaged (pits, cellars, piping, storage containers) or burial sites (garbage, compost, cult activity, human or animal remains). After the on-board imager locates a suspect, the air crew directs the ground units, substantially reducing their danger. Remaining overhead, the air crew provides illumination and security until backup arrives.

As calls for service increase, fewer patrol cars are available for response to air-initiated observations. The high volume of priority calls in most cities also impacts air support to outlying divisions. "There are no extra cops anymore." "By the time someone calls the police on a gang shooting, it's over in seconds or minutes, so you stay where the calls are." Even with helicopter speeds exceeding 150 mph, a 5-minute response can be too late. Used in conjunction with K-9 units, the airborne FLIR can rapidly clear a perimeter, thereby freeing ground units for other tasks.

Many suspects are knowledgeable about infrared procedures and limitations. Some are experts in the technology. They have learned to use insulation or cold packs to block heat transfer. They know how to hide near or under other heat sources so their image blends with an identifiable source and becomes indistinguishable. Many are aware that deflecting their image to disguise human body shape sometimes works, especially in urban areas where a camera typically sees many *hot spots* or *heat prints*. They know detection is harder during certain daytime conditions and more likely under certain nighttime conditions. Infrared is harder to beat in combination with K-9 searching because each capability checks and balances the other.

Helicopter infrared videocamera records a K-9 team capture.

CALIFORNIA HIGHWAY PATROL

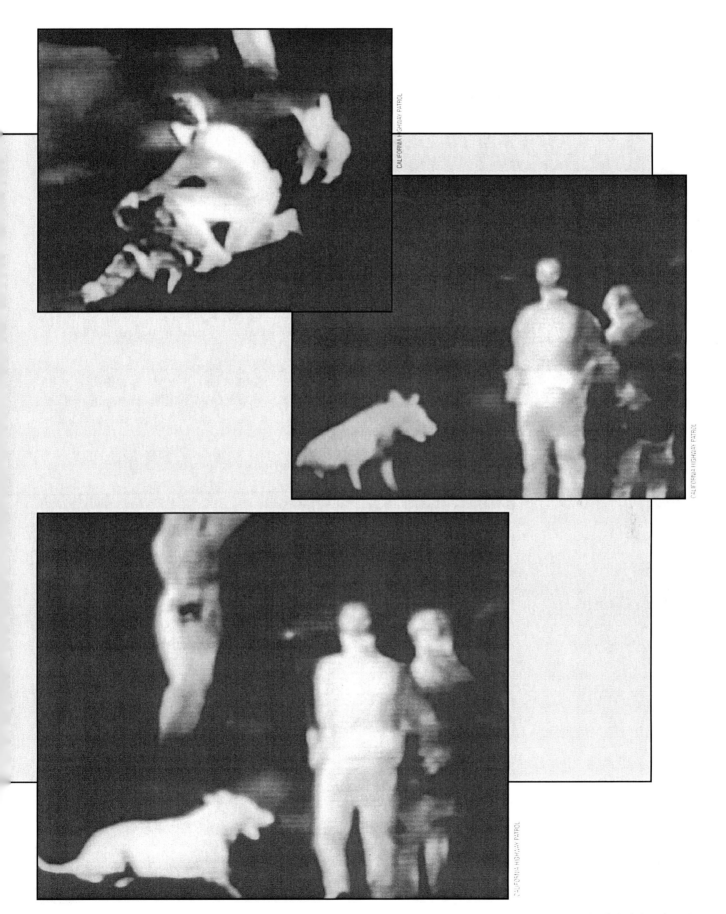

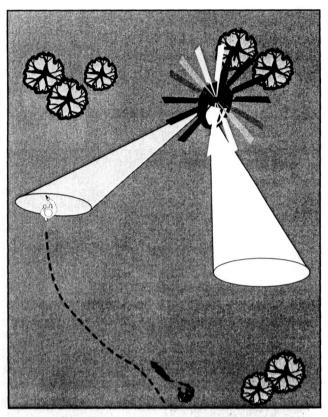

K-9 in tracking mode.
The helicopter sets up a rolling perimeter to contain and immobilize the suspect along the indicated direction of travel. FLIRing ahead of the tracking team, the helicopter may locate the suspect or see a hot spot that the dog is approaching or that can be investigated by another team. FLIRing the area surrounding the tracking team, the helicopter may locate the bad guy who has doubled back.

If the suspect has a substantial lead but there is no track, scent trail, or any other information giving a direction of travel, the police dog teams will be deployed to search concealment areas within the area of operation. Suspects who appear to have fled a crime scene frequently creep back into the area. One or more dog teams may be held back, prepared to act on sightings by the helicopter or other reporting parties.

Fugitives typically hide from helicopters, waiting for the ship to leave in order to escape. Except in wide-open terrain, they know the helicopter cannot immediately take them into custody. The handler can take advantage of this tendency for suspects to freeze-then-flee by coordinating the K-9 search pattern with the air search. There are many ways to do this depending on the terrain and how the helicopter is configured.

For example, the dog alerts into a strong wind across a deep ravine. Scoping the ridge, the handler sights the suspect. To prevent detection, he takes cover with the dog, contacts the helicopter in order to coordinate tactics, then makes his approach.

Searching for a combative robbery suspect, the K-9 alerts at the door of a shed. Helicopter-mounted FLIR sees a hot spot or thermal signature diffusing through the far wall of the shed. The helicopter advises ground units to coordinate for officer safety prior to entry.

The dog alerting high against the side of a building may indicate suspects on a roof. The helicopter can quickly check this out. If you think that a fugitive is hiding under a semitrailer in a freight yard, the pilot may fly a wider orbit and *peek under* the rig. If a suspect has climbed a tree in an orchard, the ship can fly directly overhead aiming the infrared or the searchlight straight down to penetrate the trees or foliage (works equally well to find cannabis or plastic water piping).

In tall grass or bushes, the rotor wash is sometimes used to *part* the growth and reveal the hiding suspects. The resulting turbulence sometimes helps the dog scent the offenders. More often low-level flying interferes with scenting. If the dog is not able to search effectively, take cover and maintain surveillance until the aircraft moves off or ascends.

We work very closely with the airship. Most of the time, those guys in the airship are very good. They hear the foot pursuit going down, they get the request, they're in the air setting a perimeter for the officers. The patrol units aren't even there yet.

They'll go, "Where're you at?"

I'll go, "I'm at 54th and Figuaroa, and he was last seen runnin' north." The airship knows where he is. We go to an available tac frequency.

He says, "Let's get a unit over on 53rd, a unit on Hoover ..." you know, he can basically set it up and not even be there yet.

We were on hillside searches looking for an armed robbery suspect. The airship finds a real big hot spot, as big as a human, right down in a gully. We go through these bushes. We're down there at least half an hour looking for this place. Where is it?

The ship says, "Man, you're standing right on top." We're looking around.

What happened, it was a pool of water. The water had warmed up and was giving off more heat at night than the cooler land.

I was searching for this suspect in the area of a large estate. The airship figured they were seeing nothing but rocks. When I came on the scene, I said, "Let's go up the road to the ranch and work back down to the original area."

As soon as the dog hit the grounds of that estate, he was in full-blown alert. He took off running down the property line, over a fence, and across the hillside.

Looking down, I could see a plain white tennis shoe lying there. I said, "Was this guy wearing white tennis shoes?"

Sure enough, he was. Before I know it, the dog is digging down into the dirt, and up he comes with the suspect, who had buried himself to evade detection.

Officers said, "You know the airship came over and hovered over that spot trying to figure out what they had." As it turned out, they did have the suspect in view.

Nothing is fail-safe.

—K-9 Officer

Location and direction of travel. Helicopter radio transmissions are concise. The K-9 officer has to use the same language to radio locations and directions of travel. It is important to be able to transmit rapid, frequent changes in direction, to think in terms of bearings, elevations and landmarks, and to estimate distances accurately. Simple, clear communications are essential to prevent air and ground teams from conflicting.

It is important to know where you are. Although this seems self-evident, handlers assisting other agencies sometimes find themselves working in unfamiliar areas. North-south may be difficult to figure out in a metropolitan area or an outlying area at night. Taking the time to get oriented initially will facilitate the whole operation.

If you are coordinating K-9 deployment with the helicopter, ask the pilot questions. If possible, select a cover officer who knows the area. One officer had neither advantage. The helicopter dropped the K-9 team off in a large dark field behind an extensive industrial complex to track a suspect who had knifed a convenience store manager. The handler had never been there before, he was 60 miles from the police station, and the helicopter left to respond to an officer-involved shooting.

Searchlight. The powerful helicopter spotlight is typically used to clear and secure the perimeter, to immobilize and search for suspects, to act as a decoy while FLIR or NVGs are focused in a different direction, to assist the arrest procedure, and to assist landing where necessary. The searchlight should typically not be used to illuminate the area in advance of the search dog team (destroys night vision) or to light up the K-9 or the officers (makes them targets).

DECOY TACTICS 2:
K-9 in air scent mode. The helicopter clears a perimeter around the area of operations to contain and immobilize the suspect within that area. FLIRing inside the area, the helicopter may locate the suspect or see a hot spot that the dog is approaching or that the air ship can direct the dog team to investigate.

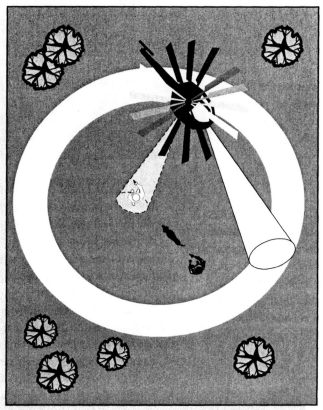

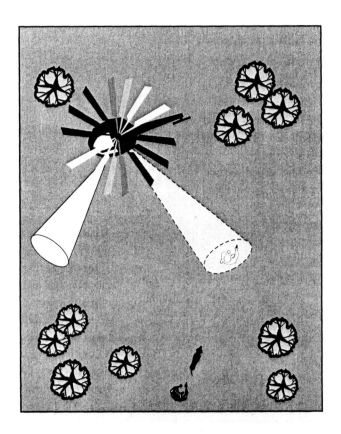 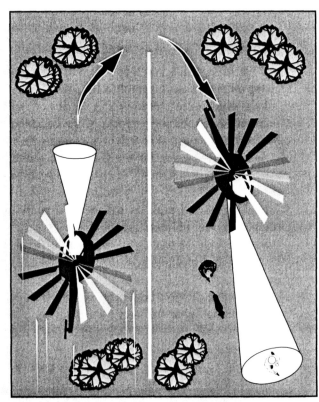

DECOY TACTIC 3:

Night. The helicopter flies
a search pattern with the
searchlight pointing in one
direction and FLIR in
another direction. The suspect believes the aircraft is
searching the area illuminated by the searchlight.
K-9 is typically deployed
in the area being FLIRed.

Day. The helicopter flies a
search pattern at a distance
from the area of operations
while FLIRing the target
area. The suspect believes
the aircraft is searching the
area below the helicopter.
K-9 is typically deployed
in the area being FLIRed.

K-9 alert. If the dog alerts, the handler has to *coordinate* his request for the helicopter to hover over the area in order to maximize the surprise and safety factors for the search team. FLIRing in the direction the dog is alerting may reveal the suspect or a bigger problem requiring reinforcements or different tactics.

K-9 apprehension and arrest. The search team advises the helicopter if there are shots fired. The handler requests the helicopter overhead to illuminate the area and provide airborne assistance. Orbiting above the scene, the helicopter watches for more suspects who may appear or attempt to flee. If the suspect fights, the helicopter is directing other units to the area to assist. In a remote area capture where the deputy and his dog were losing, the highway patrol helicopter dropped off the observer to help the handler wrestle the crankster into restraints.

INCIDENT REVIEW

The K-9 operation does not end until the handler reviews the dog's performance to determine how the incident will affect future operations and completes any necessary remediation.

Police dog behavior shaping continues throughout the dog's career. The handler either takes command of the process or lets outside forces dominate. Drives that are positively reinforced on the street will strengthen. Drives that are negatively (or never) reinforced diminish or produce unreliable behavior.

Was the experience positive or negative for the dog? If negative, what retraining is needed and how soon can you do it? If the dog was injured, recreating the incident in training after the physical recovery will be the best indicator of the dog's resilience and future behavior.

Experienced handlers refer to the downtraining that occurs on some missions. For example, on the nth alarm call to the same address week after week, the dog starts losing focus as he searches the building for an intruder. A limited number of searches without finds build drive. Has the

DECOY TACTIC 4: *Run and return.* The helicopter makes a low pass over the area (searchlight on at night). Assuming the observer does not spot the suspect, the aircraft leaves the scene and throttles back a few miles away. Then, as the K-9 team searches through the area, the same helicopter, or a second ship, returns at about 100 knots (searchlight on at night) for another pass. Used by San Diego Police and other departments, the idea is to encourage the bad guy to leave his hiding place, then surprise him. Moving suspects attract police dogs.

handler's behavior changed? Has the dog's perception changed from *somebody is hidden in this building* to *nobody is in here?*

"We've had two incidents where our own officers have shot dogs on a search. In one the dog was killed. In these instances, I know how sensitive the handlers are to their dogs, but it stresses the need for the handler to maintain constant visual contact with the dog. If the dog turns a corner, you've got to command him to down or come back, and you move up to the corner to get him in sight.

"We were conducting an area search without briefing patrol officers as thoroughly as we should have: 'O.K., here's what we're going to do, these are what the responsibilities are, here's what you need to be careful of.' Tell the cover officers what to do: 'I'm going to watch the dog. Your job is to look at the surrounding areas and cover me.'

"The dog got separated from the handler and ended up attacking a patrol sergeant. His only defense was to shoot, which he did. He ended up killing the dog. It was like mixing oil and water between the two officers for a long time. Eventually they worked it out.

"The other incident involved some burglary suspects in a used car lot that was completely fenced. Somehow two officers were inside this fenced lot. They shouldn't have been there. That should have been spotted by the aero unit, or if you do a thorough roll call in briefing of perimeter people before you deploy the dog, they should have known. The handler made his announcement and conducted the search.

"A helicopter overhead saw what took place. The handler had lost sight of the dog. Aside from that issue, *he believed only suspects were inside.* He had no idea cops were in the perimeter. *The officers saw the dog and ran.* Immediately when they ran, the dog alerted, chased and bit one officer on the butt. The officer fired.

"The dog suffered a through-and-through gunshot wound and was down for about three weeks. He has come back and is working fine now. The officers have patched up their differences. As emotionally tied as the handler is to the animal, that is like shooting one of your children. I work with this guy. We joke about it now. I am sure if the dog had died it would be a different situation.

"Any time we have a bite, a K-9 supervisor needs to be briefed as soon as possible concerning: 'These were the circumstances of the search, this is why the guy got bitten, this was his medical care.'

"Then we can evaluate it from a tactical standpoint, a procedural standpoint, make sure all the documentation which needs to take place is actually done. It gives us a better opportunity to evaluate our handlers and their dogs in the way they do their job on a daily basis."

—Police K-9 Administrator

Sustaining reliable fugitive pursuit, search, and apprehension skills requires more training on a regular basis for corrections teams than for police teams. What happens nightly on the streets of Sacramento is an unusual occurrence inside the walls of Folsom Prison.

CHAPTER 5

PRISON PATROL

"The dog teams will be watched closely.

Not only by the inmates but by their friends on the outside.

Any chance to eliminate the dog will be taken

if it is believed to be necessary."

—K-9 Trainer

The tactics of deploying a prison service dog in the corrections setting are basically the same as the tactics of deploying police K-9. Teams generally have the same basic K-9 detection and enforcement training. The corrections environment, however, is different from the street. Certain modifications of strategy and tactics are warranted, both in daily security tasks and in emergency situations. Sustaining reliable skills in certain areas will be more difficult for corrections teams than for police dog teams. Recognizing the potential areas of conflict is essential to keeping canines viable inside institutions and camps.

KNOW YOUR MISSION, KNOW YOUR *BEAT*

Implementing dog teams in daily corrections operations is good news for the public, although many inmates do not think so. Trained for prison service to work "in the walls" around prisoners, the dogs operate under tighter control than most police dogs on the street. They must be stable, friendly canines who go home with their handlers, play with the kids, work out with a ball or toy as often as possible, and go along fishing on weekends. They don't do paperwork, but they do maintain a comprehensive task capability.

Defining that task is the responsibility of the administration. Some institutions and camps employ specialist dogs for narcotics detection, explosives detection, or tracking escaped prisoners. Some departments employ protection trained dogs exclusively to assist correctional officers in preventing and controlling disturbances. Several departments define the prison dog team: A dog team trained to search for escaped or hidden prisoners, evidence, drugs or other contraband, to pursue and stop fleeing or aggressive prisoners, and to provide protection for the handler, other correctional officers, and the public.

Corrections canines have sniffed out contraband ranging from a .22 caliber shell hidden in a sneaker, to pounds of marijuana coming through the postal system, and kilos of cocaine concealed in delivery trucks. Conducting housing unit shakedowns, dog teams have turned up tattoo machines, homemade knives and pipes, explosive materials, drugs, hypodermic kits, and other contraband. A typical visitor vehicle search resulted in the arrest of two women charged with introducing contraband into a correctional center when cocaine was found in a makeup kit inside one visitor's purse. Interestingly, some visitors choose not to stay when they see the canine teams.

The dogs can escort combative inmates, as well as help transportation units escort high risk inmates off prison property for medical treatment. The major advantage of a prison canine program is the deterrent effect on the inmates. Dogs enhance the safety and security of the staff and the inmates. They have a role in the response to "calls for assistance" or red lights.

K-9 programs can generate good public relations for the facility through the media and personal appearances locally. Corrections dogs can also supplement police K-9 response to felony searches and task force operations outside the facility.

If the dog's mission includes protection or high risk search, it is important to emphasize *basic enforcement capability*, because corrections officers are typically not police academy graduates, nor do they typically have street experience. For example, handlers need practice in arrest techniques incorporating the presence of the dog. They need tactical training for deploying the dog to search buildings and open areas. For institutions that maintain a SWAT team, regular training with the K-9 unit enhances the proficiency of both specialties.

K-9 teams are under scrutiny in prisons. Inmates watch every reaction of the canine. Skilled at reading other people, they learn to read the dogs as well. Prisoners identify the weaknesses and strengths of each animal then broadcast this information. Some offenders can read the dog better than the handler can. A dog the inmates do not respect because they perceive him to be flawed or weak is vulnerable in much the same way as an officer they disrespect. Conversely, a dog that is perceived to be strong may be challenged as a display of machismo.

Inmates will try to turn this perception against the officer. Attempting to distract or bait the dog (catcalls, hissing, staring at the dog, offering food to the dog, leaving food out for the dog), inciting him to be aggressive, perhaps to bite, becomes part of the con game. It will cost the institution major lawsuits if allowed to proceed unchecked through the population. *The institution should establish clear guidelines for dealing with subversive activity against prison dogs using procedures similar to dealing with actions against officers or guards.* The dog is the officer's partner. Any action against the dog constitutes action against the handler.

> Yesterday, I overheard several kitchen inmates while passing, talking about techniques for disabling a guard dog (K-9) if attacked. Mainly they discussed putting their arm out for him to grab, then hitting him (the dog) hard in the windpipe with their other hand.
> —Kitchen Steward reporting to the Food Service Manager

The prison dog must be aware but relaxed on patrol in close quarters with inmates (entryways, service elevators, loading docks). The K-9 that is tense or has high body sensitivity, grabbing or growling at whatever touches him, will be a liability inside an institution. If the dog is basically unstable, he will become a control problem. Such a team will be a target for traps set by the inmates. One inmate "fell" around a corner into the K-9 team, claimed the dog's teeth grazed the site of an old scar, and promptly sought legal redress. Inmates will systematically harass the dog in an attempt to build a jacket on him to support *the big lawsuit*.

Maintenance training should emphasize handler control of the dog in high-stress situations: physical agitation by inmates, fights, crowds or mass movements, narrow corridors, crowded cells, rambunctious children, cats, emotionally disturbed persons, traffic, loud machinery, projectiles, and gunfire. Interior patrols and code responses demand that the dog be approachable and controlled. He must alert on command but also shut down completely on command.

An officer and his K-9 were leaving the main office area. Walking down the hallway toward the gym door, the handler was confronted by inmate Joe. Joe started yelling about not liking dogs. He said, "These fucking dogs don't belong here. Keep the fucking dogs away from me. One of these days I am going to kill these fucking dogs." Bracing both arms against the doorjamb, he blocked the doorway. The dog alerted but did not bark.

In a calm monotone the handler told Joe to back away from the door. Swearing loudly, the inmate backed away, giving the officer room to exit. The handler then warned Joe not to harass him or the other K-9 teams in the future. Persistence and control paid off. Soon after, the department installed more comprehensive procedures for confronting harassing inmates. Specific correctional disciplinary offenses must be designed for abusive language and threatening acts towards the department's prison service dogs.

Rap—talk—is part of institutional life. Verbal threats may be overt or covert, requiring familiarity with a particular culture or language. Distinguishing what is actual and imminent from what is merely talk is part of every correctional officer's job. Although the dialogue may descend into the arena of the ridiculous, the K-9 officer cannot afford to ignore what might lie behind the talk:

> While making my rounds in the no-man's-land between perimeter fences, I went up to the inner fence to speak to the officer overseeing inmates performing rock detail in the yard. We were talking when an inmate named French began harassing the K-9 by whistling at him and making squeaky noises with his lips. I ordered French to stop harassing the dog or his activity would be terminated.
>
> French: Did you hear that fuckin' bullshit, we can't whistle at the dogs.
>
> Inmate Gray: Fuck you and your dogs. I've got some relatives that just love to shoot dogs. I think I'll call them up and have George hunt your dogs down.
>
> French: Shit. I'll have my mom bring down my pit bull and he'll take care of all of them.
>
> Gray: Fuck you, I'll get rid of your dogs. They shouldn't even be in a penitentiary. They'll be gone soon. I've got something in the works right now.
>
> I told Gray his activity was terminated, to return to his house.
>
> Gray: Fuck you and your fucking job. I don't need to move any more of these fuckin rocks.
>
> Gray threw the shovel down and took 4 or 5 steps off the sidewalk towards the fence. I ordered him back onto the sidewalk. He complied and went back to his [prison] house, yelling obscenities on the way.
>
> [Rock detail was terminated for the day. The officer recommended inmate Gray be suspended from work detail pending classification.]

Prison dog teams have the advantage over police K-9s in their potential *knowledge and control over the patrol area.* Integrated into the existing security system, the canine unit supplements and enhances the surveillance capabilities of the institutional staff. Areas that the canine team patrols regularly on foot, inside or outside the perimeter, become very familiar to the dog. Changes in the scent picture frequently cause a readable behavior change, even where the dog has not been commanded to search and the handler is not expecting an alert.

Rap—talk—is part of institutional life. Verbal threats may be overt or covert, requiring familiarity with a particular culture or language.

KEEPING THE EDGE v. USING RESTRAINT

It is very important that prison dog handlers be armed while on duty outside the institution, especially on escape duty, when teams will be called upon to work their dogs not only in the vicinity of the facility itself but also in the surrounding metropolitan or rural area. Based on the requirements of their specific job assignments, canine officers must be firearm qualified with semi-automatic handguns, shotguns, and rifles. Each officer should be assigned his own duty weapons, properly stored for rapid accessibility.

The potential for violence by an escaped prisoner is high based upon the number of offenders serving time for violent crimes. According to the "Institution Population Characteristics," California Department of Corrections, 1993:

Total Population	Offense	Number/Percent
114,275	Violent Crimes (Murder, Manslaughter, Robbery, Assault, Sex Offenses, Kidnap)	48,779/42.7

Other offenses included Escape (223) and Possession Weapon (2,290).

A youth authority ward or prison escapee can be armed with a handgun left in a surrounding field by friends. He can be armed with a knife, stabbing tool, or impact weapon taken from the institution. Or, he can be armed as a result of a residential or vehicle burglary committed shortly after the escape.

Based upon the figures above, the chances of meeting an escapee who was serving time for a violent crime are quite high. As the prison service dog team will most often be the first to encounter the escapee, the protection of the handler and the dog are of utmost importance.

Once it is known that the department will use dogs to search for escapees, the team will become vulnerable, not only to those inside the institution, but also to the inmate's friends on the outside.

"C'mon doggy, bite me! Gimme a million bucks. I wanna sue this place." California Youth Authority teams reinforce control.

What should a handler do if he and his dog are attacked by an armed fugitive? What should a handler do if his dog is attacked by another dog, a dog trained to fight? What should a handler do when his dog locates an escapee, the escapee panics and puts the welfare of private citizens in danger? If he is not armed, he is useless in those situations.

The investment made by the department for the prison service dog is many thousands of dollars. If another dog can render it useless or permanently injured, the investment is lost.

Also, personnel are now uniformed and appear to the public as law enforcement officers. This greatly increases their visibility.

Arming the dog handler does not mean he is going to shoot someone. Many law enforcement officers go through an entire career and never fire their weapon, except at the range. However, they are armed because they face the potential for life threatening violence while they are working. Prison dog handlers face that same potential.

The department has to decide what defensive weapons will be authorized for the canine officers inside the institution. Different locations at the facility may have different requirements, but administrators should remember that violence can erupt anywhere, regardless of the landscaping, building design, or designated activity. A doctor was stabbed at the institution hospital. A staff member in the laundry was raped, taken hostage, and abducted from the institution. An officer in the kitchen was hit over the head from behind by a heavy steel pan. An offender brandishing a shop tool took on a K-9 officer in front of the superintendent's office. It is noteworthy that all of these incidents took place in youth authority institutions.

There is a clear and convincing argument to be made for deploying unarmed officers inside institutions. The collateral argument in favor of the canine is his effect as a deterrent and as an instrument of control that cannot be turned against the officer. Typically when a K-9 program starts, officer assaults go down. Whether chemicals or impact weapons are to be employed inside the institution, and under what circumstances, are matters each state and each prison system must decide.

The key to successful weapons deployment is realistic training. On a regular basis the team practices apprehending offenders armed with sticks, bedding, water hoses, or firebrands. Quarterly or more often, the K-9 officer should qualify at the range with the dog at his side.

The bad boys of Spring Creek Correctional Center, Alaska, include moose and brown bear. The max security prison invaded their property, and they do not fear dogs.

Fitness is typically an underrated tactic in corrections. Walking or standing around the institution tires the officer and gives the illusion he or she has exercised. Throwing a kong, ball or other retrieve toy for the dog does not exercise the handler, and tugging exercises done improperly strain the handler's back. Boredom, overeating, or smoking will contribute to the problem.

Competent K-9 teams make rigorous physical conditioning, endurance and strength training, a regular part of their program. When performed correctly, narcotic detection is surprisingly hard work for both the dog and the handler. Teams responsible for searching fugitives need to conduct extended exercises (half day and full day) in likely escape areas, not only to practice the tactics and maintain familiarity with the terrain, but also to increase their fitness. These exercises should be carried out at night as well as during the day, winter and summer, in all kinds of weather. The dog teams will be expected to take the lead in pursuits, searches and apprehensions. Not just keep up. Lead.

Have the prison dog teams present a day of training for the department at each basic correctional officer's academy. Officers need to know how to work with the canine teams, their

capabilities and limitations in physical altercations and searching. New officers will have questions about the group. Some will be interested in assisting with the K-9 training.

Some officers, as well as some members of the prison staff, will not like the dogs nor the concept of canines working in the prison. It will be up to the handlers to keep the lines of communication open and to maintain positive relationships with people on both sides of the K-9 issue. Elitist tactics usually damage dog programs. As in law enforcement, the unit that polices itself, and stays friendly and professional has the best chance of survival.

Outfit at least two vehicles for canine transportation and deployment. Although prison dogs spend most of their time inside the institution or working the perimeter on foot, dedicated vehicles facilitate normal deployment. K-9 teams can jump into any vehicle or aircraft if necessary for rapid response to code calls.

K-9 SECURITY PATROL

Prison dogs can be very effective finding weapons or other evidence bearing fresh human scent (see evidence search chapter). Shortly after responding to a large fight at an institution school, a youth authority K-9 was deployed to detail the landscaping outside the building where the fight had taken place. In seconds the dog located a 5-inch sharpened steel stabbing weapon with a taped handle hidden on the grounds near the room where the wards had fought.

Take a fresh look at familiar agility equipment. How far away can you stand while directing the dog to scale the wall?

Deploying the team on random patrol patterns familiarizes both the handler and the dog with the normal configuration of areas inside and outside the perimeter of the institution. Once the dog knows what is normal in an area, he will quickly perceive contaminating scents (tracks, evidence). On patrols outside, use discretion commanding the dog. Part of the time, he should be allowed to run off lead, to relax and relieve himself or play with a toy. He should not be out of the handler's sight, however. Part of the time, the dog will be actively searching under command, on- or off-lead, depending on his training. Part of the time, another officer or staff member will have hidden articles for the dog to find during the patrol in order to provide opportunities for reinforcing the dog's evidence detection capability.

Perimeter foot patrol, walking outside and inside the boundary of the facility:
1. Checking for contraband (dog alerts to concealed drugs, weapons, articles)
2. Checking the fence and all security systems for damage or disturbances (dog indicates locations of concentrated human scent)
3. Checking for any fresh digging, tracks, markings, items or evidence of an escape attempt (dog indicates locations recently contaminated by human or other scent)
4. Visible deterrent to inmates thinking about escape

In order to use the dog most effectively and to maintain emergency response capability, the dog team should not be placed on a stationary post except for planned surveillance operations.

Interior patrol, walking inside the buildings and grounds of the facility:

1. Checking designated buildings, equipment and areas for contraband, damage, or disturbances (dog as detector)
2. Observing (not supervising) prisoner movements or work details (dog as deterrent)
3. Assisting inspections (dog as detector or deterrent)

Transporting inmates inside or outside the facility (court, medical, work detail) is not recommended as a general K-9 function.

Called to an institutional school area, the dog handler was met and briefed by the superintendent who expected a large disturbance between the inmates of two dormitories during the school movement. They had extra staff placed throughout the school and would release classes one at a time. The superintendent requested the dog team stand by in the middle quad area for visual effect. The assistant superintendent asked that no biting take place if any fights were to break out unless weapons or life threatening situations occurred.

During the movement, the dog team stood by for 35 minutes. Inmates exited the classrooms loud and unruly only to become quiet and cooperative upon seeing the K-9. The school movement was completed with no incidents to report. Use of the dog was well received by the staff and had a positive impact on the inmates.

Patroling jail grounds and work crews. How many did not run because the dog was there?

Whether you are dealing with mass movements or one-on-one situations, have a plan for what happens next. If, in the case above, a group of inmates had decided to "take on the dog" and handler, what was the plan? Were backup canines available? Who was going to handle the fight? Two female administrators were wearing dresses and high heels. Where were they going to go and who would cover their retreat? Numerous supervisors were scattered around the grounds. Did they have a plan of action?

OFFICER PROTECTION AND DISTURBANCES

Use the best methods available. Deploying the dog may or may not be the recommended tactic in any given situation. If available, one of the best methods for stopping fights or counteracting a potentially deadly situation is high pressure water. Chemical agents with various delivery systems (sprays, grenades, ferret rounds) are another method of choice. A wide range of projectiles, from pellets to rubber rifle slugs, will quickly and effectively handle a variety of situations. A surprise rush with blankets may stop an incident from turning deadly. Surprise and speed in general are effective tactics when officers are challenged.

A prison dog team was dispatched to an institution school for added security during the movement. There had been a fight at the facility during an earlier school movement involving several inmates. With the K-9 present, no problems arose. Near the middle of the movement, a living unit notified security they had a prisoner refusing to move to school. Moments later a second call broadcast that the prisoner was now

Practice detection and protection in kitchens and food preparation areas of the prison as well as warehouses. What is the loss of a few loaves of bread or a few pounds of meat in training compared to sniffing 2 kilos of cocaine in a delivery truck? Or locating an inmate hiding with a 10-inch blade?

threatening staff. The handler was asked to take the dog to the living unit to assist security with this situation. At the living unit the prisoner was in a room sitting on the bed, refusing to move. A group supervisor told the prisoner to get up. He refused.

The dog team entered. The handler ordered the inmate to stand up, place his hands behind his back, and back up to the doorway. The dog was on lead and at the handler's order began barking aggressively. The man looked at the dog, stood, and complied. Another officer handcuffed the inmate and walked him out the door. During the escort, the prisoner became loud and argumentative. Moving closer to him, the handler ordered the inmate to keep moving and to be quiet. The prisoner complied and was placed in lockup without incident.

What was the next step if the prisoner had failed to comply? Confrontations require strategy for changing tactics as the situation changes. Basically, this incident was the same as an offender on the street refusing to comply with police officers. What did this department want the handler to do? What was the handler's plan? If the inmate had continued passively sitting on the bed, would the K-9 officer have placed his dog in a cover position and moved in to handcuff the inmate? Or stepped back, allowing one or several officers to take custody of the inmate?

If suddenly the fight was on, would the officers have engaged (fought) the inmate or disengaged to let the K-9 team handle it? The handler calling the shots as the lead officer is a third option: "Stay back," putting the dog into a watch position and moving toward the prisoner, or, "You guys take it," moving with the dog into a cover position. Frequently the confined space of an institution forces the closest officer to take charge of the individual causing the incident. Practice clear communications and flexibility deploying the dog team.

The multi-trained prison dog performs a variety of tasks in sequence. Responding to a large disturbance in progress between gangs, the K-9 team and an officer with a 37-millimeter gas gun were used to escort inmates involved in the dispute from classrooms to a search area then through a metal detector. At first the inmates were loud. When the dog team arrived, they moved quietly and calmly. A few inmates tried making loud noises, the dog barked, and they calmed their behavior. Searching the grounds outside, the dog located a 5-inch metal shank concealed in the grass.

Good tactics often produce results short of having to deploy the dog:

I received a call from the security sergeant to come to House No.1 with my K-9. Entering House No.1, I saw the inmate in the dayroom area with a mop wringer and glass on the floor from three windows he had broken out. The assistant superintendent gave the order to go in on the inmate. Two officers were to go through the side entrance first, the rest through the front entry. I was the first through the front. Four times I ordered the inmate to put down the mop wringer. He did not comply. He was in a threatening, offensive stance. My dog growled and barked at him.

Meanwhile, officers approached from the rear. The inmate did not see them and took a baseball batter's stance, ready to strike out at me. As the inmate was watching my dog, the officers approached from behind and took him to the floor. I secured the dog and assisted the other officers applying restraints and getting the inmate into a cell.

Cell extraction techniques generally lack the element of surprise. The prisoner knows you are coming through the door, and his back is secure. The number of inmates inside the cell and whether you have a hostage situation developing are critical factors. By policy some departments never deploy dogs in this role. Other techniques (water, chemicals, projectiles, SWAT) may be safer and more effective.

To use the dog, it is imperative this tactic be practiced on a regular basis. The training must involve all the officers who will be working together with the dog. If deployed as part of an entry team, the dog and handler enter first so the dog targets the offender, not intervening bodies. Sometimes officers get lucky:

We were called to help remove an inmate from his cell in D-Mod to C-Mod. Three officers, my dog and I approached the inmate's cell after he had refused to move. As the sliding door opened, the inmate shouted threats at us and made threatening gestures. He held an edged weapon in each hand. He began to kick through the opening at one of the officers.

Opening the door enough to fit through, one officer entered holding a protective shield. The dog and I were the last to enter. The inmate backed to the center of the cell where he fought, kicking and stabbing. As the four officers tried to restrain the inmate, his right arm remained free, and he stabbed repeatedly at two officers.

I sent in the canine. Dodging the officers, he bit the inmate on the right leg above the knee. The inmate fell over backwards with two officers on top of him. I called the dog off, and he backed right out.

As soon as the inmate was restrained, I requested medical personnel to examine him then took the dog out.

If high pressure water, chemical weapons or other control tactics are not available, deploy K-9 with the entry team to save an inmate. Train in advance. Cell space is tight, the dog is easily confused, and the officers have no advantage of surprise.

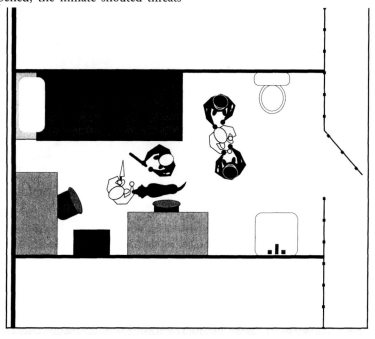

Protection trained prison dogs must meet the same reliability standards apprehending and calling off inmates that qualify police dogs for the street, including a clean calloff:

> Operations advised me an inmate had pruno in his cell and was refusing to come out so officers could conduct a shakedown. We responded with the tactical team. An officer warned me the inmate said he had something to take out the dog and he was ready. He had soaked the floor and soaped his body.
>
> At 2010 hours the order was given and we entered the module. At the cell door, I asked the inmate if he would come out peacefully. He replied with swearing to the effect that he was ready to take us out. He was holding a spray bottle in his right hand and an unidentifiable object in his left hand. He sprayed my dog in the face through the cell slider.
>
> In we went. The K-9 made contact with the inmate, biting him on his left side under his arm. I made contact with my PR-24 on his left shoulder and upper arm area. The inmate kept wrestling with us until an assisting officer and I restrained him against the bunk with the minimum force necessary. I called off my dog. He immediately released his hold and came to my side. Other officers took control of the inmate.

One negative experience in training or deploying dog teams can convince a department not to use K-9's in that context again, regardless whether the teams used appropriate tactics:

> We tried using the dogs inside in training scenarios, because the dog is an intimidating factor. When I was a watch commander at the jail, we staged a riot and had the dogs in there. Because of all the noise and hysteria, the dogs are barking. The only person who suffered a bite happened to be a young deputy.
>
> We realized those are pretty bad actors in there. Unless you are going to sacrifice the dog. There's strength in numbers. Go down a cell block with 50 inmates and they've all got mattresses up to shield themselves. They know, "Let's just pounce on the dog," the same as throwing a deputy in there. Somebody might get bitten, but the odds are in their favor they can kill or disable that dog. So it's useless.
>
> A couple years ago we did have a jail riot. What we found out were real effective were sting ball grenades. We would toss one of those things and 100 BB's go everywhere. It was over like that. We don't use the K-9s in crowd control situations at all.

Disturbances are by nature confusing incidents that make a straightforward response difficult, especially when there is a fire or equipment breakdown or both. An incident described by a non-K-9 officer puts this problem into perspective:

> At 0130 hours, I was conducting a shakedown of the industries building when called to respond to operations. The sergeant advised us inmate Smith was refusing to lock down. He had a weapon, was breaking glass, and had started a small fire in the day room. Entering House 1, I walked by D-Mod and saw inmate Jones in C-Mod pick up the weight lifting bench and smash the day room glass. Walking over to B-Mod, I saw inmate Smith breaking the dayroom glass with a wooden table leg, yelling, "I'm going to kill you." I ordered him to lock down, and he said, "You murdering motherfucker, I'm going to kill you." He kept breaking glass with the table leg and a sharpened wooden broom handle.
>
> The house sergeant told us to outfit into protective gear, but there were only three sets available. Additional responding personnel had to bring the gear with them. I suggested chemical agents, but they were kept in the armory, so the sergeant went to get them, leaving me in charge. I split the staff into two teams of 4 and 5 officers.
>
> At 0158 I radioed the sergeant the fire in B-Mod had flames 18 to 20 feet in the air

and appeared to be burning chairs. The fire had activated the sprinkler system, which we could not shut off due to the fire in C-Mod. Ambulance, city fire, K-9 teams, and chemical agents were en route to the house. The arriving chemical agents were two cans of mace, which leaked and had to be thrown out.

Entering two separate doors of B-Mod at 0215 in an attempt to restrain inmate Smith, one team was overcome with heavy smoke. The K-9 entering with the second team backed off and refused to enter the smoke-filled module. I advised the sergeant of our failed attempt in B-Mod.

The fire in C-Mod was still burning, endangering other inmates. Ordered to restrain Jones, we lined up two teams behind another K-9 team and entered C-Mod. Visibility was almost zero. Inmate Jones had pulled a burning wooden handle and burning plastic garbage can from the fire. He threw the burning can on the dog team. Stepping forward, the handler was stabbed by the inmate. At the same time the dog, apprehending Jones, also bit the handler on the left leg. Finally we got Jones into hard restraints. I put the fire out with a dry chemical extinguisher.

At 0232 we entered B-Module. Inmate Smith was standing in front of Cell 20. He threw a long metal bar at the officers then retreated into the mop room and closed the door. We formed a half circle in front of the door. An officer was getting ready to open the door when Smith charged out, slamming into the line of officers. We restrained him, got him outside, and conducted security checks of both mods.

How it was possible to start two fires under the guards' noses in a maximum security prison? Were high pressure water hoses available? Had either of the dog teams ever trained in heavy smoke with the handlers wearing masks and other protective gear? Had the dog teams previously trained with the tactical teams in battle? *Practice tactical entry with the K-9 on a regular basis.* To be safe and effective, entry is rapid, coordinated, the handler and each officer knows his objective. The dog is familiar with the officers' actions and responds to the handler's commands.

Incidents that escalate beyond the dog team's capability require changing tactics. Inside a maximum security prison officers in the glass control room had a ringside seat for the following incident. They videotaped everything. No orders were ever given to use the other weapons at their disposal to prevent the injuries received:

Inside a prison, an inmate ties off both upper level entry doors to a module. He soaps down the stairs. He pulls off the 25-pound bar from a weight set. The bar is 54 inches long. The man tries to assault other inmates by breaking into their windows and rooms.

Officers are ordered in. They can only gain access from the bottom floor. As they struggle to climb the slippery stairs the dog and officers fall repeatedly. When the dog team and a shield man reach the top stair, the inmate swings the bar.

The shield man takes the first blow. The top platform is littered with shattered glass from the cell windows. Pieces of glass in the soap solution make traction difficult. The inmate swings again.

This time the dog handler deflects the blow with his PR-24. Striking downward, the bar hits the dog on the top of the head between his ears. Although injured, the dog remains conscious. The static pressure injures the handler's right forearm. The handler and other officers take the inmate to the floor and handcuff him. The inmates are locked down. Dog and handler go to the hospital. The team is out of service for several months.

CROWD CONTROL

Police agencies and prisons have different policies regarding K-9 deployment in crowd situations. Some departments prohibit the use of dogs for control, apprehension, or protection during any type assembly. Other departments define a role for the K-9 unit, frequently as part of their tactical team deployment.

Confronted unexpectedly by multiple adversaries, a K-9 team may not have the option of cover or retreat. A group of approximately 200 brick and rock throwing violent rioters were dispersed in Richmond, California, by one gas man, one sergeant, one canine unit, and one follow-up radio car unit. The show of organized force, although small, had a profound effect in favor of law enforcement.

Deploying police dog teams in a face-off against a violent crowd is a high risk tactic. Where law enforcement or prison officers are heavily

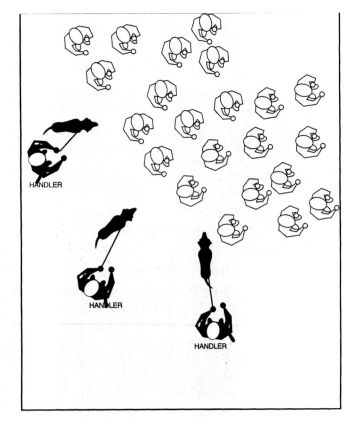

outnumbered by a gang or a mob, police dogs are typically ineffective, or they confuse and endanger the situation. Vehicles deployed as part of a tactical team are much faster, safer and usually highly effective. Helicopter support is invaluable for surveillance, insertions, and extractions. Chemical and impact weapons in addition to full protective gear are essential for tactical teams.

Where a mass riot is in progress, a war zone exists. Perpetrators may be armed with automatic weapons. The dog loses his deterrent value in such lethal force situations. His value apprehending and arresting perpetrators is restricted.

If dogs are to be integrated into riot strategy, particularly where lethal force is being used against officers, keep the K-9 units mobile in the background in order to deploy rapidly out of vehicles to control specific targets. Efficient communication with air and ground units is necessary.

Prison dog teams deployed strategically (typically on the perimeter) have proved effective to *direct the flow of large groups* of inmates or to prevent passive groups from becoming aggressive. Before isolated occurrences turn into mob psychology and mass violence, the presence of quiet K-9s as a show of organized force typically *prevents large group disturbances*. The dogs also *prevent escapes*. Groups that are passive or passive-resistive do not warrant active deployment of the dog.

Plan for reinforcement or retreat if the crowd goes out of control.

The police dog (prison dog) may be deployed actively to *rescue an officer down* or in need of assistance. Practice this tactic regularly in riot gear with the SWAT team, inside buildings and outside, so every dog and officer can perform under high stress conditions (weapons discharge, pyrotechnics, chemical agents). Sound, including the barking dog, ricochets off walls, as do bullets and projectiles. Noise disorients the teams. Hand signals are essential. Again, plan for reinforcement or retreat if the rescue becomes unfeasible.

Officer rescue tactics:

1. Scene safety—Assess risks versus resources. Do not throw away lives to save one.
2. Deploy K-9 team(s) to the front of the tactical formation (line, wedge, echelon). The dog is on lead, the handler riot-equipped.
3. Platoon commander/squad leader directs the advance to the victim.
4. K-9 and tactical teams advance beyond the victim. Rescue teams package and transport the victim.
5. Tactical teams establish control and clear the area.

Ordering everyone to lie down is a sound tactic to restore order and to identify the primary instigators of a disturbance or riot.

I responded to a disturbance in a classroom and found a fight in progress with about 20 to 25 inmates involved. A female teacher was near the entry door behind her desk with several inmates throwing chairs, broken chair legs, books, and other loose objects in her direction and toward other inmates. I placed myself with my K-9 between the inmates and the teacher to act as a barrier and directed her to leave the room.

Once she cleared the room, I ordered the inmates to stop fighting, get on the floor, and place their hands on their heads. Several inmates refused to comply. At this point, I let my K-9 out on the full six-foot lead and began a sweeping motion with the dog directed at the wards. At the same time I ordered them to the floor inmate Miller struck another inmate, Scully, in the lower back with a classroom chair. Scully was removed from the room by other responding staff. Miller attempted to fight my dog and was bitten on the lower right arm. He then complied and got on the floor.

After all of the remaining inmates were placed on the floor, staff placed them in restraints. I remained in the room with my dog until all inmates were placed in restraints. I then provided security coverage with my K-9 in the school area until all inmates were removed from the area. There were no further incidents.

I then proceeded to the medical ward to check on Miller (refer to medical report). I informed him the bite was not punishment and asked if he understood why he was bitten. He stated that he understood and that he had heard the warning but continued to fight.

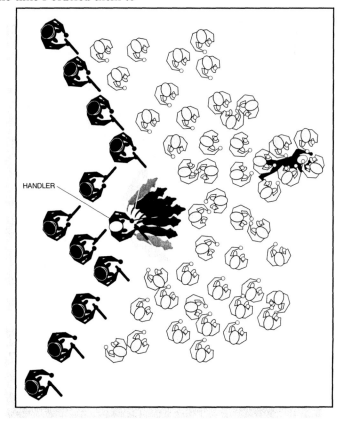

HANDLER

HOSTAGE INCIDENTS

What if an inmate had grabbed the teacher? The situation encountered by the K-9 team would have changed. Suppose the inmate had a knife to her throat? The taking of a hostage by a prisoner puts into motion a set of procedures that are entirely different from controlling a disturbance. By itself, the act removes the dog team from the lead role and places it on the perimeter, usually out of sight and hearing, in containment and support roles.

Initially in a prison hostage taking, the K-9 team will be needed to assist with lockdown and to secure the facility according to rehearsed procedures. The more rapidly and uneventfully this occurs, the better. The handler who wastes time trying to play hero and get the inmate back onto a reasonable track, either by prolonged conversation with the abductor or by a show of canine teeth, is making a mistake that may cost lives. Take whatever immediate defensive action is necessary, then get the dog out of there.

Once lockdown is achieved, security has the related tasks of bringing the incident to an end inside while preventing compromise from the outside. The K-9 unit can play an effective high profile role in the latter. Temporarily assigned to perimeter patrol, evacuations, or escort duty, the dog teams operate unattached as rover units in case they are needed for protection, search, or weapons recovery after the incident is resolved.

If the inmate escapes with the hostage, crossing beyond the institution boundary into the real world, the mission changes to a law enforcement operation conducted by the agencies charged with handling hostage taking incidents on the outside. With the exception of the prison negotiators or officers who can directly assist in formulating plans for the capture, corrections officers typically fall back to a support role, turning the leadership and ground maneuvers over to county or city SWAT. Prison dog teams play a role only if they are currently capable of working with local tactical teams outside.

If the inmate escapes alone on foot (highly unlikely but possible), the K-9 unit and tactical teams will switch to the escape apprehension mode.

DETECTING DRUGS

A primary function of the prison dog team is to perform routine and special searches of the institution for controlled substances. Each institution will have its own search policy and procedures based on department regulations, state law, and the type of facility. Security officers maintain liaison with local law enforcement agencies and narcotic task forces for current information about the drugs circulating in the community, typical packaging and methods of concealment, sources, sales, and distribution. Related information about gangs and weapons trafficking helps corrections anticipate what might be discovered coming into the facility, update priorities for searching, and indentify individuals who may be involved inside the institution.

Security of the search is important. All information concerning the preparation and execution of these searches must be held confidential on a "need to know" basis. Areas designated to be searched must be cleared of all prisoners and staff not participating in the actual search.

Equally important are emergency veterinary procedures, either a veterinarian close to the institution or doctors or qualified staff at the institution hospital. More than one police or prison dog's life has been saved by the timely intervention of an internist or surgeon who did not expect his patient to have four paws and a tail. Do these professionals the favor of (1) providing them up-to-date supplies of drug antidotes and veterinary products they might need for your K-9s, (2) setting up standard EMS (emergency medical services) procedures in case, for example, a dog ingests a narcotic during a search, and (3) at least 4 times a year training with the medical personnel you will be relying on.

Ambulance crews in a medium-sized city liked one K-9 so much that they said, "Just call us. We'll do the transport, and we'll work on him until the vet is ready to take him."

Keep a comprehensive emergency medical kit available to the handler during every drug search.

Drug search tactics are the same for prison and parole dogs as for narcotic detector dogs on the outside. Corrections dogs search vehicles, buildings, parcels, and outside areas. The safety precautions taken are the same. Deployment tactics are basically the same. The canine's job as a detection tool is the same. The difference lies primarily in the search environment. The world of the convicted offender gives narcotic dog handlers more latitude in some areas while placing more constraints in others.

In *Estes v. Rowland* (1993) 14 Cal.App.4th 508, a group of visitors had challenged California Department of Correction's (CDC's) visitor-vehicle search program, specifically at San Quentin State Prison. The court held the prison dog search program was not unlawful as exceeding the limits of a proper administrative search or violating prisoners' rights to receive visitors. A legitimate administrative search (1) must be clearly necessary to a vital governmental interest; (2) must be limited, and no more intrusive than necessary to accomplish the governmental interest; (3) must be reasonably effective in accomplishing its purpose; and (4) must be conducted for a purpose other than the gathering of evidence for criminal purposes.

Prison officials testified that drugs are the central problem confronting California prisons. They described how drugs contribute to prison violence because various gangs fight over control of the drug trade in a particular area. Moreover, an inmate with a drug debt he cannot pay may be attacked or killed. Inmates and their families are sometimes forced to participate in drug smuggling under threat of physical harm.

Because existing search procedures were inadequate to detect drugs, prison officials decided to employ drug-detecting dogs to search visitors' vehicles. In December 1984, a dog-assisted search was conducted at the Correctional Training Facility at Soledad using dogs provided by the United States Customs Office. Every car was searched and a "considerable amount" of narcotics discovered. Due to the success of its experiment, the Department purchased two dogs that were first employed at Soledad in August 1985. The dogs were not only used to inspect vehicles, but to search work and recreation areas and living units within the prison.

At the entrance to each prison a sign is posted warning that possession of weapons, alcohol or drugs on prison property is a felony. On the day of a search a prison staff member advises incoming cars that a random vehicle search is being conducted using dogs trained to detect narcotics. Visitors are told they may decline the search and leave the grounds, but that they will lose the chance to visit that day. As vehicles approach the prison, randomly selected cars are directed to the search area. All occupants are obliged to leave the car and directed to a table on which they must place their personal belongings in a basket for inspection. A staff member obtains identifying information from the driver and records the date, time and results of the search.

Once the occupants of the car exit the vehicle the dog search begins, and normally takes only a few minutes. At some prisons, the search ends if the dog does not find anything; at other prisons correctional officers conduct a manual search regardless of the results of the dog's search. If the dog alerts to the presence of narcotics, but none are discovered, the visitor may be asked to submit to an unclothed body search. If the visitor does not consent to such a search he or she is denied a visit for that day.

If drugs are discovered on a visitor or in a car, the visitor is generally arrested or turned over to local law enforcement. If weapons are discovered, the visitor may be arrested or cited, and may be denied a visit for that day. When the search reveals alcohol, the visitor may be arrested or cited, or may simply have the alcohol confiscated and then be allowed to visit.

The appeals court upheld the following conditions:

1. All persons eligible to visit inmates must be mailed written notice (in both English and Spanish) of the dog search policy, the reasons for the policy, and the consequences of finding contraband in the vehicle or on the person of a prison visitor.

2. Immediately prior to a proposed search, the driver of each vehicle must be informed orally and in writing (again, in both English and Spanish) of what the search will entail, the reasons for it, and the consequences of finding contraband. The notice must advise the driver that he or she has the option of leaving and returning without the car without losing visiting privilege for that day. Searches may be conducted only after written consent for the search is first obtained from the driver.

3. If the driver decides to leave, passengers may stay and cannot be denied their visit.

4. Local police officers may not be involved in the search process, and may not be present at the search *unless there is some valid reason for their presence* (emphasis added). Violations of the Vehicle Code may not be reported to any law enforcement agency.

5. It is reasonable for dog searches ordinarily to be limited to 10 minutes, given the expert testimony that a dog only requires one and one-half to two minutes to search a car. At the same time, unusual factors beyond the control of the Department may in particular instances render it impossible to commence or complete a dog search within the period prescribed by the court. A tired or otherwise distressed dog may refuse to

If drugs are discovered on a visitor or in a car, the visitor is generally arrested or turned over to local law enforcement. If weapons are discovered, the visitor may be arrested or cited, and may be denied a visit for that day.

cooperate with his handlers. Additional time may also be required in connection with the search of an unusual vehicle, such as a van or a motor home. In unusual situations such as these, where the exigency is not created by the Department, the search may exceed 10 minutes. In no instance, however, may the wait for search to commence or the search itself exceed 30 minutes.

6. Once a dog alerts to the presence of narcotics, the search is no longer an administrative search, confined by the limits of that doctrine, but a probable cause search limited only by "general principles of detention and arrest." The Fourth Amendment imposes no fixed time limits on a search founded on probable cause.

    It is recognized that evidence of criminal activity unrelated to the purpose of the search may be disclosed by legitimate, limited administrative searches. Although the dog searches were conceived to discover contraband intended to be or at least capable of being smuggled into prisons, they may unearth evidence of other criminal activity. Department officials do not exceed the proper limits of an administrative search if they undertake further investigation based on the discovery of such evidence. Because it is a crime to bring drugs onto prison property, regardless of how it is packaged, peace officers cannot be limited when conducting a search incident to a valid detention or arrest based on such a violation. The discovery of such evidence provides probable cause to continue the search, limited only by relevant constitutional principles.

7. Dogs must be kept at least 20 feet from visitors at all times. Former CDC Director Daniel McCarthy instituted the policy of keeping the dogs 20 feet away from visitors to prevent visitors from getting too close to the dogs, and not the reverse. The court ordered the Department to resume compliance with this previously imposed condition.

8. There may be no reading of books, letters or other documents in possession of visitors that are not reasonably suspected of being contraband.

9. A limited administrative search of prison visitors aimed at restricting the flow of contraband into a prison is among the unusual situations in which a strip search request (which, it must again be emphasized, can be refused) is justified based solely on a dog alert. If a dog alerts, but no contraband is found in the vehicle, officials only may ask to conduct a strip search; the visitor is free to refuse and leave the premises.

10. A strip search may be requested where the contraband discovered during the search, although not packaged in a manner suggesting the entire amount was intended to be smuggled, exists in a form that can be secreted on the person of a prison visitor. Further, the duty of a peace officer is to arrest a person in possession of contraband on prison premises.

11. Department officials conducting the searches will avoid unnecessary damage to visitors' private property and treat it with the respect it deserves.

12. The Department must adopt regulations encompassing the conditions and must distribute them to all institutions prior to any future search.

In its brightline ruling, the court said the evidence demonstrated that smuggling drugs and weapons is the central problem confronting prison administrators. Because visitor searches provide an effective means to address this problem, they qualify as administrative searches. The dog search program was designed to intercept drugs before they make it into

After removing the occupants, start the search on the downwind side of the vehicle. If the blower system has been activated, interior searching will typically be unnecessary.

the prison. Regardless whether the dog searches are used regularly, they provide a strong deterrent to attempted smugglers, since a visitor should never know when he or she may be subjected to a search.

Prisons across the U.S. must of course establish procedures in accordance with their own state's laws. In California, it is a felony to bring contraband onto prison property, and there are large signs in English and in Spanish so stating.

Preparing for Visitor Vehicle Searches

- Select the posts where tactical team members will give visitors the initial advisement far enough away from the search site to facilitate the departure of those electing to leave as well as to prevent any disruption of ongoing searches.
- Select a search site en route to the prison entrance but out of the normal traffic flow. The site must be large enough to accommodate the necessary vehicles, tables, and to maintain the required separation between the visitors and the dog teams. Shade and protection from high winds are important where the dogs will be working in temperatures over 90 degrees Fahrenheit or wind velocity over 25 miles per hour.
- Satisfy the legal requirements regarding notifying eligible visitors of the search, including any requirement to announce that trained dogs will be used to sniff vehicles or property for contraband

Visitor Vehicle Search Procedures/Briefing

Searching includes local law enforcement agencies assisting the search.

- Personnel duty assignments
- Visitor/vehicle selection process
- Procedure for those visitors exercising their right not to be searched
- Maximum delay time of the visitors selected for search
- Search procedures, including K-9 (if there are multiple stations searching vehicles simultaneously, provide the necessary personnel and materials)
- Arrest/citation, escort, and referral procedures (including consent forms, strip searches, handling passengers)
- Evidence/contraband processing

Visitor Vehicle Search Procedures/Searching

TEAM LEADER TALKS TO THE VISITORS

"Roll your window down, please. Is this your vehicle?"

Advise again of the search. Instruct driver to turn engine off.

"Driver's license and vehicle registration, please?"

"Do you have any weapons, drugs, prescription drugs, or alcohol?"

"Who are you visiting today?" (Write down inmates' names.)

Have occupants leave the vehicle: "Leave the glove box open."

"Remove the keys, and step out of the vehicle."

"Open the trunk for me." (Team leader's hand holds trunk lid down but ajar. Driver's act further establishes ownership of vehicle.)

"Please take all your personal belongings, place them in the box on that table and have a seat." (Tactical team member assigned to each table is in charge of searching personal belongings and persons. Handheld metal detectors are used on all persons, who remain seated unless told otherwise.)

TEAM LEADER PREPS THE VEHICLE

Closes all windows

Unlocks and closes all doors

Checks for open glove compartment

Heater off, cooling system off, ventilating system on high

Checks for hazards to dog

Closes exit door gently

Steps away from vehicle and signals 1 minute wait period

Signals ready to the handler

HANDLER STARTS THE DOG DOWNWIND

For a large vehicle (motor home, truck) start 5- to 10 yards away

HANDLER NOTIFIES THE TEAM LEADER OF FINDS AND ALERTS

All evidence collected must be marked and the chain of evidence maintained by the assisting staff member. After the dog team is finished, security personnel may search the vehicle.

"On this date at 1436 hours, my K-9 was searching a vehicle driven by Joe Johns when she alerted to the passenger door. While searching the interior of the vehicle, the dog alerted to a container filled with what appeared to be 5 marijuana cigarettes under the front right seat.

"I removed the dog from the vehicle and instructed the tactical team to photograph the container of cigarettes and their location. One cigarette tested positive for marijuana.

"The police department took possession of the contraband, and the driver was placed under arrest."

"On this date at 1030 hours, my K-9 was searching a vehicle driven by Mary Jane. While sniffing the exterior of the vehicle, the dog alerted to the left rear of the vehicle where the trunk lid was open about a quarter inch. Opening the lid I directed the dog to search the interior of the trunk. He leaped in and alerted to a purse on the driver's side of the trunk. I immediately removed the dog from the vehicle and instructed the tactical team to hand search that area of the trunk. In the bottom of the purse the tactical team found a match book containing a folded piece of magazine. Inside was a whitish powder. The powder was tested by a Valtox test kit, and tested positive for cocaine.

"The police department took possession of the substance and photographed the evidence. A police officer then took the driver into custody."

Visitor searches do not stop the flow of drugs into corrections institutions. Typically, only small amounts will be discovered this way unless the individuals are exceptionally stupid. Even if the dog alerts to a seat, giving rise to the suspicion that the visitor is body packing narcotics, strip searches are frequently not productive. Alert guards in visitation areas, anatomical inspection devices, and controlling or eliminating contact visits have more potential effect. The value of visitor searches is their visibility and the message they convey to the community.

Delivery vehicles are a primary route for narcotics and weapons to enter institutions. Large loads of dope have been found in every type of packaging: ice cream, toilet paper, soap flakes, bedding, steel pipes. The prison dog is the logical interdiction tool to use against this trafficking method. But he must be deployed as part of a fully supported program to perform random inspections at gates or inside sally ports at loading docks. Searching large delivery trucks hauling food (especially frozen or refrigerated products), dry goods, office supplies, or industrial materials is difficult and will be limited in scope by the volume of deliveries to a large institution. *Randomness*, as well as informant-based searching, increases the deterrent effect.

The prison dog needs extensive training and experience detecting drugs through masking scents, sealed containers, cold containers, and concealment in cargo palettes. Dogs should examine the trucks themselves separate from the cargo. Screen delivery searches from inmates working in the service areas. They do not need continuing education in narcotic detection methods. Also, prisoners do not need to know the style or proficiency of the K-9 team. A maximum security prison did nothing to prevent inmates from watching the dogs search shipments on the freight dock behind the kitchen. This lapse of consciousness by the administration almost cost

Check vehicles thoroughly, even unlikely locations on staff vehicles.

them a K-9 when poisoned narcotic "bait" was planted by an inmate who had targeted a particular dog. The alert handler quite literally saved the dog's bacon. Secure delivery searches will heighten the perception that anything coming in may be searched at any time.

All daily incoming flat mail and parcels are typically searched by prison staff. The dogs can assist with the initial screening process and can also detail the packages. Mail or parcel search procedures incorporate the same basic concepts of controlled sniffs employed at a public postal facility. *Officers, not inmates or wards, must have control over the receiving area. The area where parcel searching is to be conducted must be cleared by the dog prior to parcel placement.* And the area where the sniff takes place must be a comfortable work area free of contamination or distractions to the dog.

"At 1445 I was called to the mail room by the K-9 officer to check a package received with today's mail. The dog had alerted on the package. Inside were six magazines. Dismantling one titled *Street and Smiths College Football,* I discovered page 143 folded over and sealed. Inside were thin packets of a white powdery substance. The powder tested positive for cocaine."

Some institution staff are involved in the drug trade. Departments have various policies based on individual state laws regarding detector dogs sniffing staff vehicles and property.

Shakedowns of any part of the facility can be screened by the detector dog before hand searching: living units/modules, weight rooms, recreation yards, libraries, shops, laundry, kitchen, lockers, warehouses and other storage areas, garages, grounds—any areas accessible to inmates. Coordinate these inspections through the security unit without advising the staff in advance. *It is unbelievable how fast drugs disappear if the inmates know the dogs are coming.*

In a northern adult corrections facility, the K-9s searched mods, dorms, staff vehicles. The search uncovered several caches of high-THC marijuana. In the gym, one of the dogs alerted to a corner, clawing and biting at the new hardwood floor. The handler had difficulty believing what his dog was doing. Later, officers got a tip that a major stash for sale had been located underneath the floor where the dog alerted, but was moved the day before when inmates learned dog teams were arriving to search the institution.

Select the areas to be searched realistically based on how much the K-9 teams can accomplish in the time available. Secure all inmates away from the search areas (out of the area or in lockdown). Staff involved in the search should be made aware that scent travels, therefore to extend their search in the vicinity of the dog's alerts:

> At 1315 hours I called the K-9 officer and his dog to assist in conducting a routine shakedown of Room 14, H Mod. At 1325, the handler told me his dog had alerted to the desk area of this cell. I then began a detailed search of the immediate area and the entire cell. I found the following items which were seized as evidence:

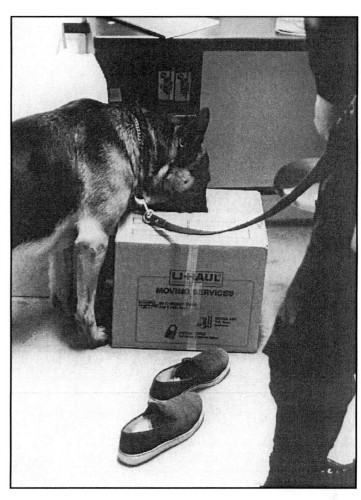

Prison dogs tasked to sniff mail need parcel search training. On property searches use an efficient pattern and be prepared to read an actual alert v. curiosity.

1. A homemade smoking bowl with debris (burned) made out of a metal eraser end, a 4-inch length of copper wire burned on both ends, a package of "zigzag" cigarette papers in a "Miller High Life" mug
2. A plastic baggie with vegetable debris and a 2-page list of institution telephone extension numbers and officers' names inside some paperback books
3. Probable marijuana residue on the desk top
4. Three packages of "C&H" sugar, a metal "X-ACTO" type cylindrical marking instrument in a property box containing papers belonging to (offender)
5. Two homemade knives wrapped in a pair of institutional blue jeans
6. A homemade hypodermic kit in the left front pocket of jeans found in the false bottom of a wooden 4-shelf bookcase located between the desk and the bunk in the room.

—K-9 Officer

In another prison tar heroin was found smoothed into envelope seams. Marijuana, meth, and pennies for weight were found in soup cans soldered under normal looking labels, undetected by prison guards or the drug dogs.

Where time permits, the K-9 officer following up indications or high alerts gives both the handler and the dog the reinforcement of pinpointing the source of the odor as well as identifying the narcotic the dog detected:

"At 1310, I received a request to come to House 4. Arriving at 1315, I was told my K-9 was needed to perform cell searches. All inmates were locked down, and I proceeded into the Bravo section to start searching.

"Entering the first cell, I searched the lower areas first. My dog alerted high in the corner of the cell underneath a high window. I pulled 5 books from the windowsill and laid them on the floor. Instantly, my K-9 alerted to a hardback book. Inspecting the book, I found a piece of blue paper wedged into the binding. I pulled the binding back and pried out the paper. The paper was an Equal packet with brown, grassy-like material inside. It had the odor of 'pot.'"

Mutual Aid

Lay the proper groundwork for mutual aid assignments. When K-9 teams are sent to assist another institution, the department should brief the requesting facility fully:

In October, a drug sweep of the CENTRAL corrections facility was conducted using a dog handler team 'on loan' from MAX I. Housing areas on Unit 6, parts of Unit 4, the Kitchen, Food Storage, Maintenance, Laundry, Shops, and Programs areas were all swept. Results were negative for location of current drugs, although the dog discovered some places where drugs had probably been stashed in the past. The dog was efficient and located all his 'test stashes' successfully.

At the time the request for the search was initiated, we had a problem with drugs coming into CENTRAL. Transfers of certain prisoners, combined with placing others in Segregation, had pretty much "cleaned house" before the dog arrived. Informants report that CENTRAL has "dried up" in the last two weeks. We have also heard that there were "A lot of toilets flushed when the dog hit the hall." The negative results of this search should not discourage future projects of this kind.

Security on this project was very tight, with the result that there was an initial lack of coordination as to how the search should be handled. Our CENTRAL staff was not familiar with the methods or capabilities of the dog, although we had a general idea from MAX I's policy on dogs. We had to improvise search plans and patterns, and coordinate evacuation of inmates from housing areas on short notice, with no real idea of how long searches would take. This was an initial experiment. Future projects of this nature should go better.

Facilities should prepare contingency plans, instructing staff just how a dog search should be handled. Extra officers will be needed to thoroughly search areas the dog 'hits.' Details such as where to move prisoners while an area is evacuated for search need to be pre-planned. Large facilities need to prioritize search areas—the entire facility is usually too large for even 3 or 4 detector dogs to cover in the time available.

This planning should be coordinated with the K-9 staff providing the sweeps, so that general ideas of the time needed to sweep an area, how long the dog can work without resting, etc., can be incorporated in the planning.

If possible, new handlers should tour the facility prior to the search, so they are familiar with the layout and know what to expect. This could be done as a 'courtesy tour for a Department employee' for security reasons, with facility staff not being aware that a dog search is pending.

The search should be as complete a surprise as possible. If a random sweep program is established, dog-handler teams simply appear at an institution and search without warning, on a random basis.

Conduct seaches frequently. The impact of a search is lost if prisoners feel "it's a one-time shot." As an alternative to the single-sweep method (covering as much area as possible at one time) more frequent searches of smaller areas will not tire the dogs and will prevent massive disruptions of facility operations. *Searching one wing, mod, unit, or work area at a time is easier on everybody, and more frequent searches of different areas at random will prevent the prisoners, and corrupt staff members, from considering themselves safe for a time after a search.*

Urinalysis of inmates whose property caused a detector dog to alert frequently gives results indicating drug ingestion.

———————■

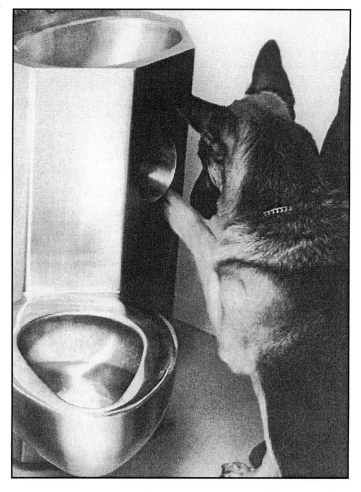

Searching one wing, mod, unit, or work area at a time is easier on everybody, and more frequent searches of different areas at random will prevent the prisoners, and corrupt staff members, from considering themselves safe for a time after a search.

THE GREAT ESCAPE

Escapes are unusual occurrences at most institutions and camps. As a result, the prison dog handler may feel as if he is merely training to train. He may privately wish a prisoner would make a break in order to experience a real search. Or to validate his training. The military deals with this dilemma every day. Police dog handlers typically do not have this problem, because in the world at large offenders are free, initially, to flee buildings or vehicles. So they do. By contrast the incarcerated person is supposed to be secured or under surveillance. Escape requires diligent effort.

Corrections regards an escape as a system failure. Until the system actually fails, there is little incentive to practice repair (the government does not normally fund preventive maintenance). Immediately after an escape, new razor wire goes up, fences are mended, holes filled in, new detectors are installed, personnel shift, funds shift, there may be a brief period of attention to prevention, then daily life returns to the institution with demands that supersede emergency preparedness training.

Few prisons devote enough training time to escape scenarios. Lack of funding and personnel are the most frequently cited reasons. Preparedness requires a strong collective resolve on the part of both the administration at the highest level and the tactical personnel, including the dog handlers. The money and time must be set aside and held inviolable for this purpose. The training must be of such quality that, even if they never work an actual escape during their K-9 careers, the officers will feel confident and ready. If the department cannot provide this level of training, the prison should exclude fugitive search and apprehension from the K-9 program. Instead they may rely upon the nearest law enforcement agencies for mutual aid.

From a tactical standpoint, felony searching is an order of magnitude more demanding than routine prison duty inside the walls. Ideally, the handler will have the psychological advantage of understanding how his adversary thinks, probably a more comprehensive understanding than the cop on the outside. The handler may even *know* his adversary. However, *the movement and the reliance on the dog to locate the adversary* are the critical components that can only be learned by field work.

Escape training, parole searching, and mutual aid response affect protection trained canines in a positive way. Spending substantial time outside performing field searches relieves much of the stress the dog (and the handler) experiences inside the institution. Departments deciding to eliminate escape training and outside agency assists should carefully weigh the pros and cons of deploying aggressive breeds inside. The department may find nonaggressive breeds fill the need for detecting contraband and interfacing with the public.

Police K-9s have caught many fugitives from jails and prisons. Deputy Mike Lydon of Butte County Sheriff's Department, California, had the classic experience. Starting his shift that day, Lydon was a little uneasy. His K-9 was returning to the street after a major operation that left the dog with one kidney. The handler wondered how his partner would perform. Driving his patrol car out the front of the jail complex, he heard radio traffic advising an inmate was going over the fence to the rear of the jail. A custodial officer was chasing him. The inmate was heading toward the freeway at a dead run.

Accelerating around the complex, Lydon drove out through the field between the jail and the freeway. Here came the inmate. He tried to make it to the freeway. The deputy sent his dog. The K-9 hit him head-on. The jail officer slammed into him from behind. Inmate sandwich. In less than five minutes it was over. One in custody. One sheriff's deputy no longer wondering if his dog would perform.

When prison dogs come on line at an institution, escape attempts may drop. If there have been other security upgrades at the same time, it is difficult to say how much the K-9 teams have contributed to the lower statistic.

Many times fleeing inmates are apprehended without direct contact by the dog. When the dog approaches, the inmates give up so fast there is no need for biting.

Doing a fence check at the Northern California Youth Center in Stockton, K-9 handler Bill Buhk saw three wards running south from the facility. Radioing central security, the handler started foot pursuit with his German shepherd Heidi. Security officers from other schools at the center were responding and taking positions around the perimeter of the field. As the wards ran, the handler kept calling to them to give up.

Twice they dived under cover in the wheat field, crawling on their hands and knees. When they disappeared, the dog would locate their track and stay in hot pursuit. Just as Heidi got close, all three gave up, so the handler called off his dog.

The custody facility of a large sheriff's department used to be a small honor farm for a bunch of drunks. That same facility now holds over 30,000 inmates, of whom 25% are pending trial for murder:

> In part of the facility we don't get as many escapes as we get walkaways. The guy is just up there for drugs or lightweight burg. They've got the freedom of the ranch, not behind hard doors, and they just walk away. So if it's a walkaway that is discovered quickly enough, they will send the dog.
>
> We have another jail 10 minutes away from here. Every now and then somebody will climb the fence. They get the bird up and we send a dog up there. The area involves a lot of hillsides and brush. We get out there and search. The helicopter will FLIR (infrared) the thing.
>
> —K-9 Administrator

When does an escape attempt become an escape? Officers radioed an escape in progress from the central kitchen of a major institution. The direction of travel was given as southwest of the kitchen across McNeil Road into the bushes. Another officer reported the inmate was now running from the bushes north across McNeil at Third Street. The K-9 team had arrived at the end of the bushes at Fourth and McNeil. Dog and handler started running toward Third Street.

Seeing the inmate, who was still running north on Third, the handler called, "Don't move or I'll release the dog!" The inmate did not break stride.

The handler released the dog. As soon as the inmate saw the dog approaching, he stopped. Moving behind cover, the K-9 officer called the dog back to a heel and placed him on a slip lead. Meanwhile the inmate was waving a 12-inch butcher knife, saying, "Keep the dog away from me."

"Put down the knife and walk away from it. Do it."

After five commands, the offender complied, lay down on his stomach, and was handcuffed by another officer.

Although technically the inmate never left the borders of the institution, the department concluded he was headed that way and, without the K-9 intervention, would have, however briefly, escaped.

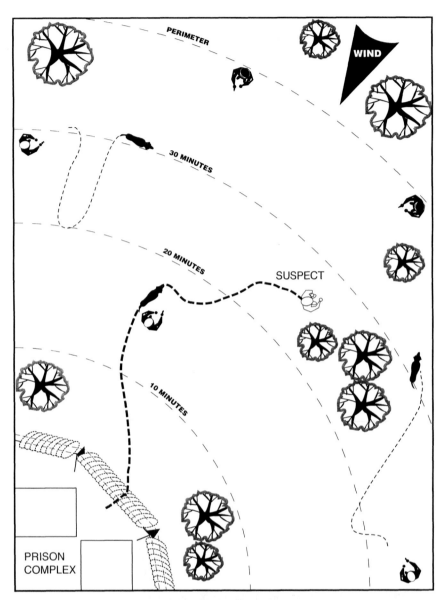

ESCAPE TACTICS

Fugitive search tactics are basically the same for police and prison dog teams. Launching a search from the corrections environment, however, distinguishes 1) the starting strategy and 2) what the fugitive might do.

First, long before corrections officers discover the dummy in the bed or the hole in the fence, every facility has developed a plan for what they intend to do before, during, and after an escape. From the K-9 unit perspective, every escape does not call for a prison dog response. The helicopter snatches the inmate from the yard, for example. The ward hides in a dumpster to make his getaway and gets crushed in a garbage compactor instead, for another example.

As shown by the illustration, current aerial photographs and topographic maps clearly marked with *escape time contours* (radial distance a fleet person can run for fixed intervals) help security place

Create a master map showing how far an athlete can run in all directions from the prison, timed in advance. When a breakout occurs this big picture *will help set realistic perimeters.*

the first perimeter. Revise the map any time the scenery changes around the institution (roadways, buildings, or other features). Obviously there are *leaks* in the plan (inmate runs like hell down the highway and hijacks a car), and no map like this is totally accurate (bare stubble field in the winter, tall cornfield in the summer). Or at Alaska's maximum security prison in Seward, it is deep snow in the winter, moose and grizzly bear in the summer.

If the idea is to field K-9 teams, though, it is better to have a plan for three primary reasons: 1) the dog has efficiency requirements for tracking and air scenting, 2) safety, and 3) explaining to the court what you were doing out there and why you did not find him in time, before he hung himself from a tree as one lifer did.

As soon as the escape is discovered, the department requests *air support and mutual aid from local law enforcement agencies.* At the same time, security officers are manning *perimeter positions.* Remember, the K-9 officer immediately dons his *tactical field gear and checks his dog.* This takes time. Unlike a police officer, the corrections officer has to retrieve his weapons, water, flashlights and other tactical equipment from a secure area. *Cover officers for the K-9 teams must be armed and equally well equipped.* Search teams must have clear *communications on a tactical frequency.* Coordinate *transportation* to the staging area to prevent response delays.

Secure any area where the prisoner was last observed until the canine unit arrives. Do not allow the staff or prisoners to contaminate the area. Once a dog starts searching, do not allow assisting facility staff to forge ahead and either contaminate the track, interfere with the air scent, or risk being mistaken by the dog for the fugitive.

Brief each dog handler as fully as possible about the offender: description (physical, medical, criminal history, survival experience), sentence (does he have anything to lose), status in the local community (friends or relatives outside, access to money, places to stay, places he might hide). It is particularly important to find out the escapee's survival training, prior escape experience, and his knowledge about the local area in order to anticipate what he might do. Two or more inmates escaping together double the danger.

Keeping in mind that many inmates practice deceit as a way of life, condition yourself to maintain a high degree of suspicion about everyone and everything during the search. Cons are artists at changing clothing and appearances, manufacturing weapons, stealing weapons and drugs, and concealing themselves near the action, waiting for opportunity. Some offenders have learned that stealth is the most effective weapon of all.

Especially against search dogs. For this reason safety is the handler's top priority. While other officers are standing at the hole in the fence gazing at the tracks across no-man's-land, do not forget about those bushes 50 yards away. You are exposed. He is concealed. There is a tendency to conclude the offender is trying to get away as far and as fast as he can. Especially after time has elapsed, "The guy's gone. He's outa here."

Escape is a crime, sometimes a crime of opportunity, sometimes premeditated. The fugitive might have good reason to stay close to the location where he disappeared. Perhaps revenge, a stash, a confederate. Perhaps simple fear. Fear motivates but also paralyzes.

Fear emits scent too. Believe your dog if he is tracking away from the scene of the escape and suddenly alerts off to one side. Conduct felony searching—tracking and air scenting—off lead, employing the safest possible tactics of movement and verbal control of the dog.

Attach a clearly labeled field map to every search report. The map can be an original drawing (drawn post-search from field notes and sketches) or an overlay to an existing map. Prepare the map immediately after the search as part of the report to avoid a quagmire of words and to provide accurate recall months or years later in court.

> This date at 1900 hours, I was called out from my residence to report to the prison for mutual aid with our K-9's for an escape in progress. I arrived at 1940, along with the sergeant and the other dog team, and reported to the incident command center. We were briefed by the prison on the two escapees and shown an aerial photograph of the area. We were then briefed on where prison officers were placed and the areas that had and had not been searched. The lieutenant, who is the SWAT commander, requested we use the dogs to clear the large fields to the east of the prison up to the river. This was a large area (1000 acres) they had been unable to search, yet they did have a perimeter guard set up around the area. After a brief discussion of the type of terrain, surrounding areas, weather conditions, it was decided we would work both K-9s from opposite ends, toward the north and south. A high easterly wind was blowing at this time. Conditions were harsh with the wind, rain, cold and lots of mud.

Escapees typically travel near highways, hiding motionless if approached. Use full felony arrest procedures.

Each K-9 team was provided one armed backup officer from the prison. Each backup officer, along with the lieutenant, was briefed on how the K-9s work and what assistance would be needed during the search and during an apprehension, if one occurred. We then proceeded into the fields with the other team (K-9 #2) at the south end, and myself (K-9 #1) at the north end.

After fording a canal filled with water, we began an area search of our assignment. Shortly after deploying, we found two sets of footprints, one barefoot, the other a boot, coming out of the field the two escapees had been seen earlier running into. We decided to follow these tracks and radioed this information to the lieutenant. The tracks led back along the east side of the canal, down into the water at the northwest corner, and up to the railroad tracks running east-west, parallel to the prison on its north boundary. We continued to work these tracks along the brush and tree lines bordering the railroad tracks up to the river.

Meanwhile, K-9 #2 continued searching the field. Farther away, they located the footprints, confirming by direction of travel they were those we had found exiting the field. A search of the railroad tracks and surroundings along the banks of the river on both the east and west side proved negative. We then searched the railroad tracks from the east end from the river to Kelly Road on the north side of the tracks. The K-9s found nothing further, and we returned to the command center.

At this time, there was a strong feeling the two inmates had hopped one of several freight trains that had passed through and were holed up somewhere, and that the dogs should be called out of the search until there were more leads to go on.

At 0230 hours, it was reported both inmates were apprehended along the railroad tracks approximately fifteen miles south at the city's railroad yard.

—Escape report

Coordinated action among different search units—the leapfrog technique—typically has the best chance of success.

"At 1420 hours this date, central security was notified of an institution forestry crew escapee. The inmate escaped from a soil conservation work crew at Lowell. I was directed by the sergeant to go to the escape area with my dog. The inmate was believed to have crossed the river north of the work site.

"Arriving at the site, I contacted the crew chief who said he had located where the inmate had crossed the river and attempted to come out of the river bottom. He had lost the inmate's tracks and was not sure what direction he headed.

"My dog and I searched a large barn near the location as well as some tall weeds to ensure the inmate was not hiding in the immediate vicinity. The K-9 cleared the area with no results.

"At this time, I noticed an area in the drainage farther downriver where it appeared someone had gone through the tall grass and matted it down. Following the matted grass, we located the prints of a forestry-type boot heading west through a grape vineyard. The dog and I continued tracking, accompanied by one cover officer, while the chief of security returned to his vehicle and drove ahead of us, searching visually. The tracks continued on through a second vineyard. We were joined by two officers who started leapfrogging ahead of us to gain ground on the escapee.

"At this point, the chief of security began placing arriving units along the river up toward the freeway attempting to get a sighting. Throughout the escape, we were assisted by patrol units of the sheriff's department whenever it appeared the inmate might be headed toward any buildings or residences in the area.

"We continued tracking the inmate along the river's edge on the north bank heading west. A second K-9 team began a search of the river bank from the freeway, heading east toward the inmate's direction of travel. The escape units were now being assisted by a St. Stevens Medivac Helicopter that began to fly between the K-9 teams on the ground along the river.

"At 1653 hours, the second K-9 team sighted the escapee on the north bank of the river approximately 3/4 mile above the freeway bridge, running east away from him. We responded to the area via a sheriff's patrol unit to assist the K-9 team in the chase. The helicopter flew overhead attempting to keep the inmate down and immobile.

"Arriving at the location, I began assisting the second K-9 team with a search of the brushy river drainage, as the inmate had disappeared from sight. The second K-9 alerted on the inmate, who was now across the river, and swam the river toward him. The inmate, seeing the dog enter the river after him, began waving his hands to surrender.

"It was not possible for the helicopter to land on that side of the river, and access by ground would have been extended, so the handler commanded his dog down to watch the inmate while he waded the river. After he got across, I followed with my dog. The river had many holes and was thigh deep in places. The inmate was taken into custody. We hiked out and transported him back to the prison.

"The entire escape covered about 12 miles. My dog tracked approximately 4 of those miles where the tracks were not visible. When the second team located the inmate, the dog obeyed the commands and did not make physical contact with the inmate. Seven agencies were involved in the search."

Where searchers are mantracking an escapee, K-9 teams can be sent out ahead to work back, another leapfrog maneuver. If the units fail to find the fugitive, perimeter units may be moved, areas re-searched or expanded.

Our two K-9 teams were dispatched this date to assist a prison work camp with an escape near the lake. We left the central facility at 1725 hours, arriving at ranger headquarters at the lake at 1805.

Directed to the work site staging area where the inmate had departed at 1600, we waited for 30 minutes, unable to meet with staff due to poor radio communications. Making contact with another staff member, we were taken to an area where tracks had been located. At that time, I was informed a staff member had a good set of tracks heading to the water line at the lake's edge.

We were joined by two officers who started leapfrogging ahead of us to gain ground on the escapee.

We decided to go to the area ahead of the mantrackers and work the dogs back, to box off and clear the area. The area we searched with the dogs contained tall grass, caves near the shoreline, and heavy brush leading to the back of a mobile home park.

Ten minutes after we started, at 1855 hours, my dog alerted about 100 yards away into a heavy brush and rock outcropping. As I approached and worked the K-9 into the brush, I spotted the inmate hiding in the rocks. I called to him to freeze. At this point my dog came out of the brush heading toward the inmate. Seeing the dog, he raised his hands to surrender. I called the dog off. I told the inmate to put his hands on his head. Placing the dog on a down, I handcuffed the inmate and searched him. In custody at 1905, he was taken to the prison for lockup.

—Escape report

Integrating citizen sightings into the search process can bring quick resolution of the escape.

"At 1933 hours, I responded to an officer's call that she was observing an escape in progress from the prison industries complex toward Oldtown Road. Requesting they get a helicopter airborne, I responded via vehicle to the area of Oldtown Road and Slater Street. I then continued on to the area of Post #3 on institution property.

"Dispatch said the subject had run into the tree line on the east side of Oldtown Road and institution property. The sergeant radioed me to begin a search of the tree line. My dog and I began searching south from Post #3 toward Slater Road. At this point, we had contained the treeline.

"While searching the treeline, dispatch received information from a citizen that the subject had just run through their yard and out into the field on the west side of Oldtown Road. Two officers entered the reporting party's property on the east side from Oldtown Road. I teamed up with another officer, and we drove around the homes on Oldtown Road, effectively closing off the west end of the field behind the reporting party's property.

"After securing the field, I gave an announcement that I was a correctional officer with a dog, and that if the subject did not surrender and show me his hands, I would enter the field with the dog. After waiting 30 seconds and receiving no response, I entered the field. The field was contained by institution staff, who remained in their vehicles. I made a pass across the north end of the field heading east.

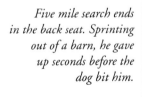

Five mile search ends in the back seat. Sprinting out of a barn, he gave up seconds before the dog bit him.

"Sweeping back to the west, my dog alerted to the southwest corner of the field approximately 200 yards away toward a blue plastic tarp next to a pile of barrels. Commanding the dog down, I approached the tarp, pulled it back, and found the escapee lying face-up on his back. I ordered the inmate to roll over onto his stomach and place his hands on his back, then I hooked my dog on lead. I instructed the inmate not to make any moves as the dog would bite him. My cover officer handcuffed and searched him. The inmate was in full custody at 1942 hours."

The decision to recall the dog versus commanding him to go to source is the handler's responsibility. It is the handler who will have to articulate the reasons for his actions, provided he is alive to do so. In this case, injury to all parties, the handler, the cover officer, perimeter units, and not least the dog was averted. Had the inmate been lying on his back, weapon in hand, ready for that tarp to be pulled back, the handler, even with gun aimed, could easily have been killed. The dog could not have protected him. Had the dog been commanded to apprehend whatever was under the tarp, the dog could have been killed.

It was the third day of an escape search involving dozens of corrections officers, highway patrol officers, sheriff's deputies, and two helicopters. The search area covered almost 200 square miles and two townships with rough undeveloped terrain and scattered housing. The escaped felon, who had extensive survival experience, had walked away from a work camp at night and disappeared into the thick oak, berry brush, and steep rocky hills, leaving behind no detectable track and no probable direction of travel. The inmate had been everywhere throughout the camp and the surrounding area, his scent mixing with that of the officers and other inmates. The sheets on his bed lay fresh and untouched that night. All his personal belongings were gone. Officers were following up all citizen sightings, but public anxiety resulted in numerous false calls, sometimes putting the man in two places at once.

By the third day, the fugitive was believed to have performed at least two burglaries, taking a backpack, clothing, food, survival gear including a stove, a 22-calibre pistol, a .45 automatic, a sawed-off shotgun and ammunition, and a large cache of drugs, including marijuana, methamphetamine, and heroin (reported by a citizen who was more afraid of getting caught by the criminal than by the police). That day a police K-9 team and cover officer carrying a rifle started at first light searching yards, woods, vacant buildings, and homes in the vicinity of the highest probability sightings.

At 1330, in response to a sighting of a bicyclist wearing blue jeans and a T-shirt with a backpack pedalling fast down Clinton Road, the K-9 and other teams jumped in a patrol car to find him. After an hour of high speed driving, nobody saw the subject.

Meanwhile a highway patrol officer took the report of a motorist driving up Highway 88 who had seen a tall figure dressed in camouflage pants and carrying a backpack standing in a small meadow near a creek south of the highway.

Ten minutes later the dog team responded to the area, entering the creek drainage from the highway. Instantly, the K-9 alerted in the meadow, put his nose down, and began tracking upstream to a talus pile. Crossing the creek, he headed uphill through the woods toward the southwest. A few minutes later, the dog lifted his head from the track and began working air scent. He went straight uphill.

Following the dog at a fast pace for several hundred yards, the handler kept looking up. Finally, about 50 yards ahead of the dog the handler saw what appeared to be a *disembodied human head* placed on the ground, eyes staring straight ahead.

At the same time the handler saw the dog break into a run toward the head, growling. Calling the K-9 off and back to a heel, the team took cover. Shouting at the head from 25 yards away produced no visible response. Moving across behind another boulder, the handler was relieved to see that the subject's body, still attached to its head, was in a deep hole next to an uprooted stump.

It was the missing inmate, so far out on drugs that he had not even blinked at the police dog. The officers shouted for him to show his hands. He showed no motor response at all. The dog would have targeted the head. It took four officers to lift the slack body out of the hole, cuff him, and haul him out to the highway. The doctor at the hospital reported the find probably saved his life.

Searches that end with an uncompliant but unmoving subject are common in law enforcement. Prison inmates in particular frequently react, or rather fail to react, this way. Although the offender may not have taken any drugs, he may fail to respond. What should the K-9 officer do? Send the dog?

The answer has two parts. First, and this is difficult for inexperienced officers to accept, there is no prescription, no hard-and-fast rule telling officers what to do. Real life incidents are complex, and they call for intelligence and street sense in equal parts. *The officer has to make a judgment.* Second, *the officer has to articulate that judgment.* Mere passive resistance where there is no articulable threat does not justify sending the dog to bite someone. Use the dog or whatever measures you believe are necessary to counteract a threat you can describe. In the end, the handler, the cover officer, or someone has to move in and take the person into custody. No dog can make an arrest all by himself.

PAROLE & PROBATION

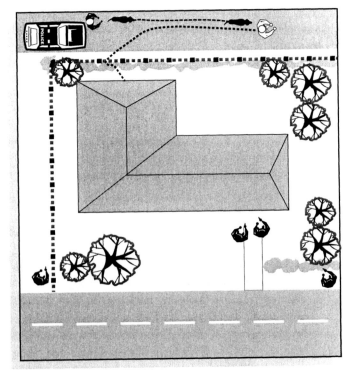

Parole knocks at the front, parolee goes out the back, K-9 is waiting in the alley.

The probation department in Santa Barbara County, California, initiated a two K-9 team program that conducted 264 narcotic searches in the first year of operation. Sixty-six offenders were arrested for drug violations as a result of the searches. Asset seizures totalled over $975,064 and 43 weapons. There were 92 controlled substance seizures. Other California counties deploying drug detector dogs with probation officers include Madera, King, Orange, and San Diego. Probation and parole agencies have even borrowed narcotic detector dogs for operations across state lines.

The task force concept has made it possible for departments that cannot fund detector dogs on their own to have their services available as needed. Prison dogs can be effective performing outside agency assists. For these operations, full safety and tactical equipment is necessary, the handler needs to be briefed and debriefed along with the parole and patrol officers, participating officers need to be briefed about how the dog works, and the parole officers themselves must have the required training in officer safety tactics.

A mile behind landscaped, middle income homes, where the highway curves to a plateau, a dirt road leads east through piñon pine that used to be high desert wilderness. Residents to the west probably still think of it that way. Purple lupine flowers and deer, clear streams running through the red rock, foxes and coyote, and the occasional bear. The parole officer driving through the rocks and dust knows it isn't so. This federal land now bears the fruit of a social system out of control. Filthy trailers parked at random in hundreds of acres of scrub pine hacked almost to death. Mangy dogs tearing at old sofas and mattresses. Stacks of deer carcasses, black hooves jabbing at the sky.

Out of these trailers unspeakable toxins leak into open ditches. Human waste, battery acid, motor oil, and the residual chemicals of methamphetamine labs or, for drug users whose brains cannot follow a recipe, would-be meth labs. The man the parole agent has come to see has one of those brains. After doing hard time in the neighboring state, he moved here to set up another drug operation.

The agent steps up the rickety platform to the front door of the trailer and knocks. She hears scrambling in the rear of the trailer. Finally, the door opens to a heavyset wreck of a woman in her early twenties, six months pregnant. She insists the parolee isn't there, but the agent knows otherwise from an informant. Forcibly moving the female, the agent gets past her and finds the man buck naked in the filthy refuse of the back bedroom. More task force officers roll into the site, keeping the two people under observation outside while a narcotic dog team begins searching the debris inside the trailer.

It is a disgusting job, but the happy Labrador blows up in the little side bedroom, obviously used for preparing narcotics. He alerts to a hash pipe and some white residue, then stands on his hind legs sniffing toward the walls, upper shelves, the ceiling. A card table and workbench hold scales, pipes, tools, radios and tapes, a PDR. Even the officers can smell marijuana and acrid chemicals.

Based on a rock taken off the man, the pipes the dog finds, and the dog's strong alerts, they arrest the parolee and begin prying paneling off the walls. Duct tape, rough boards, and nails everywhere indicate the paneling has been removed many times in the past. The handler comments that in his experience meth users keep their supply handy, hoarding it so nobody will steal it, also so they can remember where it is. Despite the dog sniffing all the junk in the trailer, sheds, old vehicles, dirt piles, and stinking refuse on the property, they find no more drugs.

Until the handler says, hey, why isn't the female hooked up, and they walk her out to a marked sheriff's unit to arrest her for obstructing. The agent proceeds to search her baggy clothing. Every time the agent reaches into a pocket she finds paraphernalia or baggies or bottles or other containers with narcotics. The whole time the K-9 unit was working the trailer and grounds, this woman was sitting loaded outside the trailer. Keeping liability in mind, the handler was careful never to let the dog get close to the offenders or sniff them. More important, the officers could have all paid with their lives for failing to frisk the woman. Was her pregnancy a factor?

The narcotics piled on the hood of the patrol car gave this woman a free ticket to

The officers could have all paid with their lives for failing to frisk the woman. Was her pregnancy a factor?

hospital delivery and neonatal care. Probably future child care and welfare as well. In the end, she complained about the discomfort of having her hands cuffed behind her back, considering her pregnant condition. Despite officer safety considerations, the officer obliged, handcuffing her in front for the ride to the station.

On Thursday this date, my K-9 and I accompanied parole agents to apprehend missing parolees at six locations in two cities. My primary functions were to assure that the suspects did not flee out the back when parole entered the residence and to search for drugs in the residence.

At two of the residences, we found weapons—one butterfly knife and one Rambo-type knife. No drugs were found at these locations.

At one residence, the suspect would not come out. When he found out there was a K-9 present, he turned himself in.

Out of the six stops, we netted three parolees and two stashes of marijuana. One stash was a shoebox of pot packaged for sale. The other was a bureau drawer containing three rocks of cocaine.

For the three-day period indicated, the prison K-9 unit provided two K-9 teams to the state narcotic enforcement bureau in a large-scale drug raid throughout the metropolitan area. A total of 22 separate locations were searched. All entries and search warrant services were performed by the sheriff's department SWAT team, who also secured all locations prior to our entry for drug searches. Our dogs located narcotics with a total estimated street value over $275,000 and were directly responsible for the recovery of over $42,000 in cash. The entire operation was a year long in preparation by undercover agents with the state bureau. A large group of foreign nationals had been making buys with this group for over a year. Our searches assisted them in the apprehension of parties involved as well as narcotic detection.

Contact the NIC Information Center for corrections research, policy formulation, and professional standards. Special collections and publications facilitate networking among administrators in state corrections agencies, jail systems, and community-based corrections; staff trainers in federal, state, and local correctional agencies; and correctional educators.

U.S. Department of Justice
National Institute of Corrections
Information Center
1860 Industrial Circle, Suite A
Longmont, Colorado 80501
(800) 877-1461

CHAPTER 6

EVIDENCE SEARCH

"You do not want the wrong person,

like a kid, finding the gun.

Whoever did this, we can't let him walk."

—Officer at the scene of a homicide

Set up security, access routes, and plan documentation of the search area (or crime scene) and collection of physical evidence before starting the canine search.

Police dogs searching for evidence can reduce the time to clear crime scenes, fugitive escape routes, or other high probability areas. They also increase the probability of detecting evidence in missing person cases.

Typically, the dog alerts to human or other special scent on the article, not to the article itself. If you touch something, human scent transfers to that item. Large or small, a vehicle or a credit card, human scent attaches to the door handle, the car seat, the money, or the underwear. How long the scent may be detected depends on the initial deposition, the environment, the chemistry and surface area of the item.

Plan the K-9 training program to anticipate the types of cases the dogs will most frequently work. Patrol dogs need the ability to find general human scent. Tasks requiring the dog to discriminate for a particular person or chemicals demand greater proficiency, therefore more training. Time (time of day and lapsed time), temperature, weather, *evidence composition, contamination, and concealment* affect scent diffusion. In addition, area size, terrain, hazards, and distractions all affect the level of difficulty. Typical evidence:

- Personal effects (pager, clothing, wallet, credit card, bills, or coins)
- Weapons or projectiles (gun, shell casing, knife)
- Signs of criminal activity (burglary tools, drops of blood or semen, accelerant)
- Dead body (cadaver)

"We were searching for a burglary suspect. The dog had penetrated heavy brush. We could hear him snarling and tearing, but we didn't hear any screaming, grunting, or other human sounds. Finally, the dog backed out of the bushes yanking and tugging a large duffel bag containing a shirt and other clothing. And a gun."

—San Francisco Police K-9 Officer

Dispatch K-9 teams to search for evidence without delay. Get the right team for the right job. The untrained dog "taking a shot at it" can destroy rather than discover evidence. Or the team may not perform a definitive search. Delays work against the dog. Human scent diffuses away from objects with time. Desiccation changes scent. Precipitation washes scent away. Bacteria, insects, rodents, coyotes, raptors or other scavengers plunder evidence. A bear scattered a pilot a mile beyond his wrecked plane the first week after he crashed.

Mills *searches among the charred timbers and bent pipes of Davis Community Church, California, for the origin of a $1 million arson. Investigators called the ATF National Response Team, handler Greg Liddicoat, Deputy State Fire Marshal of Nevada.*

DAVIS ENTERPRISE/ALISON PORTELLO

As perceived by the dog, there are basically three types of evidence, all requiring scent discrimination:

1. Generic human scent
2. Other scents the dog has been trained to detect: gun products and shooting by-products, decomposition chemicals, accelerants, illegal game or fish, agricultural or other contraband [see other chapters for narcotic and explosive detection]
3. Scent matching a scent guide [see other chapter for tracking]

Some dogs can work only one or two types. Of all K-9 teams in service, relatively few maintain type 3: Reliable scent discrimination, based on prescenting, to detect or identify a particular person.

Deep in the animated network of the cell nucleus lies the molecule of heredity, DNA. Its twin spirals are built from four interlocking chemical bases: adenine paired with thymine and cytosine paired with guanine. Code messages, genes, are stored along a chromosome in sequences of these chemical bases. Genes define the unique characteristics of each living thing. It is here, for example, that people are assigned eye color, and dogs are assigned coat color. Except in cases of identical twins, DNA patterns vary distinctively from person to person, creating a *genetic fingerprint* that has become a valuable technique for investigating crimes in which biological clues—white blood cells, hair roots, traces of semen, bone, or other nucleated cells—are left behind.

Experiments indicate that dogs can identify an individual through their recognition of each person's unique *scentprint*. The verification of genetic typing, which has its basis in unique chemical patterning, supports the existence of unique scent, since scent is, after all, only chemicals diffusing through the air to the dog's nose. Complex individual human scent points to the uniqueness of each human scent pattern, like a fingerprint.

Convincing a court that a dog is capable of making this distinction requires accurate training records. The dog establishes credibility through controlled testing based on scent collected from known individuals. After evidence is located at a crime scene, investigators may decide to retain some of the evidence for K-9 discrimination purposes before sending it to a laboratory for analysis. Special materials (adsorbents or absorbents) are used to collect the scent. *To conduct a test, the trained, presented dog sniffs the scent diffusing from a set of controls, including the test subject, in a controlled environment.* Examples: lineup of typical people, including the suspect; array of typical items, including the item of evidence. The court will require adherence to proper testing procedures and training records that show the dog is a reliable instrument to isolate the uniqueness of the scent.

EVIDENCE SEARCH EQUIPMENT

Required handler equipment includes water, plastic gloves, lights, flagging, notebook and a camera. Carry water on your person for the dog. Unless water is at hand, you will typically not water the dog as frequently as he needs to rehydrate. Disposable plastic gloves are the minimum. More protective gloves, masks or clothing depend on the task. The emergency medical services rule: "Do not put your hands where you cannot see."

Multiple flashlights are essential, even for daytime searches. Carry the appropriate flagging, chalk, or other marking systems on your person. Investigators have to be able to locate and identify the flagging after you have completed the K-9 search. Use different marking systems to distinguish search area boundaries from evidence locations. Pocket knives, scissors, clean handkerchiefs, sterile gauze, evidence collection bags, jars and cans are also valuable.

The handler records observations in a notebook or voice recorder. Diagrams and descriptions made at the scene, without distracting or obstructing the dog, will be valuable for the report and for court. A camera with flash and low light capability will be important to the K-9 officer even if investigators or others are photographing the scene. Establish a procedure for shooting that does not interfere with working the K-9. Even if an assisting officer will be taking the shots, give the dog experience in advance around cameras.

TACTICS FOR EVIDENCE SEARCHES

Maintain officer safety. If a K-9 team is searching for an offender and the dog alerts to evidence, the officers have to make an emergency decision. Assess the immediate threat level. If high, redirect the dog to search for the live suspect. Evidence the dog finds may inform officers the suspect has left the area. Locating unexpected evidence, such as a cache of stolen items or a weapon, can change the mission totally.

Experiments indicate that dogs can identify an individual through their recognition of each person's unique scentprint.

Secure the search scene. Do not destroy evidence while trying to detect it. Although this seems obvious, some K-9 officers are lax in their approach to a search scene, particularly after they perceive all danger is past. Cover officers may not provide much support for the evidence search phase after the action is over and the bad guys have been led away in handcuffs. The politics of patrol versus investigations can also make the handler's job harder. The dog figures into this equation as well. After an arrest where the dog found the suspect or contacted the suspect, he may be too excited or too tired to perform an evidence search.

The patrol dog who has just had a nose full of the suspect's scent is actually the best candidate to detect evidence involving that suspect. Rest the dog, give him time out, put him away in the patrol car, remove him from the media or the public. Use that time to plan the evidence search.

If possible, do not assign officers to search areas in advance of the dog team. Every time an officer picks something up and puts it back down, his scent transfers to it. When an officer digs around, moves things, sifts through material, even with gloves on, his scent adheres to those materials. Officers not trained in evidence recovery sometimes destroy latent scent on objects before the dog sniffs them.

Although officers have searched through an area (thus contaminating it), the dog can still work. Be aware, if he is not discriminating for a particular person or item the dog may alert to places other officers have touched.

Designating the search areas and assigning priorities are the basic elements of evidence search strategy:

- Typical search areas include fugitive flight paths, locations where the offender has hidden, extensions of a crime scene, the offender's residence or vehicles, locations provided by a witness or an informant, and public areas where the offender may plan to return later to retrieve evidence.
- If there are multiple areas to search, set the priority for each area. Subdivide large areas.
- The handler must be able to describe precisely each area his dog searches. When setting the boundary, do not contaminate the search area. Distinguish natural landmarks (tree, rock) and manmade landmarks (fence post, light pole) that are part of a search area perimeter from other trees, rocks or posts in the vicinity.
- If more than one K-9 will be searching, assign the areas in order to minimize distractions. Eliminating interference takes priority over searching the highest probability areas first. When the dog's concentration is compromised, he may not search effectively.
- Anticipate the need for special equipment to access areas, dig or retrieve evidence.
- Ensure that investigators are realistic about the dog's capability. After a 15-mile pursuit over a mountain pass at night, an armed robbery suspect was arrested out of his car, but he had tossed the gun. The sergeant on duty dispatched the K-9 team to locate the weapon. The sergeant said it would take about an hour.

The patrol dog who has just had a noseful of the suspect's scent is the best candidate to detect evidence of that suspect. Detection requires fine grid search patterns penetrating the micro-climates of scents vaporizing from small objects.

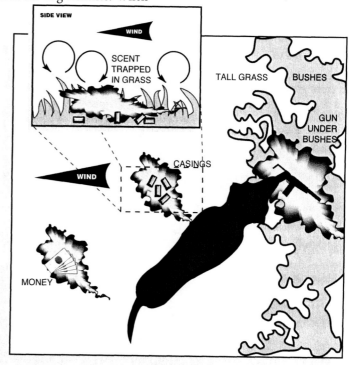

Protect K-9 scent guides from contamination. Use the same collection and security procedures employed to protect other evidence (weapon, article with prints, human tissue or secretions). Pick up the guides with scent-neutral tools (stick, pliers, screwdriver, knife-edge) and store in evidence bags or sterile glass jars at room temperature or colder.

Early one morning deputies attempted to arrest several suspects for narcotic sales. The address on the warrant was a house at the edge of open fields. When the deputies made entry, the suspects fired shots then fled out the rear of the house across the fields. Several were caught immediately. Others disappeared into irrigation ditches and brushy wind breaks heading toward the main highway.

Deputies searching the house found weapons in every room. The suspects in custody said one fugitive had buried a 9mm MAC-11 automatic weapon in a 40-acre field southwest of the house. Sheriff's deputies and one K-9 made several passes over the area but found nothing.

A few days later, after a storm moved through dropping light rain, three other dog teams responded and began searching systematically at the south end of the field into a north wind. Each team worked a separate section of land. Fifteen minutes into the search, one of the police dogs alerted several yards from the missing weapon. Pinpointing the source, the dog found the assault pistol buried under an inch of dirt and sprouting wheat. Officers secured the area to wait for an evidence technician to shoot photos and dust for prints. The gun was loaded and ready to fire.

K-9 EVIDENCE ALERT

The dog's reaction to the pistol was aggressive behavior (digging, scratching, barking, attempting to retrieve). The handler read the dog's behavior as an alert. Other police dogs are trained to perform nonaggressive behavior (sitting, lying down) or a complex of behaviors (sitting and barking). Although the aggressive or actively alerting dog can disturb evidence unless the handler intervenes, the advantages include:

On lead or under close control, the dog works calmly, no hectic behavior, with frequent breaks and appropriate reinforcement. Presenting, with discrimination training, links found objects with the suspect.

Officer Janelle Squires, Kalispell Police Department, Montana

- the alert itself reinforces searching
- the dog tries to go to source to get reinforcement, and his actions typically locate the evidence precisely

At 3 a.m. after a busy night, a police officer had been home asleep an hour when she was called out to a warehouse near the freeway 20 miles north. Containment units were reporting they had "a live one" inside. Driving at high speed, the K-9 officer arrived on scene a short time later, exiting the freeway a block past the warehouse. A chain link fence surrounded the warehouse and its service yard. A witness had seen a man with a ball cap trying to force entry into the main building. The witness immediately called police. He was sure nobody had come out through the front gate.

Two officers walked to the entry door with the K-9 team. On the ground in front of the door lay a ball cap and bolt cutters. The dog sniffed the cap.

There is one problem, said the handler. This door is locked. The padlock was in fact secure.

No problem, said the assisting officer, I'll cut it open, and he proceeded to cut the lock with the bolt cutters.

For drill the K-9 team made entry and cleared the building. Afterward the team was searching through equipment stored outside the warehouse when the dog leaped off a platform into a vat of axle grease. The handler now had a police dog covered with axle grease.

Completing the search, they moved out toward the fence. Halfway across the yard, the shepherd lifted his big head, alerted, and trotted toward the fence bordering the freeway. Jumping against the fence in the darkness, he grabbed something and ran back carrying a work glove.

To avoid climbing over triple-strand barbed wire on top of the chain link fence, the team passed outside the enclosure and proceeded north through the landscaping along the freeway.

As soon as the dog cast downwind of the first glove, he alerted again and dived into the shrubbery. The handler expected yelling or worse. Nothing. Just the dog's tail wagging as

he backed out of the shrubs with a second glove in his mouth.

The suspect had apparently fled across the freeway. The handler commented she probably came close to running over the suspect on her way to the call.

CADAVER SEARCH TACTICS

Dogs trained to alert to generic human scent typically transfer this recognition to recently dead or even long dead persons. Annie Lerum, search dog handler and trainer, commented in the *SAR Dog Alert:* "Because of current laws governing the disposal and dispersal of remains, they become difficult if not impossible to procure for training. Time after time on real-life searches, dogs that have only experienced live finds in the past easily and consistently alert on dead bodies. The alert will often differ from a live find, but the dogs still have no problem working this scent."

Treat all firearms as if they are loaded. Beware of improvised explosive devices (IEDs). Reconstructing the crime scene may involve determining what happened in 1 event (shooting distances, weapons, projectiles) or a sequence of events (bloodstain patterns).

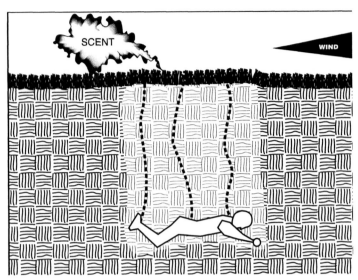

Regrowth or surface cultivation conceals grave sites. Irregular terrain conceals depressions or mounding. Once digging begins, loose material, rock scars, or substrate disturbance may indicate a burial site. Train with hydrogen sulfide, hydrogen phosphide, carbon dioxide, ammonia, and methane gases (decomposition). Sniff probe hole patterns in dirt (steel roads, shovel blades) or holes drilled in concrete.

The same is true for evidence work. You need not expose your dog to every possible article in order for the dog to find a specific one on a search. Research indicates that after a certain point of decay the proteins that make up our bodies break down to form simple proteins. These simple proteins are the same in humans as in animals. The rate of deterioration depends on many environmental factors. Old bones are difficult to identify in the field as human or animal. The crime lab may request a forensic anthropologist to make the determination.

On a bone search in a national park, Lerum's dog found 20 bones. The body was believed to have been dumped there one to three years earlier, and the search area was a popular feeding ground for animals. The dog's alerts on all the bones were very similar. In most cases park rangers could not tell the difference in the field between human and animal bones. There was no skull. Later, about half the bones were determined to be of human origin, but the dog's reaction did not differentiate among the bones.

Trooper Andy Rebman of the Connecticut State Police, who teaches cadaver detection, points out that a person changes from live, to freshly dead, to "full-bloom" putrefaction, to a skeleton. The time it takes a body to "melt down" depends on the time of year, the weather, and the deposition materials. Decomposition slows down if a body is buried, generally giving it a "longer shelf life." The slower diffusion rate, however, may force the dog to detail the area to locate the body. The available information is largely anecdotal because few scientific studies have been conducted. In most cases where trained dogs have made finds, even bleached bones at high altitude in Wyoming, the handlers have been able to read their alerts.

Wear gloves when working with any of these substances. Chemical byproducts include the hazardous materials putrescine and cadaverine. During the putrefaction of flesh, cadaverine is the syrupy colorless poisonous ptomaine formed by the decarboxylation of lysine. Also poisonous, putrescine, the crystalline substance formed by decarboxylation of ornithine occurs in putrid flesh. Carbon dioxide, hydrogen sulfide, and methane are gas products of decomposition. Rising through the soil, these gases are carried by the prevailing air currents. Scent travels at the speed of the wind and tends to pool and remain in low or sheltered areas. These gases are water soluble, so ground moisture and light rain help the air scenting dog.

In the language of forensic anthropology, there are three types of burials:
- PRIMARY INTERMENTS: Bones lie in anatomical relationship approximating the normal bone articulation when the person was alive
- SECONDARY INTERMENTS: Bones are collected after the decomposition of soft flesh then buried
- MULTIPLE INTERMENTS: Several bodies located in one grave

Police investigators have to deal with a fourth type as well:
- DISMEMBERED INTERMENTS: Bodies are cut apart and the parts buried separately

The four layers of interest to the K-9 team:
1. Surface of the grave exposed to the world
2. Fill above the body
3. Buried body and associated artifacts
4. Substrate or natural soils below the grave itself

When a body is in deep burial, below four feet, it is usually in long term storage and changes are relatively slow. Surface-laying or shallow-buried bodies may deteriorate rapidly depending on the climate and other environmental conditions.

The advantages of deploying air scenting dogs to locate interments are they are inexpensive, rapid and definitive in covering relatively large areas, they do not damage subsurface evidence and do minimal damage to surface evidence. Dogs adapt to many types of terrain, and they can work in most weather conditions. The K-9 search is not intrusive since there is little or no penetration of the ground surface. Dog teams are easy to manage and supervise, can be used day or night, or after other search methods have failed. They can sometimes detect a snow- or water-covered body or burial site (covered in the rescue chapter). K-9s can be brought in to re-sniff an area periodically without mounting a major search effort each time.

The disadvantages are the limited availability of trained dogs, the burial must be fresh or decomposition must be underway, and dogs have limited reliability in extreme weather. Gale force winds, intense heat, or heavy rain tending to wash scent into the substrata represent poor scenting conditions. Besides the danger of hazardous materials, frequently sewage systems, swamps, and manure sumps generate false alerts. Organic decomposition releasing methane and other gases, or inorganic toxins may produce anosmia. The dog handler wishes for safe moist ground, loose soil texture, a light breeze to move the scent, and cool air temperatures.

LOOK FOR
- mounds or depressions
- loose soil, sand, gravel
- disturbed or displaced earth, rocks, vegetation
- ground markings or tracks
- scraped or broken rock
- area hidden from view
- ease of access (serial and other type killers revisit sites)
- available concealment (structures, natural features)
- recent construction (unusual size, location, design)
- unusual signs (cults, gangs, markers to help killer relocate site)
- unusual materials (transport, storage of remains)
- unusual odors or colors (masking chemicals, decomposition catalyst)
- unusual activity (person watching the investigation)

Searching a broad, sandy floodplain for a missing little girl, the handler noticed a white male drive by the area in a gray jeep. She noticed him because he appeared 4 times in the same vehicle during the 3-day search, and each time he slowed to a stop and watched for several minutes as she worked the dog. The third day, when her dog located the child's remains at the base of a bridge, he was gone.

Desperate for clues, investigators decided to suppress information about the find and field the canine team again. It worked. Along came the gray jeep. The driver was not happy to see the investigators.

August 1995, Larry Moore, a former West Yellowstone contractor, led authorities to the body of Brad Brisbin, a sheriff's deputy whom he was convicted of killing in 1990. The only person ever convicted in Montana in a bodiless murder case, Moore is serving a 60-year sentence in the Montana State Prison. He disclosed the location of the body and directed Gallatin County Sheriff Bill Slaughter to the murder weapon as part of a plea

At a homicide, avoid focusing on the body. Search the entire scene systematically. Watching where the dog sniffs could determine a bloodstain pattern, a place the offender touched, or body secretions, such as semen. Fogging or hydrating an area may enhance scenting.

bargain concerning his role in a bombing plot at the prison earlier this year.

DNA from bits of human tissue found in the pickup camper where Brisbin was supposedly shot November 1990 was used to convict Moore.

The body with a wallet and ID were buried 5 feet deep in a narrow trench at the corner of a 10-acre gravel pit. Before his trial, Moore had repeatedly driven a white Cadillac past the areas dog teams were searching. The .357 pistol was 2 feet deep under a tree on the east side of U.S. 191 about 10 miles away.

As winter hit one of the northern states, a graduate student telephoned police saying he had murdered his girlfriend in a jealous rage two weeks before. The student claimed he stuffed the clothed body into a garbage bag and put it in a dumpster near the university. After calling the police, he killed himself.

All the city garbage is trucked to a major dump site west of town. It is immense, hundreds of acres of rotting refuse piled 40 feet high. Since it is a port city, fish offal contributes to the scent picture. Based on the date of her disappearance, the young woman's body could be buried as deep as 18 feet. Police faced the prospect of sorting through tons of rank material.

The question to be asked in this type of case is how effective can a dog be, even a dog trained to detect cadavers in debris? The area is large, the scent picture complex. What are the chances of success? To answer the question the agency must weigh the potential for success against the cost in dollars and risk. There is significant risk of disease or injury to the handler and dog. Deployment under these circumstances demands justification.

MURDER INVESTIGATIONS

The Half Moon Bay *Review* reported that police suspected Ronald Middleton of killing longtime resident Henry Olson, who ran a carpet cleaning business in the oceanside community. Investigating Olson's disappearance, officers served a search warrant for Middleton's home on the 10-acre rural property he leased 6 miles from the coast. Executing the warrant, police discovered an indoor marijuana grow with $4300 worth of rotating grow lights, a thermostat-controlled heating system, and more than 200 plants of a potent Hawaiian seed stock. Three plants were over 10 feet tall.

The property lay in rolling coastal meadows at the base of higher hills. The suspect, in a week, had the orchard rototilled, had hired people to clear areas of grass, and had dug around the house. He said it was fire prevention. He hired a tractor to plow different areas and to put a pond in a drainage off Purissima Creek. That summer the pond site was dry, waiting for the winter runoff to pool against the new earth dam.

Suspecting Olson's body was somewhere on the property, police requested search dog teams from the California Rescue Dog Association. The responding handlers, Shirley Hammond, Eva Cecil, and Adela Morris and their Doberman pinschers were assigned various areas to detail. They were on the lookout for mounds, depressions, discard piles, or other evidence of a burial site. The time from Olson's disappearance to the K-9 search spanned almost a month, late July to August 23rd.

Working the pond dam, Shirley's dog Spice alerted, giving the typical signs: sniffing the ground, digging, and lifting her head to sniff as high as she could. Then they brought Adela's Brandy in, who also indicated. The third dog Shasta also showed interest in the area the first two dogs had indicated, but she went around to the downhill side of the dam and started to tunnel there.

On the basis of the three canine alerts, the department brought in a front end loader which started digging up the area. Each time they uncovered another layer of rock and dirt, they stopped and called a handler over from another assignment to re-check the site. The dogs' alerts intensified.

Although there was a slight downhill draft with some vertical movement, the air flow over the pond area was calm to light. The air temperature during the search was estimated in the 70's.

Biological materials degrade with time. This process is accelerated when items are wet and sealed in airtight containers, such as plastic bags.

Surface temperatures in the dam area, which was rapidly turning into a pit, were much higher. The cat driver was sweating. Searchers had stripped to their T-shirts.

Farther down, to everyone's surprise, they uncovered construction-type garbage: flashing, gypsum board, insulation. Up to this point everybody was excited. A dozen officers from different agencies stood watching intently. Then they got into real garbage. In the scrap were a couple of plastic grocery sacks filled with rotten meat. When they got to the sacks of meat, some officers walked away saying, aagh, it's just garbage.

Hammond, however, had many years' experience working search missions, including major disasters and serial killings. Her first dog had found charred bones at the infamous Wilseyville site in Calaveras County, California, where a serial killer had butchered people then used a magnesium-like compound to incinerate the parts. Searching hillsides with pungent mountain misery in full bloom, "The dogs would poke their noses down in the stuff and come up with a question on their faces, walk farther, poke their nose down, then look at us like, hey. So we started looking every place they put their noses down, and every place they put their noses down we'd see a piece of charcoal. Handler Peggy Emrey picked up one of the pieces and said, my god it's a scapula. The paper said they ended up with 43 grocery bags of bones. One find was in a chicken pen, about 26 inches deep, the body encased in lime."

So when they discovered the putrefying meat on the Olson search, Hammond asked, "Why would somebody do this?" They dug the garbage out of the pit. While they were clearing the debris, the dog teams were working several different areas of interest elsewhere on the property.

"I was searching the creek bed when they called and said you need to come back to check the area again. They had removed the meat. I put Spice back in the area, into the hole, and sniff, sniff, sniff. Then she turned, came out of the hole, jumped up onto the bank where the meat bags were, sniffed the pile, and lowered her shoulder like she was going to roll in it. I made a noise. With that she whirled around, came back into the hole and dug again. To me she had eliminated that bag of stuff, said no, that's not what she was looking for." The dog's reactions were typical: sniffing and pawing the dirt, giving the body language, scenting up into the trees.

Beneath, the loader uncovered a 4X8 sheet of plywood. Breaking that apart, they saw the body of the victim rolled up inside a tube of carpet. A carpet cleaner buried in a 20-foot roll of carpet. The body was recognizable. Searchers could see the man's tattoo when they removed the carpet. His company shirt had a readable logo. His head was bagged. He had been shot in the head, and the murderer probably bagged it to contain the dripping fluids.

By the time they dug up the body, they had effectively destroyed the earthen dam. It was a deep find. From the top of the dike, the body was buried 10 feet vertically and 10-15 feet laterally from the outside low point where the third dog began digging into the dam.

"I think the killer's actions helped, instead of hindered, the dogs. The things he did to camouflage the body (construction materials, meat) actually called it to their attention." Rather than acting as a barrier, the debris created voids for scent diffusion. The rotten meat proved a distraction for some of the investigators but did not stop the detector dogs.

COMPANY MEADOWS

Rudiger "Rudy" Hack was very well liked in the Amador County town where he lived. His disappearance that November, a bloody garage and other evidence of a homicide indicated a suspect and started a search for Rudy's body that lasted five months and covered five counties in California and Nevada. The killer had only a few hours' driving time to dump the body between leaving the scene and showing up at an address near Lake Tahoe.

Days after the incident, in the season's first snowstorm, climbers from three agencies and a K-9 team gathered at the top of Carson Pass Spur in a whiteout. Tire tracks and footprints

"I think the killer's actions helped, instead of hindered, the dogs. The things he did to camouflage the body (construction materials, meat) actually called it to their attention."

Hobo alerts to dismembered torso of Rudy Hack, Company Meadows, Alpine County. Biological material must be considered hazardous. Follow universal precautions for handling stains or biological materials.

matching the suspect's had led searchers to the cliffs at 8000 feet along Highway 88 overlooking the old Kirkwood dumpsite. It was possible the suspect had shoved the body off one of these cliffs, figuring no agency would consider rappeling four hundred feet straight down to investigate.

The weather interfered with the investigation more than the geography. Teams rappeling down into the couloirs where a body could have been thrown set off fresh snow slides. The dog triggered his own avalanche that sent him riding over a 60-foot cliff. But he came up swimming and kept on searching. Searchers found nothing but bedsprings and old tin cans. In a few hours they were forced out by the storm.

Mid-winter saw the same crew together with avalanche hunter Dick Reuter directing the search across the higher ledges of Carson Spur. Reuter shot snow off the ledges with explosives. They found an old tarp but no body.

As a result of another murder charge and plea bargaining, searchers looking for Rudy Hack had new clues when the suspect, Jerry Taylor, admitted he dismembered and buried the body on Leviathan Peak in Alpine County. A late March snowstorm found deputies and detectives from two agencies, Caltrans highway crews, and the K-9 team driving snow machines seven miles from snow line to Company Meadows at 8200 feet.

"The guy's attitude was incredible," one of the deputies yelled over the engines. "First he had us drive past that area down there," pointing at cliffs to the south. "He led us over the pass then back down past here on a wild goose chase. He was trying to get us to promise him a contact visit with his wife and kid. Finally we came to an understanding. He took us to the place we're headed. He said he buried the torso under some trees. He buried the feet, the hands, and the head in five different places. Absolutely no emotion. Just matter-of-fact, like it was sort of interesting to him. Like he was proud of having done the whole thing."

Taylor could not pinpoint the sites because everything had changed from November with bare ground, to March with three feet of snow. The man had lied so often, it was hard to believe his story.

When the searchers reached the area, wind and snow blew across the high plateau. After the long ride, the handler let the dog air out his nose and relieve himself. A deputy showed her the aspen grove where the suspect had indicated he buried the torso. Picking up a shovel, the handler deployed the dog about 50 yards downhill from the target area the detectives had flagged.

The mid-morning air temperature was zero degrees Fahrenheit, winds erratic, gusting to 25 miles per hour. Working the crusty snow in a pattern ahead, the dog lifted his tail almost at once, straining toward the aspen. The handler released him, and he trotted to a lumpy, yard-square area and began sniffing intently. This was a campsite often used by deer hunters in the fall.

The dog needed no encouragement. He began moving snow, dirt and stones with both paws.

He paused to sniff, relocated to the north, then resumed digging. As he shoved his nose under football-sized rocks, the handler pried them loose with the shovel and dug beside the dog. About a foot down, she felt the blade hit something soft.

Clearing dirt, she saw pink flesh. She reinforced the dog and moved away from the hole to let other officers take over digging. As the other deputies approached, the dog started to defend his find, so the handler let him sniff the body again then distracted him away from the site.

After getting water, they were ready to search again. The easy part was over. They had a torso.

To identify the body they wanted a head for forensic dentistry or hands for prints. Investigators showed the handler where Taylor indicated he had buried the extremities, an area the size of several football fields now lying under 2-3 feet of wind slab snow. The temperature had dropped. The wind was gusting to 40 miles per hour as another storm rolled across the Sierra. Several officers were cold.

The dog was active and frisky. He worked steadily, nose down. In one spot, he sniffed hard, pawed briefly, then drifted, nose down, in a wide circle. The handler turned snow with the shovel. The dog worked back in. He developed the same unfocused reaction. The handler and dog moved off to search elsewhere while shovelers removed several yards of snow. When brought back in, the dog gave the same reaction. Despite repeated sniffing, he could not go to source. The icy slabs were so hard, shovelers were wishing for pickaxes. The handler knew if her K-9 did not find the head, he was less likely to find the hands. There was no sign of animal activity in the area.

The Caltrans driver suggested blading snow away with his snowcat. Although compaction and exhaust fumes were negative factors, the storm was getting worse fast, and it was clear they could not move enough snow and earth with hand tools alone. While the cat bladed the area, the handler took the dog away, watered him, and prescented him again on the torso hole.

Returning, the dog worked the three-foot depression the cat vacated. Interested only in a six-foot square area, he pawed and sniffed vaguely in the dirt. The handler and other officers dug holes here and there, finding nothing. Repeatedly, they backed off so the cat could scrape away more earth. The results were the same. The handler heard talk in the wind, Wait 'til spring, Let's get the hell out of here.

Trying one more time, the handler dug where the dog was nuzzling the dirt. The blade hit a skull. Winter had arrived the day after Taylor murdered Hack. Hair and skin were fully preserved. The dog got to play, and everybody got off the mountain.

In June, the K-9 team returned to the burial site. The air temperature was about 70 degrees Fahrenheit, the ground surface about 90 degrees. Vegetation in the search area was sage, skunk cabbage, mules ears, and rabbit brush—all in bloom. Less than a minute after the dog began searching, he alerted into the dirt, sniffing and digging. The hard dry ground resisted even the sharp shovel blade. About a foot and a half down, they uncovered pieces of slimy black, apparently baked skin. Praising the dog, the handler took him out of the sunlight to lie down under the aspen. Returning, she dug up enough small bones and connective tissue to determine what the dog had found was a hand.

EVIDENCE RECOVERY AFTER FIRE

The out-of-control wildfire that ripped through Oakland, California, October 20, 1991, was a disaster mission for law enforcement and fire crews. The firestorm destroyed more than 3300 houses and apartments and blackened 1900 acres. Immediately afterward, it became an evidence search operation for dog teams assigned to locate missing human bodies, or pieces of bodies. There was no expectation of life in the ruins left by heat in excess of 2000°

F. Heat that crystallized concrete block into sharp sugar. Heat that melted expensive sports cars into small puddles on the roadway. Heat that burned human and animal bodies beyond recognition, leaving only broken shards of bone.

At least 26 people died in the fire. Many of them were still missing when the dog teams searched three days later. Much of the rubble and ash was still hot. Hot spots and debris collapse threatened the search teams.

The experiences of the teams who worked the search were remarkably different from routine evidence searches for weapons, contraband, stolen articles, or homicide victims. Handlers Muse and Sjoqvist reported their dogs, trained for both evidence and disaster searching, had highly positive alerts on material later identified as human remains. The first day of K-9 search, officers made a piece of burned human skull available for prescenting in a brief practice session with each team. The dogs reacted with a "natural response" to bite, to eat the material. While not dramatic, the alerts to the foreign smell were readable—the dogs would mark the odor, go toward it, sniff it, then try to bite it. Seeing the alert, the handler had to be close to the dog to reinforce the behavior while preserving the evidence by reinforcing the dog at the source.

The fire had a sterilizing effect on everything. There were no bad smells typical of an earthquake or flood. Absent also was the heavy equipment used in urban disasters to remove large sections of collapsed offices or industrial buildings. So little was left standing in this residential area that rescuers assisted the dog teams by turning over the rubble with shovels, drawing maps and noting the locations of alerts. There were still many unstable structures, walls and chimneys leaning perilously, and danger of falling through hot ash into basements or other holes.

The dogs proved incredibly durable negotiating the rubble. Their training had given them confidence and directability. They searched over fallen walls hairy with nails sticking upright. They searched through broken glass and gingerly stepped off hot metal. They sensed hollow, hot areas and searched around them. They disregarded burned animal carcasses. Sewer pipes and vent stacks proved a distraction. They sustained no major injuries and worked in the way only experienced search dogs can work. It was not a search for new dog teams.

Disaster detection dog teams searching for live victims usually work in four K-9 strike teams accompanied by a safety officer. In this case they worked in two K-9 pairs with eight or more assisting rescuers canvassing the rubble. Where possible, the dogs worked alternately to confirm alerts, the opposite handler acting as spotter. Alerts were recorded and reported for further investigation. The miles of rubble would have been impossible to cover thoroughly for such minute evidence. However, friends and relatives gave addresses to target potential victim locations. Dog teams detailed inside the perimeter of those properties.

Searching through bathroom-type debris, a dog alerted to fragile pieces of bone verified human by the police. Working through boulders that had crashed downhill into somebody's backyard, a dog found a femur-type bone and later half a jaw bone. These and other finds eventually accounted for all the missing fire victims.

ACCELERANT DETECTION

Arson, like terrorist bombing, is sabotage. Whereas bomb dogs are typically deployed before the explosion, the accelerant dog goes to work after the fire is out. In 1991, according to the National Fire Protection Association, 98,000 arson fires in the U.S. caused $1.5 billion damage to structures and claimed 490 lives. Accelerant dogs have proved effective detecting the source locations of many fires. Laboratory analysis of evidence collected as a result of the trained dog's alerts can, in many cases, identify the chemical used to start the fire and in some cases can point toward the offender himself.

Flammable liquids are used most frequently, particularly gasoline, although arsonists are becoming more sophisticated in the compounds they select and their deployment techniques.

The types of compounds accelerant dogs commonly train to detect include gasoline, diesel, kerosene, and over 17 products including some plastics.

Except in rare cases of a total burn, some accelerant product is left. Even explosions do not totally consume the product. There is residue left over. The dog is trained to air scent to the location of that residue.

In 1986, the Connecticut State Police and Bureau of Alcohol Tobacco and Firearms (ATF) trained a Labrador retriever named Mattie to detect accelerants. She was highly reliable. Laboratory analysis of material selected by the dog consistently identified chemicals she was trained to detect. In some cases, the dog's nose was shown to be more sensitive than the laboratory instruments.

Unlike rescue, narcotic, or bomb dog handlers, accelerant dog handlers typically do not receive laboratory verification of an alert for several weeks. At the fire scene, when the dog alerts into the debris, investigators dig out the section of material indicated by the dog and ship it to the lab. Usually it comes back positive. If the accelerant has dissipated or burned, the concentration may be insufficient for the lab test to verify.

After a four-fatality townhouse fire, investigators took 80 samples of materials. After setting up controls, they deployed an accelerant dog to sniff the samples and controls. The dog responded positively to five samples. Without the dog, investigators must use a shotgun approach. With the dog indicating *it's right here,* agencies save time and reduce the cost of lab testing.

STRATEGY

People running around at a fire is the biggest problem. Not the human odor. If a truck has a leak, firemen track fuel around the scene on their shoes. They fuel generators, spill fuel on the ground, step in it, then walk through the fire scene. Every step with gasoline the dog will hit.

By talking to the chief, the handler can attempt to find out where the apparatus (fire fighting equipment) was parked. Were generators or power saws used? Did they refill them? Where? If firefighters filled up a chain saw, that area can be eliminated. A K-9 hit will be attributed to the chain saw. If it was something else, the handler cannot tell. If the dog alerts, something was there. Although fire departments cannot prevent fuel spillage altogether, firefighters who are aware of the dog's reaction may be able to prevent or track some of these occurrences.

Departments can also assist the accelerant dog by mapping the fire, incorporating the major sections to scale and indicating the progression of the fire if known. For a structure fire, this means rooms, hallways, floors. For a wildland fire, it means contours of the land, natural and manmade features. Prior to the arrival of the dog, the agency can have a crew member or officer at the scene draft a diagram before the K-9 team starts. For structure fires, a floor plan obtained from the city or county is valuable. For forest or wildland fires, topographic maps are essential. The handler can plan the search, and when the dog deploys, can relate the alerts to the diagram or map.

In the rubble of structure fires, it takes a lot of time for investigators to determine where the walls, doors, and hallways were located. Heavily trafficked areas many times look like floor patterns, burning in corridors because of the concentrated foot traffic. If investigators know the floor plan, they can eliminate false patterns.

TACTICS

Arriving at the fire scene, the handler typically leaves his dog in the vehicle and goes out to assess the search scene. Safety comes first. Besides electric, gas or other utilities, the dog team may encounter hot spots, areas ready to collapse, or hazardous materials. The handler looks for indicators of arson, the burn pattern, the areas he wants to search, Fire scenes, from

People running around at a fire is the biggest problem. Not the human odor.

forest fires to structure fires are often complex and multi-layered. Walked through the upper levels of collapsed debris, accelerant dogs can detect the presence of flammable liquids through the debris. The detection process strips away layer after layer until the incriminating material is discovered. The handler-investigator is part of that layering process.

The fire investigator makes notations on indicators he observes. The dog is a tool, part of the whole process. The fire investigator has to be there. It is not sufficient to send the dog, the dog alerts, and officers pull that one spot for lab analysis. Even if it comes back positive, laboratory testing must be verified by substantiating information, primarily the observations of the fire investigator.

When he is ready to use the dog, the handler goes out somewhere near the fire scene, or part of the fire scene he knows has no potential for containing flammable liquids. There he flakes the scene, taking an eyedropper of gasoline, and putting one drop out in the debris. He knows the exact spot. "Ready to go to work?" starts the dog searching. He works the dog past the known spot. As soon as the dog alerts, he gets reinforced. The handler calibrates the dog on that one drop.

Accelerant dogs are trained on obstacles and rubble. They also learn on the job. After a large structure fire, firemen had to use a 24-foot extension ladder to get into a hole. The handler got on the ladder, called the dog over, put her on his shoulder and climbed down. The dog quickly got used to the routine.

For the dog trained with food reinforcement, the officer places his hand with food in it right down on the spot where the dog is alerting. The dog eats out of his hand. Getting another handful of kibble, he asks the dog to show me. Where the K-9 puts his nose down, the investigators are looking at a spot about 4 inches in diameter where they will recover material. That is precisely where the handler reinforces the dog.

When the handler sees that his dog is fatigued or has found nothing for a while, he hides a training aid to reinforce and recalibrate the dog. He places the dog back in the vehicle, letting him cool down, water, relax, then brings him back out again. Some fire scenes take many hours or days.

Greg Liddicoat, Deputy State Fire Marshal of Nevada, responds throughout the west with his accelerant dog Mills. As an experienced fire investigator and handler, Liddicoat is an authority on working an accelerant dog in conditions ranging from high altitude cold to desert heat:

"In southern Nevada I did a fire during the heat of mid-summer. I hosed my dog down, watered her, took her out. Three minutes was the maximum I could search with her before she needed a break. I put her back into the air conditioned truck to cool off then got her out again to work. As soon as she starts panting, that's it. She is not using her nose. As soon as you see the tongue come out, you're done.

"The Davis, California fire scene took two days. I worked for a long time there. We would work 20-30 minutes. The dog was alerting, getting fed. We kept going over different areas. To verify the alert, I feed, move on, then come back from a different direction. You bull's-eye the target area. When I get a hit, I feel positive that something is there.

"Say you have a pool of gasoline. The center of that pool will be gone, but the edges will determine a pattern the dog sniffs. The dog sniffs along the cracks. Say a floor is gone but the gasoline dripped onto the dirt below. The dog will alert to the dirt."

In the Meeks Bay fire at Lake Tahoe, news video caught Mills alerting at the back door of the building. It was raw gas. There was no burn there. When Liddicoat pulled the sill, he could smell it. The gas had soaked up into the sheetrock, inside the wall.

In the past, most accelerant dog handlers were not fire investigators. Departments did not want to contaminate the dog work. The handler went to court, said what the dog had done, and left. Now many handlers are investigators. If other officers are investigating the fire, the dog handler might only have the responsibility of working the dog. However, his investigative skills increase his ability to set priorities, recognize factors that affect the dog's behavior, and interface with personnel at the scene. If no other qualified person is at the scene, the handler may have to do the complete investigation, including the evidence recovery. During the recovery of evidence, the dog sits in the vehicle.

Where the dog has alerted, the investigator takes measurements to determine the position and location of the materials. He photographs the scene, documents the collection of evidence, and follows standard crime scene investigations procedures. The accelerant dog handler carries everything he needs to perform an investigation in his own vehicle or on his person.

One drawback: the dog that is getting frustrated by finding nothing at a fire scene intensifies his search until his nose detects turpentine leached out of the wood by the fire. Pitch is a petroleum product. If there is nothing else, the dog finally discriminates to that level of sensitivity and starts hitting turpentine.

The nose is not wrong. It is too good. A good handler recognizes this behavior. Almost all buildings have some wood, and today almost all of it is soft. Hardwoods are cost prohibitive. Melted plastics do not give the same effect.

Greg Liddicoat: "I can look at the debris, watch how she's doing the alerts, and pretty much say, OK, that's probably turpentine, not a flammable liquid. If we have no burn patterns indicating flammable liquid in a particular area, and she alerts on wood, we take up the wood. I run her past the area underneath, and she doesn't alert. I take her back and she alerts on the piece of wood. It's probably turpentine."

Any hidden areas, cracks or cavities where gas could seep (under furniture legs, tight places where the gas will not burn) are places to search. The dog team typically searches the outer walls first, because flammable liquids commonly flow underneath a wall. If the dog detects nothing there, the interior walls are next, searching the sill plates. Then back and forth in a pattern. If there is enough residue, the dog will catch it and alert to it.

Liddicoat: "I let her wander on lead as much as possible. If she gets off-pattern, I put my hand down and point out where I want her to sniff. She is trained to follow my finger down cracks. She is so used to it now, she will follow a crack until it ends.

"For instance we had a sill plate where a basement had been. I directed her down the sill plate. She hit three different places on the sill plate. I brought her around on the other side of the sill plate, and she hit once directly opposite where she hit on the other side—a good indication something was there. In two other places I didn't get anything.

We routinely collect samples from anything the dog hits. We pulled up the sill plate. A crack ran in the concrete almost the full length of the building.

It ran under the sill plate. I ran her down the crack. As soon as she hit the sill plate she stopped and alerted. I got four hits in the same exact spot. We actually dug up the concrete.

The whole thing is motivation. When I let her out of that truck, she knows it's time to go to work. She sees the burned-down building, smells that odor of burned materials, and she knows immediately it's time to go to work. She's ready to go. Doing training, it's "Yeh, OK, time to go eat..." But when I get to a fire scene, she's bouncing all around, can't wait to get out of the truck. When I walk to the back of the truck, she is excited in anticipation. As soon as she comes out, her nose goes right to the ground. She starts working right there.

The court con-cluded the man had no reasonable privacy interests remaining in the ash and ruins of the fire scene.

November 2nd at night in Iowa, an explosion and fire destroyed a suspect's apartment building. A basement located under part of the building was now a gaping hole with the retaining walls exposed to the elements. The deputy fire marshal described the site as having been hit by a horrendous explosion. The body of a woman who was in the basement was found 29 feet from the house. The debris of a wall scattered over 144 feet. After the fire was extinguished, what remained of the building was mostly ash and charred timber.

Arriving at the scene two hours later, the fire investigator supervised the removal of the woman's body, made general observations of the fire scene, and arranged to have the area secured. A complete investigation was impossible that night due to fire, smoke, and darkness. When the investigator left the scene at 2 a.m., firemen were still extinguishing the blaze.

Returning early the next morning, the investigator continued to probe for the cause and origin of the fire. Accumulated water prevented him from inspecting the basement until afternoon. His accelerant dog then alerted at what had been a bathroom. Samples collected from the area carried a strong smell of gasoline. He left the scene to notify the state fire marshal the explosion might involve arson. Returning to the scene with a search warrant, agents found several containers buried in the debris that had held gasoline.

Although he was out of state, the owner was accused of arranging for the destruction to collect insurance. The state charged him with arson in the first degree, and a jury convicted him. The court concluded the man had *no reasonable privacy interests remaining in the ash and ruins of the fire scene*. After the fire and explosion, the apartment complex was virtually destroyed. Little remained. Because the offender could have no reasonable expectation of privacy in a gaping hole in the ground filled with ashes and rubble, no violation of such an expectation could have occurred by the fire marshal's entry onto the premises.

STATE V. BULLER[9]

The Supreme Court of Iowa ruled in *State v. Buller* that evidence of the reaction at a fire scene of a dog trained in accelerant detection is a type of specialized information that will assist a trier of fact. Accelerant detection by a trained dog is probative in arson cases in that it provides direct evidence that a crime has been committed. The State offered evidence strongly indicating that the laboratory analysis was considerably less reliable in detecting fire accelerants than trained dogs. Foundation for expert testimony was shown by evidence establishing: (1) the dog handler's expertise; (2) the dog's training; and (3) the general accuracy of the dog's reaction during investigations. The court held that the dog's alert proved the criminal act of arson.

STATE v. ACRI, 277 Ill. App. 3d 1030, (Illinois, 1996)

The fallibility of dog sniff evidence requires lab test confirmation. There is no "general acceptance" of the reliability of uncorroborated alerts in the field of arson investigation. Dog alerts which are not confirmed by laboratory analysis do not meet the Frye test and are properly barred.

9. *State v. Buller*, 517 N.W.2d 711 (Iowa 1994)

AIR CRASH INVESTIGATION

A single engine plane flying from Seattle, Washington, to Oxnard, California, malfunctioned at 17,000 feet south of Reno, Nevada, went into a steep dive, exceeded the stress limits of the airframe, and broke up in mid-air.

Skiing nearby in the snowstorm, the local sheriff and a K-9 handler had heard the plane's approach. They stopped skiing to remark that anyone would fly in such a whiteout. Then they heard the whine of the aircraft going into a steep dive. A loud explosion. Then engine noise. Then silence.

Turning in their tracks, the two officers skied back out to the highway with the dog. They said little, knowing from experience the scene on the side of Pickett's Peaks a couple of miles away was not going to be pretty.

First they had to locate the crash. Residents six miles down canyon from Pickett's heard the Beechcraft break apart. Two skiers on the side of the Peaks heard the plane directly overhead and felt the impact. Unable to locate the crash in the storm, they skied out to report it. Over the next 12 hours, three feet of snow fell on the mountain.

Sheriff's deputies, rescue volunteers from three counties, and California Highway Patrol worked from Saturday to Monday afternoon trying to find the pilot, his wife and adult son who were on board the airplane when the accident occurred. In fact the entire nose section, the instruments, engine, and propeller were missing almost that long and provided the only real clue leading to the missing bodies. What began as a disaster rescue ended as an evidence search of immense proportions.

When Oakland air traffic control radioed the plane was off course over the high Sierra, the pilot responded he was having difficulty taking his aircraft off autopilot. Shortly after, they disappeared off the radar screen, plummeting 9500 feet in seconds. A National Transportation Safety Board (NTSB) investigator said the wreckage had the signature of an in-flight, airborne separation of major structural components. There was no fire. The plane just disintegrated. Debris spewed over a mile across the mountainside. Big intact pieces, little hard-to-identify pieces. Fiberglass, metal fittings, Plexiglas, clothing, toilet paper, but no bodies.

Initially, the K-9 deployed on area search to locate the wreckage. Once they found the first few pieces of fuselage and a door section, other volunteers were called in the first evening to search primarily for victims. Searchers were cautioned to leave evidence in place, to be aware NTSB would be conducting an investigation. Items were flagged until they ran out of flagging. The avalanche hazard and limited visibility prevented searching at night.

As more dogs and grid searchers worked on Sunday, a pattern emerged. The plane had been flying south. Perhaps coincidentally, the path of debris scattered from 7500 to 9500 feet across Pickett's Peak indicated the plane's final orientation was also toward the south. A door and other large sections of fuselage lay close to the middle of the wreckage. Working a pattern northward, searchers discovered items probably stored in the tail section and finally pieces of the tail section. Lighter items scattered farther. Paper, cloth, or bits of foam padding had apparently floated on the storm winds coming out of the southwest. Small dense items that probably fell like a rock were the most reliable to establish a profile of the crash.

Once they found the first few pieces of fuselage and a door section, other volunteers were called in the first evening to search primarily for victims.

By the end of the second day, agencies were working diligently to complete the profile, to find any evidence of persons on board the aircraft when it went down. Stories circulated about all three occupants parachuting out of the plane. Searchers working in the deep snow and cold did not have time for stories. But it did not help when they found the rear seats of the aircraft intact, buried upright in the snowpack, safety belts securely fastened, both empty.

The dog teams were valuable finding evidence at the crash site. Prevailing conditions, including the size and elevation of the search area, made hand-sifting through the rubble difficult.

Finding the rubble was the biggest problem, since everything was covered by deep snow. Items that landed on the surface of the pack immediately after the crash were covered by 2-3 feet of snow during the storm. Items buried on impact lay under 5-6 feet of snow. Searchers wading around found large pieces. Some debris hung up in the trees. But the dogs indicated or dug up hundreds of items.

When a dog alerted, the handler investigated with a shovel, did a hasty search with the dog in the immediate area, then flagged it or had other searchers follow up by digging in that section. Although not trained to detect aircraft materials, several dogs, once rewarded for finding a piece of wing or fuselage, learned to do so on the spot. Some dogs made so many finds, the handlers had to give them breaks by changing locations.

The second night everyone was called out of the field to rest for a major effort at daybreak. At home the tired K-9 handler spread out the topographic map and tried to make sense of the evidence. Where were the bodies? Even more strange, where was the front end of the aircraft?

The north area, Area A shaped like a triangle, contained lightweight, large surface area materials: canopy cover, sleeping bag, clothing, paperwork, interior upholstery, rear baggage door and materials. Area B to the south contained large and small pieces of the fuselage, wing, and interior, baggage, eyeglasses, pieces of glass, and further south the tail section, including the ELT (emergency locator transmitter), the right wing in two pieces, the pilot's chair, the top of the fuselage and some windshield, the four seats with nobody in them, flooring, and the left wing. Nothing searchers had found lay south of that left wing.

The handler applied mechanical physics to the aerodynamic properties of that nose section. Suppose, as the plane broke up, that nose section, in the process of disengaging from the rest of the fuselage, went its own way. What would it do? One propeller could rotate in only one direction. Suppose the centrifugal force of that propeller, like an unguided missile, led the free nose section off course. Where would it end up?

The next morning, the CHP helicopter sighted tree damage and wreckage at tree line, 8000 feet, one half mile east and 400 feet higher than the last evidence. It was the aircraft nose. Ripping branches off the tops of old junipers as it came down, the prop had literally drilled into the forest floor at the base of a 150 foot tree. A piece of the fuselage waving in the wind caught the helicopter pilot's eye. Less than 50 yards away, the missing pilot's boots stuck out of the snow. Lacerated by the trees, his body was in a sitting position, right arm cocked as if still holding the stick, still flying the aircraft. No doubt he flew it right to the ground.

The K-9 assisted in locating the son's body, buried under 3-4 feet of snow in a seated position less than 20 yards away. There was little visible damage. The woman's body was located halfway downhill toward the rest of the aircraft, also surprisingly intact, under 3-4 feet of snow. Autopsies of all three victims showed that immediate internal injuries probably caused instantaneous death.

Suppose, as the plane broke up, that nose section, in the process of disengaging from the rest of the fuselage, went its own way. What would it do? One propeller could rotate in only one direction.

Explosion with fire is more typical of air crashes, particularly commercial aircraft that come down outside an airport and impact the ground or other obstacles. The victims of accidents involving urban areas are usually located in the aircraft and on the ground. In these cases the K-9's primary job is locating small pieces of bodies, frequently burned beyond recognition, to assist the NTSB, FAA, FBI, and other agencies in charge of the investigation. Federal agencies have an established protocol for conducting aircraft accident investigations and will advise K-9 teams how to work within their procedures.

MISSING PERSON EVIDENCE

Tom Vines, Training Director of the Carbon County Sheriff's SAR Team, Red Lodge, Montana, and co-author of *High Angle Rescue Techniques*, describes in *Response Magazine* how a small piece of evidence found by a dog drove a large scale search down the right track. Typical of national park searches, the area involved was challenging. Coordinating the many agencies involved was equally challenging. The range and scope of this case shows that no evidence search is trivial, and most are not easy.

Fall in Yosemite National Park. A security officer for the Park concessionaire reported that one of the company's employees was three days late reporting to work. The employee, Michael Kalantarian, had a good attendance record. On Tuesday and Wednesday, his two days off, the man had gone on a solo climb to Mt. Clark, a peak several miles east of the Valley, and had not returned. Another employee had driven him to the trailhead Tuesday morning. She knew he intended to climb Mt. Clark but could not recall if he had mentioned his approach route, what face he would climb, or his intended route back to the Valley.

Meanwhile, Yosemite Search and Rescue (YOSAR) gathered a physical description and photograph to post a flier throughout the Park. They interviewed acquaintances for a personality profile indicating how the man might behave if he had trouble on the trip. An experienced backpacker with good equipment, Kalantarian was familiar with the Mt. Clark area through previous solo hikes. Although he was not a rock climber and had no climbing equipment, he liked scrambling and said he would probably do some on this trip. On a previous attempt to climb Mt. Clark, he had run short of time and opted to climb the closer Mt. Starr King. Nothing in his personality profile indicated the man had any physical or emotional problems.

Mt. Clark, 11,500 feet high, sits at the north end of the Clark Range. Considered a pretty mountain, its summit offers a panoramic view of the Sierra. Two scrambling routes ascend the peak from the west: one Class 3 (steep but easy climbing, requiring the use of the hands but not requiring a rope), the other Class 4 (not difficult climbing, but use a rope). Complicating the search area were hiking approaches from the Mono Meadows Trailhead to Mt. Clark. With 20 miles round trip, a steep climb in the middle of it, and only two days to do it, Kalantarian would be pressed for time. Knowing he had no ride waiting at the trailhead, he would probably return direct to the Valley, each cross-country route containing Class 3, 4, or 5 (rope required) climbing, all hazardous.

The weather had been cold but clear with only one brief snowstorm in the high country. Patchy ice and snow from the major September storm lay in shaded areas.

Search planners considered the most likely scenarios:

a. Kalantarian had fallen on Mt. Clark and was still in the area.

b. He was injured on one of the return routes, expanding the search area to 50 square miles.

c. He got sick or changed his plans (less likely possibility).

d. He left the park without telling anyone (remote possibility).

With 20 miles round trip, a steep climb in the middle of it, and only two days to do it, Kalantarian would be pressed for time.

In any case, he was now three days overdue. This, combined with scenarios _a_ and _b_, called for urgent response. It was Saturday after dark, too late for a hasty search or air search. Bypassing those steps, the search management team decided to mount an all-out search on Sunday.

That Saturday night, the team continued organizing and gathering information, managing via the Incident Command System (ICS), with the usual positions of Incident Commander, Plans Chief, Operations Chief, and Finance Chief. Local and statewide dog teams, ground teams, and two commercial helicopters were called out. Combined with the Park's contract helicopter, one aircraft would perform air searches while the other two inserted K-9 and ground searchers. The Investigative Unit Leader managed background investigations, searching the wilderness permit file for one from Kalantarian (proved negative) or similar routes by other hikers who may have seen him (also negative). An attraction team flashed lights and sirens from Glacier Point Road viewpoint eight air miles from Mt. Clark (no response).

The Plans section prepared the search plan for the next day, using trails to define perimeters, siting trail blocks at intersections and sweepers to clear trails and locate witnesses. Teams would be assigned to search Kalantarian's most likely approach and return routes, developing a moderate Probability of Detection (POD). Flights over Mt. Clark would examine climbing areas on the peak to achieve high POD's as soon as possible. All teams were briefed to search carefully for tracks or evidence establishing his presence or route.

Early Sunday morning, scent articles collected from Kalantarian's residence were supplied to arriving dog teams. At first light, the plans chief and helitack foreman flew over the search area for orientation, to scout for landing zones, and to do the initial air search. Air searching continued throughout the day. The victim's co-worker accompanied an investigator, a dog team, and a mantracking team to the Point Last Seen (PLS), a small meadow beside the trail. Identifying Kalantarian's bootprint, they copied it to issue to search teams.

Helitack crews established landing zones in the search area for helicopter insertion of ground teams. In the Clark Fork drainage, teams established a spike camp for searchers returning down the west flank of the Clark Range. On the summit of Mt. Clark, a communications team established a radio relay base. Checking the summit register, they found no entries during the relevant period. During the day, over 40 ground searchers entered the area on foot or by helicopter insertion. These teams soon began finding occasional tracks but were unable to identify them as Kalantarian's. One helicopter developed mechanical problems and was replaced by two more commercial helicopters. With so many experienced overhead personnel gone from the Park at this time of year, the search managers requested additional help.

Monday, helicopters worked all day inserting ground teams, shuttling field teams to new assignments, and searching by air. At noon, air crews searched the Merced River Canyon. Teams searched drainages leading north into the Merced River Canyon as a possible return route for Kalantarian.

The Plans Section assumed anyone approaching Mt. Clark from the west would have left a campsite or a pack somewhere in a two-mile strip on the west slope in order to climb the peak with a lighter day pack. Finding that pack or campsite would: 1) provide evidence he had been in the area and probably had not left it, and 2) identify his intended climbing route. Plans assigned a dog team, a grid team, and a helicopter to this "Camp/Pack" zone.

Climbers ascended the two most likely summit routes. Other teams checked the summit register of nearby Grey Peak. Interviewed under hypnosis, the co-worker provided additional details about Kalantarian's equipment but no details about his planned route.

That afternoon, a team approaching the northwest arête of Mt. Clark found a line of tracks following the approach to the Class 4 section that appeared only a few days old. At the base of the steepest section, where the teams needed ropes, they found a cap with a Yosemite logo. A search in the immediate area turned up no other evidence. Although it was too dark to fly the cap back to headquarters, investigators in the Valley discovered a photo of Kalantarian wearing this popular style cap.

During the day, additional resources had continued arriving in the Valley. New overhead management personnel were given orientation flights then assigned to assist Plans or Operations. The additional helicopters relieved logistics and transport problems.

Early Tuesday morning, a helicopter carrying infrared detection equipment flew the area but found no evidence. Search assignments continued, with teams checking hazards on possible return routes and additional summit registers.

The baseball cap was flown to search base. A CHP helicopter took the cap along with hair samples from Kalantarian's residence to a forensic lab in Fresno. Initial tests showed the samples to be the same general type. Additional tests would determine if the hair samples matched specifically.

The POD immediately surrounding Mt. Clark was now fairly high. Evidence—tracks and the cap—on the northwest ridge coupled with the failure of air searching to find Kalantarian, made the "Camp/Pack" zone increasingly important. The questions remained: Was the evidence his? Was he still in the area?

12:11...

At 12:11, the camp/pack team found a single leather boot, its sole matching the missing man's track, lying in a rock alcove about three-quarters of a mile west and downhill from the baseball cap.

12:26...

Fifteen minutes later, a search dog found Kalantarian's pack hidden in rocks about a mile and a quarter north of the boot on the northwest summit ridge.

13:22...

At 13:22, the grid team discovered drag marks leading west and downhill.

13:48...

Picking up the same drag marks, a second team farther downhill began following them and at 13:48 found Michael Kalantarian in the Clark Fork drainage, conscious and in stable condition but unable to stand.

Traveling late and cross-country with limited survival equipment (no flashlight or matches) and no climbing gear, Kalantarian's route forced him onto more and more difficult rock until finally he fell about 70 feet down a slab. Regaining consciousness in a shrubby pine, he had a cut on his head and what he perceived to be a broken right wrist and right ankle. He could not walk. His water bottle, cap and glacier glasses were gone. Night temperatures dropped into the 15 degree Fahrenheit range.

To survive, he knew he had to reach his pack, about a mile and a half northwest of the accident. Crawling, trying to stay warm and find water, he heard the helicopters but had no signal mirror. A low, slow search helicopter passing overhead on Monday did not spot him. Instead of contouring west, his worm's eye view threw him 90 degrees off course.

Evidence detection kept the search teams on course. Kalantarian later lost both legs below the knee and half of each of four fingers on his left hand to frostbite. He kept his life.

CHAPTER 7

DRUG SEARCH

"No dope or money is worth your life."
—Sgt. Tony Alvarez, L.A. IMPACT

"A clear night in the desert outside Las Vegas. The new car is cruisin'. Eighty, eighty-five. The dope's secure. Down south you watched them put it in there. Seal the container, seal the tank, fill the tank with gas.

"Without warning, the night lights up behind you. In your rear view mirror strobe lights shoot out from a highway patrol car, like a space ship. Like a damn avenging angel.

"Fighting panic, you pull over. One trooper gets you out. The other trooper walks his partner around your car. His partner is a blond dog that sniffs, suddenly flips upside down, wiggles under the sedan and starts pawing and biting *at the gas tank*. Your knees buckle.

"The trooper calls the dog, the angel, Duster."

—K-9 Trainer

Agencies large and small are employing dogs to detect narcotics and dangerous drugs. We are developing programs to improve the efficiency and effectiveness of canine enforcement teams by combining canine operations with technology, training, testing, and by conducting research to determine canine limitations and to develop new detection techniques. Besides monitoring and evaluating canine team employment, supervisory personnel need to receive technical training to insure maximum coverage, including mutual aid assistance to agencies that do not have dog teams.

Instruments exist that are capable of detecting drugs and other evidentiary materials. Technology has yet to develop practical devices for all necessary field applications. Until these devices become available, the dog has a job.

Large departments typically have a special investigative unit dedicated to narcotic enforcement. Narcotic detection dog teams generally work under that unit. Detection dog teams perform their training under the direction of the department K-9 trainer or a specialist drug dog trainer, who also arranges for periodic evaluations. Detection teams may train or be evaluated by qualified trainers outside the department.

Small- to medium-sized departments may have one or more specialist narcotic dog teams where the handler has multiple duties and therefore has the added responsibility of adequate utilization and training. Some of these agencies crosstrain patrol or protection dogs for drug detection, which significantly increases the total training time required. Crosstraining, especially in rural departments, can enhance successful employment provided the officer and dog are strong and highly motivated.

The trained dog's alert or positive reaction is used to establish probable cause to search or to obtain a search warrant. Narcotic detection dogs are trained to use their scent discrimination capability to memorize the scent of specific drugs. Like a computer, on command they bring up the scent schematic of these drugs and discriminate or search for a matching scent picture. When the dog recognizes the scents of specific drugs, he *alerts, that is, he exhibits behavior changes the handler can read and identify as indicative of drug scent.* Depending on the scent density and rate of diffusion, the dog can detect drugs despite masking scents, intervening structures, vehicle bodies, or multiple layers of packaging.

COURT DECISIONS AFFECTING THE USE OF TRAINED CANINES

A K-9 officer cannot be tactically effective unless he is aware of the possible legal implications of his conduct. An illegal search by a K-9 officer may lead to the suppression of evidence and possibly the dismissal of charges against a guilty individual. Well-trained dogs have a significant role in drug enforcement, and that role can be enhanced by an awareness of Fourth

Amendment proscriptions concerning the use of detection dogs. Supreme Court and lower court cases have established Fourth Amendment guidelines for the use of specially trained dogs in the following areas: (1) Public places or third-party controlled areas, (2) motor vehicles, and (3) persons, private residence, or areas where society attaches a high expectation of privacy. Adherence to these guidelines will help insure the admissibility of evidence discovered as a result of dog sniffs and the continued vitality of drug detection dogs in law enforcement. Law enforcement officers should consult their legal adviser. Some police procedures ruled permissible under Federal constitutional law are of questionable legality under State law or are not permitted at all.

PUBLIC OR THIRD PARTY CONTROLLED AREAS

The role of detection dogs in law enforcement has been made more secure by the decision of the U.S. Supreme Court in the case of *United States v. Place*.[10] In *Place*, law enforcement officers at New York's LaGuardia Airport lawfully detained the defendant on a reasonable suspicion that he was carrying a controlled substance. Reasonable suspicion had previously been established by officers who had talked to Place before he boarded his plane for New York. When the defendant refused to consent to a search of his luggage, the officers gave him the opportunity to accompany his luggage to the office of a Federal judge where a search warrant would be sought. The defendant declined the offer but requested and received a telephone number where the officers could be reached. After the defendant left the premises, his luggage was taken to Kennedy Airport where, 90 minutes after the initial detention, it was subjected to a "sniff test" by a trained narcotic detection dog. In response to the dog's positive reaction to one of the bags, a search warrant was secured. The subsequent search of the bag revealed a substantial quantity of cocaine. The defendant was later arrested and indicted for possession of cocaine with intent to deliver.

Although unnecessary to the resolution of the dispute in Place, a majority of the Court took the opportunity to address the constitutionality of *"dog sniffs."* Specifically, the Court considered whether the use of a dog to detect odors emanating from the defendant's luggage constituted a search requiring compliance with Fourth Amendment dictates. The Court engaged in a two-step analysis to determine whether the officer's actions violated any expectation of privacy that was both subjectively and objectively reasonable. This two-step test for determining the existence of a reasonable expectation of privacy was first announced by the Supreme Court in *Katz v. United States*.[11]

Finding first that the defendant had a subjective expectation of privacy in his luggage, the Court then considered the more important question of whether that expectation of privacy was objectively reasonable. In other words, did the use of the dog violate any expectation of privacy that society as a whole was willing to recognize and protect. Of particular significance to the Court was the fact that the dog sniff did not require the opening of the defendant's luggage: "The 'dog sniff' does not expose noncontraband items that otherwise would remain hidden from public view, as does, for example, an officer's rummaging through the contents of the luggage. Thus, the manner in which information is obtained through this investigative technique is much less intrusive than a typical search. Moreover, the sniff discloses only the presence or absence of narcotics, a contraband item. Thus, despite the fact that the sniff tells authorities something about the contents of the luggage, the information obtained is limited. This limited disclosure also ensures that the owner of the property is not subjected to the embarrassment and inconvenience entailed in less discriminate and more intrusive investigative methods."

"In these respects, *the canine sniff is sui generis—unique*. We are aware of no other investigative procedure that is so limited both in the manner in which the information is obtained and in the content of the information revealed by the procedure." In view of the

10. *United States v. Place,*
462 U.S. 696 (1983)
11. *Katz v. United States,*
389 U.S. 347 (1967)

limited intrusiveness of this dog sniff which only revealed one thing (e.g. whether there was contraband in the item tested), the Court concluded that this single fact is something society is not willing to protect. Consequently, under the circumstances present in *Place*, the use of a trained dog, although foiling the defendant's subjective expectation of privacy, did not violate any objectively reasonable expectation of privacy and, therefore, *was not a search* under the Fourth Amendment.

In *Place*, the Court did not go so far as to say that no dog sniff would ever be considered a search. Rather, the Court was careful to limit the impact of its decision by narrowly concluding that "the exposure of [defendant's] luggage, which was located in a public place, to a trained canine—did not constitute a 'search' within the meaning of the Fourth Amendment." The obvious implication of the Court's narrow ruling is that if the location of the article subjected to the dog sniff was changed, then the conclusion that the sniff was not a search could also change.

As a result of the limited application of the Court's pronouncement in *Place*, lower courts have had to consider anew the constitutionality of using specially trained dogs in other than public places. In certain cases, the courts have held that *the dog sniff is not a search*—Gamble v. State,[12] State v. Snitkin,[13] and Stout v. State.[14] Other courts have held to the contrary—*United States v. Tartaglia*,[15] Crosby v. State,[16] and Commonwealth v. Johnston.[17] The distinguishing factor appears to be the degree of privacy the individual defendants have had in the "other than public places." For example, if the nonpublic place where the dog sniff occurs is controlled by a third party and the defendant has no reasonable expectation of privacy in the area, then the sniff of the defendant's property found at that location does not constitute a search. However, *if the dog sniff takes place in an area where the defendant has a reasonable expectation of privacy, such as his home or automobile, then the sniff does amount to a search and it must be reasonable under the Fourth Amendment*. The following cases demonstrate this distinction and illustrate different courts' approaches to the legality of dog sniffs in various nonpublic places.

In *United States v. Lovell*[18] the Fifth Circuit upheld the legality of law enforcement officers subjecting a passenger's luggage to a sniff test once it has been entrusted to the care of a third-party common carrier.

Benny Lovell's nervous appearance piqued the interest of U.S. Border Patrol Agents at the El Paso International Airport. The agents observed Lovell for the brief time it took him to check his luggage with a skycap and walk to the airline terminal and noted that he was visibly shaking and frequently glanced over his shoulder. The agents decided to remove Lovell's luggage from the airline conveyor belt and to subject the bags to a dog sniff. Prior to the dog sniff, the agents compressed the sides of the suitcase and both got a faint smell of talcum powder and a strong odor of marijuana. The court found no fault with the agents' actions.

After a positive alert from a trained narcotic detection dog, a search warrant was obtained. Pursuant to the warrant, agents opened Lovell's luggage and found 68 pounds of marijuana. Lovell was subsequently arrested and charged with possession of a controlled substance with intent to distribute.

Prior to trial, Lovell moved to suppress all the evidence obtained from his luggage on the grounds that the bags had been seized and then searched in violation of his Fourth Amendment rights. The U.S. Court of Appeals for the Fifth Circuit was asked to decide whether: (1) The removal of Lovell's bags from the airline conveyor belt was a *seizure* under the fourth amendment, and (2) whether the *sniff* of the luggage was a *search*. The court also considered whether squeezing or "prepping" the bag was a Fourth Amendment violation. On this issue, the court stated, "...while we could hypothesize a 'prepping' process so violent, extreme and unreasonable in its execution as to cross the bounds of constitutional propriety, we are not confronted by such a process here."

In response to the first query, the court distinguished between luggage taken from

> *If the dog sniff takes place in an area where the defendant has a reasonable expectation of privacy, such as his home or automobile, then the sniff does amount to a search and it must be reasonable under the Fourth Amendment.*

12. *Gamble v. State,* 473, So.2d 188 (Ala. App.1985).
13. *State v. Snitkin,* 681 P.2d 980 (Sup. Ct. Hawaii 1984).
14. *Stout v. State,* 688 S.W.2d 1188 (Tex. App. 1985).
15. *United States v. Tartaglia,* 864 F.2d 837 (D.C. Cir. 1989).
16. *Crosby v. State,* 492 So.2d 1152 (Fla. App. 1986).
17. *Commonwealth v. Johnston,* 530 A.2d 74 (Pa. Sup. Ct. 1987).
18. *United States v. Lovell,* 849 F.2d 910 (5th Cir. 1988).

the custody of a traveler and luggage taken from the custody of a third-party common carrier. Finding the latter to be much less intrusive, the court concluded, "...momentary delay occasioned by the bags' removal from the conveyor belt was insufficient to constitute a meaningful interference with Lovell's possessory interest in his bags. As a result, the Agents' actions did not constitute a seizure.

The court also rejected the defendant's contention that the sniff of his luggage was a search. The court began by recognizing that "when airport security concerns are not implicated, every passenger who has luggage checked with an airline enjoys a reasonable expectation of privacy that the contents of that luggage will not be exposed in the absence of consent or a legally obtained warrant." Nonetheless, the court concluded that the passenger's reasonable expectation of privacy did not extend to the airspace surrounding the luggage; the use of a drug detection dog to sniff luggage in the custody of a common carrier is not a search and, therefore, neither probable cause nor a reasonable suspicion is required to justify the action.

Lovell is just one of many cases holding that the use of a drug detection dog to sniff items placed in the care and custody of third parties is not a search under the Fourth Amendment. The same result has been reached in cases where dogs have been used to detect the odor of drugs emanating from safe deposit boxes, packages shipped through Federal Express, cargo stored in the facilities of a private carrier, and parcels traveling in the U.S. mail. The common thread running through each one of these cases is that the particular defendants involved had *no reasonable expectation of privacy* in the area in which the drug detection dog was used and, therefore, the dog sniff was not subject to Fourth Amendment constraints.

U.S. v. England:[19] "A person who deposits an item in the United States mail retains far less of an interest in the mailed item than does a person who checks his luggage for transport with a common carrier." The U.S.C.A. 9th concluded that the U.S. Postal Service's brief detention of packages prior to their inspection pursuant to a warrant is not an unreasonable seizure for fourth amendment purposes.

Coleman England placed a package in the U.S. mail for delivery from Los Angeles to Birmingham, Alabama, by Express Mail. The package was set aside by postal inspectors who suspected the package contained narcotics.

A narcotic-sniffing dog alerted positively to the presence of narcotics in the package. The package was sent on its regularly scheduled flight to Birmingham where authorities had obtained a search warrant.

Federal agents seized the package on arrival in Birmingham and found cocaine after searching the contents. Approximately 10 months later, England placed a second package in the U.S. mail for express delivery to Birmingham.

The package was transported to a nearby police station for a dog test. After a positive response from the dog, a warrant was obtained, cocaine was found, and England was later arrested.

If no drugs had been found, the package could have been returned to the post office in time to make its scheduled flight to Birmingham. England was convicted of 2 counts of possession of cocaine with intent to sell and 2 counts of intentionally using a communication facility to aid in the offense.

England contended the trial court erred in denying his motion to suppress the evidence as an unlawful fourth amendment seizure. The 9th Circuit rejected his contention citing *U.S. v. Jacobsen*[20] and *U.S. v. Beale*.[21] The fact that the postal inspectors in England's case first moved the packages before the dog sniff test was of no consequence, especially in light of the fact that the packages would have arrived at their destination on time if no drugs had been found. The reasonable articulable suspicions of the postal inspectors justified the brief detention of England's packages to allow a more thorough inspection. Consequently, no seizure occurred.

People v. Wieser:[22] the owner of a public storage facility contacted Officer Johnson, reporting a co-lessee in the facility was engaging in suspicious behavior, explaining the defendant had visited

19. *U.S. v. England*, 971 F.2d 419 (9th Cir. 1992).
20. *U.S. v. Jacobsen*, 466 U.S. 109 (1984).
21. *U.S. v. Beale*, 736 F.2d 1289 (9th Cir. 1984).

Lovell is just one of many cases holding that the use of a drug detection dog to sniff items placed in the care and custody of third parties is not a search under the Fourth Amendment.

his locker for about 5 minutes on each of the previous 5 or 6 days, riding a motorcycle and carrying only a backpack—3 different motorcycles, each exhibiting the same California license plate. Linking the story with other information about the defendant's activities, Off. Johnson brought a drug-sniffing dog to assist in the investigation and "twice walked the dog past several lockers in the public storage facility, including the defendant's, and on each pass the dog alerted to the defendant's locker. Officer Johnson testified that the dog's behavior indicated that narcotics were present in the locker." Obtaining a search warrant, the officer discovered marijuana concentrate and psyilocyn, a hallucinogenic substance, in the locker. The defendant filed a motion to suppress evidence obtained as a result of the execution of the search warrant.

The court concluded, "...that the canine sniff of the storage locker did not constitute a search is supported by the manner in which Officer Johnson conducted the search." The owner of the facility had contacted Officer Johnson to report suspicious behavior. The locker was adjacent to a roadway that was accessible to all persons visiting the lockers. The police officer himself had a locker at the facility which gave him the same right to use the roadway that was afforded to others who rented lockers. The dog sniffed a locker rented by the defendant in the public storage facility. Officer Johnson walked the dog past the defendant's locker and several other lockers, using multiple lockers as controls in order not to isolate the particular locker under investigation. At all times the dog remained in a public walkway outside of the defendant's locker. Johnson testified that the dog merely sniffed the air outside the locker. Under the facts of this case, the police had the right to be outside of the locker and did not violate the defendant's right of privacy by having a trained dog smell the odors emanating from the locker.

U.S. Customs is employing drug detector dog teams to walk among travelers in the public airspace of airline terminals. These dogs do not invade the privacy of persons but rather sniff the designated locations of common airspaces and perform passive, nonthreatening alerts whenever they detect narcotic scent. Similar methods are used by teams deployed in corrections facilities, such as visitation or delivery areas where members of the public enter, contact inmates, and exit.

While *Oliver v. United States*[23] does not deal with dogs, the concept of open space is important for area searches using K-9. Two police officers, acting on a tip that marijuana was being grown on the defendant's farm, went to the farm to investigate. While there, the officers drove onto the defendant's property and, ignoring a "No Trespassing" sign and a locked gate, located a marijuana field approximately 1 mile from the defendant's house. The marijuana was seized and the defendant was arrested and indicted for manufacturing a controlled substance. Prior to trial, the defendant moved to suppress the marijuana seized from his property on the grounds that it was discovered as a result of an unreasonable, warrantless search.

The U.S. Supreme Court determined that no search had occurred based on a two-part analysis. First, the Court recognized that the Fourth Amendment "does not protect the merely subjective expectation of privacy, but only those expectations that society is prepared to recognize as reasonable." In other words, for an expectation of privacy to be reasonable, it must be an expectation that society as a whole is willing to recognize and protect. The purely subjective intent of the individual is not controlling. In the second step of its analysis, the Court, speaking for society in general, stated that it was not willing to either recognize or protect an expectation of privacy in an open field. In reaching this conclusion, the Court first looked at the traditional "overriding respect for the sanctity of the home" and compared it with the open fields as follows: "Open fields do not provide the setting for those intimate activities that the Amendment is intended to shelter from government interference or surveillance. There is no societal interest in protecting the privacy of those activities, such as the cultivation of crops, that occur in open fields. Moreover, as a practical matter these lands usually are

> *The defendant had visited his locker for about 5 minutes on each of the previous 5 or 6 days, riding a motorcycle and carrying only a backpack—3 different motorcycles, each exhibiting the same California license plate.*

22. *People v. Wieser*, 796 P.2d 982 (Colo. 1990)
23. *Oliver v. United States*, 466 U.S. 170 (1984)

accessible to the public and the police in ways that a home, an office, or commercial structure would not be." On balance, the Supreme Court found open fields unworthy of protection under the Fourth Amendment.

In practice, the Supreme Court's determination that there is no reasonable expectation of privacy in open fields has effectively removed all physical entries into such areas from Fourth Amendment scrutiny. Law enforcement officers with trained dogs can, when the situation dictates, confidently make warrantless entries into open fields without fear of contravening fourth amendment proscription. What must be remembered, however, is that the home and the curtilage, that is the area immediately surrounding and associated with the home, remain under the protection of the Fourth Amendment. Consequently, any governmental entry into the home or curtilage must comply with Fourth Amendment standards by being conducted under the authority of a valid warrant or by falling into one of the recognized exceptions to the warrant requirement.

MOTOR VEHICLES

Dog sniffs may occur in motor vehicles or other areas where defendants are afforded a reduced expectation of privacy. In *United States v. Whitehead*[24] law enforcement officers noticed the defendant as he arrived at the Miami, Florida, Amtrak Station 10 minutes before the scheduled departure of the morning train to New York City. The defendant called attention to himself by carefully scanning the front of the station before entering. The officers initiated an investigation by speaking to the taxi driver who drove the defendant to the station and the ticketing agent who sold the defendant his ticket. The taxi driver advised that the defendant had been picked up at a Miami hotel well known to the officers as a common meeting place for drug traffickers. The ticketing agent informed the officers that the defendant paid cash for a first-class sleeping car ticket to New York, the reservation for which had been made only a few hours before. With this knowledge, the officers approached the defendant, and after identifying themselves, asked to speak with him. Although the defendant agreed to talk to the officers, he immediately broke into a profuse sweat. When asked to identify himself, he produced a pair of military dog tags but claimed to have no other identification. In response to further questioning, the defendant advised that he had been in Miami for 2 days to play tennis with friends. The officers then informed the defendant that they were conducting a narcotic investigation and asked for consent to search his bags. When the defendant denied his consent, he was permitted to board the train with no further interruptions.

After the defendant's departure, the officers in Miami contacted Amtrak officers, who boarded the train when it made a scheduled stop in Washington, D.C. More officers boarded the train in Baltimore and with them were 2 drug-trained dogs. One of the officers knocked on the defendant's door. When the door was opened, the officer identified himself and was given consent to enter. Once inside, the officer asked for permission to search the defendant's bags. The defendant again broke into a profuse sweat and asked what would happen if he objected. The officer indicated he had dogs available to sniff the luggage. At that point, the defendant told the officer to "bring on your dogs." The dogs were brought into the roomette, where they both alerted to one of the defendant's bags. The defendant and his luggage were detained while a warrant was obtained. The subsequent search of the suitcase revealed 3 kilograms of cocaine.

Prior to trial, the defendant moved to suppress the cocaine found in his luggage on the grounds that the dog sniff of his luggage, which was located in his roomette, was an unlawful search under the Fourth Amendment. The trial court rejected the motion and found the defendant guilty of possessing cocaine with intent to distribute. On appeal, the defendant renewed his Fourth Amendment claim.

Recognizing that the roomette in question was not a "public place," the U.S. Court of Appeals for the Fourth Circuit first considered whether the roomette was the equivalent of the defendant's

Although the defendant agreed to talk to the officers, he immediately broke into a profuse sweat.

24. *United States v. Whitehead*, 849 F.2d 849 (4th Cir. 1988)

home or hotel room where his expectation of privacy is heightened, or instead more akin to a motor vehicle where the privacy interest is diminished. After pointing out that trains, like cars, are subject to pervasive government regulation and their mobility creates the same "law enforcement exigency...and...potential for immediate flight from the jurisdiction," the court made the following observation: "Whitehead's roomette was moving swiftly in interstate transit. Whitehead's status therein was that of a passenger, not a resident. Although Whitehead had no ability to direct the train's movement, its continuing journey imposed practical constraints on the officers' ability to mount a full-fledged investigation within jurisdictional boundaries. Moreover, Whitehead could leave the train at any stop, and unlike a hotel guest, he had no authority to remain on the train once it reached its destination." Based on these observations, the court rejected the defendant's contention that the roomette was the functional equivalent of a hotel room or a temporary home that deserved the most scrupulous protection under the Fourth Amendment.

The court's review, however, did not end there. The defendant countered with the argument that even though motor vehicles are given less protection under the Fourth Amendment, probable cause is still required to justify the warrantless search of such vehicles. Again, the court disagreed. Because the dog sniff is so much less intrusive than a traditional search, the court reasoned that a prior showing of probable cause was unnecessary. Instead, the court found that such a limited and discreet intrusion as is caused by a dog sniff could be justified on the basis of a reasonable suspicion. In light of the facts known to the investigating officers in *Whitehead*, the court found that a reasonable suspicion existed at the time the dog sniff was conducted.

Many cases have adopted the rationale used in *Whitehead* and have upheld the use of dogs to detect drugs in motor vehicles when a reasonable suspicion can be articulated. The fact that a warrant based on probable cause is not required is attributable in large part to the reduced expectation of privacy attached to motor vehicles.

U.S. v. Trayer:[25] a train case where a dog trainer with 16 years experience training dogs to detect narcotics testified *on behalf of the defendant...unsuccessfully*. Since a dog sniff of a train compartment is not a Fourth Amendment search, see *U.S. v. Colyer*,[26] the narcotic dog's presence sniffing down the corridor was not disputed. In fact, "...the dog alert in combination with the information obtained from Amtrak's train manifest supported the search." At issue in Trayer was *whether Ben II's alert was reliable*.

"It is argued that Ben II, who had been trained to exhibit aggressive behavior on detecting drugs, instead froze and pointed at the compartment as would a bird dog. Officer Buss explained, however, that Ben II alerted in that fashion 'on a majority of occasions' and had alerted correctly (finding drugs) in 58 out of 60 alerts. On the other 2 occasions, Ben II alerted to packages in which money was found. Officer Buss testified that, in his view, the dog was alerting to traces of drugs on the money. That Ben II's behavior is idiosyncratic (perhaps a triumph of genetics for a Golden Retriever) does not diminish its reliability so long as the dog's peculiar brand of alert is a trustworthy method of communicating the presence of drugs."

During the 1970s, there was much confusion among court decisions about when, if ever, police could search the contents of a car without a warrant. Many cases expressed the view that when it came to "personal" containers, such as a tote bag, briefcase, or a suitcase, the police could seize the container, but were required to obtain a warrant before they could open it and search it.

Then, in 1982, the United States Supreme Court created a "bright line" rule regarding the searching of cars on the basis of probable cause during a roadside stop, *United States v. Ross*.[27] According to the *Ross* rule, if the officer had probable cause (the same standard required to obtain a search warrant), he was entitled to search any part of the car, or anything

25. *U.S. v. Trayer*, 898 F.2d 805 (D.C. Cir. 1990).
26. *U.S. v. Colyer*, 878 F.2d 469 (D.C. Cir. 1989).

At issue in Trayer was whether Ben II's alert was reliable.

inside the car, where it was reasonable to believe the object of the search might be located. This included any type of "personal" and/or locked container or compartment inside the car, such as the glove compartment or a briefcase.

Despite this seemingly clear rule, one exception developed, or remained, which became known as the "specific container" exception. Under this rule, if the police had pre-existing probable cause which related to a specific container only, rather than the entire car generally, they had to obtain a warrant before searching the container. In other words, the higher level of privacy in personal belongings prevailed over the diminished level of privacy in automobiles. This meant, for instance, that it was not legal for officers to wait until the suitcase was placed in an automobile, then make a vehicle stop and search the suitcase without a warrant, *Arkansas v. Sanders* [28] and *United States v. Chadwick.* [29]

This exception to the *Ross* rule persisted until *California v. Acevedo:* [30] Federal drug agents intercepted a package in Hawaii which contained marijuana. It was addressed to J. R. Daza in Santa Ana, and was to be delivered via Federal Express. The agents made arrangements with the Santa Ana police officers, who obtained the package and were watching when Jamie Daza claimed it from the local Federal Express office and took it with him to his apartment. Officers observed Daza toss away the wrapper and take the package inside.

Less than one hour later, Acevedo arrived at the apartment, stayed for about 10 minutes, then left carrying a brown paper bag which looked full and which was the same size as one of the wrapped marijuana packages sent from Hawaii. Acevedo walked to his car, placed the bag in the trunk, and started to drive off. Fearing loss of the evidence, officers in marked police cars stopped the car, opened the trunk and bag, and found marijuana.

The California Court of Appeal ruled that the search was illegal, based on *Chadwick* and *Sanders*, because the officers' probable cause pre-existed and related specifically to only the paper bag, as opposed to the car generally. The court ruled that they were required to obtain a search warrant before opening the bag.

The United States Supreme Court reversed and held that the warrantless search of the bag was proper. It held that there is no meaningful distinction, either with regard to privacy or exigent circumstances, between a container in the typical *Ross* situation and a "specific container" under the *Chadwick/Sanders* doctrine: "Until today, this Court has drawn a curious line between the search of an automobile that coincidentally turns up a container and the search of a container that coincidentally turns up in an automobile."

Accordingly, and also to make life easier for law enforcement, the court terminated the anomaly and announced that henceforth only one rule would apply: "The police may search an automobile and the containers within it where they have probable cause to believe contraband or evidence is contained." There is now a single, straightforward rule for the warrantless searches of vehicles based on probable cause.

INVESTIGATIVE DETENTIONS

K-9 officers must maintain current knowledge about the body of case law dealing with *investigative detentions*. When the police temporarily detain the holder of a container in order to expose it to a dog, or when a police officer, through a show of lawful authority, causes a motorist to stop his car and requests a consent search, decisions of the U.S. Supreme Court make warrantless stops of this sort lawful where an officer is in possession of facts amounting to at least reasonable suspicion that the individual is engaged in some type of criminal conduct. [31]

In the landmark decision of *Terry v. Ohio,* [32] well known to most law enforcement officers, the Court constitutionalized the investigative stop and the attendant frisk as an intermediate police response between inaction and overreaction. The Constitution does not require a police officer confronted with possible criminal activity to choose between the 2 alternatives of making an arrest (when probable cause may be absent) or walking away (allowing a crime to occur or a criminal to escape). The investigative detention doctrine provides an intermediate response which, in the

27. *United States v. Ross*, 456 U.S. 798 (1982).
28. *Arkansas v. Sanders*, 442 U.S. 753 (1979).
29. *United States v. Chadwick*, 433 U.S. 1 (1977).
30. *California v. Acevedo*, 500 U.S. 565 (1991).
31. *U.S. v. Trayer*, 898 F.2d 805 (D.C. Cir. 1990)
32. *Terry v. Ohio*, 392 U.S. 1 (1968),

appropriate circumstances, constitutes the "essence of good police work."

To determine whether reasonable suspicion exists, officers should examine the circumstances before them critically, employing previously acquired knowledge and training, and make a common sense assessment. Officers must also be prepared to relate the fact upon which they relied in the likely event that their actions are legally challenged at a later time. These demands obviously favor officers who are observant, take careful notes, and who are articulate on the witness stand.

While it does not deal with dogs, *California v. Hodari D.*[33] points toward the use of narcotic dogs where a fleeing suspect is believed to have tossed contraband. As 2 Oakland police officers rounded a corner onto 62nd Street in their unmarked vehicle, they saw 4 or 5 youths huddled around a small red car parked at the curb. When the youths saw the officers' car approaching, they apparently panicked and took flight. Hodari D. and one companion ran west through an alley; the others fled south, as did the red car.

The officers were suspicious and gave chase on foot. One officer circled around the block and was heading south on 62nd as Hodari, who had gone through an alley, was running north. Looking behind as he ran, Hodari did not turn and see the officer until the officer was almost upon him, whereupon Hodari tossed away what appeared to be a small rock of cocaine. A moment later, the officer tackled Hodari and took him into custody.

The issue was whether Hodari had been "seized," i.e., detained, within the meaning of the fourth amendment at the time he abandoned his drugs.

There had been no "seizure" at the time the drugs were discarded because a person is detained only at the time physical force is actually applied, or at the time the suspect submits to the officer's assertion of authority. Here, no physical force had yet been applied, nor had Hodari "submitted" to the officer's authority at the time he threw down the cocaine. Accordingly, the drugs were voluntarily abandoned and did not constitute "fruit of the poisonous tree." Because the contraband is not the "fruit" of an illegal seizure, it does not have to be suppressed and can be admitted into evidence.

Money furnished "in exchange for a controlled substance" or "traceable to such an exchange" is subject to forfeiture, 21 U.S.C. § 881(a)(6). In a civil forfeiture action, the government must introduce evidence showing probable cause to believe the money falls within section 881(a)(6) or another provision of the forfeiture laws. A case involving cocaine-laced money found in luggage, *U.S. v. $639,558.00 in U.S. Currency,*[34] contained a footnote alleging a cocaine/currency connection that could be a major issue. Expert testimony argued a high percentage of money in circulation is contaminated by narcotics, calling into question whether a positive K-9 reaction or alert should be sufficient to constitute probable cause for a search.

To overcome this argument, a handler should be prepared to testify that his dog is *trained to alert to a greater quantity of a narcotic than mere residue.* Further, the handler must show the dog has performed reliably to detect drugs in training exercises using scientific controls, where the dog must distinguish between drug contaminated money and money itself. The dog trained to find drugs, not money per se, sniffs found cash according to a controlled procedure. The dog alert in combination with other information enables seizing the money as drug sale proceeds depending on individual state laws.

Criteria for performing a K-9 sniff test on money seized by narcotics agents:
- The money has not been contaminated by handling (dope-scented hands)
- The money has not been put through a money counting machine
- The money has not been stored in a contaminated area
- The chain of evidence has been preserved with respect to contamination ("Do not disturb this scent picture.")

If any of the above criteria have been violated, a sniff test would be invalidated.

A handler should be prepared to testify that his dog is trained to alert to a greater quantity of a narcotic than mere residue.

33. *California v. Hodari D.*, 499 U.S. 621 (1991)
34. *U.S. v. $639,558.00 in U.S. Currency*, 955 F.2d 712 (D.C. Cir. 1992)

$170,000 cash proceeds from sales of methamphetamine plus 20 pounds of meth inside a safe. Agent Les Lovell and Jake.

PERSON OR HOME

Law enforcement officers may wish to use a detection dog in areas where there is unquestionably a reasonable expectation of privacy, such as sniffs of a person, a private home, or hotel room. In *State v. Boyce*[35] the court held that a canine sniff of a person or of objects being carried by the person is "...offensive at best and harrowing at worst to the innocent sniffee" and requires a reasonable suspicion. Using a dog under such circumstances generally implicates a person's reasonable expectation of privacy requiring prior judicial authorization or other appropriate justification under one of the exceptions to the warrant requirement.

In *United States v. Thomas*[36] the Second Circuit Court of Appeals held that simply using a dog to detect odors emanating from the defendant's apartment constituted a search even though no entry into the premises was made. In *Thomas*, the defendant claimed that the warrantless use of a drug-trained dog outside his apartment to detect odors originating from within was an illegal search that tainted the subsequently issued warrant. The court acknowledged the precedent established in *Place*, but noted that the use of a dog to detect odors in a suitcase is quite different from using a dog to reveal the contents of an individual's home.

Emphasizing the fact that an individual has heightened privacy interest in his dwelling place, the court made the following statement: "[A] practice that is not intrusive in a public airport may be intrusive when employed at a person's home. Although using a dog sniff for narcotics may be discriminating and unoffensive relative to other detection methods, and will disclose only the presence or absence of narcotics, it remains a way of detecting the contents of a private, enclosed space. With a trained dog police may obtain information about what is inside a dwelling that they could not derive from their own senses...Here the defendant had a legitimate expectation that

35. *State v. Boyce*, 723 P.2d 28 (Wash. App. 1986)
36. *United States v. Thomas*, 757 F.2d 1359 (2nd Cir. 1985)

the contents of his closed apartment would remain private, that they could not be 'sensed' from outside his door. Use of the trained dog impermissibly intruded on that legitimate expectation." In keeping with this rationale, the court in *Thomas* concluded that the use of a dog to detect the odor of drugs coming from the defendant's apartment was a search which required both probable cause and a search warrant.

Drug detection dogs are effective tactical weapons to use in the war on drugs. Traffickers have attempted to thwart the efforts of these dogs by packaging drugs in containers filled with mothballs, garlic, coffee, perfume, baby powder, and gasoline. When these attempts at concealment fail, drug cartels, acting out of fear, have put contracts out on the lives of certain detection dogs. The fear exhibited by the drug traffickers is itself a signal to the law enforcement community that we are using a weapon that works.

To keep this weapon working, law enforcement officers must be careful to use detection dogs within the boundaries set by the courts. Those boundaries can be summarized as follows:

- If the dog is used to sniff an item located in a *public place or a place controlled by a third party*, then no search will occur and Fourth Amendment proscriptions regarding searches need not be a concern.
- If the sniff is to occur in an area of *reduced expectation of privacy*, then a mere showing of reasonable suspicion is all that is required.
- If the dog is used to sniff an area where the defendant has an *extremely high expectation of privacy*, then a warrant based on probable cause or an exception to the warrant requirement is a prerequisite.
- *If in doubt, get a warrant.*

An alert or positive reaction given by a trained dog to a location or a container can provide probable cause for a search and the subsequent arrest of an individual. If the search or arrest is then challenged in court, the officer will have to demonstrate to the court both his personal expertise and his dog's reliability and training. The K-9 officer must be prepared to testify to the training history of his dog in the field of narcotics detection. The officer should also describe to the court the dog's past work experience. Most importantly, the officer must testify that his dog's alert or reaction to the location or container in question was a reaction which in the past had consistently and accurately detected the presence of narcotics. The K-9 officer will have to show his own training and any continuing education, as well as his experience with that particular dog. *Remember, the dog's excited behavior, by itself, is not enough proof that a controlled substance is present. The District Attorney must be able to present a strong foundation of the dog's reliability and the handler's expertise.*

People v. $48,715 et al., California 1998
Consent to search included movement of the truck and use of the dog. Forfeiture proceedings are easily instituted against property discovered or used in narcotics transactions.

The People v. David Santana, 63 Cal. App. 4th 543, 1998
The act of "poofing," i.e., squeezing luggage and smelling the expelled air does not amount to a search within the meaning of the Fourth Amendment.

People v. Reyes (1998) 18 Cal.4th
Parole search does not require suspicion.

State v. Benton, Ohio Supreme Court, 1998
Condition requiring parolee to submit to warrantless search "at any time" does not violate Fourth Amendment.

REQUIRED TRAINING

Before starting street work with the narcotic dog, the team must successfully complete an initial training academy and a performance evaluation that demonstrates they meet the department standard. New teams need 320 to 400 hours of training, including the following academic and field work:

1. Basic on-lead obedience and agility training to control and direct the dog.

2. Canine transport, housing, basic care, and emergency veterinary medicine, including the use of antidotes and high quality insulated medical storage containers.

3. Training aids: Actual narcotic substances, typically 5- to 2000-gram quantities. Under DEA license, the department obtains court orders for the use of these substances as required. Street drugs scheduled for destruction should be analyzed by a criminalistics laboratory then packaged, identified, and properly transferred to the department, maintaining the chain of evidence. Scientific investigation conducts quantitative analysis on the narcotics in order to verify the purity level of each substance.

    Narcotics must be stored separately (safes located in separate rooms for marijuana or methamphetamine) with controlled temperature and ventilation to prevent contamination. Storage in scent-sterile containers (glass) prevents contamination by metal or plastics. The handlers need 24-hour controlled access. Transport the aids in padded metal camera-type cases that can be secured easily inside the patrol car. Each department must establish procedures for the accountability, destruction, and replacement of all narcotic substances. Renew the aids every 4-6 months. Repackage aids as frequently as needed, depending on the contamination factor and whatever proofing you need to do during your training.

    Random audits insure proper procedures are being implemented.

4. Training in the use of all handling equipment (leads, collars, gloves, emergency medical gear) and specialized tactical equipment (communications as well as protective gear and investigative tools).

5. \Department policy and procedures for narcotic dog teams, including reporting incidents and recording the dog team's rolling resume for court testimony. When preparing an affadavit, reference the schools you have attended or taught, your participation in narcotics investigations, the publications you have read or authored, your responsibilities as a dog handler, the dog's training, certification, and service record, including the controlled substances he has found.

6. Drug detection capability: Typically *marijuana* (cannabis sativa, containing THC—tetrahydrocannabinol), *cocaine* ($C_{17}H_{21}NO_4$), and *heroin* ($C_{21}N_{23}NO_5$), also the scent-related derivatives of these drugs, such as hashish, rock cocaine or tar heroin. Some departments train *methamphetamine* ($C_{10}H_{15}N$) despite the potential for false positive alerts, either to precursor chemicals or to legal compounds with similar scent properties, such as compounds containing ephedrine. Most of the time, meth and herb are used together, methamphetamine as the upper, marijuana as the downer to end a speed trip. Cross-contamination is the rule. For this reason the marijuana trained dog will typically find meth also. The toxicology of certain drugs, such as LSD, contraindicates training dogs to find them.

*Officer Dave Kain and
K-9 Günnar.*

SNIFF SEMANTICS

Scent or odor: Airborne molecules that activate the sense of smell upon contact with the individual's nasal receptors. The structure and density of these molecules determine how neurotransmitters code or chemically identify them to the brain.

Applying this definition of scent to K-9 drug detection, each drug we train the dog to detect diffuses special molecules the dog learns to recognize when he sniffs them. Each drug has a *scent signature.* Street drugs are typically complex compounds. In terms of physics and chemistry, the scent is not the drug. By analogy, human scent is not a person. *To a trained dog the scent of each drug is distinctive.*

We shape the dog's behavior to perform the same *alert* for all the drugs he is trained to recognize. We reinforce the K-9 alert to minimize error, in laboratory test terms, to reduce the number of false-positive alerts (the dog alerts where there is no drug scent), commonly called a false alert or *false hit,* and false-negative alerts (the dog fails to alert to available scent), commonly called a failure to find or a miss. The standard scientific terminology describes the K-9's investigative procedure. Various terms (non-narcotic alert, non-seizure alert, unknown alert) have been used to describe the detector dog's alert in cases where the dog alerted but no drugs were found. The language of biomedical research is clear. Inventing new terms is unnecessary and can cause confusion where we need clarity.

Every time a trained narcotic detector dog sniffs for drugs he is performing a *search, or an investigative procedure.* In training, the handler can partly control the environment. On the street, he cannot. The terminology describing the dog's reactions are standardized as follows:

DETECTOR DOG ALERT

Common Term	Technical Term	Meaning
Alert	Positive alert	Dog exhibits behavior indicating he recognizes drug scent
No alert	Negative alert	Dog does not alert
False alert	False-positive alert	Dog alerts in absence of drug scent
Miss	False-negative alert	Dog does not alert in presence of drug scent

The first two terms (positive alert, negative alert) apply to both training and streetwork. Reliability means the dog will alert if he detects narcotic scent, not otherwise. The last two terms (false-positive alert, false-negative alert) apply to training, where the handler has control over the environment and the odor of interest, and knows if the dog is sniffing in the target area. There are several reasons for the false-positive alert (reinforcement, learning) or false-negative alert (distraction, dysfunction) that have to be changed through training or medical treatment. Cognitive deployment, realistic maintenance training, and evaluations are important to maintain K-9 team reliability.

Scent cone describes *odor diffusing from a source*. Scent does not diffuse in straight lines or neat shapes. Nor is the scent pattern usually continuous. Discontinuity and randomness are the rule, not the exception. Considering the effects of turbulence, we could refer to scent plume, cloud, pool, bloom, or scent puffs, like smoke signals. Scent cone signifies the dog targeting the source of the odor. When the scent cloud does break up into isolated puffs, the dog may not be able to sniff to the source. *Understanding these concepts is critical to reading your dog and using effective tactics.*

Canine accuracy, like that of every animal including police officers, is less than 100 percent. The dog's nose may be dysfunctional. For other reasons, he may not be working that day. Errors attributed to the dog are frequently either training problems or handler errors. The dog that misses 80 kilos of dope in a closet, for example, might never have trained on large quantities before, a training problem. Scent overload, the rapid adherence of scent to the mucosa reaching a saturated or steady state, may surprise the dog. He may exhibit a reaction or behavior change the handler fails to read as an alert, typically handler error. Scent presents to the detector dog as a function of the surface area, not the weight, of the narcotic.

The dog may detect scent when the dope is gone. Four skiers toke up in the parking lot before going up the mountain. Five minutes later a narcotic detector dog alerts to the car. There is no dope inside. However, the dog has performed correctly. A reliable narcotic detector dog's alert signifies the *presence or recent presence of dope*.

The handler is responsible for directing the dog to sniff the scent cone or airspace where drug scent might diffuse. Good search tactics employ patterns that detail or provide thorough coverage of the area being investigated. Packaging, masking scents, chemical interference, lacing, inaccessible caches, precursor chemicals, heat, supercooling, booby traps, poisons, and other distractions are all challenges to K-9 teams. Some problems can be solved by training. Some hazards are too deadly to risk the dog. We will deal with these issues in the drug search environment.

Typically the dog is trained to signal a find in one of two ways: the *aggressive alert* or the *passive alert*. Either style requires a dog with strong search drives that reacts reliably when he detects drugs. The dog trained to alert aggressively *tries to contact the scent source* (biting, scratching, penetrating, attempting to retrieve), while the dog that alerts passively does not try to contact the scent source but instead *performs trained behavior* (sitting, looking at the source, sniffing toward the source, looking at the handler). Different searching and alerting styles reflect different training philosophies, different dogs, and the demands of the police officer's work environment. Canine safety and minimal privacy intrusion are typical arguments for the passive alert. Reinforcing the drives and locating the scent source are typical arguments favoring the aggressive alert.

For nearly all detection training, the handler should not know in advance where the narcotics are hidden. This compels the handler to read his dog. He develops proficiency and confidence reading the dog and can clearly describe the dog's behavior for investigators and later for his report. These methods require behavior shaping supervised by a qualified trainer, but they typically create a handler who acts consistently, whether training or conducting an actual search. Sensing this consistency, the dog usually performs reliably too.

Learned behavior that goes unrewarded will extinguish. Scientists know that a variable schedule of reinforcement is more powerful than a constant schedule. Suppose the narcotic dog searches a house without finding any drugs. Agents find no drugs in the house. The dog gets no positive (or negative) reinforcement. He does not need reinforcement on every search. In fact, random *dry* or unrewarded searches build drive. The next time the dog is deployed to search a house, he hits a bureau in the master bedroom. His typical alert. Reinforce the alert: play, praise or other method. Time the reward to reinforce the alerting behavior.

For nearly all detection training, the handler should not know in advance where the narcotics are hidden. This compels the handler to read his dog.

Solving a problem or test, such as discriminating for drug scent, the dog needs to know he did it right. Reinforce him with play or praise. Praise is a conditioned reinforcer, as powerful as play if used correctly. If the dog does a number of actual searches without detecting narcotics, an assisting officer hides training aids, the dog searches, alerts on the aid, and the handler reinforces his behavior. If the dog does a number of actual searches where he detects narcotics in the same type packaging, for example, cocaine wrapped in plastic with duct tape, *proof him* later in training with controls to prevent alerts to packaging materials.

Here are 4 common errors: 1) Never reinforce your dog's alert on an actual search unless he is finding a training aid. 2) You don't know what he is alerting to. 3) If he alerts, just praise him. 4) Or wait until you see the dope, then reward him.

Here is what to do:

Reinforce your dog when he alerts on an actual search. The background scents are the variables eliminated by changing the training environment and by proofing with controls. The drugs are the constant components.

Praising the dog is a powerful conditioned reinforcer. Restaining the alerting dog while you check for dope is equally powerful.

Time the reinforcement to coincide with the behavior—the alert— or do nothing. At least do no harm. Do not reinforce the wrong behavior if the dog is distracted.

What if there is scent but no dope? When removed from a location, drugs leave detectable scent behind for a *brief period of time*. Take the dog away for a break. Later, set up exercises to determine if you have a training problem.

K-9 tactics vary depending on the type of search: outside areas, vehicles, buildings, parcels, luggage, aircraft, vessels, or, for U.S. Customs and other agencies, on or about persons. Dogs are capable of detecting narcotics buried underground or submerged, depending on the conditions. Challenge the team with increasingly difficult assignments: distractions, masking scents, obstacles, and larger, more complex search areas.

Search patterns:
- *Area search:* The handler directs the dog back and forth across an area (yard, flight path of a fugitive) in a z-pattern.
- *Perimeter:* The dog searches in linked patterns around the outside of an object (vehicle or building exterior, pallet of cargo) or inside a confined space (room or vehicle). The dog can examine small items (shoe box) in a few sniffs, moving only his head. Or he may walk past an array of parcels, sniffing each one in turn.
- *Assigned location:* The dog has a limited range of motion at a location, such as an airport concourse, where the objects or individuals he is searching move past him. Or the K-9 searches on an active conveyor belt, such as airport baggage, a technique that forces him to keep moving but that dogs typically like.

Maintaining reliability: Regular, supervised training exercises reinforce the desired search behavior. Exercises with controls *proof* the dog's search capability and verify his reliability as a detector dog. Rigorous training pushes both the dog and handler to the max to discover the team's limitations. Advanced training scenarios extend the time and conditions under which the dog will work reliably. Periodic evaluations conducted by qualified trainers outside the department show that the team meets the department's standard of performance.

If the K-9 handler's experience is in patrol, he will need training in narcotics investigations: recognizing indicators for narcotic enforcement; high risk warrant service; search and seizure law; narcotic asset forfeiture law; narcotic officer safety; drug pharmacology.

If the handler is a narcotic officer, he will need skills in canine behavior shaping, surprisingly similar to managing informants, and support from the administration for ongoing canine training. If he works the only narcotic K-9 in the department, getting support can be a frustrating job. Underutilization in some departments shuts down the dog unit before the teams optimize their performance.

WHAT DRUGS ARE BEING USED IN YOUR COMMUNITY?

Drug task forces and local narcotic officers are the best source of information about street drugs. Patterns of drug use change rapidly. To be effective, the drug dog handler who is not a narcotic officer has to educate himself about drug use and trafficking, at least on a local basis.

Publications are valuable for training and reference. Narcotic officer association periodicals, such as *The California Narcotic Officer*, are relatively current. Narcotic K-9 officers need to maintain access to the following information:

1. Name of the drug (including slang terms)
2. Physical appearance (color, texture, odor, liquid, powder, rock, tablet, etc.)
3. Packaging (plastic bags, bindles, balloons, etc.)
4. Use (smoke, inject, swallow, inhale, and tools)
5. Price per unit measure (wholesale or retail per gram, kilogram, ounce, or pound)
6. Psychophysical effects (stimulant, depressant, hallucinogen, toxin, dose), including effects on police dogs
7. Chemicals used to manufacture the drug (example, ephedrine as a precursor for methamphetamine) and cuts (substances added as adulterants)
8. Distribution pattern (source, courier, shipper, route, destination)

As new drugs appear on the street, or old drugs reappear, each agency has to evaluate the threat and train their dogs accordingly. Is the narcotic manufactured, sold, or shipped in the area? How much is involved (pounds and price)? Is this a short term trend or a long term threat? Can a dog detect the narcotic safely? Reliably? What is the drug's pharmacology—toxicity, chemical stability? What is the potential for inducing false alerts on chemically related non-narcotic compounds? Is the training feasible if "What you train you must maintain"?

DRUG IDENTIFICATION BIBLE
Revised 4th Edition

Leading reference to identify controlled drugs. Hundreds of color photos of illicit drugs, packaging and paraphernalia. Product markings of over 10,000 prescription and over-the-counter drugs. Officers carry this 6 in. by 9 in. paperback on patrol. 750pp

Order:
Amera-Chem
P.O. Box 518
Grand Junction, CO 81502
Tel 800-772-2539 or 970-256-7038
Fax 800-852-7870 or 970-256-7308

OFFICER SAFETY

Officer safety is as much an issue for drug dog teams as for patrol dog teams. When a drug dog is searching a vehicle on a car stop, for example, the team needs a cover officer in charge of the occupants. The K-9 officer has to concentrate his full attention on his dog without worrying about getting shot in the back or people running away. The handler is fully occupied working his dog and, if he sees a behavioral change or an alert, taking appropriate action.

When conducting consent searches by himself on the highway, one officer asks the occupants to handcuff themselves voluntarily to a stationary object. Another agency asks the occupants to seat themselves voluntarily in the back of the patrol car for the officer's safety. What is *the department's liability and the liability of the officer* under these circumstances?

First, on difficult searches, the handler whose attention is diverted will miss a higher percentage of behavioral changes by the dog. Under stress the handler may even fail to read a clear alert. Missing a dog's quick *mark*, indication, or sniff of interest on scent he cannot immediately target may mean missing a find because the officer will not have enough information to change his tactics and get the dog's nose in a position to make the find. Failing to read alerts, where the result is negative reinforcement, can actually detrain the dog.

Second, the handler has to watch the aggressive-alert dog to prevent narcotic ingestion. If a K-9 contacts any hazardous substance, start emergency medical procedures right away to minimize contamination and absorption.

Do not conduct searches at the expense of officer safety. No drugs or cash are worth the officer's health or professional welfare, let alone his life. High risk encounters are part of street work. But exposing drug search teams to unnecessary risk is negligence. When making a car stop, serving a warrant, or entering a building, officers are trained and ready to use the force necessary to save lives and secure the scene. Once that is done, and only then, can drug search proceed. Searching for drugs or other evidence while the scene is not yet secure is irresponsible and may place not only officers' but also innocent citizens' lives in jeopardy.

Felony stop. K-9 detected hidden narcotics.

TEAM TASKING

Especially in rural communities where a trained drug dog team is available, it is important to train all the patrol officers to *think dog*. When an officer makes a vehicle stop and he has reason to believe the vehicle contains drugs or he obtains consent to search for drugs, the department should facilitate calling the dog team to the scene. After officers hand shake a vehicle—open it up, search through it, take items out of it—the drug dog may not work effectively.

The same holds true for searching buildings or residences. Once the location is secure, officers should wait for the dog to search before doing a physical search. If an officer finds drugs in a bureau drawer, for instance, takes the drugs out, turns the drawer and its contents onto the bed, then handles the door knobs and washes his hands on his way outside, he has just distributed drug scent throughout the apartment. The incoming drug dog will probably alert to the door knobs, the sink fixtures, the towel, the drawer, the bed—all the contaminated surfaces—and generally drive his handler crazy. Sometimes this post-search procedure is unavoidable, notably where officers find drugs unexpectedly. K-9 awareness by the patrol force will increase the team's effectiveness.

A physical search by officers after the K-9 search is important whether the dog came up dry or found drugs. The bad guys know about dogs and try to outsmart them. Masking scents, double shrink-wrap packaging, freezing, they're doing everything you can imagine to fool the dog. The more the handler can learn about his dog's limits, the better man and dog will function as a team. Some areas are inaccessible to the dog—a hot engine compartment or an 18 foot ceiling, to name two. Scent detection in these circumstances will be affected by the air flow, the quantity and concealment of the drugs, and the experience of the dog team. The good team is not foolproof and will not claim to be 100 percent.

Patrol cooperation will do two more things. Once the dog's effectiveness is recognized by the court, his alert and other evidence gives officers reason to believe drugs are present, to obtain a warrant, and to search. Second, departments that use drug dogs efficiently have found asset seizure to be a significant benefit of the dog program. Discoveries by the dog do not deflect credit from narcotic officers but rather enhance the record of narcotic team effectiveness.

The U.S. Customs experience gained by deploying hundreds of canine detector teams has relevance for every department using dog teams to locate narcotics and dangerous drugs. Proven Customs training methods are in fact the basis on which most police K-9 teams train and test. *Since high quality proficiency training is critical to performance reliability, its importance cannot be overemphasized.* The basic requirement to maintain drug dog team proficiency is straightforward—the team must be used on a daily basis. Results of all deployment, including training, must be recorded to maintain the canine's *rolling record* to support court testimony.

The *Gangs 2000* intelligence report released by the California Attorney General in 1993 forecast gangs becoming more vicious and violent, committing predatory crimes and serious felonies, becoming more ethnically diverse, involving more females and better organization. Gangs will continue to traffic and sell cocaine, heroin, marijuana, and methamphetamine. State and nationwide integrated narcotics systems will be designed to meet the combined information needs of the narcotics enforcement anti-drug analysis functions of participating law enforcement agencies, spanning jurisdictional boundaries throughout the country. Major system components include: intelligence and case management; geographic mapping, photograhic imaging; drug data analysis; integrated access linkage; remote/mobile access. Effective narcotic K-9 teams become an active part of these systems.

The Gangs 2000 *intelligence report released by the California Attorney General in 1993 forecast gangs becoming more vicious and violent, committing predatory crimes and serious felonies, becoming more ethnically diverse, involving more females and better organization.*

DRUG DETECTOR DOG UTILIZATION REPORT

Date	Case No. Training	Search Area	Alert/Location	Drug/ Qty.	Other

Search warrant service can be one of the most
dangerous activities a police officer faces.

BUILDING SEARCH

Detectives and patrol officers of neighboring city police departments executed a search warrant on a warehouse. Inside officers found a large *heat-seal machine and heat-seal bags.* The machine was on with marijuana residue on a table along with a large digital scale preset to 15 pounds. Twenty-five bags of high quality manicured bud, empty bags with the name Great Northern Bean emblazoned on them, six guns, including a semi-auto Uzi, a case of NI-712 *odor suppressant*, $920 in case, and pictures of the operator drying and manicuring weed on the floor of his business. Two vehicles were seized inside the location, based on the odor of marijuana detected in large duffle bags found in the vehicles. A Dodge motor home had been modified with a series of sophisticated hidden compartments capable of transporting over 200 pounds of marijuana. Documents found inside the warehouse led officers to other locations in the area where search warrants were served, other drugs recovered, and more vehicles seized.

Smart crooks mean cops have to work smarter. Increasingly, the sophisticated traffickers, even illegal aliens, expect the same rights accorded law-abiding U.S. citizens. Depending on circumstances—who is involved, what profits are at stake, what they believe the cops know, what legal advice they have obtained—these individuals will be demanding to see search warrants or will be actively uncooperative with law enforcement. The K-9 officer needs to be knowledgeable about developing probable cause, requesting permission to search, obtaining search warrants, particularly telephonic warrants, and warrant service.

Search warrant service can be one of the most dangerous activities a police officer faces, and not only in terms of physical harm, even death, to officers or suspects. Searches may subject narcotic investigators to civil suits, departmental discipline, or criminal charges. Despite competent planning and execution, warrant service can quickly get out of control due to circumstances beyond anyone's control.

Search warrants on small to middle level dealers have proved extremely dangerous. The suspects are well armed, they worry about rip-offs, are involved in territorial disputes, and they frequently use drugs themselves. Because they lack the sophistication of the major violators, they are quick to shoot it out with the cops.

These people generate the most complaints from residents. Patrol personnel as well as citizens who call in with information expect narcotic officers to run through the suspects' front door shortly after they hang up the phone. This attitude encourages narcotic investigators to take action when common sense might call for another approach. This attitude can also affect whether a narcotic detection K-9 is requested and how the dog team deploys.

In one medium-sized city where department procedure involved using a tactical entry when serving drug-related search warrants, officers with high powered weapons made their announcement then pried the gate and rammed the door of a house in the middle of the night. Family members were in their bedrooms. It was the right district but the wrong house. Apparently, an informant had given officers bad information, or unverified information, that became the basis of the warrant. Nobody in the house spoke English. Bursting into the parents' bedroom, the first officer through the door was felled with a shot from a handgun fired by the surprised father. Cover officers then killed the man in his bed. The detector dog deployed after the shooting incident found a few grams of marijuana.

Dog handlers, especially officers performing interagency assists, must guard against deploying in a manner detrimental to the agency in charge. While the K-9 officer will generally not be knowledgable about intelligence underlying the mission, he does control deploying the dog. Do not become overzealous in response to pressure from individuals at the scene, even from officers of higher rank. For example, one group of narcotic officers requested a crosstrained K-9 make the initial entry with them even though the teams had never trained together before. The handler declined. Instead he took a position on the perimeter. Ironically, before officers could enter the house, the subject emerged from a side door, jumped a hedge along the alley, and walked into the K-9 unit on the perimeter.

SLEDNET Task Force. Carson City, Nevada

Who wins? How would your dog react to narcotics hidden under an 8-foot Burmese Python?

NARCOTIC CANINE TACTICS

Brief the investigators as necessary in the use of narcotic dogs. Officers at the scene may not be experienced in K-9 search tactics. Explain how the dog works, what you need them to do, and ask for their questions before the operation gets started.

Before deploying the dog at the search scene:

Secure the building and surrounding property. Remove all unauthorized persons, including owners or occupants, from the location(s) to be searched. First, if anybody is holding narcotics or is contaminated with narcotic scent, the dog may alert to that person. Second, if you are searching by permission, for example, as a result of a knock and talk, individuals are more likely to rescind that permission when they see the dog getting close to the stash. When doing a permissive search on a residence, get permission to bring the dog in also. Many people do not envision having a dog in their home. They think it will be just a couple of officers with flashlights looking around.

Pay attention to unconscious investigators walking around with found drugs. Request they move out of that area before the dog starts searching it.

A lieutenant who was critical of detector dogs loaded his suitcoat with narcotics and stood in the center of a room watching the K-9 work. When the dog alerted to the lieutenant, the handler corrected him back to the search pattern. The dog kept alerting. The handler kept pulling him back. Finally, after the handler announced his dog was not working and left, the lieutenant displayed his suitcoat to the other officers present.

Do a walk-through. Inspect the area to be searched, removing or avoiding dangerous items such as exposed chemicals, broken glass, hypodermic needles, or other hazards. Remove dogs or other animals from the premises (drugs have been hidden in dog houses occupied by very large dogs). In one house, an 8-foot Burmese Python had his own bedroom where he lurked under piles of boxes, clothing, and other debris.

Test the air flow in the building. Estimate the turbulence effect of heating and ventilating units, windows and doors, or other conditions affecting scent diffusion. Determine how air spaces such as rooms or hallways are breathing, that is inhaling *(air diffusing inward)* or exhaling *(air diffusing outward)*. In some cases, close the doors or windows to reduce turbulence. In other cases, ventilate to control the temperature or to increase the diffusion rate. Turn the heating or ventilating systems off or on to the dog's advantage. After changing the environment, wait for the system to stabilize before starting to search.

If possible, have at least one other officer present during the search to *record alerts, investigate potential finds, handle the narcotics, and maintain the chain of evidence.* Handling the narcotics puts the K-9 officer in the chain of custody.

Hide the drug training aids as needed using uncontaminated instruments (e.g. tongs, forceps, sticks). Do not rely on gloves to prevent scent contamination. Scent diffuses through gloves, even plastic or rubber gloves. Also, gloves transmit their own scent. Use different assistants to hide the aids. Have the assistant distribute his personal scent throughout the search area to prevent the dog from keying to locations of concentrated human scent.

Change the type of concealment frequently to prevent the dog from anticipating a find and giving a false alert. One handler—this is hard to believe—reinforced his dog's vehicle searches by hiding narcotics behind the rear license plate, every time. Guess where the dog anticipated finding narcotics? Change the drugs and the packaging. One handler—even harder to believe—carried the same drug samples around with him in the same 35-millimeter film cans for two years.

Wear gloves to protect yourself from chemicals, diseases, needles or other sharp objects. If you have to sweep your dog's mouth in a hurry to keep him from swallowing something, you will not have time to put on gloves. Human skin is inadequate protection. *"On is in"* describes the risk of absorbing anything from hallucinogenic drugs to deadly viruses through the skin or tiny cuts or breaks in the skin. No barrier is perfect. However, the less permeable the material, the more protection you have. The more you sweat also.

Searching with the dog:

Divide long searches into shorter intervals to give the dog breaks and reinforcing finds. *Plan these search segments* before starting to work the dog so the investigators and patrol officers at the scene know where the dog will be working, what you need from them, and how to work around the dog. Nobody wants to stand outside for 30-45 minutes waiting for a narcotic dog to search the interior. Systematic K-9 deployment enables narcotic officers to re-enter rooms or areas as soon as the dog completes his search.

Carry water, extra gloves, the appropriate leads (6-foot, 15-foot or both), flashlights, and flags or tags with you. Do not rely on returning to the patrol car for these items. Water will start the emergency wash if the dog picks up drugs or other poisons. Carrying water assures better hydration for the dog. Do not permit the dog to drink or eat anything from the premises. Work the drug dog on lead for efficiency and safety. The assisting officer can tag the alerts.

A corrections team searched a large warehouse with a high steel roof. Only the entry door was open. Inside, the air was so hot and dusty and still that the officers said it felt fuzzy. Cockroaches, dead mice, and rabbit droppings littered the floor. Repeated trips outside convinced the handler to carry water on his person. Better ventilation would have improved the team's performance. When the dog did alert to drugs secreted in shrink-wrapped computer equipment,

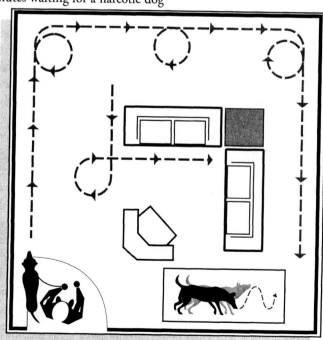

Consistent search patterns: the sine wave or multiple passes at different levels. If the dog is distracted or at corners, rotate as a unit into a new angle of sniff attack. Crawl or climb to check every likely area.

he tap-danced for minutes among the pallets in a 40-foot section, caught in a large pool of scent, unable to go to source *or pinpoint* the narcotics.

Use standard search tactics (whatever you do, just do it...reliably).

Start the dog sniffing outside the boundaries of the search area to ensure he covers the entire designated area. Cops get tunnel vision on entry. Three major concealment areas are entryways (to buildings, to rooms, to closets), hallways, and stairwells. The dog tends to rush through entries, eager to get on with the search. Do the workup and start the dog searching well outside the building, room, or area to be searched. Get the dog focused on the task so that he will detail entrances and exits. Crosstrained police dogs are particularly guilty of fast entry on drug searches.

One house had been under surveillance for months. Officers knew drugs were being sold out of the house. They had observed a delivery. Where were the drugs? Where had the drug dog rushed in and out? Where were all the narcs standing around talking? On the welcome mat covering loose floorboards at the front door, of course.

During another search in an apartment, a bedroom closet looked clear, but the narcotic dog kept biting the doorjamb impatiently. Finally, casting his light inside the closet above the door, the handler saw unusually thick molding nailed over a hole in the sheetrock. Officers retrieved five bricks of marijuana from the hole.

Do not let the dog relieve himself in the search area. Train in buildings with distracting scents (cats, dogs, rabbits) that may incite canine crime in order to correct this type of problem. If the dog lifts his leg, he is not searching. Get him out of there.

Typically, dogs work the perimeter of each room or section first, then search interior objects. Direct the dog to search across any areas of the floor where drugs could be hidden. Pay attention to blank walls, molding, partitions, window and wall covering, electrical outlets, heaters, ducting, carpet, tile, ceiling panels. Sniff appliances, computers, and file cabinets.

Do a rapid or hasty search only if time or resources prevent conducting a detailed search. This tactic saves time but reduces the probability of detection.

Do not give up. If it appears on entry that the subjects left the day before and took everything with them, search anyway. If the dog fails to alert to an apparent load of dope in plain view (or in plain sniff), get on with the search. If the dog appears to be working, find out by making controlled hides. Find out later if the item the dog did not indicate was in fact dope, or if the packaging prevented detection. If you discover a training problem, determine if you can work around the problem, then proceed on that basis.

The West Sacramento K-9 handler, whose dog is crosstrained for narcotic detection, said, "We did a house search with the task force. In a bedroom closet was a locked cedar chest. The dog hit on the chest. He grabbed hold of it, tore at the wood. The narcotic officers unlocked it, and the dog flipped up the lid with his head. Inside we found a bunch of pot, crank, and big rolls of cash. In the same room was a waterbed frame with a regular mattress. The dog burrowed between the mattress and frame. I asked them to lift up the side of the mattress. I knew something was underneath. There was a big freezer bag full of crank.

"In another room the dog almost pulled over a desk. Inside the drawer were a couple of scales with marijuana. In the bathroom he kept alerting high, standing on his hind legs. I told them, hey, check high. There is something up high, but he can't pinpoint it. In one of the cabinets near the ceiling were scales and more pot.

"It was a typical crankster pad. In a storage area of the garage, clothes and boxes were piled everywhere. The dog kept alerting but I couldn't see what he was hitting on. He kept throwing his head up, and going into a pile of boxes. When he gets frustrated, he starts biting at other stuff. In one of the boxes were glass pipes with residue.

"It totaled out a couple pounds of pot, about two pounds of crank. I explained to the guys that it's just a matter of targeting. There was a lot of shit in there. You can imagine how overwhelming it is to the dog when he walks through the door. Every place the dog alerted there was a bunch of dope."

Know when to quit. The handler's job is to direct and read the dog's performance, to maintain reliability by giving him breaks and reinforcement, and to stop before his reliability declines. Always quit if the dog quits searching.

Investigative tools and medical kit in the patrol vehicle:

- Emergency medical equipment
- Camera and film
- Tape
- Phillips and standard screwdrivers
- Extra batteries for flashlights and camera
- Steel probe
- Magnifying glass
- Air gauge
- Coat hanger, slim-jim
- Piece of carpet or plastic pad for crawling under vehicles
- Drug test kits
- Knife
- Tape measure
- Hammer and pry bar
- Drill and assorted bits
- Magnet
- Mirror
- Scales
- Evidence bags

The dog's drug detection record should include:

- Time, date, case/cite
- Search location (the address and the area, building, vehicle, or object the dog searches)
- Location of the alert (precise but brief—for example, left front hubcap)
- Drug and quantity found (*zero* if nothing found)
- Other item found (e.g. money, tools, paraphernalia—amount and type)
- Document and photograph the concealment area/method, any scent masking material used, including other types of drugs, and any other apparent attempt to reduce the effectiveness of the detector dog
- Photocopy all agency reports on the case and maintain them in the dog's performance record. If there are any questions later about details of the case, you have them at hand. Also, the 3-ring binder of the training records and incident reports for a dog being used on a regular basis soon weighs a few pounds and provides substantial evidence of the dog's capability.

Building searches frequently include vehicles containing drugs and cash ready for transport. In one case, task force officers served a search warrant at a stash pad where they deployed a narcotic K-9. The dog hit on a Chrysler Laser vehicle parked in the garage. Hidden inside a secret compartment protected by plastic molding, they recovered $333,300 in cash. When officers simultaneously executed a warrant at another location, a K-9 alerted to a Ford Mustang convertible parked in the garage. Detectives recovered $42,532 from a compartment behind the rear seat of the Mustang. These dogs were detecting drug scent contaminating the money handled by traffickers. Investigation results totaled 11 arrests, including 10 federal indictments, the seizure of 144 kilos of cocaine, approximately $950,000 in cash, 16 firearms and 7 vehicles. Without the use of the K-9s, it is unlikely the money would have been recovered from any of the vehicles.

Sometimes what is absent in a warrant search becomes as significant as what is present. A deputy feeding his horse in a backyard corral looked across the yard through a neighbor's window and saw three marijuana plants about five feet high growing in the sunlight. The next morning the task force served a warrant on the house, placed the owner under arrest, and deployed a narcotic dog. The dog dragged his handler through the front door to pounce on a

bag partway under the coffee table in the living room. In their haste to go for the green, detectives had not noticed a plastic shopping bag filled with over a pound of dried herb packaged for sale. The house itself was new, over $200,000 paid in cash by the jobless suspect. Apparently the owner was not a user. Nothing in the house suggested drug use—no ashtrays, no peraphernalia, nothing in the garbage. The dog showed no interest in any of the bedrooms nor on any of the bedding. The handler noticed the conspicuous absence in the kitchen and elsewhere of common packaging materials, ziplock bags, plastic wrap, tape. There were, however, suitcases with Honduran baggage tags attached. A brand-new fax machine broadcast greetings from a satisfied customer thanking the suspect for a recent narcotics delivery.

Neighbors asked a teenaged male to pick up the papers, feed the dog, mow and water the lawn and garden while they were away on vacation. While performing these duties, the young man observed that not all the plants in the garden were legal vegetables. He notified the sheriff's department.

Arriving officers obtained permission from the owners behind the residence to surveil the garden over the back fence. They could see through the chain link. From their vantage point in the adjacent yard, they could plainly see greenery that looked like mature marijuana plants growing in the garden.

They obtained and served a search warrant for the residence. A little girl answered the door. She said her parents were in the back bedroom. Entering the master bedroom, officers discovered mom and pop sharing a joint. The room was filled with smoke from burning marijuana.

If the dog alerts where you would not expect to find dope, expect dope.

Brought into the residence to search, the dog entered the daughter's room and alerted high, stretching his neck toward the ceiling as soon as he entered the room. Nothing about the ceiling or walls suggested concealment. The handler found a floor vent at the side of the room opposite the door and directed the dog to detail the vent. The dog instantly went crazy, pawing and clawing at the grate. Removing the grate, the handler reached down as far as he could into the air duct but felt nothing. After probing the ducting, the officer concluded it was venting the parents' bedroom into that room. The dog also found a woman's leather wallet containing narcotic residue lying on the little girl's bureau.

Entering the master bedroom, the dog immediately hit the bottom drawer of a 6-drawer bureau to the left of the door. The drawer contained packets of snapshots and a photo album. The dog insisted. Paging through the album, investigators discovered a page displaying a mature marijuana leaf. Detailing the rest of the bureau, the dog alerted high on top, indicating a small wooden box with dope inside. Next, the dog alerted to the third drawer down of another chest of drawers. Inside were the father's T-shirts, below that a piece of cardboard, below that the bottom of the drawer was totally covered with packets of dope labeled for sale, neatly wrapped and price-tagged. The dog did a strong alert on a cabinet containing many pounds of dope packaged for sale, paraphernalia, and money. On each find the handler reinforced the dog. Several times he removed him from the house to give him a break.

A west coast DEA agent received information a suspect was in possession of two tons of marijuana stored in a warehouse. The caller indicated the suspect owned or operated a company that leased the warehouse. The caller gave the agent directions to the suspect's residence, stating he drove a white Ford van which would be parked in the driveway. Following the directions, DEA located the residence, the white van and surveilled two men making repeated trips to the warehouse and other residences. The warehouse was one of 30 to 35 units in a light industrial complex. Each unit had an office entrance in front and a roll-up door in the back. A public alleyway ran along the rear of the units, where the roll-up doors were located. At 7:30 p.m., a narcotic canine team arrived at the warehouse. The officer led his dog along the public alleyway, sniffing the roll-up doors of the unit next to the warehouse, then the warehouse. The dog alerted to the warehouse.

Later that night the agent obtained a search warrant for the warehouse, the suspect's residence, and the van. Attached to the affidavit in support of the search warrant was a two-page expertise statement concerning the dog's reliability that the agent had obtained from the handler. Executing the warrant the next day, agents found 1445 pounds of Thai marijuana in the warehouse. The search of the suspect's residence and van uncovered additional evidence of narcotics trafficking.[37]

The suspect did not have a legitimate expectation that the contraband stored in the warehouse would not be detected by a canine sniff. The key principle is *the dog is an extension of the officer's own senses in* much the same way that a flashlight enhances the officer's sight. The dog is a tool. *If the officer is where he has a right to be*, the dog sniffing at that location is not a violation of the fourth amendment.

A spectacular demonstration of that basic principle happened in Chicago. The Chicago Police Department's Gang Crimes South unit began surveillance of a suspect. Police followed him to a garage located on a grassy vacant lot with no visible address directly abutting a public alley. An overhead door swung out into the alley. Another door was boarded up and nailed shut. The overhead door was secured with both a standard key-lock in the door and a large padlock.

The suspect unlocked the garage door with keys, raising it only high enough to enter by crouching down, and quickly closing the door behind him. He entered the garage empty-handed but emerged minutes later with a partially filled green plastic garbage bag. Thus began a series of furtive delivery trips, the tireless suspect returning repeatedly to the garage and departing with green garbage bags with unknown contents. For several days the officers observed the suspect perform the same covert ritual. No one else entered the garage during the entire surveillance period.

When a confidential informant advised them the garage contained a large amount of cocaine, they enlisted the aid of a DEA narcotic detection dog. The dog sniffed along the alley. At the garage he barked and pawed excitedly, alerting to the overhead door the suspect had used. Confident the garage contained drugs, the police obtained a search warrant based on the dog's alert and the informant's tip.[38]

37. *U.S. v. Lingenfelter*, 997 F.2d 632 (9th Cir. 1993).
38. *U.S. v. Vasquez*, 909 F.2d 235 (7th Cir. 1990).

Case No: _____ ‗

CONSENT TO SEARCH

I, _____ , hereby grant my consent to _____

_____ , officers of _____ ·

Department to search the following vehicle described below including luggage, containers, and contents of all.

_____

Color   Year   Make   Body Style   License Plate

I understand that I have the right to refuse to consent to the search described above and to refuse to sign this form. I further state that no promises, threats, force, or physical or mental coercion of any kind whatsoever have been used against me to get me to consent to the search described above or to sign this form.

Date: _____ Time: _____

Signature: _____

Signature: _____

Yo, _____ , por medio del presente doy mi consentimiento a

_____ los oficiales de la _____

para que registren el siguiente vehiculo, incluyendo equipaje, paquetes de todas clases y sus contenidos.

_____

Color   Ano   Marca   Estilo de Carroceria   Numero de Placa

Entiendo que tengo el derecho de negarme a consentir que se registre lo que se describe aqui arriba y negarme a firmar esta forma.

Ademas declaro que ninguna promesa, amenaza, fuerza, o coercion fisica o mental de cualquiera clase se ha usado en contra mia para obligarme a consentir al registro aqui descrito o para firmar esta forma.

Fecha:_____ Hora: _____

Firma: _____

Firma: _____

*Handle every search area as
a crime scene. Suspect vehicles
are rolling crime scenes.*

HIGHWAY INTERDICTION

In one year Officer Joe David of the Needles California Highway Patrol Area seized over 25 million in drugs, currency, and assets. Officer David and his narcotic K-9 interdict drugs on remote southwest highways where high speed commercial traffic as well as private vehicles flow to and from the Los Angeles Basin. Through his advanced highway drug interdiction program *Desert Snow*, Joe David has instructed hundreds of law enforcement officers throughout the nation in the most effective methods for interdicting drugs on vehicle stops. His methods have provided the basis for many successful investigations.

Automatic authorizations: Once an officer has lawfully stopped a vehicle, there are certain actions he may take with no additonal factual justification. These authorizations include:

1. Ordering the person or persons reasonably suspected of criminal conduct out of the vehicle
2. Asking the driver for his driver's license and vehicle registration
3. Separating the driver and occupants *immediately* and asking them questions individually
4. *Seeking consent to search the car*
5. Locating and examining the vehicle identification number
6. Examining the exterior of the car and portions of the interior that may be viewed without entry, including deploying the dog to sniff the exterior
7. Controlling the car and its occupants for the brief period of time required to accomplish the purpose of the stop

When the K-9 officer investigates a highway stop, he should have the necessary documentumentation depending on current search and seizure law:

- Consent to Search
- Disclaimer of Ownership of Assets & Waiver of Rights to Notice of Seizure
- Asset Forfeiture Financial Tally Sheet
- Highway Interdiction Seizure Report—DEA

In *U.S. v. Ross,* if probable cause exists, you do not need a search warrant. Most states parallel this federal court decision. For telephonic search warrants, set up procedures in advance with your local district attorney.

Handle every search area as a crime scene. Suspect vehicles are rolling crime scenes. On the freeway with cars speeding past, or on the highway at night with no cover is not the time to be in a hurry or to forget the danger in your determination to find dope.

Learn the vehicle configurations for various makes and models of automobiles and trucks. Learn to recognize what is normal (like examining your K-9 on a daily basis) so you will notice what is abnormal. Are you suspicious that something is wrong? Can you articulate the reasons for your suspicions? Look at the subjects themselves. Look at the cities of origin and destination, how they are traveling, the purpose of their trip, where they stayed, the time there, even that good friend whose name the subject can't remember. How about the odors you can smell? Could you say the people appear to be involved in some activity not completely consistent with normal behavior? Dispatch runs a wants check on the vehicle. While waiting for the return, you again question both subjects and ask *clarifying questions concerning the circumstances of their trip.*

As your cover unit arrives, you fill out a consent to search form. After each subject appears to read it, you explain it verbally and record this exchange. You ask them to sign it. If they refuse but you are still legally detaining them to accomplish the purposes of the stop, the dog may be deployed to sniff the outside of the vehicle. After moving both subjects to a designated location on the right shoulder with your cover officer, you go back to your patrol car to get your K-9.

Your cover officer has an important officer safety role as you and your dog search the vehicle:
• Taking a position of advantage to overlook the entire scene
• Staying within talking distance of you and the subjects
• Keeping the subjects away from you, the dog, and the vehicle as you are searching
• Watching for approaching vehicles or subjects
• Preventing the subjects from talking to each other or moving around, and watching their body language while you search (they may create a disturbance if you are getting close to concealed items)

Wind and traffic permitting, start sniffing as you approach the vehicle. Detail seams, cavities, and underbody. Inside, remove hazards and ventilate, patterning the doors, overhead, seats, and floor.

Observing a vehicle exceeding the speed limit on the Florida Turnpike, a trooper stopped the vehicle. In anticipation of issuing a traffic citation for speeding, the tooper obtained the driver's license and the rental agreement for the car. Within three minutes of the stop, a second trooper arrived with a narcotic detection dog to sniff for evidence of illegal drugs. The dog alerted to the car's trunk, *at which point the driver tried to flee.* He was soon apprehended, and the trunk of the car was searched. Six kilos of cocaine were discovered. The entire incident transpired within some six minutes after the initial stop.

The defendants were charged with trafficking in cocaine and possession of the drug. The driver was also charged with resisting arrest. The appeals court upheld the evidence discovered as a result of the dog sniff. The court found, "...the three minutes between the initial traffic stop and the point at which the dog began to work was, if at all, a de minimis intrusion into the defendants' liberty interest. Thus their Fourth Amendment rights were certainly not infringed...the arrival and use of a sniff dog during a vehicle stop for a traffic infraction must take no longer than the time necessary to write the traffic citation." *However, if reasonable, articulable suspicion of criminal activity develops, that time extends as long as the officer is diligently pursuing a lawful investigation.*[39]

39. *Florida v. Williams,* 565 So.2nd 714 (Fla. 1990).

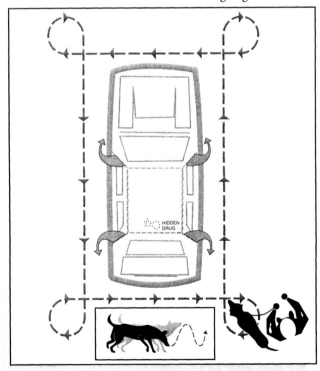

When possible, prepare the vehicle for the initial *outside* search by activating the ventilation system (heater off, air conditioning off). Close all doors and windows and wait 60-90 seconds to allow air pressure to build inside. When the dog starts working, interior scent will be flowing out the seams and vents. The car exhaling (scent diffusing to the outside) circulates air in peripheral areas (trunk, engine compartment, underbody), helping to make scent from these areas available to the dog. This technique enhances safety if the dog gives a strong alert and it does not become necessary for him to enter the vehicle. This technique does not generally apply to trucks, buses, vessels or large aircraft, where the dog sniffs parts of the exterior but typically searches the interior as well.

Case No: _____

DISCLAIMER OF OWNERSHIP OF ASSETS
&
WAIVER OF RIGHTS TO NOTICE OF SEIZURE

Name: _____ __ D.L. #: _____

Address: _____

Date: _____ Time: _____ Location: _____

1. I acknowledge that the following described assets were seized from me by Officers of _____ _
_____

2. I hereby state that I am NOT the owner of the listed assets and have no claim for its return to me.

3. The name and address of the owner of the assets is:
_____
_____

4. The assets came into my possession under the following circumstances:
_____
_____
_____

5. I further state that no promises, threats, force, or physical or mental coercion of any kind whatsoever have been used against me to get me to sign this form.

6. I understand that I have the right to refuse to sign this form.

7. I have been advised and understand that by signing this disclaimer of ownership of assets I am waiving my right to a notice of seizure of the assets and that I do not have a right to file a petition or claim for return of the assets since it does not belong to me.

Signature of property holder: _____
Signature of seizing officer: _____
Signature of witnessing officer: _____

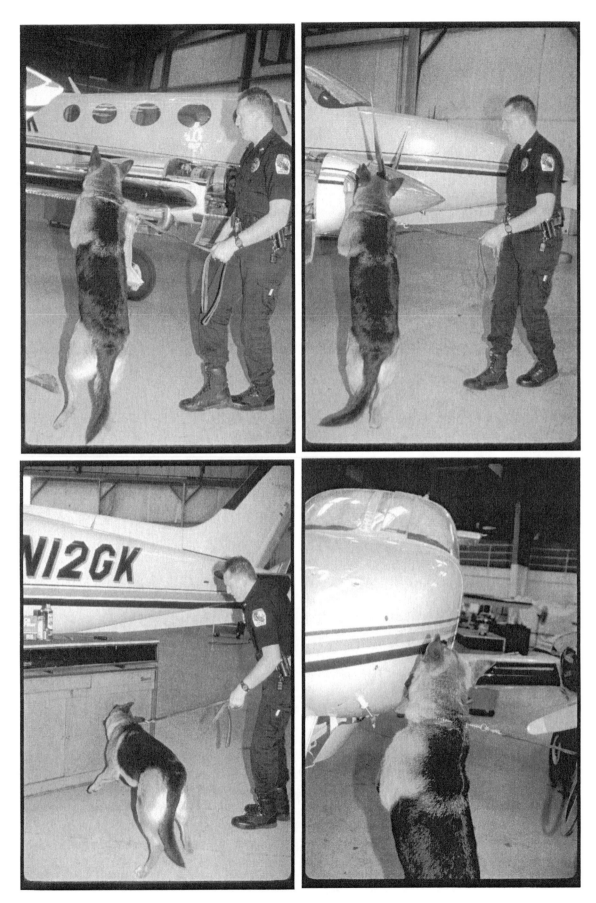

Detail the outside of the vehicle, deploying the dog around the exterior in a routine pattern checking all the seams, vents, cavities, corners, and tires. Use caution around hot engines and hot exhaust pipes. If other vehicles are running nearby, remember vehicle exhaust can impair the dog's scenting capability. Searching the exterior of a car typically takes 1-3 minutes.

If you decide to deploy the dog inside the vehicle (to investigate an alert, or on a permissive search the ventilation system is not working, or you have no alerts but many indicators), use caution:

- Hazardous materials: You don't want your dog in there.
- Excessive heat: You don't want your dog in there.
- Unstable cargo: Stabilize or don't send the dog.
- Narcotic ingestion: Watch your dog.

Take time to detail. The K-9 should examine all the key concealment areas, including the seats, dash and wheel, flooring, roof liner, door jamb, panels and consoles, trunks, pickup beds and tailgates—natural voids, specially constructed voids, and personal property. Don't forget the spare tire (release a little air for a sniff). Finish the task (be persistent). If you do not find drugs pursuant to the dog's alerts, put the K-9 in your patrol car and do a visual search (set up *control* exercises later to resolve any training problems).

If the dog does not alert anywhere, put him away and follow up with a visual inspection: Scratched screw heads, funny wires, bulges or hollow spaces, removal marks (gas tank straps—tap the tank), whatever appears abnormal. Or normal things that appear out of context: Baby seat, diapers, no baby. Size 13 hi-tech tennis shoes, new, occupants are Mexican-American males barely five feet tall. Box labeled "100 Musical Favorites on CD" but no disk player in the car. You want to find the drugs if they are there. You also want to find out your dog's limitations. Maybe a particular concealment method prevents your dog from detecting the dope. If you discover it during your hand search, you win. You win two ways. First, you get the dope or the money. Second, you find out what prevented the dog from detecting the dope.

Every professional canine handler should recognize and deal with his animal's fallibility. It is reality. It is the way we learn. Chances are, the handler in the agency up the road needs to know what you have learned. Sharing K-9 information with other officers and handlers is critical to developing high standard performance.

Take reasonable care to protect the subject's property during the search. Be sure to count promptly any money found and record the amount by completing the Financial Tally Sheet. If you seize cash as illegal drug money, base your report on the following:

1. All Indicators.
2. Subjects' reasons for not claiming the money at first.
3. Subjects' reasons for signing the Disclaimer.
4. All phone calls made, including numbers, names, and statements
5. Location of the money found.
6. Subjects' statements claiming how they got the money.
7. Give a receipt for the money.
8. If in doubt, contact your District Attorney's office.

When you have a subject with money, vehicle, suspicious items typically evolving from drug sales, and he claims he knows nothing about anything, he may sign away a large amount of cash, or vehicles, or anything, writing it off as a business expense to avoid prosecution. Depending on applicable state or federal law, law enforcement may take the items through the seizure process. A state highway patrol seized almost one half million dollars this way with a

Sharing K-9 information with other officers and handlers is critical to developing high standard performance.

Cover officer occupies the driver while observing the search procedure.

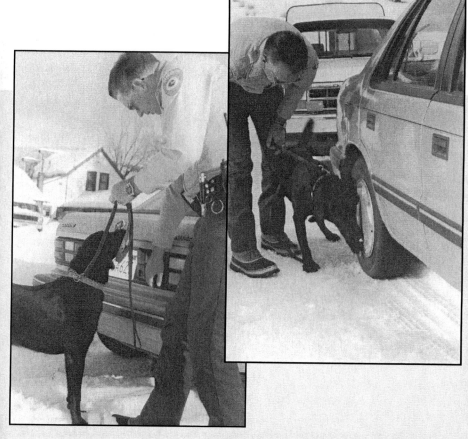

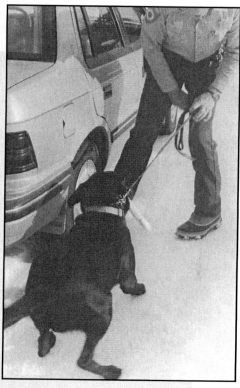

■

Tapping the exterior of a small vehicle can help direct the dog sniff inside. Keep the dog on lead in case he dives under the seat to grab a load of narcotics. Alpine County Deputy Everett Brakensiek and Deke.

suspect who had completed a large heroin sale between the U.S. and Mexico immediately prior to the stop. He signed the disclaimer voiding all further claim to the money.

Develop your knock and talk and permissive search techniques. Many crooks grant a search request even when they are holding. Near midnight, a highway patrol officer stopped to assist motorists west of a large mountain resort. Two male Hispanics stood in front of a brown pickup with its hood up. Pulling alongside, the officer saw cash on the floorboard through the open passenger door. "Just checking the oil," they said. Returning to their city of residence after doing poorly at the casinoes, they accounted for the cash as traveling money.

Talking to the passenger, the officer noticed his bloodshot eyes, slow speech and dry mouth. The suspect said he had been smoking pot about two hours before. He also had no driver's license and two FTAs. Obtaining permission to search, the officer saw a clear plastic baggie of white powder in a casino money bucket, which turned out to be methamphetamine and which the suspect claimed. Both men denied there were more narcotics in the vehicle.

Radioing for the assistance of a drug detector dog from the area drug task force, the highway patrol intercepted a sheriff's deputy leaving the town after a three hour K-9 training session. Always happy to do a search, his drug dog hopped out of his patrol car, began sniffing, and quickly alerted to the money still lying inside the suspect's vehicle. Tail wagging furiously, the K-9 made another active hit near the heater duct on the floorboard where officers retrieved a cardboard box wrapped in black tape. It contained several ounces of meth.

Highway patrol placed both suspects in custody and towed the truck. A task force agent responded to the scene and took custody of almost $1000 cash, later released, and the suspected drugs. The two suspects reported having the package of drugs in their vehicle *for safekeeping*. It seems when they left home they were afraid the family would help themselves to their stash. Who do you trust?

Highway patrol agencies or task forces may require that traffic stops resulting in arrests other than traffic arrests be turned over to the agency with the expertise and ability to do follow-up investigations. Before you turn your case over to another agency, collect whatever evidence you need to justify your stop, detention, search, and arrest. Keep in mind that *you* will have to justify what you did and why. When turning the scene over to another agency, turn it over to one person and state that name in your report. Tell that person you are turning the scene over to him.

If you are called out as a dog handler to assist on a highway stop and the dog alerts, request the highway patrolman or investigator recover the evidence. You and the dog act as a tool to aid their investigation. "We came, sniffed, alerted" requires only a concise one-page report appended to the primary agency's report. If you are assisting a single officer, he should provide cover while you search. Then you put the dog away and cover him for evidence retrieval. In every case on follow-up, contact the investigating agency to obtain as much information as possible about what was found or not found, and where.

The narcotic detector dog is not a trivial tool. Many cases would, without a doubt, have ended differently had a trained dog been present to build probable cause. A case in point occurred when an Ohio Highway Patrolman observed a red automobile exceeding the posted speed limit and signalled its driver to stop beside the highway. Leaving his marked cruiser, he walked up to the passenger side of the vehicle. The passenger opened the window: "I asked for driver's license and registration. I told them they were stopped for speeding. The driver produced a valid license but not a registration. I asked him who owned the car, and he said his wife. I asked him where the registration was. He started looking through his wallet and coat pockets but did not find it. He seemed to be a little bit nervous at that time.

"I asked him if the registration was possibly in the glove box. He said, yes, that it was in the glove box. But he didn't open the glove box. He seemed reluctant to. At that time I asked him if he would get it out of the glove box. So he reached over, and in a very quick manner he opened the glove box, reached in and retrieved the registration and slammed it back shut. Now prior to that

I had asked him if there was, if he had a gun in the glove box, because of the reluctance that they showed. He said there wasn't a gun in there. But when he opened the glove box, I got down to a position where I could see the entire glove box when he opened it. I wanted to make sure there weren't any weapons in there.

"When he opened it, in the right corner of the glove box, I could see a package about the size of a baseball wrapped in duct tape. Based on my experience working narcotics, I immediately recognized that as possibly a package of narcotics. Another trooper had pulled in behind my car. It's common practice to back up another trooper. I told him what I had observed. We got both people out of the car, patted them down for weapons. Neither subject had a weapon. At that point, I went back to the car and retrieved that duct taped package.

"I smelled it, and it smelled of coffee grounds. In my training as a drug dog handler for the highway patrol, we learned drug traffickers will use coffee grounds to disguise or to mask the odor of drugs so that a drug dog cannot detect it. The coffee smell tipped me that that package contained some type of narcotic. Both suspects denied knowing what the package contained or any knowledge of the package. They disclaimed the package.

"I opened up the package and found a zip lock bag containing a lot of coffee grounds. Inside the bag, down in the coffee grounds, was a smaller package also wrapped in duct tape. Opening up the second package, I found a good-sized chunk of what appeared to be cocaine. It was still in brick form, like it had just been chopped off a kilogram of cocaine. It appeared that it hadn't been cut yet. A third and fourth trooper had arrived, and we secured both suspects in handcuffs."

Although the court found no merit to the suspect's complaint that the initial traffic stop was a pretext to detain him and search for contraband, it did hold that: "Duct tape has become the universal packaging and repair material replacing the baling wire and electrician's tape of earlier days, so that baseball-sized objects wrapped in that substance are not peculiar to the packaging or transportation of illicit drugs or other unlawful pursuits. We do not believe that probable cause exists for warrantless seizure and search of a package wrapped in a common wrapping material sometimes used to wrap packages of illicit drugs, merely because it is so wrapped, in the absence of other qualifying information or circumstances disclosing the probable illicit nature of the package in question. Nothing in the record discloses the circumstances of the driver's appearance or conduct to fit some pattern or profile of illicit drug possession. Indeed, one's merely fulfilling the profile of a drug courier, standing alone, does not give probable cause for arrest and search."

The courts want more than suspicious packaging commonly used to ship illicit drugs. The dog offers a minimally intrusive, practicable means of detecting crime.

The court gave something more, though, to the troopers. It suggested what tactic could have succeeded: "We do not say, of course, that a seizure can never be justified on less than probable cause. We have held that it can—where, for example, the seizure is *minimally intrusive and operational necessities render it the only practicable means of detecting certain types of crime,* reference the seizure of a suspected drug dealer's luggage at an airport to permit exposure to a *specially trained dog.* No special operational necessities are relied on here, but rather the mere fact that the items in question came lawfully within the officer's plain view. That alone cannot supplant the requirement of probable cause."[40]

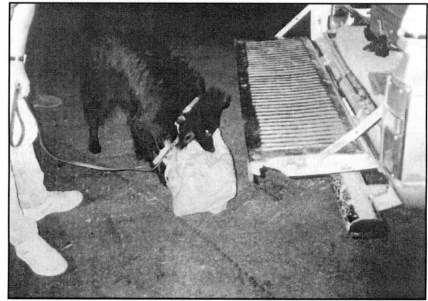

DEA TASK FORCE

In one case the court went out of its way to point out that a K-9 could have been used to good effect. "LOST TAG" scrawled on a cardboard placard taped to a Ford Bronco with no license plate got the attention of a Florida deputy. He stopped the vehicle to investigate. A check revealed the driver had several prior felony convictions, including firearm, drug, and burglary offenses. Contrary to the driver's story that the tag had been lost a few days (not to mention the passenger's "two or three weeks" version) there was no record the vehicle had ever been issued a license plate. Asking a series of investigative questions, the officer asked if they were transporting any illegal drugs, narcotics or firearms, specifically, was anything in the truck that should not be in there. The driver responded sarcastically, "Us." (As events unfolded, his answer was absolutely correct.)

After writing and explaining the warning cite, the officer and his partner informed the suspects they intended to "put a dog around the truck", referring to a canine sniff. Parrying the deputies' questions, the driver would not consent to a search but let slip that his uncle's gun, a nine millimeter, was in the truck. He refused to say *where* in the truck the gun was located but, incredibly, asked the officers to allow him to go back to the Bronco for a minute. Request denied.

About ten minutes later the suspect was arrested for being a felon in possession of a firearm. A search of the vehicle discovered: 1) over 200 grams of crack cocaine; 2) a quantity of powder cocaine; 3) two .9mm pistols and ammunition; 4) counterfeit $20 Federal Reserve notes; 5) and other drug-related items, such as scales and razor blades.

First, the court found the stop justified. Second, there was nothing impermissible about the officer's intention to "put a dog around the truck" to detect illegal drugs since a canine sniff is not a search within the meaning of the Fourth Amendment (*Place*), and police do not need particularized reasonable suspicion of drug-related criminal activity before subjecting an otherwise lawfully detained vehicle to a canine sniff. The court stated, in fact, it is hard to understand why the officer did not subject the Ford Bronco to a canine sniff, since a police dog was present at the scene during part of the detention.[41]

Despite the progressive building of probable cause by the officer, a canine alert can prove valuable to clear a logjam at a particular step in the investigation. This proved true when a Texas Trooper made a U-turn to stop a brown vehicle for the driver's failure to wear a safety belt. The incident escalated into almost identical brown vehicles travelling side by side, both with Tennessee plates (one a paper tag), the passenger of the second vehicle throwing a package of marijuana out the window, the trooper's discovery of a marijuana cigarette butt in the rear ashtray of the first car, the arrest of three suspects, and the clear indication of contraband when a detector dog sniffed the backseat of the first car. When officers removed the lower portion of the backseat, the dog alerted strongly on the right side panel. Using a screwdriver, the trooper pulled apart the right rear quarter-panel, revealing a package which he identified as cocaine. Money was found in the left rear quarter-panel through the same procedure. The driver of the first vehicle was arrested on felony drug trafficking charges. Later at the detention center a search of the second car discovered identical secret compartments accessed in both cars by electronically controlled trap doors.

The appeals court held the car stops were not pretextual because the officer had a legitimate reason to make the initial stops. Referring to the Fourth Amendment as black letter law forbidding the introduction of illegally seized evidence in a federal prosecution, the use of the dog as a tool in the course of the search did not raise any further constitutional issues, as *the dog acted as a mere extension of the officers' sensory faculties*. The dog alerting inside the vehicle provided the officers with probable cause to conduct a further search of the back seat area. Removal of the backseat did not involve the destruction of property such that the procedure was unreasonable. Finally, the intrusive searches accomplished by the use of a screwdriver to pry back the exterior side panels so that the suspected contraband would be visible were reasonable under the circumstances of the dog's very strong alert in that area of the automobile.[42]

41. *Ohio v. Lamar*, 621 N.E. 2d 1232 (Ohio 1993).
42. *U.S. v. Williams*, 784 F. Supp. 1553 (M.D. Fla. 1991).

The dog will alert when you least expect it.

Hiding narcotic training aids, take into account scent diffusion, concealment and temperature changes.

A *spontaneous alert* is a gift. New Mexico State Police stopped a vehicle for speeding on the interstate highway. While writing the citation, the officer smelled an odor he thought was either cocaine or crystal methadrine coming from the car. The driver reacted nervously when asked about carrying narcotics. When the driver refused to consent to a search of the car, the officer escorted him to a nearby police station in order to get a search warrant.

At the police station, the officer called an agent of the Drug Enforcement Administration requesting a background check on the driver. The agent told him the DEA "had been doing surveillance on [suspect] for drug trafficking." With these facts, the officer went before a state magistrate and requested a search warrant for the suspect's car. The magistrate refused to issue the warrant. The officer then released the suspect.

When the DEA agent discovered the suspect had been released, he telephoned a detective of the Albuquerque Police Department to ask if they could obtain a narcotics sniffing dog and stop the vehicle as it came into Albuquerque. A police unit proceeded to the interstate east of the city and set up his radar. The radar detected the suspect traveling 65 miles per hour in a 55 mile per hour zone.

When stopped, the suspect told told officers he had been stopped earlier. The radar officer asked to see the ticket. The suspect replied it was in the rear of the hatchback. When the officer reiterated he would like to see the citation, the suspect got out of the car, opened the hatchback, and retrieved the ticket. Sometime during this encounter, several other police officers arrived at the scene and engaged the suspect and his passenger in conversation. Within a few more minutes, another police officer arrived with the dog. Circling the car, the dog showed interest underneath the rear area of the car and at the passenger door, then jumped into the open hatchback where he "keyed" on a duffel bag. The police then searched the entire car and the duffel bag, which contained approximately 33,000 methaqualone tablets.

Police may stop and detain an automobile and its occupants if they have an articulable and reasonable suspicion that the car is carrying contraband (*Sharpe*). First, here the judge found there was the presence of the Patchouli oil, a substance emitting a very strong, distinctive odor that is used to shield or mask other smells. The officer had learned it was sold and used in California, mainly to cover up the smell of marijuana. Second, a DEA computer indicated the suspect had been "involved in a case in Tucson," had suspected involvement in a cocaine smuggling ring, and had associated with known methamphetamine dealers. In sum, the finding of reasonable suspicion supported the stop and the call for the narcotics dog.

The judge found further that the dog's leap into the back of the car did not vitiate the seizure, regardless of whether or not it was a search. The judge found that the defendant voluntarily opened the hatchback to retrieve the citation requested by the officer. Then the dog came along and "on his own, apparently jumped into the back of this car and immediately found what is sought to be suppressed here." The court held the dog's instinctive actions did not violate the Fourth Amendment. Once the dog alerted, the police had probable cause to believe the automobile contained narcotics.[43]

The K-9 hit becomes *one element along with multiple indicators* linking the suspect to the crime. During the late evening, two deputies stopped a Mercedes Benz for speeding. The driver was very nervous and diaphoretic (sweating). He could not produce the vehicle registration or proof of insurance. He tried to block the deputy's view of the car's interior. Radioing for a criminal history check, the deputy learned the subject had been arrested for illegally carrying a weapon and for possession of marijuana. The deputy asked for, and was denied, consent to search the car. The officer removed his narcotics dog from his police car and let the dog walk around the subject's car. The dog, who had proven reliable many times, alerted on the suspect's car. Again the deputy asked for, and was denied, consent to search. He arrested the suspect and called a tow truck.

42. *U.S. v. Thomas*, 787 F.Supp. 663 (E.D.Tex. 1992).
43. *U.S. v. Stone*, 866 F.2nd 359 (10th Cir. 1989).

The vehicle was towed to the police station and a search warrant issued. The search revealed six marijuana cigarettes in the passenger compartment, 13 zip-lock bags, each containing one pound of marijuana in the trunk, $1746 cash under the carpet, and a vial containing cocaine. The car was stolen from Houston.

Here, the deputy had probable cause to stop the vehicle for speeding. He was confronted by an abnormally anxious driver who could not produce the necessary documents and who tried to keep the officer from seeing inside the car. The officer diligently pursued a means of investigation that was likely to quickly confirm or dispel his suspicions (*Sharpe*). A routine and quickly conducted check disclosed the suspect's drug history. The narcotics dog was readily available. The K-9 alert, coupled with the officer's observations and his ten years of experience, eight or nine of which were involved in working narcotics cases as time permitted, gave the officer probable cause to arrest the suspect at the scene of the traffic stop.[44]

Conflicting stories between vehicle occupants, among other indicators, may build the requisite reasonable suspicion to call for a detector dog even though it may mean a significant time delay. A Kansas Highway Patrolman stopped a slow-moving Ford for failure to indicate a lane change and asked for the driver's license and proof of insurance. Unable to produce proof of liability insurance, the driver nervously accompanied the trooper to await the written warning. In response to the officer's routine questioning, the driver said he was en route to Dallas from Kansas City, Missouri, where he had been for two days and had attended an auto auction and a basketball tournament game. He stated the vehicle was leased. Checking registration, dispatch advised the officer of a different rental company in a different state. Asked about a large box in the back seat, the driver said it contained a cooler.

Checking the VIN numbers on the Ford, the officer spoke with the passenger, who said they were returning to El Paso, Texas, from Kansas City. He gave the length of their stay as four or five days, denied attending a basketball game, and appeared confused at the mention of Dallas.

Returning the driver's license, the officer was suspicious. He asked if the driver had any weapons, drugs, contraband, or large sums of money. Appearing more nervous, the driver said he did not. When the trooper requested permission to search the vehicle for such items, the driver said he was welcome to look in the trunk but did not want to sign anything. He stated, "Let me open the trunk, yes." In the trunk was another large box containing a 100 quart cooler and a tan bag containing a large amount of money.

Placing both men to the right of the vehicle, the officer advised them they were not under arrest but he was seizing the money to determine its legality. Advising them both of their rights against self-incrimination, the officer questioned them about the money. The driver said the money was his but he did not know how much money there was, later stating he buys and wholesales cars. The officer radioed for assistance. Meanwhile he questioned the passenger, who had a previous drug arrest. At this point, the trooper suspected the men were involved in transporting and distributing drugs and requested the closest drug canine unit to respond. They were over fifty miles away.

Arriving over an hour and a half into the stop, the K-9 alerted aggressively to both boxes containing the coolers and to the bag of money as well. He did not alert to anything else. The suspect was permitted to drive his car to the highway patrol office, where the K-9 was employed to sniff the entire car. Finding nothing of interest to him there, the dog went into the building through an open door and ran off with some of the suspect currency from the table where the troopers were counting it. The dog refused to let the money go until he was given his ball (his reward for performing his job).

The handler testified the dog was never trained to find currency itself but had been trained to alert to the odor of three drugs, marijuana, cocaine, and methamphetamine. The dog had

44. *State v. Arrington*, 556 So.2nd 263 (La.App. 2 Cir. 1990).

been used to sniff currency before. The handler testified the dog had over 90% accuracy in training situations *(indicating high reliability but not claiming perfection)*.

Despite concluding that the initial vehicle stop was a pretext to question the occupants about illegal activity, and despite the officer returning the license to the driver prior to asking questions, the appeals court found the investigative detention was justified because *specific and articulable facts and rational inferences from those facts gave rise to reasonable suspicion the person had committed or was committing a crime.* The court did not suppress the money, the boxes and coolers, the officer's testimony about the search, the suspect's statements, or any tangible evidence seized before the suspect went to the patrol office.[45]

Conflicting stories between two individuals ostensibly returning from a Florida fishing vacation alerted a Georgia State Patrolman who stopped them for speeding and discovered the driver had no identification, the car was titled to the driver's wife in Indiana, the two men could not identify each other's surnames or occupations, and they told markedly different versions of their trip. Activating a video camera in the patrol car, the officer asked for consent to search the automobile. The driver objected. The passenger demurred. To dispel his suspicions, the officer informed the men he was detaining them on the highway until he could obtain a narcotics dog to sniff the car and also run a more extensive computer check on persons wanted for drug offenses through a DEA clearinghouse.

Arriving from 30 miles away about 40 minutes later, the dog alerted to the car's trunk. Concluding he now had the right to search the car without the driver's consent, the officer opened the trunk by pushing the electronic release button on the dashboard. In the trunk he found a small suitcase and a small blue travel bag. Inside the blue bag were three plastic bags containing a substance the officer believed to be marijuana. He formally arrested the two men, placing them in the patrol car. Further search revealed a brown paper bag containing three kilograms of cocaine, another paper bag containing $2000 in cash, and a long butcher's knife.

Denying the suppression motion, the appeals court noted it had reviewed the videotape and was persuaded the officer's brief attempt to secure consent to search the automobile was entirely noncoercive. The court held the officer's participation in Operation Nighthawk, a professional program of heightened awareness of drug trafficking on interstate highways, had no bearing on the case. Further, a "drug courier profile" played no role in this calculus. In a concurring opinion, one judge observed, "Just because an officer is pleased that a suspicious car violates traffic laws so that a stop is justified does not make the stop unconstitutional. One who violates traffic laws is not, because he appears to be a drug courier, immunized from arrest."[46]

Arizona officers patrolling the interstate south of Tucson stopped a vehicle with no front or rear license plates and only a portion of a temporary paper registration visible. Asked for his driver's license and vehicle registration, the driver had no license, although he produced an Arizona identification card and a sales slip indicating the car belonged to a third person. While the first officer conducted a records check, a second officer asked the driver if he was carrying any illegal drugs, currency, or weapons. The man replied he was not. The officer then asked if he could look through the vehicle. The driver said yes. The officer walked around the vehicle then retrieved a narcotics detection dog from the squad car. Standing next to the vehicle the suspect had been operating, the K-9 alerted to the trunk. Placed inside the vehicle, the dog alerted to the back seat. Opening the trunk of the vehicle, the officers found approximately 150 pounds of marijuana.

Indicted for unlawful possession of marijuana for sale and unlawful transportation, the defendant filed a motion to suppress the evidence, claiming he was not told of the thoroughness of the search or that a dog would be used in the search. Citing the bright line rulings from *Terry* through *Place* et al, the appeals court found that the use of the drug detection dog under the circumstances presented did not result in a search exceeding the scope of the defendant's consent.[47]

Further search revealed a brown paper bag containing three kilograms of cocaine, another paper bag containing $2000 in cash, and a long butcher's knife.

45. *U.S. v. $83,900, in U.S. Currency*, 774 F.Supp. 1305 (D.Kan. 1991).
46. *U.S. v. Hardy*, 855 F.2d 753 (11th Cir. 1988).

Before performing a permissive search of a vehicle, *record* (tape or disk) suspect statements as you are obtaining permission (if possible, written permission) to search. *Ask the questions and record both your questions and their verbal responses. To a jury, eliciting the subject's comprehension this way is evidence that he or she understands.* Later he cannot say, "I can't read." Then you have to prove he can read. Or, "I did not consent," or even, "I revoked my consent." Then it becomes your word against the suspect's.

Two men stopped on an interstate for weaving back and forth in the lane were driving a rental car without authorization, making a straight-shot trip to a known *source city* (from Kansas to Detroit), giving conflicting stories about each other and their trip, and showing extreme anxiety. Acting diligently to prevent the possibly ongoing crime of car theft, the officer detained the suspects with their vehicle at a nearby patrol post while he contacted Hertz rental agency. Suspecting that drug trafficking might be involved, the officer called for a trained drug dog to check the vehicle. The dog arrived and alerted to the trunk of the vehicle just minutes before the officer obtained authorization to release the vehicle to the suspects. Searched under probable cause, the trunk contained heroin being transported for distribution.[48]

On the hound: Rhode Island Police observed a Toyota northbound on the interstate with the passenger leaning head, arms and shoulders outside the window screaming at a northbound Chevrolet. Thinking an altercation between two moving cars was brewing, the troopers took up dogged pursuit, radioing for backup. When stopped, the Chevrolet driver produced a valid license and registration and explained the passenger in the Toyota was asking directions to Boston. Officers allowed the Chevrolet to depart.

Meanwhile the Toyota driver produced an expired Puerto Rican license that looked suspect, gave conflicting birthdates, and could not identify his passenger except as Sammy. He told the officers he was going to Boston to visit his aunt but could not provide either her address or telephone number. Questioning the passenger out of earshot, another officer was told they were travelling to Boston to visit the passenger's hospitalized mother. The passenger's driver's license was suspended.

To the pound: Accompanying the two men to state police barracks for further inquiries, the officers called a special agent fluent in Spanish who spoke with the men in Spanish over the telephone and basically confirmed their roadside stories. Asked in Spanish to sign a form consenting to a vehicular search, the driver refused. Officers then arranged for a trained drug dog to perform a canine sniff around the Toyota's perimeter.

What they found: The dog's alert initiated a chain reaction: Driver and passenger were placed in a restricted-egress conference room; the Toyota was moved into a garage on the premises; and the troopers obtained a judicial warrant enabling them to search the car. Given access to the passenger side of the car's interior, the dog alerted to the door jamb. The police pried it open, uncovering several bundles of cocaine. Cocaine was also found inside the driver's door. A total of about two kilograms of cocaine were recovered. Both men were arrested.

Tail's end: The courts found that here, as elsewhere in community caretaking cases, reasonableness has a protean quality. The term embodies a concept, not a constant. It cannot be usefully refined in order to evolve some detailed formula for judging cases. The police had a legitimate reason for stopping the car and a strong noninvestigatory justification for removing it from the highway. *Place* applied full bore to this case. The canine sniff around the vehicle's perimeter was not a search and did not implicate the fourth amendment. Upon receiving a positive indication that drugs were present, the officers had probable cause to procure a warrant and carry out the detailed search of the vehicle's interior, disclosing the cocaine cache.[49]

Once you lawfully impound a vehicle, there is no requirement that an inventory search

47. *State v. Paredes,* 810 P.2d 607 (Ariz.App. 1991).

48. *U.S. v. Kalu,* slip opinion. (6th Cir. 1992).

policy detail the specific method by which a search is to be conducted (flashlight, canine, et al). The requirement for a standardized procedure appears to be directed at criteria for deciding when to impound a car and conduct an inventory search in order to prevent arbitrary use of the power. A man was stopped in California for two vehicle code violations as he was driving a car registered in Washington state. The officer arrested him when it was determined he was wanted on a warrant for cruelty to animals.

Departments should be on-line with the national narcotic intelligence exchange system for real time trafficking information, including dog- and officer safety advisories.

The vehicle was not registered to the suspect, and there was no one to take charge of it. The area in which the suspect was arrested was an area "rampant with illegal drug sales." Therefore, the arresting officer called a tow truck to take the vehicle to an impound yard. Prior to the arrival of the truck, the officer conducted an inventory search of the interior, discovering an envelope containing $2326 in the glove box. He also observed a cellular phone and a nationwide users' guide. He was aware the suspect had been carrying a pager on his person when arrested. The officer was not able to search the trunk area or the area behind the back seat as he did not have a key to the trunk.

Called to the scene, a narcotics K-9 alerted to the envelope of money. The dog then entered the vehicle and alerted on the center rear seat area inside the passenger compartment. He clawed at the base of the seat belts.

The vehicle was then towed to the parking lot of the police department. A second canine unit was called, and that dog also alerted on the back seat of the vehicle.

Based on the actions of the dogs, the officer obtained a search warrant so that he could go into the locked trunk. Gaining entrance to the trunk, the officer found a lever which when pulled released the back seat to fall forward. After the back seat fell forward, the officer found a loaded nine millimeter pistol and additional currency.

The officer testified that use of a canine was not specifically addressed in the department's policy on inventory searches. However, he considered his use of the dogs as part of the inventory search.[50,51]

Do not use two dogs to sniff the same area or objects. If the dog is reliable, a "confirming" alert by another detector dog is not necessary. Multiple dog sniffs invite problems. For example, one dog alerts in a particular location but the other does not (the air flow changes). Or the question arises whether the second dog is merely following the scent of the first. Or the question of precedent arises. If the handler determines that his dog is not working properly (dysfunction, distraction), a functional canine may re-cover the area. In that case the first dog team withdraws, and the second dog's actions form the basis for the report about the areas he sniffs.

The effective use of detector dog teams requires current intelligence and deployment in high risk areas involving large quantities of narcotics. Quantitative performance measurement is one of several factors that must be considered in determining the allocation of canine program resources. Other factors include threat analysis, changes in smuggling trends, and the productivity of other teams in the same or similar locations. The Federal Highway Administration's Drug Interdiction Assistance Program (DIAP), DEA and other agencies track source locations, destinations,

49. *U.S. v. Rodriguez-Morales,* 929 F.2d 780 (1st Cir. 1991).
50. *Ohio v. Riley,* 624 N.E.2d 302 (Ohio 1993).
51. *People v. Roberson,* (Calif. Ct. of App. slip opinion, 1993).

typical peak periods of trafficking, highways used most frequently, and typical travel routes. *Departments with narcotic dog teams should be on-line with the national narcotic intelligence exchange system for real time trafficking information, including dog- and officer safety advisories.* The more the handler knows, the higher is the canine's potential for success.

Profile of the profile: The notion of a "drug courier profile" first surfaced in the plurality opinion of Justice Powell, joined by Chief Justice Burger and Justice Blackmun in *U.S. v. Mendenhall,* 446 U.S. 544 (1980). The Supreme Court has made it clear that the undergirding legal and constitutional issue involved is simply the presence of articulable suspicion for a stop and/or frisk. The so-called profile is something that may have investigative and factual significance but not legal significance *per se.* It is but one of the ways in which an officer accumulates articulable suspicion.

Since a stop and frisk based upon a profile is but an instance of the broader phenomenon of stop and frisk generally, it would never suffice for an officer to make the blanket and conclusory statement that the suspect "fit the profile." It would be required, as it always is when an officer must articulate his articulable suspicion, that the officer recite the observed characteristics. Reference to the profile might then explain why he, on the basis of his own or the collective experience of the police team, could attach significance to the observed characteristics that an ordinary layman could not.

Commenting in *Mendenhall:* "In reviewing the factors that led the agents to stop and question the respondent, it is important to recall that a trained law enforcement agent may be 'able to perceive and articulate meaning in given conduct which would be wholly innocent to the untrained observer.' Among the circumstances that can give rise to reasonable suspicion are the agent's knowledge of the methods used in recent criminal activity and the characteristics of persons engaged in such illegal practices."

That the source of the expertise could be collective experience rather than requiring each officer in the field "to reinvent the wheel" for himself is the special investigative virtue of the profile: "Federal agents have developed 'drug courier profiles' that describe the characteristics generally associated with narcotics traffickers."

The Maryland Special Appeals Court observed: "The only legal significance to this umbrella term called 'the profile' is that the expertise of the police will be legitimately taken into consideration when we assess the significance of observations that might to the untrained layman seem completely ambiguous. The establishment of the profile by the Drug Enforcement Agency simply gives us the *benefit of the collective working expertise of many investigators working nationwide in this sensitive area of law enforcement.* The special significance that a given observation might have to a trained and experienced policeman could always be established on a case-by-case basis, even if the 'profile' did not exist."

A profile, any profile, is simply an investigative tool. It is an investigative tool, moreover, that the officer who uses it may describe to the court as he explains the special significance that otherwise innocuous observations may have for him. Although in recent years special attention has been lavished upon the drug courier profile in the special setting of airports, it by no means the only profile utilized. There are pickpocket profiles, especially valuable for use at racetracks and other crowded areas. There are airplane hijacker profiles and terrorist profiles. Customs officers regularly select individuals for personal attention by using smuggler profiles. In the special world of drug smuggling, there has even been a "balloon swallower" profile.

There are also, as this case illustrates, drug courier profiles for highways and streets as well as for airports. In *U.S. v. Sharpe,* 470 U.S. 675 (1985), the Supreme Court affirmed the finding of articulable suspicion to stop a motorist essentially on the basis that a congeries of apparently innocuous driving characteristics were tell-tale indicia of couriers carrying drugs north and south along the Atlantic coastal highway.

It is important to remember that a profile is, in essence, a fact and not a legal principle. As a fact, it is as susceptible to change as the seasons. Tell-tale characteristics in one region or milieu may be very different from those in others. *As countermeasures are constantly devised to meet the tactics of the opposition, the tell-tale characteristics of last year may not be the tell-tale characteristics of next year.* Because of this inherent fluidity, it is particularly unfit for being frozen into a legal principle.

What the dog does on the street may not be his typical alert. Circumstances may force a behavior change.

The detector dog handler (and the patrol dog handler) in particular needs to be aware that suspects will attempt to use the facts of a case to assist in the suppression of evidence. Like narcotic officers, dog handlers vary in ethnicity, sex, and socio-economic condition. Likewise the dogs vary in perceived levels of aggression according to breed and size. Handlers typically enounter accusations of racial bias, gender bias, of using the dog to initimidate, to harass, or of making false claims for the dog's detection capability. *Officers making vehicle stops are particularly exposed because of the risks inherent in these encounters.* For example, the officer who has current intelligence that drug cartels are using white females of a certain age bracket wearing designer clothing driving expensive late model sedans to ship large quantities of dope and cash on a highway through his area would be foolish to ignore these facts or fail to articulate them if he stops a vehicle for a traffic violation. These facts are critical during the officer's approach to the vehicle (the woman can shoot) and also in the officer's report (the woman was talking on a cellular phone, was extremely nervous, and the dog alerted on the outside of the vehicle at the trunk latch).

Some lament the fact that the Supreme Court has not yet told us whether meeting the so-called "drug courier profile" is an adequate predicate to establish either articulable suspicion for a stop or probable cause for an arrest or search. Of course, the Supreme Court has not told us that and they never will. Indeed, they cannot, for there is no such thing as a single drug courier profile; there are infinite drug courier profiles. The very notion is protean, not monolithic.

In the last analysis, it is never a profile *per se* that is the object of appellate review. The data to be scrutinized by the suppression hearing judge and appellate judge alike are the factual observations of the policeman. They may, to be sure, be interpreted through the collective police experience reflected in a profile. *The ultimate issue, however, is whether the factual observations in combination, refracted through the trained eye of the policeman, yield articulable suspicion.* Except as a guide to interpretation, the existence of a profile neither adds to nor subtracts from that computation.[52]

What the dog does on the street, may not be his typical alert. Circumstances may force a *behavior change* the handler will interpret as an alert based on his training and experience. One dog sniffing the exterior of the car after a vehicle stop jumped up on the driver's side window, left partially open because the door was broken. The handler interpreted this action as an alert to the interior of the vehicle. Placed into the passenger compartment, the dog alerted on the ashtray and an area between the front seats concealing a glass pipe containing cocaine residue.

Once inside the passenger compartment, the officer noticed the backseat had been modified so that a piece of plywood could be raised allowing access to the trunk area. Raising the plywood, the officer peered into the trunk, where she discovered a loaded .22 caliber Marlin rifle. Next the dog was directed into the trunk, where he alerted on a liquor box. Opening the box, the officer found a plastic bag containing 14 smaller plastic bags of crack cocaine. This is a classic case of the detector dog opening doors with his nose, figuratively speaking—sequentially developing probable cause to enlarge the search as he finds more and more dope.[53]

The handler never explained whether the initial alert by the dog encompassed the entire area of the car including the trunk. The court therefore concluded the first alert applied only to the passenger compartment. Subsequently, when the glass pipe with the cocaine was discovered, the officer had probable cause to search the entire car. Actually, *the officer had probable cause to search the entire car based on the first alert.* Scent diffuses easily through the interstices (seams

52. *Derricott v. State*, 578 A.2d 791 (Md.App. 1990).
53. *U.S. v. Seals*, 987 F.2d 1102 (5th Cir. 1993).

and voids) of a typical vehicle. The handler would have contributed to the government's case by explaining that *when a narcotic detector dog alerts to a car, narcotics could be located anywhere in that car.*

The dog may be able to help locate the source of diffusing scent. As part of a larger investigation, DEA agents seized a vehicle and removed it to an agency garage. At the garage, the car was exposed to a drug-sniffing dog, which alerted to the trunk area of the car. Searching the car without a warrant, the agents found and removed from the trunk approximately three kilograms of cocaine. Three days later, after receiving a tip that a more intense search of the car could yield more contraband, another sniff test was conducted. Again, the dog alerted at the car. The agents removed carpeting and moved the back seat and a portion of the rear deck, revealing what appeared to be a secret compartment. The agents then removed the back seat and found nine additional packages of cocaine. Using the dog to *particularize the area to be searched* facilitated the agents' more thorough search of the car body.[54]

The Kansas Highway Patrol set up a traffic checklane as a local multijurisdictional law enforcement effort to focus on checking drivers' licenses and reducing "accident-related causative factors." The checklane was implemented at a rest area such that all traffic on the interstate, whether eastbound or westbound, could be funneled into the rest area and stopped. Signs were posted approximately 500 feet from the entrances to the rest area, advising motorists of the checklane. There was no advance publicity regarding the checklane.

The suspect entered the checklane in his car early in the morning. The trooper who was checking the suspect's driver's license smelled alcohol and asked the driver to submit to a preliminary breath test. The suspect agreed to do so and went to the patrol car to take the test, which indicated his blood alcohol level was below the legal limit. During the suspect's detention, another officer walked a narcotics-detecting dog around the suspect's car. The dog "alerted." After the dog's response, the trooper searched the front seat area of the suspect's car and found a bag containing what appeared to be marijuana. The suspect was arrested, and an inventory search of his automobile was conducted. Because it was cold on that night, the trooper took a coat from inside the suspect's automobile and gave it to the suspect to wear. Prior to giving the suspect his coat, however, the tooper checked the pockets for weapons and contraband. In one pocket, the trooper found a white envelope containing a white powdery substance. The suspect said it was his cocaine from a year ago.

The suspect moved to suppress the physical evidence and his statement to the trooper. The court held the suspect was not unlawfully seized for the purpose of allowing the drug dog to sniff the exterior of his car. If probable cause existed to search the automobile, the seizure of the suspected marijuana and the arrest of the suspect were lawful. However, no evidence was introduced from the handler of the dog as to the training, background, characteristics, capabilities, and behavior of the dog that would justify the officer's intrusion into the suspect's vehicle.

In order to establish probable cause for the search of the vehicle, some foundation testimony is necessary to establish that the alert of the dog provided probable cause for the search of the vehicle. On a proper showing, a narcotics dog's reaction to a vehicle may supply the probable cause necessary to justify a search of the vehicle, but there must be some evidence that the dog's behavior reliably indicated the likely presence of a controlled substance: "Obviously... a description of the dog's conduct, training and experience by a knowledgeable person who can interpret the conduct of the dog as signaling the presence of a controlled substance would constitute the minimum requirement for finding probable cause." Thereby the court suppressed the physical evidence and the suspect's statement concerning the evidence.[55]

The suspect entered the checklane in his car early in the morning. The trooper who was checking the suspect's driver's license smelled alcohol

54. *U.S. v. Rivera*, 825 F.2nd 152 (7th Cir. 1987).

Compare this with two other similar searches. In the first a woman and her seven-year-old son were traveling north on the interstate when she was stopped at a police department roadblock. The stated purpose of the roadblock was to check drivers' licenses, vehicle registrations, and proof of insurance. The woman produced her driver's license, registration, and proof of insurance as requested. While one officer was checking her documents, another officer walked a trained narcotic detection dog around the exterior of the car. Before the document check was finished, the dog alerted to the car. A search of the car revealed over a hundred pounds of marijuana hidden in luggage in the car's trunk.

In the second case a suspect with one passenger was driving a van north on the interstate. They encountered a police roadblock. While waiting in line before anyone had checked their documents, a narcotic detection dog alerted to the van. After the suspect stepped out of the van, an officer frisked him and found a .25 caliber handgun in the front right pocket of his pants. A subsequent search of the van revealed 30 pounds of marijuana concealed in a false compartment under the van's chassis.

The Supreme Court has upheld the constitutionality of brief roadblock detentions not based on an individualized reasonable suspicion of criminal activity in the context of a twenty-five second average detention at a sobriety checkpoint and a 3-5 minute average detention at an immigration checkpoint. Finding the factual circumstances of the two searches to be legally indistinguishable from *Place*, the court found the well trained canine sniffs were made of the exterior of the suspects' vehicles and did not invade their homes or bodily integrity. The vehicles were detained lawfully in a public area, and the sniff took place in that public area. The sniffs did not subject the suspects to any embarrassment, inconvenience, or delay. In each case the dog alerted to the vehicle before the officer's inspection of the driver's license, vehicle registration, and proof of insurance had been completed.[56]

A U.S. Border Patrol agent cross-designated as an agent of DEA and U.S. Customs stopped an automobile at a permanent checkpoint between San Diego and Los Angeles. The vehicle contained a driver and two passengers whose nervous behavior indicated to the agent they could be concealing undocumented aliens or perhaps narcotics. At the secondary inspection station, another cross-designated agent approached the driver's side of the vehicle and asked the driver to stop his engine. After ascertaining the driver was a U.S. citizen, the agent asked permission to inspect the hatchback-trunk area of the vehicle. The driver complied and opened the trunk. The agent discovered no undocumented aliens, nor did he find any drugs or contraband. At this point, the agent's immigration inspection lasting 3 to 4 minutes was completed.

Observing the driver becoming increasingly nervous and uneasy, the agent decided to use a detector dog trained to alert to hidden persons or narcotics. He walked the dog around the outside of the vehicle. The dog alerted positively. The detention for this portion of the inspection lasted about 60 seconds. Searching for contraband pursuant to the dog's alert, agents discovered about 800 grams of methamphetamine, two handguns, money and drug paraphernalia. The court held the brief continuation of this otherwise proper checkpoint detention for purposes of the canine sniff did not violate the fourth amendment.[57]

A subject may be detained to wait for a narcotic detection dog. One evening on the interstate a Louisiana State Police Trooper stopped a driver for speeding and improper lane usage. The driver hurriedly exited his vehicle—unusual because 99 percent of the persons the trooper stops for traffic violations remain in their vehicles until told to exit. Upon request, the driver produced his driver's license and vehicle registraton. The trooper asked the driver if he had ever been arrested. There was a long pause before the driver stated that he had only been arrested for traffic violations. The trooper then radioed for a check on the vehicle and the information provided by the subject.

By this time the trooper and the driver were seated in the patrol car. The trooper noticed

55. *State v. Barker*, 850 P.2d 885 (Kan. 1993).
56. *U.S. v. Moralez-Zamora*, 914 F.2d 200 (10th Cir. 1990).
57. *U.S. v. Taylor*, 934 F.2d 218 (9th Cir. 1991).

the man was extremely nervous, more so than the average person receiving a traffic citation. The officer noted the driver's stomach flutter such that his shirt moved. Additionally, the blood vessels in his neck protruded. Further, he was very talkative and continually rubbed his hands together.

Receiving information that the subject had been arrested in another State for possession of methamphetamine with intent to distribute, the trooper asked permission to search the vehicle. The suspect, gasping, refused, becoming visibly more nervous. Fearing for his safety, the trooper radioed for backup and another officer arrived on the scene. The trooper filled out a consent to search form, but the suspect refused. They were now twenty minutes into the stop. The trooper then requested a narcotics detection dog be sent to the scene.

At this point, according to the trooper, the suspect consented to a search of his vehicle. Nevertheless, fearing that consent may have been coerced by the suspect's expectation of a narcotics dog, the trooper decided to wait on the dog. Thirty minutes later, a sergeant arrived with a detector dog trained to find marijuana, cocaine, and methamphetamine. The dog alerted

The K-9 sniff must be done, or at least called for, within the timing of the stop. Interagency cooperation can be productive.

to the suspect's vehicle, indicating the likely presence of controlled dangerous substances. A vehicle search resulted in the recovery of three ounces of amphetamine, a spoon, a set of scales, and a .357 Magnum. The court said the trooper diligently pursued his investigation in a manner likely to quickly confirm or dispel his suspicion. The cause, method, and 50-minute duration of the suspect's detention were reasonable.[58]

Timing the dog deployment is especially critical for vehicle interdiction. The K-9 sniff must be done, or at least called for, within the timing of the stop. This does not mean officers have to use stopwatches. The courts have consistently held in favor of due diligence, reasonable

suspicion, and common sense. Unless you have *articulable reasonable suspicion*, continuing to detain suspects at the scene after completing the purpose of the stop (issue traffic citation) is illegal, thereby rendering a subsequent search of the vehicle improper.

The ultimate short sweet sniff took place in Florida, where a highway patrolman pulled over a vehicle with the intention of issuing the driver a citation for speeding. After examining the subject's driver's license, the officer asked the driver and his passenger to exit the car. The patrolman then released a dog from the cruiser. The dog was directed to sniff around the vehicle for evidence of drugs. The dog alerted to an odor in the car's trunk. Upon opening the trunk, two kilograms of cocaine were found. The defendant was placed under arrest. "Just as no police officer need close his eyes to contraband in plain view, no police officer armed with a sniff dog need ignore the olfactory essence of illegality." *In plain sniff.*[59]

Vehicles are drugs on the move. Your job requires that you be *uncommonly observant*. Observing a car being driven on the New Jersey Turnpike at a speed in excess of 55 miles per hour, a trooper clocked its speed, put on his overhead flashers and pulled the vehicle over. When asked for a driver's license and registration, the driver produced his license but said the rental agreement, in lieu of registration, must be in the trunk. The subject opened the trunk to get the registration and consented to the trooper's peering into the trunk. Doing so,

58. *State v. Fikes,* 616 So.2d 789 (La.App. 2Cir. 1993).
59. *State v. Taswell,* 560 So.2d 257 (Fla.App. 3 Dist. 1990).

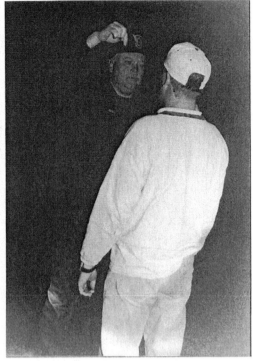

the trooper caught a glimpse of a black suitcase in the fleeting view he had of the trunk's interior, before the disconcerted driver abruptly closed it. When asked about the suitcase, the driver said he "had no knowledge of what was in the trunk." Noting this curious profession of ignorance along with other curiosity-arousing circumstances (the passenger professed he did not know the driver, and the driver stated he did not know who had rented the car), combined with the subject's nervous demeanor, the trooper was impelled to form a reasonable suspicion that criminal activity was afoot. He placed the passenger in handcuffs, and to restrict the motion of the driver, put him in the backseat of the police car.

Another police car arrived, a tow truck was requested, and the vehicle towed to trooper barracks two-and-a-half miles from the stop site. Half an hour later a detector dog arrived, began the sniffing procedure, zeroed in on the trunk of the car, and clawed at it violently, manifesting that its trained olfactory sense had focused upon a controlled substance. Results of the dog test were placed into an affidavit and a search warrant issued. Inside the suitcase officers found a "goodly quantity" of cocaine.

The appeals court judge was incredulous at the suspect's claim he was driving at 50 miles per hour, taking great care not to draw attention or breach the law: "It is not easy to go 50 miles an hour on the New Jersey Turnpike and not attract attention." He concluded there was a sufficient array of articulable facts to justify the dog sniff, and the transportation of the vehicle from the Turnpike to the barracks was not such an intrusive procedure as to violate constitutional mandate, but, rather, was reasonable. Requiring the government to bring the curious and clever canine out to the Turnpike would have been dangerous, risking not only the dog along that busy thoroughfare but potentially causing a chain collision of catastrophic proportions. To take the car to the dog rather than take the dog to the car was the only reasonable alternative. Once the dog's snout had hit paydirt, so to speak, the proper exterior search finding the drugs to be within "plain smell" was sufficient to give rise to probable cause leading to the constitutionally obtained and executed search warrant.[60]

An officer first observed a vehicle carrying two occupants following too closely and appearing to have illegal window tint. He then signaled the driver to stop. He cited the driver for the illegal window tint as well as for driving without a driver's license. The officer detained the suspects after they gave him conflicting stories at the scene as to the nature of their travels and their recent activities, and as to the ownership of the vehicle. The driver was not licensed. Further,

60. *U.S. v. Cruz*, 1992 U.S. Dis. Lexis 13188 (Pa).

A few feet away from the stop, the ultimate K-9 distraction hits the fence.

the officer's routine check with DEA indicated that the suspect and certain members of his family were involved in the crack cocaine business. The driver had been involved in drug related seizures or charges in two states.

The vehicle was stopped at approximately 7:00 am. The officer summoned the K-9 unit, which appeared at the scene at 7:36 am. The trained narcotics dog alerted on the trunk of the vehicle. Opening the vehicle's trunk, the officer found it contained $23,811. Because of the manner in which the money was packaged, the lack of either visible or stated means of either of the suspects acquiring the money, the conflicting explanations about the money, who owned it and other factors, at 7:41 am, the officer reported seizing the vehicle and currency. Also seized were a pager in possession of the driver and a Rolex watch.

The discovery of large sums of money without credible explanation can provide the necessary circumstantial evidence that the money was furnished or intended to be furnished in a drug transaction. The officer's determination of probable cause is derived from the totality of the circumstances, not from "a minute parsing of each item of information that leads to a finding of probable cause."

Despite the barking pit bull, CHP Officer Dennis Nissen's Osti makes the hit.

The appeals court found the detention of the suspects until the K-9 unit conducted a dog sniff was valid. The dog's alert, when viewed in light of the totality of the circumstances surrounding this stop, provided the officer with probable cause to believe that the vehicle, specifically the trunk, contained contraband or other evidence of criminal activity. These facts provided sufficient probable cause to justify the issuance of a search warrant, justifying the officer's warrantless search of the vehicle.[61]

A vehicle drove into a permanent border patrol station in New Mexico, where the occupants produced valid resident alien cards. When questioned about her destination by a Border Patrol Agent, the nervous driver, who avoided eye contact, responded she was traveling to a town in the States for two days. Asking and receiving permission to inspect the trunk of her vehicle, the agent found it contained no luggage.

Another agent then squatted down and looked under the vehicle. Using a mirror and flashlight, the agent saw shiny bolts on the gas tank support straps. Suspecting the gas tank had been altered to conceal narcotics, he referred the driver to the secondary inspection area and obtained verbal consent to conduct a dog search of the vehicle.

After the dog alerted, the driver signed a written form consenting to a full search of the vehicle. Agents retrieved approximately 25 pounds of marijuana from the vehicle's gas tank.

Before the suppression hearing, the suspect filed a motion for pretrial production of the training file for the dog that sniff-searched her vehicle. Specifically, she sought "training records, veterinary records, false-positive/false-negative alert records and all other records establishing the dog's ability to smell." The suspect argued the dog search was suspect because the dog had been recovering from a serious injury (fractured leg) and (she claimed) had false-alerted upon initial contact with her vehicle.

The agent who handled the dog testified that although the dog had been injured several months earlier (an injury unrelated to his nose), the dog was certified on the day the suspect's vehicle was searched. He also stated that the dog had never false-alerted during its three years of service. Though the court ultimately denied the suspect's motion for pretrial production, it nonetheless required the government to produce the canine log for the day of seizure.[62]

Handlers should keep in mind that courts are not looking for the dog "who has never false-alerted." One hundred percent proficiency is not believable and actually casts doubt on the reliability of the team. The suspect does not have the authority to say how the dog performed. The handler has the responsibility of articulating to the court what the K-9 team did.

In 1993, California enacted Health and Safety Code Section 11366.8:

(a) Every person who possesses, uses, or controls a false compartment with the intent to store, conceal, smuggle, or transport a controlled substance within the false compartment shall be punished by imprisonment in a county jail for a term of imprisonment not to exceed one year or in the state prison.

(b) Every person who designs, constructs, builds, alters, or fabricates a false compartment for, or installs or attaches a false compartment to, a vehicle with the intent to store, conceal, smuggle, or transport a controlled substance shall be punished by imprisonment in the state prison for 16 months or two or three years.

(c) The term "vehicle" means any of the following vehicles without regard to whether the vehicles are private or commercial, including, but not limited to, cars, trucks, busses, aircraft, boats, ships, yachts, and vessels.

(d) The term "false compartment" means any box, container, space, or enclosure that is intended for use or designed for use to conceal, hide, or otherwise prevent discovery of any controlled substance within or attached to a vehicle, including, but not limited to, any of the following:

(1) False, altered, or modified fuel tanks.

Handlers should keep in mind that courts are not looking for the dog "who has never false-alerted." One hundred percent proficiency is not believable and actually casts doubt on the reliability of the team.

---

61. *$23,811. In U.S. Currency v. Kowalski*, 810 F. Supp. 738 (W.D.La. 1993).
62. *U.S. v. Gonzales-Acosta*, 989 F.2nd 384 (10th Cir. 1993).

(2) Original factory equipment of a vehicle that is modified, altered, or changed.

(3) Compartment, space, or box that is added to, or fabricated, made, or created from, existing compartments, spaces, or boxes within a vehicle.

K-9 can be used to develop probable cause for a traffic stop on suspects under surveillance or part of a larger investigation. The suspects are then arrested for drug trafficking, none the wiser to the ongoing case. When the agency presents their case in court, specialized training enables officers to maintain the integrity of the larger investigation in progress. This is called *walling off* the investigation.

Chicago Police were surveilling an individual pending his indictment as the ring leader of a drug trafficking organization. The police surveillance was designed to keep track of the main man and the other indictees so they could be arrested when the indictments were issued. Early that afternoon detectives saw standing on a corner a suspect they knew was one of the persons about to be indicted for alleged participation in the West Side drug ring. Parked half a block away for 30 minutes, the detectives observed the suspect on five separate occasions leave his car to engage in hand-to-hand transactions with various individuals on the street corner. After each exchange, the suspect would return to his car until another person approached the corner. He would then re-emerge from his car to meet the person for another hand-to-hand exchange. Both parties walked away immediately after the exchange.

When the suspect drove the Cadillac northbound, the detectives followed and made the vehicle stop, guns drawn. They knew of the suspect's prior record, including numerous arrests and convictions on charges from battery to robbery. Numerous weapons (40 handguns, 23 hand grenades and a cluster bomb) had been found at his house. In the front passenger seat with the suspect was another individual the officers knew was part of the drug organization. Ordering the suspect out of the car, an officer conducted a pat-down search. The frisk revealed a thick, hard bulge in the jacket pocket. Removing it, the officer opened a wad of currency consisting of 45 bills all folded in half. The suspects accompanied the officers to the police station.

An hour later, a drug-sniffing dog arrived and alerted positively to the currency. Detectives then prepared an inventory report on the currency. At the same time DEA phoned to inform them the indictment against the suspect was returned. A detective then placed the suspect under arrest, gave him his Miranda warnings, and asked no further questions. The courts upheld all the evidence, including the dog sniff test in the police station. Probable cause to arrest was not necessary for the dog sniff because the police had reasonable suspicion of drug activity.[63]

In another Chicago case, DEA stopped an Oldsmobile, placed the driver under arrest, seized his car, and permitted the car to be sniffed by a trained narcotics dog. Five and one half hours after the canine sniff, a warrant was issued for the search of the vehicle. Officers located cocaine in the trunk of the car. The suspect claimed fourth amendment rights violation, rendering the arrest subject to quash and the seized evidence subject to suppression.

A government informant had provided detailed information relating to a planned drug deal enabling the government to conclude the suspect was delivering cocaine. *Based on the information the government had in its possession prior to the stop and subsequent dog sniff, there was probable cause to arrest the suspect without warrant.* The court held even if this information did not amount to probable cause, it certainly amounted to a reasonable suspicion of criminal activity justifying an investigatory stop. When the canine alerted after the momentary detention, the police then had probable cause to execute a full and formal arrest.[64]

U.S. agencies and the Federal Government of Mexico have reportedly used the *narcomobile*, a mobile drug detection system to discover large loads of marijuana in cars as well as trucks. A vehicle moving along the highway trails a pattern of air, like a speedboat wake or a jet contrail.

Five and one half hours after the canine sniff, a warrant was issued for the search of the vehicle.

63. *U.S. v. Moore*, 1992 U.S. Dist. Lexis 16440 (Ill).
64. *U.S. v. Yokana*, Slip opinion (N.Dist. Ill 1986).

Air escaping from the vehicle diffuses according to this partly laminar, partly turbulent flow. You experience this phenomenon when you smell smoke and see the driver of the car ahead smoking a cigarette. Moving a narcotic detector dog on a platform through a scent cone is the same in principle as walking the dog through the scent cone, provided he is trained to search under these conditions. The concept makes no intrusion into a reasonable expectation of privacy.

Suppose a dog on foot can detect a kilogram of marijuana 50 yards upwind in a 25 mile per hour breeze. Theoretically, driving the dog through the slipstream of a truck traveling 55 miles per hour carrying 100 kilos of marijuana, again provided the dog is trained to search this way, will cause an alert. In practice, K-9 detection also depends on the density and distribution of scent escaping the source vehicle, the speed and distance of the source vehicle, and the efficiency of the system presenting the air to the dog's nose.

Police agencies have modified vans and other vehicles to scoop oncoming air through a system of high-grade steel pipes. *Y* joints direct the air into a steel collection box inside the vehicle. Vent holes in the box are accessible to the dog's nose. A forward-looking videocamera mounted behind the dog's platform surveys the collection box as well as the highway ahead of the vehicle. As the unmarked K-9 unit moves along the highway, the dog examines air venting from the collection box. When he detects narcotic scent, the dog alerts. The camera records the dog alerting, the vehicle ahead, and the date-time or other programmed information. To isolate the target vehicle in heavy traffic, the K-9 unit may make two or more passes around several vehicles, recording both the dog's behavior and the traffic ahead.

In the U.S., the dog's alert in the narcomobile has typically not been used to establish probable cause but merely to identify vehicles that should be investigated by other officers. Officers stopping the target vehicle and obtaining consent to search may then call in the mobile K-9 if needed to conduct a standard vehicle search. Air conditioning keeps the dog comfortable summer and winter while working inside the K-9 unit.

Highway testing with hundreds of different target vehicles and variable quantities of marijuana or other drugs—5, 10, 20, 30, 40, 50 kilograms—has reportedly shown what procedures are most effective. Configuration of the source load, speed, and distance of the target vehicle produce variations in the time to obtain an alert from the K-9. One study determined the average effective distance for the dog unit at speeds up to 45 miles per hour was 50 feet behind the suspect vehicle. Faster than 45 miles per hour required 40 feet. Distance and speed do not appear to affect the dog's response to larger loads. One dog hit on a truck carrying a 750 kilogram load of marijuana in its walls 10 seconds after the truck had passed. The same dog took 90 seconds to detect 5 kilos in a bag in the back of a sedan. One dog accumulated a 2-week record of 16 different vehicles, enabling the seizure of 1.5 tons of marijuana. The dog hit buses with marijuana in suitcases, cars with marijuana in gas tanks, floors, roofs, side panels, and engine compartments.

This type of interdiction targets large quantities of narcotics. The dog will probably not detect small quantities secreted in glove compartments or center consoles. One advantage seems to be the absence of alerts where there is odor but no dope.

"Go for the *big* hauls...
searching for gram-quantities is like trying to turn the tide."
—California Highway Patrol Officer

LARGE VEHICLES

At a Texas border patrol checkpoint, two agents approached a truck to determine the driver's citizenship. Showing intense interest, the drug detector dog belonging to one of the agents started toward the vehicle. Walking around the tractor-trailer rig, the dog's interest developed into a full alert. The driver told the agent he was a citizen of the United States. The agent noticed he appeared nervous and, as he was watching the dog "work odor" around the vehicle, became increasingly nervous. Based on the handler's observations about the spontaneous alert, the other agent asked the driver to move his truck to the secondary inspection area.

While at secondary, the dog was worked in a pattern around the vehicle. The agents saw several items in the trailer bed, including a toolbox, which they asked the driver to open. The dog jumped up and alerted to the bed of the trailer. After further discussion with the driver and further investigation of the contents of the trailer (all with the driver's consent), the agents discovered 330 pounds of marijuana in a compartment behind a trap door, under a diesel tank, hidden in the bed of the trailer.[65]

Semitrailers and other large trucks offer traffickers opportunities to transport up to several tons of drugs rapidly across the United States. The great volume of commercial vehicles entering and crisscrossing the States daily and the relative difficulty of thoroughly searching them, especially when laden with legitimate, perhaps even perishable or hazardous cargo, presents a formidable challenge to law enforcement. The size, weight, and configuration of large commercial motor vehicles, recreational vehicles, buses, large aircraft, or vessels makes searching with a narcotic dog difficult, sometimes infeasible. Customs dogs have better access at some border checkpoints and airports. Large vehicles used by smugglers include van semitrailers, propane tankers, petroleum product tankers, vacuum tankers, single hatch liquid tankers, water tankers, dry cement hopper trailers, stake bed trucks, moving van trucks, flatbed trucks, flatbed trailers, car carrier semitrailers and tractor trucks.

Common concealment techniques include false compartments interior to trunk walls, wheel wells, flooring, truck beds, side walls, doors, rocker panels, seats, dash compartments,

Even with technology to detect defects and irregularities, the high volume of container shipping means some illicit loads get through. Dogs at ports of entry, weigh stations, and highway stops screen vehicles that would otherwise go unchecked.

65. *U.S. v. Dovali-Avila*, 895 F.2d 206 (5th Cir. 1990).

front firewalls, tires with "quick breakdown" modified rims, modified bumpers, axles, differentials, shock absorbers, gas tanks, engine compartments, modified roof "dents" filled with narcotics then refinished, tool boxes and other accessories, camper or travel trailer modifications, and airtight containers, such as hermetically sealed tin cans.

The commercial officer will be observing the driver and examining his documentation and the truck itself for indicators of drug trafficking. Commercial vehicle driver indicators—detection of the impaired driver, a cursory examination to determine evidence of drug impairment, the driver's demeanor and his knowledge about the contents of the trailer. The paid courier is likely to know nothing about the load he is hauling, to be unarmed and very cooperative with law enforcement, to be an owner-operator with a property crime history, and to be receiving pay in money or drugs. Many are foreign nationals. Traffickers who have a vested interest in illegal cargo are more likely to be dangerous, to be armed, to have a criminal record as a major violator, to be very knowledgeable about the cargo and the operation, to be above the industry standard in dress and hygiene, and to refuse a search. Ask the driver who "has nothing to hide" to sign a written consent form then detain all occupants separately away from the vehicle while officers conduct the search, including the detector dog sniff.

Look for fraudulent documentation (or lack of required documentation), such as operator's license, tractor and trailer registration, medical certificates, record of duty status (log book), manifest (bill of lading). Perform a criminal record and national narcotic intelligence check.

Origin versus destination—typical supplier locations for narcotics and other dangerous drugs, typical shipping routes, and buyer locations.

Modification of structure—either the truck or the trailer—to accommodate concealments, to give "legitimacy" to the trip, and to discourage physical inspection. Alterations may be immediately visible to the observant officer, such as amateurish construction or lettering, disturbed areas, fresh glue or paint, or new connectors, or the changes may be highly professional and therefore difficult to discover. Airfoils and other customized equipment further complicate observation.

Equipment—missing, or legitimate but malfunctioning, such as pressure gauges registering zero, or items that contradict the claimed purpose of the trip or the destination.

Questionable commodities—transportation cost compared to maximum profit potential, such as a partial load of perishable products that are unusual or poorly loaded or spoiled.

Semitrailers, doubles or triples may conceal thousands of pounds of contraband in specialized compartments in the top, sides, or floor. K-9 response to high concealment may be unusual behavior at a distance from the vehicle.

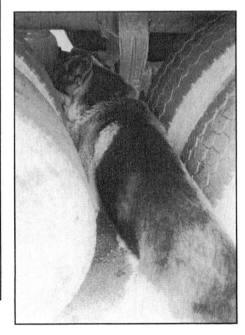

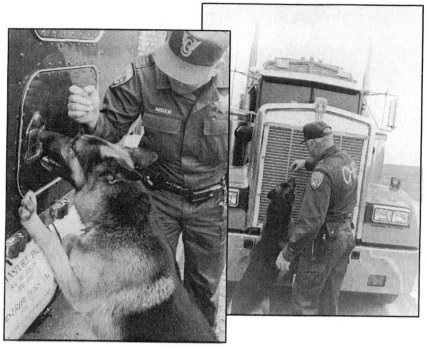

The nose of an experienced officer can detect indicators for follow-up by a K-9 sniff. Scent detected by the human nose:

- Marijuana (raw, burned)
- Chemical (acid)
- Spoiled produce (rotten, decayed, sour, putrid, rancid)
- Substances with strong characteristic scents frequently used to mask drug scents, e.g., coffee, perfumes, air fresheners or deodorizers, baby powder, cedar shavings, mothballs, gasoline or other petrochemicals, derivatives of alcohol
- Materials used to install hiding places, e.g., bondo or fiberglass, glue, paint, putty, sealants, fresh tar

The inspector investigates load dimensions, resonance changes, dimensional discrepancies, thermal properties (radiant heat emissions), temperature and pressure readings, tare and actual weights, distribution and content.

Stopped at an immigration checkpoint, the driver consented to a search of the refrigerated tractor-trailer rig he was operating. Before arriving at the checkpoint, he knew law enforcement agents were using drug detector dogs. At the checkpoint, he observed the dogs. After he consented to the search, officers hoisted a dog into the trailer and the dog alerted to boxes containing cocaine. On appeal, the defendant argued that his consent was involuntary and that the agents' use of a dog during the search exceeded the scope of his consent because he had anticipated only agents would conduct the search. In rejecting the defendant's argument, the court ruled the search did not exceed the scope of the defendant's consent because (1) the defendant knew before he arrived at the checkpoint that drug sniffing dogs were used to examine vehicles, (2) dogs were present when he gave his consent to search the tractor-trailer rig, and (3) the defendant said nothing when the dog was lifted into the trailer. The court ruled that the use of the dog did not constitute a search.[66]

If placed in the truck cab, the dog should search the sleeper unit and radio speaker system.

Hot engine compartments diffuse scent but make targeting difficult for the dog.

For K-9 safety and hazardous traffic conditions work the dog on lead.

66. *U.S. v. Gonzakez-Basulto*, 9898 F.2d 1011 (5th Cir. 1990).

COMMERCIAL MOTOR VEHICLE DEPLOYMENT TACTICS

Working a drug detector dog successfully in some cases of concealment is extremely difficult. In these cases the handler has to be aware and be trained to assist the investigation more actively than merely deploying the dog around the truck. If not trained to recognize and examine indicators, the handler needs the assistance of highway patrolmen or other experienced officers.

Approach large vehicles into the wind if possible. Initiate the sniff 50 to 75 feet away, depending on wind conditions. Contraband with a high rate of vaporization may be detected at a considerable distance. Dogs need experience detecting scent at these distances. The dog that is used to scratching, pawing, or biting an object at the location of highest scent concentration may be confused or uncertain when he detects odor 50 feet from the target vehicle, with nothing to paw or bite nearby. The handler also needs experience reading his dog's behavior in these situations. A brief behavior change may be the only canine indicator, particularly where the concealment is high on a large vehicle. Some dogs are more aggressive, walking on their hind legs sniffing the air like a bear, or racing forward toward the target.

Turbulence increases as the canine team approaches the vehicle. Air that was moving in a smooth laminar flow pattern 50 or 60 feet away from the vehicle typically rolls into vortices close to the vehicle. As a result, scent diffusing from concealment high on a truck may be detectable at ground level 50 feet away but not at 5 feet. The shape of the vehicle and wind velocity determine scent diffusion patterns around vehicles just as air deflects off surfaces in a wind tunnel. There may be pockets of low velocity or rising air, for example between the tractor and trailer, as well as high velocity flow, for example along the sides of a trailer. Sharp edges generally increase turbulence and require a closer sniff.

Trucks parked in parallel also affect the patterns of scent diffusion. Alerting, a detector dog

False compartments are welded to support I-beam chassis beneath van trailers.

Although trucks traveling with the van box removed appear empty, they may be transporting hundreds of pounds of dope concealed in metal tubing or under plates covering the voids between I-beam supports.

crossed underneath a row of 8 tractor-trailers (the handler ducking and weaving at the end of the lead) to locate a kilo of cocaine concealed inside the false wall compartment of a trailer. The handler should anticipate how multiple trucks at a weigh station or check site will affect scent diffusion. It may be necessary for the detector dog to perform random searches of vehicles isolated from the main stream of truck traffic.

To maximize canine efficiency and safety, work the narcotic dog on lead. For commercial motor vehicle searches a 15-foot lead allows the dog to cast crosswind safely or to investigate under the vehicle without dragging the handler along. Do not work the dog off lead on the highway or at a busy check site.

Conduct the initial search around the entire vehicle. The dog may alert or show a behavior change right away. This is your lucky day—there is probably a big load of drugs on board. If the dog does not alert on the first pass and it is necessary to detail the exterior, work him more slowly, sniffing all exterior compartments, the grill area, tanks, I-beams, and other possible areas of concealment. Without special equipment, the dog cannot sniff areas higher than his nose while standing on his hind legs. Besides the narcotic itself, the method of concealment, traffic, wind, temperature, weather, and time of day all affect scent diffusion. On big rigs, as on other vehicles, the dog may not be able to go to source.

The inside of a truck cab resembles the interior of a passenger vehicle or small recreational vehicle (RV). Searching inside the trailer of an 18-wheeler is like searching a building. Often cargo intervenes and can be moved only by special equipment. If the dog cannot balance confidently, he will stop searching. Unstable platforms, metal grids, hot or freezing metal flooring, slippery flooring, palletized cargo, or piles of loose materials may distract the inexperienced or fearful dog from detecting narcotics. Palletized cargo wrapped in plastic is slippery. Falling between the stacks of pallets is a risk. Steel bands securing the cargo may cut the dog's pads. Rain or ice increases these hazards.

The handler assigned the task of working highways, borders, or traffic check points where he will encounter such big rigs needs tools, or access to tools, beyond the standard K-9 patrol equipment. He will need a variety of flashlights, screw drivers, pliers, drills, saws, pry bars, test rods, mirrors, and other investigative tools. Concealment methods as well as found drugs should be photographed and submitted to the national narcotic intelligence exchange system.

Dog and handler are at risk searching a trailer filled with cargo. Plastic wraps make surfaces slippery. Loose cargo shifts. Refrigerated trailers require specialized training.

COMMON CONCEALMENT AREAS TO SNIFF

Tractor trucks—In aerodynamic tractor models, modifications include factory created void areas under floorboards, and front kickboard areas that can only be detected visually by removing the floor carpeting, metal flooring, or cutout metal access plates. Sleeper compartments are refabricated to create a false rear wall compartment. Remote electronic release of the roof air deflector or other device serves as access and entry to these compartments. Compartments may be constructed of aluminum and the exterior of the sleeper unit professionally modified with fiberglass painted to appear normal.

Drugs have been concealed in all the following common features of tractor trailers:

- Hitch plate or "kingpin plate" (fifth wheel connection point) connecting the trailer to the tractor truck, as an access or entry point to the inside of the tanker/trailer, or as a concealment device in itself for small quantities of drugs
- False walls, roofs and floors of van semitrailers, large trucks, and air, sea and land shipping containers
- Cab of tractor, sleeper unit used to conceal narcotics in console area, dashboard padding or cavities, in radio and stereo equipment, under seats or bedding
- Cabinets to house emergency valve operators, tools, or other equipment
- Refrigerated or box trailers may appear empty with a few pallets or boxes in the nose of the trailer
- Tires, spare tires
- Fuel tanks or false compartments inside tanks
- Bumpers (regular and large cattle guard type) filled with narcotics then welded shut
- Tractor-truck oil bath air cleaner
- Engine compartment of the tractor
- Axles, underconstruction, chassis frame (I-beams), and supports

Air brake tanks—Cylindrical air brake tanks are unwelded on one end and sealed and welded metal containers loaded with drugs are inserted into the tanks. Caps of the tanks are welded back into place and compressed air is pumped inside, allowing the tanks to function normally. An excessive number of air tanks on the tractor and trailer, such as 7 or 8, would be a suspect indicator. The dog should sniff each tank. Apply the brake pedal several times to force air to exit the airbrake system through the trailer's various air release points, including the circular rear brake chambers. Work the drug dog past these points immediately.

Metal boxes in semitrailer roof—A semitrailer's roof is filled with metal boxes containing drugs. Silicone-sealed boxes also contain coffee grounds, a typical attempt to deter narcotic detector dogs. Expect long distance alerting or high alerts outside or inside the trailer.

Corrugated metal false front wall compartment—A corrugated metal false front wall installed in a van semitrailer duplicates the original front wall and creates a large false compartment approximately 2 feet deep extending the full height and width of the trailer's front section. The dog may alert along any exterior or interior seams, or around bolts or screws used to secure the false wall. Where drilling the front trailer wall from the inside fails to show sunlight, indicating a false compartment, deploy the dog to sniff the drill holes.

Propane tankers—Liquid propane gas is a highly volatile and dangerous product. Tankers loaded with this commodity are rightfully treated with respect and a measure of fear by most people who come in contact with them, even by police officers who inspect the tankers. Empty tankers can be as dangerous as loaded ones, sometimes more dangerous. A tanker full of propane gas must be treated carefully to avoid a possible explosion or fire. Here the experienced detector dog can be valuable if properly deployed.

Drugs are secreted inside the tank. Bogus gauges, scrapes, chipped or new paint, plates out of position, new nuts and bolts, absent or fraudulent identification are all indicators. Wherever possible, let the dog sniff all vents and inspection holes. When scaffolding or platforms give the dog access to high places on trucks, familiarize the animal with the equipment before actually searching so that he is accustomed to climbing, traversing, and detecting scent in typical locations.

After using the appropriate precautions to rotate the gauge handles of tankers (or separate tanks), direct the dog to sniff near the valve (including bleeder valves, emergency valves) or cap immediately after venting. This technique has to be practiced. The dog needs experience with the noise and air blast created by the discharge of a pressurized tanks. Keep the dog's head away from valves during the initial release. Pressure valves are dangerous because the vapor may be extremely cold. Toxic liquid may jet out. *Any tank may be carrying hazardous materials.*

The dog should sniff around the inspection manholes, threaded caps, inspection pipes, fittings, flanges, connectors, plates and seams of the tanker belly or trailer to detect scent diffusing from false compartments or tubing. Pay attention to wheel mud flaps and fenders, special bottom load and discharge manifolds, and, for liquid bearing tankers, the metal tubes designed to house discharge hoses.

The security seal and inspection plate may be removed intact and the tanker filled with drugs. The plate is then replaced and the severed security seal reattached to appear authentic. Although the driver claims the tanker is empty, comparison of the tare versus actual weights reveals significant overage. Tapping the underbelly produces different sounds from tapping the upper side. Deploy the dog to sniff all seams and valves.

Petroleum product tankers are seldom inspected due to the noxious and caustic contents. Deploy the drug dog to search the tanker belly and sides for scent diffusing from the cutout hole.

Vacuum tankers have independent, sealed compartments. All hatches must be opened and, if possible, sniffed by a drug dog, for a thorough inspection.

The internal design of most single hatch tankers consists of 3 compartments separated by 2 bulkhead walls with manhole passages through the middle of each wall. Smugglers install watertight doors on these manholes to create 2 concealment areas, one in front and one in the rear of the tanker. The middle compartment can then be filled with a bona fide liquid in case officers inspect it by opening the single top hatch. Deploy the drug dog at all seams and orifices.

Water tanker trucks have considerably lower liquid capacity than the large semitrailer tankers, but their ability to conceal drugs is substantial. On this type truck, deploy the dog to detail the tanker.

Closed hopper pressure vessels—Tarps are laid over the drugs, then the bins are filled to the top with powdered cement or other commodity. Belly dump hopper tankers develop internal pressure when gases diffuse from commodities or actual gas being transported. In the case of dry powder cement hoppers, spontaneous reaction builds up pressure and heat inside the hoppers. Inspect these pressure vessels only after taking specific precautions and releasing pressure valves. Where pressure and heat build up inside the hoppers, the accelerated rate of vaporization from the concealed drugs may aid the detector dog.

Hopper commodity or aggregate hopper trailers can be discharged in a few seconds. Large gravity discharge hopper openings on the belly of the trailer release the entire load in 3-4 seconds. Scent typically diffuses from the clam shell gates, control valves, and seams.

Flatbed and stakebed trucks are the common types of cargo carriers that can be modified in many ways to conceal drugs, including creating false beds and compartments between I-beam frame supports. Detection is made more difficult by overloading the cargo bed, covering the entire commodity load with a heavy tarp, and tying it down. Normally, the false bed or compartment's trap door cannot be accessed until the entire load is removed and the trap door is lifted from the top surface of the bed. Wooden sides and rear gates conceal the false bed compartment. Planks, mats or grating used as additional flooring above the false bed further hides the concealment. Hay, manure or tires strewn on top of the planks discourage inspection. False compartments can run the length and width of the bed, concealing surprisingly large drug shipments in ordinary

Where pressure and heat build up inside the hoppers, the accelerated rate of vaporization from the concealed drugs may aid the detector dog.

looking trucks, *trucks that may appear empty*.

Note discrepancies in flooring planks and subflooring. Deploy the drug dog to search the surface of the stake bed as well as the sides and underbody of the truck. The dog should have prior experience finding drugs hidden in flooring so *the handler can read the alert* if the dog starts pawing and scratching the stake bed flooring, especially where excrement, garbage, ostensibly legitimate loads of vegetables or fruit, or other distractions are evident.

Trailers hauling livestock or baled hay present special distractions to the inexperienced detector dog.

Oil drum-within-an-oil-drum fuel tanks--Cylindrical side-saddle fuel tanks of a stakebed truck may be modified by inserting a sealed drug-filled cylinder. Diesel is held in the interior space between both cylinders. While a drug dog may be able to scent drug residue or odor exiting seams or holes, drilling may be required to disclose the drugs in the inner drum.

Moving vans or rental trucks—Construction typically consists of aluminum walls with structural support beams running vertically along the inside of the cargo area and horizontally across the roof. Many have several wooden boards running horizontally at staggered distances on the inside walls. A simple false-front wall compartment can hold multi-thousand pound quantities of narcotics. Some modifications perfectly mimic the bona fide appearance of interior walls and are very difficult to detect.

Drilling has typically been been the conclusive method of detection after depth discrepancies are noted between the outside and inside cargo areas. Position the dog at the rear of the truck to sniff the airspace immediately when the doors are first opened. Remove cargo as necessary to give the drug detector dog access to inside walls as well as the outside of the cargo area. Deploy the dog to check suspect packages or other cargo.

Metal/wood false front wall with access by roof trap door—A roof plate is installed as the access door to the false front wall compartment in a 24-foot cargo truck. The false front wall mimics the side walls in construction, for example sheet metal supported by vertical metal I-beam ribs and staggered wooden rails attached horizontally top to bottom, identical to the side walls. Deploy the drug dog to search the seams and openings.

Smugglers fill furniture, appliances such as refrigerators, or commercial product cardboard boxes with drugs to carry them cross-country in rental trucks. Taking advantage of police reluctance to offload, they load the containers of narcotics first, forward of the rest of the cargo. Deploy the drug dog to sniff as the rear cargo doors of the truck are opened. A behavior change may warrant offloading enough cargo to give the dog and handler access to the interior.

Narcotics are concealed in the hollow framework of semitrailer superstructures, including car or boat carriers. Tubing or beam-type structures should never be ignored. Amazing quantities of potent narcotics, such as hash oil, have been found inside. Detail the drug dog along the framework of the superstructure and at ends or angle seams where he may detect escaping scent.

Prepare the interior of a bus for the narcotic dog by operating the ventilation system or by allowing the front and rear doors to the passenger seating area to remain partially open. Air circulating slowly will aid the dog. The dog enters the bus and is taken directly to the rear where he begins a detailed search. He examines any lavatories or other compartments in the rear. In the passenger compartment, he sniffs the floor, seats, seatbacks, jumps onto the seats, sniffs the overhead compartment, then crosses the aisle to perform the same sequence, then moves ahead to the next row. The dog executes this figure-8 pattern throughout the seating area. Finally, he sniffs the driver area, dash, and compartments in the front of the bus.

AIRCRAFT

Commercial aircraft interiors should be searched immediately after passengers and crew deplane. K-9 tactics are the same as for a bus, starting/entering at the rear, detailing accessible overhead compartments, lavatories, galleys, storage and passenger seating areas. Detector dogs have alerted to aircraft seats previously occupied by a narcotic body carrier. In such cases, the handler notifies the appropriate officer who attempts to identify the person or persons previously occupying the seat(s) in order to search the individual(s) and all accompanying baggage. If the dog has to search the cockpit, a pilot or qualified ground crewman should be present to ensure instruments are not moved or damaged. Baggage and freight compartments can be searched when empty. Search the baggage and freight after unloading in a secure area to give the dog better access. Bags the dog alerts to on the conveyor belt should be placed under surveillance until reclaimed by the owners.

Aviators with a pilot services company informed DEA about their suspicions that one of their customers was involved in smuggling illegal narcotics. Company employees told DEA investigators the suspect had arranged for one of their pilots to fly him in a Piper Navajo plane, which the suspect provided, on a round trip between Pennsylvania and Florida. This method of transportation for one passenger going to one destination was far more costly and more time consuming than taking a commercial airline. The suspect paid all expenses, about $2000 in cash. He was not in communication with the pilot, who was paid $150 per day for four days before the

Search small aircraft like vehicles, sniffing all seams on the wings, engines, and fuselage, in particular the doors and wheel wells. Do not jump the dog onto the wings.

return flight. The suspect carried more luggage on the return flight than he did on the flight to Florida. In addition, DEA knew that the listed owner of the aircraft, a construction firm, did not exist where it was purportedly registered.

A month earlier, an associate of the suspect informed DEA the suspect was involved in cocaine trafficking between Florida and Pennsylvania. According to the associate, the suspect received his cocaine in South Florida and had contacted him on at least two occasions to help transport the cocaine and act as a bodyguard.

When the suspect (he was using an alias but DEA knew his real name), requested that the company provide a pilot for a round trip to Florida, DEA arranged to have the reporting pilot assigned to the duty and also provided extra compensation. As before, the suspect provided the plane and maintained possession of the plane's keys. The pilot telephoned DEA during the trip several times to report the suspect had changed the destination of the plane en route, paid all expenses in cash, and failed to give the pilot the name of his hotel or a contact number. He also failed to arrive at the planned departure time, instead arriving later that night eager to leave immediately even though the pilot told him it would be safer to wait until morning.

The flight from Florida landed at the Pennsylvania airport at 7 a.m. After the suspect placed his suitcases on the ground, armed DEA agents, who had been informed of the plane's scheduled arrival by a telephone call from the pilot, approached both the suspect and the pilot and requested identification. Several other armed DEA agents were nearby. The suspect identified himself by his real name but refused to consent to the search of his suitcases. Shortly thereafter, without the suspect's consent, a brief dog sniff of the suspect's suitcases was conducted by a trained narcotics dog. Although the dog did not isolate which of the suitcases contained narcotics, he alerted to the presence of narcotics among the suspect's suitcases. The dog also made an attempt to board the aircraft. As a result of the positive dog sniff and the other information previously received, the suspect was immediately arrested, the suitcases and airplane secured, and a warrant to search the plane and suitcases was obtained from a Pennsylvania District Justice.

Pursuant to the search warrant, the DEA agents found 10 kilograms of cocaine in a suitcase in the locked baggage compartment of the airplane. The agents also recovered a trace amount of cocaine from one of the suspect's suitcases placed on the ground and subjected to the dog sniff. No keys to the cabin of the plane or the locked baggage compartment were found in the suspect's possession, a fact he tried to use in court to distance himself from the incriminating evidence.[67]

The Federal Aviation Administration conducts ramp checks for registration and other violations. The FAA typically looks for drug trafficking indicators, such as provisions or equipment for long distance flights, extra security precautions, aircraft modifications, damage or other evidence of landings at substandard airfields. A drug detector dog can assist these checks. The tactics for searching small aircraft are primarily the same as for passenger vehicles, except for the airflow system (not available), entry/exit (protect the wings from the dog jumping on them), and restricted cabin space (protect the instruments). For small, high wing planes, it is a good idea to cast the dog through the area 10 to 20 yards downwind of the aircraft. Knowing the construction of particular aircraft can help. In most small aircraft, except for the front firewall, the compartments are not airtight. The skin fits over a skeletal framework that allows scent from any area inside the fuselage to diffuse through the door or vent seams, or even into a wheel housing, depending on the design and the airflow. Deploy the dog to sniff the door seams, vents, especially pop-open vents, the underside of the wings and fuselage.

Based on evidence from an informant, Customs agents believed a suspect was transporting drugs between San Diego, Ft. Lauderdale, and Boston. The suspect was about to fly out of San Diego one night when an agent rapped on the window of his privately chartered plane and asked to board it for inspection. The door was opened, and the agent entered. He asked the suspect if he could search his bags, but was told to get a warrant first. The agent replied he would try to obtain a warrant but told the suspect to wait a moment while he took the bags off the plane to have a trained dog sniff them for contraband. The positive sniff test was completed within thirty minutes of the beginning of the suspect's detention. He was then held for an additional ninety minutes before being released. His bags remained with the agents, who eventually obtained a warrant to open them. The bags contained 210 pounds of marijuana. Two weeks later the suspect was captured on a freeway, fleeing from his car after a forty minute pursuit.

VESSELS

In most situations, narcotic K-9s should deploy with Customs vessel search teams, especially when searching large seagoing vessels. Ships have enormous concealment potential. It is not possible to routinely search an entire vessel. Seaport inspectors will determine the priorities for searching areas where drugs are typically seized—crew quarters, lavatories, galleys—and a member of the vessel's staff or Customs officers will accompany the dog team. Consider high air temperatures and hot metal surfaces (engine rooms) before deploying the dog to search such areas. Many locations on vessels are accessible only by ladders, requiring a *harness*, bag or crane to lift or lower the dog. Searching small craft or recreational boats requires familiarization but should not be difficult for the dog. Dogs deployed frequently to search vessels need strong agility and swimming skills.

67. *U.S. v. Bausman*, 1987 U.S. Dis. Lexis 692 (Pa).

PARCEL SEARCH

A Colorado police detective assigned to a narcotics enforcement team interviewed a cable TV employee who identified some local drug traffickers. A month later a confidential informant told another investigator the same people were making frequent trips to New York to obtain cocaine, which they brought back via the airlines to Colorado. After the first detective learned of the information from the confidential informant, he contacted the private mail carrier in the area requesting they be on the alert for packages addressed to the suspects because they might contain cocaine.

A couple of weeks later, the clerk noted that a package coming through the express office was addressed to one of the suspects at a local address. The security officer in Denver told the clerk to contact the detective and allow him to inspect the package. The detective asked the clerk to hold the package until he could get a narcotics-sniffing canine to the office to inspect it. The officer then brought his dog trained to sniff for cocaine and marijuana to the office. When allowed to sniff an array of five packages, including the one addressed to the suspect, the dog alerted on the suspect's package several times, indicating it contained a controlled substance.

Equipped with this information, the detective swore out an affidavit and obtained a search warrant to open the package. The substance inside field-tested for cocaine. A controlled delivery was then attempted (at approximately the same time the package would have been delivered in the normal course of events), but no one was present at the residence (suspects often do not want to receive packages, or they have a neighbor receive the package for them). A note was left saying that delivery would be attempted again on the next business day.

After the package was delivered, the police executed a search warrant for the residence. The suspects were charged with possession of cocaine with intent to distribute, as special offenders, and with tampering with physical evidence.[68]

> "What is the incentive for private parcel carriers to cooperate with law enforcement? They can lose their operating rights. A private carrier cannot carry contraband."
> —Jim Pullis, Loss Prevention Representative, United Parcel Service

Mailing contraband is illegal. Drugs fall into the same category as shipping an Uzi. One gun dealer who is allowed to ship automatic weapons can send the gun to another dealer. A pharmaceutical company can ship prescription drugs. Any time you have a controlled substance not coming from a legitimate source, such as a pharmaceutical company or a medical practitioner, then it is considered contraband.

The U.S. Postal Service knows they are transporting narcotics. The private carriers are aware narcotics are going through their systems. What is their responsibility in this regard? They are caught in a Catch-22. If you start opening up everything coming through the system, or single out a parcel, then you have transgressed into violation of privacy. If the carrier knows they are being utilized and does nothing about it, they are an accessory to a crime. The carrier must show he is policing himself without transgressing into violation of privacy. Certain private carriers reserve the right to inspect and open packages.

Because a local police department is frequently the agency contacted first when a postal crime

68. *People v. Boylan*, 854 P.2d 807 (Colo. 1993).

is committed, cooperation between local police or sheriff's deputies and Postal Inspectors or private carrier representatives is required. If the police are first on scene, officers follow standard investigative procedures: Aiding the injured, protecting the crime scene, gathering and preserving evidence, locating and questioning witnesses, and so on. A postal employee should telephone the Postal Inspection Service (PIS). The private carrier employee contacts his loss prevention or investigations representative.

Postal Inspectors are federal agents who carry firearms, make felony arrests, and serve federal search warrants and subpoenas. They work closely with the Internal Revenue Service, the Drug Enforcement Agency, the Customs Service, United States Attorneys and with state, county, and local prosecutors in investigating postal cases and preparing them for court. Postal Inspectors spend about two-thirds of their time investigating and solving postal crimes. Postal Inspectors assist law enforcement agencies in obtaining federal search warrants, and making controlled deliveries of mail containing illegal narcotics. *Once a person releases a package into the mail, until the package is received, it is under the federal Postal Inspector's jurisdiction.* The postal carrier can answer some of the of the police officer's questions, such as who lives at an address or a box number, but not mail cover details for a felony investigation. A controlled delivery has to be delivered by a U.S. PIS or a regular postal employee. Federal crime laboratories provide forensic analysis of evidence for departments working a joint investigation with the Postal Inspection Service.

The parcel sniff must occur in an uncontaminated environment with clean control parcels, and the handler cannot know which parcel is suspected.

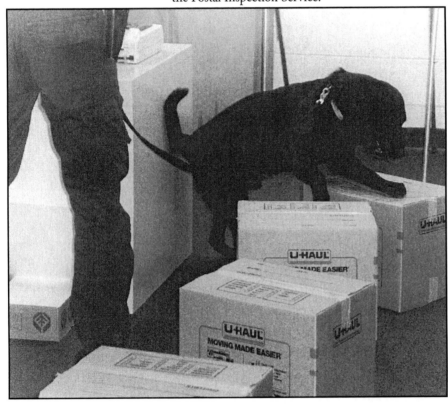

Inspectors investigate alleged violations of about one hundred different federal laws relating to the U.S. Mail and in the postal system, including the following crimes:

• *Controlled substances*, the mailing of illegal narcotics (21 USC 843b) or the possession, use, and dealing of such drugs by a postal employee in a postal facility or while on duty (21 USC 841(a)(1) and 844)

• *Money laundering*, the concealment of taxable income or the proceeds from an illegal enterprise by engaging in certain monetary transactions, including the purchase of postal money orders to help disguise such income or proceeds (18 USC 1956 and 1957).

Should a police officer receive information that illegal drugs are being sent through the U.S. mail to a suspect, the Postal Inspection Service can provide a *mail cover* on the suspect. This alerts the local agency as to when the suspect's drug letter or parcel is received at the delivering post office. Since a federal search warrant is required to open mail, if a state narcotics violation is also a violation of federal law, the Inspection Service may be able to assist in developing the probable cause needed to convince the U.S. Attorney's Office to seek a federal search warrant to open and test the contents of a suspect letter or parcel prior to its delivery.

If the mail contains drugs, Postal Inspectors will work with officers on a *controlled delivery* to insure receipt by the suspect so appropriate action can then be taken. This includes such things as providing a Postal Inspector who will dress as a postal letter carrier, placing electronic beepers in the mail, and obtaining any *Karo* search warrant necessary under the circumstances (*United States v. Karo, et al*, 1984, deals with monitoring a beeper in a private residence). The Inspection Service will assist to interdict illegal drugs originating from both foreign and domestic sources which enter a major postal facility to be processed for delivery, including working with narcotics-trained canines in a mail screening and profiling program for illegal drugs.

Frequently, *dirty* or illegally obtained funds generated through activities like drug trafficking are transferred through one or more bank accounts or transactions, including those where postal money orders are purchased in the *laundering* process. In order to better trace laundered funds, 31 USC 5325 requires that any financial institution which issues a bank check, money order, cashier's check, or traveler's check to any person must collect certain information from that person, if the transaction is made in United States coins or currency in an amount greater than $3,000. This includes deposits, withdrawals, currency exchanges, or other payments or transfers by, through, or to the financial institution, unless the individual has a trasaction account with the institution and certain efforts are made to identify the person making the transaction. Multiple transactions must be treated by the financial institution as a single transaction if the institution knows these transactions are by or on behalf of a specific person and if they result in cash coming into or cash going out of the financial institution in an amount greater than $3,000 during any one business day.

Where the $3,000 transaction floor is exceeded, the financial institution processing the transaction must file IRS Form 4789, Currency Transaction Report, reporting certain details about the transaction. Civil and criminal penalties are provided for failure to file the required report, or for filing a false or fraudulent report. Any property involved in a violation of 18 USC 1956 (Laundering of Monetary Instruments) or 18 USC 1957 (Engaging in Monetary Transactions in Property Derived From Specified Unlawful Activity) can be seized if it is subject to forfeiture under federal law.

Carriers do not want their clerks removed from the job to testify in court, nor subjected on the witness stand to the pitfalls of cross-examination that requires an expert in narcotics investigation. Equally important is protecting the clerks or other employees from the perception that individuals who are identified as drug couriers by surveillance techniques will retaliate against them.

A package sent by a private courier service bears many similarities to a letter sent via the United States Postal Service. Mail being sent by first class postage traditionally has been defined by statute as "matter closed against postal inspection" that may not be opened except pursuant to a search warrant or to determine an address for delivery. Other types of mail are not closed to inspection. Some private carriers reserve the right to inspect and open packages, a contractual operations right which is outside the bounds of the federal and state constitutions. Private carrier representatives may act according to their own charter in handling parcels. Recall, however, that when the representative acts at the direction of a law enforcement officer, thus becoming an *agent* of law enforcement, he is subject to the same constraints against unreasonable searches and seizures as the U.S. Postal Service. The carrier does not want to lose the right to inspect *at will* the parcels they are transporting.

In one case, the deliverers are unaware they have a next-day air letter going to a major dope dealer. The letter is addressed to a PO box, and the company cannot deliver to a PO box. They cut the parcel open to see if there is something inside indicative of the address. If there is nothing inside, they will send out a postcard to the PO box saying, you have a package at our office, what do you want us to do with it? They cut the package open, and what are they looking at? Twenty thousand dollars in cash. You cannot ship hard cash via the private carrier. The company investigator calls the local drug task force to say, hey, I got a package with $20,000. going down to such-and-such address. The task force calls back in five minutes, hey that's a major dope dealer. The reverse address, when they call back to the East Coast is a major dope dealer the troopers have been after for 5 years but have never been able to peg down. They bring a (U.S. Customs) dog in, and he hits it. They do a double bust.

While investigating one individual, police narcotics investigators became aware of another individual frequently observed at an airline ticket counter making cash purchases of round trip tickets to the Los Angeles area, always for very short stays. The suspect used various aliases purchasing round trip tickets between Pittsburgh and L.A. Using multiple names for residences, employment, and vehicle registrations, his activities fit the profile of one trafficking in narcotics.

Allegheny County detectives shared their information with the Los Angeles Police Department (LAPD), who set up a joint investigation of the suspect. Setting up a mobile surveillance, LAPD observed the suspect mail a parcel with a fictitious return address at a private carrier office. After the suspect exited the office, detectives removed the package from the roller conveyor and summoned a canine officer with a narcotic detection dog to the scene. The dog picked out the specific package dropped off by the suspect from a number of different packages. The dog did this several times despite the officers moving and mixing a number of different packages. Detectives then applied to a Los Angeles Superior Court judge for a search warrant for the suspect package. Upon issuance of the search warrant, detectives opened the package in the presence of the judge and found five kilograms of cocaine inside. A second search warrant for premises in California netted further evidence. LAPD apprised Pennsyvania detectives of their findings, and a controlled delivery of the original package resulted in the suspect's arrest and the seizure of more evidence.[69]

Successful investigations are a product of outstanding cooperation among law enforcement agencies and private companies. Typically, all federal, state, and local law enforcement agencies that directly participate in a federal investigation are entitled to an equitable share of any seized or forfeited assets. The share given to the participating agency depends on the extent to which that agency was involved in the investigation. *Narcotic detector dog units have the responsibility of employing K-9 tactics that further the operation at every level.*

A Texas police department notified DEA New Orleans that their officer was working the airport with his trained narcotic dog when the dog alerted to drugs on certain boxes. The K-9 bit one of the boxes. The officer marked the boxes, notified the private carrier, and allowed the boxes to be shipped to New Orleans for interception by DEA. DEA confirmed the box bitten by the dog emitted an aroma associated with drugs. Opening the boxes at the carrier terminal, they found 21.5 pounds of marijuana. When the U.S. Attorney's Office declined to investigate, agents contacted detectives of the New Orleans Police Department. Working together, DEA and NOPD arranged surveillance with a controlled delivery and arrested the suspect.[70]

Major metropolitan centers, source cities and transshipment centers, have integrated narcotic detector dogs into their interdiction programs, some prior to the 1970s, with many variations depending on they way they operate. K-9 officers who work in jurisdictions that do not have special investigations units need to know how to proceed in parcel cases, from working the entire investigation with local agents to requesting experienced investigators from outside agencies to advise or conduct the investigation.

Before responding to perform a parcel investigation, the K-9 team's training and performance record must be current and relevant. The dog should have experience with mail—envelopes of various types and sizes, rolled newspapers, magazines, and boxes. Dogs doing freight searches need exposure to large quantities of narcotics, different containers, such as palletized cardboard, wood or metal boxes holding aromatic chemicals or produce, and the distraction of noise and specialized equipment, such as forklifts in warehouses, horns and engines in garages, at storage yards, loading docks at airports or distribution centers. The K-9 may need to work a conveyor belt, sniffing parcels, freight, or baggage. He has to be confident working stairs, catwalks, or drain covers.

A U.S. Postal Inspector, assigned to investigate transportation of illicit drugs through the

K-9 officers who work in jurisdictions that do not have special investigations units need to know how to proceed in parcel cases.

69. *U.S. v. Chapple,* 1991 U.S. Dist. Lexis 19977 (Pa).
70. *State v. Rose,* 607 So.2d 974 (La.App. 4 Cir. 1992)

mail, became suspicious of two Express Mail package receipts. The receipts were addressed to a person in Maine, sent from two locations on the west coast. On each, the sender's name coincided with a previously investigated sender. The originating addresses were false. The Postal Inspector directed the postmaster in Maine to watch for future Express Mail packages addressed to the same individual from the west coast.

Such a package arrived from Oregon early one morning with a guaranteed delivery time of 3:00 p.m. that day. An hour later the postmaster was able to contact the postal inspector, who directed him to hold the package pending further instruction. At 10:00 Maine time, the inspector called the Oregon officer, learned the originating address and the sender's name were fictitious, then arranged with the state police for a trained dog to sniff the package for drugs. The dog was trained to find marijuana, cocaine, hashish, and heroin in all of their forms.

When the state police arrived at the post office at noon, the postmaster closed the office for lunch, taking the police officers to his nearby house to conduct the test in privacy. Four times, the police hid the package in the garage and sent the dog to find it. Each time, the dog located the package and indicated the presence of drugs.[71]

Although the court did not dispute the K-9 tactics used in this case, officers should employ procedures conforming to standard scientific investigative procedures. It is important to use controls. Also, once the dog alerts to the parcel, conclude the sniff test. It is not necessary or desirable to perform instant replays. In this case, what if the dog had alerted the first two times but not the last two? Further, it is arguable that, instead of testing for narcotic content, repeated testing actually *trains* the dog to find a particular parcel.

The concept of parcel searching is a controlled test: A lineup or array of parcels where the dog sniffs each item in sequence and identifies the presence of drugs by alerting to individual item(s). There are primarily two types of searches. *In the first type, the K-9 sniffs all designated incoming (or outbound or in transit) parcels with no controls.* Any item may contain drugs. U.S. Customs K-9s search aircraft luggage and air freight this way. Prison dogs typically search all mail and deliveries entering institutions this way. *In the second type, the K-9 searches a special lineup of a profiled parcel placed among controls, that is parcels similar to the suspected parcel but not contaminated by narcotics.* K-9s perform this type of search when investigators have identified a particular parcel as suspect. The handler does not know which parcel is suspect to prevent him from keying his dog to that parcel.

If the parcels are flexible (e.g. envelopes, cardboard boxes, luggage), the skilled handler *breathes* or *compresses* each parcel for the dog just before he sniffs it to increase scent diffusion. The handler must be alert to prevent the dog from perforating parcels containing dope and ingesting the narcotic.

Through control exercises in training, the dog should be *proofed* on cash—bills and coins—to verify he does not alert to money per se but rather to the narcotic scents he is trained to detect.

Offenders keep trying to defeat police dogs. They attempt to make parcels undetectable by elaborate wrapping schemes (heat-seal packs, multiple layers of plastic wrap and tin foil, taping, specialized containers) or by hiding narcotics in other compounds with strong characteristic scents they hope will mask the odor of dope (coffee, baby powder, perfume, absorbent materials soaked in rubbing alcohol, disinfectant, polish, gasoline or other petroleum derivatives). Dangerous chemicals are the worst. Illicit drugs may be concealed in corrosive or caustic agents, compounds prepared to injure or kill the unsuspecting clerk, inspector, agent, K-9 officer, or dog who opens the parcel.

Be cautious with the detector dog. Do not let him penetrate the parcel. The trained dog has characteristic alerting behavior that precedes biting. React quickly to reinforce the alerting behavior and remove the dog from the scene.

Officers should employ procedures conforming to standard scientific investigative procedures. It is important to use controls.

71. *U.S. v. Allen*, 990 F.2d 667 (1st Cir. 1993).

Request the detector dog team respond to the location. Do not transport the parcel to the K-9. Get the turnaround time nailed so the handler and dog do not have long to wait. Conduct the search in an area you believe is *clean* or *clear*, that is not contaminated by narcotic scent or other scents with the potential for distracting the dog. As soon as the dog arrives, before placing parcels in the test area, deploy him to sniff the room or outside area to verify it is uncontaminated. If K-9 teams have conducted previous searches in the same area, be sure previous alert sites do not distract the dog. The area should be free of outside interference, and the dog comfortable working there.

Ensure a qualified investigator will be present where the sniff takes place. That officer will take control of the parcel based on the result of the dog sniff and will continue to develop the parcel interdiction case.

Has the parcel been isolated from all other suspected parcels? Avoid *commingling* to eliminate any possible contamination issue with the suspected parcel. If you have parcels that you believe have contraband and some you believe to have money, keep them separate. This also pertains to keeping suspected parcels separated to prevent cross-contamination. If you discover a package under investigation has been commingled with contraband, other suspected parcels or has been contaminated in handling, do not use the dog to search that package.

Treat every parcel search as a scientific investigation with controls. Request the case agent place the suspected parcel among control parcels (similar but uncontaminated parcels) to maintain the credibility of the sniff, eliminating any argument that the suspected parcel was the only one presented to the dog. It also helps the dog quickly identify the type search he will be doing. *Fingers that have touched dope or a suspected parcel do not touch control parcels.*

If the dog exhibits aggressive behavior on parcel searches, place the suspected package label-side-down to protect it. For a highly *boxy* dog, place the parcels inside uncontaminated desks, lockers, file cabinets, or other containers so he does not destroy evidence. Determine the air circulation wherever the parcels are placed to insure the dog sniffs into the scent cone of *each parcel he is supposed to search.*

When feasible, avoid using only the K-9 alert for probable cause on warrants. If all else fails, however, the K-9 alert is sufficient.

A suspect deposited two packages in the U.S. mail for Express Mail delivery from Los Angeles, California to Birmingham, Alabama. The second package was mailed from a different postal station ten months after the first. Postal inspectors at each station suspected the packages contained narcotics.

The suspect's first package was set aside and presented to a trained narcotics-sniffing dog. The dog alerted positively to the presence of narcotics. The package was then sent on its regularly scheduled flight to Alabama—the same flight it would have been on had no detention occurred. Pursuant to a valid search warrant, federal agents in Alabama opened the package when it arrived and confirmed that it contained cocaine.

The suspect's second package was taken from the postal station where it had been deposited and transported to a nearby police station for a dog-sniff test. The test was positive. A search warrant was obtained, the package was opened, cocaine was discovered, and the suspect was later arrested. Had the sniff test been negative, the package could easily have been returned to the postal station and put on its regularly scheduled flight to Birmingham. The suspect was convicted of two counts of possessing cocaine with intent to distribute, in violation of 21 U.S.C. § 841(a)(1), and two counts of intentionally using a communication facility to aid in that offense, in violation of 21 U.S.C. § 843(b). He was sentenced to sixty months in prison, plus four years of supervised release.[72]

Gang affiliates, drug cartels, defendants who read court affadavits, and thousands of other intelligence sources have made offenders aware that K-9s are searching parcels. Countermeasures taken by suspects have included mailing bogus packages containing *legal items contaminated by*

72. *U.S. v. England,* 971 F.2d 419 (9th Cir. 1992).

Fingers that have touched dope or a suspected parcel do not touch control parcels.

narcotic scent in attempts to discredit the K-9 search. Your team's ability to fully document each search will maintain your credibility.

Acting upon information from two informants that a suspect was receiving shipments from Florida of cocaine concealed in teddy bears via private carrier, the sheriff's department confirmed that four packages, all bearing a return address from Miami, Florida, had been delivered by the carrier to the suspect during a two-month period.

Shortly thereafter, the carrier notified the sheriff that another package from the same Florida address had been received for delivery to the suspect. The carrier was instructed to hold the package so a Customs Service dog trained to alert to marijuana, cocaine and heroin could sniff it. The dog did alert. An X ray of the package revealed the outline of a packet contained within what appeared to be the shape of a teddy bear. A warrant issued. The court ruled that, inasmuch as the Customs dog's alert itself constituted probable cause that the package contained narcotics, they did not need to determine whether X raying the package constituted an illegal search.[73]

In 1992, the *Los Angeles Times* reported a highly profitable drug trafficking technique whereby chemists outside the country combined narcotics with common product materials (plastics, fiberglass), shaped them into ordinary-looking products (in that case, ironically, K-9 flight kennels), and shipped those products to the U.S. very economically, separating the narcotics out of the compounds in clandestine chemical labs here.

"This investigation demonstrates cocaine can be molded into any imaginable shape or form and shipped into any port in the United States," said Charlie J. Parsons, special agent in charge of the FBI's Los Angeles office. "The case also demonstrates how sophisticated the cartels have become."

Once the certified narcotic dog alerts on a parcel, and that parcel is going to be sent on to its destination for a controlled delivery, contact the other agency to advise them you have a positive K-9 alert on the parcel and will provide them with verification of the team's expertise. Some jurisdictions require an additional dog alert to verify for their magistrate. The procedure of multiple dog searches can create problems. There have been occasions when one dog alerted and one did not (positive v. negative alerts), thus clouding the issue and the case. In general, if the judge at the destination wants a dog hit there, disallow the first hit. Typically, U.S. mail gets opened in the destination city, while packages being sent through private shipping companies are opened in the source city.

> "The biggest thing, though, is a person expecting narcotics...*they're piggy.* They want
> it, and they're not going to screw around with it. If they're going to move narcotics,
> they're more than likely going to do it in the air, because it's quick."
> —Narcotic investigator

A midwest sheriff's detective received a telephone call from an LAPD detective informing him they had used a narcotic detrector dog as part of a routine investigative procedure to examine packages being shipped from the Los Angeles airport by private carrier. The detective said the dog identified a package being shipped to a Kansas address. The detective believed the parcel was suspicious because the seams were covered with duct tape. Then the dog indicated it contained narcotics.

Telephoning the carrier's headquarters, the sheriff's detective arranged for a controlled delivery. Obtaining a warrant, the detective and his sergeant opened the box and found it contained newspapers and a clear plastic bag containing a white, powdery substance that tested for cocaine. Bag and parcel were then resealed.

Police detectives performed the controlled delivery, identified the suspect, obtained a completed affidavit and search warrant for the location, found evidence, and arrested the suspect. The court held that the parcel was not seized under the fourth amendment. The suspect's

73. *People v. Offen*, 585 N.E.2d 370 (N.Y. 1991).

possessory interests were affected minimally, if at all. The detentions by the Los Angeles and Kansas officers did not last for an unreasonable length of time, and the parcel was delivered within the time deadline established by the carrier. The suspect's fourth amendment rights were not violated by the use of the narcotics detector dog and the officers' actions subsequent to executing the first search warrant.[74]

The Search Warrant and Affidavit, and Statement of Probable Cause provide the foundation for valid parcel searches leading to successful criminal prosecutions. The search warrant clearly describes the package to be searched (size, wrapping, weight, address, and shipping identification) for a controlled substance or the proceeds from the sales of a controlled substance. The statement of probable cause describes the location of the investigation, verification that officers were lawfully present at the location, details about the parcel and why it came under investigation, including relevant surveillance information (for example, strong odors, heavy taping, fictitious address, shipper profile and activity). The statement references the search conducted by a qualified narcotic detector dog, attaching the team's record of expertise. The officer also describes how his training and experience provided the basis for his observations and finally what procedures will be followed after opening the parcel.

U.S. Postal Inspectors in New Orleans, Louisiana intercepted an Express Mail Parcel that "fit the profile of an ongoing Inspection Service Express Mail Narcotics investigation, which includes fictitious return addresses." Indeed there was no such business at the New York City address indicated. Inspectors placed the suspect package with several other packages, and two certified narcotics detection dogs separately alerted on the package. Obtaining a warrant to search the parcel, the inspectors opened it and discovered a pound of marijuana. Contacting the police department, they taped up the box. A controlled delivery resulted in the suspect's arrest. The appeals court upheld the evidence, but the use of two dogs was unnecessary and could have damaged the case.[75]

In a North Dakota post office a parcel mailed from the west coast did not itself cause suspicion; however, a series of prior events led the postmaster to believe the parcel contained drugs. On previous occasions, the recipients had mailed registered letters to the west coast. A short time later a package would arrive for them. From one package, employees noticed unusual odor, commenting it smelled like marijuana. Directed to cooperate with local authorities, the postmaster notified the police department who called in a drug detector dog team from another town. Brought to the post office, the dog was presented with a number of packages, including the suspicious one, spread out on the floor. When the dog did not positively identify the suspect package, it was put back into the flow of mail and delivered to the addressees.

Later in court, testimony indicated the dog's failure to positively identify the package "may have been due to the manner in which the package had been handled." What does this mean? *Officers should not speculate or offer reasons why a narcotic detector dog does not alert.* Make sure conditions are right before deploying the dog. If the search area or the package is contaminated, do not deploy. If the conditions are well controlled, you deploy the dog, and he does not alert, put the parcel back into the flow (as they did in this case). End of test. *Why* is irrelevant to the case. It may be relevant to your caregiving (you discover the dog is sick) or your training (you need to conduct remediation), but the court does not need theory, it needs facts.

Subsequently, the same suspects sent another letter to the west coast followed by another parcel arriving at the North Dakota post office. A dog trained to detect drugs came to sniff the array of packages. This time the dog "reacted in a manner indicating the package contained a controlled substance." Put back on lead, the dog was again commanded to "search pot." Again he alert on the suspect package. On the basis of the dog's alert, the police obtained a search warrant. The next day, the suspect was taken into custody. The state supreme court upheld the dog sniff.[76]

74. *State v. Daly,* 789 P.2d 1203 (Kan.App. 1990).
75. *State v. Philippoff,* 588 So.2d 778 (La.App. 4 Cir. 1991).

When you conduct a search (sniff) and the dog alerts, reinforce your K-9 partner and end the test. Repeating the test has no evidentiary value and may negatively affect the dog's training. The dog's performance reliability should give the handler the confidence to believe the first alert.

A private delivery service parcel with a Phoenix, Arizona return was mailed to a suspect at his girlfriend's address in Chicago. A confidential source who worked at the apartment building where the package was sent informed a DEA special agent that two "Latins" residing in the apartment where the suspect was staying were dealing drugs from that apartment. The informant also told the agent other tenants had observed many people going in and out of the apartment, staying for short periods of time, and buying *boy* and *girl* (cocaine and heroin). Over a span of seven months, the informant provided identifying information about the subjects. When the private carrier Next Day Air package for the suspect arrived at the apartment building one morning, the informant, who accepted packages for the tenants, promptly contacted the agent. Stating in his affidavit that drug traffickers often use private carriers to send narcotics, which are "easily transported in a small package," the agent said Phoenix is "a known source city for narcotics."

Based on this information, the agent met the informant and took the package to a Chicago police station. Within two hours, the agent and other officers placed the parcel among three others and brought in a trained narcotic detection dog with a recorded 95 percent accuracy rate in 80 cases. The dog reacted positively for drugs in the parcel.

The court found no constitutional improprieties with respect to the limited investigative detention of the suspect's package. The agent acted diligently to confirm his suspicions about the package's contents by locating a drug detection dog. Eighty-five minutes passed from the time the officer took the package until the dog detected narcotics. Further, the package was not in the suspect's possession at the time of the detention.[77]

> "A rising tide lifts all boats. When contraband absolutely, positively has to get there overnight, the incessant commercial messages which inundate our society's channels of communication *guarantee* felons, like other entrepreneurs, prompt delivery."
>
> —Circuit Judge Selya

Maine police received anonymous calls claiming a suspect was selling cocaine and marijuana received via private carrier from Florida. Parcels arrived weekly for several months. Finally one morning, advised by the carrier that another suspect parcel had come in, police held it for a state trooper and his dog to conduct a sniff test. After the canine alerted to the parcel, a search warrant was issued, and the parcel was found to contain a substantial quantity of cocaine.

Assaying the intrusive impact of the police action, the appeals court delineated three presumptively-relevant factors: 1) investigatory diligence, 2) length of detention, and 3) information conveyed to the suspect. Both the case officer and the dog handler, though off duty when the call came, readily agreed to help. *The decision to probe for probable cause by using the sniff test itself suggested an attempt to reduce any intrusion.* The sniff was timely (a one hour and forty-five minute detention). After the owner relinquished control of the inanimate object to a third party, the last factor had little relevance because there is no law obligating the police, within the early hours of the incident, to telephone the parcel's intended recipient and tell him the nature and cause of the delay.[78]

Perhaps the ultimate test of reasonable detention for a dog sniff came out of Emmonak, a small bush community on the Yukon River, located 700 air miles northwest of Anchorage. Emmonak, like most of Alaska's bush, cannot be reached by any road. Small aircraft are its lifeline to the outside world. All mail to and from Emmonak must travel by air.

One autumn Saturday, a suspect mailed an express delivery package from Emmonak. The postmaster was suspicious because the local Trooper had informed him the man was suspected of

The decision to probe for probable cause by using the sniff test itself suggested an attempt to reduce any intrusion.

76. *State v. Kesler,* 396 N.W.2d 729 (N.D. 1986).
77. *U.S. v. Mena,* (slip opinion, Illinois, 1986).
78. *U.S. v. LaFrance,* 879 F.2d 1 (1st Cir. 1989).

trafficking. When the postmaster called the Postal Inspector in Anchorage, he was directed to send the package to the PIS by registered mail. Three days later, the suspect and his girlfriend mailed three additonal packages in a manner that again arroused the postmaster's suspicion. Reporting to the PIS, he was again directed to send the three packages by registered mail.

Because of the mail schedule, all four packages left the village three days later sealed in a registered pouch. Mail leaving Emmonak travels to St. Mary's, where it is sorted, then forwarded to various destinations. Because of aircraft maintenance, the usual flight from St. Mary's to Anchorage was canceled. Sent on a substitute flight, the mail did not arrive until late Thursday.

Immediately on receipt, the Postal Inspector called the Alaska State Troopers K-9 Unit to arrange a drug detection canine sniff but was told no dogs were available that evening. Friday morning, the packages were subjected to a drug sniff by a reliable dog, that gave a positive alert on all four parcels. Completing the required mail cover forms and drafting affidavits and search warrants for the three packages mailed the previous Saturday, the inspector presented them to a federal magistrate who issued the warrant. All three contained marijuana. A warrant, subsequent search, and lab analysis of the express delivery package disclosed cocaine. In upholding the dog sniff and other evidence, the court said the time consumed in transferring the packages from Emmonak to Anchorage simply reflects the facts of life in the Alaska bush. The magistrate concluded it was unreasonable to expect postal authorities to procure the presence of drug-detecting dogs in a small bush community. Flexible standards are necessary to permit enforcement of anti-drug laws in remote communities.[79]

Delivery truck offloaded for a sniff at Stateline, Nevada.

Receiving information that a suspect was using and selling cocaine, an Alabama officer determined packages with fictitious addresses were being shipped on a regular basis via private courier express. He alerted the carrier about the investigation. Soon the carrier's branch manager determined a typical parcel had been missent and was coming back in for rerouting. The manager gave officers and a drug dog permission to enter the express truck when it arrived. Inside, the K-9 alerted to a particular parcel. Based on the dog's alert, the dog team's training and demonstrated reliability, the suspicious nature of the parcel itself, and patterns of behavior uncovered by the investigation, a warrant, issued for the vehicle where the suspect placed the parcel after picking it up. The parcel contained cocaine.[80]

Enlist the cooperation of the private carrier to screen incoming air deliveries with the drug dog. Typically, all air deliveries arrive in one vehicle, picked up from the airport and transported to a distribution center. During transport, the parcels are *contained*, locked up inside the truck. Scent molecules diffusing from the parcels, including parcels with drugs, are largely trapped in the vehicle. No vehicle is perfectly sealed of course. As the molecules seek equilibrium, scent *loads up* (diffuses) throughout the air space. The carrier is going to be under a time frame, because they have to move the parcels and move them quickly. Depending on how your dog is trained, you do one of two things. Coordinate

79. *U.S. v. Aldaz*, 921 F.2d 227 (9th Cir. 1990).
80. *Gamble v. State*, 473 So.2d 1188 (Ala.Cr.App. 1985).

with the carrier's investigator to have the dog there to meet the vehicle when it pulls in. The vehicle is closed, locked, and scent has diffused inside for a minimum of 15 minutes or longer, depending on the location. Your setup is loaded. Bring the dog in at that point. *Put the dog in the vehicle.* If there is anything of interest, the dog will alert within a few minutes. If he alerts inside the truck but cannot pinpoint, you know something is present. Now you let the dog detail. Or, they have to unload those parcels one at a time. The dog gets a chance to *sniff each parcel as it is being offloaded* until boom, he hits one. An experienced dog, even in the face of a hundred-odd parcels, will zero in on contraband. If the dog would be overwhelmed working inside a concentrated space but knows how to work a conveyor belt, offload the parcels onto the conveyor belt so he can sniff each one as it goes by.

Scientists refer to the *absolute threshold* of canine scenting as the minimum quantity of substance a dog can detect, and the *discrimination threshold* as the minimum quantity a dog can detect in a contaminated environment (real world). *Scent overload* is the rapid adherence of scent molecules to the olfactory mucosa to a steady state or saturated state. Entering a closed space, such as a mail truck, containing a large quantity of narcotics, the dog may react with behavior indicating he is experiencing scent saturation.

An airline employee in Tennessee called a DEA investigator, reporting a suspicious package, noting this was at least the second such package shipped by the sender to the same address in a single week. The employee also noted the private courier's shipping fee ($55) was rather expensive for such a small package that could just as easily have been mailed for a fraction of the cost. Arriving at the airport within an hour, the investigator examined the small cardboard box addressed to a beauty salon in Mississippi from California. The addresses on the box were handwritten, and the return address did not contain a zip code. All the seams were sealed with masking tape. According to the receipt completed by the sender, the box contained "parts." Shaking and squeezing the box, which did not rattle, the investigator questioned if it contained parts of any type and shared the employee's suspicions it contained illicit drugs.

To confirm his suspicions, he summoned another DEA investigator, who handled a narcotic detector dog. Shortly after, the dog alerted to the box, indicating it contained narcotics. Taking possession of the box and obtaining a search warrant, the investigator opened the box and discovered plastic bags filled with methamphetamine. Making a controlled delivery, other agents arrested the suspect.

The DEA investigator's affidavit established that he was an experienced drug investigator, that the package was suspicious for a variety of specific reasons, that it came from a source city for drugs, that the dog alerted to the package, and that drug dealers often ship drugs via private common carrier. The affidavit also specifically explained the dog was trained to detect the presence of controlled substances. The information clearly constituted substantial basis for a warrant.[81]

Traffickers are wise to interdiction methods. They are now sending well-packaged or professional-looking parcels through the mails. *As crime parallels increasingly rapid, efficient shipping technology, the detector dog's role could become even more important in narcotics investigations.*

81. *U.S. v. Daniel,* 982 F.2d 146 (5th Cir. 1993).

Tactically, unless
deployed for
apprehension,
the narcotic dog
is better left out
of the picture
until employed for
the sniff test.

BAGGAGE—AIR, TRAIN, BUS

Police detectives in Pennsylvania were assigned to a narcotics interdiction detail at the Greater Pittsburgh International Airport. At 5:00 p.m., a detective observed an individual disembark from a flight from Florida. He carried no luggage, and the officer noticed bulges in the pockets of his jeans. The city of departure was a known source city for drugs, and officers had previously made many airport arrests of persons arriving from that city carrying drugs.

Detectives watched the man enter a restroom, exiting 15 seconds later, a common counter-surveillance technique. When he emerged, the man looked around furtively as though determining if he was being followed, also pulling down his T-shirt, as though concealing something on his person. Following along the public corridor, detectives observed the man's activities, including another quick trip to a restroom.

At 5:20 p.m., the detectives approached the man, identified themselves as police officers, and asked, "Is it okay if we talk with you for a few minutes?" The man agreed to speak with them, relating his destination and producing his ticket folder upon request. The officers noticed there was a baggage claim check attached to the ticket folder. Recording the information, they returned the folder. When asked who paid for the ticket, the man said his uncle paid the fare. Shortly thereafter, he said he bought the ticket himself. Later, he said again his uncle had bought the ticket. The man grew nervous, shifting from foot-to-foot and wringing his hands. He said he was in Florida to visit his uncle and, upon request, produced identification. The detectives inspected then returned the identification.

Stating they were narcotics officers, the detectives asked the man to show them what was in his pockets, also stating he was under no obligation to comply. From his pockets, the man voluntarily produced large rolls of cash, mostly in ten and twenty dollar bills, totalling over three thousand dollars. He also produced a sky pager, commonly used in drug trafficking, and while withdrawing the pager from his pocket, turned it off, effectively erasing the telephone numbers recorded inside.

This case typifies thousands of encounters, some more some less consensual, that have occurred between travelers and law enforcement officers in airports, train and bus terminals, and ports of entry throughout the U.S. When such an encounter builds, rather than allays, the officer's reasonable suspicion, the consensual encounter can develop into an investigatory detention. Factors giving rise to a reasonable suspicion that a suspect has committed or is committing a crime must be considered in light of the *totality of the circumstances—the whole picture* of each case.

Sometimes the investigating officer is himself the K-9 handler. At other times, the K-9 handler and his dog will be called into the case as a tool of the investigation. Either way, all officers on the case need the narcotic investigation skills to navigate the legal minefield that exists *from the time of the initial encounter*, through the escalation of suspicion, to the time of the arrest, and beyond. As the incident unfolds, officers need to pay attention—to their own perceptions during the encounter as well as to the suspect's probable perception. If the investigator is a dog handler, he has the third, complicating *perception of the dog* to add to the investigatory picture. Tactically, unless deployed for apprehension, the narcotic dog is better left out of the picture until employed for the sniff test, not as a matter of secrecy (Newsman Daniel Schorr: *"There is something corrupting about secrecy."*) but rather to prevent suspects from claiming coercion by a police dog.

In the case at hand, at 5:27 p.m., the detectives asked the suspect to accompany them to the airport police station in order to investigate the matter further. He agreed. A detective retrieved the checked suitcase. In the interview room, the suspect identified the suitcase as his own but claimed he did not know how a padlock had become attached. Asked if he would consent to a search of the suitcase, he refused. At 5:55 p.m., a detective told the suspect they would call in a drug-sniffing dog to inspect the suitcase and the money, and they would attempt to secure a search warrant for the suitcase. A prior marijuana conviction was verified by computer.

The detectives informed the suspect he was free to leave or remain while they sought a search warrant. The man said there were no narcotics in the bag, threatened to file a lawsuit against the officers, then stated he wanted to catch the next flight to Michigan. The detectives gave him receipts for the suitcase, the cash and the pager, and told him how to retrieve the items if they failed to get a search warrant or if no drugs were found. Leaving the station at 6:55 p.m., the suspect boarded a flight for Michigan.

Minutes later the detector dog team arrived. The dog sniff took place at 7:00 p.m. The dog alerted to the cash, but not the suitcase. The detectives then drafted and signed an affidavit to be submitted in support of an application for a search warrant. The affidavit mentioned the dog alerted to the cash, but did not mention the dog was exposed to, *and did not alert to*, the suitcase. The affidavit also mentioned the suspect's prior felony arrest was for a "large amount of marijuana." A district justice issued a search warrant at 7:55 p.m.

The detectives searched the suitcase and found ten one-kilogram packages of cocaine. Each package was sealed in a plastic bag, covered with tape, sealed in another plastic bag, wrapped in a layer of aluminum foil and a layer of duct tape, smeared with axle grease, and wrapped in yet another layer of plastic wrap and duct tape.

The suspect was then removed from his flight to Michigan, which had yet to depart, and returned to the airport police station at 9:15 p.m., where he was advised of his Miranda rights. The suspect signed a written waiver of his rights and gave a detailed statement admitting he had been a cocaine courier for about one year, earning $150,000 to $180,000 profit.

Finding no lack of diligence by the officers and no violation of the suspect's rights, the court upheld the evidence but had to address the omission from the affidavit of the fact that the dog was exposed to, but did not alert to, the suitcase. The detective who prepared the affidavit gave uncontroverted testimony that he omitted this fact because he did not feel it was relevant to a probable cause determination, explaining that, in his experience, drug couriers often mask the scent of drugs by packaging in materials such as coffee or pepper or, as in this case, axle grease and dense plastic. Reviewing the totality of information, the court found probable cause remained.[82]

The security procedure on certain commercial flights of matching every piece of baggage with a ticketed, boarded passenger increases safety, not only from sabotage but also from drug trafficking. The ability to link a passenger with particular baggage enhances law enforcement's potential of prosecuting narcotic offenders.

Five minutes before a flight was scheduled to leave Los Angeles International Airport (LAX), a man bought a one-way ticket to Kansas City for $209 cash. Two narcotics officers were watching and saw him make the purchase. Nervously looking around, he asked several times whether his luggage would make the flight and completed special luggage forms for people who check their luggage late. The officers did not speak to or interfere with the man as he boarded his flight, which took off as scheduled at 5:20 p.m.

At that point, the officers got permission to go onto the tarmac to see if the man's luggage had made the flight. It had not. Finding the luggage, the officers asked an airline representative if they could take it inside. Refusing to relinquish custody of the luggage, the representative accompanied

82. *U.S. v. Frost*, 999 F.2d 737 (3rd Cir. 1993).

the officers to the DEA office for a drug sniff at 6:45 p.m. The test was performed in the hallway. At 7:00 p.m., the dog indicated the presence of narcotics. The airline yielded custody to DEA. All these events took place prior to the 7:20 p.m. departure schedule for the luggage.

Based on the dog's alert, a search warrant was executed, revealing three kilograms of cocaine base in the luggage. Here the suspect's only interest was that the airline, as his bailee, would place his luggage on the next plane two hours later. The entire process of removing the luggage from the cart, taking it from one office to the other, and having the dog sniff it, was completed prior to the time the luggage would have been placed on the airplane. The airline did not give up custody of the luggage to the narcotics officers until after the dog had indicated the presence of narcotics. *Because nothing the officers did interfered with the suspect's possessory interests in his luggage prior to the dog sniffing, there was no seizure of the luggage.* Because no seizure occurred, it was unnecessary for the court to reach the issue of whether there was reasonable suspicion for a seizure.[83]

The spontaneous K-9 alert is a gift. A multi-agency group of certified narcotic detector dog teams were conducting a training exercise on the tarmac at a western airport. A state investigator was working his yellow Labrador past a row of luggage. In one of the bags a DEA agent had concealed a kilo of cocaine. Before reaching the training aid, the dog unexpectedly alerted to a briefcase on a nearby luggage cart recently taken off an arriving flight. Noting a description of the briefcase, the officers let it go in the flow of bags placed on the conveyor belt, meanwhile hurrying out to the baggage claim area. There, what to their wondering eyes did appear but a high ranking individual from the department of justice, who picked up the briefcase off the carousel and headed out the door. When the dog handlers gathered around him in the parking lot beside his car, he said not a word but went straight to the hood of the car, opened the case to reveal the narcotics inside, and asked to make one phone call to resign.

A man boarded a train in Los Angeles destined for Chicago, paying over $700 in cash for the ticket on the day of departure and leaving a disconnected callback phone number. Kansas City police advised Chicago DEA they had arrested two people on the train's sleeper car in an unrelated drug investigation and were told by Amtrak attendants about the man's suspicious activities. At a brief stop in a town outside Chicago, the man jumped off the train, leaving his suitcase on a luggage rack in the sleeper car. It was a Samsonite oyster suitcase with hard sides and a rubber gasket seal. It had no identification or tags.

In Chicago, the crew chief and DEA agent removed the suitcase from the train and used a pocket knife to pop it open on the platform. It contained 18 kilos of cocaine. Ten minutes after the agent carried the suitcase to his office in the train station, Amtrak employees came in to report seeing the suspect on a lobby pay phone excitedly waving his hand in the air. After his arrest, in court the suspect testified he had no intention of leaving the station or his bag. At that point he knew he would be arrested but preferred arrest to showing up without the drugs: "...the people might think that I just—that I'm lying and I took off with their drugs."

Once the suspect abandoned the suitcase, and as a result had no legitimate expectation of privacy in it or its contents, the agent determined it was unnecessary to use the narcotic detector dog kept available a block from the station. "The only reason that we have the dog is if we have enough facts to detain an individual's luggage and he does not give us consent to search the luggage and if we have enough reasonable suspicion to detain the luggage, we have the dog examine it at that time." If a case arises where there is doubt about abandonment, a trained detector dog may assist by providing information for further action.[84]

On another Amtrak train from Los Angeles, detectives in the Kansas City station observed the suspicious conduct of a disembarked passenger, approached the man, identified themselves, and engaged him in typical conversation. The man appeared very nervous, seemed to have difficulty swallowing, lacked any identification, said he was visiting his favorite aunt, and said no, the detectives could not search his luggage for narcotics. One of the officers then told the suspect he

At that point he knew he would be arrested but preferred arrest to showing up without the drugs: "...the people might think that I just— that I'm lying and I took off with their drugs."

83. *U.S. v. Johnson,* 990 F.2d 1129 (9th Cir. 1993).
84. *U.S. v. Rem,* 984 F.2d 806 (7th Cir. 1993).

would order a narcotics-trained canine to sniff his luggage. The suspect said he did not want a dog, and told the officer to go ahead and look in the luggage. The officer told him he did not have to give permission to search the bags, but the suspect said he could search the bags. Inside, a wrapped, glued Purex box held a plastic bag of cocaine.

The court majority said, just as a statement by a law enforcement official that he will attempt to obtain a search warrant does not automatically vitiate an otherwise consensual search, so the detective's statement that he was going to order a canine sniff did not automatically vitiate the suspect's consent. "[The suspect's] knowledge that a dog sniff and resulting search would inevitably prove incriminating does not mean his consent was involuntary and coerced."[85]

Chicago police possessed more than reasonable suspicion necessary to briefly detain a train passenger's luggage for a sniff test by narcotics dogs, when the passenger arrived from Los Angeles, a major narcotics distribution center, carrying a bag secured with a combination padlock. Multiple indicators included traveling under an assumed name, stating his destination was Chicago even though his ticket listed his intended destination as Detroit, giving conflicting answers to the detective's inquiry whether he had been given items to carry in his suitcase, appearing furtive, nervous, and avoiding eye contact while carrying his baggage and during the short period of general questioning. The detective told the passenger his bags would be subjected to a sniff by trained dogs for the presence of narcotics which he could witness if he wished. If the search proved negative, the luggage would be returned. The passenger was given a receipt for his luggage and told he was free to leave if he chose. The passenger decided to leave and exited the train station.

Taken to the DEA office in Union Station, the passenger's bags were placed in a line with three non-suspect bags. Two separate sniffs, each by different dogs trained in narcotics detection, resulted in reactions indicating the presence of narcotics in the locked bag. The first sniff occurred within 30 minutes of the initial interview, and the second 40 minutes after the first sniff. A search warrant executed 24 hours after the sniffs revealed 9 kilograms of cocaine with an estimated street value in excess of $1,800,000. Also found in the locked bag were mothballs and other evidence of drug trafficking. Tried by a jury, the suspect was found guilty of violating 21 U.S.C. § 841(a)(1) and sentenced to 121 months in prison to be followed by 5 years of supervised release.[86]

A detective's attention was drawn to a passenger arriving from New York City into Union Station, Washington, D.C. Based on her responses to general questions and a commercial identification card, the officer requested permission to search her totebag. She refused. He requested permission for a narcotics dog to sniff the bag. That, too, she refused. He then informed her he was detaining her bag for a canine sniff, but she was free to leave. He gave her his name and a number where she could later reach him to retrieve the bag. Still holding her bag, she started getting into a taxi. At that point, the officer detained the woman as well as the bag.

A 20- to 30-minute canine sniff ensued. The first dog's handler reported the dog showed some interest in the bag, but the handler did not want to call an alert because he felt *the dog was not working properly*. Within a few minutes, another detective brought over a second dog, who in fact alerted on the bag. Placed under arrest and taken to the Amtrak Police Office, the suspect was given two options: wait for a search warrant, or consent to the search. The consent search revealed four kilos of cocaine and several bags of crack.[87]

The handler has to read his dog and call the shots. If you believe the dog is not working, it is better to back off the investigation than to stumble through, hoping something is found in the parcel or at the location in question. Extending yourself frequently leads to more trouble—suddenly there are three more packages or two more houses they need the dog to search. Most small- to medium-sized departments do not have the luxury of backup detector dogs, making it difficult for the handler to quit once deployed. Where the dog has proven to be a high-calibre scenting dog and the other officers on the force have learned to rely on him, the handler may face resistance or resentment when he pulls off an operation. Stay calm and explain to other

A search warrant executed 24 hours after the sniffs revealed 9 kilograms of cocaine with an estimated street value in excess of $1,800,000. Also found in the locked bag were mothballs and other evidence of drug trafficking.

85. *U.S. v. Robinson*, 984 F.2d 911 (8th Cir. 1993).
86. *U.S. v. Fergonson*, 935 F.2d 1518 (7th Cir. 1991).
87. *U.S. v. Nurse*, 916 F.2d 20 (D.C. Cir. 1990).

officers what has happened rather than blowing up at the scene or venting your anger on the dog ("Don't shoot the dog!").

Conducting an undercover drug-dealing investigation, a Virginia officer got a tip from a reliable informant that "ready rock" was coming to town from New York on a bus the next night. The officer met the bus, joining the queue of passengers waiting to embark. From his position he saw four black males, including a suspect, get off the bus. He overheard them speaking with Jamaican accents. Two wore pagers. The driver advised they had come from New York.

The men walked down the street from the station carrying luggage. One bore a large radio. Drawing their weapons, the officers identified themselves, told the men to drop their bags, and frisked them, finding no weapons. They were "going to Lisa's." Asked "what's happening," an officer said he suspected they had drugs. Meanwhile another officer radioed the state police to request a drug detector dog be dispatched to the scene.

When the dog arrived, the officer placed the luggage and the radio in a line on the ground. On his second walk past the bags, the dog showed interest. On his third pass, the dog alerted to the radio. At the station, executing a search warrant to open the radio, police discovered crack cocaine inside. All four were arrested and charged with conspiracy and possession with intent to distribute.[88]

Pay attention to the search environment just as you would on a vehicle stop. Is the pavement hot in direct sunlight? Is the night cold with 40 mile-per-hour winds blowing down the city street? What is the turbulence effect of nearby buildings? Is traffic exhaust diffusing onto the search area? Are passing vehicles churning slush ice onto the search area? Is a crowd gathering? Is anything likely to distract the dog? The undercover officer or case agent in charge at the scene and the dog handler need to *confer and control the test site*. Baggage or other articles the dog is called to examine may have to be removed to another location to perform the test.

Monitoring a bus station for narcotics smuggling, a narcotic dog team inspected the baggage area in the underbelly of a bus parked for cleaning and refueling. After the passengers got off to stretch their legs, the dog and detectives boarded the bus. As the dog was walking down the aisle, he lifted his head, sniffing high, alerting to narcotic odor above head level. Opening some of the doors to the overhead baggage compartment, detectives removed some of the bags, placed them at the dog's level, and allowed him to sniff them. The dog alerted to two bags. The officers then returned all the bags to the overhead storage area and exited the bus.

The passengers returned to their seats on the bus. Before it departed, the detectives re-boarded, retrieved one of the bags to which the dog had alerted, and asked the owner to identify himself. A woman admitted it was her suitcase. The officers asked her to take it and wait outside the bus. Repeating the procedure with the second bag, they identified another female suspect. Off the bus, the claimants requested the detectives get a search warrant, so they got advised of their rights and a ride to the police station.

Placed in an interview room at the station while a search warrant was obtained, the women waited a short time then consented to a search of their bags. Uneasy with this change in attitude, the officers asked their lieutenant to enter the room to witness reading the women their rights again. Both consented to a search of their bags in order to "get out of the room." Each bag contained five pounds of marijuana.[89]

The officers acted on *articulable, reasonable suspicion* caused by the dog's initial alert in the aisle when they retrieved baggage from the overhead for the K-9 to examine more closely. This action corresponds in part to removing parcels from the flow of mail in a post office to set up a sniff test, but the passenger's greater privacy expectation in carry-on baggage (as contrasted to mail) was overridden by that first alert. Canine intelligence prevailed.

88. *U.S. v. Sinclair*, 983 F.2d 598 (4th Cir. 1993).
89. *U.S. v. Harvey*, 961 F.2d 1361 (8th Cir. 1992).

Investigators were on patrol in the Buffalo, New York, bus terminal when the morning express arrived from New York City and parked at Gate 5. All the passengers entered the terminal through Gate 5 except a man who entered through Gate 4. Separating himself from the main flow drew the attention of the officers, who observed his nervous demeanor, his counter-surveillance activity, and who began a consensual encounter that graduated into the man shaking and sweating and refusing the officer's request to search his bags, stating the *officer did not have "probable cause"* to search his luggage.

Agreeing to accompany the officers to the office for a further check on his identification, the passenger again refused a request to have his bags searched. He lied about his criminal history. One of the officers then informed the man his bags would be detained until a narcotic detection dog arrived to conduct a sniff test. He was free to leave, but if the dog reacted postively to the bags, the officers would apply for a search warrant. The man vehemently refused to leave, to make sure the officers obtained a warrant.

When the narcotic canine arrived, the officers conducted a controlled inspection involving several different pieces of luggage. The dog *hit on* the suspect's bags. Informed of the dog's reaction, the suspect picked up his shoulder bag, threw it onto a desk, and told them to search it. It held a quantity of marijuana. The other bag contained cocaine.[90]

The cop's job gets harder every year. This was but one case of thousands showing how legal terms have become part of the language of the street. The bad guys memorize and rehearse *police procedure*. "Source city"—not a title of honor—has been tagged on every city with a population over one million, most with over 500,000, and many with over 100,000. Offenders, especially wealthy drug traffickers, are looking like, talking like, and acting like regular citizens. They make a practice of *looking normal* to escape identification by typical interdiction methods. Enter the trained drug dog, who will not be fooled by cool looks.

90. *U.S. v. Glover*, 957 F.2d 1004 (2nd Cir. 1992).

The Customs dog must learn to ignore thousands of pungent odors. Transoceanic passengers themselves usually emit strong body odors after sitting confined in an airplane for many hours.

PERSON SEARCH

Two Nigerian males were arrested by U.S. Customs Inspectors at the San Ysidro POE Pedestrian Lanes attempting to body carry white heroin into the United States. Both Nigerian males were brought to a local hospital for X-rays and examination. The X-rays revealed at least fifty balloon shaped objects in each of their abdomens. 625 grams of white heroin were recovered from one Nigerian male while 810 grams of white heroin were recovered from the other Nigerian male. Couriers are typically paid $3,000 to $10,000 to smuggle the heroin.

Couriers entering the United States through border checkpoints or airports frequently carry the narcotics they are trafficking on their person—in their personal property, their clothing, or inside their bodies. Using a narcotic detector dog trained to perform aggressive alerts around suspects holding drugs on their person risks a violation of civil rights if the dog detects the narcotic scent. Depending on the quantity of drugs ingested and the time of ingestion, it may or may not be possible for a K-9 to detect narcotics inside a courier. Drugs carried inside body cavities, such as the stomach or abdominal area, are not normally detected by the K-9s.

U.S. Customs has trained nonaggressive breeds or mixed breed dogs, usually small and friendly looking, to perform air space sniffs surrounding deplaning passengers and luggage at international airports. Passenger or person searches by federal K-9 teams are conducted by the dog sniffing the free air space surrounding individuals as the team walks past or among the passengers. The Canine Enforcement Officer (CEO) handling the dog does nothing but work the dog. A second officer follows immediately behind to observe, record alerts, locations and other pertinent information. Sometimes, the dog needs to be as close as 12 to 18 inches to recognize small quantities of the hard drugs. When the dog detects drug scent, he is trained to perform a predetermined behavior not directed at the source subject(s), for example, looking at the handler for food or a conditioned reinforcer. Such noninvasive, nonaggressive searching does not violate the civil rights of the suspected individuals. Customs does not need probable cause to perform these searches.

Teams usually have four checkpoints where people must pass in single file or form lines as they travel the jetway to the luggage carousel, passing through immigration and customs. The dogs move on lead with their handlers through these areas. If a dog shows interest, for example targeting a businessman with a briefcase going down a concourse, the handler may wait until the man appears at the baggage carousel and walk the dog by him again to see if he alerts. Often, the handler who can read his dog well does not wait until the dog goes into a full passive alert. He will reinforce the dog while moving out of the area. The inspector following him will detain the man along with his luggage.

The Customs dog must learn to ignore thousands of pungent odors. Transoceanic passengers themselves usually emit strong body odors after sitting confined in an airplane for many hours. Passengers may bring unusual items such as dried fish or other food to eat on the plane or give to friends. Children and babies have their own particular odors the dog has to learn to ignore. Soap scents, perfumes, hair dressings, deodorants...the dog works through these potential distractions seeking the particular scents he is trained to detect.

The average international flight carries 300 passengers. One arriving flight represents a big job requiring rapid deployment. K-9 teams do not have much time as people hurry down the concourse to collect their baggage and leave the terminal. The average bag rotates six times on the carousel before pickup. Agents try to identify suspects as quickly as possible in order to obtain several confirming alerts in successive locations before they reach the baggage claim area. It is not unusual for an entire family to be taken at once.

Narcotic detector dog searching of persons is typically not permitted nor recommended. If the dog alerts spontaneously in the presence of people, the handler will typically advise pursuing alternate routes of investigation to confirm or clear the source of the reaction.

OUTSIDE AREA SEARCH

A rural task force executed a search warrant for the sale of marijuana at a residence. The search led officers to the seizure of about one ounce of marijuana. The county had just acquired two new narcotics detection canines who then got their turn. The canine search led to the seizure of over 9 1/2 pounds of marijuana, which was found packaged in ziplock bags, hidden in metal cans with lids then buried about a foot underground in a flowerbed.

At 7 o'clock one morning, officers of a middle-sized city police department's Probation Compliance Team, their Vice Narcotics Unit and Metro Team ended a six-month investigation regarding the sales and distribution of tar heroin and cocaine in the area with the service of three search warrants. Officers serving the warrant at J Street received no answer at the door and so forced entry.

Inside the residence they located an undocumented alien male. While securing the residence, an officer practically tripped over a canvas bag lying on the floor in the middle of the back bedroom. The bag contained a half pound of tar heroin, a one-pound bag of cocaine, and a two-pound bag of marijuana. In the same bedroom, officers observed a chair in the bedroom closet directly under a cooler down-draft vent. Standing on the chair, officers gained access to the vent, where 13 kilos of marijuana were secreted out of view in the upper part of the vent. Officers searching the kitchen area of the residence located a container in the trash, a liter beverage bottle with its top cut off wrapped in black electrical tape. Mud adhering to the container suggested it had been previously buried.

A drug dog team met detectives in the back yard and conducted a systematic search. During the search the dog did not alert but did show area interest in four separate locations. Probing with a metal rod, officers felt soft pockets of dirt two-to-three feet deep. Removing the dirt with a posthole digger, they uncovered a glass jar containing 9 ounces of tar heroin in the first hole. Seizures from the other holes totaled over 30 ounces of cocaine and two more ounces of tar heroin.

Searches for narcotics hidden outside are sometimes the most useful of the narcotic detector dog's tasks. Outside searches are difficult in terms of the dog's ability to concentrate on his task. Where do you walk your dog? Where does he play? Relieve himself? Chase squirrels? Where does the wind blow? Rain and snow fall?

Unlike human scent on articles of evidence, narcotics diffuse their distinct odor for a long time, weeks, months or years. This works to the dog's advantage. There is, however, a lower bound to detectability, when the rate of vaporization is too low for the dog to recognize the scent. Detectability depends on concealment as well as the surface area of the narcotic. If the offender packages the drugs in clean, uncontaminated containers, nesting the packaging in multiple layers, sealing in airtight containers, burying the package underground, masking the narcotic scent with other chemicals, and camouflaging the site, he makes the detector dog's job difficult, not necessarily impossible.

These methods are not news to the bad guys. Offenders have been packaging and burying narcotics for years. Effective concealment requires work, something few offenders like to do. Detection also depends on the dog's search drive, his experience with similar tasks, conditions at the time he is searching, and the handler's ability to read behavior changes in his dog. A slight behavior change in the K-9 may alert the handler to probe an area or to investigate further.

Tactics for searching narcotics outside are the same as for other types of evidence. Safety is the first consideration. The area must be secure and free of hazards or distractions to the dog. Carry water, flashlights, and flagging, and the 15-foot lead. Tools to have available include a 4-foot steel rod for probing, a sharp shovel and a posthole digger. Partition the search area into clearly designated sections. Work patterns, into the wind if possible, detailing each section. Isolate intervening structures such as sheds or tanks, searching them separately.

Flag locations where the dog alerts or indicates interest for further investigation. A camera is important for the canine team working alone. When an assisting officer is following the handler, he can take notes or photos. Always record where drug training aids are placed.

Called out one night to execute a warrant with the task force, the handler started working his dog in the garage. On entry, the dog raised his head and blew around the car parked inside. He alerted near a tank and tool box against a wall. Inside the tool box was a kilo of methamphetamine and a black funnel dirty with crank. Inside the house, the dog searched the ground floor with no alerts. Upstairs, he alerted to a briefcase on the bed which contained a pistol and $8,000 cash. Task force officers seized the briefcase.

Outside, while watering his dog at the patrol car, the handler turned around to find a 120-pound Rottweiler that had broken off its chain and was challenging the police dog. Seeing what was happening, another officer drew his pistol and took aim at the Rottweiler. A young neighbor girl stepped out of the dark in front of the dog. "Don't shoot him! He's a good dog. I'll tie him up." Recovering from this near-accident, the officer holstered and helped the girl tie the dog back onto his run line with some rope. This didn't last. The next time the K-9 team came out of the house, the Rottweiler was waiting at the door.

After completing warrant service or securing the property, request animal control to remove dogs or other domestic animals that could interfere with the drug dog team. Cats are often a problem. Drugs have been found in horse stalls and tack rooms, so do not discount barns, sheds, pump houses, tractors, generators or other outlying buildings and equipment.

Recreational vehicles, including boats, and junk cars, construction waste, or other trash are candidates for drug caches also. One department searched a house and garage with the drug dog but failed to check the trunk of a broken-down sedan sitting on blocks in a field near the property. Weeks later an informant told them they missed the stash. Returning to the scene, they recovered a half million dollars in cocaine from the abandoned wreck.

On large estates or housing complexes, drug caches in landscaping are difficult, even for the adequately trained dog. Narcotics are buried in containers under bushes or dirt, behind loose stones in walls, underneath sidewalk paving, inside hot tub covers, in pump systems for swimming pools, among hay bales, beneath driveways, everywhere that can be imagined. One coastal grower hid his dope in what appeared to be a child's tree house about 40 feet up a Douglas fir. The ten pound block of bud brought the K-9 up on his hind legs sniffing 50 feet away from the base of the tree, causing the handler to look up. Crude boards nailed to the rotten bark made climbing the tree a memorable experience. The suspect was nimble. The officers were not.

One coastal grower hid his dope in what appeared to be a child's tree house about 40 feet up a Douglas fir.

Distractions play a major part in the dog's effectiveness on outside searches. Stray cats, dogs, squirrels or other animals. Fertilizers. Gas powered mowers and trimmers. Garbage. The male dog typically lifts his leg against trees, bushes, trash cans, and poles. When the dog starts minutely sniffing the base of a fence post while he is supposed to be drug searching, what is the handler going to think and how will he react? How secure is a sealed cooler that is filled with twenty kilos of cocaine and buried under a foot of dirt next to a fence post? Near a boulder in a flowerbed?

Limited experiments have shown that the narcotic dog's ability to detect green growing marijuana is directly related to the plant's age or stage of development as well as environmental factors. The amount of THC (delta-9-tetrahydrocannabinol) available in the plant affects the scent diffusion and therefore the dog's potential for finding it. We know the dog can locate mature live, recently cut, or dried (most common) marijuana.

At issue is whether it is cost effective to field K-9 teams to actually search out marijuana growing operations. Except for limited applications, probably not. Cases where the dog may be deployed effectively include locations where terrain or weather prevent air reconnaissance within a well defined area, and situations where growers have camouflaged offensive positions designed to ambush investigators. In the latter case, crosstrained police dogs can serve important protection and detection functions for officers attempting to find the plants and arrest the growers.

Strong leadership is required to keep the SAR operation under control, to target the objective, the victims, while performing safe, efficient operations. Ultimately, every mission has limits, and every mission has an end.

Oklahoma City bombing.

CHAPTER 8

SEARCH AND RESCUE

"Evidently it was going to be one of those days

when one of the biggest problems in facing danger was to figure out

the biggest danger

and not to have a change of mind too often or too late or too soon."

"When it comes to racing with death,

all men are not created equal."

—Norman Maclean, *Young Men and Fire*

Burglaries, armed robberies, stolen vehicles, escaping fugitives—police dog teams across the nation make hundreds of arrests every day. The dogs save officers' lives. They protect the public. Typically, their work is little noted nor long remembered.

"My dog helped me make 48 major felony arrests in a 6-month period, and I was just doing my job. Nobody except the department really noticed," a policeman explains. "Then came the night my dog found a little two-and-a-half year old who had wandered a quarter mile from her house. Suddenly my dog's a hero. I'm a hero. People sent cards and donations. It was a pretty simple track, actually. Three years later, though, people still remember. They still ask to see my rescue dog."

Search and rescue, SAR, is incredibly popular in the United States: helicopters (including news media helos), ground searchers on foot or skis (including news media crews), search dog teams, horse posses, patrol and off-road vehicles, technical climbers and cavers, rescue divers and boat drivers, fixed wing aircraft, disaster rescue specialists, incident command specialists, communications specialists, emergency medical specialists, support specialists, law enforcement, fire, corrections, or other public agencies, private corporations, and associations.

The agency or group of agencies in charge are under pressure from every direction, first to obtain resources quickly, then to field as many resources as fast possible for as long as possible. Tremendous pressure is exerted by parties close to the victims, by the media, by resources anxious to participate, and by members of the departments in charge trying to do their job in a responsible manner. Strong leadership is required to keep the SAR operation under control, to target the objective, the victims, while performing safe, efficient operations. Ultimately, every mission has limits, and every mission has an end.

The first step in any rescue is finding the missing person alive. As a detection tool, the trained dog's nose still ranks with fiber optics, infrared imaging, acoustic sensors, and sniffing devices. As in other disciplines, such as drug searching, the full time rescue dog specialist is the best resource. Where specialized teams are not available, the on-duty police dog team has a chance of responding quickly and finding the person alive, before the search area expands exponentially, or before drowning, disaster rubble, or avalanche claims the person's life.

Crosstraining police dogs for rescue work begins at the initial police K-9 academy where the dog learns first to search, then to make rescue finds, evidence finds, then to locate and apprehend suspects. The canine can perform both police and SAR search *if the training is consistent and the team performs each type of task on a regular basis.* When a dog team that already has street experience intends to begin rescue work, adjustments have to be made in the training to establish reliable rescue search behavior.

Realistically, few police K-9 teams have the time or support to develop and maintain rescue search capability in addition to street work. The dog team participating in search and rescue needs the special skills and equipment required by these types of missions. Perhaps the most important concept is the *scope* of a rescue, typically larger than the average street incident, both in the number of people who get involved and in the time expended.

The trained police or rescue dog team performing hasty search can reduce time and manpower, increase coverage, and increase the probability of detection. Fast response minimizes the search area size. The dog team works rapidly using paths of least resistance in an attempt to overtake the victim.

The principles of scent diffusion and canine detection are the same for SAR as for a police action. Human scent given off by lost or trapped victims diffuses identically to the way scent diffuses from fleeing or concealed suspects. Turbulence, precipitation, and darkness are typical conditions for both types of operations.

The primary difference between a criminal search and a rescue is what happens at the end, a live find. Or, if the victim is dead, at least the resolution to the incident for the family or loved one, so they can suffer the grief such a personal tragedy causes and afterwards get on with their lives.

Few officers can devote the time necessary to train and maintain their dogs in search and rescue.

The difference, however, is not only the end, save the good guys. It is also the search strategy and tactics. The environment often threatens the whole operation: time (find him before he dies), extreme weather (the victim succumbs to exposure), and difficult terrain or disaster rubble (the wrecked human body). The trained K-9 team uses standard high profile tactics to detect the missing person. A notable difference between rescues and criminal searches is the difference of scale: days versus minutes, miles versus city blocks. The equipment also differs, survival gear versus protection gear.

MELISSA DAY SEARCH

At 1900 hours, Officer Todd L. Daugherty of Susanville Police Department, California, responded to North Street on a report of a missing child. Upon arrival, he learned that the 4-year-old girl was missing from the McCoy Flat area along Highway 44, in the county's jurisdiction. An arriving sergeant requested the officer and his K-9 Zeus respond to the scene and attempt to track the child.

When he got out to the scene, 18.7 miles from town, the handler harnessed his dog and began trying to locate a trail. About 50 yards south of the victim's pickup, the dog hit a track and worked it for a mile, primarily toward the west. When the track crossed a cindered road, the police dog lost the track. By that time it was dark. They returned to the point where the child went missing, which became the command post. The K-9 team stayed on scene, assisting by searching meadows and wooded areas until 0330 hours. By then the dog was too tired to be of any further use, so the officer took him home.

The next day at 1130 hours, Officer Daugherty contacted the sheriff's department from his home and asked if they had found the child yet. He was advised they had not. He told them the dog would be available if they needed him again. At 1200 hours, dispatch called to advise that Sheriff Ron Jarrell was requesting he bring the dog back out as they had found some tracks. Responding to the location with his dog, the handler looked at the tracks they had found. Discovering they were too old for his dog to use, Daugherty spent the rest of the day deploying the dog on area search in various open meadows.

At 1930 hours one of the horse units found a fresh set of footprints on a dirt road near the camp. Responding to that area, the K-9 team found that the prints were no more than a few hours old. The dog clearly took the track. As the dog worked the track for 7 miles in a southward direction, the officers had periodic visible confirmation of the print. At the Goodrich Meadow near Highway 36, the dog and mantrackers lost the track. The dog indicated that the child had left the road and gone out into the meadow, but he could not track her past this point. At 0200 hours, the K-9 team began a grid search of the large Goodrich Meadow area. At 0230 hours, advance grid searchers located the child on the south side of Goodrich Meadow. Search parties credited the dog with making the find.

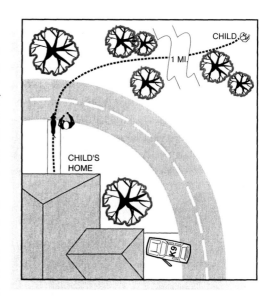

Total time on the search was 5 hours on the first day and 16.5 hours the second day. Total miles outside the city limits were 84.9 miles.

The police dog that has mastered nonaggressive off lead searching can perform area searches in separate sectors at the same time as the rescue dog teams. Once the dog teams are at the scene, the paid on-duty officer should be prepared to work the roughest terrain and get his uniform as dirty as necessary. He should expect to be assigned to a lower probability area if qualified rescue teams are working other, perhaps higher probability areas. Performing this role of diplomat for the department sometimes pays the extra dividend of a find.

SIERRA SEARCH

The highway patrol found an abandoned pickup truck on a remote backcountry road near Stampede Reservoir, its front wheel broken, apparently by a large rock. Tracing the vehicle to a subject in Reno, police learned the man had left a bar drunk several nights before. He was reportedly wearing blue jeans, brown cowboy boots, a gray sweater and windbreaker. He was described as tall and thin with sandy brown hair, and was a smoker. They found cigarettes and a locked briefcase in the truck. The night the man disappeared a snowstorm had moved rapidly through the area. January winds effaced any track, leaving 10-inch snowdrifts on the northern slopes and scrubbing other areas bare. The exposed rock, manzanita, buckbrush and mountain misery were shades of gray, blue, green, and brown similar to the man's colors. A search helicopter saw no sign of him.

Tahoe Nordic ski teams and snowmobiles worked grids north and south of the place last seen in addition to the outlying roads, trails, and shorelines around the reservoirs. The two search dog teams, one a volunteer rescue team, the other a police dog team, were assigned to the areas west and east of the road respectively. To the west the rescue dog checked onshore wind for scent diffusing from Stampede Reservoir and searched the open land surrounding the reservoir. To the east the K-9 team searched the steep forest with its brush and rock.

The K-9 team made two sweeps through the western half of their sector then followed a 6100-foot contour line northeast to an old pipeline. Continuing along the pipeline northwest to the 6200-foot elevation, they reached a knoll overlooking the forest to the south. Alerting, the dog traced the air scent to the body of the man lying against the hillside, his body dusted by snow. He appeared to be a victim of hypothermia, his cowboy boots placed neatly beside him, his jacket folded on the ground near his right ear. The man's legs and arms were extended, a peaceful expression on his snow-covered face. There was no sign of injury. After briefly licking the man's face, the dog picked up a boot and, wagging his tail, came running back to the handler.

ORANGE COUNTY SHERIFF'S DEPARTMENT

Tracking on lead, the police dog can establish a direction of travel, locate evidence, or possibly find the missing person.

Crowding resources into an area, theoretically to locate the victim by saturation, blocks the operation at various levels. Every resource has operating limits. Exceeding those numbers significantly reduces effectiveness.

One western sheriff's department experienced chaos the fourth day of a search in the mountains for a 10 year old boy. They had a 25-square-mile expanding search area from 7- to 11,000 feet elevation in rugged terrain with lightning storms. The boy was reportedly shy and had developmental disabilities. Few searchers were told that he had a long stride and a fast, strong gait.

By the third day 5 helicopters were searching and transporting searchers in the immediate airspace. Over 150 ground searchers, 50 mounted units, and more than 30 dog teams of varying capability were assigned within a small area. Unknown numbers of 4-wheel drive units, hikers, hikers with dogs, horseback riders and several private helicopters occupied the same territory.

Dog teams on scene included a man with his bird dog, a retired dog borrowed by a neighbor, and teams not fit for hard work or high altitude. At night network TV broadcast a plea for help that ran, "If you are a trained SAR team, call (sheriff's department). If you have no training but have the desire to help, call (sheriff's department)."

The fourth day saw jammed phone lines, jammed radio frequencies, jammed air space, sick and injured searchers, busloads of friends and neighbors crowding the command center, aircraft lining the local airport, mounted unit wrecks, and traffic accidents. By the end of the sixth day the focus of the search had changed several times on the basis of unverified clues. A handler radioed, "My dog has scent, and I estimate the track to be 12 hours old." That evening the sighting of a boy reportedly evading searchers in the forest turned the mission into a guerrilla operation. The boy was not found during the search.

He was found many days later, lying in the open, by hikers walking a wide exposed ridge less than 2 air miles from the place he was last seen. A pathologist determined the probable time of death to be the first night. The evidence indicated he lay down to sleep. Forever.

The agencies congratulated themselves on a job well done.

Proliferating resources can stampede the mission, leading to faulty reasoning like:
• If 1 helicopter over an area is good, 4 must be better.
• If 4 dog teams in an area are good, 16 must be better. And 50 additional searchers in the same area on foot would be even better.
• "Hey, a dog is a dog."
• We have 10 ground pounders to put in that area. Put a dog team in with them to increase the odds.

Conversely, there are large area searches where the agency requests only two dog teams when the operation could use ten. Or three days into an intensive search effort, the request goes out for "a tracking dog" to search an area where hundreds of ground searchers have failed to find anything.

Overzealous claims by handlers have led agencies to believe dog teams can do amazing things, like track six days later through a car wash. "My dog has scent" has diverted more than a few SAR missions off course.

The right tool for the right job. Every law enforcement agency intending to use dogs as well as other resources needs to maintain key personnel who know how to contact *reliable* search dog teams. Know how these teams work before deploying them. Like other resources, trained search dog teams must deploy efficiently in order to work effectively in the field. Dog teams have a responsibility to apply a basic medical principle to canine search: "First do no harm."

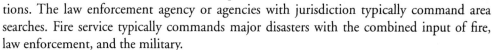

ICS

Search and rescue typically operates under the Incident Command System, applicable to fire, rescue and other law enforcement opera-tions. The law enforcement agency or agencies with jurisdiction typically command area searches. Fire service typically commands major disasters with the combined input of fire, law enforcement, and the military.

AFRCC

If a SAR operation goes beyond the capability of local and regional search and rescue resources, agencies in the U.S. can call the Air Force Rescue Coordination Center. The RCC will activate the closest available resources and will authorize air transport of teams on an "as available" basis where travel distances are greater than four hours' driving time and the mission is to save lives. Individual states maintain agreements with the Air Force regulating the procedures for SAR missions within their boundaries.

AFRCC - 48 States: (800) 851-3051

The K-9 unit relies upon the patrol force or other rescue resources to set up a perimeter immediately when notification of a missing person has been made. Setting a perimeter is appropriate where the person has been missing for a short time or has a known route of travel or has a high probability of being in a defined area. When circumstances call for setting a perimeter, it is important to do so in order to limit the area that dog teams and other resources will have to search to locate the missing person.

Adequate communications are essential. Although the handler does not set the perimeter, he must know where it is being manned to prevent air scenting the SAR personnel. *For the same reason command should advise handlers in advance of activity in adjacent sectors so the dog does not waste time finding rescuers.*

SAR incidents require specialized training for both the handler and the dog. As in flying aircraft or fighting fire, the team must be trained to a recognized standard of performance. A dog is not just a dog. The pet dog, the hunting dog, the police dog not trained for SAR will be a liability to the mission. The agency would not send a field trial dog to a bomb call. Deploying a team with insufficient training puts the missing child's life at risk also.

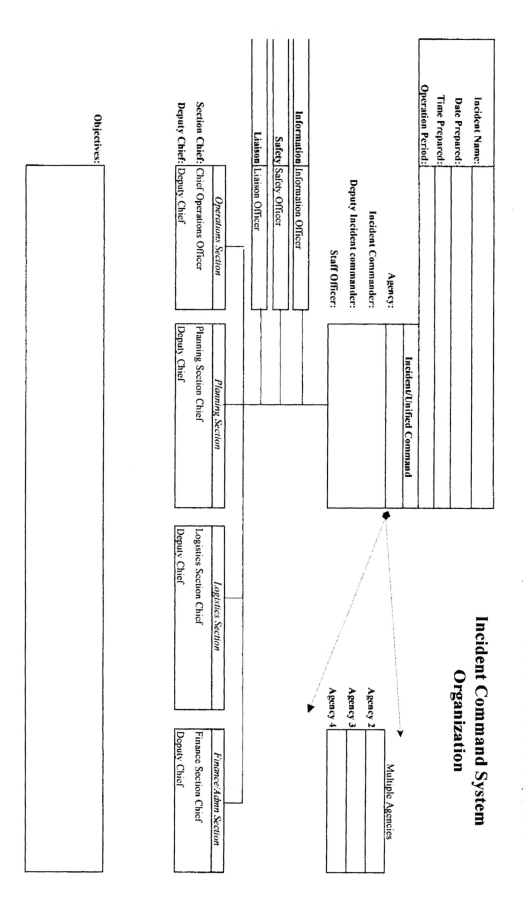

Incident Command System Organization

Incident Name:
Date Prepared:
Time Prepared:
Operation Period:

Agency:
Incident Commander:
Deputy Incident commander:
Staff Officer:

Incident/Unified Command

Information Information Officer
Liaison Liaison Officer
Safety Safety Officer

Agency 2
Agency 3
Agency 4

Multiple Agencies

Section Chief: Chief Operations Officer
Deputy Chief: Deputy Chief

Operations Section

Planning Section Chief
Deputy Chief

Planning Section

Logistics Section Chief
Deputy Chief

Logistics Section

Finance Section Chief
Deputy Chief

Finance/Admn Section

Objectives:

CICS®
Computerized
Incident Command
System

CICS® is a computer application tool for law enforcement, fire, and military to develop plans and budgets for emergency management as well as scheduled events or training scenarios. Compatible with standard ICS (Incident Command System) and LEICS (Law Enforcement Incident Command System). Identifies, tracks and updates personnel and equipment location, contact information, status, time and cost—estimated and actual. Enables rapid planning as well as accurate after action analysis and reporting. Available at k9tactics.com.

When dog teams with unknown capability show up at a search, command personnel who have limited experience with K-9 need rapid assessment methods to develop intelligent strategy. Look at the dog team. Are they equipped for this type search? Do they appear fit for this type search? Are they capable of searching at night (absent hazardous conditions)? At this altitude? In this weather? Ask the handler questions. Has the team met a standard of performance recognized by the agency in charge?

Type incidents where a rescue dog team would typically be useful:

- Area searches for lost or missing person(s) (child, hiker, fisherman, skier, found vehicle, depressed or dysfunctional individual)
- Disasters where person(s) might be buried under rubble, water or snow (earthquake, rock or mud slide, flooding or drowning, plane crash)
- Evidence search for dead bodies (cadavers) or body parts, or any items bearing fresh human scent, such as a plane crash, clues relevant to a search, or a crime scene.

Type incidents where a rescue dog team would probably not be useful, or may obstruct or endanger other personnel:

- Fire while hot or hazmat situation
- Missing person in populated urban area, except to check specific locations for a potentially concealed person, for example, to check back yards for an elderly patient with Dementia of Alzheimer's Type
- Tactical police mission, unless the dog is a police K-9
- Inside a perimeter or section where another dog team or other ground searchers are actively deployed
- Using dogs to follow right behind or mixed with foot searchers
- Only specialist police dog teams should be deployed for criminal apprehensions, drug searches, bomb searches, arson investigations, or potentially violent suicides

Incident commanders in missing person searches rely on lost person behavior profiles for the initial deployment of resources and development of objectives. These profiles may be generalized statistical studies or information from experts who have worked similar missions in same-type areas, or a combination of both. The best source of information may be an observant local resident who spends time outside and is familiar with the area or remembers previous incidents.

Search planners initially gather information to construct all scenarios of missing person(s) behavior that have a non-trivial possibility of being valid, accounting for alternative directions of travel, last known locations, or places last seen (PLS). Competing scenarios leading to markedly different POA (probability of area) and ROW (rest of the world) calculations must be analyzed rapidly and ranked by priority in order to begin the strategic deployment of SAR teams.

When an agency makes the decision to conduct a full-scale search, the Incident Commander or Search Manager must immediately do two things before resources are deployed: (1) divide the search area into manageable segments, and (2) coordinate the establishment of a Mattson Consensus.

Clear descriptions of the theory underlying the search management function are co-authored by John Bownds, Ph.D., Mathematics, Oak Ridge National Labs; Michael Ebersole, Park Ranger/Pilot, Grand Canyon National Park, Arizona; David Lovelock, Ph.D., Mathematics, University of Arizona; and Daniel J. O'Connor, Helicopter Pilot, Load Research Analyst, Massachusetts. In their articles, and as creators of the widely-used non-copyprotected CASIE (Computer Aided Search Information Exchange) search software series, these men have made a valuable contribution to area search efficiency. The application to search dogs is based directly on their work.

It is useful for the K-9 officer to examine search theory at least at the basic level because the field tactics fall into a logical order. Later he will be able to describe the incident to his administration, the victim's relatives, or the court.

Although used many different ways, POA usually means, "What is the likelihood that the victim is in this particular search segment?" POA changes for each segment (sector) after any portion of the total search area is searched.

POD (Probability of Detection) often refers to a measure of a search team's effectiveness after coming in from a period of searching. "How well has this segment been searched?" PODs can be applied to resources or segments.

POS (Probability of Success) is a product of a search segment's POA and POD (POS = POA x POD). POS has limited predictive value.

A Mattson Consensus establishes initial POAs for a new search, allowing incident commanders to deploy resources as they see fit. The Mattson Consensus is an averaging of opinions, and is actually an educated guess (based on victim behavior, lost person characteristics, and the experience, knowledge, and hunches of the search experts) of where the victim is most likely to be. The experts rank each search segment based on 9 choices (*very likely to be in this area, even chance...,* to *very unlikely...*), which the computer converts to a numerical value.

At the end of each operational period, if the victim is not found, the search dog handler is debriefed to find out how well he searched his assigned segment, producing a POD. PODs and POAs from all the search segments are then used to generate updated POAs. To maximize the use of resources for the next operational period, command allocates the resources so that after the next operational period the POA for the ROW (region outside the designated search area) will be as large as possible. The dog team is assigned a new sector. The sequence repeats until either the victim is found or the probability that the victim is in the ROW is so large that

After the find, if the handler is treating the patient, secure the dog away from the scene.

JUDY SALVIOLO

the search is suspended.

Calculating the optimum resource allocation is a job for a computer once the numbers exceed 2 or 3. For s segments and r resources, there are s^r cases to deal with. So a scenario with 10 segments and 6 resources would require checking one million (10^6) cases. If a computer is not available, or if the number of segments and resources exceeds the computational capability at the command center, either the search must be segmented differently or it must go forward using subjective estimates (recognizing that search and rescue is still an art, not a science).

AREA SAR TACTICS

Air search in concert with search dog teams rates the highest initial priority. The helicopter, if available and weather permitting, is the number one resource:

Reconnaissance	Observe the area and advise Plans
Transport	Insert, extract K-9 teams and other SAR resources
Communications	Airborne intelligence for emergency transmissions
Detection	Air unit may detect the subject independently or by advancing the path of the ground units
Rescue	Perform the rescue or direct technical rescue to the site
Transport	Airlift patients to medical facility or other location

Operations coordinates the deployment of search dogs with the air and ground units in order to prevent interference. Typical precautions include not fielding a grid search team in a segment directly ahead of a dog on track (helicopter or mantrackers are options), not fielding a tracking dog without prescenting into a sector recently covered by grid searchers.

Dogs typically get used to helicopters on searches. Noise is rarely a factor. Rotor wash creates turbulence that can break up a scent cone or disturb the continuity of track or trail scent. If the helicopter has to operate in the vicinity of a sniffing dog, staying as high above ground-effect as practical usually helps scenting. In some cases helicopters have helped the dogs by stirring up dead air or by creating a temporary backwash to drive scent being blown in the opposite direction back into the dog's face.

Area safety must be evaluated, and constantly re-evaluated, by each dog team in the field regardless of clearance from Command. Weather changes, sometimes rapidly. On a large search Command may be unaware of a storm cell over the handler's sector. Rain changing to ice, wind shifting to generate a firestorm, rising temperatures exceeding the dog's tolerance, local fog, high winds, the list is long. Similarly, Command cannot anticipate every possible hazard (mine shafts, wells, construction, refuse, cliffs, or unstable ground). Indeed the Incident Commander and Plans Chief need feedback from field personnel who discover problems that affect their tactics and that could affect search mission strategy.

The tracking dog detects and follows track and trail scent leading from a location where the missing person was last seen, from found evidence or a verified footprint. The dog may be trained to discriminate among multiple tracks if presented by a scent guide. If the dog loses the track, the handler has to select tactics to either relocate the track or change to air scenting.

If the K-9 team is working a track, possibly using a leapfrog confirmation technique with mantrackers, they are defining and redefining the highest probability area as they go. The tracking or trailing dog may cross many other search sectors. When this happens, ground searchers in those areas may have to stand by for the canine to exit the area. If the dog sniffs out of the scenario altogether, proceeding into the ROW, mission command may be forced to analyze alternative scenarios, re-draw the search sectors, and re-deploy some or all of the search resources.

The air scenting dog works patterns through assigned sectors to detect human scent. If no scent guide is available, he will be sniffing for general human scent. If an uncontaminated scent guide is available and the dog is trained to discriminate, presenting allows him to detect one among several human scents as well as to increase his effective range of detection. In the early

HEAVENLY SKI PATROL RESCUE DOG

stages of an operation dog teams are efficient hasty searchers, rapidly covering trails, roads, paths of least resistance, and attractive hazards. The K-9 team may work a perimeter to discover the victim's track or trail, or to detect the victim inside the boundary.

Detailed area searching increases the probability of detection significantly but takes more time than the hasty search. Crosswind search patterns which overlie the perimeter are ideal. Convection during daylight hours destabilizes the air, increasing turbulence and forcing more detailed sniffing. Contouring down hill from ridges and hilltops, the handler must maintain a low rate of descent to keep his dog focused on searching. At night, early morning or late evening, normal air patterns are more stable than during the day. Laminar air flow permits detection at greater distances. The handler contours up hill from valleys and drainages. Scent may pool or concentrate in depressions or plant life.

Access to the sector, the slope, aspect, and terrain features may prevent using the wind to the dog's advantage. Atmospheric inversion layers or precipitation holds the scent at various elevations and makes detection more difficult.

Night searching, although typically advantageous to the dog, restricts the handler visually. The decision to search at night considers the emergency versus the tactical problems and risks to the searchers. The risks to a missing child usually justify searching at night.

When searching for lost or missing persons, the police dog handler whose dog is not trained to perform nonaggressive off-lead search has to keep the dog on lead. The dog should not be allowed out of the handler's sight during the search or released to search dense underbrush where the handler cannot see the dog's actions or movements. While searching for evasive persons, the handler should use a cover officer to assist in the search in case the victim, once found, attempts to flee. The cover officer remains with the handler and follows his directions. *Be aware that young children or mentally impaired individuals may suddenly run up to rescuers when located.* Muzzling the dog while searching has to be practiced in advance during training and must take into consideration the decreased searching ability and increased fatigue factor for the dog.

Changing sectors to reach another search assignment is typically easier for dog teams than for dozens of grid searchers. Helicopters can transport K-9 teams efficiently so they can get to work fast.

For air scenting, the search sector should be realistic in size so that the dog team can search it in a single operational period. If the team is unable to do this, then that search segment will

The ballistic nylon K-9 rappel harness can be used to evacuate a child or small person.

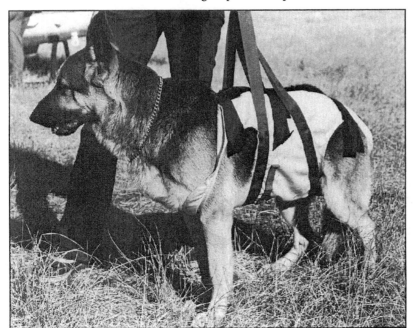

have to be split for planning purposes, indicating that the segment should have been made smaller at the start of the search. Sometimes throwing a search dog team into a large area is unavoidable. For example, the weather is bad, it is night, the canyon is big, and there is only one way in and one way out. If the handler is able to transmit a report of his coverage at the end of each operational period, he will contribute more to the operation than if he accumulates information for, say, three days. Changing POAs, for example a high probability clue found in another area, may change the optimum deployment area for the dog team. Command may direct the handler to hike out of the canyon as fast as possible so the dog can be used elsewhere.

An area search, by definition, is two-dimensional, not three. Handlers generally do not give much thought to this. For example, imagine a victim is buried "in" the search area. Unless the region under the earth is specifically designated as a search segment, the victim is actually in the ROW with respect to visual searching. Sniffing, however, *may* add a third dimension to the search tool. We have to say "may" because the pace of a dog team on area search is typically much faster than on a disaster, which calls for three-dimensional detection. Where an area search victim is actually under dirt or water and the vaporization rate is low, the dog deployed on area search may not detect the scent.

Frequently, not much thought is given to caves, mine shafts, outbuildings, or other isolated points in the initial segmentation of a search area. If there are many such points in an area, it might be appropriate to lump them together as one search segment, with one initial POA for all of them. This requires careful application of search theory, however.

It has become somewhat standard procedure to create segments out of trails. Dog teams are frequently deployed to search trail systems. Such a segment should only contain the trail, not something on either side of it or under it. A search of the trail will probably have a large POD since the search is being conducted *only* on the trail. It is important that search credit taken for the trail *not be extrapolated* to include segments or areas adjacent to the trail, even though the dog can sniff scent sources off the trail upwind. If the dog alerts off the trail and finds the victim, nobody will be worried about the POD.

Search segments often contain a mix of trails and terrain. Many times a team will only have time to examine the trail. In this case, the trail should be split out from its original segment and made into its own segment. A high POD for the trail does not imply a high

Attached with carabiners to the handler's descent system, the dog is controlled by the handler's legs en rappel, and promptly released on landing.

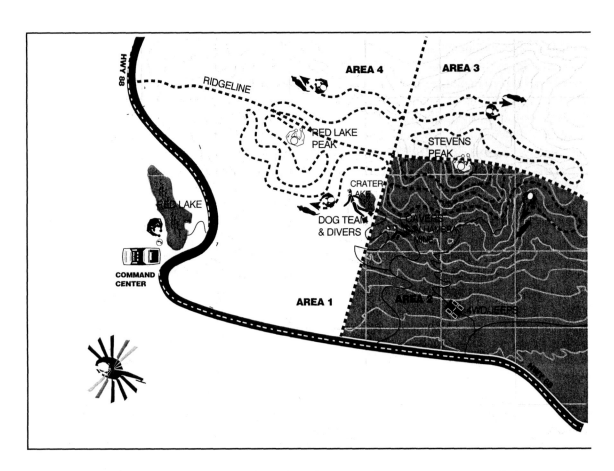

On large area searches
teams need clearly
defined sectors. Do
not miss areas where
resources interface.

POD for segments or areas near the trail. Such areas need separate treatment, with their own POAs and PODs. Sending a dog team along a trail route, especially through tall trees in still air, does not confer a magical blessing of special coverage to the off-trail areas.

This method assumes the victim remains in the same sector throughout the search. If the victim is mobile, computed values can be useful to the search command, but the underlying search theory is much more complex. Game theory to model a series of scenarios is relevant in cases where the subject is moving. *The evasive victim, who is actively avoiding detection, may behave with some predictability. The dysfunctional victim may move randomly, difficult to impossible to predict.*

Robert J. Koester and David E. Stooksbury analyzed five years of search and rescue data from Virginia to characterize the behavior of lost Dementia of Alzheimer's Type (DAT) patients. This disorder leads to such problems as wandering, pacing, aggression, irritability, withdrawal, fear, and anxiety. DAT subjects differ significantly from other lost subject behavioral profiles. Hikers, hunters, and other groups venture into the woods with both a purpose and equipment. The type of clues they leave often involve multiple physical objects. Containment is an effective tactic where the lost subject recognizes and follows a feature such as a road, trail or string barrier. The subject is aware he is lost and wants to be found. DAT subjects may simply wander into the woods and tend not to leave physical clues other than signs of passage and scent.

Dogs deployed on DAT-type searches have typically found victims in drainages, creeks, and heavy brush, deceased or suffering from hypothermia and dehydration. Many patients cross roads, or are in somebody's back yard where they end up after traveling a *path of least resistance* until they get stopped or get stuck. Then they frequently succumb to the environment.

The mobile subject will typically be detected more readily by a search dog than by a human searcher, particularly at night. The dog's superior hearing and eyesight are designed to detect motion.

The tactic of calling out to the missing person, as grid searchers frequently do, is a matter of handler discretion. First, if the victim is unlikely to respond (DAT, hearing impaired person) calling out is a waste of time. Second, the dog needs previous experience in training with his handler shouting people's names, *and with the people at some distance shouting back.* Calling is also wasted effort unless the team stops, and both the handler and dog listen for a response. Finally, a searcher calling out may distract a search dog in the area or confuse other searchers ("Who was that?"). Handlers should reserve calling out for victims who are likely to respond and locations where no searchers are within range.

Topograhic maps are necessary for back-country searches.

"My dog has scent." An irresponsible statement that gets everybody excited believing a find is imminent. Every dog has scent.

"My dog is alerting." Don't get excited. Get the facts. Is this interest or a full bore alert? What is the dog doing? What is the direction of the alert? The trained handler will give the operations commander relevant information, not merely say, "I have an alert." Many people, alive and dead, have been located because one or more search dogs alerted in the same direction or showed interest in converging directions, even though the dog could not pinpoint or access the source. Turbulence or terrain may prevent the dog from following the scent directly to the victim.

Distractions may prevent the dog from finding the victim at all. Two male juveniles and their dog were snowboarding. Their father was videotaping them. The camera captured an avalanche burying the young men and the dog. Only one brother survived. The dead dog was found quickly and was slabbed out on the surface of the avalanche like a body at the morgue. When an inexperienced search dog handler arrived, rescuers asked if they should move the dead dog off the avalanche. The handler politely declined. When the search dog sniffed the avalanche, he alerted toward the dead dog. The handler pulled him away. When the dog alerted again, the handler again pulled him away. Later probers found the son's body under several feet of snow, near the dead dog.

"The victim got in a car and left." The reliable team will not make creative statements about what the victim did. If the dog quits tracking when he hits a paved road, as in this case, the handler will read the dog and note the location. He will change tactics. First he may advise command to dispatch patrol units on roads leading out of the area. He may call for air support. He may examine both sides of the road for some distance to see if his dog can relocate the track. Depending on circumstances, he may call for mantrackers to examine the roadway in both directions.

Down or recall the dog alerting into a dangerous area.

"We cleared that area. He's not there," or "Hey, the dog covered it 100% (or 99%)." Send the team home. No dog is that good.

Verify all clues. The handler who prescents his dog (directing the dog to sniff an object, supposedly for discrimination purposes) using an unconfirmed clue or an unconfirmed object of evidence to "see if the dog has scent" or to "see what the dog does" is not reliable. This is very different from a controlled sniff test. If a found object has not been identified as having anything to do with the subject of the search, and if the dog has nothing he can associate as the desired scent, his reaction tells the handler nothing. In fact if

Returning from a 200-yard find, Cirque gives a clear alert and refind.

the dog shows interest, receives reinforcement, and later the object proves unrelated to the incident, the handler has just reinforced his dog for responding to the wrong odor.

A clue is any information, in any form, which, in the judgment of the search command, may reasonably relate to the whereabouts of the missing subject. A clue is authentic if it originates from a reliable source and is clearly related in an important way to the missing subject. For example, a clue may be the subject's intended direction of travel (DOT). Weighted mathematically in each search segment through which it passes, the DOT clue *influences* the POA, that is the likelihold that the subject is in a particular segment.

The potential influence of a clue is directly related to its authenticity. The potential influence of clues (5-level option, from *clue strongly suggests subject is in segment*, to *clue strongly suggests subject is not in segment*) and authenticity ratings of clues (5 levels, from *clue is very likely authentic*, to *clue is very likely not authentic*) are integrated into mission planning by the CASIE software. If necessary, the effects of a 'bad' clue can and should be canceled at any stage in the search.

A week into a large search for a missing child, a grid searcher walking the highway radioed he saw a white sock 6 feet down the embankment overlooking a lake. He would guard the area until a dog team arrived. The first handler to arrive looked down at the muddy, weathered sock and asked if anyone had identified it as belonging to the missing child. Nobody had. The officer in charge refused to send a family member out to identify the sock but requested the dog "sniff the sock to see what he'll do." No scent guides were available.

Just then a second handler rolled into the scene with a massive dog. "I'll handle this," the man said. Snuffling along the highway, the animal dragged its handler over the berm, past the sock, down the talus and into the bushes out of sight. Minutes later the man radioed he had located a barefoot print near the lake pointing toward the dam, which discharged down a steep canyon, but the dog was tired so they were discontinuing. On the basis of that one report, the officer in charge sent grid searchers down the 20-mile canyon in the cold afternoon rain. Weeks later the victim was found miles away in the opposite direction.

Multiple dog alerts may indicate a victim's location, although other teams actually make the contact. This commonly occurs during disasters: the dog alerts from the boat and divers find the body; the dog alerts into the debris and rescuers uncover the victim; the dog alerts into the snow and shovelers dig to the victim. It is less common in area search situations for the dog to be unable to get to the source after he alerts. If this happens, it is important that the handler read the details as well as the dog. In one case involving a night search for a 9-year-old girl, three dogs alerted briefly from three different positions beneath a wooded ridge. Reporting the direction of the dog indications, the location, elevation, and downslope winds, the handlers collectively provided the information needed for the incident command to deploy a fourth canine team up the ridge. Within minutes the fourth dog detected the girl's track and located her.

An obvious example of inaccessibility is a wall or cliff where the dog alerts from above or below but cannot get to the victim. Although the cliff itself may be obvious, finding a victim on it may be very difficult. A detailed search may require climbers. Do not be in a hurry to attribute the dog's alert to other activity going on above or below the wall.

KINGS CANYON, CALIFORNIA

A photograph shows Wolfe Kirson shaking hands with the President. The California Representative, rises to speak:

"Mr. Speaker, I rise today to pay tribute to an outstanding young man, and, with great sadness, to announce his death.

"Wolfe Kirson was a good and inspirational young man who cared deeply for others. He sought to help those in need and was willing to share his life for this cause. His most noteworthy community service was through the Santa Monica Boys Club. Indeed, he was named Young Man of the Year, and went on to receive national recognition.

"Tragically, Wolfe Kirson lost his life in a fall at Sequoia National Park. Though only 20 years old, he had touched the lives of many...

"...it is no small thing to say of someone that he was good, was loved and shall be missed greatly."

It was no small thing, either, the task facing Paul Fodor. In front of him sat Sam Kirson, Wolfe's father. Behind him rose dozens of peaks over 10,000 feet, some over 12,000. Somewhere up there was Wolfe. Probably. Paul was the park ranger in charge of running the search.

Sam Kirson's face showed the strain of driving all night from Los Angeles to Tulare

The team that found Wolfe Kirson, Zeke boulder hops with handler Marty Cross.

County Sheriff's Office where he contacted a deputy about his missing son. Tulare notified Sequoia-Kings Park dispatch at 11:30 pm, and at 8 o'clock Monday morning, September 19th, Kirson walked in the door at Park headquarters saying, "My son's lost in your mountains."

Fodor pieced together the information. Wolfe's friends were doing a loop trip out of Mineral King starting the 10th. Wolfe planned to drive to the Park on Monday the 12th, hike up to meet his friends in Lost Canyon, then hike back out with them to the Sawtooth Trailhead on the 16th. Young Kirson was tall, lanky, handsome, blue eyes, brown hair, mentally and physically healthy, with eight years of backpacking but little technical rock experience, primarily in Southern California and the eastern Sierra Nevada. He had never backpacked in Mineral King before. Ten miles would be an easy day for Kirson, while 18 would push it. He liked bagging peaks with friends and might decide to try an attractive climb alone.

Details about Kirson's equipment were sketchy since nobody had actually seen him pack or load his car. They assumed he had food for 5 days, was carrying a medium gray external frame pack, maybe a tarp or tube tent, a light green down bag, possibly a map, stove, compass, or rain gear. Usually he carried a sleeping pad, water filter, cup, fishing pole and tackle, flannel shirt, reading glasses, and a first aid kit. The clothing description included size 9-10 hiking boots, jeans, and a blue down jacket. None of the colors, the rangers knew, would be easy to see from the air.

But the weather was not helping the aerial search anyway. On the 12th when Wolfe started out, clear weather had given way to low overcast and a cold front. Fog hid the summits and passes down to about 11,000 feet.

"I don't know if he knew how difficult the terrain is," said Steve Goon, his UCLA roommate. Wolfe was definitely eager to do the hike. Delayed from leaving L.A. on the 12th, he would have gotten to Mineral King late. He had not locked the pickup door of the tan Nissan he was driving. He filled out the self-issue permit hikers are supposed to leave telling which way they are going, what they plan to do, and when they plan to leave. What he said on his permit, though, did not match what he was supposed to do.

Right there the rangers had a problem. Suddenly the search area became 400 square miles instead of one trail. Kirson's permit said he was going to go over Timber Gap and exit Farewell Gap, which did not make sense geographically. It meant checking the whole Great Western Divide.

Why had the party Wolfe was supposed to meet in Lost Canyon not reported him missing earlier? They looked for him Tuesday the 13th, then on Wednesday, when he did not show up, they left, thinking he canceled his trip. The Nissan Wolfe drove belonged to his dad, so his friends did not recognize the truck when they drove out of the Park.

Wolfe failed to show up for a fraternity retreat in Palm Springs over the weekend of the 17th. When Sam Kirson stopped by the fraternity house Sunday night, he found out his son was gone. At that point the father put the pedal to the metal. A week had passed since his son left for the Park.

Paul Fodor phoned the party Wolfe was supposed to have met, while other rangers used wilderness permits to contact people who had been in the area in case anybody saw him. The party reported they had penciled their route where he was supposed to go on a map before leaving L.A. They also left a note at the only trail junction saying, "Wolfe, take the right trail, come into Lost Canyon." The note was gone when those folks came out. But he could have gone over Timber Gap, Glacier Pass, or several other routes. The backcountry ranger for the Columbine Lake-Sawtooth Pass area did a trail search. A Jet Ranger flew the Divide area, landing the helicopter to interview any hikers they spotted.

Late in the day, Park rangers talked to a backpacking party who said they had seen a guy

Right there the rangers had a problem. Suddenly the search area became 400 square miles instead of one trail.

looking like Kirson about 4 pm the 12th on the trail below Monarch Lake. He told them he was headed over Sawtooth Pass to meet his friends in Lost Canyon at Columbine Lake. The point where they saw him became the PLS (place last seen). Many people miss the Sawtooth Pass trail and go over Glacier Pass without realizing what they have done. There are hundreds of social trails on the west side in the steep decomposed granite. The east side is cliffs and boulders and headwalls of cirques. The Divide itself is a high, winding snake of awesome proportions and jagged rock. On September 12th, a singular low pressure cell of clouds hung across the Divide.

The afternoon of the 19th, the Park called in all the troops to review their first search day and hold a plans meeting for the following day. Clearly they had to escalate to a major search. Searching big, rawboned wilderness called for all the resources they could find: helicopters to transport as well as to search; infrared or other hi-tech tools, many foot searchers; rescue dog teams. Rangers sectored topographic maps for the next day's mission and made phone calls throughout the state. Responding to the urgent request, dog teams drove through the night to Sequoia Park.

On Tuesday the 20th, everything that could go wrong did. It started out okay. Headquarters was located at Ash Mountain, west of the Mineral King parking lot where Wolfe had departed. Paul Fodor was the IC (Incident Commander). At the recreation hall, he set up an Operations Section Chief and a Logistics Section Chief, Communications in the old dispatch office, a Timing Unit, a Planning Unit in the fire office, and all in-Park personnel. Well not all. About 15 fire crews were supposed to go out searching that morning in teams of two. Except they had been sent off to a fire during the night. So the Park had to call in standby people. Then one helicopter died, so they had to operate with only one Bell 206-3.

Some teams got deployed. Ranger Anne Walsten and her dog were fielded early to search from Glacier Pass to the area below Empire Peak, following the ridge around on the ledge above Spring Lake to the saddle above Columbine Lake. Marty Cross and his dog flew to Columbine Lake. They searched the shore and nearby areas while waiting for a Park person to fly in on the next flight. There was no next flight. Clouds moved in at 10 am. Marty interviewed a backpacking group headed toward Lost Canyon. The weather deteriorated to the mid 20s Fahrenheit, visibility 50 yards, and a strong northeast wind driving graupel at first, then snow.

Rod Meagher, his search dog, and a Park ranger hiked from the Mineral King helipad to Sawtooth Pass. The primary search area was both sides of Sawtooth Pass. But by the time they reached the pass, the weather had shut it down. Command was recalling all the search teams. By noon it was snowing.

Wolfe's mother Rebecca had arrived at Sequoia separately with her husband. A Park liaison stayed with her at a location away from the command center. The father sat right in front of Paul Fodor and was helpful thinking of names and phone numbers for more information. Going through the process with Paul, he remarked, "This is real detective work, isn't it?"

Meanwhile in the high country, when Anne Walsten completed her search area and saw the weather moving in, she began hiking out. After six years as a ranger in Mineral King, wintering alone in a cabin up there, she knew about leaving ahead of storms. South of her, Marty and his dog searched about three hours until it started to get cold. He did the north end of Columbine Lake down to the headwall of Lost Canyon. Up-canyon winds were strong. The dog found a hand axe, so the team worked in a circle looking for other evidence. As the temperature dropped, Marty put on more clothes and set up a bivouac tent for the night. Then he got a radio call to hike out. By the time he and his dog crossed the 11,500-foot pass and

But by the time they reached the pass, the weather had shut it down. Command was recalling all the search teams. By noon it was snowing.

reached Mineral King four miles away, it was 6 pm, dark and snowing.

Wednesday the 21st was worse. Everything above 4,000 feet was in clouds, rain, and snow. Rod and his dog searched up Monarch Creek to Monarch Lake, checked out an arrow somebody had found traced in the sand, then worked back down. Other dog teams went up to Mineral King to stage. Dogs teams arrived at the Park that either were not trained appropriately or were not physically appropriate for the mission.

The Park had scent articles they had lifted with tongs and bagged individually for the dog teams. Some teams used these, some did not.

N.A.S. Lemoore Angel 3 *in Little Slide Canyon.*

Eight two-man foot teams who went out that afternoon said they were not effective in the heavy fog and rain. They were able to cover only a quarter of their area with only 25% POD (probability of detection if the subject is there).

A search for missing Outward Bound students at Lodgepole grew into a red herring for the Kirson search. The Park had to divert some of their own personnel and several dog teams to handle that search also. The missing students returned at six that evening.

Thursday the 22nd, the weather broke. In a series of morning flights, helicopters lifted dog teams and foot searchers to their assignments. Finally the search was going the way Fodor and his crews had tried to do it on the 20th.

One unit worked their tracking dogs on the west side of the ridge and trails. But with the solar radiation at that altitude, the time interval since Kirson went missing, high wind, hard rock, trail use by dozens of other people, and previous precipitation, tracking was actually not feasible. However, the Park had no K-9 advisers to manage the search dog operations, so they had to rely on the teams being able to do what they said they could do.

Other teams prescented their dogs with the scent guides the Park provided. While they did not expect highly accurate scent discrimination, they were hoping to intensify any alert on the missing man. If Kirson was still up, moving around, and laying a fresh track, they would be able to work a track. Meanwhile the strategy had to be clearing individually assigned areas with the dogs working air scent.

By 10 am, Anne Walsten was up in a helicopter searching with FLIR (Forward Looking Infrared). Already the rocks were reflecting enough heat (versus human body heat) that the instrument could not even isolate the searchers that the helicopter crew could see with their own eyes. Under those conditions, the chance of infrared finding Kirson was low, especially if he was hypothermic or dead.

Marty Cross and a Park ranger worked the pass southbound along the ridge toward Sawtooth Peak. Winds were upslope on both sides of the Divide. Asking his partner to stay on top of the ridge, Marty and his dog Zeke dropped off on a lower contour, picking their route through the boulders. The ridge was massive, with a sheer wall on the east side and giant spires. All they could do was traverse the tops of the boulders. It was treacherous for both the men and the dog. Working in advance of his partner on the ridge, Marty came out on top of a north-facing couloir about 50 yards from the peak. Climbing down through a hole beside a boulder, he had to call his dog back from a high angle snowfield. Regaining the ridge, he had difficulty keeping his partner in sight. He glassed the north face of Sawtooth Peak with his binoculars thinking if Wolfe went up there and fell off, it was sheer cliff below. Just then the dog moved out to the edge of a boulder and looked down, sniffing.

Lowering his binoculars, Marty went "Zeke!" The dog's ears were perked up. At first Marty thought he was alerting to searchers on a trail descending the east side of the pass a quarter mile away. The dog started pounding his paws like he was about to jump off. Flame from the handler's lighter showed an up-wall wind. Climbing down to his dog, Marty matched his gaze straight down and saw the victim 300 feet below. The body was contorted and motionless. Stuff sacks and other debris were scattered on the ledge. He had taken a long fall. There were no signs of life.

It was 11:50 am. Marty stayed in place to direct the helicopter to Kirson's location. The body was not visible from below or from any other point on the ridge. An hour later the helicopter crew evacuated Kirson from the mountain.

MONO COUNTY—YOSEMITE NATIONAL PARK, CALIFORNIA

"A case of bad weather, high altitude, broken helicopters, dual command centers, tin can-and-string communications, hypothermia, worst-on-worst conditions," said John Dill. The Yosemite SAR ranger, a veteran of big wall rescues did not exaggerate, "Mountain rescue teams had become 99% convinced Lester Needham wasn't in that canyon. Then to have the dog team go through, the dog go 'Arf, arf!' and find him—that's one for the comic books."

Sawtooth Ridge is the high jagged border between Yosemite National Park and the Toiyabe National Forest. Little Slide Canyon runs northeast off the ridge. At 8 am Saturday, July 19th, two Reno businessmen were on the second day of their trip, climbing above 9500 feet in the canyon. Rising 2500 feet in a mile, the canyon is steep and narrow with a mountaineer's route instead of a trail. The stream originating at Maltby Lake flows fast and loud. Lester Needham and Bruce Raabe had to scramble around boulders and cross snow bridges above deep chasms and waterfalls.

Both men were in good shape. They had full packs with camping gear. Needham wore lightweight trail boots. They intended to go up past Maltby Lake to the top of Sawtooth Ridge, then down the source of Slide Canyon Creek to the trail on the southwest side behind Matterhorn Peak, and hike out to Twin Lakes over Burro Pass. At 9500 feet they split up below a fork in the canyon to climb past a rock point.

Ten minutes after he left Raabe, Lester Needham was working his way up the other steep snow chute. At that altitude in the morning everything was still frozen. Needham's boots could not get a grip on the hard snow. He slipped.

Sliding down the slope out of control, it looked like he would crash into the rocks. A human toboggan, he hit the rocks and dropped into a hidden crevasse, falling 30 feet into Little Slide Creek.

One of his legs and his back broke. His left heel shattered. Breaking on impact, his backpack saved his head. He was alive, he was conscious, but he could hardly move.

Hours later Raabe was looking for him. He searched all day around Maltby Lake, over the ridge, and across the plateau into Yosemite. Then he hiked out to get help. That night, leaving a note on Needham's car, he notified Mono County Sheriff's Department. June Lake Mountain Rescue and Yosemite Park took reports. Immediately, the search became large scale. A multi-jurisdictional unified command ICS had to be set up to operate at long distance. The potential search area involved hundreds of square miles ranging from 4,000 to 13,000 feet elevation, and highly variable weather systems across the range.

Sunday, a California Highway Patrol helicopter flew the area. The winds were high. They could not fly the canyons. On Monday, Command put foot searchers into the prime area, Little Slide Canyon. Yosemite became the primary rescue coordinator for logistical support under the direction of Ranger John Dill.

Thirty-foot crevasse where Lester Needham fell.

Doug McGee of June Lake Mountain Rescue said, "Sunday at the time of the SAR callout, we didn't feel we had a search. The victim, Lester Needham, was in good health with no indication of problems, marital or legal. Often this sort of thing happens. People get separated and search for each other. Eventually the missing person shows up.

"Monday though, I felt the helicopter being used for SAR was only operating at about 10-to 20-percent efficiency. So we started running it full bore on Tuesday. We moved up to the back of Mono Village. The Park and Mono County had the ability and people ready to go. We had false sightings of the victim in the Park, as usual on these things."

The search was obstructed initially by lack of air support and resources committed to an earthquake exercise in Bishop, California. Mono County had lost its Mobile Command Center to the exercise. National Guard helicopters were out of position also. As a joint operation affecting two large jurisdictions with a remote backcountry search area, the mission presented classic difficulties. The major part of the search area lay above 9000 feet, limiting the capabilities of both ground and air searchers. The primary search area, Little Slide Canyon had to be eliminated first. After that the search area expanded to hundreds of square miles.

Units involved in the SAR included Mono County, National Park Service, U.S. Navy, U.S. Air Force, California Air National Guard, California Army National Guard, California Officer of Emergency Services, June Lake MRA (Mountain Rescue Association), China Lake MRA, Bay Area MRA, California ESAR (Explorer Search and Rescue), California Youth Authority, Federal Aviation Administration, California Highway Patrol, Careflight, and the Wilderness Finders, Inc. search dog unit. At the command center, Needham's wife Mary Jo encouraged the searchers who came and went and provided photographs of her husband.

The weather was not cooperating. Clouds hung over the crest late Monday morning bringing afternoon thundershowers down at the Bridgeport elevation and lightning with hail on the mountain range. This pattern continued through Tuesday afternoon.

Monday night, Mead Hargis of the Park and Doug McGee of Mono got together to set up a planning session. From the pay phone at Twin Lakes, they contacted the sheriff's office then set up a link with Dill in the Valley and Park rangers at Tuolumne Meadows through a speaker phone and extension hookup. They had to coordinate three operations centers: Yosemite Valley, Tuolumne District, and Mono's Twin Lakes. They developed a comprehensive search strategy. "The guy was lost in Mono County but headed toward the Park," Dill said. "Since he was reported as 'fairly expert with pretty good gear,' we saw two alternatives. Either he was moving around, probably in the Park, or he was down, probably in Little Slide Canyon."

"The Tuolumne effort tried to pinch off Needham if he was still hiking around." Rangers set out confinement teams for the Yosemite search area and interviewed hikers. The two agencies agreed the Park would search its part of Needham's route, establish confinement on trails leading out of the Park, and provide planning and logistical assistance to Mono County.

"The prime area was the Little Slide. Mountain rescue teams searched that area." Raabe accompanied these teams and ended up climbing the canyon several times. "Their consensus was if a person had been in the canyon able to respond, they'd have found him. They called in reporting snow bridges, high stream flow and crevasses."

The CHP helicopter continued searching the area until the aircraft had mechanical problems. Dill and McGee "wanted to do a Type 3 (*detailed* or tight grid) air search using a helo with an experienced crew." But helicopters were not available. An H-3 helicopter from Moffett Field in San Francisco could only search the lower elevations due to operational ceilings. The 60 miles per hour it had to maintain was too fast.

McGee wanted to get at least two dog teams up high to search Ice and Maltby Lakes. Vertical rock borders these lakes. Needham could have fallen in the water. The idea of using a helicopter to transport an inflatable boat up to the lakes was brought up, but Command did not know how much air time they had. The clouds were already coming in.

McGee and Hargis calculated flying times, weights, and predicted weather. "Mead and I agreed on our decision afterwards," McGee said. "We had one helo trip left, and we used that trip to put dog teams on the ridge plateau."

When the dog teams deployed at Ice Lake, they met two mountain rescue teams who briefed them. The men had spent the night at Ice Lake. They had spent the previous day working up the canyons with two other searchers. They covered Little Slide Canyon four-abreast. They felt they had covered Little Slide well. It was narrow. The path of least resistance lay along the stream. Steep on both sides, the route up was not actually a trail. They had found footprints south of Ice Lake that wandered all over the plateau, heading south, north and back. They felt maybe Needham had wandered around waiting for Raabe to show up. Raabe had not searched higher than Maltby Lake, so the prints could not be his. In fact, they matched Needham's shoe size.

Incident Command radioed they would like a dog to work Little Slide Canyon.

Meanwhile Lester Needham lay in the icy water for over three days. He stared up at the hole he had fallen through and watched the melting snow enlarge the hole from four to six feet. At one point, a big piece of ice hung ready to fall on his head. He banged a metal cup against the rocks to signal, but realized nobody could hear him above the cascade.

His determination, however, was strong. He pulled all the fiberglass tent poles out of his pack and connected them. Tying a bandana on the end, he slowly lifted the assembly toward the hole, got it just to the edge, and God, it was not quite high enough. One more. He fished it higher...and the whole thing collapsed.

He saw the helicopters flying up the canyon looking for him. He kept waiting for them to fly over at night so he could beam his flashlight through the hole.

"I just lay there looking at the sky. I really didn't think about anything. The only thing I was concerned about was that my wife would not know what happened to me. I didn't think anyone would find me. I knew I would die. I couldn't make it another day. I kept dozing off."

Two of the four dog teams inserted near Maltby Lake began searching down Little Slide Canyon. Marty Cross

Rescuers cover Lester to protect him from the icy water and package him for transport.

JUDY SALVIOLO

directed his golden retriever to check out granite cracks and other traps. He sent the dog into snow tunnels beneath the snowfields undercut by the stream. There were many tracks from mountain rescue teams that had searched up and down the Little Slide.

Several hundred yards down the canyon, they reached a steep snowfield about 150 feet wide and 225 feet long, extending from wall to wall in the canyon. They started glissading. "I was a third of the way down when the dog just took a hook," Cross said. "He went over to this rock wall on the south edge of the snowfield and poked his head down this opening, this crevasse. There was an obviously steep overhang. I didn't know how strong the snow was, so I laid myself out on my belly, crawled to the edge and looked down. I was looking right down at Lester."

It was now Tuesday at 12:15 pm. Lester responded with his eyes to the men giving a thumbs-up above him. Problems for the rescuers were just beginning.

Handler Bill Macaulay climbed down to do the patient assessment while Cross radioed base. Needham was alert, oriented, and had a pulse of 120. He did have capillary refill in his hands but could not move his left leg. He complained of severe back pain and leg cramps. Also, his left foot was numb. He was shaking uncontrollably.

Lester was immersed in the water from the knees down. There was water flowing underneath him from his head down, and the waterfall gave off a constant spray. He was totally saturated. He had pulled his Polarguard™ sleeping bag and tent over himself, but it was all saturated with water. Without a hat, his head was lying right on the granite.

Handlers put a wool balaclava on Needham's head. The third handler to reach the site, Judy Harper, was a nurse. Considering his strong pulse and alert state, she decided it would be safe to attempt rewarming him with sips of clear warm fluids. Meanwhile the fourth dog handler, Chris Salisbury, hauled each team's cached gear from the ridge down to the site and started building a camp. The handlers radioed for a backboard, a litter, IV, and oxygen.

Eight mountain rescue teams started hiking up with all the requested gear. From base, their ETA was four to five hours. Rescuers knew they might have to spend the night on the mountain with the victim. McGee recalled, "When the news came down that the dog had found him, there were instantly 13 guys ready to haul up that hill with all the equipment they needed."

After doing the primary survey, handlers pulled wet material off Needham and tried to protect him from the water. They propped his broken pack underneath his legs. A dry sleeping bag was put over him, with the one foot they could move placed inside the bag, and a space blanket over the top.

A C-130 was now in the air above the search area with broad spectrum communications, acting as an airborne radio relay for the helicopters, ground teams and the three operations centers.

During the five hours they were with him, the dog handlers kept a running conversation going with Needham in order to monitor his status. He still had renal function, but his carotid pulse varied from 104 to 120. His feet were numb from being in the water. His upper left thigh kept cramping. Rescuers were careful about the possibility of a broken back and hip. Up to the time he was found, Needham had managed to eat some Sweet & Low® and

Unable to winch Lester from the crevasse, teams had to force the litter through the narrow access tunnel.

JUDY SALVIOLO

drink a lot of water, which probably helped control his shock and general body chemistry. He had a huge, open sore on his buttocks from pressing against the wet granite.

Racing darkness, the Navy helicopter Angel Three from Lemoore landed in Yosemite Valley late that afternoon. Offloading gear to reduce weight, the aircraft took off toward the stormy high Sierra.

"We had cloud-to-cloud lightning," recalled Lt. Larwood, mission co-pilot. "We went across Hetch Hetchy Reservoir because the weather seemed to be better toward the north." They sneaked among thunderheads and came out over Twin Lakes.

The helicopter couldn't land at the rescue site, which was on a steep narrow slope with pinnacles on both sides. Rescuers gave the crew an estimate of how high they would have to be to have a 75-foot clearance for the rotor blades. They reported wind, temperature and periodic precipitation. Long streamers of orange surveyor's flagging were strung up in trees and bushes nearby to indicate wind direction.

Angel Three flew into the tight canyon nose-first, with no alternatives for a wave-off. Pulling into a hover a few feet above the snow, they dropped off a crew member, a backboard, a Stokes litter, then turned around and flew back out.

Extracting Needham from the crevasse was a difficult exercise. The hole above him was too small to winch through. The access route dog handlers had been using to reach Lester was only a rescue litter wide, a tunnel of boulders and ice. They logrolled him onto the backboard. With the help of arriving mountain rescue teams, Needham was lifted through the long corridor out to the surface, treated with oxygen and covered with a blanket.

Angel Three returned, hovering about three feet above the rock. Rescuers lifted the litter onto the chopper deck, the crewman jumped in, and Angel Three flew to Bridgeport, where Needham was transferred to a CareFlight helicopter and flown to St. Mary's Hospital in Reno.

The dog teams and other ground crews packed their waterlogged gear and began the long downclimb. They got out about 10 pm.

"The doctors say I shouldn't be alive," smiles Needham, walking and working again after successful spinal surgery that restored feeling and movement to his legs. "If you're going out there and backpacking, you expect to take certain risks. I don't think I'd change anything because I like to be out there. Bruce and I separating was probably an error, but Bruce and I are the type of people that would probably do it again. I'll still go out and hunt and fish by myself. Raabe'll go out by himself. The real mistake was crossing a steep snowfield like that without an ice axe. I wasn't careful enough."

Angel 3 ferried to safety a man few expected to see alive.

JUDY SALVIOLO

DISASTERS

From the standpoint of the trained dog team, a disaster is any search to detect people buried, immobilized, or injured in wreckage debris, urban rubble, water, snow, rock, or other material. An earthquake causes a disaster search when buildings collapse on the people inside or nearby. A snow avalanche causes a disaster search when it buries a skier. A disaster search starts when an aircraft crashes into a hillside. A lake becomes the scene of a disaster search when a fishing boat overturns and two men disappear. In each case the search dog team has received specialized training to perform detection in that particular environment.

AIR CRASH

When an aircraft disappears off the Airway Traffic Control (ATC) screen, controllers are frequently able to designate a several-square mile area with a high POA for the missing aircraft. Via satellite Russia, France, and other countries have pinpointed Electronic Locator Transmitter (ELT) signals from aircraft crashed inside the U.S. More commonly U.S. military or commercial aircraft detect the ELT signal and provide location coordinates to rescuers. In cases where the ELT is destroyed or never activated, or for low-altitude flights, detecting the air crash may require investigating the flight plan and mounting an air search.

If the crash is not visible from the air (deep snow, tall trees, bad weather, night) but an area has been identified, dog teams should be deployed. Hasty area search tactics are typically effective. Although the aircraft may have broken into many parts in the air or on impact, there will be a high rate of scent diffusion from large surface area materials, including body parts. If the aircraft has burned, the dog will detect scent from the debris.

Have at least one K-9 team standing by during an air search. When the crash is located, the dog team goes in with the first rescue crew. The handler then becomes the first person to approach the site. He can determine if victims are missing without contaminating the site for the dog. If the plane breaks up in the air, people may separate from the fuselage and end up a considerable distance from the main site. These people are unlikely to survive. Higher priority must be given to survivors who have left the main crash site attempting to get help.

Highest priority is given to the survivors at the crash site. Rescuers move in to secure the site, provide medical care and evacuate survivors. Officers notify the Federal Aviation Administration/National Transportation and Safety Board (FAA/NTSB), check for fuel or freight hazards or contraband, place guards as necessary, take photographs, and take appropriate measures to preserve all the evidence. The bodies of any persons killed in the accident and all property should be left as found until the position and condition of the bodies are noted by a trained investigator. If it is suspected that the aircraft may have on board any dangerous cargo such as radioactive materials, explosives, ammunition, corrosive liquids, gaseous materials, poisons, or even bacterial cultures, special precautions should be taken to maintain a safe distance and protect rescuers from the wreckage. The department will need the names and addresses of all available

Freel Peak air crash. Climbing to the 11,000 foot summit in a 60 knot wind, the dog team and rescuers found burned bodies trapped in the smashed cockpit. They filled 2 body bags and dragged them to a saddle, stowing them in the rocks, then downclimbed in the dark.

witnesses to aid the accident investigation.

The handler, relieved of duty to those who are alive at the scene, prepares to deploy the dog to find the missing people. If there is a large wreckage trail, the handler does an initial survey to obtain as clear a picture as possible. Primary considerations are the point of initial impact, probable flight path, impact angle, impact speed, whether or not the aircraft may have been under control, and if structural failure occurred prior to impact. Markings on trees, rocks, and the ground help determine the aircraft's path. The handler then deploys the dog on a hasty area search.

Air scenting across the path of wreckage, the dog may alert to bodies, blood or other evidence. Although the handler's initial objective is locating live people, he should reinforce all the dog's finds. Praise is a good tactic, keeping the dog moving in a pattern and reserving special reinforcement for live finds. After dog teams have covered the area to detect survivors, they can focus on evidence recovery.

If it appears survivors have walked or crawled away from the wreckage, deploy a dog capable of tracking to sniff the vicinity of the site. If there is only one missing person, prescent the dog on the plane's interior. A blood trail may help the dog track. What could a survivor see and hear from the crash? Which way would he go to get help?

Icing brought a single engine aircraft down at the 7000-foot elevation near Tinker's Knob. The ELT broadcast briefly then quit. An airliner pass,ing overhead picked up the signal and fixed its position, but storms kept rescue teams out of the area for several days. The morning it cleared, the highway patrol flew the area and located the aircraft.

The plane's fuselage was largely intact. The wings and wheel struts were ripped off. The plane had struck with force but was amazingly intact on the rocky mountainside. Landing the highway patrol helicopter nearby, the driver kept the ship hot while the other patrolman ran back to find out if there were survivors. Pilot and passenger were gone. The cracked windshield and bloody interior indicated head injuries.

Lifting off, the helicopter circled above the crash site looking for the man and woman. Minutes later they swung off toward the north to pick up SAR personnel in a meadow seven miles away.

Three dog teams were flown in first. Scented on the aircraft passenger seat, the German shepherd police dog began tracking a trail of blood spots leading down the rocks toward the river. The trail led to a lady's high heel then disappeared into a steep band of willow and alder brush several hundred yards above the river.

Standing at the crash site, the second handler listened to the river below, looked up the mountain, and decided both victims would have gone downhill. He started his dog working an air scent pattern downhill. The third dog team did the same farther to the south. All three handlers realized after getting down into the brush and cliffs that there would be no going back uphill. The crash victims also would have been unable to climb back out. Although he lost the track on their falling descent through the brush, the police dog found the female passenger yards away from where they emerged on the river. The river flowed deep and fast. The second dog team located the pilot on the river bank several hundred yards downstream. Both had died of their injuries and hypothermia.

Search the area for survivors first, then conduct a thorough on-lead search for wreckage. Retrace the projected flight path, leaving all finds intact. Small objects found hundreds of yards or several miles away may give investigators key information.

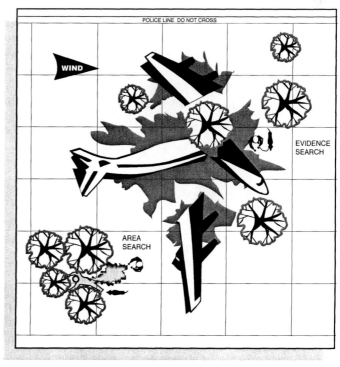

WATER SEARCH

The Salmon River is 425 miles long from its source on the southern flank of the Sawtooth Range to its confluence with the Snake River at Lewiston. It is the longest river contained within any one state in the United States outside of Alaska. The Salmon drains an area of more than 13,000 square miles in central Idaho. Its main tributaries are its East, Middle and South forks and the Little Salmon. In addition to the Sawtooths, the Salmon drains the White Cloud, Lost River, Lemhi, and Salmon River ranges. Most of the Salmon River system, including the Middle and South forks, drains the Idaho batholith, deep-seated intrusive igneous rock.

Deb Tirmenstein and Choteau.

The section of the Salmon from North Fork to Riggins, where it crosses the state from east to west, has been named "The River of No Return." The river flows through a deep forested canyon for that entire 165-mile stretch. Massive ponderosa pine and vertical granite slabs adorn the scenic drive up the Salmon above Riggins. During runoff, several huge rapids, Vinegar, Ruby, and Lake Creek get "way gnarly" (commonly above the 40,000 cubic feet per second range, with a record flow of 130,000 cfs). The river is treacherous at these high-water flows.

In July, 1993, Tony Bradbury, Sr. lost his life to the Salmon River. Bradbury's family operates Exodus-World Class Outdoor Adventures, a whitewater rafting tour company and The Lodge at Riggins Hot Springs in Riggins, Idaho. Driving back to the lodge for the evening, Tony had pulled his car to the shoulder of a one-lane road to allow oncoming traffic to pass. As he edged to the side of the road, the soft shoulder gave way, catching the front tire of the car. Tony lost control of the vehicle. It rolled down a 40-foot cliff into the main Salmon River below.

Emergency personnel and divers arrived at the accident scene but could not find Bradbury, who had been thrown from the wreckage into the swiftly moving water. The windshield had broken out and the body was gone. Volunteer divers from Clearwater, McCall, and Boise spent the next three days attempting to locate and recover the body. The divers found a dead horse that had plunged through the ice months before into a hole 57 feet deep.

Norm Klobetanz, friend of the family, whitewater boatman, and guide for Exodus, suggested they bring in an experienced canine team, Debbie Tirmenstein and her black Labrador Choteau from Missoula, Montana. Gallatin County Sheriff's Department in Bozeman, the dispatch agency for Western Montana Search Dogs, called Tirmenstein. She loaded up their gear and drove the 200-plus miles to Riggins.

"When I saw the place the vehicle went off the road and checked out the river, I was *sure* it was going to be a wasted effort," said the handler.

"The Salmon is one of the most challenging rivers to dive because of its depth, size and power," said Klobetanz. "It *averages* Class III water, a large pool-and-drop river, averaging 100-150 yards across, 1-2 significant rapids in a 4-mile stretch with smaller riffles and holds in between, offering big, slow eddies in places over 60 feet deep. It is not the kind of river where you go to the bank and wade out. It gets very deep very quick. In the summertime it gets warmer, but it is the kind of river that is on a larger scale than we typically think. Like the Green, the Yampa, the Snake, the Colorado—big western rivers with these characteristics. It is not like the Madison, Yellowstone, Big Horn, Flathead, Arkansas. That larger, deeper, trenched size that swallows vehicles. In smaller rivers people get hung up. In these rivers they can disappear."

This particular year, with a wet, cold spring and summer, the river stayed colder than normal all summer. *Bodies drowned in these larger rivers do not gas up as fast as in warmer waters. Typically 14-30 days in the high cold water.* In this case the pickup truck dropped down the steep bank in a violent roll and crashed upside down.

When Tirmenstein arrived, the fourth day, the divers wanted to know if the dog would alert on the dead horse in the hole. From reading the literature on animal and human cadavers, the handler stated it was possible, although she had never observed the dog alerting on dead animal carcasses either on land or in water.

They put in just below the PLS (point last seen) at Spring Bar in a whitewater raft. Klobetanz rowed, and a support member for one of the dive teams sat in back with a radio to contact the sheriff and rescuers ashore. Riding the front of the raft were Debbie and Choteau.

Klobetanz recalled the search: "One of the first things Debbie said, 'The dog rarely makes a mistake. It's usually the people or the handler.'

"I sent that rolling with OK. I said there was a dead horse the divers had identified at a depth of about 55 feet, several hundred yards downstream from fast water. The fast water went through a relatively shallow fastwater spot into a long, deep, but at the same time turbulent pool that led to a very big rapid. In that long, deep, turbulent pool divers had identified the horse. We got from the fast part through the riffle into the deep turbulent pool right where the river got real deep.

"Choteau grabbed the bow line that was bundled up very much like a throw dummy for retrieving. Debbie said, 'What's that! He's alerting.'

"I said, 'Ten feet off on my right hand is where the dead horse is.' We told everyone later that's where the dog first alerted, maybe that's it. We continued on 100 yards or so to the end of the pool where it continued into a rapid.

"The victim's brother, whom I knew, arrived on the scene at that point saying he'd had a dream, and motioned back up the river to where the dog first alerted, 'My dream says he's there. Can you get back there?'

"In a raft that's sort of difficult. But I worked the eddies and the side soft water for a long time, went back upriver, side-ferried across and caught the eddy, maybe a hundred feet below where the dog first alerted, below and on the far bank. We caught an eddy there, and I saw the dog alert again. It was not as strong an alert, but we were a hundred feet below the first alert. The currents were coming from where he had first alerted.

"Leaving that spot we went down through a large rapid. Much further on, a half mile at least, the dog alerted in another eddy area. In my bird dog experience with a game bird nearby, the dog went birdie. We got out of the boat, and the dog went up and down the shore. In a certain area, the dog got birdie, got excited. We called the divers in. A jet boat came in with the divers and we discussed everything that had

International Scale of River Difficulty

If rapids on a river generally fit into one of the following classifications, but the water temperature is below 50 degrees F., or if the trip is an extended trip in a wilderness area, the river should be considered one class more difficult than normal.

Class I   Moving water with a few riffles and small waves.

Class II   Easy rapids with waves up to three feet, and wide, clear channels that are obvious without scouting. Some maneuvering is required.

Class III   Rapids with high, irregular waves often capable of swamping an open canoe. Narrow passages that often require complex maneuvering. Many require scouting from shore.

Class IV   Long, difficult rapids with constricted passages that often require precise maneuvering in very turbulent waters. Scouting from shore is often necessary and conditions make rescue difficult. Generally not possible for open canoes. Boaters in covered canoes and kayaks should be able to Eskimo roll.

Class V   Extremely difficult, long and very violent rapids with high congested routes which nearly always must be scouted from shore. Rescue conditions are difficult and there is significant hazard to life in event of a mishap. Ability to Eskimo roll is essential for kayaks and canoes.

Class VI   Difficulties of Class V carried to the extreme of navigability. Nearly impossible and very dangerous. For teams of experts only, after close study and with all precautions taken.

happened up to that point.

"They decided to dive in that spot. The handler said, 'I don't want to get a lot of bodies in the water with the dog here,' indicating she would go on down river. The diver said, 'First show us what your dog can do.'

"Debbie brought Choteau in, had the dog run up and down the shore again, and he got excited within this one range. They wanted to know where he was alerting. Standing with her arm angled about 45 degrees upriver, the handler showed them, 'It's on this line where I'm pointing.' The dog swam out into the murky eddy, stuck his head underwater, and circled, biting at the water. 'Let us get back in the water and disappear beyond the bend before you get into the water.' We floated on down river. The dog sat beside her sniffing the air, intent at his search work.

"We went through another long, long slow pool. We heard nothing over the radio. Went through another big rapid, searching. Nothing and nothing. Heard chatter over the radio about finding nothing.

"Debbie turned to me and said, 'Norm, there's something back there.' I said OK, whatever, and we kept searching.

"We were at least a mile down river, we hear over the radio, 'We have a jacket.' On the line where Debbie had pointed, where the dog alerted, approximately 30 feet out and 15 feet down, they found a jacket in the sand, the same color as the sand. Relatives identified it as belonging to the victim. (Diver Larry Hill of Hailey, Idaho, said the coat was three-quarters covered by sand and gravel in the area pinpointed by the dog.) In hindsight, that jacket had washed out of the wreck site.

"We continued on that day and, nothing. The dog did not alert again. We tied the raft up as far as we got. The jet boat picked us up, and we came back upriver through it all.

"We all got together, and we described what had happened with the dog that day. They talked about it all, about the dead horse, the dog's reaction below. That was a very difficult part of the river. Divers had been in there several times. The visibility was poor. The horse was in a pothole at 55 feet. The current falls into a big hole. Big boulders and turbulence.

"The next day we started out right where we had tied the raft up and continued on. The divers involved decided to wait. After finding Bradbury's jacket, they had become believers in the dog. We went on and on until past noon ten miles down river. The dog did not alert again. Meanwhile, looking at the river, the divers had decided the first possible place was where the river gets real ugly, the deep turbid pool. They had decided to go back in there.

"We didn't have a radio person in the boat that day. Somebody came along the road, waved us over and said they just found somebody. We had no idea where. We pulled over, tied the raft up, climbed into the vehicle and drove all the way back. Both Debbie and I are going, well we don't know where it is, but we feel sort of defeated.

"We ended up back at the site of the first alert, in the same big deep area where the dead horse drew us off. At that moment there they were with the body bag on the far side of the river.

"According to the divers, Bradbury's body was 45 feet down, under a rock. At the point of the original alert, where I had reached out with my right hand to fix the location

Smooth laminar flow carries submerged victim scent downstream. In the vortices of an obstruction or base of a waterfall, scent diffuses into the air. Divers who know the river can help predict diffusion patterns.

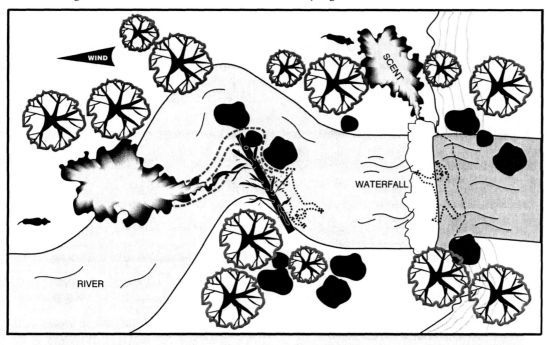

of the dead horse 10 feet away and down, if I'd reached out with my left hand, 10 feet out and down was where Tony lay. The dog's second alert had been 100 feet down river in that strong current, just below the location of the body. The dog had a total of 3 alerts, the first two on the body of the victim, the third on his jacket."

In 1988, a fact sheet was compiled based on 122 water search reports sent to the National Association for Search and Rescue (NASAR) from search dog units around the country. Twenty-six different SAR dog units—from Maine to California and from Washington to Georgia, as well as one in Canada—were represented. Of the 130 victims involved, 84 were found by trained dogs, 24 were recovered out of the area searched and 22 have not yet been recovered. Of the 22 victims not found or recovered, the dog alerts in 9 instances could not be followed up by divers or draggers because the location was too hazardous to the divers, too deep (150 feet), or, in the case of flooded valleys, the remaining trees, buildings and bridges underwater were not suitable for dragging. Information from the source searches was tabulated against seven water types:

1. Rivers, creeks, streams (normal flow)
2. Lakes, ponds, reservoirs (contained)
3. Rivers, creeks, streams (flooded)
4. Catastrophic floods
5. Flooded valleys
6. Tidal areas
7. Other (floating bog, marsh, quarry)

The rate of success using trained dogs was 84% in lake, pond, and reservoir situations. Sixty-eight percent of the victims found were recovered by divers (or in some cases by dragging operations) from the bottom. Dogs have been effective in a wide variety of circumstances: fresh, brackish and salt water, still and moving water, and at various temperatures and depths. *The deepest K-9 detected submersion reported to NASAR through Spring 1994 was 175 feet.*

The statistics for flooded rivers and streams showed 42% of the victims were found outside the area searched by dogs or others. Forty-two percent compared to 16% (normal flow rivers) and 14% (lakes) may be significant. The finds in the flooded river situations were at 23, 40, 10, 13, 12, 17, 3/4 and 1/2 miles from the PLS or point of entry. Victims were located an *average* distance of 13.3 miles from the PLS in flooded rivers, creeks, or streams, while in their normal flow the average distance was 1.1 mile. For contained lakes, ponds, or reservoirs the average distance was 50 yards.

BEAUFORT SCALE

Beaufort Number	Name	Miles Per Hour	Description
0	Calm	<1	calm, smoke rises vertically
1	light air	1-3	direction of wind shown by smoke but not by wind vanes
2	light breeze	4-7	wind felt on face; leaves rustle ordinary vane moved by wind
3	gentle breeze	8-12	leaves and small twigs in constant motion; wind extends light flag
4	moderate breeze	13-18	raises dust and loose paper; small branches are moved
5	fresh breeze	19-24	small trees in leaf begin to sway; crested wavelets form on inland waters
6	strong breeze	25-31	large branches in motion; telegraph wires whistle; umbrellas used with difficulty

Beaufort Number	Name	Miles Per Hour	Description
7	moderate gale	32-38	whole trees in motion; inconvenience in walking against wind
8	fresh gale	39-46	breaks twigs off trees; generally impedes progress
9	strong gale	47-54	slight structural damage occurs; chimney pots and slates removed
10	whole gale	55-63	trees uprooted; considerable structural damage occurs
11	storm	64-73	very rarely experienced; accompanied by wide spread damage
12	hurricane*	74-136	devastation occurs

* The U.S. uses 74 statute mph as the speed criterion for hurricane.

FORCE OF WATER

The force of water against an obstacle such as your legs or a swamped boat increases in proportion to the square of the velocity of the current.

Current Velocity (cubic feet per second)	**Average Total Force of Water** (foot pounds)		
CFS	on legs	on body	on swamped boat
3	16.8	33.6	168
6	67.2	134.0	672
9	151.0	302.0	1512
12	269.0	538.0	2668

Trying to stand hip deep in water would be very difficult even at a current velocity of 3 cfs, particularly if you were trying to cross a stream with a slippery, uneven, rocky bottom.

ESTIMATING CURRENT SPEED

An estimate of the current speed can be made by first measuring a 100 foot length of a river's downstream flow and then observing the time it takes a stick to travel this distance.

Distance: 100'	**Current Speed**		**Distance: 100'**	**Current Speed**	
Seconds	**Feet per Second**	**MPH**	**Seconds**	**Feet per Second**	**MPH**
5	20.0	13.60	25	4.0	2.72
10	10.0	6.80	50	2.0	1.36
15	6.7	4.56	80	1.3	.884
20	5.0	3.40	140	0.7	.676

BUOYANCY AND BOYLE'S LAW

Buoyancy was first described by Archimedes as follows:

"A body immersed in a liquid, either wholly or partially, is buoyed up by a force equal to the weight of the displaced liquid."

Which means that:

- If the weight of displaced liquid is greater than the weight of the immersed object, buoyancy will be positive and the object will float.
- If the weight of the displaced liquid equals the weight of the object, the buoyuancy will be neutral, and the body will remain suspended in the liquid at any depth.
- If the weight of the displaced liquid is less than the weight of the immersed object, buoyancy will be negative and the object will sink.

Boyle's Law states

"The volume of a gas varies inversely with the absolute pressure, while the density varies directly with the absolute pressure provided the temperature remains constant."

National Water Search Report

The Incident -

Show PLS, location of containment techniques, location of clues, and areas of water recovery activities(#)on copy of topo map or diagram.
Date: _____ ; Time: _____ ; Weather: Clear ____ ; Stormy ____ ; Other _____
PLS: _____
Type of incident: boating ____ ; swimming ____ ; storm related ____ ; other _____
Type of water: lake/pond ____ ; marsh/swamp ____ ; tidal water⁺ ____ ; quarry ____ ;
               creek/stream*_ ; river* ____ ; Other _____
        *: Normal flow ____ ; in flood ____, rising stage ____, receding stage ____ .
        +: High tide ____ ; low tide ____ ; slack ____ ; current strong ____ ; other _____
Bottom characteristics: mud/muck ____ ; snags ____ ; rocky/ledges ____ ;
               sand/gravel ____ ; other _____
Water temperature: _____
Clues found: shoe(s) ____ ; hat ____ ; clothing ____ ; other _____
Containment techniques: Monitor downstream dams ____, water falls ____, "holes" ____ .
               Set cross stream/river traps ____ . Other _____
Recovery attempts#: divers ____ ; dragline ____ ; sonar ____ ; other _____
Previous drowning history of area: _____

The Search -

Show location of alerts and clues found on copy of topo map or diagram.

Date(s): _____ ; Time: _____ ; Weather: Clear ____ ; Stormy ____ ; other _____
Unit Name: _____
Water temperature: _____ ; Thermocline(s)? : Depth(s) ____ ____ ____
Air temperature: _____   Estimated wind force: _____ (Beaufort Scale)
Dog alerts and wind direction:
            alert#1, bearing ____ ; alert#2, bearing ____ ; (continue on back).
Dog alerted: from boat ____ ; from shore ____ ; swimming ____ ; other _____ .
Alerts on clothing: yes ____ ; no ____ . Clothing found on surface ____ ; on bottom ____ ;
            on snag ____ ; other _____
Follow up recovery activities: divers ____ , dragline ____ , other _____
Distance searched from PLS: by shore _____ by boat _____

The Find -

Show where body found on copy of topo map or diagram.

Date: _____ ; Time: _____ ; Weather: Clear ____ ; Stormy ____ ; other _____
Location: _____ Distance from PLS _____
Body found: on surface ____ ; floating between surface and bottom ____ ; snagged ____ ;
           on bottom ____, depth _____ . Found by: divers ____ ; dragline ____ ; other _____
Distance of alert to location of body _____ .

Prepared by: _____   Date: _____

Enclose: Copy of annotated topo map or diagram
Send to: NASAR, c/o Marian Hardy 4 Orchard Way N.   Rockville, MD 20854
Rev. 2/88

The Search -

Show location of alerts and clues found on copy of topo map or diagram.

Date(s): _____ ; Time:_____ ; Weather: Clear _____ ; Stormy _____ ; other _____
Unit Name: _____
Water temperature: _____; Thermocline(s)? : Depth(s) _____ _____ _____
Air temperature: _____   Estimated wind force: _____ (Beaufort Scale)
Dog alerts and wind direction:
        alert#1, bearing _____ ; alert#2, bearing _____ ; (continue on back).
Dog alerted: from boat _____ ; from shore _____ ; swimming _____ ; other _____
Alerts on clothing: yes _____ ; no _____ . Clothing found on surface _____ ; on bottom _____;
        on snag _____ ; other _____
Follow up recovery activities: divers _____ , dragline _____ , other _____
Distance searched from PLS: by shore _____ by boat _____

Prepared by: _____   Date: _____

The Search -

Show location of alerts and clues found on copy of topo map or diagram.

Date(s): _____ ; Time:_____ ; Weather: Clear _____ ; Stormy _____ ; other _____
Unit Name: _____
Water temperature: _____; Thermocline(s)? : Depth(s) _____ _____ _____
Air temperature: _____   Estimated wind force: _____ (Beaufort Scale)
Dog alerts and wind direction:
        alert#1, bearing _____ ; alert#2, bearing _____ ; (continue on back).
Dog alerted: from boat _____ ; from shore _____ ; swimming _____ ; other _____
Alerts on clothing: yes _____ ; no _____ . Clothing found on surface _____ ; on bottom _____;
        on snag _____ ; other _____
Follow up recovery activities: divers _____ , dragline _____ , other _____
Distance searched from PLS: by shore _____ by boat _____

Prepared by: _____   Date: _____

The Search -

Show location of alerts and clues found on copy of topo map or diagram.

Date(s): _____ ; Time:_____ ; Weather: Clear _____ ; Stormy _____ ; other _____
Unit Name: _____
Water temperature: _____; Thermocline(s)? : Depth(s) _____ _____ _____
Air temperature: _____   Estimated wind force: _____ (Beaufort Scale)
Dog alerts and wind direction:
        alert#1, bearing _____ ; alert#2, bearing _____ ; (continue on back).
Dog alerted: from boat _____ ; from shore _____ ; swimming _____ ; other _____
Alerts on clothing: yes _____ ; no _____ . Clothing found on surface _____ ; on bottom _____;
        on snag _____ ; other _____
Follow up recovery activities: divers _____ , dragline _____ , other _____
Distance searched from PLS: by shore _____ by boat _____

DYNAMIC HYDROLOGY AND SCENT DIFFUSION

Hydrology is the science of water. Search missions are complicated by the dynamics of this unbreathable medium. Many variables affect the *rate of diffusion* of human scent from a submerged body through the water into the air where the dog is sniffing. Hydraulic flow, geomorphology, chemistry, and temperature of the water conspire with the body chemistry, mass, and surface area, time to rescue, and wind above the water to determine, first, if the dog can detect the victim and, second, if the operation becomes a rescue or a recovery.

Tactically, the knowledge of water and recognition of hazards are essential tools for the handlers as well as the divers, boatmen and technical teams who perform searches in this environment. *Reading the water* increases operational safety and identifies good places to look for a victim.

Nobody knows this better than two experienced water searchers with diverse professions who have written articulately about water search and rescue. Surviving more than a few exciting SAR incidents on rivers and rocks from Alaska to Yosemite, first as a ranger, later as a chief ranger in the National Park Service, Tim J. Setnicka wrote in his comprehensive book, *Wilderness Search & Rescue:* "There *are* much better ways of performing whitewater search and rescue operations than grabbing a rope and jumping into the froth. Whitewater is any stream, river, creek, waterfall, or other rapidly flowing body of water which creates turbulence as it flows over, around, and through natural or manmade obstacles. Anyone involved in whitewater SAR should have a basic knowledge of whitewater features."

Marian Hardy, a kayaker and dog handler with Mid-Atlantic D.O.G.S., has authored K-9 water search articles, prepared the National Water Search Report, and has been active nationally encouraging the use of dogs as a water search resource. In "How to Develop and Train a Water Search Dog Team," *Response* (Winter 1993), Hardy concludes: "An agency requesting water search dog teams should expect to get teams that can search from a boat or shore for one or more drowned victims in extensive areas of water, such as lakes, ponds, quarries, reservoirs, rivers, streams, estuaries and bays. Dog teams should be comfortable and experienced in searching from various types of boats under various weather conditions. Dog handlers who search rivers and streams with fast currents should be knowledgeable about river hazards and the necessary safety precautions."

Scent diffuses from the submerged body in three forms:

1. Soluble solids, liquids, and gases (peptides, amino acids, carbon dioxide, hydrogen sulfide, methane) dissolve and diffuse in the water. Scent diffuses into the air by evaporation (dog sniffs the air).
2. Insoluble molecules lighter than water rise to the surface and float (dog bites the water).
3. Gases diffuse directly into the air (dog sniffs the air).

General rules for scent diffusion in water:

↑ Turbulent flow (vortices)   = ↑ Rate of diffusion into the air

↑ Laminar flow (currents)   = ↑ Rate of diffusion through the water

In general, we would expect a high rate of diffusion directly above an area of turbulence or vertical mixing, while a strong laminar flow would probably carry the scent downstream before it diffuses into the air. These values change for each incident. Predicting the combined effect of these processes (rate of diffusion in water and air) is tricky to impossible during a search. The dog may not indicate the precise spot where the body is, or he may detect scent at two different locations, neither directly above the victim. The body may be moving during the search operation. In a river the dog will generally alert downstream from the victim. Once the scent diffuses into the air, however, the air currents take over. Studying the types of water and typical hazards will help the handler deploy his dog most effectively.

The term *river* is broadly defined as any rapidly flowing body of water moving through a channel characterized by numerous rapids or waterfalls and obstacles. *Rapids* are any area of rough, turbulent water flow. The sizes and types of rapids are infinite in number. They are formed by the interrelationship of river gradient (elevation change or slope); the number, size, and type of obstacles; the narrowness of the channel; and the rate and volume of fluid flow.

Frequently, as water surges into a rapid, large waves form that seem to be fixed in place. These stationary *standing waves,* unlike the progressive motion of ocean waves, are generated by water continuously coursing over fixed obstructions. Normally arrayed in rows perpendicular to the current, they usually mark the river's deepest and fastest pitches. The largest of these, up to 9 feet, are commonly called haystacks. Turbulence causes a high rate of diffusion.

Eddies are pockets of calm water, often moving in a circle or even upstream, located on the downstream side of obstructions like rocks. For kayakers and rafters, they provide ideal resting spots in the middle of rapids, and allow time to recover from one set or problems and to chart the route through the next. A vacuum is created by fast-moving water flowing around an obstacle, much like the dead spot behind a large trailer truck that encourages slipstreaming by small cars. This low pressure area is a haven of calm water in the midst of the flow. A low rate of diffusion occurs directly above or downstream of the body.

The boundary between an eddy and the fast downstream current is sharp. Unless handled properly in a strong current, a boat can get into difficulty at this boundary. Imagine that you are in a boat that either leaves the eddy or leaves the fast downstream current. Either way, there are opposing pressures on opposite ends of the boat. If the maneuver is not executed properly the boat may capsize.

Entrapment is the pinning of someone in or under the water. Even if the victim can keep his head elevated, he can quickly

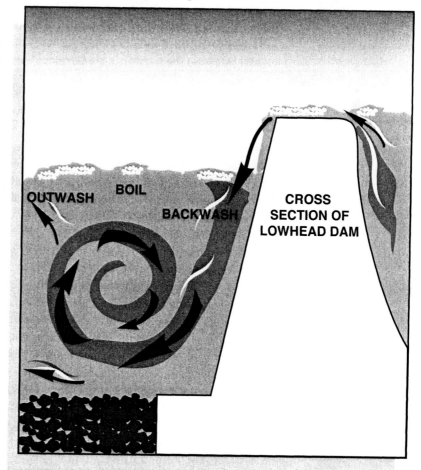

Fluid flow over low-head dam. Victims sucked into the hydraulic backwash current are recycled until they escape at the bottom downstream, swim across to shore, or disintegrate.

OUTWASH   BOIL

BACKWASH

CROSS SECTION OF LOWHEAD DAM

come under the influence of immersion hypothermia and eventually drown. If trapped underwater, the results are obvious. Entrapment can happen in relatively shallow water, measuring at least above the knees, when a person who is walking across a current loses his balance and, for example, catches his foot between two stones or snags his clothing. Pressure on the victim's body forces him downstream while the jammed foot or snared clothing anchors him, and he cannot free himself. The other type of entrapment pins the boater between a raft or canoe and a rock or bridge abutment. Scent diffuses at a high rate downstream or at the surface of the obstruction.

At any place along a river's course, a *strainer* may develop. Anything that combs the water passing through it and can block the passage of an object in the current, such as a swimmer or boat, is a strainer: trees, bridge abutments or pillars, pipes or cables. In the early seventies, several rafters were killed in an accident while floating the Snake River in Wyoming with professional guides when their raft was pinned against a bridge piling.

If a strainer is approached incorrectly, the rescue boat could swamp and get stranded or pinned against it by the force of the current. If you find yourself in the water, probably the best thing to do (depending on the circumstances) is to try to climb up and wait for help. Do not try to swim down and under. If you become entangled under water, the current will hold you there, with obvious consequences. Fast current can carry a boat into overhanging branches, trees and undercut banks on the outside curves of a stream with much the same hazard and outcome as being caught by strainers. Scent typically diffuses at a high rate along the strainer and downstream.

Strainers are one of the best places to look for victims, particularly those in flood-related incidents. There are underwater strainers, too. They do not have any effect at the surface, of course, but they are effective collection areas for submerged bodies. In a flood situation, the river has probably exceeded its banks and may have taken a shortcut across the bends and curves of its normal course, so the search area also includes the land area over which the water flowed. Strainers then might be a riverside forest, fences, hedgerows or buildings.

Probably the most potentially dangerous features that form in whitewater, Setnicka writes, are *reversals*, also known as *holes* or *hydraulics*. When water flows over an object beneath the surface, it curls upward and back upon itself. The largest holes, usually behind large, steep rocks, can hold a swimmer or boat in suspension. Holes are readily identified by floating debris circling in one spot instead of moving downstream in an area of strong currents and rapids. The most serious occur wherever water falls the quickest over a barrier—at dams and waterfalls. Holes can easily trap a body, and very often are too dangerous to search. Scent diffuses at a high rate above the hydraulic, and wind direction will affect detectability.

Waterfalls of any size pose obvious hazards by greatly increasing the probability of upset craft, traumatic injuries, and entrapment in large hydraulics. The handler whose search dog alerts into shallow riffles downstream of a turbulent falls may expect the body to be trapped in a hydraulic or held down by eddies at the base of the falls.

Low-head dams, usually man-made structures 6 inches to 10 feet high across a river or stream, present a great, insidious threat to swimmers or boaters. From upstream these dams may be undetectable. If an engineer designed an efficient, unattended, self-powered drowning machine, it would be hard to come up with anything more effective than a low-head dam, writes Canadian Virgil Chambers, chief of the Fish Commission Bureau of Waterways Boating Education Section. Hazards exist, not only from going over the dam, an obvious source of danger, but also below the dam is the backwash, where the power of the water is frequently overlooked.

Anything caught in this backwash below the dam is trapped and recycled round and round, making escape or rescue most difficult. A person (or boat) caught in the backwash of a dam will be carried to the face of the dam, where water pouring over it will wash him down under and back beneath the boil. When the victim struggles to the surface, the backwash again carries him to the face of the dam, thus continuing the cycle. This process can continue for many hours or days until the water volume over the dam or something downstream changes the character of the backwash. Scent diffuses at a very high rate from bodies churning in the backwash.

To complicate matters, these dams are usually loaded with debris (tires or logs on the surface, rocks or steel bars on the bottom) posing another serious problem for the circulating victim. If rescue is not immediate and the victim is to survive and escape this water trap, he may go down with the current coming over the face of the dam, stay as close to the bottom as possible, and try to get past the crest of the boil before resurfacing. This maneuver is very difficult, and few have done it.

Another method of escape, with rescuers available, is for the victim to try lateral movement across the dam after each cycle. This involves proper breathing control and great endurance. If the victim is able to work his way to the side of the dam, rescuers may then be able to assist him out of the powerful backwash. In either case, the chances of survival are much greater if the victim is wearing a PFD (personal floatation device).

Dams do not have to have a deep drop to create a dangerous backwash. During periods of high water and heavy rains, the backwash current problems get worse, and the reach of the backwash current is extended downstream. Small low-head dams that may have provided a refreshing wading spot at low water can become a monstrous death trap when river levels are up.

K-9 teams searching from boats are at risk here too. Avoid the hazard and search the backwash zone from the shore if possible, but never from a boat downstream of the dam. Even with a strong motor, writes Hardy, the backwash is stronger, and the boat may be sucked upstream into the drowning machine. There are fast water rescue groups that are trained to handle this sort of rescue and know the techniques that work. Let them do it.

Ledges, natural forms of a low-head dam, are exposed edges of rock strata in the water that may stretch across all or part of a river or stream. Depending on the variation in rock strata, the continuing vertical action of the water may have carved out an underwater cavity that can collect debris, including the victim. Specific local knowledge of these features is important. Ask questions.

Tidal waters or estuaries have an ebb and flow of the tide as well as their own various currents, all of which may affect the victim's location. The circulation patterns in estuaries may be linear (horizontal or vertical) or vortical (angular velocity), depending on the shape and gradient of the bottom. Tidal marshes may be deceiving because of the changing water levels affecting the logic of where a victim might have gone. These marshes may have deep, foot-holding mud, which has trapped small victims. Tidal waters are typically not contained, and local knowledge and drowning histories of the area are critical to determining where to search.

Non-tidal marshes and swamps may be associated with streams or lakes, but they can be as hazardous to the searcher as to the victim: poisonous snakes, unstable footing, thick vegetation that obstructs scent diffusion. Under some conditions, the searcher can actually be up to his ass in alligators, but he can't drain the swamp. Discussing a mission in Southern Maryland, Marian Hardy said, "Apparently the man's scent was pooling along the water surface. It dissipated and went all over the place, up all the little creeks that fed into the marsh. The dogs consistently alerted on the water in general."

Lakes and ponds can be large or small, natural or man-made, deep or shallow, weed-bound or clear, spring-fed or still, and there may or may not be scent-inhibiting thermoclines. The one characteristic that lakes and ponds have in common is they are a natural containment feature. If the victim is there, he will stay there for the searchers to find. Quarries are usually rain-filled or spring-fed, are deep, cold, and may have underwater or submerged caves. They are also natural containment features.

The water in lakes, ponds, and reservoirs usually does not have fluid flow like a river. Dam release of the water is an exception. The earth's rotational force (Coriolis force) has a slow drift

Even with a strong motor, writes Hardy, the backwash is stronger, and the boat may be sucked upstream into the drowning machine.

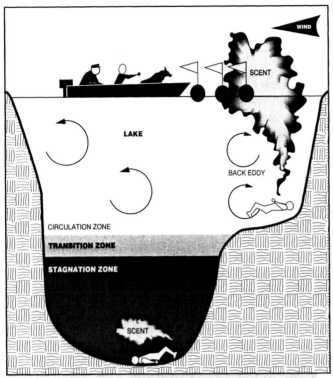

effect in large, deep bodies of water. The force of wind on the surface causes circulation and the mixing action constantly at work in confined bodies of water. The propellers of motorboats add a mixing effect.

We have all heard, "We'll wait until the body floats, if we can't find it soon." What happens in relatively deep water? What about gases formed by decay? Will the volume of water displaced by the body increase until a neutral state of buoyancy is achieved and the body starts to float? This process does occur when the water temperature reaches 38°F or warmer and the water is not very deep. At temperatures below 38°F, there is preservation by refrigeration. Depending on temperatures and other factors, the time for a body to surface ranges from immediately, to days (warm water) or weeks (cold water), to never.

Understanding *pressure principles* clarifies what to expect. Water has weight because the force of gravity pulls on each molecule of water. Water pressure is equal in all directions at any given depth and is measured in pounds per square inch (psi). The pressure increases by 0.433 PSI for each foot of depth in fresh water (fw) (0.445 psi in salt water). In other words at 34 feet, the water pressure alone has increased by 14.7 psi (fw), or one atmosphere of air pressure at sea level. At 68 feet, the water pressure is two atmospheres. Where the body is submerged 150 feet or deeper, close to 4.5 extra atmospheres of water pressure hold the victim down.

Scent diffusing from a body submerged in the circulation zone will surface. Depth, water temperature, and turbulence determine scent density. If too low, the dog will not alert. Scent diffusing from a body submerged in the stagnation zone of a deep lake may not escape the hydrostatic layer to reach the surface.

Therefore, the deeper the victim descends, the less likely he is to rise to the surface. As the depth increases, the pressure increases and the body density increases because the body cavities collapse. Boyle's Law states that in order to *inflate* the cavities sufficiently to increase the body's buoyancy, the pressure of the gases in the cavity would have to exceed that of the surrounding water—not likely to happen naturally.

Water density changes with temperature: most dense at 39.2°F, less dense for higher or lower water temperatures. For lake, pond or reservoir-type systems, two factors determine temperature: 1) incident solar energy, 2) wind mixing of the warmer surface water with the colder water below.

In temperate lakes over 200 feet (60 meters) deep (first order), the bottom water is at the temperature of maximum density, 39.2° F (4° C), year round. After the ice cover thaws in spring, the surface water gradually warms from 32°F to 39.2°F (0—4°C), within which temperature range its density increases. Vertical circulation commences as the surface reaches the bottom water temperature. After this *spring turnover*, the surface rises above 39.2°F and its density decreases as it continues to warm through the summer.

As a result, a sharp division forms between the upper and lower waters of the lake. The deeper, colder layer is sealed off from the top by a zone of rapid thermal transition, called the thermocline. Oxygen cannot diffuse through the thermocline from the warmer layer. In some lakes, hydrogen sulfide, a toxic gas, forms in the stagnate bottom layers. During the period of summer stagnation, vertical circulation is induced by wind, but this force is not strong enough to cause mixing of the bottom water, the hypolimnion. *Scent from a body on the bottom or suspended in the hypolimnion may not penetrate the thermocline. If it cannot diffuse into the circulation zone above, it will not reach the dog's nose.*

The fall and winter cooling again reduces the surface temperature to its maximum density, and the *fall turnover* occurs.

A similar turnover occurs in lakes of the second order, 25—200 feet deep. In the second order lake, the bottom temperature changes measurably but is never far from that of maximum density. In lakes of less than about 25 feet deep (third order), vertical circulation is induced almost exclusively by wind action rather than density differences, so there is little difference between surface and bottom temperatures.

If a person dies by inhaling water, a *wet drowning*, the rule-of-thumb is the recovery will be made within a circle whose radius equals the water's depth. Water intake reduces the victim's buoyancy, and the victim alternates between negative and neutral buoyancy, either going to the bottom or hanging submerged. If the body is not located, the reported point last seen (PLS) may not be accurate and the use of dogs could be helpful. If a search dog alerts out of a boat or starts swimming in circles over one spot in a calm lake, divers should search down at that point.

If the dog detects nothing, the body may have descended beneath a thermocline into the hypolimnion or stagnant area. *The thermocline acts as a barrier to scent diffusion.* Unless the force of high wind or artificial mixing (boat propeller, high pressure hose) *breaches* that barrier, the rate of diffusion may be too low for scent detection. In these cases, underwater cameras or other technical search methods may be more effective.

Dry drowning (little or no water enters the lungs) is less frequent. The victim experiences an automatic physiological blockage of the breathing passage associated with a traumatic incident before entering the water or the shock of entering cold water. Lung volume maintains buoyancy and the body will float on or near the surface. In cold water near-drowning, if the mammalian diving reflex (MDR) occurs, and if rescue arrives in time, the person may survive.

Handlers should be aware of the condition of the water system at the time the incident occurred. Conditions may be different by the time the search operation begins. Those changes will affect your search tactics.

K-9 WATER SEARCH STRATEGY AND TACTICS

Preplan: Current maps of the area (river or lake and surrounding topography) should be available to search units. Indicate potential or known water hazards on the maps. Aerial photographs of the river or lake and the shorelines provide references for planning. Annotated photos at low, medium, high, and flood levels will help identify differences in hazards and accessibility. All of these support documents need review and revision on a regular basis.

The SAR history of the area, both from mission files and local annecdotes, will help shape future search strategy. Compare past search techniques with the presently proposed SAR plans. Many water searches where the body of water is contained can be preplanned better than general area searches or other types of disasters. The ICS, whether a single command (river, lake, or bay in one jurisdiction) or a unified command (multi-jurisdictional or multiple agencies share responsibility), can be quickly established in order to maximize the operational effectiveness of the reconnaissance and hasty search.

K-9 team training prerequisites:
- Swimming skills (handler and dog)
- Safety training

  "If you don't want to swim in it, don't boat on it," boatmen say. Learn the basic self-rescue techniques for the type water you will be searching, still or fast water. If the boat capsizes, the tactics of searching change to the tactics of survival. People come first. Let the dog go. Dogs seem to instinctively know what to do in a current. Do not let the K-9 become a liability.
- Boating (typical boats and waterways) safety and navigation

Learn the operations and limits of the boats that may be used as a K-9 search platform. Speed, range, the best places for the dog in the boat, getting the dog from the water into the boat, communicating with the driver, all these should be worked out in advance of the mission.

- K-9 water search capability (from shore, boat, swimming)
  The dog has trained with divers and gives a readable alert to submerged bodies under various conditions. Typical K-9 water alerts: trying to jump into the water, rapid shifting in the boat, tail wagging, head ducking, sniffing deeply and rapidly, barking, grabbing things in the boat, biting at the water. The handler is able to read, reinforce, and report his dog's alerts. The dog team has shown reliability performing to the certifying agency's standard.

Equipment:

- PFD (handler's own personal floatation device)
- Dry bags (positive buoyancy, water tight) for radios, first aid, camera, personal gear (tie gear to the boat, not the handler or boat driver)
- Radios (K-9 team, divers, boat drivers, technical SAR, shore personnel)
- Whistle (secured to handler)
- Knife (one-hand access)
- Thermometer (air and water temperatures)
- Light (waterproof, also secured to handler)
- Small map case (record alerts)
- Boat (dog can sniff near the surface of the water, minimal exhaust fumes)
- GPS unit (global positioning system) or compass (report location and direction of alert)
- Buoys/flagging (mark location of alert)
- Small throw rope

Reconnaissance and Hasty Search

The urgency of a water incident calls for a firehouse response. Trained dog teams may react as part of this initial phase, or they may be held at a staging area ready to deploy. The incident operations chief begins tactical operations immediately. Hasty search teams leapfrog to quickly survey both sides of the river or the lake shore for someone in immediate danger, hanging onto a rock or a branch, or who has made it to safety. The K-9 searching during this rapid response period may alert downwind of a live victim who can then be rescued, or he may sniff evidence that will lead to finding the victim. A strike team of three boats may run the entire watercourse where the missing person could have gone down, taking one dog team along. Divers may immediately search the PLS. Hasty teams should be noting likely catchment areas for dogs to check if a detailed search becomes necessary.

Calculating the time lapse before notification, perimeter units should be dispatched downriver beyond the distance the river could have carried the victim after immersion. Confinement boundaries can be calculated by multiplying the time that has elapsed since the accident times the river's velocity. Slow shallow water may form a natural perimeter. If no obvious slack water is evident, a lookout with minimal rescue gear may be posted at a clear observation point like a bridge or road intersection.

A helicopter is highly advantageous for a fast and complete hasty search. Large aircraft that cannot fly *low and slow* make less adequate aerial observation platforms. Hovering or landing capability is needed for insertions or extractions. Leapfrogging by heli-inserting dog teams at intervals along a river course or lake shore increases hasty search effectiveness. Canyon winds and whitewater are special hazards for K-9 teams attempting to debark helicopters or negotiate rocky riverbeds. It is not possible to overstate the importance of good judgment in these situations.

Nor can we overstate the importance of good communications among all the functional units, single resources as well as task forces. Aircraft, divers, boatmen, and K-9 teams have to be able to talk to each other, or else they can quickly put each other at risk.

Detailed Search

If a hasty search and repeated sweeps of the helicopter and boat crews reveal nothing, the incident command triages the search area and dispatches resources for an extended search effort. A dog team can work from accessible shoreline or from a boat. Scent rising from the victim to the water surface is first acted upon by the various currents in the water, then diffusion into the air subjects the scent to air currents. The size and depth of the body of water to be investigated, wind direction and force, as well as air and water temperatures determine what approach to take. Ideally, dog teams should search downwind of high probability areas first.

Small lakes, ponds, or creeks can often be searched from the shore. Boats should deploy to

grid search large bodies of water. Alerts marked with a buoy and located on a map give divers a reference point to start underwater search operations. Human scent from a buoy, people on shore or in other boats can distract the dog. For the same reason, as soon as divers arrive to search a location, reassign the dog team to another area.

The oarsman or driver must be proficient with his boat. A search is not a training session in this regard. But he may need instruction from the handler about air scent strategy, where to go, how fast, how far away, when to drift, and to keep the motor exhaust downwind of the dog. *Part of the handler's training is guiding the boat driver and the divers.* All three are integral to a successful rescue and, working together on the water, become members of the same task force. A fourth element, the technical search team (camera or other detection devices), may provide essential information, particularly in deep lake water.

Depending on availability, helicopters can be useful in the detailed search phase transporting search crews and equipment while continuing to look for the victim. Light changes throughout the day. When sunlight penetrates a hole or overhang or crevasse, an airborne observer might be able to see a body that is undetectable from any other point. Air search may be critical to pinpointing a location when the dog is alerting toward a high risk area. Obviously, a low altitude helicopter inspection of the alert location must be coordinated, because the propeller wash will break up the air flow carrying the scent to the dog's nose. An experienced pilot can sometimes direct his rotor downdraft to *part the water*, making a body visible or even bringing it to the surface. There have been cases where the blade turbulence has increased the rate of diffusion, changing a weak K-9 indication into a strong full-blown alert.

Give the boat driver clear directions.

Have a harness or other plan to get the wet dog back into the boat.

The K-9 may swim safe areas of water that cannot be searched from shore or from a boat. Swimming the dog requires the ability to direct the dog at a distance, including calling the dog off an alert when he is headed into unsafe water. This too should not be tried for the first time on an actual search.

Debriefing

Recording as precisely as possible where each dog searched and the location of every alert may be the only way the dog teams can ever estimate how effective they were. Without real time feedback, behavior shaping is difficult. Even when the agency calls three days later and says, "The body came up right where the dog was indicating," there are too many variables to erase all doubt. Often the handler never knows the final disposition. Once in a great while the handler is rewarded by a *hands-on* recovery.

A 36-year-old man was flyfishing the Truckee River east of Reno, Nevada. When he failed to return home to his 5 children and pregnant wife, the next day, a deputy located his truck, his fishing pole, and his line snagged across the river. That is all they knew. He had been wearing a white T-shirt with "No. 1 DAD" on the front, blue jeans, and hip waders. The river bottom was rocky and slippery, only 3 feet deep in most places except for intermittent deep holes, but it was rushing. It averaged 40 yards wide. The air temperature was in the high 70's during the day. On the third day, the department called out a search dog team.

When Judy Salviolo and her German shepherd Silas began searching the river, the dog had the initial confusion of divers upwind. Part of the time the team worked along the high bank, then from a small boat:

"He had this bomber alert. He jumped off the bank but lost it. So he came back up and again alerted way up high. The wind was blowing diagonally from a large hole in the river below a dropoff. I told the divers the dog was really interested in something. By then they were all out of the water, and I was confident it wasn't them.

"The water was so swift. We went back upriver, got in the boat, and floated down to the small island where the water was flowing over the rocks into the hole. Coming down, the dog jumped out of the boat, swimming right to where he had the alert. Two of the divers came through but found nothing. We worked all along the edge of a rock bar, but the dog just boom alerted in the one area and kept returning to it. He was pawing and biting the water. In between he ran to the bank and grabbed sticks, playing, grabbing every stick he could grab.

"The water was swift on both sides but calm in the middle. The divers swam back. They found him 10 feet down at the entrance to the hole. His body was at a point where it was very still. The scent was diffusing laterally and up where the water was coming over the rocks. The divers expected him to be hung up somewhere, but apparently his waders sank him like a stone. The dog's strongest alerts were about 50 yards downstream of the body. He also had strong alerts about 30 yards away. There was no chance the body could have been spotted from the air because the water was so turbid. We were working in a strong breeze, maybe 15 knots. But it was squirrelly. You'd walk 10 feet and it would be different. Trying to put all that together was interesting.

"The victim was face-down when found. When the divers brought him up, as soon as they turned him over, he let out an air bubble with the strong scent of rapid decomposition. Three times Silas ran over to sniff him. I was glad for the opportunity to reinforce the dog."

The National Association for Search and Rescue (NASAR) is a resource center for education and training worldwide in many rescue disciplines. To obtain information or to contact fast water trainers or urban disaster specialists:

NASAR
4500 Southgate Place, Suite 100
Chantilly, Virginia 20151
(703) 222-NASR (6277)
FAX (703) 222-6283
www.nasar.org

DISASTER SEARCH

Natural forces—avalanches, earthquakes, floods, fires, storms—continue to prevail over our environment. These natural phenomena are compounded by what we do to ourselves—air crashes, explosions, structure collapse, hazmat incidents, and man-caused fires. Past disasters have demonstrated to the agencies in charge of the aftermath that major urban disasters demand an order of magnitude higher level of training and response capability for the 21st century.

> You must realize that when dealing with building collapse, very little can be done to control the environment. One false move during the evolution could result in an injury or fatality to rescue personnel. A good friend of mine, James Gargan said it best, "You either do it right or you will wear the building."
> —Battalion Chief Chase N. Sargent,
> Virginia Beach, Virginia Fire Department

The task is rescuing people from pain and saving their lives. The key is *reliability*. Vital to saving people who are alive but invisible under tons of debris are reliable detection tools to pinpoint the victim locations, so that heavy rescue teams can do their job effectively. Random rubble removal costs time, manpower, and millions of dollars.

Ben Schifrin, MD, FACEP, Medical Team Manager for the Sacramento USAR (Urban Search and Rescue) Task Force compiled these earthquake rescue data for the Tenth Annual Scientific Meeting of the Wilderness Medical Society:

USAR:

Evolution of USAR in USA
- Threat of nuclear war (Cold War)
  — Civil Defense System
- Earthquakes — Birth of USAR
- Foreign service
  — Armenia, Philippines Quakes
- Hurricane Hugo and Loma Prieta Quake
  — Development of graded response

Structure collapse victim rescue scenarios
- Injured but not trapped
  (struck by falling debris)..................... 50%
- Non-structural entrapment
  (by furniture and debris) 30%
- Void space entrapment
  (inside collapsed structure) 15%
- Entombed
  (pinned by structure itself).................. 5%

Sixty percent of all structure collapse deaths are rescuers

Armenia Earthquake:
- Entrapped victims who did not get medical aid in the rubble went on to die — usually from Crush Injury Syndrome
- Experience repeated in other disasters is rationale for ALS (advanced life support) care at the rescue scene

Mexico City Earthquake:
- 135 rescuers died • 65 rescuers drowned
Causes of rescuer death
- Underground and ditch drownings
- Heavy equipment used over rescuers

Survival rate of entrapped victims gives rise to the concept of a "Golden 24 Hours" in confined space medicine
- 30 minutes 99%
- 1 day 81%
- 2 days.. 33%
- 4 days 5%
- 5 days 7%

Confined space and heavy rescue is slow, each live entrapped victim requiring 3-4 hours and 8-20 rescuers for extrication

Northridge Earthquake:
- The event: Monday, January 17, 1994: 4:31 a.m.: Martin Luther King Birthday holiday
- Magnitude 6.8; duration 40 seconds;
- Shallow epicenter and vertical thrust
- More damage than Loma Prieta, magnitude 7.3

The human tragedy:
- 61 deaths
- 7757 EMS and ED treated in LA County (2004 in first 24 hours)
- 736 injuries: Ventura County
- 1496 admits (506 in first 24 hours)
- 10% of all households: at least 1 quake-related medical emergency
- No murders reported for 48 hours!

Handler Vikki Fenton's Cher *finds pieces of flesh and teeth after a fiery jet crash near downtown Billings, Montana.*

BILLINGS GAZETTE/ JAMES WOODCOCK

Structural damage:
- $30 billion damage
- 30,000 structures destroyed
- 250,000 structures significant damage
- 100 major alarm fires: 3 hours for control
- 3000 major water main disruptions
- ARCO pipeline spills oil into 12 miles of Santa Clarita River
- Train derailment: sulfuric acid spill

Impact on SAR and EMS response
- Collapse of Highway 101 and Interstates 5, 10, 210, and 405
- Hundreds of overpass closures; multiple landslides
- Loss of LA County Dispatch Center computers
- 3 Fire/ALS stations destroyed
- 8 of 12 local hospitals heavily damaged: 18 hospital closures
- 8 hospital evacuations with 928 patients; 2500 acute beds lost
- Only 136 ICU beds in LA County for first 24 hours

Major Northridge USAR rescue scenes

Northridge Mall Parking Structure
- Adult male in mini-streetsweeper
- 20,000 pounds of concrete pin victim under 3 stories

Northridge Meadows Apartments
- 163 units; 3-story wood frame
- Pancake collapse of bottom floor
- Over 35 live rescues
- 16 dead, all on first floor
- 8 extrications by fire rescue services
- 3 fully entombed require full USAR tools for rescue

4-story home: 1 live, 1 dead extrication

Federal response:
- 10 FEMA/OES USAR Task Forces activated for rescue
- 10 OD/PHS DMAT Hospital Teams supplement damaged hospitals
- FEMA Management Teams oversee response and recovery efforts

But, hey, it could have been worse:
The Tangshan Earthquake in rural China

- July 28, 1976; magnitude 7.8
- Early morning: most victims in bed
- Pre-Quake: victims sat up
- Quake: falling debris struck heads
- 242,769 dead
- 361,300 injured — high incidence of lumbar compression and neck injuries
- 20% injuries Crush Syndrome

The disaster finds that have been credited to dogs are newsworthy. Less well known are the ineffectual dog searches due to inadequate training or inappropriate dogs or handlers. The dog that digs up objects *hot* with human scent. The dog that wastes valuable time and resources alerting to dead animals. The dog that does not give strong, clear alerts or is unsure on rubble, or tires prematurely. The handler who is not prepared for disaster search.

Achieving reliability in disaster detection means training and maintaining *strategically located, full time professional Task Forces*. The search and rescue teams, including disaster dogs, must be transported to the disaster site within hours of the incident occurrence. If possible, such strike teams should be flown to the scene, and must operate effectively at any hour in any weather. They must be fully qualified and completely self-contained with all necessary personnel, equipment, logistics, and security in order to operate independently without support from the affected area. There can be no freelancing. *Everyone must have the tactical training to deploy through an organized Incident Command System with a reportable chain of command.*

Police dogs typically have the drive, search capability, and trainability for urban disaster search. The police dog or candidate canine with the drives for suspect searching quickly understands the disaster discipline. The K-9 is typically eager to target victims' scents and give a barking, digging alert. Although the rubble encountered in disaster work is much more difficult than the standard police obstacle course, the confident dog can learn to move about in a safe manner to prevent injury. Handler ability to control and direct the dog at a distance and a strong canine drive to penetrate small spaces to reach the target are both necessary for disaster search. The amount of training required is formidable.

The challenge for law enforcement agencies is *time, training and deployment time, and costs*. Dedicated tasking is critical to the success of K-9s in USAR, just as in narcotics or any other special detection function. The partially qualified dog will waste time and resources and will ultimately affect the outcome of potential survivors. Disaster dog teams need an academy period of supervised clinical training and certification followed by regular maintenance training and operations, including remediation as needed, and periodic recertification.

Disaster response teams, like firefighters, law enforcement officers, and emergency medical responders, incur considerable liability for their actions in the field. The agencies that deploy these teams are also held liable for the actions performed while search and rescue teams are working within the scope and course of their employment. *Failure to train* due to lack of professional support for K-9 teams will cause accidents that will result in damaged lives and extensive litigation.

CANINE SEARCH SPECIALIST

The FEMA (Federal Emergency Management Agency) US&R System is the federal organizational structure for urban disaster search and rescue. Individual state agencies cooperate with the federal agency and have developed their own standards and procedures based on the federal requirements. Following are the General and Specific Requirements and Criteria for the Canine Search Specialist (1994):

FEMA
CANINE SEARCH SPECIALIST

GENERAL REQUIREMENTS AND CRITERIA

1. Must be at least 21 years of age.

2. Must be physically fit according to the standards of the sponsoring organization. However, there cannot be any physical or mental handicaps, limitations or conditions which would preclude the ability of an individual to safely perform any required tasks.

3. Must be currently certified in at least American Red Cross First Responder and Cardiopulmonary Resuscitation—Basic Life Support or equivalent.

4. Must have successfully completed the First Responder Awareness Program for Hazardous Materials—NFPA 472.

5. Must be aware of the signs, symptoms and corrective measures of critical incident stress syndrome.

6. Must be available on short notice to mobilize within 6 hours of request and be self-sufficient for at least 72 hours for a response assignment of up to 10 days.

7. Must be capable of improvising and functioning for long hours under adverse conditions.

8. Must have a working knowledge of FEMA's US&R Response System, organizational structure, operating procedures, safety practices, terminology and communications protocols.

9. Must understand the needs of and provide support to their counterparts within the task force for specific operations, techniques and application of tools and equipment.

10. Must understand and adhere to safe working practices and procedures as required in the urban disaster environment.

11. Must maintain current inoculations for Diphtheria/Tetanus (or Tetanus only if there is a contra-indication to Diphtheria), Hepatitis B, Measles/Mumps/Rubella (if born after 1957), and Polio.

FEMA
CANINE SEARCH SPECIALIST

SPECIFIC REQUIREMENTS AND CRITERIA

1. Must currently be an operational search dog handler recognized by a state or local government organization responsible for search and rescue.

2. Practical knowledge of general search strategy and tactics, including:
   A. One year search and rescue experience, with a minimum of 5 actual search missions.
   B. "Probability of Detection" analysis.
   C. Victim behavior patterns in various situations.
   D. Search pattern selection criteria including terrain, structures, wind, weather and air circulation characteristics.
   E. Search team organization and operational procedures.
   F. Understanding of canine search operations including team size, check/recheck procedures and observer responsibilities.
   G. Understanding of the general capabilities and limitations of technical/electronic search equipment.
   H. Understanding of general rescue strategy and tactics.

3. Practical knowledge of the technical aspects of search theory, including:
   A. Map and compass techniques.
   B. Ability to accurately sketch a search area.
   C. Ability to apply and interpret search area marking techniques for perimeters, alert areas, hazards, etc.
   D. Understand search area sectoring.
   E. Recognize and identify victim location clues.
   F. Practical knowledge of night search techniques, including increased hazard awareness and applicable air circulation characteristics.

4. Practical knowledge of the theory and techniques of searching collapsed structures, including:
   A. Recognizing and identifying hazards associated with structural collapse and its environment.
   B. Structural features and conditions that contribute to a high probability of victim survival in a collapsed structure.
   C. Understanding the need for flexibility and coordination during multiple search operations.
   D. Understanding of air circulation characteristics in various environments.

CANINE SEARCH SPECIALIST

SPECIFIC REQUIREMENTS AND CRITERIA (continued)

5. **Practical ability to apply search strategy, tactics and procedures at collapse sites, including:**
   A. Understanding of US&R mission operational procedures.
   B. Understanding of the size-up and reconnaissance considerations of an affected area.
   C. Understanding of specific size-up and reconnaissance considerations of an assigned work site.
   D. Understanding of US&R equipment and tools utilization.
   E. Able to integrate with local resources and other teams.

6. **Able to conduct search activities in an adverse environment, including:**
   A. Awareness of the hazards associated with various disaster search environments.
   B. Able to function safely at heights and on or around rubble. Have experience and training in personal safety in confined spaces, and in below-grade, compromised conditions.
   C. Able to interpret different canine alerts and areas of interest.
   D. Able to perform as a secondary observer.
   E. Understand the parameters of the work time limitations for canines and determine rotation periods.

7. **Must be competent in canine search handling skills, to include:**
   A. Must have a close rapport and effective working relationship with the canine.
   B. Must be able to accurately interpret the canine's different alerts and indications of areas of interest.
   C. Must be able to work canine off lead.
   D. Able to direct canine into voids, tunnels or restricted spaces.
   E. Must have a good understanding of the capabilities and limitations of the canine.

8. **Knowledgeable with and able to provide first aid for canines.**

9. **Must be familiar with Basic Rope Techniques/Rescue System 1 or equivalent.**

Does your dog have the drive to penetrate and search voids?

FEDERAL EMERGENCY MANAGEMENT AGENCY
500 C St., SW, Washington, DC 20472
TEL (202) 646-4335 FAX (202) 646-4336

The employing agency should provide search dog handlers with the highest practical level of emergency medical training (paramedic, EMT). Medical skills are a necessity for handlers as they may be called on to assist in the primary treatment of partially covered victims.

Extreme missions require extreme training. Dogs performing disaster search need much more extensive physical training than the agility obstacles. Dog and handler need intensive fitness training throughout their career. While focusing on the search task, the disaster dog must be able to:

- Ride in various aircraft, vehicles, boats, containers or lifting systems
- Climb up and down ladders
- Jump from one level to another without falling and with very little forward momentum
- Traverse unstable, uneven, and slick surfaces
- Hold his position while the material under him is moving
- Maneuver under low obstacles
- Traverse narrow, elevated structures, and reverse direction
- Penetrate voids, tunnels, or restricted spaces
- Search rubble piles at a distance as directed by the handler

Handler confidence is equally important. The handler who acts tentative or uncertain can destabilize the dog. The handler who talks at the dog to relieve stress may create dependency or lose control of the animal. Searching unstable or hazardous rubble is the biggest threat to the disaster dog handler. Like urban firemen, the handler needs full time professional support in order to do the job safely and to have the assurance of full compensation should an accident in training or on a disaster mission end his career.

Searching unstable or hazardous rubble is also the biggest threat to the disaster dog. Beams shift. Walls collapse. Voids close. Leaking gas explodes. The handler may be helpless to aid his dog. His own life and the lives of other rescue personnel are in jeopardy. Fear makes a search dog dysfunctional. Acquired skills must overcome some of his natural instincts. It may be dangerous to jump off moving objects. The dog must learn it is possible to balance or gain control over a moving object by using his body weight and gravity. To maintain traction on slippery surfaces, the dog learns to spread his toes, not dig in with his toenails. He places each paw deliberately and independently on the rubble. Specialized agility training gives him the confidence to search rubble safely. The handler must be able to direct his dog over the rubble at different speeds, from a stand to a very rapid, flowing motion. The dog moving too fast may not be searching the rubble thoroughly. The dog moving too slowly may lose focus.

The disaster dog candidate can begin on rock piles, wood piles, piles of tires or other debris and never *see* a traditional agility setup. Neither is the agility course a *sufficient* condition for training a disaster dog. A dog that wins K-9 trials may fall apart trying to search rubble. In fact, the goal of the agility course is for the dog to achieve competence then advance to rubble search. Controlled movement is a necessary tactic for disaster search.

The alert signals detection. The dog's alert as performed in training must be easy to read (aggressive, sustained barking, digging, attempting to penetrate to source) so that even rescue personnel not trained in K-9 are able to recognize it: "That dog's got somebody!"

Training a *visible and audible alert at the location of strongest scent* has three important functions:

1. *Gives rescuers a point to deploy technical search teams and begin selected debris removal.* This happened many times after the Mexico City earthquake in 1985, a watershed for U.S. international disaster response. Dogs indicated dead bodies and live trapped people, uncovered in the rubble after the search teams moved on through 60 buildings reportedly searched.

2. *Gives the strongest possible alert* by that particular dog. The dog's alert on a disaster mission may be weaker or more difficult to read than in training. If the dog gives only weak or diffuse alerts in training, he may not perform a readable alert under the stress of a mission. This happened after a propane explosion when a dog trained for the *bomber* alert gave a subtle indication on a live 4-year-old. The handler did not see it (between searchers on their knees, scratching the dirt with a paw, sniffing toward the wall). The observer, fortunately, caught it and acted upon it. The dog team moved on through the scene of elbow-to-elbow fine grid pickers and scrapers, airborne dirt and loud noise. The observer made his way over to the wall the dog had indicated, saw a patch of hair he thought was a cat, reached down and touched it, and it moved. "When I found her alive, it scared the hell out of me. I'm not used to finding live people." The emergency room reported to the mother, "They've found her. She's breathing, she has a pulse and she's one minute away." And she survived.

3. *Gives rescuers a fresh objective* in rubble that has been searched repeatedly or has produced multiple victims. This happened at the 1994 Northridge Earthquake (Richter 6.6+) north of Los Angeles where air bags lifting 94 tons each pried apart the

Strong, readable alert into the rubble.

concrete floors of a 3-story apartment sandwiched to one. The bomb-like explosion of the temblor dropped a man's bed 12 feet, fused his doors so he couldn't open them with a sledgehammer, and forced him to crawl down from the balcony with his wife on his chest. Twenty thousand people were instantly homeless, 55 died, and the damage climbed above $8 billion. Responding firefighters and rescue teams saved dozens of victims. Fiberoptics televised buried victims. Sonar listened for breathing and heartbeats in primary voids under the second floor. There were hundreds of aftershocks. The morning after, a search dog found the 16th victim in a 3-foot space where the house-of-cards apartment had toppled on him.

Although some dogs reportedly perform distinct alerting behavior detecting live v. dead bodies, others perform the same alerting behavior detecting both live and dead bodies. Scientific testing has not been conducted to determine precisely when a person passes from live to dead in the dog's perception (unconsciousness, deep hypothermia, recently dead) or if in fact the dog can make that distinction reliably. The question also arises whether the dog can reliably distinguish a live person located beneath dead bodies. Using only live persons for disaster dog training does not necessarily produce two distinct alerts (live v. dead) on disaster missions. Other unknowns are the effects of canine age, time in service, mission experience, and the search environment itself. Some dogs have given a strong, enthusiastic barking-digging alert to a dead body. Some dogs have given atypical alerts to live persons.

Establishing the status of victims as efficiently as possible is an important US&R objective. However, the canine search specialist should not be responsible for making this assessment based on his dog's alerting behavior unless he has documented high reliability. Neither should any other task force member triage sites based solely on differential alerting behavior. If the dog alerts, the location could be investigated by technical search specialists, rescuers removing selected debris then repeating the K-9 or technical investigations, or deploying a second dog, depending on the circumstances of the search.

30 Earthquakes of the 20th Century*

	DATE	LOCATION	MOMENT MAGNITUDE	DEATHS		DATE	LOCATION	MOMENT MAGNITUDE	DEATHS
1.	1906	San Francisco, California	7.7	3,000	16.	1980	El Asnam, Algeria	7.1	2,590
2.	1908	Messina, Italy	7.0	110,000	17.	1985	Michoacán, Mexico	8.1	9,500
3.	1920	Gansu and Shaanxi, China	8.3	200,000	18.	1988	Armenia	6.8	25,000
4.	1923	Tokyo, Japan	7.9	142,810	19.	1989	Loma Prieta, California	7.0	62
5.	1927	Qinghai, China	7.7	200,000	20.	1990	Western Iran	7.5	50,000
6.	1935	Quetta, Pakistan	8.1	30,000	21.	1992	Landers, California	7.3	1
7.	1939	Erzincan, Turkey	7.6	32,700	22.	1993	Latur, India	6.2	9,750
8.	1948	Fukui, Japan	6.9	5,390	23.	1994	Northridge, California	6.7	60
9.	1960	Southern Chile	9.5	5,700	24.	1994	Northern Bolivia	8.3	10
10.	1964	Southern Alaska	9.2	131	25.	1994	Kuril Islands, Japan	8.3	10
11.	1970	Northern Peru	7.9	67,000	26.	1995	Kobe, Japan	6.9	5,200
12.	1971	San Fernando, California	6.7	58	27.	1995	Sakhalin Island, Russia	7.0	1,989
13.	1976	Mindanao, Philippines	8.1	8,000	28.	1995	Aiyion, Greece	6.3	26
14.	1976	Guatemala	7.6	22,780	29.	1999	Izmit, Turkey	7.4	15,000
15.	1976	Tangshan, China	7.4	655,000	30.	1999	Taipei, Taiwan	7.6	3,000

*Adapted from "Notable Earthquakes of the 20th Century," *National Geographic*, April 1995, with updates by USGS, Golden, Colorado.

EARTHQUAKE DANGER IN URBAN STRUCTURES

Earthquakes are complex, different in scope and effect, and produce surprises. Urban damage can occur from a moderate quake if the fault is nearby as well as from great quakes along large faults. Quakes can produce sudden horizontal or vertical shifting, rolling wave motion, local upheavals, pits or crevasses, or can change the elevation of an entire mountain range. There are a thousand ways to contort the earth. Few are currently predictable.

Plate tectonic theory explains seismic zone mechanics. An estimated 16 major plates, each about 45 miles thick, form the earth's crust. These plates ride on the softer and generally hotter mantle called the athenosphere. Where the plates collide, separate, or strike-slip past each other earthquakes frequently occur. In California, the San Andreas is a strike-slip fault, running southeast from San Francisco to Los Angeles. Along this fault the Pacific Plate underlying Los Angeles moves northwest toward San Francisco, while the North American Plate rides southeast. Where the crustal masses collide head-on, for example north of Los Angeles, the force of impact lifts mountains and creates cracks in the earth known as thrust faults.

Different types of plate movement damage surface structures in different ways depending on the type and location of the structure, the magnitude, direction, frequency and duration of the seismic force. The energy released during a magnitude-8.1 tremor may collapse a hospital and freeway overpass, leaving wood frame homes between intact. The *way* these structures fail, as well as the extent of the damage, determines how effective a search dog can be.

The effects of earthquake shaking on buildings, highways, bridges, or other structures are functions of the quake magnitude, the elapsed time of strong shaking, and the fault length. Local intensity is often not related to the magnitude recorded for the quake. The strongest effects tend to be near the quake epicenter, the forces attenuating as the distance increases. The rate and pattern of attentuation is a function of the geology of the region, dampering slowly in some regions, dropping off sharply in others. There are site-specific effects that will, for example, bring down the 8-12 story buildings in one city, or flatten the low frame structures in another town. Various types of vibration have different effects on a range of building sizes and shapes and can be demonstrated using simple pendulums. In certain types of quakes the effects are much stronger on the top floors of tall, swaying buildings than at ground level. In other types, the lower floors collapse,

Loma Prieta Earthquake, San Francisco. Primary seismic waves expand and contract the earth's crust. Secondary, slower, more powerful waves shake the ground as they pass through the rock. Soft, wet soil may liquefy, successive waves producing a quicksand that cannot support heavy structures.

leaving more survivors at the upper levels.

Buildings are currently designed in offices by engineers using mathematical models, assuming straight sound materials, and competent construction forces. Older buildings are more brittle, often poorly interconnected and not designed to resist earthquakes. Masonry and concrete walls that have little or no reinforcing steel can crack and fall. Native stone and earthwall structures are very dangerous. Where roof and floors are not well-connected to walls, the walls can fall away. Entire structures may be weak and unable to withstand the prolonged shaking of a major quake. Weak structures may barely withstand moderate quakes and they frequently collapse during strong aftershocks. Structures may contain fatal flaws, such as lack of symmetry in plan or height, low strength materials (short columns), unplanned openings cut in walls or beams, or uncalculated walls (property line walls).

Modern buildings are intended to provide stiff resistance to moderate quakes but crack and soften to resist great quakes while still holding together. Concrete and masonry should be well reinforced. All structures should be well connected together. Interior partitions, ceilings and contents can suffer extensive damage, yet the structure can perform well. Even new buildings may have fatal flaws, caused by poor design and/or construction. The ideal structure would be light, tough, and fireproof.

EVALUATION OF DAMAGED BUILDINGS

During the search phase of an urban disaster, mathematical analysis of structures is typically not feasible. The integrity of the building or other structure and the relative danger must be assessed by a systematic series of value judgments that should be performed by field experts. As first responders, building officials should be contacted to provide floor plans for the structure or set of structures involved.

Highly trained teams are available from the *Structural Engineers Association of California* and the *American Society of Civil Engineers*. One of the most important personnel to have on site at any structural collapse is a qualified structural engineer and architect. These personnel routinely design, build, and work with all forms of concrete and ordinary construction. Many of the engineers who are drawn to the emergency end of the spectrum have done research in earthquake effects on structures. These personnel can provide technical expertise to the heavy rescue team, advising which parts of the building may be unsafe to move or potential danger areas of secondary collapse zones. Movement of certain parts of the building without proper evaluation may result in parts *several blocks away* moving, or worse, *secondary collapses* occurring at the site. Their knowledge of construction materials and their properties can prove to be a valuable safety tool for the entire team. This engineering component can also provide good pre-entry or arrival briefings dealing with the types of construction the SAR teams can expect to encounter.

General building types can be rated according to their probable need for SAR if damaged. Lowest on the list, therefore safest, are wood frame dwellings and light frame buildings, commercial or industrial wood structures. Steel buildings (wood or concrete filled metal deck floors) with steel moment resisting frame, braced steel frame, or steel frame with cast-in-place concrete shear walls are also low. Medium hazard is presented by steel buildings with light moment frame and light X bracing, cast-in-place reinforced concrete buildings with concrete or wood floors/roof. Buildings with precast concrete walls or unreinforced masonry are safer if they have wood floors/roofs. The highest hazard types are reinforced or unreinforced masonry buildings with concrete floors/roof.

At the search site, an experienced structural engineer can better identify the type of construction, which will aid in making value judgments about the relative degree of danger. The danger of urban building search cannot be overstressed. SAR teams try to avoid areas of potential instability and sudden failure hazard (brittle failures). There is a high probability of at least one aftershock. The aftershock hazard is greatest after quakes where weak structures have been partially damaged but

STATE OF CALIFORNIA

OES/PEO **BUILDING/STRUCTURE** Assessment
Report No. _____

Facility Name _____

Address _____

Ref. Dwgs.
Mo/Day/Yr _____ Time _____
use 24 hr

Type of Disaster _____

OES/PEO ID No's. _____
Other PEO Reports _____

No. Photos _____ No. Sketchews _____
Co.-City-Vic _____

Facility Status [   ]

SAFETY INSTRUCTIONS: The possibility of the presence of toxic gases in confined spaces or of fuel leaks should be recognized as potential hazards.

CAUTION: This report was made for the California State Office of Emergency Services. The prime purpose of the report is to advise of the condition of the facility for immediate continued use/occupancy. REINSPECTION OF THE FACILITY IS RECOMMENDED. AFTERSHOCKS MAY CAUSE DAMAGE WHICH REQUIRES REINSPECTION. The conclusions reached by engineers who reexamine the facility later should take precedence. The assessment team will not render further advice in the event of conflict of engineering recommendations.

A. PLACARD POSTING

1. Existing: None ☐   2. Recommended posting: Green ☐   3. Posted at this assessment: Yes ☐
   Green ☐   Gold ☐   No ☐
   Gold ☐   Red ☐
   Red ☐

Posting Authority: _____

B. RECOMMENDATIONS

1. Shoring and bracing

   Needed to protect public ☐

   Needed to protect adjacent building ☐

2. Barricades needed   Yes ☐   No ☐
3. Monitor building movements   Yes ☐   No ☐
4. Monitor weakened components   Yes ☐   No ☐
5. Structural Report by CE or SE

   recommended Yes ☐   No ☐

C. COMMENTS _____

_____
_____
_____
_____

OES/PEO Form No. 11   II-41

D. FACILITY DESCRIPTION   Assessment Report #_____

	Lateral support system	Exterior walls	Roof diaphragm	Horizontal bracing	Interior bracing and/or shear walls	Non-bearing partitions	Floors	Stairs	Other	Undetermined
Concrete										
Precast concrete										
Reinforced masonry										
Unreinforced masonry										
Steel frame										
Metal deck										
Wood										
Other										
Undetermined										

1. Number of stories _____
2. Number of basement levels _____
3. Pre-1934 design?
   Yes ☐   No ☐   Unk ☐
4. Primary occupancy:
   Government ☐   Hotel/motel ☐
   Hospital ☐   Commercial ☐
   School ☐   Industrial/mfg ☐
   Office bldg. ☐
   Other _____

E. STRUCTURAL DAMAGE OBSERVATIONS (D.O.)

Damage Scale	0 None (0%)	1 Slight (1-10%) D.O.	2-3-4 Moderate (11-40%)	5 Severe (4-60%)	6 Total (Over 60%)	NA Not Applicable	NO Not Observed

1. Exterior walls _____
2. Frame (general condition) _____
3. Frame members _____
4. Frame connections _____
5. Roof framing _____
6. Interior bearing/shear walls _____
7. Partitions (non-bearing) _____
8. Floor(s) _____ _____ _____ _____
9. Stair(s) _____ _____ _____ _____
10. Elevator _____ _____ _____ _____
11. Glass _____
12. Mechanical equipment supports _____
13. Electrical equipment supports _____
14. Other _____ _____ _____ _____

F. ESTIMATE OF DAMAGE
1. Approx. bldg. area (   )
2. Est. % of bldg. damaged _____
3. Est. damage valuation $ _____
   _____

G. FALLING HAZARDS

	Appar. Hazard	No Appar. Hazard	Unknown
1. Parapet walls	_____	_____	_____
2. Ornamentation	_____	_____	_____
3. Chimney (s)	_____	_____	_____
4. Floor _____	_____	_____	_____
5. Roof structure	_____	_____	_____
6. Equipment	_____	_____	_____
7. Other _____	_____	_____	_____

H. SOIL OR GEOLOGICAL DAMAGE

	Appar. Hazard	No Appar. Hazard	Unknown
1. Settlement	_____	_____	_____
2. Liquefaction	_____	_____	_____
3. Landslide	_____	_____	_____
4. Faulting	_____	_____	_____
5. Other _____	_____	_____	_____

E. REMARKS (Including identification of "Other" items in sections D, E, G, and H)

_____

_____

_____

_____

_____

OES/PEO Form No. 11   II-42

still stand. It is high where there are previously observed hazards:
- Partly collapsed multi-thickness brick walls
- Unsupported roofs and floors
- Unstable concrete frames and walls
- Unconnected precast concrete walls and slabs
- Postensioned concrete slabs
- Leaning buildings and corner buildings
- Partly collapsed buildings with many floors lying on one
- Groups of buildings laterally supported by one
- Floors (with or without beams) supported by loose building parts and furniture
- Falling hazards (parapets, heavy roof tile, chimneys)
- Brick (stacked bond worst)
- Hidden brick (plaster covered)
- Hollow tile infill can almost explode out (plaster covered)

HEAVY RESCUE TEAMS

Heavy and tactical rescue personnel are the *rescue* component of the disaster SAR function. They are responsible for gaining entry, disentanglement, and retrieving those live and dead patients associated with building collapse. These personnel, along with their associated fire and rescue skills, need to be specialists in several areas. They should have a good knowledge of building construction, shoring techniques for both structures and trenches, technical rope rescue knowledge, confined space entry skills, and the ability to interface with other components of the team. Most of these personnel should also have some skills in crane and heavy equipment operations as well as sling and

Pull the dog back if his weight is crushing a victim.

clamshell bucket rigging. While heavy rescue personnel should leave the actual heavy equipment operations to those experts associated with that function, they should understand how to work with heavy equipment and the physics and mechanics of rigging.

These personnel should also be able to work closely with engineers, search dog teams and emergency medical personnel. For example a roof breach evolution involves breaching the roof or top slab with a variety of saws, hand tools, hydraulic equipment, and, if you are working in concrete, the use of Bristar and water wedge. The rescue team can then enter and begin shoring operations if necessary to make the entrance safe. With the assistance of a heavy rescue member as their safety, the dog team can be placed in the hole to search. It may be necessary to keep the handler in a safe zone while the dog works. In pancaked areas rescue teams will be working in close quarters tunneling, shoring, and cutting re-bar, conduit, and other debris to create open spaces for the dog teams to search.

The amount of equipment and logistics needed to perform these tasks is staggering. Depending on the type building and incident, equipment needs will differ. Some considerations: a variety of shoring materials; saws, cutting torches, and other tools for breaking, breaching and burning;

a variety of hand tools, invaluable for removing debris and tunneling operations; heavy lifting equipment for slab lifting and rigging (cranes, clamshell buckets, air bags), requiring a qualified heavy equipment operator; entry equipment (IDLH, immediately dangerous to life and health, atmospheres require air breathing apparatus and atmospheric monitors), tripod and packaging equipment if you plan to move victims around; support equipment for man and beast, especially adequate amounts of *fluid replacement for both dogs and man.*

Detector dogs increase the effectiveness of skilled heavy rescue teams. Dog teams need the expertise of heavy rescuers to carry out their search strategy safely and effectively. Realistic training precedes successful tactical operations. That means the first time a 4-dog strike team works with a heavy rescue crew should not be at 3 in the morning in front of a 6-story building that is now 30 feet high.

> Train as a team. Use as many disciplines as possible to make up your team. While components of the team may be separate entities, they must train together and be able to come together in the event of an emergency. To simply think that we can grab personnel with some expertise up from all over the country or state when a collapse occurs and call them a team, and then expect them to function as one, safely and efficiently, is idiotic!
>
> —Chief Sargent

CALIFORNIA RESCUE DOG ASSOCIATION/SHIRLEY HAMMOND

Handler Shirley Hammond's Cinnamon *finds man alive in train wreck, San Bernardino, California.*

Although search dogs should be deployed to investigate some holes or areas of rubble too small or too risky for a person, there are situations where a dog is clearly ineffective and could jeopardize the lives of many rescuers besides his own. W. J. Anderson, *SAR Dog Alert* (October 1992):

"Dog handlers who train their dogs to search through foam are playing with a ticking time bomb. When it goes off, and it eventually will go off, they will be lucky if they only kill their dogs.

"A fire is a chemical reaction involving the rapid oxidation of a combustible fuel producing heat and flame. Three elements must be present to have a fire. They are: fuel, oxygen, and heat. These three elements form the firefighting triangle. The fire goes out if one or more legs of the triangle are broken by removing or isolating that element. It will reignite if the missing element or elements are reintroduced.

"The foam itself is not the issue. The danger lies in why the foam is there. There are several types of firefighting foams; all work to break the triangle by smothering, separating, suppressing vapors, and, to a certain extent, cooling the three elements of the fire triangle. The persistence of foam blankets varies. Some start to decay, or ghost, in as little as five minutes. Agitation, caused by a dog going through the blanket, will accelerate its decay. One type of foam used in some U.S. communities is relatively self-healing; most foams are not. The uninitiated—and that category fits a dog—cannot tell from observation if a foam blanket is or is not self-healing. The dog also cannot tell the depth of a foam blanket. It could be covering a surface spill with virtually no depth, or a fuel sump several feet deep.

"Liquid fuels have three basic characteristics that are important to fire fighting. They are flash point, fire point, and ignition temperature.

"The flash point is the temperature at which a liquid fuel gives off enough vapors to form an ignitable mixture with air near its surface. The vapors will flash, but not continue to burn. *Although the liquid fuel will not continue to burn, the vapors can ignite with explosive force.*

"The *fire point* is the temperature at which a liquid fuel produces enough vapors to support combustion once ignited.

"The minimum temperature at which fuel in an air mixture will initiate self-sustained combustion is the *ignition temperature.*

"The flash point for gasoline is *minus* 45 degrees Fahrenheit. (Water freezes at *plus* 32 degrees F.) Its ignition temperature is 536 degrees F. The flash point and ignition temperature for other light fuels approximates that of gasoline. Gasoline vapors are heavier than air and can flow along the ground like a river looking for an ignition source. Other fuel vapors may be lighter than air and will flow along ceilings or collect in overhead pockets.

"One pint of gasoline in 100 cubic feet of air has the explosive force of five sticks of dynamite. A pint is 16 fluid ounces, a can of beer is 12 fluid ounces. A closet two feet deep by five feet long by ten feet high is 100 cubic feet.

"There are seven firefighting phases. Only the last three are important to dog handlers. These are overhauling, ventilation, and salvage. The meanings of ventilation and salvage are obvious. A fire is overhauled by breaking up fuel sources, opening walls, etc. which could hide smoldering ashes, and otherwise ensuring that the three elements of the fire triangle have been neutralized. Heat is transmitted by conduction, convection, and radiation. The heat generating source does not have to be in the immediate vicinity of the fuel and oxygen for there to be a fire. For example, a fire burning around a metal pipe or other conductive or convective object in the basement of a building could transmit enough heat to ignite a fire several floors above. Until a fire has been overhauled, there are no guarantees that it could not recur if a foam blanket was broken.

"Foam blankets also can be used to contain and isolate hazardous materials. Search is part of the initial recovery phase of an urban disaster. During this phase, only defensive HAZMAT actions, in which potentially hazardous materials are only contained and isolated, will be feasible. There is no way for a dog or handler to know by inspection that there is nothing hazardous under a foam blanket. A dog that has gone through a foam blanket covering a hazardous material could very well contaminate an entire team, especially if the material was a biological agent."

People are not sent through foam blankets. Dogs cannot be more effective in this type situation. This single example, only one of many, illustrates why, beyond specialized dog training, handlers must have all the current safety and operational experience provided urban disaster rescue technicians.

The major confined space search and rescue hazards are chemicals, like CO and H_2S that are toxic, flammable, and asphyxiating. The only way to know what atmospheric concentrations exist within a confined space is to meter it with the proper instruments. If the lethal concentration is there, and the handler or dog takes one breath of it, either or both will be DRT—dead right there. Professional firefighters said it years ago: "You only do well what you do full time."

When incoming task forces arrive at an area severely affected by a disaster, they could possibly be faced with thousands of persons trapped beneath the rubble. Some may still be alive, others are probably dead, and many simple rescues may have already been accomplished by the local people. The combined use of physical, canine and electronic search tactics will enable the task force supervisors to better establish priorities and focus emphasis on the most important rescue activities.

Data compiled by Professor Niu Shi-ru, Acting Director of the Institute of Health and the Chinese Academy of Medical Sciences at the time of the great 1976 Tangshan, China (PRC) earthquake contrasts the relationship between post-earthquake time of rescue and victim survivability. Shi-ru determined that the survival rate of victims rescued within 24 hours—*the golden day*—was quite high (81.0 percent), but dropped precipitously to 33.7 percent when rescued between 24 and 48 hours.

The incident management system is illustrated by the FEMA TASK FORCE Flowchart and Rescue Site Management on the following page.

Specific groups or divisions are the search division, a rescue division, a medical division, and a technical division. They all interact horizontally. The first action of first-responding companies should be to *isolate the numerous incidents* that may be occurring simultaneously within a given area during a large scale disaster. The assignment of single company members to these sites requires the *establishment of some type of perimeter*, which will help prevent a mass flood of volunteers from entering the area and possibly getting injured.

From a functional standpoint, the technical division actually makes many decisions during the reconnaissance or size up, where the initial damage assessment is made and witnesses give information. This information is based on life threat identification, incident control, and property protection in order to determine the extent of damage and the need for personnel and equipment.

To determine victim locations in collapse situations, experience has shown that: 1) most victims will, to some degree, delay before exiting a building, causing many to be caught in the building's transportation routes during collapse, and 2) those same transportation routes (corridors, stairwells, and vertical shafts) are much more likely to form void spaces in steel reinforced concrete buildings than other areas of the building.

It is important for rescuers to understand that disaster victims typically do not delay exiting structures because of some lack of preparedness or because they do not want to get out. It is because they *cannot get out.* Anybody who has experienced 15 seconds or more shaking at the epicenter of a 6.0 or greater earthquake understands this. The noise alone, a thunderous grinding, is disorienting. Waking up at night to roaring and shaking so severe that it is impossible to stand up or get out of bed forces the victims to await their fate. If everything around them collapses, they will be caught. Disaster preparedness has limited, after-the-fact meaning in these situations. Nobody spends his life sleeping in a bomb shelter wearing combat boots and a helmet. Every person spends some part of his life endangered.

It is equally important for rescue dog handlers to understand that the dog himself must have the courage and search drive to prevail over the disaster environment. Aftershocks shake the rescue site. People scream. Generators and large earthmovers are trucked onto the site. The dog whose nerve fails, who is not curious about every new thing, should not be subjected to disaster search.

Incident command personnel in consultation with the engineering staff will triage buildings and make assignments of teams. The structural engineer along with several search and rescue personnel from the various disciplines will conduct a walk-through or size up to determine problems, ingress and egress routes. This triage process, based on construction type and occupancy along with the type of collapse can provide a tool to guide the decision about what buildings to search first, thereby

Disaster victims typically do not delay exiting structures because of some lack of preparedness or because they do not want to get out. It is because they cannot get out.

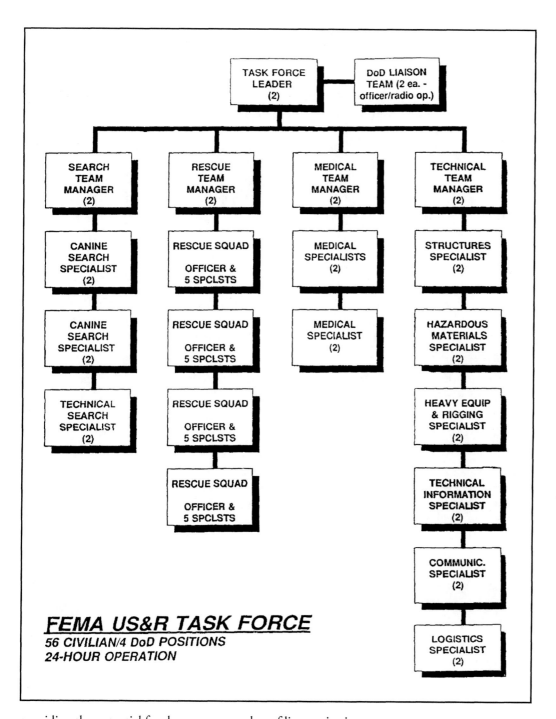

FEMA US&R TASK FORCE
56 CIVILIAN/4 DoD POSITIONS
24-HOUR OPERATION

providing the potential for the greatest number of live extrications.

The specialized task forces will have the task of dealing with the most difficult rescue situations. Depending on the complexity of the search and rescue activity, they will have to spend a greater amount of precious time on a smaller number of difficult cases. Obviously, it is always important to establish whether or not the team is involved with a live victim rescue since time should not be wasted in unproductive missions (removing bodies) while other live victims might still be saved.

Accordingly, it is essential that every possible search method be employed to enable task force supervisors to locate viable victims before committing rescue resources to any prolonged (although well-intentioned) operation. Body recovery is not the primary mission of a task force. Normally, such recovery operations should only be undertaken when a body is readily (and safely) accessible or when its location would prevent rescue personnel from extricating a live victim.

Task force supervisors must ensure the close interaction of the Structures Specialists and Hazardous Materials Specialists in the Technical Team with the search and rescue personnel during search operations. The Structures and Hazardous Materials Specialists provide initial assessments of relative building stability and safety in relation to the ongoing search operation. In addition, recurring assessments should be performed throughout the operations.

Initially, a team of two handlers and two dogs goes out with a search team manager, who is responsible for helping coordinate the K-9 activity, channelling that resource based on the structure triage, the hazard marking system, what preliminary searches have been done, and what victims have been removed. One rescue squad individual is assigned as a safety officer, responsible for looking for secondary collapse potentials, identifying hazards, keeping the dog and the handler as safe as possible.

The search team component is responsible for 3 things. First, they typically go out on the preliminary strike on a large-scale incident with the recon team to do *initial search markings and to identify high-probability areas to put the resources*. Second, once resources are committed to that location, they help distribute the resources, depending if it is a single- or multiple-structure event. Use of the technical or K-9 search components is going to change relative to that. Third, they go to work to locate victims at each designated site.

> Let's take an Alabama tornado or hurricane disaster for example. Say we've got 80-100 structures that are down and they want to search these structures. We would send a reconnaisance team out, a structural engineer, a rescue team individual, a search component with a search team manager. They would evaluate the structures for three things:
>
> 1. What is the structural integrity of the building? Can we actually get in it, or is it a writeoff from a safety standpoint?
> 2. Because most of the surface victim rescues will be done, we will be looking for concealed victims trapped beneath the debris. Based on the search component's evaluation, we will assess, where is our greatest potential for live recoveries? The search marking system will indicate a preliminary search has been done of this building. Search teams have evaluated 40-50 buildings or structures and identified 4 that have potential.
> 3. Of those four, based on our current resource capability, we can work two of those sites. The two we recommend to work are based on the potential for live extrication. At that point, when we go into rescue operations, as opposed to just a cursory search operation, the search team will come back and work side-by-side with the rescue teams identifying exactly where the victims are.
>
> —Chief Sargent

At the scene, the K-9 team searching to pinpoint is directed by a rescue squad member. Where possible, for example a 60- x 60-foot building, the K-9 team first does a *perimeter search to see if any scent is diffusing out around the edges of the site.* Searching the perimeter also gives the handler a better chance to evaluate the site, including the potential rate of scent diffusion. If the dog alerts into the debris from the perimeter, teams must decide whether to send the dog onto or into the rubble at that point.

Searching the rubble, the handler directs the dog up on top of rubble and into crawl spaces, working in a careful, methodical manner. The handler may have to boost the dog up onto ledges and enter some of the deeper crawl spaces or voids to observe the dog. The team may have to call for a ladder to access higher or lower areas, or rappel into holes. The dog will work in and around workers on the rubble. The handler may request workers to step back 10 or 15 feet while checking a hole, but it is not reasonable to expect all work on the site to be held up. Equipment will continue to work in the vicinity unless it is a hazard to the workers, and smoke from smoldering fires may persist in the area. The dog may show interest in contaminated clothing or food but will typically not alert.

On the rubble pile the handler has to be able to work his dog from remote locations because he may not be able to go everywhere the dog goes. Unlike searching areas or intact structures, the handler will typically not be able to deploy the dog in a pattern based on air flow or scent diffusion rates. Safety determines coverage. Where possible, use *cold nonflammable smoke* such as commercial cold smoke or unscented talcum powder to analyze the local air flow at the entry to voids, crevices, or elevations where the dog cannot go. If these spaces are inhaling (scent diffusing away from the dog), breaching to an adjacent area may be necessary.

Do not overcrowd the work site. Do not put 3 dog teams into a small collapsed house, for example. Overcrowding distracts the canine, and overloading could hasten further collapse. Too many people and dogs is also dangerous when searching voids and tunneling through debris. If conditions worsen, jammed egress routes may injure or kill rescuers.

Still, a spotter for the K-9 team performs the valuable role of watching for a change in the dog's behavior that the handler might not see.

> When I use a trained disaster dog: 1) the dog is going to cause less disturbance than a person; 2) from a safety standpoint, a dog is more expendable than a person. I can get away with smashing a dog a lot easier than I can get away with smashing a dog and a person. In that risk-benefit analysis, taking all the emotions out of it, simply looking at it from a tactical perspective, the person is worth a lot more to me than the dog.
>
> The rescue technician may say, "This thing is not supported. You can't go in there. However, the dog may be able to get in and out of there safely. Watch out for these electrical hazards. Watch out for these water hazards. Here on the side of this building is a big lean-to collapse. Let's do a good search up here. Let's check out the footing. Let's see if we can get the dog to work this 10 x 10 section. Let's get him up on the rubble pile here and see if we get a positive alert. Let's get him in this void and see if he alerts."
>
> It is important that the search component not work independently any more than the rescue component work independently, throwing in resources at a place where there may not be a viable find. These types of resources are limited at best. When you start wasting time, say, to get through a concrete structure, you may spend 24 hours trying to breach to get to one person. If you're screwing around trying to get to a dead body, you've wasted 24 hours. Or if you are going after one when you could potentially get ten, you've really wasted your time.
>
> —Chief Sargent

An important consideration in the middle to latter stages of a mission is the need to reassess previously searched structures. That is, if the profile of a building/structure has been significantly reduced because of debris removal by heavy equipment or secondary collapse, it may become necessary to treat the structure as a new opportunity and to repeat the various search procedures.

Reference the **FEMA US&R Response System** *Field Operations Guide* (*FOG* Manual).

FEMA US&R RESPONSE SYSTEM
URBAN SEARCH & RESCUE TASK FORCE

TASK FORCE OPERATIONS SITE SKETCH

SIDE THREE

SIDE TWO

SIDE FOUR

SIDE ONE

TYPE OF OPERATION: _____

DEPICT:

[ ]   BUILDING/STRUCTURE(s)   [ ]   SECTORS (team/squad assignments)
[ ]   OPERATIONS POST   [ ]   MEDICAL TREATMENT AREA
[ ]   EQUIPMENT STAGING AREA   [ ]   PERSONNEL STAGING AREA
[ ]   ACCESS/ENTRY ROUTES   [ ]   CRIBBING/SHORING WORK AREA
[ ]   CONTROL ZONES (Collapse/Hazard Zones, Work Zones, etc.)
[ ]   PERSONNEL HAZARDS (Live Utilities, Haz Mat, Collapse Potentials, etc.)

EMERGENCY SIGNALLING

o   **EVACUATE THE AREA**   3 short blasts (one second each)
o   **CEASE OPERATIONS/ALL QUIET**   1 long blast (three seconds)
o   **RESUME OPERATIONS**   1 long and 1 short blast

FEMA US&R RESPONSE SYSTEM
URBAN SEARCH & RESCUE TASK FORCE

TASK FORCE OPERATIONS REPORT

TASK FORCE DESIGNATION: _____

DATE: _____

START TIME: _____   COMPLETION TIME: _____

TF TEAM: _____   TEAM MANAGER: _____

TEAM/SQUAD MEMBERS:

1 _____   2 _____
3 _____   4 _____
5 _____   6 _____
7 _____   8 _____
9 _____   10 _____

OPERATIONS SITE: ADDRESS: _____
                     SECTOR: _____

DESCRIPTION OF OPERATION: _____
_____
_____
_____
_____
_____
_____
_____
_____

COMMENTS/EVALUATIONS/RECOMMENDATIONS: _____
_____
_____
_____
_____
_____
_____
_____

TEAM LEADER/SQUAD OFFICER:

FEMA: US&R OPERATIONAL PROCEDURES

LARGE SCALE SEARCH STRATEGY

What area should be searched first? When the disaster affects large geographic areas, many structures over a widespread area may be involved with many people requiring attention.

At the inception of a mission, supervisory personnel use two general strategies to deploy Task Force search resources:

1. Sector the area in question. Depending on the size of the damaged area and the search resources available, an area may be sectored by city block or other easily definable criteria. Divide and apportion each sector for search operations.

2. For larger areas, such as all of a city or jurisdiction, determine the search priorities in terms of the type of occupancies affected. Those presenting the highest likelihood of survivability and the greatest number of potential victims receive attention first. Survivability is based primarily on type of building construction. Occupancy relates to the function of the buildings and the time of day, or day of the week. Midday during the week, for example, schools, hospitals, nursing homes, high rise and multi-residential buildings, office buildings, hotels, etc., would be searched first.

SEARCH AND RECONNAISSANCE TEAM

Task Force staffing allows for two 9-person search and reconnaissance teams. If necessary, both can be deployed at assigned locations when the Task Force begins operations. For sustained operations, these teams subsequently alternate operational periods. During the mission, it may be necessary to deploy a search and recon team to a remote location.

A full Task Force search and reconnaissance team should be staffed as follows:

(1) **Search Team Manager:** Supervises teams, sketches/records information, communicates details/recommendations to the Task Force Leader

(2) **Canine Search Specialists:** Conduct canine search operations, including redundant verifications of alerts

(1) **Technical Search Specialist:** Conducts electronic search operations

(1) **Medical Specialist:** Provides treatment for survivors and Task Force members

(1) **Structures Specialist:** Provides analysis and advises building stability, shoring, and stabilization

(1) **Haz Mat Specialist:** Monitors atmospheres in and around voids and confined spaces; identifies, assesses, and flags hazardous materials dangers

(2) **Rescue Specialists:** Provide assistance to the search/recon team including drilling/breaching for electronic viewing equipment, fiberoptic devices, and/or deployment of listening arrays, acoustic/seismic devices

SEARCH OPERATIONS TACTICS

Once a viable specific work area (group of buildings, single building or separate section within a building) has been identified, hazard zones should be conspicuously cordoned off and flagged. Identify individual hazards, such as overhanging building components, structural instability or secondary collapse zones, hazardous materials, live utilities, etc. using the structure triage, assessment and marking systems.

The properly trained search dog can cover large areas in a relatively short period of time. Two canine teams work under an overhead coordinator, who monitors their safety and directs their operation to ensure thorough coverage of accessible areas. Task Force staffing deploys 2 separate canine teams initially, rotating them into rest cycles and using them alternately during extended, continuous operations.

The overhead coordinator sketches the general features of the search area, noting all significant information. He communicates findings and recommends priorities to the Task Force Leader.

If a dog alerts, the handler notes the location mentally but does not physically mark it. The overhead coordinator pulls that team away and directs the second canine team into the same general area.

If the second dog alerts at the same location, it is marked, and the overhead coordinator informs the Task Force Leader and Rescue Team Manager for subsequent action. The search team continues its assignment.

Electronic, fiberoptic, and physical search operations may be conducted separately or in conjunction with the canine operations.

Throughout the operation, Structures Specialists should reassess building stability and safety, including previously searched structures. If the profile of a structure has been significantly reduced because of debris removal by heavy equipment or secondary collapse, searchers may have to treat the structure as a new opportunity.

OKLAHOMA CITY

Sabotage of the Alfred P. Murrah Federal Building in Oklahoma City killed 169 people at 0904 on April 19, 1995. Police and rescue dog teams from Oklahoma and other states were immediately dispatched, first bomb squads deployed to clear the area of explosives, then disaster task forces deployed to find survivors.

Unstable rubble, weather, and hazardous materials endangered the teams throughout the search and rescue operation. Firefighters performed technical shoring, insertions, and extractions. In the aftermath of the terrorist act, officers labored to process the area as a crime scene at the same time rescuers were extricating victims.

Search and Rescue Dogs of Oklahoma handler Steven E. Powell and his dog Bronte, a 6-year-old rottweiler, found four victims in one location, among them the last person found alive. John Hnath, President, and his 20-month old German shepherd Mickey responded along with 4 support personnel, Anna Powell, Debra Hnath, Laurie Price, and Shannon Buhl. In the handlers' own words:

> Powell: After receiving an emergency page about 0930, we left our respective jobs, gathered our dogs and equipment and left in a caravan. When we reached Oklahoma City, we reported to the Incident Command, the Oklahoma City Fire Department. The suspicion of additional bombs and a passing storm prevented all rescue teams from entering the building.

> At 1800 I entered the south side of the Alfred P. Murrah Federal Building. We saw widespread destruction and death. All the training of a lifetime could not prepare you for what we saw. We were walking among the dead and wounded. Flesh and blood flowed freely, mixing with water from the rain and broken pipes.

> Our previous missions had been much smaller in scale. Typically a local agency had put us in charge of the mission. We had developed a small level of expertise making decisions in crisis situations.

> Now my assignment was to locate any possible survivors and let the rescue workers excavate them from the debris. Cooperation on the search was the best I had ever seen. We welcomed the help of others as they arrived.

> The fresh scent of flesh and blood everywhere potentially overwhelmed the human scent of live victims. Finding an unconscious victim buried in the center of several bodies with profuse bleeding would be nearly impossible, especially those areas covered by debris, where the blood was not evident.

> The opening to the first floor was a 6- by 12-foot hole, triangular in shape with concrete flooring dangling by rebar at 45 degrees. Looking into the hole, I asked a Marine sergeant if anybody has been down there searching. He yelled down. There was no response.

> We entered the first floor. It too was destroyed. The only lights were my helmet light and a flashlight.

> Bronte immediately alerted to a pile of debris that we would later learn held Brandy Ligons, barely alive, and the bodies of 3 people.

Search and rescue K-9 Zeus, New York Task Force 1, indicates a find at Oklahoma City.

NYPD Officer Robert Schnelle and his dog find the homeless in rubble nightly on city streets. In 1993 they worked the collapsed structure and 20-foot crater of the World Trade Center bombing.

The debris determined our path. I looked up through holes a man could easily fall through hidden by debris. Nothing was recognizable.

Hnath: I was used to working Mickey off lead, but the damage was so extensive, we had to work very close. Every step had to be tested. Searching a 10 x 10-foot area effectively took 15 to 20 minutes.

Mickey kept showing interest in 3 areas, but the firefighters working these areas were not finding anything. I asked if someone who had been here just after the bombing was available. A few minutes later a U.S. Marshal came and talked to me. When I showed him where Mickey had indicated, he said children had been removed from all 3 areas. While we were talking, a firefighter found another body part where Mickey had alerted.

Powell: Late that night on our second deployment a storm attacked, pelting us with cold rain. High wind shoved the building. Debris fell from precarious ledges. The Fire Department called everybody out of the building.

Our third deployment at 0300 was the front of the building on the 3-story high debris pile. The FBI asked me to scale the pile and search it. Not familiar with what had been done up to that point, I asked them for boundaries. Safety was everyone's biggest concern. Large chunks of concrete were flapping 9 stories up above the pile.

John and Mickey along with Shannon Buhl tried to scale the western edge of the debris pile adjacent to some of the intact floors. Mickey had to be hand-carried over the jagged debris. The shepherd alerted strongly where a body was later recovered.

I removed Bronte's collar and vest to search a 2 x 20-foot hole. She searched left and right deep into the hole but had no significant alerts.

After much difficulty scaling the debris, we loaded into a crane basket for a lift to the top of the pile. The debris was so unstable it was almost impossible to search. Wires connecting each floor to the debris were poised to pull tons of rubble down on our heads.

Bronte worked carefully, going everywhere I asked. We had a minor cadaver alert on the west end of the debris pile. We had a strong alert on the center of the pile. The next day 3 bodies were removed from that spot.

Hundreds of rescue teams converged on Oklahoma City over the following days. Canine Search Specialists Robert Macaulay with his golden Quasar and Annie Lerum with her German shepherd Colter flew in April 20 with the California Task Force. They worked the same 2-day marathon with few breaks that most of the searchers experienced. Their observations, together with those of Powell and Hnath, gave valuable insight for future disaster missions:

Search recon was zero, a big problem. The communication level on the early end of the search was very poor. This is symbolic: a firefighter would search a pile; another set of firefighters would come in and wouldn't know if that was the pile the previous firefighter had just stacked or the pile they needed to search. That translated over to the dog teams.

We debriefed ourselves because we are used to working with each other. But at first we were not getting information to help us work. Even with all the folks, we had to make all the decisions about where to go.

Things settled down a little bit after the first 12-18 hours. The communications improved. You have to realize that the people briefing us had just carried 90 people out of the building. To them it looked pretty clear! There was no impression that the people left could be alive.

As a team, we usually work together with a field navigation communicator (FNC), the support person. You have the dog, the handler, and the FNC, proven to be effective. At Oklahoma City, instead of our FNCs, we had firefighters who had no idea how we work.

There were a thousand people, and nobody knew anybody's name. The FBI guy wants to know who the sheriff was, or the firefighter wants to know who the FBI guy was, or you said *he said this*…that was a problem

We should not have been eating in the building. Everybody was. We should never have rested or slept in the mouth of the building on the back side. They should not have set up a firefighter base inside the mouth of the building. Later they learned, after moving the debris, that almost every column in the entire building, if not decimated instantly, had a crack at the base. They did not know this because debris piled around each column. The debris wasn't paperwork, it was pieces of concrete. They discovered the building was actually ready to collapse.

Broken glass was everywhere. The sheets and shards of glass were not much of a hazard, but the fine powder of glass caused by the blast wave was. It was like working the dogs on sandpaper. It wore their pads down.

We breathed fiberglass and dust. The doctors rigged saline flushes for the rescuers and dogs each time we finished a shift. The first couple of days we worked in blue surgical masks and ate a lot of dust. Day 3 we received top-of-the-line duo filtered masks that took care of organic vapors, asbestos and other dust. You have to move the mask to give verbal commands.

Additional safety equipment included coveralls or specialized clothing, steel toe and shank leather boots, leather gloves over rubber gloves (for bio-hazards), helmets, safety glasses, and light sticks for night work. Warm gear was needed in the Sunday morning wind-chill of 19 degrees. The main trick is remembering to use the gear you bring.

Training exposure paid off in Oklahoma City. The unstable rubble—ceiling panels, insulation, papers, cabinet, huge piles of assorted junk—moved when the dogs stepped on it. The dogs' variety of experience carried them through. The key lesson is the dogs learned to handle new experiences. You cannot imagine everything you might encounter, but if you train so that new situations are not a menace, they will not slow you down.

We were in close contact with other people and dogs the entire time. Many people came up to touch the dogs, some even found socializing with the dogs to be therapeutic for them! This clearly shows that our dogs must be highly social with other dogs and people. A dog that cannot handle this type of interaction should be washed from the program early.

The canine handlers and the search team leaders need to get together more frequently to discuss how the dogs are working, both individually and as part of the Task Force, and to establish specific goals for the next operational task. As dog handlers, we are used to independent operations. We need to do a better job of integrating our efforts with each other and with the Task Force.

The US&R Task Force response to Oklahoma City underscored the importance of rapidly deploying light, highly mobile, professional search teams.

AVALANCHE SEARCH

A 1993 survey by the American Association of Avalanche Professionals reported the following distribution of avalanche rescue dogs at U.S. ski areas:

More than 20:	California
10 to 15:	Colorado, Utah
5 to 10:	Montana
1 to 5:	Alaska, Idaho, Oregon, Washington, Wyoming

The total number of dogs trained for avalanche rescue in this country includes a significant number of rescue dog teams stationed outside developed ski areas. Still the total number is small. Although avalanches claim few lives compared to other types of natural disasters or accidents, the victims buried under snow and slide debris generally have only minutes to live and are seldom able to free themselves. Survival depends on detection by rescuers on the surface. It is a race against time.

KIRKWOOD AVALANCHE

Kirkwood Ski Patrolman Dave Paradysz: "It was a little after noon January 4th. Another patrolman and I were out digging a snow pit for layer analysis in another part of the ski area. We had just gotten to the bottom of a 10-foot hole when the avalanche call came over the radio. We jetted over to the bottom of Chairlift 2 and rode that up. My dog Doc was at the station at the top of Chair 2. The avalanche was a few hundred yards from the station south of the top of Chair 2, well within bounds, in an area called Button Bowl south of the groomed trail leading to the bottom of Chair 3. Two snowboarders and a skier had been on the hill. The skier, Jeff Eckland, was the one caught. He is a groomer at Kirkwood Ski Area. He was on his day off.

"At the top of Chair 2, the patrolman I was with drove my dog and me up the ridge on the snowmobile. Meanwhile Dave Allessio was also working the station with his dog Woody. He was one of the first patrolmen to get the call and traversed into the slide path. He started searching the bottom part where most of the debris was.

"When we traversed into the slide, Doc was obviously feeding off my stress. He was pretty excited about the whole deal. It didn't take much to put him to work. It was fortunate. There was a big pile of snow in front of a stand of trees. We started right there and, boom, the dog hit it. Within 10 seconds, he was digging and found him.

"There was a patrolman named Louie with a hasty pack ahead of me skiing in. Before Louie could even get his pack off, Doc was digging and I was telling him to dig there. I clicked out of my skis and went over where the dog was. Between the trees Doc had uncovered this guy's back.

"I couldn't immediately tell how he was oriented, up or down. I was pretty much digging frantically. I thought I had his head, but it was his elbow. That clued me which way he was facing. So I dug to his face and was able to get him air. I could not see his face, but I was able to talk to him then. He was conscious. I asked him where he was hurt and if there was anyone else he knew of who was caught. He said his left side was hurting. It turned out he had a broken rib and bruised liver. I called for a sled with a backboard. Oxygen arrived with the other patrollers. We were able to put him on oxygen right away while uncovering him."

Dave Myers, ski patrol director: "The dog dug to Jeff by himself. Everything worked right. Fifteen minutes from the call to the find. We had two avalanche dogs located at the top of the hill. Everything that was done was appropriate and expedient."

"Apparently Jeff knew he was in the slide, tried swimming, tried to cover his face up, and it looked like just the position of his body might have aided in that. I think everything combined helped. It looked like he had been swept to the side of the avalanche into the trees. He was under about 3 feet of compacted snow. He was not able to move at all. They estimate he was found in 15 to 20 minutes, by 12:27. It took quite a few minutes to actually dig him out.

"As other patrolmen got the oxygen on him I was able to reward the dog. He had already grabbed a stick. He was pretty happy about the whole deal. He was the true definition of a hero—he had no clue what he had done. Happy as can be, same old Doc. Then we went back to work and helped clear the rest of the slide path to make sure there was nobody else. Probe lines got established."

Myers: "We had about 12 patrollers on the scene and about 30 volunteers."

Paradysz: "I worked Doc for about an hour. Pretty intense. The dog was beat. I brought him down to the bottom, got him some water, let him rest while I went back up and probed.

"Jeff was found approximately 100 feet below the crown, swept into some trees from above. We were guessing it ran 500-600 feet total. It was hard slab. I don't know if anyone did a fracture line profile afterwards. Jeff lost both skis, his pole and a glove in the slide. Originally we thought the slide might have been ridge deposition, but up there later we saw the sliding surface was pretty close to the ground. The crown was a 3-foot fracture. It had been shot the day before, the last time it snowed."

Jeff Eckland, after the rescue: "I knew I was going to be all right when I felt the dog on top of my head."

AVALANCHE SAR TACTICS

Safety and speed are the dual tactics for successful avalanche rescue. Safety comes first. If *the area itself or the access route to the area are in danger of re-avalanche*, rescuers may have to wait until control work has been performed or conditions change. This is hard to do when the operation is set to go and every minute ticking by reduces the victim's chances for survival. Flipping the rescue helicopter in a powder slide is not a good idea, one agency discovered while inserting teams on a backcountry accident. At another ski area avalanche two search dogs had alerted to two different locations on a 400-foot slide. Two young skiers were missing. Patrolmen had driven long poles to mark each location and were shoveling snow when the lookout posted above the slide called out *avalanche*. Dogs and people ran for their lives. Later in the spring the two bodies were recovered a few feet uphill of each marker pole. The poles had moved with the melting snowpack. The dogs had detected the skiers under 15 feet of wet compacted snow.

Speed and safety are maximized by the following search tactics:

1. Avalanche safety and communications equipment and training for both the dog and handler are basic requirements.

2. If the handler and dog are first on the scene, the handler must make the initial safety assessment prior to deploying the dog. If professionals are on scene, get an advisory from them. If falling snow, wind deposition, or loaded slopes threaten release, be ready to leave the area.

3. Work a regular pattern from the point of access, preferably up the slide from the bottom of the deposition, preferably into the wind. Sniffing up the slope takes precedence over searching into the wind if the handler has discretion. The dog's search style must be rapid and efficient. The dog may be trained to work out across the avalanche while the handler climbs up one side, or the handler and dog may work the pattern together across the slide.

Avalanche hunter Dick Reuter (right) prepares to throw a hand charge for avalanche control, Carson Spur, California.

4. Detail the slide below every known PLS, all likely areas, and the locations where other victims have been found. The place where tracks (snowboard, snowmobile, skis, snowshoes, boots) enter the avalanche may be *below* the victim's buried location if he climbed up the avalanche path before it released.

5. The handler should be trained to operate an avalanche transceiver or handheld detector while working the dog. He should be prepared to help the scenting dog by probing or shoveling as necessary. Unless he has an assistant, the handler is responsible for flagging his dog's alerts.

6. When the dog alerts, unless he digs immediately to the victim, the handler reinforces him with praise, directs shovelers to the location, and redeploys the dog. The team should be trained in reindication procedures for deep snow. If the handler is the only rescuer on scene, he will in most cases attempt to make the recovery at the location of the alert.

7. Multiple dog teams should coordinate their deployment. The size of the slide will determine how many dogs can search effectively at the same time. It is usually better to have fewer dog teams working the slide at once with frequent rotations than to crowd canines onto the site. Briefing procedures are important for replacement teams.

8. If the dog alerts off the avalanche, teams should check the trees and the snowpack, including tree wells, rocks or crevasses where an airborne avalanche may have blown the victim. If the avalanche had a known airborne component, off-slide areas should

be segmented for search. The victim may have been killed or disabled by the violent flight then covered by falling snow.

9. Scent diffuses laterally as well as vertically where there is a channel, such as a water course or plant life near the source. The dog that alerts and digs to a tree branch or flowing ground water may be detecting scent from a victim buried somewhere else on the hill. Investigation may require tracing these scent channels to discover the source.

10. Resting the dog is an essential tactic too often disregarded in the stress of the emergency. If dehydrated or fatigued, the dog may be sniffing while he is actually incapable of detecting the source scent. Regardless how the dog appears to everyone else, it is the handler's responsibility to read his dog's viability: *look good, search good.*

Although a killer avalanche is by definition a disaster, urban-type avalanches where buildings are hacked apart and swept downhill by the snow, the rocks or the mud are much less common in the U.S. than in countries like Chile or Nepal. Credit goes in part to building codes, but the 21st

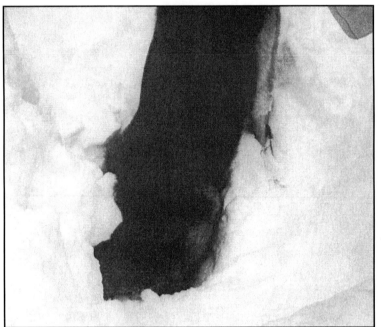

century will see more development in steep-sided mountain valleys. To the detector dog it is all the same. His job is typically made easier by voids in the rubble. Scent concentrates there, and air spaces tend to increase the victim survival rate. However, the handler and other rescuers face more hazards in the urban avalanche (collapse, explosion, fire, toxins) than in a simple snow slide where the biggest threats are typically re-avalanche or backcountry access. Deployment procedures must take these hazards into account despite the possible net effect of slowing the entire rescue operation.

TWIN LAKES AVALANCHE

The area was still not safe. A week after major avalanches destroyed several homes in 1986, the eastern Sierra had hundreds of unstable slopes still loaded with snow ready to go. No place was riskier than Twin Lakes in Mono County, California. Crossing the icy lakes in boats, search and rescue

Digging to the scent source. Train with equipment scattered in the snowpack to reduce the chance of gear diverting the dog from finding people.

personnel saw slides continuing to rake the mountainsides that rise above the shoreline at 7000 feet to 8- and 9000-foot summits. The steep east- and south-facing slopes, largely barren except for scrub sage and a few trees in the gullies, represent ideal avalanche terrain. The previous week sheriff's deputies had warned residents to evacuate, but they did not go. Plows worked Lower Twin Lake, cutting through 25-foot deep slides to open up the road along the lake.

Missing was John Aaron, 28, occupant of a house caught in the slide. Playing pool at a neighbor's house, February 15th, he went home in the early evening. At 8:30 pm his friends were concerned about the avalanche danger and called him. He said he would be safe in the basement. At 9:08 pm the electricity failed. Dual avalanches had hit the two power poles behind Aaron's house then crashed into the 3-story structure, driving the upper two stories 300 feet downhill, shredding and tearing everything in its path and sending debris across Twin Lakes Road. The 20-ton rock fireplace inside the house was destroyed. A vacant house below Aaron's was destroyed as well.

The main avalanche was a Class 5, 1500 feet long, 70 feet wide, cleared to ground. It released from an elevation of 8500 feet. A feeder gully joined the main path high on the slope, adding snow to the flow.

For a week the avalanche danger was extreme. The day after the avalanche the neighbors went

WOOF dog Zeke *alerting in 30 foot snow pit to the body of John Aaron.*

outside briefly to dig where the foundation should have been. Aaron's dad and brother arrived. They dug and dug and ended up with a 6-foot hole. The snow was hard and over 35 feet deep.

On February 21st the first rescue crews to enter the area brought two rescue dog teams to search the avalanche path. One team worked high, one low. Chris Salisbury and German shepherd Lance began searching the lower half of the debris where the top two levels of the house lay in ruins. Judy Cross and golden retriever Zeke searched the upper half directly above the foundation. Each dog alerted in his area. Personnel from Mono County SAR and Marines from the Mountain Warfare Training Center shoveled and probed. The dog teams switched areas. Each dog confirmed the previous alert. The locations were flagged, and shoveling continued.

The handlers controlled the dogs as they sniffed the unstable debris. Climbing through the voids, the dogs made each move carefully, sniffing constantly. The alerts were unmistakable. Each dog would dig and paw and bark, trying to penetrate the rubble. At the lower site they recovered the source of the scent, the victim's boots and gaiters. The dog teams searched the rest of the avalanche with no other alerts.

Late that afternoon, Marines digging above the north wall of the basement thought they heard whining. They dug a small round hole toward the sound. Suddenly, a dog popped out of the hole. It was John's German shepherd Sadie. She had survived in a runway behind the back wall of the foundation, uninjured except for a few cuts on her face and side. After greeting everybody, she went away and relieved herself, something she had not done for 6 days. Finding Sadie, Aaron's best friend, renewed hope that he was still alive.

Day 2 of the search was dedicated to excavating the primary alert area, periodically putting the dogs back into the rubble to check for reindications. They developed a routine: put a dog in, get the strong digging alert, pull the dog out, shovel. Put the dog back in to determine what direction to dig, then pull the dog out and shovel again. It was temperature gradient, scent permeable snow throughout with the exception of ice layers and debris that shifted the scent pattern. Aaron's scent was evidently diffusing along the collapsed flooring. While digging, Zeke cut his paw on a piece of glass invisible in the snow. That did not stop the dog. The dogs were not distracted by the 50 or more people on the surface of the site, the food, the chainsaws, the snowmobiles, the D-8 Caterpillar working the lower half of the slide—nothing broke their concentration.

The Marines dug and dug. The Cat rolled up to assist and bladed 25 feet of snow and debris off the site. They hit timbers that had fallen near the fireplace. The dog went back in and gave a strong alert. The Marines dug. The handler probed something soft. Sent back into the hole, the dog brought out Aaron's powder pants then dived back into the hole digging furiously until he was upside down. He produced Aaron's balaclava, tearing it to shreds. The handler said, "My dog knows where this man is."

Rescuers dug. The more they probed and dug in that one spot, the more the dog got into it, digging while standing on his head. Six feet more, totaling over 35 feet, a shoveler said, "We got him." The dog had reached Aaron's head. Aaron was on his side in his sleeping bag. He had probably heard it coming and had brought his hands up over his nose and mouth. An ice mask encased him. They had to chainsaw through the debris to make the recovery.

"Check and see if there's any warmth," said his father Walter Aaron. "Just check and see."

His other son, a medic, shoved his way to the hole saying, "Get out of the way!" Touching the solid, frozen body, he recoiled, "Let's get out of here!"

The father went over and sat down. Looking into the distance, he said, "That mountain killed my son, didn't it?"

PETERS RIDGE AVALANCHE

The following avalanche accident account is compiled from reports by Stan K. Bones, Northwestern Montana Avalanche Information System, and rescue dog handler Terry Crooks of the David Thompson Search and Rescue Team in Libby, Montana.

During the last two weeks of December 1993, prior to the accident, western Montana had been covered by a high pressure weather system and temperature inversions. Colder heavier air had settled in the Flathead Valley, producing low clouds and fog. At the higher elevations conditions had been mostly dry and clear. Although dry conditions had dominated, the areas exposed just above the cloud deck were receiving deposits of surface hoar.

On Thursday morning, December 30th, a locally heavy snowfall moved into the area. The Peters Ridge—Jewel Basin is a moisture favored area receiving a strong influence from nearby Flathead Lake. The Noisy Basin SNOTEL site just a couple of drainages south of the Peters Ridge location recorded 3.4 inches SWE (snow-water equivalent) during the 24 hours from 4 am Thursday to 4 am Friday. This translates to 24 inches of new fallen snow being deposited upon the surface hoar layer.

Friday a group of 14 were snowmobiling in the Peters Ridge area near Bigfork, Montana. Their objective was to make the crest of the Swan Range and snowmobile in the Strawberry Lake area. The party was mixed Canadian and local U.S. citizens. The Northwestern Montana Avalanche Information System backcountry avalanche advisory issued at 8 am that morning rated the instability in this area as *moderate* on slopes having terrain with vegetative anchors and *high* on slopes lacking anchors. The slope that failed was mostly devoid of anchors.

Around 11:30 am, snowmobilers Pierce, Brazda, and the Canadians rode their machines up Peters Ridge Forest Service Road through 4-5 inches of new snow. At the point where they left the road, the head count was 12 with Buls and Anderson ahead of them. They overtook these two at a draw above an avalanche path. The new snowfall depth at that point was 16-18 inches. Buls and Anderson were having trouble breaking trail through the moderately heavy powder. It was snowing, but visibility was good with the cloud layer still above them.

Catching up with Buls and Anderson, Brazda and Pierce continued to lead the group and break trail with the larger and more powerful machines capable of setting the track. There were 13 machines in the group with 7-year-old riding double with his father Miles Merrill. All the snowmobiles were specially modified machines with 2-inch traction cleats. The machines were designed to operate in steep powder and heavy going.

Up the draw, the entire party circled their machines, stopped and collected on a flat area in the first avalanche path of the Strawberry Mountain Basin. On previous trips Brazda and Pierce had seen evidence of this slope avalanching. On this day moderately thick alder brush was sticking 5 feet out of the snow. Visibility was still good, but the cloud layer was just above their heads. From that point, the draw bottom turns left, climbs 30-35 degrees for 400 feet to a bench in the draw.

Leaving the group on the flat, Brazda climbed the steep pitch and slowed, turning and stopping on the bench, the site of the eventual avalanche accident. Popping sounds from his snowmobile indicated the clutch and belt were getting hot from pushing the machine through the heavy powder. Brazda estimated 24 inches of new snowfall at that location. Visibility was now down to 100 feet. Waiting perhaps 30 minutes for the rest, he removed his helmet and opened the hood to cool the clutch.

Bart Nelson drove up the slope in Brazda's track, circled above him, dropped down and stopped alongside. Ten machines crowded on the bench. Finally, some rode back down to the large flat, including Brazda, Pierce and Jim Baird. Brazda intended to run back uphill, forging to the crest of the Swan Divide, 300 vertical feet above the bench.

Six machines with 7 riders remained on the bench. Miles and son Jamie Merrill were doubled. Brazda remembers he had stopped below on the flat waiting with other machines when he heard Pierce call out, "Hey! Look out!" Turning to look up the draw toward the bench, he saw an avalanche coming down out of the fog. Turning to start his machine then turning back again to see the avalanche, he realized the lower edge of the deposition was stopping above them. The avalanche would not reach them on the flat.

The avalanche was estimated to be 900-950 feet slope distance from the highest point to the draw. After the flow entered the draw it turned left and flowed down the draw another 350-400 feet. Total elevation drop from top of crown to toe of debris was estimated to have been 750 feet. The slide was 350-400 feet wide.

After what Brazda believed were seconds but may have been longer, he remembers someone repeatedly yelling up to the bench asking if anyone was there. The eventual reply was only one. Indicating to the other six riders he was going back up to the bench, he got two-thirds of the way when his machine became unbalanced on the avalanche debris. Turning left around a couple of small trees, he was unable to continue climbing. He descended the slope again in order to make another run at it. Anderson had left to get a shovel. The avalanche snow was compacted, so Brazda's snowmobile had good traction.

On the second attempt he succeeded in regaining the bench. Sandra Sherman stood along the west edge of the debris. She appeared okay. When hit by the slide she fought and swam against the flow. After she came to a stop buried in 3 feet of snow, she pushed and dug her way out. She sustained fractured ribs, probably from impact with the tumbling snowmobile she had been riding. Baird transported Sherman to Base II Camp. An ambulance took her to Kalispell Regional Hospital, where she was treated and released the next day.

Continuing to the upper edge of the debris, Brazda saw a sea of white snow and fog broken only by a few small trees. Pierce followed on his snowmobile. Nearing the top of the debris, Brazda saw the bottom of a snowmobile

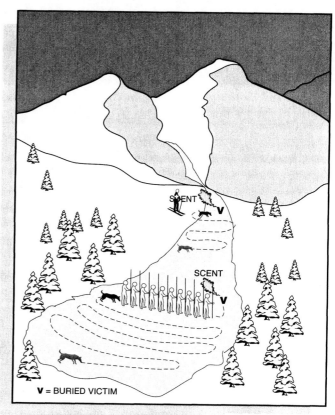

Train the dog to sniff probe holes. Deep, dense snow and ice are barriers to scent diffusion. Post lookouts to warn of re-avalanche.

V = BURIED VICTIM

Marie Sjoquist, WOOF Search Dog Unit.

ski he recognized as a Polaris. Stopping, he began digging with his gloved hands around the buried machine. He became exhausted rapidly, however, and realized the futility of his efforts.

Pierce was carrying a cellular telephone. At 1252 hours he called 911, alerting the Flathead County Sheriff's Office. Dispatch alerted East Valley Quick Response Unit, a volunteer medical emergency unit, and Creston Volunteer Fire Department. The ALERT helicopter, an advanced life support unit, was dispatched with a flight EMT and RN aboard. Flathead SAR, Flathead Nordic Ski Patrol, and Big Fork Quick Response Unit were notified. Kalispell police and ambulance were asked to assist. The call went out for responders with snowmobiles to report to the Peters Ridge Trailhead. North Valley SAR was initially placed on standby as they had responded to another reported avalanche in the Lost Johnny drainage on the opposite side of the Swan Crest Divide.

The ALERT helicopter was unable to fly anywhere near the incident because of low clouds and landed at the trailhead site, later called Base 1 Camp. Some individuals that worked with Creston Fire or East Valley QRU lived near the Peters Ridge Trailhead and were able to respond rapidly. A Flathead County motor grader plowing snow in the vicinity was dispatched to clear Peters Ridge Road to the trailhead, later called Base II Camp. Ambulance units followed the grader as it plowed a single lane up the Peters Ridge Road. Responders lacking snowmobiles were paired with those that had machines. An initial concern was rescuer avalanche training and safety equipment. More avalanches threatened the site and the approach route.

A transceiver search was conducted at the scene. The Canadians had three transceivers. Jamie Merrill was wearing one when he was buried. Baird and Sandra Sherman also had transceivers but were unable to detect any signals from Merrill's buried unit. Although Gordon Sherman owned a transceiver, he was not wearing it that day.

Members of the snowmobiling party and some of the first rescuers to arrive had no probes. They cut sticks and small trees to use as probes in hopes of finding buried victims. They probed some buried snow machines but could only penetrate 6-24 inches. Except for Sherman, all the victims were buried 5 feet or more. Once rescuers arrived with conduit probes and shovels, productive digging was possible.

Approximately 2 hours after the avalanche, Jamie Merrill was found by digging, buried between 2 snowmobiles. His location between the machines probably prevented dense packing of the snow. He was found with his head beneath one of the machines. Heat from the engines may have helped provide an air pocket that allowed Merrill to survive his 5-foot burial. When recovered, he was hypothermic but quickly warmed and aided in the search for his 7-year-old son Miles.

When flight EMT Anderson and RN Wardle arrived on scene, they administered to the victims as found. Radio communications from the avalanche site to Kalispell Regional Hospital were not possible, the first indication of the radio communication problems that plagued the search effort to its conclusion. Only one of the 4 victims found that afternoon showed any signs of responding to CPR. Pat Buls, victim number 3, was transported to Base II Camp while CPR continued. He was pronounced dead there. The other 3 victims were all pronounced dead on site.

Buls was found by rescuers digging further around the 2 snocats where Merrill was found. Victim number 4, Bart Nelson, was also found by rescuers digging in the area around his buried snowmobile.

Victim number 5, K. Smith, is credited by the accident site commander as a dog recovery. Two German shepherd police dogs from the Kalispell Police Department arrived at the avalanche scene at about 1645 hours. One of these dogs is credited with finding Smith, who was pronounced dead at 1706 hours. The dogs alerted to several other sites, but probing and digging at these locations produced no further finds. These 2 dogs were joined later that night by a Golden Retriever, also unsuccessful at finding the last victim.

Victim number 6, Gordon Sherman, was found by random probing about 20 feet downslope from a snocat found uphill of some small trees. The last victim that day, Sherman was pronounced dead at 1736 hours, 5 hours after the avalanche.

On that Friday four of the victims were found near their snow machines. Sherman and Smith, the apparent exceptions, were found 75-100 feet uphill of their machines. All members of the party wore helmets on the trip. Air temperatures were mild at the time of the accident, estimated at 30 degrees Fahrenheit. Some of the victims may have removed their helmets while their machines sat on the bench. Two of the fatalities were found without helmets. One victim was found without a face shield. His helmet was packed with snow. No ice masks were found on any of the victims. The four fatalities were buried 5-6 feet. All died from asphyxiation.

As darkness fell a small generator and 2 lights were brought to the accident site, allowing the search for the boy to continue well into the night. Tired searchers leaving the site were replaced by incoming better trained probers. After nightfall the number of rescuers at the avalanche scene stabilized to 75 persons split among two 20-person probe lines, shovelers, several random probers, and various support personnel. Base III Camp to provide rescue support was initially set up on the flat in the runout zone of an avalanche path that had not yet slid. The camp was later moved to a safer location.

Heavy snowmobile traffic ferrying rescuers and supplies compacted and iced the steep hill, obstructing the flow, and forcing the installation of a pulley system using a powerful snowmobile to pull downhill and tow less powerful cats to the top.

Afterward searchers reported that the confusion, the trash, the people and machines all over the surface of the avalanche made it very difficult for the dogs to work. The incident command and ski patrol probers did their best to search in an orderly fashion, but scent contamination preceded the arrival of most trained rescuers and there was apparently little overall strategy. The K-9 teams were deployed without much plan. Because of fatigue, the search for Miles Merrill was suspended at 0045 hours.

Saturday dawned snowing. When the recovery crew arrived on site at 10 o'clock, 5 inches of new snow covered the accident scene. The new snowfall was accompanied by light southwest winds. Visibility was limited by snowfall and clouds. During the search period the new snowfall rate was measured at 1.25 inches per hour. Only searchers with transceivers were

allowed on site because of the increased avalanche hazard. Members of the Flathead Nordic Ski Patrol, Missoula SAR, Lake County SAR, David Thompson SAR, Flathead SAR, Forest Service, and a few individuals made up the 27-person search group this day.

Handler Terry Crooks and his black Labrador *Jess* (certified by the Canadian Avalanche Dog Association) of the David Thompson SAR Team went by ambulance to the staging area where snowmobiles were lining up to drive to the scene.

"There was no briefing. I was asking questions to gather information. I asked one of the rescuers if there were any witnesses to the PLS of the boy. The fellow next to me said, 'I was standing next to him. He is my son.'

"The father was one of the best snowmobilers. To prevent the dog getting a lot of fumes in the face riding to the site, we got on a snowmobile with the dad. I rode the back, and he drove standing up, straddling the dog the whole way. He said it would be an easy 2.5 miles, but it was wild. What's rough to us is no big deal to a snowmobiler.

"There was a lot of confusion. The rescue crews had little experience working with dogs. The slide was heavily contaminated with food, snowmobile emissions, and human waste." The activity concentrated on random probing, dog searching, and coarse probing of the deposition below the central portion of the slide, between the position where the Merrills were caught by the avalanche and the area where Jamie Merrill was found the day before.

"We started working from the bottom up. The slide had not been flagged, there were no markers. Seventy-five people had loaded the slide the night before. There were 6-foot pits. The process of recovering four bodies, one live victim, and five machines, had left holes everywhere. Basically the slide came down and made a break or elbow to the left. Most of the deposition, where the snow machines and people were found, was in that curve. My dog indicated on the old holes where they had found people. I was with a fellow who was there the day before. I would ask him if somebody had been found here. He would say yes, somebody was found there. The dog made her way up, indicating several places here and there. I dropped flags at a total of six places where urine or other human contamination was found.

"Those who had not worked with dogs before did not understand that with dog indications you go all the way to the bottom to check it out. At the upper end where the depth was over 10 feet, searchers were reluctant to check it to the bottom as the probes were only 10 feet long. At the top of the slide area, my dog had two indications, one where the wind was blowing across the pack to the base of a tree and the place where the boy was found. She persisted in returning four times to alert at the site before it was excavated. I flagged it and pulled people in saying this needs to be checked. They would probe it then leave. Finally one of the guys that knew dogs committed to digging out the hole.

"Time was running out. The site commander directed his effort toward the dog's repeated alerts. It was snowing heavily, the pack was wind loading again with poor visibility. We were working below several loaded avalanche chutes. They had to make the decision that if we don't make the find by 1 pm, we're out of here. They had talked to the dad.

"Ten minutes before we pulled out the boy was found where Jess had repeatedly alerted. He was 12 feet down, 30-40 feet from his last seen area. The dad was grateful. He really believed in the dog and gave credit to the people that were there. He had worked by our side courageously throughout the rescue looking for his son. A lot of parents don't care enough about their kids to take them out and spend time with them."

All personnel organized quickly to evacuate the avalanche site.

"We worked 2.5 hours on the slide. The dog comes out of field trial stock and was so fired up. She is relentless and will never stop. After a couple hours, I finally dropped down the slope and put her down to rest. That was why I did not go back into the hole until the find was verified. The dog could read the intensity of the actual search and was working extremely well. After the find, I rewarded Jess by giving her her favorite retrieving dummy. She enjoyed it as always, playing without a care."

Sunday, January 2nd, the Flathead Nordic Ski Patrol held an incident debriefing. On Wednesday the 5th, Flathead Sheriff Jim Dupont held a debriefing for all organizations involved in the incident. Several critical incident stress syndrome debriefings were held after the accident for operations personnel.

This accident was preventable. The party did not call the avalanche hotline, a free 800 number, to check on backcountry snow and avalanche conditions before departing. They lacked the knowledge and experience to evaluate the weather and snow conditions to determine the stability of the snow. While traveling in avalanche terrain they failed to practice safe travel techniques. The party grouped in a draw at the base of an obvious slide path. The bench location where the 7 snowmobilers were caught is not only threatened by avalanches from the path that released but is also at risk from releases farther up the draw or from slides on the slope opposite the fatal slide.

It is probably impossible to determine if the fatal avalanche was a natural or artificial release. The avalanche could have been a natural release as the result of heavy new snow loading onto a buried weak surface hoar layer. It may also have been triggered by the 7 riders on 6 snowmobiles overloading the buried surface hoar layer or a more deeply buried layer of faceted or cup-shaped crystals. Snow depths along the side of the avalanche were measured at 5 feet, while the debris depth was estimated to be 15 feet maximum in the deepest portions of the draw. Water content of the avalanche debris snow was measured at 38%. The avalanche was rated SS-N or AO-3-O (soft slab, natural or artificial-other release, medium size path, old snow running surface).

Visibility at the time of the avalanche was very limited. The party below was unable to observe the victims as they were caught in the slide. No one was able to identify the last seen points or areas of the victims. Only a limited number of the party were wearing transceivers. Of the 3 beacons utilized that day, only 2 appeared to be operable. All members of the party should have been wearing transceivers, and the frequencies of those units needed to be compatible. The party was not carrying sufficient, if any, shovels and collapsible probe poles. These pieces of safety equipment are needed by all members of such a party. These people were all accomplished and skilled snowmobile riders. They lacked, however, avalanche skills in risk assessment and safe travel and route selection techniques. Their riding equipment was top notch. They lacked safety equipment.

Concerning the rescue and recovery operation, the county sheriff's office, the search and rescue organizations, and the county office of disaster and emergency services needed to adopt the Incident Command System. The county needed to develop an avalanche response plan identifying resources and trained personnel. The plan would include notification procedures for agencies and entities bearing responsibility for managing public and private lands.

Search dog teams specifically need to be trained and certified to a recognized level of performance. Particularly in disasters, like this incident, common practice has been to field whatever dogs are available. As Crooks and Jess demonstrated with their find, reliable detection tactics are critical and are only achievable through training. This accident with 5 fatalities matched the Mt. Cleveland climbing accident during Christmas holiday in 1969 as one of the most serious avalanche accidents in Montana.

CHAPTER 9

BOMB DOGS

"As terrorist tactics change,

it will become increasingly important to be proactive

rather than reactive

in developing technologies to protect the public."
—Congress of the United States
Office of Technology Assessment

"We always underestimate the dog.

Only he knows what he's smelling.

We can only be guided by his body language.

You have to pay attention to him.

You miss a bomb, and it lets you know."
—Detective Bob Noll, Bomb Squad,
New York City Police Department

At 7:17 p.m., December 21, 1988, Pan Am Flight 103 disappeared from the radar screens of Prestwick, Scotland. Bound from Frankfurt to New York, the Boeing 747 *Maid of the Seas* exploded at an altitude of 31,000 feet and crashed onto Lockerbie, Scotland. The blast was felt 2.5 miles away and killed all 259 passengers and crew along with 11 people on the ground. Police and rescue dog teams from many parts of Britain went into action. Andy Colau and Bill Parr, handlers with search dog units in Southern Scotland, reported the following.

Subsequent to the crash, all rescue services were summoned to the locality following activation of the local authority's emergency/major incident scheme. By 9 p.m. two police dog teams and one local SAR dog team were deployed to search the main impact area and ruins of domestic properties, and to ensure that the immediate area had been cleared of all non-essential personnel. The first sortie of the rescue mission had the number one priority of *finding anybody alive.* At this time fires were still burning and the streets were littered with glass, rubble, etc. The whole area reeked of aviation fuel.

Spewing burning fuel, a large chunk of the fuselage had struck a hill outside Lockerbie, then careened into a gas station and two rows of houses, gouging a 20-foot-wide crater in a roadway. In the center of town, an aircraft engine lay embedded in the street. The wings and attached fuselage section dug a crater 140 feet long, 80 feet deep, and 40 feet wide. Two houses disappeared. The impact caused the fuel to explode into a fireball towering 10,000 feet. Twenty-five miles south the

main highway was littered with dirt and pebble-sized pieces of rubble. Honeycomb insulation was found on the coast of England, 80 miles distant.

The initial search concentrated for 10 miles along the fight path. Bodies were distributed in an east-west line. Two police dogs found 61 bodies in one-half hour on a nearby golf course. They were taken to the town hall, which had been turned into a makeshift mortuary. Scotland Yard opened a separate murder inquiry for each body. One body was found on a back porch, another entangled in the branches of a tree. Three miles away, the plane's blue-and-white cockpit segment containing the 19 bodies of the flight crew had landed, fully recognizable, on the hillside of a farm. Hacked off the fuselage, it lay on its side like an ill-fated fish.

Search dog teams were dispatched in police transport to investigate a report of possible survivors. The report turned out to be incorrect. During searches of the country roads and fields, the dogs located aircraft wreckage. A chance meeting with a farmer resulted in a search of debris on open moorland in sleety conditions. Compass bearings of the general debris trail were taken at known grid references and reported to police control.

By 11:30 p.m. 21 additional search dog teams had arrived, having traveled up to 150 miles from their homes. After consultation with police it was decided that search dog teams working in groups and in combination with local and Royal Air Force mountain rescue teams would search the urban area immediately out of the fire zone and rural areas indicated by the previously-found debris trail. Temperatures dropped throughout the night to 5-10°F. The smell of aviation fuel hung in the night air. Some of the dogs sustained chemical burns on their feet.

By 8:00 a.m. the teams had located over 100 bodies but no survivors. After a short break 18 dog teams were redeployed to cover the forest and wooded areas, with foot search teams and helicopters covering the open ground to determine the location of bodies, personal effects, mail and aircraft wreckage. Canine team searches were terminated one hour after darkness.

On Friday, December 23rd, the search took on what was to be the general theme until December 31st, comprising open moorland and forestry searches, searches in the area of the explosion and fire, and searches in rubble and fuselage debris located in the urban area remote from the initial fire and explosion. Generally dog teams were used to locate human remains, personal belongings, mail, aircraft wreckage, anything that had been on board Flight 103. Canine teams worked directly with police and accident investigators locating bodies under debris up to 4 feet deep. Finds included bags of U.S. mail and an exquisite cut glass vial of perfume. All finds were treated as confidential because the police suspected they were dealing with sabotage.

A total of 46 volunteer search dog teams were used, peaking at 40 teams on December 26th. Teams were drawn from most parts of Scotland, England, Wales, and Northern Ireland, some traveling more than 350 miles. Several dogs were injured. Three handlers suffered minor injuries searching ruins and from exposure to aviation fuel fumes. Stress played an important role in determining handler and dog suitability for certain tasks. Every handler and dog was restricted to a maximum of three 9-hour days within the impact zone, working up to 20 minutes and resting away from fumes for at least 15 minutes.

Wreckage was scattered over a vast tract of land stretching from Lockerbie to the North Sea. At least ten houses were destroyed. The agency ended up with hundreds of bags of fragmented, unidentifiable human remains. The cost of the aftermath to the local authority was estimated at nearly 5-million pounds, not including the assistance provided by the armed services.

What brought about the worst security-related disaster in aviation history involving a U.S. civilian air carrier?

> A small battery sends a small current through a wire. A fuse is ignited. Approximately 14 ounces of a plastic explosive called *Semtex* is detonated. The explosive force of the blast is sufficient to penetrate through the luggage container and pierce the plane's fuselage just below the left wing. A catastrophic chain reaction begins, combining the force of the blast with the high pressure inside the cabin and the low pressure of the environment outside the plane. Cracks in the fuselage are created and began to spread out. Holes are poked in the roof and the belly of the plane. The hydraulic systems are cut and the craft becomes uncontrollable. But there is nothing left to control as the plane disintegrates and falls to earth in and around Lockerbie.
> —Ralph Nader and Wesley J. Smith in *Collision Course*

Nearly 1000 aircraft passengers throughout the world have been killed in the past 8 years because of terrorist bomb attacks on civilian aircraft. "How could this happen?" ask the families.

Nader and Smith describe two ways to significantly reduce the possibility of such calamities:

1. Sufficiently stringent *security checks* in place to prevent any bombs from being smuggled on aircraft
2. *Aircraft hardening*: building bomb resistant planes.

The problem: Very small bombs that are difficult to detect have enough power to potentially destroy an aircraft that is in flight. According to the study, *Technology Against Terrorism: Structuring Security*, by the U.S. Congress, Office of Technology Assessment (January 1992), "Explosive devices of the size used in airline terrorist events to date are deadly not because they directly cause catastrophic failure (blow the aircraft to pieces), but because they start a domino effect where the aircraft destroys itself." For example, necessary electronic or hydraulic systems can be destroyed, causing the plane to crash. Or radiating cracks in the fuselage can be caused by the explosion, causing the fuselage skin to peel back; hence, the plane disintegrates, which is what happened to the Boeing 747 that was flying as Pan Am Flight 103.

It is difficult to develop detectors that can discover a bomb that is physically small, but contains enough explosive material to cause an airliner to crash after detonation. Research is

The problem: Very small bombs that are difficult to detect have enough power to potentially destroy an aircraft that is in flight.

seeking a way to "harden" the aircraft and the cargo storage equipment (or harden only the cargo bins), so that the smaller bomb cannot create the domino effect of plane loss-of-control or disintegration. The FAA and aircraft industry are looking at manufacturing bomb-resistant removable containers that hold luggage.

Civilian aircraft continue to be an inviting target to saboteurs, extortionists, and the mentally deranged. Accordingly, passengers and members of the public who wish access to a gate are screened for weapons and explosives. According to the Department of Transportation publication, National Transportation Statistics (June 1992), in 1990, 1,145 billion people were subjected to airline passenger screening. From that screening process, 2,853 firearms and 15 explosive/incendiary devices were detected. During this same time period, more than 400 bomb threats were directed against airports and more than 300 bomb threats were directed at aircraft in the United States. *Nationwide, in cities and other areas, bombing incidents are on the order of tens of thousands and are increasing.*

> We know that there is a lot of thievery out of luggage at airports. If something can be taken out of a suitcase, something can also be put in.
> —Caroline D. Gabel, House Subcommittee on Aviation

Billions of pieces of luggage and mail annually carried on domestic flights create a security nightmare. Saboteurs are paying particular attention to *looking normal* in order to foil any profiling procedures. Subversives also use dupes to evade screening systems.

The security measures taken at Ben Gurion Airport in Israel are instructive. At Ben Gurion, a highly motivated and well-trained security force performs a personal in-depth interview and profile evaluation of all passengers. The profiling looks at things such as passenger travel documents, their responses to an established set of questions, and the trained observations of the security personnel. (Passengers at Ben Gurion must report two or three hours in advance of their flight.) The aim of the system is to eliminate a large fraction of the passengers who do not appear to represent any possible threat from the time-consuming hand search imposed on those passengers who fit the suspect profile. This system is *augmented with a positive luggage and passenger match before the plane leaves the airport* (emphasis added).

> —Ralph Nader and Wesley J. Smith

The FAA and law enforcement agencies must maintain awareness of basic civil liberties. In the application of current intelligence to recognize the indicators of potential sabotage, security personnel must not be overzealous or base screening procedures primarily upon race or ethnic appearance. During the Persian Gulf War it was widely reported that many people who ostensibly "looked" like Arabs were subjected to vigorous and harassing security checks. In the interest of public safety the courts have upheld that if used responsibly, *procedures that recognize indicators and direct luggage, parcels, or individuals to greater technological screening are not unwarranted intrusion into people's privacy.*

One technology, thermal neutron activation (TNA) detects plastic explosives by bombarding the items being examined with slowly moving neutrons that are absorbed by nitrogen nuclei, emitting characteristic radiation that is read by detectors. Another technology employs blowing controlled air past the item or person being examined, collecting the diffused gases, and chemically analyzing them.

Bomb dogs sniffing the air are another technology. Louis A. Turpen, Director of San Francisco International Airport, stated that an effective security program should include a "systems approach." "Mix the tools at each point in the system. Include redundancy. Change the routine on a regular basis so that security measures are not predictable. Play the 'what if,' game. Try and anticipate weaknesses so that they can be filled. Adequately fund your security forces and have a program that

Model Explosive Detector Dog Team Performance Record

AGENCY: _____

_____   _____
OFFICER   ID NO.

_____ _____   M F   _____
DOG   BREED   SEX   AGE

1. I have been a police officer for ___ years. During this time, I have had the following training and experience:

_____
_____
_____
_____
_____
_____

__ Resume attached

2. I have been a K-9 officer for ____ years. During this time, I have had the following training and experience:

_____
_____
_____
_____
_____

__ Resume attached

3. I have worked with the dog named above for ____ years. During this time, we have had the following training and experience:

_____
_____
_____
_____
_____

K-9 TRAINING/TESTING REPORTS   __ Attached   __ Available
K-9 INCIDENT REPORTS   __ Attached   __ Available

4. My dog is trained to detect the following substances: _____

_____

When the dog recognizes a scent he is trained to detect, he *alerts,* typically exhibiting the following behavior:

_____

can respond to individual circumstances. *Bring people into the program who are excited about their work and want to do a good job (emphasis added)*. Mandate federal law enforcement and security agencies to communicate with the airports about the current threat assessment. Take these steps and the security of aviation would be greatly enhanced."

The bomb dog teams of the San Francisco Airport Police are representative of the high level of enthusiasm and professionalism necessary for reliable explosives detection. Trained and evaluated through Air Force contract to FAA, the teams undergo yearly recertification.

The handlers are trained in bomb recognition and are trained to execute safe procedures in deploying the explosives detector dog (EDD). In addition to conducting security searches at the San Francisco Airport itself (federal property, aircraft, cargo, and for visiting dignitaries, including the President of the United States), the bomb squad responds throughout the Bay Area.

Implemented in 1972, the FAA has an extensive program in the U.S. to protect the airports. The United States Air Force (USAF), through a reimbursable agreement with the FAA, provides initial training at Lackland Air Force Base, San Antonio, Texas. The USAF also provides follow-up evaluations and refresher explosives detection training for civilian law enforcement officers and dogs. All teams assigned to this program must be familiar with aircraft and automobile search procedures, baggage and related containers, and air operations areas. Every team is evaluated at least once a year and must qualify or return to Lackland for additional training. Participants in this program have been dispatched to locations throughout the world.

Most of the large departments in the U.S. (New York City, Miami, San Diego, Seattle) and the military have explosives detection dogs or rapid access to them. FAA bomb dogs are required to maintain a minimum 30 minute response time to their airport. The Secret Service and several other federal agencies, normally those with personnel protection responsibilities, have explosives detection dogs. The dogs are also used 1) where a device has been located and a search is necessary for a secondary device, and 2) where intelligence indicates an explosive device may be used, for example a highly charged gathering of public figures or a postal facility. Federal protection searches, for dignitaries and state department officials, are followed up with technicians.

Handlers themselves are typically not Department of Defense certified bomb technicians. *If the bomb squad trains and deploys its dog teams adequately, they will be fully occupied performing canine training and operations* and will not have time to maintain expertise in removing and/or disarming, and disposing of bombs, fireworks, improvised explosive devices, dangerous chemicals, nor investigating bomb threats or explosions after the fact. *Bomb dog reliability depends on this. Reliability also demands that bomb dogs be specialist EDDs*, not crosstrained patrol or narcotic dogs.

Narcotics or patrol is one thing. If I miss a burglar, "Gee, I missed a burglar."

If I miss a shipment of drugs, "Gee, I missed a shipment of drugs." In narcotics, if you miss it, the guy that gets hurt is the one trying to buy it anyway.

If I miss a *bomb*, a lot of innocent people can be hurt. It's *imperative* that the bomb program be conducted properly, with great seriousness. The lives of too many people depend on what you're doing.

—Sgt. Kenneth Burger, Chicago Police Department

Typically operating as the lead search team, the bomb dog handler can never forget the mind-focusing phrase: "It's a bomb until it's not a bomb." The concept shapes all the tactics for deploying bomb dogs.

Bomb dogs are Labrador retrievers, Malinois, German, and other breeds that exhibit the same high social and search drives needed for the best narcotic or accelerant detector dogs. Precisely because the alert is passive—the dog locates the source, sits, looks at the source—the bomb dog has to have exceptional drives to carry through a productive career. His attitude must be, figuratively speaking, that the work is to die for.

The dog needs to be confident, agile, and fast in his responses. For searching aircraft or vehicles the dog must be comfortable climbing on seats, stretching to the overhead and tilting his head back to check it. He must willingly penetrate and back out between seats, aisles, restrooms, and other tight places. Climbing ramps or metal stairs onto aircraft, jumping onto palletized cargo, or riding utility vehicles is part of his routine.

The dog is trained to recognize and respond to a distinct set of chemical compounds. Security prohibits listing the compounds used by any given agency. Some explosives are legal to possess but are common components of improvised explosive devices (IEDs). Highly sophisticated, powerful explosives are being developed worldwide. Shaped charges, acid bombs, fire bombs, submersibles—the list is limited only by the saboteurs who build the devices. Agencies train various explosives, depending on the threat to their area of operations. *From a tactical standpoint, bomb dog deployment is dictated by the type of area that must be searched, not the type of explosive.* The dog will perform the same alert behavior to each explosive he has been trained to detect. System constraints are the availability of time to train as well as the availability of the explosive training aids.

The Secret Service has 12 substances they train. Some are less common, European-type explosives. The bomb and arson units supply explosive materials for training. You have to expose the dogs to what they can possibly come into and to what is out there. If you are going to give the dog a half stick of dynamite in training and he gets keyed on that, and someone makes a six-stick bomb, you may not get the appropriate response.

A nitrate fertilizer with some oil could create quite an explosive. You get into some high concentrations of nitrates in some cosmetics which may cause your dog to alert. There are some greases used on switch boxes in railroad yards that use a base that may attract explosive detection dogs. If the dog makes a mistake, it is better he makes it on the right side than by not indicating, then an explosion goes off.

—Detector dog trainer

Directability on search and reliable alerting behavior in response to the odor of specific chemicals is the basis of bomb dog operations. Canine units rise or fall on the issue of reliability. The task force concept is integral to successful operations. When the bomb squad receives a threat or develops information leading to the possibility of a bomb, the bomb technician and handler work together. If the dog alerts, the bomb technician takes over. Asked what he and his dog do post-alert, one handler answered, Get the hell out!

A bomb dog handler from an island in the Caribbean described his experience. Called to search for a bomb in an office building, they went down a stairway into the basement. The dog alerted immediately and hard, dragging the handler through the doorway, across a room, and into another room where they both stopped short. The dog sat. The officer saw TNT dynamite "stacks as far as the eye can see. My head it says go, but my feets they do not move!"

Bomb recognition (typical concealment, detonators, and devices) as well as explosive recognition (typical chemical compound appearance and explosive characteristics) require current intelligence and must be part of the handler's regular refresher training. As in any other type of K-9 operation, the handler and dog are a team; the handler may recognize a threat before the dog has sniffed it. That act may save their lives.

Aircraft. Airport police bomb dogs routinely search commercial and private aircraft, and the entire airport facility, including air terminals and warehouses. The planes range in size from the largest intercontinental airliners containing hundreds of seats to 2-seaters. Although a cargo plane or a standard passenger jet presents a distinctive complex of scents (fuel, upholstery, travelers bodies) and background noises (ventilation systems, arrivals and departures), bomb dog deployment inside commercial aircraft is similar to searching buildings or large commercial motor vehicles. The Boeing 747 or DC 10 takes one dog from 20 to 40 minutes.

Small aircraft deployment resembles passenger vehicle searching. Each canine team develops standard patterns of searching the exterior and interior of small planes and motor vehicles. A small plane takes one dog from 1 to 3 minutes.

When a bomb threat is received, if the plane is on the ground, passengers take their

hand-carried items and exit the aircraft. Windows or doors fore and aft are left open with the air conditioning on auxiliary power to create laminar, flow-through ventilation. The canine searches the interior, followed by a bomb technician. Bomb techs are responsible for the exterior of the aircraft. All cargo is re-X-rayed, then set aside and checked by the dog.

Always search escape routes first. Typically the bomb dog team clears the entryways then proceeds to do a *patterned search.* Narrow-body aircraft are usually searched clockwise, while wide-body interiors are sectioned off and searched sequentially. The overhead section in commercial aircraft is difficult for the dog to sniff. Some teams place a runner or interior platform across the seats the length of the aircraft to assist the dog searching the overhead. The handler is responsible for directing the dog to sniff every likely concealment area.

You have to be aware of the air currents. You might have an explosive in the corner of a room and the dog will sit down in the opposite corner. On an actual search you have to know this. If your dog sits down on an airplane right against the window, you look around but don't find anything, you might want to look at the opposite side of the plane directly across the aisle. Scent could be rising, flowing across the roof of the plane, and coming down on the other side.
—Officer James R. Horton, San Francisco Airport Police

The same principles of physics apply to the vaporization and diffusion of explosive scent as to the propagation of human or narcotic scent. The same principles of canine scenting also apply.

The bomb dog team must achieve a 97% or better on Air Force certification testing to qualify for explosives detection. I know by reading the dog if he is smelling another animal, smelling food, or smelling an explosive. He does not false-sit because he does not get praised for it. He sniffs where I tell him. I do not let him go off on his own, wandering around. That way I know exactly where he has searched, and if he goes off-pattern, I know he's got something.
—K-9 Officer, San Francisco Airport Police

Look for multiple bombs. The first bomb found, wherever it is—on the exterior, in the entryway, near the perimeter, or inside the structure or vehicle—may have been intended to increase the kill zone effect and may not be the only, or the largest, explosive device.

Hardened containers serve to reduce the overall threat level by containing the blast. Explosive devices are, wherever possible, detonated in a total-containment vessel (TCV), a sphere of the same resilient alloy used in the hulls of nuclear submarines, which can contain a large explosion.

Shipping cargo in hardened containers would help the sniffing bomb dog by restricting scent diffusion and reducing the number of areas he must check.

Records. Accurate record keeping verifies the bomb dog's credibility and, if subpoenaed into court, establishes the handler as an expert in EDD deployment.

Cargo and mail. According to an FAA report to Congress (*Security of Mail and Cargo in Transportation by Passenger Carrying Aircraft,* 1992), approximately 6 percent of the total mail, by weight, is capable of "containing a device intended to cause catastrophic damage to a passenger aircraft." The number of individual pieces that number represents is over 1-billion pieces of priority, express, and international mail. A system to screen U.S. Postal Service and private carrier mail to reduce the threat is not yet in place.

Although it is impractical to use bomb dogs on a continuous basis to screen mail, in exceptional circumstances where the Postal Inspector or investigator in charge feels there is imminent threat of receiving a mail bomb, a "pre-delivery screening program" can be implemented for a short period of time. Bomb dogs are typically used to sniff any suspect parcels or items of mail. Any item with indicators causing suspicion (unusual packaging, odors, incorrect address, special intelligence) should be isolated and treated as a live bomb pending further investigation. The typical procedure is *evacuate, isolate, sniff, and bomb tech inspect:*

1. Do not open the article(s).
2. Isolate the mailing and evacuate and secure the immediate area.
3. Do not put the mailing in water or a confined space, such as a desk drawer or filing cabinet.
4. Unless the article(s) has been placed outside, take into consideration ventilating the search area to minimize air turbulence for the bomb dog versus venting potential explosive gases.
5. If the bomb dog has alerted near multiple articles during a screening procedure, turn all of the articles over to the bomb technician for further investigation.

During parcel or baggage searches the dog may alert to package tape with nitrate-based glue, to weapons or ammunition. One dog team found a false bomb inside a gunpowder-covered package.

Building search. When called to a scene to conduct a building search, the handler and bomb technician immediately contact the officer in charge. If a MAST Captain or Fire Department Incident Commander is on the scene, the search operation will be under their direct control. The handler 1) evaluates the type and legality of the requested search and advises the officer in charge, 2) evaluates the search area for potential hazards to the dog (sharp objects, caustic materials or animals), and 3) briefs the officers at the scene as to their responsibilities and conduct during the search.

The concept of *total jeopardy* governs bomb squad operations in general and canine deployment in particular. "I will not jeopardize lives to protect property," stressed Lieutenant Walter Boser, Commander, New York City Police Department Bomb Squad.

Robots help counteract the threat to officers by performing tasks remotely. Initial entry, surveillance, moving and lifting objects, bomb tech functions—any or all of these jobs can be done remotely if the right robot is available. Sometimes a bomb or suspicious object can be identified and retrieved by remote equipment. International police forces are conducting procedures to bring the scent stimuli to the canine for a sniff instead of sending the canine into the area to locate the stimuli. Special adsorbent materials are placed in target areas then removed, all by remote control. Where remote detection is not feasible, a search by a bomb

The typical procedure is evacuate, isolate, sniff, and bomb tech inspect.

Bomb dogs search
commercial aircraft.

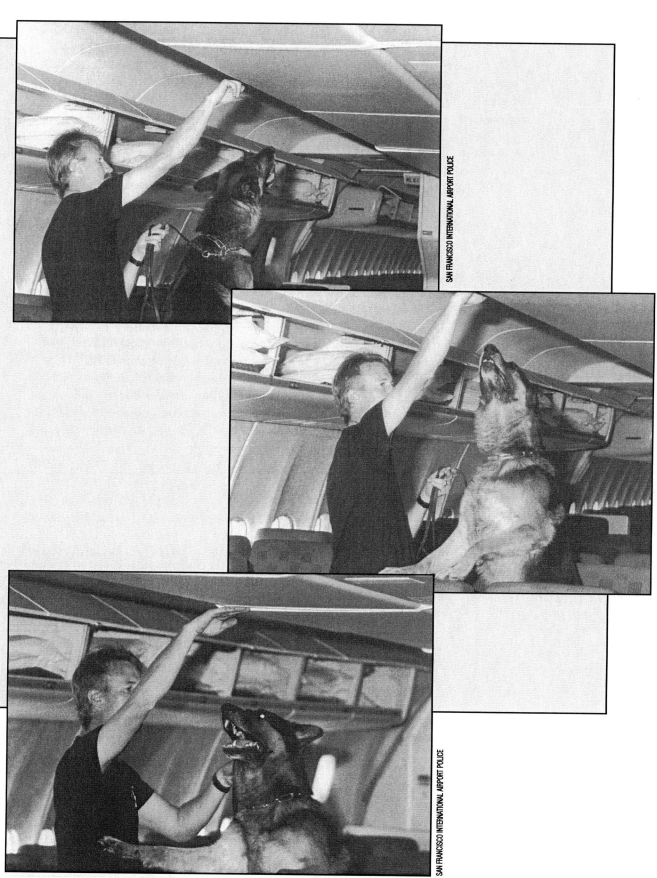

SAN FRANCISCO INTERNATIONAL AIRPORT POLICE

SAN FRANCISCO INTERNATIONAL AIRPORT POLICE

SAN FRANCISCO INTERNATIONAL AIRPORT POLICE

dog increases the probability of detection and officer safety.

Building search procedures and the time required to evacuate people and conduct a search depend on the size and type of building, the location, occupancy, and the nature of the threat. Search teams should have the proper equipment readily available and should be carrying flashlights and keys to various building areas. Using radios during a bomb search is hazardous because radio waves can detonate bombs with electric-initiator blasting caps.

1. If evacuation is necessary, people will not be permitted to reenter until a search has been completed and any suspect item has been removed or declared safe by the bomb disposal unit.

2. Before starting a search, the agency in charge should select areas, preferably outside (back loading platform, isolated area in a parking lot, secured outside area), where a bomb can be taken by a bomb disposal unit without creating undue danger to personnel, buildings, or equipment. Map in advance the safest and quickest routes to these holding areas from major locations inside the buildings.

3. Instruct all personnel (especially security and maintenance) to be alert for suspicious persons or objects. The dog may find, not only the bomb, but also the bomber.

4. Dog team and bomb tech use a patterned search to clear areas sequentially. If investigators have intelligence about where a bomb has been placed, search that location first. When the location of a bomb is not known, a bomb search should begin on the property outside the building and work inside. Among the areas to be checked outside are bushes, trees, rock work, stairways, window ledges, power boxes, storm gutters, piping or other concealment areas. The interior search should begin with areas accessible to the public, including hallways, restrooms, lobbies, stairways, and closets or storage areas. Unless contraindicated, search from the bottom (basement) to the top (including the roof) of the structure.

5. If the dog alerts, isolate and protect the area and turn the investigation over to the bomb technician.

Area search. If a bomb threat targets a large area (city park, shopping center, shipping docks), the *size* of the area is a problem. Although the bomb dog is faster and more accurate than many other detection methods, he is not invincible. Concealed explosives with a low rate of vaporization require rigorous searching, especially outside. Searching a tight pattern takes time. Look for places

SAN FRANCISCO INTERNATIONAL AIRPORT POLICE

Alfred P. Murrah Federal Building, Oklahoma City, Oklahoma.

where an explosion would do the most damage, be highly visible, or cut off access routes, and search these locations first. If the bomber is claiming a person is being held hostage to the bomb, it may be important to deploy police patrol dogs trained to detect human scent in order to isolate the target area, using caution to prevent causing an explosion.

Clandestine labs. A clandestine laboratory is a unique situation. The number of chemical substances that can be found in a lab is limited only by the imagination of the cooker and the type of product. Any chemical laboratory may contain hazardous substances. However, an industrial laboratory is designed for safety, while clandestine laboratories are designed for secrecy. Beyond booby traps set to kill anybody who enters, the lab probably contains corrosive, flammable, narcotic, carcinogenic, explosive, or otherwise toxic materials. Bare-pawed and lacking a bomb suit, the canine faces a much greater risk than other squad members. Except in cases of real and present danger to other persons, sending a detector dog into a lab, even the aftermath of a lab takedown, is rarely justified.

SEADOGS/JUNEAU, ALASKA

Search dog team Reilly Richey and Taco *in Armenia.*

CHAPTER 10

INTERNATIONAL SERVICE

"I don't *have* to save lives,

I *want* to save lives.

I *have* to bring my crew home alive tonight."

—U.S. Firefighter

Police dog teams abroad are American ambassadors. Officers accustomed to dealing with cultural diversity in the U.S. will find even greater diversity when going international. The keys to working in a foreign environment are maturity, flexibility, curiosity, and the willingness to prepare, even at the eleventh hour. The keys to doing *emergency* work in a foreign country are the same, except the final preparations are *always* at the eleventh hour.

Nobody understands this better than the cops, including the K-9 officers, who are today conducting law enforcement operations and providing consulting services through international agencies to countries all over the world. The DEA agent in Central or South America, China or Southeast Asia. The Secret Service agent hounding the President to Europe. The metro police officer tracking the development of a third world police force in South Africa or Central America. The security specialist operating in the Middle East, North Africa, or in service to the United Nations.

We have to assume that departments sending police officers overseas on law enforcement missions take the responsibility of selecting and training those men and women for successful foreign service.

It is less certain that K-9 teams considering training for international search and rescue are equally informed about what is needed to perform effectively. Here we address the needs of these teams.

INTERNATIONAL SEARCH AND RESCUE

The decision to train a dog for this kind of work should be carefully considered. This is nasty, dirty, frustrating, and frequently emotionally draining work which takes a toll on both the dog and the handler. It entails long hours, a lot of hurry up and wait. The dog will be subjected to throngs of people, unpleasant odors, loud noises, and constant agility tests. The handler will have to deal with grieving relatives, political pressures, and relentless hounding by the ever present press corps. The individual has to have enough skills to assist in areas such as medical and veterinary treatment, communications, critical incident stress, translating, media handling, hazardous materials, and structural assessment.

It is essential that the handler have a good grasp of cultural awareness, the Incident Command System, and be capable of being a good team player.

The dog must be at ease around people and other dogs, be agile enough to traverse and climb difficult terrain, be easily directed onto and into areas from a distance. The dog's alert should be vocal and positive. The dog must learn to check but not bark at areas containing clothing, sewage, food and residual scent. Fear of heights or confined spaces preclude the dog and the handler from this work.

It is essential that the handler read his canine partner accurately and not induce false alerts by using excessive pressure. We want our dogs to find live people during the aftermath of a disaster. Unfortunately we are often recruited into the tragic job of locating bodies. The training emphasis should, however, be on the finding of the live victim in order to encourage the *live find* motivation in the dog.

With experience, the animals recognize disaster scenarios and meticulously check out every nook and cranny with minimal direction. Once a dog is in the search mode, the handler commands and talks as little as possible in order to let the animal concentrate. An occasional command or word of encouragement is fine. The rest of the time, tape your mouth shut!

After a work period, it is important to take the time to help the dog unwind and give positive reinforcement. This could take the form of tugging or throwing a ball or toy or of having a person hide and rewarding the live find with a lot of praise and enthusiasm. The latter can only be done after carefully assessing the cultural and emotional feelings of the family and survivors who might be present. It is important to remain professional at all times as well as to show compassion.

—Caroline Hebard,
U.S. National/International SAR Disaster Response Team

"A disaster is traumatic anywhere," said one director of security at a major multinational corporation, "but overseas crises are compounded by distance from home, language difficulties, cultural misunderstandings, and different laws and medical or criminal justice systems."

Beyond their detection ability, police and rescue dogs play a major public relations role worldwide. At earthquakes or other disasters that endanger or kill hundreds, sometimes thousands of victims, cultures that hold dogs in low esteem fight to get live TV coverage of rescue dog teams working the rubble. Reporters press for team interviews and photos. Local people have instant rapport with the handlers and amazing faith the rescue dogs will find their loved ones alive.

Dr. Gary Weaver, Professor of International and Intercultural Communications in The School of International Service at The American University, Washington, D.C.: "While we all know that people from other cultures eat different types of food and speak different languages, we often fail to realize that they also have different values, beliefs, and thought patterns. More importantly, we seldom recognize that our own cultures also program us with a particular set of values, beliefs, and thought patterns.

"Simply mixing culturally different people together does not resolve misunderstandings and conflict. Quite the contrary. Differences usually become more apparent and hostilities can actually increase during encounters between culturally diverse individuals.

"Law enforcement professionals should also *understand the dynamics of cross-cultural communication, adjustment, and conflict.*"

Few cultures hold dogs in the high regard they enjoy in the U.S., Canada, and some western European countries. Just because an individual does not say anything, or even if he acts friendly toward the K-9 officer, he may still loathe or be terrified of the dog. A man starving in West Africa found it incredible that there are supermarkets in America where a dog can walk in with his master and help select food, toys, and a customized bed. A place where dog food, *dog food*, is stacked to the ceiling. We are wealthy beyond our own comprehension.

"Who is internationable? What are the characteristics of people who are successful overseas?

When we analyze everything we have learned from international travelers, expatriates, heads of personnel, foreigners, and diplomats, we can boil down to one word the difference between people who do especially well abroad and those who do not: *breadth*." This conclusion from Lennie Copeland and Lewis Griggs, authors of *Going International* and experts in diversity issues worldwide.

"Some people are just not cut out for international work, and some are effective and happy in some cultures but not in others. Before making or accepting an overseas assignment, careful selection and honest *self-selection* is a process warranting serious attention.

"The people who do well abroad must know not only the job and company, as they do at home, but also the cultural patterns, business norms, and national character of the assigned country. This knowledge must be founded on an understanding of the country's history, arts, politics, economic conditions, and so on."

Fine. But how is this supposed to work for the dog handler who may be called to respond to a disaster anywhere, in any country of the world? How can he possibly study the whole world?

"Those who succeed show breadth of knowledge and intellectual curiosity, but also breadth of character—an open-arms and open-eyes personality. They are what one expert calls 'geocentric' in attitude, thinking in world terms and seeing opportunities, not constraints, in the millions of differences they encounter abroad.

"Looking closely at the personalities, attitudes, and skills of people who perform at high levels of excellence abroad, we have settled on seven success traits that seem to define the person of breadth, and which make the difference, *wherever the assignment and whatever the job*. Of course, in certain countries individuals will need qualities peculiarly adapted to the demands of the particular environments, and careful attention should be paid to those unique demands."

We have applied the Griggs' seven success traits to the dog handler:

Success Trait One: Hard like water

Cops sometimes have a hard time understanding this Japanese concept. We give an order, then we say, "Do it now!" That works (usually) when arresting an America-raised individual. Many cultures do not operate this way. Martial arts training teaches officers that optimal strength lies in flexibility and resilience. Water flows in the riverbed but carves the Grand Canyon. Water is soft and takes the shape of its containers, but water can carry the load of a thousand-ton ship. Successful people abroad are not pushovers, but neither are they rigid or unimpressionable. Use the opposing force to your advantage. People who make the best out of a situation share a lively sense of humor. The ability to laugh at oneself or at a situation is most important.

Success Trait Two: Resourceful independence through people

Loners unskilled in relating to their own people are not likely to be any better with people abroad and should not be considered good candidates. People skills does not mean popularity, but rather the ability to establish communication, cooperation, trust, and respect.

Success Trait Three: Curiosity

First, why do this unless you want to learn? Also, Americans are famously poor listeners. In SAR, lives are at stake. Listen.

Success Trait Four: Positive regard for others

Why go unless you have respect for and interest in others? Foreigners will know if you empathize with them, if you can put yourself in their shoes. Lives are at stake. Walk in their shoes.

Success Trait Five: Emotional stability

International work inflicts stress. International search and rescue inflicts mega-stress,

Cops sometimes have a hard time understanding this Japanese concept. We give an order, then we say, "Do it now!"

to you and to your animal. People who are emotionally insecure and unbalanced cannot hope to do well in foreign assignments. The emotional health of your family may also affect your performance abroad. You must be emotionally secure enough to tolerate ambiguity, face the unpredictable: Can I accept not knowing everything that is going on around me, not knowing what people are laughing at, not understanding the language or the different ways they are doing things, not—and this is a big one for police officers—not being in control?

Success Trait Six: Technical competence

International expertise is no substitute for professional competence. You will not be able to get help from the specialized talent you might be able to call upon at home. Your credibility depends on your professionalism and know-how. Yours and your dog's.

Success Trait Seven: Motivation

If you really don't want to go abroad, don't. You will not do well if your family resists the training time required or your frequent travel. Nor will you do well if you are going for the wrong reasons, such as escape from problems at home, a promotion, or money. There is no shame in being better-suited to Denver than to Karachi.

WHAT TO DIAL, READ, TAKE, AND LEAVE AT HOME

If you have time before departing for the airport, make a few phone calls. The Centers for Disease Control's International Travelers Hotline (404) 332-4559 has recorded information about vaccinations (including requirements and recommendations for specific destinations), food and water precautions, and traveler's diarrhea. The State Department's Citizens Emergency Center (202) 647-5225 will let you listen to official travel advisories for specific countries, including information on disease outbreaks and other health concerns (along with details of *political violence, patterns of crime, natural disasters*, and so on). Yes, OFDA and the overhead team will be in charge of the operation and responsible for you as a U.S. disaster team member, but that does not mean they will be *taking care of you* at every moment while you are overseas. Do not assume that because you are on a rescue mission you are fully protected from terrorism. In fact the visibility of a mission might make you a target, as United Nations soldiers have discovered.

If you are single, call somebody at work, or your mother, and tell them where you are going. This person, if not your mother, should know what steps to take in case you come back in a cast or not at all.

Buy and read in advance (check online bookstores for new editions and other references):

International Travel Health Guide by Stuart R. Rose, MD
Comprehensive country-by-country listings with information to stay well while traveling.
Paperback 456 pages.
www.magellans.com
Tel: 1-800-962-4943
Fax: 1-800-962-4940

Keep your passport current. Carry several photocopies of the first page of your passport and any visas, and leave one copy at home.

Your training as a police K-9 officer or disaster rescue dog handler should have prepared you with the right operations gear (packs, duffels, tents, sleeping bags, clothing, toiletries, foul weather and safety equipment, K-9 equipment and vet medical kit), including things like radios, flagging, and at least *two* of the following: flashlights, headlamps, glasses or contact lenses, sunglasses, dog leads and collars.

Do not assume that because you are on a rescue mission you are fully protected from terrorism. In fact the visibility of a mission might make you a target.

Lock and tag your baggage unless instructed otherwise. In any case carry locks. You may be transported over there in an Air Force C-141, but the trip home may be via commercial aircraft. Always carry documents, medicines, a flashlight, some foul weather gear, basic first aid, toilet paper, a water bottle, and ziplock plastic bags with you.

Take money. Take at least one internationally accepted credit card. Travelers checks are a good idea. USG OFDA may be sending you, but you may have to function unexpectedly for a period of time on your own. Get reimbursed later back in the U.S. Do not rely on your teammates for emergency funds. First, it is not fair to them (ever notice the same guy always looks around and says, gee, I don't have any cash on me). Second, your compatriots might not be there when you are selected for the honor of having breakfast with a dignitary in a country where tipping is expected.

Take an international phone card and appropriate emergency medical insurance card. Yes I know, USG OFDA is supposed to handle this.

Carry a small camera with fast film.

Leave these things at home: All jewelry, expensive watch (wear a cheapo with a sweep second hand, readable in the dark), keys, driver's license, other credit cards or business cards, address books, anything else you don't need and might fret about losing.

MEDICAL PREPARATIONS

Medical training for the police dog handler potentially responding to a national or international disaster should at least include current Emergency Medical Technician (EMT) or First Responder with CPR. Medical training enables the handler to assess minor medical situations and recognize life-threatening situations, then respond according to his level of training. Further injury to victims is less likely, and the handler is more likely to take needed control of the presenting medical situation.

Each handler should carry a first aid kit containing emergency medical supplies he is qualified to use. Standard first aid supplies should include: cleansing solution, antibiotic ointment, sterile dressings, bandages, several sizes of bandaids, sterile eye patches, cloth and paper/plastic tape, nonsterile gloves, a pocket mask (for CPR), triangular bandages, hot and cold packs, simple splints (finger, wrist, and wire ladder splint), emergency blankets, masks to prevent dust inhalation, ultraviolet lotions to protect against the sun, and effective netting and insecticides where insect vectors are present.

For all rescue operations, several types of gloves—latex, rubber and leather—need to be available. Vinyl gloves are not protective against the AIDS virus and should probably be avoided. Industrial gloves, with spares, are needed to protect rescuers against hazmat spills and sharp rebar and concrete fragments.

Exposure to AIDS victims is a serious risk. In addition to the usual gloves, mask, and goggles protection, each team member should have his blood type and other pertinent medical data put on a military dog tag or medic alert bracelet, worn 24 hours a day while on the mission. There may be some controversy concerning the screening of team members for HIV prior to mission callout. Nevertheless, a roster of team members with their blood types will provide the medical officer ready access to a walking blood bank should the need occur for a team member to receive a transfusion while at a disaster site.

Medic Alert Foundation International: (800) 344-3226

The number of dog teams and support personnel traveling together to the disaster site determines the distribution of medical gear. Doctors, nurses, and paramedics will want extensive medical equipment. Major disasters typically call for more emergency medical supplies than it is possible to insert rapidly via air or ground transport.

Particularly in poor nations, teams must recognize the need to organize medical gear into supplies designated for disaster victims while maintaining supplies to treat rescue team injuries. If a handler or dog is injured, he may not help, and in fact may hurt, the search effort.

The following medicines apply to a wide spectrum of disasters.

Cleansing solutions and topical ointments:
- Betadine solution - kills surface germs
- Xylocaine jelly - local anesthetic applied prior to scrubbing a wound, or for road rash
- Neosporin or Bacitracin ointment - local antibiotic ointment to be applied to a clean wound prior to bandaging
- Neosporin Eye Ointment - for eye infection, check with your doctor for proper use

Antibiotics (good for strep, staph, pneumococcus bacteria causing ear infections, bronchitis, pneumonia, other common infections, and grossly contaminated wounds):
- Erythromycin (can be used by persons allergic to penicillin)
- Cephalosporin
- Doxycycline

Miscellaneous medications:
- Diphenhydramine hydrochloride (benadryl): for allergic reactions
- Diphenoxylate/atropine (lomotil): for diarrhea
- Tylenol with Codeine or Hydrocodone: pain medications
- Ibuprofen (Motrin), Advil: anti-inflammatory and pain medication
- Prochloroperazine rectal suppositories: for vomiting and severe nausea
- Scopolamine patches for air and seasickness
- Diamox tablets if traveling to high altitude areas

Carry other medications on the advice of your team doctor and personal physician.

Inadequate sanitation can bring a team to its knees. Take the standard food and beverage precautions, and drink only purified water (boiling, chemical disinfection with iodine, tetraglycine hydroperiodide, or chlorine, as well as microstrainer filters).

SEADOGS/JUNEAU, ALASKA

Regardless how prepared a police officer feels, the reality is disasters are shocking, stressful, and psychologically traumatic experiences. The sheer numbers of dead and dying can be overwhelming. Each handler has to know this and be able to admit his own feelings and emotions freely to his fellow team members—fear, revulsion, anger, and empathy with victims, especially parents of dead children.

Symptoms of stress may be obvious or subtle—sleeplessness, loss of appetite or increase in appetite, stomach pain, headaches, diarrhea, elevated blood pressure, inability to communicate, and abnormal feelings of depression or helplessness. Recognizing these signs can help reduce severe reactions. Early debriefing through EMS personnel will help relieve detrimental effects. Other methods of handling stress include consciously performing daily routines, eating a healthful diet, scheduling time to exercise daily, meditating, and practicing deep breathing exercises twice a day for 5 minutes a session. It is important to avoid using alcohol and drugs while in a stressful environment. Personal physical and mental "wellness" of the police officer is the best preparation for responding to a disaster.

Teams traveling outside the U.S. to a disaster experience the stress of a foreign culture. Officers who have never been abroad are usually impacted the most by language barriers, frequent lack of facilities, the often poor organization of the rescue and recovery effort, and always "hurry up and wait"—for transportation to the foreign country, transport to the search area, search assignments, communications, supplies, evacuation assistance, and for medical teams to help with injured or dying victims. Being a tool used by the organization in charge of the Big Picture often feels like being a pawn. Despite inefficiencies and inequities in major disasters, keeping a cool perspective is important to officer survival.

Get an "International Certificate of Vaccination" from a local or state health department. Instructions on this certificate identify some necessary immunizations. Find out what immunizations the destination country currently requires.

Record immunizations received during childhood and the dates they were administered, including polio vaccine, DPT (diptheria, pertussis and tetanus), possibly measles or the date measles were contracted.

Record the 3 vaccination dates for Hepatitis B, if received. This vaccine is strongly recommended for police officers because of potential contact with blood from criminals or accident victims.

Update tetanus if the last booster received was more than 5 years ago. Tetanus is often given in combination with diptheria, known as Dip-Tet. Doctors often advise meningococcus and gamma globulin prophylactically, effective for 30-60 days. Typhoid immunization, given in 2 injections a month apart, is valid for 3 years. Malaria risk is high for travelers to parts of the Caribbean, Central and South America, Africa, the Middle East, the Indian subcontinent and the Far East. Consult your physician about a prescription for prophylactic drugs to protect you from contracting malaria. Officers should be immune from measles either by having had the disease or by vaccination.

A Tine test should be given with a post-mission test to detect exposure to active TB. Additionally, the availability of Rabies vaccine, either carried with the team or available in-country, should be established due to the large number of domestic animals released during many disasters and the lack of uniform rabies vaccinations throughout the world.

Other available immunizations:
- Cholera I, Cholera II (valid for 6 months)
- Cholera Booster (valid for 6 months)
- Influenza
- Plague I, Plague II (valid for 6 months)
- Pneumonococcus
- Polio
- Yellow Fever (valid for 10 years)

—Prepared by Judy L. Salviolo, R.N., C.E.N., M.I.C.N.

Malaria risk is high for travelers to parts of the Caribbean, Central and South America, Africa, the Middle East, the Indian subcontinent and the Far East.

INTERNATIONAL SEARCH AND RESCUE ADVISORY GROUP (INSARAG)

"In a disaster situation, no help is as efficient as that which is locally available," writes Ola Almgren, United Nations Disaster Relief Organization (UNDRO). "Unfortunately, no matter how well prepared a country may be, or what resources it has at its disposal, it might still face a situation which requires more resources than it can deploy."

Examples of disasters where human resources and technology have formed an important part of foreign assistance are the earthquakes in Iran and the Philippines, the cyclones and flooding in Bangladesh, and the Kurdish exodus caused by internal unrest in Iraq. Such emergencies, which require the active participation of international relief teams and equipment, are examples of disasters with a service-intensive needs profile.

The need for coordination of disasters exists primarily on three levels: in international centres for humanitarian work such as Geneva and New York; in the capital of the affected country; and last but not least at the field level, where relief activities take place among the victims and within the chaotic environment at the site of a disaster. This latter level of coordination can be referred to as Operational Coordination, and it includes measures to improve the preparedness of disaster-prone countries to manage the emergency. The more service-intensive the needs profile of a disaster, the greater the importance of a well-functioning coordination of relief at the operational level.

INSARAG formed regional groups for the Americas, for Europe/Africa, and for Asia/Pacific, inviting the participation of those countries as well as international bodies, such as the International Federation of Red Cross and Red Crescent Societies (IFRC) and the International Civil Defense Organization (ICDO). Working groups were established for the exchange of information and the development of SAR technology.

DISASTER ASSISTANCE RESPONSE TEAM (DART)

The United States Agency for International Development's (USAID) Office of Foreign Disaster Assistance (OFDA) has developed a response capability called the Disaster Assistance Response Team (DART) as a method of providing rapid response assistance to international disasters, as mandated by the Foreign Assistance Act. A DART provides specialists, trained in a variety of disaster relief skills, to assist U.S. Embassies and USAID Missions with the management of the United States Government (USG) response to disasters.

The activities of a DART vary depending on the type, size, and complexity of disasters to which the DART is deployed.

During rapid-onset disasters, the focus of a DART is to:
• Coordinate the assessment of the situation and report on the needs.
• Recommend USG response actions.
• Manage USG on-site relief activities (e.g., search and rescue and air operations).
• Manage the receipt, distribution, and monitoring of USG-provided relief supplies.
  During long-term, complex disasters, the focus of a DART is to:
• Gather information on the general disaster situation.

DART Organization Chart

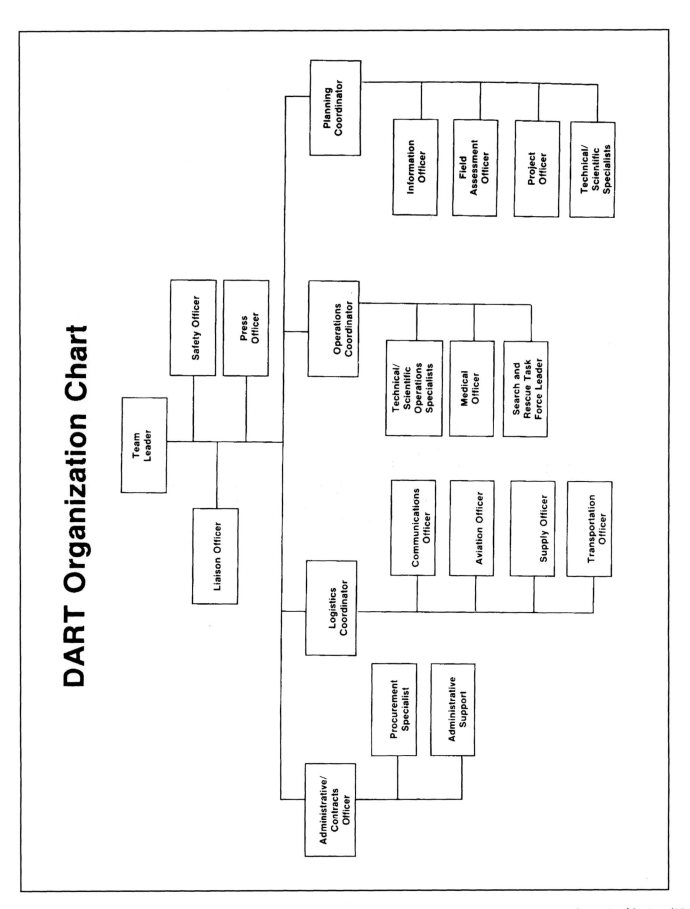

- Assess the effectiveness of the overall humanitarian response.
- Identify the needs not being met by current overall response efforts.
- Monitor the effectiveness of current USG-funded relief activities.
- Review proposals of relief activities for possible future funding.
- Advise USAID/Embassy on disaster issues.
- Make recommendations to OFDA Washington on follow-on strategies and actions.
- Implement procuring of contractual and grant services under special circumstances.

During either type of disaster response, DARTs coordinate their activities with the affected country, private voluntary organizations (PVO), non-governmental organizations (NGO), international organizations (IO), and other assisting countries. When U.S. military assets are involved with the disaster response, the DART will work closely with those assets to assure a coordinated effort by USG resources.

The structure of a DART is dependent on the size, complexity, type, and location of the disaster, and the needs of the USAID/Embassy and the affected country. The number of individuals assigned to a DART is determined by how many people are required to perform the necessary activities to meet the strategy and objectives.

A DART is composed of five functional areas;

- **Management**—Manages overall DART activities, including liaison with the affected country, PVO/NGO/IOs, other assisting countries, and U.S. military; and the development and implementation of plans to meet strategic objectives.
- **Operations**—Manages all operational activities carried out by the DART, such as search and rescue activities, technical support to an affected country, medical and health response, and aerial operations coordination. Most active during rapid onset disasters.
- **Planning**—Collects, evaluates, tracks, and disseminates information about the

disaster. Reviews activities and recommends future actions. Develops the DART operational (tactical) plan.

- **Logistics**—Supports the DART with team supplies, equipment, and services. Orders, receives, distributes, and tracks USG-provided relief supplies.
- **Administration**—Manages fiscal activities of the DART. Contracts and procures goods and services required by the DART. Provides cost accounting of DART activities.

The decisions on a DART's activation, composition, and mission are made at a disaster response planning meeting held in OFDA.

The DART is organized and supervised by a DART Team Leader selected by OFDA. The Team Leader receives a delegation of authority from and works directly for the Assistant Director of OFDA's Disaster Response Division or his/her designee. The delegation lists the objectives, priorities, constraints, and reporting requirements for the DART. Based on this information, the Team Leader in conjunction with the Assistant Directors for OFDA's Disaster Response and Operations Support Divisions, will identify the other positions needed. OFDA's Assistant Director for the Operations Support Division has the responsibility for filling DART personnel requirements, supporting DART field operations, and ensuring security for the DART throughout the operation.

Prior to departure, the Team Leader will attempt to contact the USAID/Embassy (if present in the affected country) to discuss the situation, review the DART's structure, size, objectives and capabilities, and identify the areas of support needed by the DART in country.

Upon arrival in the affected country, the Team Leader reports to the senior U.S. official or to appropriate officials to discuss the DART's objectives and capabilities and to receive additional instructions or authority. While in the country, the Team Leader advises and may receive periodic instructions from USAID/Embassy. Those instructions will be followed to the extent they do not conflict with OFDA policies, authorities, and procedures. The Team Leader maintains a direct line of communications with OFDA Washington throughout the operation.

(Remember, multiple disasters may be occurring simultaneously throughout the world.)

The duration of a DART operation will be determined by USAID/Embassy and OFDA Washington after reviewing the disaster situation and the progress of the DART in meeting its objectives.

The DART organizational chart portrays the positions and relationships described in the *Field Operations Guide.*

There are additional positions under the Search and Rescue Task Force Leader which are described in the Federal Emergency Management Agency's USAR Response System *Field Operations Guide (the FOG manual).*

Remember, multiple disasters may be occurring simultaneously throughout the world.

Out of the many international disaster rescue missions—hurricanes, floods, firestorms, volcanic eruptions, civil strife, war, and acts of terrorism—we describe one that typifies the implementation of the U.S. DART response, and some of the lessons learned:

PHILIPPINES

Luzon, the main island of the Philippines, was shaken July 16, 1990, by an earthquake measuring 7.7 on the Richter scale, the strongest quake to hit the Philippines in 14 years. It struck at 1630 local time. Especially hard-hit was the mountain resort town of Baguio, about 60 miles north of the epicenter, where it was reported that hundreds of people were trapped in the collapse of hotels and a government building. Wire services quoted a rescue coordinator in Baguio, "There were cries of children and voices of people in these hotels."

Outside Baguio, the tremor reportedly knocked down a chemical plant which then exploded. Some 130 people were said to be inside at the time. A 6-story school came down in the town of Cabanatuan, near the epicenter, and in the countryside hundreds of people were believed buried in their vehicles by landslides.

As initial tallies of damage started coming in, the U.S. OFDA activated DART. The U.S. team to the Philippines consisted of rescue dogs, rescue, medical and overhead components, a total of 24 people. There were 12 firefighters from Fairfax County, VA, and Metro-Dade, Florida, and three paramedics and an emergency physician from the Special Medical Rescue Team in Pittsburgh, PA. Dog handlers Bill Dotson (VA), Caroline Hebard (NJ), P.J. LoPresti (VA), and Heidi Yamaguchi (MD) responded with dogs. Dayton Maxwell of OFDA was team manager, with INSAR project coordinator Chuck Mills as operations officer and BFC Mike Tamillow of Fairfax County as technical rescue operations supervisor. The team also included Metro-Dade Communications specialist John Carroll and Dr. Fred Krimgold as technical specialist for evaluating structures.

The U.S. team took off from Andrews AFB at 2000 EDT, stopping over for three hours at Travis AFB for refueling. Personnel who were not current received the necessary inoculations. They were also issued malaria pills. After a 17-hour nonstop Pacific flight with two in-flight refuelings, the C-141 landed at Manila's Clark AFB at 1000 July 18, 32 hours after the earthquake. Two Huey H3s were standing by to airlift the team up to Baguio, 120 miles north of the capital.

The team's gear was shuttled by C-130 to smaller airports closer to Baguio, and then helicoptered the rest of the way, an operation that took 4 hours. The Baguio airport had been damaged in the quake, and roads into the city were blocked by landslides. In the first days after the disaster, the only way in and out of the stricken city was by helicopter. Choppers were using the fairways of the golf course as an LZ.

Temperatures in Manila were in the 100-105 degree range but 30 degrees cooler in Baguio at 3500 feet. Every afternoon at 1400 it rained.

The team arrived in Baguio at 1100 Wednesday. "The average person had gotten up about 0600 EDT Monday morning to go to work," recalled a paramedic, "so we were already up a day and a half at the time we landed at Clark. People were really starting to realize fatigue on the last stretch of the flight. But then the adrenalin would start pumping."

The U.S. team set up its base at a military resort, Camp John Hay, close to the Hyatt and Nevada hotels, which had both sustained heavy damage in the quake. On the command post wall was a map with black dots showing search and rescue priorities: "Basically the entire island," commented a team member.

At the Nevada Hotel, Filipino miners had located a number of survivors trapped between the second and third floors. The miners had been working for some 48 hours with only hand tools, shoring up the structure and cutting through floor slabs to reach them.

"You could tell they knew what they were doing," said a rescuer. "Shoring is what they do for a living." Still, they needed more than shoring skills and hand tools to bring off the rescues.

The U.S. team contributed lighting and saws, and drilled a hole for fiber-optic viewing apparatus to confirm victims' locations. While they worked from above to extricate one man whose ankle was pinned by a concrete beam, the miners worked from below to access three other people trapped nearby.

At the same time, USAF PJs crawled between the floor slabs to help locate and stabilize the survivors.

Some nine hours and at least one strong aftershock later, U.S. rescuers brought out the pinned survivor, a local man in his 30s. At the time of the quake he had been sitting in a hotel conference room. Rescuers found him still in his chair, tipped on its back. He still had his glasses on. He was dehydrated but "remarkably aware of his condition and surroundings," said Bill Gustin of Metro-Dade. The man's injured left leg was ultimately amputated below the knee.

Meanwhile the Filipino miners were bringing out a man and two women, one of them pregnant. The man died a short time later, but the women were reportedly in good condition, and the pregnant woman delivered later that night.

The search contingent had been split into two teams of two dogs with their handlers. One team was sent to the Hyatt while the other was to search the Nevada.

"Right away at the Nevada they had the rescue, which took 9 hours, so we re-deployed and worked the dogs in other buildings," a handler reported.

At about 0130 on the morning of July 19, the U.S. team called it a day. Their sleep was interrupted, a paramedic said, by aftershocks that were occurring about every 45 minutes.

A few hours later the team gathered for a briefing. Each morning Dayton Maxwell, Chuck Mills, and Mike Tamillow would meet with local officials to plan the day's work. The Air Force put a truck, two pickups, and a van at the team's disposal, so transportation around Baguio was no problem.

It was intended that the 24-person team would work in 12-hour shifts, half the group working while the other half rested. But, recognizing the magnitude of the task, the team ended up breaking into two rescue groups working simultaneously.

The search dogs worked sometimes in teams of two, sometimes all together. The two smaller dogs, a small German shepherd and an Australian Cattledog, teamed up to search one room of a school because the larger dogs could not fit into the access hole. The other dogs, a standard-size German shepherd and a Golden Retriever, were sent to search another part of the same school.

Japanese and British rescue teams also responded to the Philippines, but the U.S. team was

The two smaller dogs, a small German shepherd and an Australian Cattledog, teamed up to search one room of a school because the larger dogs could not fit into the access hole.

the only one to include search dogs. The American dogs and handlers were sometimes "lent out" to the other international groups, and also to the local miners, when they were not needed by their own team. The dogs searched several hotels in downtown Baguio with the Japanese and British, also accompanying the British to the town of La Trinidad.

The rescue contingent of the U.S. team broke into two rescue groups with firefighters from both Fairfax County and Metro-Dade, as well as medics. On July 19 one group went to the Hyatt while the other returned to the Nevada. They teamed up with search dogs, fiber-optic and sounding devices to try to locate more survivors.

As reports began coming in to the command center of people trapped in buildings and mudslides in outlying areas, American operations were redirected from Baguio City to remote villages in the countryside. Teams were transported by helicopter and truck to do search and reconnaissance. One group was airlifted to the coastal town of Agoo, where the dogs checked a municipal building and other structures that had come down. A building-by-building survey produced no victims in need of rescue.

On the night of July 20 the decision was made to demobilize. The team flew by C-130 to Clark AFB, where it held a debriefing during a layover. The dogs were bathed and dipped at the Air Force kennel, one of the largest in the world, and checked by a veterinarian.

The team arrived home by C-141 late on July 22.

Meanwhile, local rescuers kept searching for survivors. On July 27 Associated Press reported that Filipino miners heard cries for help coming from what was left of the Hyatt Hotel in Baguio. They brought out a man and a woman "in surprisingly good condition." The 20-year-old cleaning woman and 26-year-old security guard had stayed alive for 11 days in the rubble, drinking rainwater and urine, and keeping each other's spirits up by talking and praying. They said a third man who had been trapped with them died about four days earlier.

And then on July 30 came news that a 27-year-old cook was rescued from the Hyatt, reportedly one of the longest earthquake survivals on record.

Two weeks after the quake the death toll stood at over 1600, with 1000 missing and presumed dead. This compares with some 8000 killed in the 1976 quake in the Philippines. Most of those reportedly died in a tidal wave that struck the island of Mindanao.

> The U.S. mission to the Philippines showed the need for sending a large enough team: enough searchers, rescuers and overhead to split into 12-hour shifts. Responders cannot function safely or efficiently without adequate rest. During the long work shifts, rescuers tend to forget "how the effects of fatigue hamper proper decision-making and command abilities." Positions like Liaison, Safety, Press, Logistics and Planning should always be sent, as a minimum, along with at least two communications people. Rescuers who may respond out-of-country should stay current on immunizations. At the Clark debriefing it was pointed out that responding to an incident is not the time to experience the side effects of inoculations. In addition to searching, the U.S. team was able to provide significant support and assistance to the ongoing local rescue effort in the form of technical advice, damage assessments and hazard/risk analyses.
>
> —*SAR Dog Alert,* National Association for Search and Rescue

Finally, we look back, at the one terrible disaster that blew hundreds of thousands of lives apart in Central Asia just as the East and the West were moving toward each other. The world reacted to set structure and standards for tactical rescue operations, and to focus on building the communication and cooperation that we will need, beyond the next century. The events speak for themselves:

ARMENIA

December 7, l941, the skies exploded over Pearl Harbor.

December 7, l988, the earth exploded under Armenia.

Was the U.S. ready for its forced entry into World War II or the rescue response to the "disaster of the century" earthquake?

Responding under the Office of Foreign Disaster Assistance, America answered requests for large-scale U.S. aid with search and rescue task forces—dogs, medical, and heavy rescue—flown halfway around the earth to work in the aftershocks. Rescuers estimated the disaster killed 55,000 to over 100,000 people. U.S. teams joined rescuers from Austria, Britain, Bulgaria, Canada, Czechoslovakia, Germany, France, India, Israel, Italy, Sweden, Switzerland, and other nations East and West, many with search dogs. In the cold rubble, these teams worked side by side with men whose only rescue tools for days after the earthquake had been their bare hands. This difficult operation signified the beginning of new relationships among the nations of the world, and a new international role for American canine teams.

In the cold rubble, these teams worked side by side with men whose only rescue tools for days after the earthquake had been their bare hands.

The 6.9 quake struck the Caucasus Mountains at 11:41 on a Wednesday, affecting 148 cities and villages over an area the size of Maryland. Leninakan, Armenia's second-largest city with 290,000 inhabitants, was reduced to a "dust-shrouded wasteland." Seventy to eighty percent of its buildings—schools, apartments, factories and offices—came down. Similarly hard-hit were the cities of Kirovakan (population 150,000) and Stepanavan. Located near the quake's epicenter, Spitak (population 16,000) "does not exist anymore," according to correspondents for *Sotsialisticheskaya Industria*. An editor at the Armenpress news agency said he saw dozens of villages "totally destroyed."

The first U.S. contingent departed Washington DC late Friday night aboard a chartered 727. It consisted of OFDA officials, medical personnel, and an 11-member dog team: handlers Caroline Hebard (Northeast SAR K-9), Penny Sullivan (Ramapo Rescue Dogs, ARDA-NJ), Pat Yessel (Rescue 40, OH-PA), and Beth Barkley, Brooke Holt, Ed Johnson and Carol McConaughy (DOGS-East); with Bill Dotson and Steve McConaughy (DOGS-East), Ralph Wilfong (Virginia DES), and Bruce Barton (Northeast SAR) as overhead. Dog teams began working the rubble that night and were joined the next day by the heavy rescue contingent from Miami Metro-Dade and Fairfax County (VA) fire companies. They came by military C-141 along with most of the U.S. team gear.

U.S. rescuers pulled two victims from the rubble, alive: a 12-year-old girl, in remarkably good condition except for a slightly lowered core temperature, and an older woman who could only be removed after the foot of her dead daughter was amputated to free her.

As the U.S. task force got to work, another was leaving from Montreal, Canada. Six dog handlers—Bill Grimmer and Wayne Bradley (Canadian Rescue Dogs), Charlie Ek and Dick Reininger (German Shepherd Search Dogs of Washington State), Sally Santeford (DOGS-North, MI) and P.J. LoPresti (Blue and Gray SAR Dogs, VA)—joined a relief flight that included a 14-member paramedic/extrication team from Alberta and medical supplies donated by the Armenian community in Montreal.

U.S. dogs and handler were only part of the international canine rescue response. In Spitak, German and Italian teams were reportedly at work, and the *Tribune de Geneve* described the Swiss mission in Leninakan: three days of virtually non-stop work from Saturday, December 10, through the following Monday evening.

Air crashes involved relief flights in the disaster area. One crash reportedly killed 78 Soviet army rescue workers. The crash of a Yugoslav plane claimed seven more lives.

Germany's *BLICK* quoted Swiss rescuers as agreeing that Armenia was the team's "worst mission:" in the "ghost city" of Leninakan, they uncovered "an entire factory full of corpses." The Swiss volunteers worked in six teams, with three dogs and handlers per team. "We were taken to so many sites," commented one handler, "that I didn't have time to count" how many victims her dog found. *BLICK* reported that the Swiss team pulled 25 survivors from the rubble. After 70 straight hours of work, and finding mostly bodies, the 20 canines were at the limit of their effectiveness, and the teams returned home December 13.

The next day an Austrian search dog team also returned home, as reported in *Chronik*, after five days of work in Spitak and Leninakan. Like the Swiss dogs, the Austrians were exhausted by their non-stop searching. The team's work in Leninakan was rewarded with 42 people saved.

Paris Match reported that France dispatched some 500 rescue workers to Armenia, including 55 dogs and handlers. December 14, the French dogs indicated a survivor. Digging where the dogs alerted, workers finally reached a 35-year-old woman, alive.

—SAR Dog Alert

The following account is by Reilly Richey of Juneau, Alaska, a handler with Southeast Alaska Dogs Organized for Ground Search. A school teacher, Richey and his golden retriever Taco have searched the most rugged parts of Alaska. Richey was joined by Jeff Newkirk with his German shepherd Captain and liaison Bruce Bowler.

Soon after the earthquake, the Governor offered Alaskan SAR dog services to the then-Soviet Union. He made this offer in response to previous Soviet assistance in Alaska—freeing whales trapped by sea ice near Barrow and rescuing Eskimo hunters lost on St. Lawrence Island. Logistics were complicated. Alaska is exactly halfway around the world from Armenia. Working out passports, supplies, and transportation delayed their departure until December 12.

The SEADOGS teams flew Alaska Airlines to Seattle where they joined the Northwest Medical Volunteer Group. A Flying Tigers 747 carried the 52 people with tons of medical supplies from Seattle direct to Yerevan. The rescuers were primarily doctors, the search dog teams, nurses, radiologists, paramedics, interpreters, and a cameraman. With fuel stops in New York and Frankfurt and 2 flight crews on board, they probably set a civilian flight record. The quarter million dollar trip was donated by Flying Tigers. All the rescue teams and supplies were also donated. The captain said the flight was historic, the first American 747 with an American pilot to be allowed on Soviet soil since World War II. The first U.S. citizens allowed in the country without visas. And the first dog from Alaska in a long time to defecate on Soviet soil. She did it almost immediately coming off the ladder of the aircraft.

Yerevan, the capital of Armenia and its chief industrial and cultural center, is a city of 1.3 million. The U.S. teams spent the night in a Yerevan hospital 70 miles from Leninakan, their destination, close to the border of Turkey and Mt. Ararat, 16,946 feet, the Old Testament mountain where Noah's ark landed. This region is 90 percent Armenian. Forty percent speak both Armenian and Russian.

The Russian Embassy had told the Americans to take 10 days of human and dog food.

The Seattle group did most of the feeding. The plane loaded up with a hundred 5-gallon gerry cans of water in Frankfurt.

The Soviets broke almost all the rules they ever had. Besides the visa waivers, rescue teams were allowed to have radios and to use their cameras at will. Nobody searched their luggage. They were out past curfews. When a car they were in was stopped by two Soviet armed guards, the Russian interpreter rolled down the window and said, "Americanski." The officers jumped out of the way to let them go by.

They went out of their way to treat the Americans well. At the hospital in Yerevan, they would not allow the canine handlers to sleep with their dogs. They gave the dogs separate rooms. They would have been embarassed if teams had returned to the U.S. and reported they had to sleep with their dogs. It was very important to them to treat Americans like welcome guests. Very important they came back with a good impression.

Most of the medical teams stayed in Yerevan to do surgery. Sixteen paramedics left with the dog teams for Leninakan to set up a M*A*S*H-type field medical unit and to search for buried victims. They went by bus driven by a maniac busdriver.

Reilly Richey reported his experience:

The 70 miles of countryside between Yerevan and Leninakan is mostly high, big-sky country. Barren, hilly, and treeless. Group spirit seemed high but all were quietly wondering what was in store for us. Seeing no damage to the countryside, you began to think that Leninakan could not be such a disaster.

At the city limits, the first noticeable landmarks were piles and piles of rubble: metal, rocks, mattresses, etc. Trucks dumped more piles. This was evidently where they were dumping debris from the ruins.

Next we saw the homeless wandering randomly on both sides of the bus, going on in all directions. Some carried bags. Some walked alone. Others together. No one seemed in a hurry. All were expressionless. Dazed. Shocked. Some were dressed warmly. Others had little protection.

These people were everywhere. You could not escape them. Each street we turned on brought more. Although age, clothing, stature, direction varied, they all somehow seemed alike. Scenes from the movie "The Day After." Except this was real.

Initially, the bus passengers grew louder on entering Leninakan. You heard comments like: 'Look at that!' 'Oh, my God, I can't believe it! Look at that building.' But as the blocks went on, the monotony of these comments eventually led to silence. Surprisingly, there was little sound outside. An occasional whistle from a policeman or soldier, the sound of cranes, trucks, and cars, and the sound of rubble being moved. But the silence of the hordes of people was remarkable. Thousands of people roaming and thousands more on the countless rubble piles. None of them seemingly making a sound.

We also noticed the soldiers with their weapons. They were on every pile and at every corner. The bus rolled on as we stared out the windows. Tanks glued motionless. Soldiers standing equally still.

Never had I felt such an overload on my sense of sight. This would have been too much for me to grasp had our bus been still. We rolled on, and the stacks of empty coffins added to the overload. Trying to feel safe within the windows and walls of the bus, we rode into another street. Knowing everything outside was real, we felt the confines and security of the bus keep the scene at bay.

Wishing we could drive on by, I knew eventually I'd be touching and conversing with these walking wounded. My dog and I would be walking on the same piles with these expressionless, scary-looking workers. I would have to smell the air and perhaps

Thousands of people roaming and thousands more on the countless rubble piles. None of them seemingly making a sound.

touch the coffins, which seemed to come in every color. How could these people walk so easily with unchanging expressions among the stacks of black, blue, and red coffins? The degree of destruction was totally incomprehensible.

Yet many buildings were still partially or fully standing. The irony is that the oldest buildings were generally the survivors, while the newer but more shoddily built buildings had been the ones to topple. It allowed us to see a 'before' image, which unfortunately added to the reality. I would guess that 60 - 70% of the city had crumbled. Many of the standing structures were so badly damaged, they too would fall.

The region has long been a victim of warfare between Turkey and Iran. In World War I, Armenia became a battleground for Russian and Turkish armies. Nearly a million Armenians were slain or starved. Now this earthquake. Echmiadzin, a monastery near Yerevan, is said to be the oldest monastic foundation in the Christian world. The oldest branch of the Armenian church in the U.S., the Armenian Church of North America, has been under the jurisdiction of the See of Echmiadzin since 1887.

For some time, my eyes ignored the homeless, the military, and the coffins and imagined what it would be like searching these piles with my dog. A large clock hanging on one of the remaining buildings snapped me out of my daydreaming. How many buildings, people, tanks had we passed without my noticing? The clock on the building read 1140. I slipped into another daydream reconstructing the horrible scene that late morning in Leninakan—still easier than looking at the faces. My eyes looked out the window but saw nothing for several more blocks.

We'd driven miles through town, and this was the first child I'd seen. Where were the kids?

Yanking me back to the present, a child grabbed my attention. A very young, pre-school age girl holding her mother's hand. I'd not realized it until then, but children were missing from the masses of people. We'd driven miles through town, and this was the first child I'd seen. Where were the kids? Their absence left the city empty and homeless. The entire area seemed to be fatally wounded with no chance of recovery.

Later I would learn that many of the children were killed while sitting at school desks. Most of the city's multi-floor schools were now indiscernable except for the playground equipment outside. Orphans were moved to Moscow despite bitter protests by the Armenians. Others were temporarily moved to a safer or less traumatic environment. Depending on friends or relatives, this would most likely be in Yerevan. Others, of course, were in Yerevan's hospitals.

The bus continued, sometimes through narrow corridors of rubble, never escaping the mud and the ruins. A 5-story apartment building stood stripped of but one wall, exposing rooms to us. In the strange sight of the naked interior, 2 chickens were walking around in someone's former bedroom. Would these chickens be rescued? We drove by a section with tents, a man sawing wood for fires with a bow saw. We kept going by small bonfires warming only 3 or 4 expressionless people. It was cold. Down to 15° F at night. Low 40s during the day.

The bus finally stopped at the main square of town, definitely beautiful at one time. Most of the buildings were still standing. An ancient church, though, several hundred years old, was left with only one wall. Many other mortar-concrete-tufa buildings appeared warped, perilously leaning.

A truck drove by with supplies for distribution. More than 50 people ran or quickened their pace to reach it. Another army truck dispersed round loaves of bread as the crowd of people pushed forward, arms outstretched. Military vehicles tried to drive by, honking horns to get the homeless out of their way. A soldier with a billy club tried to keep order between vehicles and the homeless. Trucks honked, and glazed people meandered to the side.

The bus door opened. Bruce and 3 others left to make arrangements. Someone rolled down a window on our parked bus. My protective shell was eroding. I felt my role of spectator changing to participant. Bruce stomped back onto the bus: "Grab your gear and follow me. We got one."

Stunned that we would have a search so soon, Jeff and I stepped off the bus. Everything inside me switched gears.

We started searching with 200 workers and onlookers watching at this one site. The dogs did real well. They alerted to a corpse, which wasn't unearthed until later. After they unearthed the person, witnesses were trying to track us down to tell us. These people were super desperate.

I started out carrying all kinds of stuff, you know how that always goes. Pretty much lowered it down to a flashlight with extra batteries, cause you're always looking into tunnels or tunnel-ratting yourself through this stuff. I kept a transceiver, the hardhat, lots of flagging, radio, water for the dogs. That was the stuff I ended up using. We always had a paramedic with us. They would carry a lot of the other stuff that I would possibly need. But we were always using hardhats and flashlights and water for the dogs.

I'd heard there was a shortage of heavy equipment for moving rubble, but there were cranes all over the place. We would typically go to a 50-foot high rubble pile that used to be a 9-story apartment building, almost all of these newer buildings were 7 or 9 stories high, and all the workers would move off. The cranes would stop. We'd try to work real fast so they could get back to work. We'd go through an area, flag some spots, and leave. These piles were monstrous. Moving the rubble was a slow process. We searched a shopping center that had probably 200 people buried in it.

After they unearthed the person, witnesses were trying to track us down to tell us. These people were super desperate.

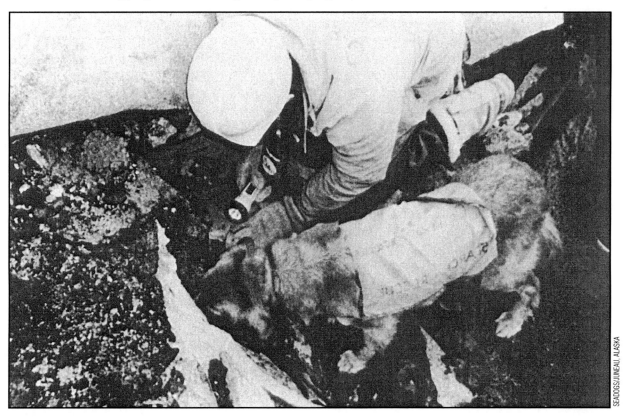

Our group worked closely with an Austrian group because they'd camped next to us. We got to know them. They had the sounding equipment, the infrared. Also search dogs, although we never worked with their search dogs. We would take alternate calls. Their dogs would go out on one, then we'd go out on the next, so our dogs got a little bit of rest. We were doing 3 or 4 searches every day, about 2 to 3 hours each. It was tough on the dogs.

We would go out right after early breakfast, usually with the Austrians. We'd do a couple searches during the day that were more independent. Then we'd go out in the early evening again with the Austrians. The Soviets supplied bus transportation. In the afternoon, we sometimes used private vehicles.

The first place we went after leaving the bus was the command center. When we first entered the country, we had heard there were 100 search dogs in Armenia. I thought "Whoa! Do they really need more search dogs?" After working piles and piles and never seeing another search dog the whole time you're there, you realize the magnitude of the disaster. I mean, Leninakan was a city of 290,000. There were 154 cities, towns, and villages reporting death (including Spitak nearest the epicenter), Leninakan being the largest of the cities. It was huge. The disaster of the century.

You could safely say that our group, although untrained in estimating casualty counts, couldn't help wondering if even the higher figures had to be too low. This was a city of over 290,000, and over half the buildings were pancakes. There could have been only a few survivors coming out of each of those buildings. That was how we felt, anyway. Every place we went, it was "There's still 25 here. There's still 400 here..." We just scratched the surface of 30 piles. There were hundreds in that one city. Hundreds and hundreds. Thousands.

I wasn't sure how my dog would do on corpses. She had only seen a couple before. One was at Deer Mountain in Alaska, and she wasn't the dog who found that person. It was a matter of reading your dog. Jeff and I felt confident when they were alerting on a corpse. It was not as enthusiastic as a live person. They would paw at the ground or sniff a particular area for an unusually long time. We'd mark it. Often people would come back to our camp grateful that we'd found their son or their daughter or mother.

We worked real fast, so we did brief praise of the dogs. Taco responded to my enthusiasm. When the dogs found a body they could visually or physically get to, we gave them a big reward.

The first body I got to was real creepy. It was this factory where there were supposed to still be maybe a hundred people buried. There were large pieces of concrete about 50 feet overhead that looked like asteroids floating in the air. Looking closely, you could see 1 or 2 pieces of rebar holding them up there. O.K., you've got your little yellow hardhat and they are 50 feet overhead. Anyhow, we were walking through this corridor. This large piece of tufa, the volcanic rock many of these places were built out of, made a long tunnel with a narrow squeeze. Taco ran down this tunnel. I could hear her at the far end. She came back all enthusiastic, did a "Show me!" I pushed my hardhat tighter onto my head, like it's going to do me some bit of good, you know. I was a little nervous that this slab might slip and sandwich me. Her alert was strong enough, though, that I thought somebody might still be alive.

I was crawling through this tunnel on my stomach, hands and knees. I had my flashlight going but had to keep shoving my body through. I shined the flashlight in front of me. Three feet away was this corpse. If I'd been able to approach it from a distance and work up to it slowly, it would have been fine. But it just popped out at me. Back home, I dreamed the whole thing. Except in my nightmare I couldn't back away from it. Anyhow, Taco was there licking the man's face, trying to wake him up. We found lots of other corpses, 6 or more later. That was the worst.

They did find a 14-year-old boy still alive in a basement while we were there. A lot of these buildings collapsed right down to the basement. They would leave the basement partially intact. This kid had some water down there. They found him 11 days after the earthquake. He was in the hospital a couple days for dehydration and feeling fine. He was pretty lucky. There are so many buildings that collapsed, so many basements. Even with the dog, on top of a 30-40-foot high pile of all this concrete-type stuff, unless there's some sort of tunnel coming up to the surface, it would be pretty miraculous to find people alive.

We were in Leninakan a week then a couple days in Yerevan. We set up a base camp near the outskirts of town. There were 19 of us, and we had 6 tents set up. We stayed there the whole time. Of the 52 that went, about 30 people got sick. I was as healthy as the healthiest person there. That worked out fine. Fatigue didn't bother me. It was more stress on the dogs. I was going on adrenaline. Very little sleep. It didn't hit me until I got home.

We saw the dogs' performance drop off as the days went on. From what we had heard, most of the foreign dog teams were pulling out after about 4 days of work on the average. You know, anywhere from leaving as soon as they saw the first rock pile. Our dogs were steadily going downhill each day. So much death permeated the place, I think even the dogs were getting bored, like, "Another one?" Not enough rewards for the hundreds of bodies they were finding. Much of our work was just confirming spots. They knew where their loved ones were buried. We would go by and say "Yeah, we think you're digging in the right place, but the dogs aren't acting like anyone's alive." They were so grateful.

The Armenian people are unbelievable. Something I hadn't been aware of, for a thousand years, they've had enemies pushing on their borders shrinking their land to a tenth of what it originally was. They faced genocide twice in the past century, once having one and a half million people killed, and the land itself has struck them now. The feeling you get talking to these people is they will persevere. For instance, their biggest holiday is New Year's Day. It's bigger than our Christmas. This year, they will not have a New Year's Day celebration. But they say that next year, they will have their *biggest* New Year's Day celebration. The message to me is they're in terrible times right now, but they can see past that. They are going to persevere.

The women were not allowed to work on these rubble piles. It was taboo. So they'd sit around the fires and wait for their children to be dug up, wait for their husbands to be dug up, whatever, trying to stay warm. It was so cold, far below freezing all the time. These two women came over and put blankets over our dogs. They didn't have hardly any food or warmth at all. They didn't want the blankets back. We managed to make them take the blankets back. But they were just so grateful. I went over and sat with them and tried to share an apple with them. They brought out two oranges! I saw this wasn't going to work. Every time you tried to give anything to anyone, they'd come back and give you more. We conversed in sign language. They cried and hugged us for trying. We really felt guilty. We really did so little. But they were so happy that people were trying.

It's like, if we'd sent a thousand 747's over there with all the supplies, the dent would have been unrecognizable. But they were just happy that someone was trying.

After a search in which I was emotionally distraught, I went for a walk. While I was walking down this street, an Armenian man pulled me by the shoulder and dragged me, led me into this storage shed, an 8- by 10-foot shack he was now living in. The

I went over and sat with them and tried to share an apple with them. They brought out two oranges! I saw this wasn't going to work.

earthquake had destroyed his home. When he opened the door, light flooded into this storage shack and you saw a portrait of his wife on the far wall. He indicated the earthquake killed his wife. Then he indicated by showing his hand off the ground at a certain level his only son or daughter was also killed.

He was all alone. The only other significant item he had left was this piece of furniture, this crate, which had some cutlery and some food items on it. He absolutely insisted that I share a can of fish with him. He hardly had any food left, but he insisted. So I ate this fish with him. I was real happy I was able to give him a little fish pin that was on my hat as kind of a gift back to him. When I gave him that, he cried, hugged me, and kissed me on the cheeks. Then he ran to his neighbor's shack, got a piece of meat, and tried to feed my dog the meat. I was relieved she wasn't hungry cause this guy needed it so bad.

Both dogs lost weight. They burned a lot of calories between staying warm and the physical work.

The magnitude of the disaster was overwhelming. We were unprepared for that. I didn't really talk about the frustration that both Jeff and I felt when people literally tugged on our shoulders. They were so desperate. They wanted us to search their apartment building or their room. It wrenched at our gut to have to tell people no, because so many people wanted us to help. There was a definite shortage of search dog teams. We could have used many, many more. People were literally tugging on us all the time. We were just scratching the surface of a few piles.

Another part that was really hard for Jeff and me was searching a rubble pile and running across children's toys or belongings. Especially those that matched the same age as my kid. You know how you get real callous about the situation...to keep from going crazy?

In one case this guy with tears coming down his eyes was trying to get Taco and me to search a spot where he thought, well, he signaled with his hands. He spread his hands about a foot and a half apart and showed me 10 fingers, then rocked his arms in front of his body like a cradle. I understood that his 10-day old baby was right there.

The lesson I learned from these people is their incredible strength. Under the greatest despair and most sobering of realities, they were still able to be so kind and loving. It was really amazing. We had Armenians around our base camp all the time. At any time they could have ripped off our food or blankets or sleeping bags or whatever. They never did. And they needed it so bad. They were holding it together.

One man said, "If this had happened to just me, I would have gone mad and crazy and killed myself. Since it happened to all my people, I could be strong and help." Another person said, "Please don't think that we're indifferent to our dead. It's just that this is not the time to cry. We will have time for that later."

You know how you get real callous about the situation...to keep from going crazy?

REFERENCE

BOOKS AND MANUALS

Adams, Ronald J.; McTernan, Thomas M., and Remsberg, Charles, *Street Survival: Tactics for Armed Encounters*, Northbrook, Illinois: Calibre Press, Inc., 1980.

American Academy of Orthopaedic Surgeons, *Basic Rescue and Emergency Care*, Park Ridge, Illinois, 1990.

Anderson, Bob, *Stretching*, Bolinas, California: Shelter Publications, 1980.

Applied Technology Council, *ATC-20-1 Field Manual: Postearthquake Safety Evaluation of Buildings*, San Francisco, California: R. P. Gallagher Associates, Inc., 1989.

Armstrong, Betsy, and Williams, Knox, *The Avalanche Book*, Golden, Colorado: Fulcrum Inc., 1986.

Bass, Rick, *The Ninemile Wolves*, Livingston, Montana: Clark City Press, 1992.

Bojrab, M. Joseph, D.V.M., Ph.D., Birchard, Stephen J., D.V.M., Tomlinson, Jr., James L. D.V.M., *Current Techniques in Small Animal Surgery*, Philadelphia, Pennsylvania: Lea & Febiger, 1990.

Bragg, Paul, N.D., Ph.D., *Healthful Eating Without Confusion*, Santa Ana, California, 1975.

Brinker, W.O., Piermattei, D.L., and Flo, G.L. (eds.), "Principles of Joint Surgery," *Handbook of Small Animal Orthopedics and Fracture Treatment*, Philadephia, Pennsylvania: W.B. Saunders, 1983.

Bryne, C.J., Saxton, E., Pelikan, P., Nugent, P., *Laboratory Tests, Implications for Nurses and Allied Health Professionals*, Menlo Park, California: Addison-Wesley Publishing Company, 1981.

Bryson, Sandy, *Search and Rescue Dog Training*, Pacific Grove, California: The Boxwood Press, 1976.

Bryson, Sandy, *Search Dog Training*, Pacific Grove, California: The Boxwood Press, 1984.

Canada, Geoffrey, *fist stick knife gun: a personal history of violence in America*, Boston, Massachusetts: Beacon Press, 1995.

Chapman, Samuel G., *Police Dogs in North America*, Springfield, Illinois: Charles C. Thomas, 1990.

Chow, Ven-Te, *Handbook of Applied Hydrology*, New York, New York: McGraw-Hill Book Company, 1964.

Cooper, Kenneth, *New Aerobics*, New York, N.Y.: Bantam Books, Inc., 1970.

Copeland, Lennie, and Griggs, Lewis, *Going International: How to Make Friends and Deal Effectively in the Global Marketplace*, New York, New York: Random House, Inc., 1985.

Doran, Jeffry, *Search on Mount St. Helens*, Bellevue, Washington: Imagesmith, 1980.

Eagleson, Peter S., *Dynamic Hydrology*, New York, New York: McGraw-Hill Book Company, 1970.

Eden, R.S., *Dog Training for Law Enforcement*, Calgary, Alberta: Detselig Enterprises, Ltd., 1985.

Fixx, James, *The Complete Book of Running*, New York, N.Y.: Bantam Books, Inc., 1970.

Garner, Gerald W., *High Risk Patrol*, Springfield, Illinois: Charles C. Thomas, 1990.

Graf, Walter H., and Mortimer, Clifford H., *Hydrodynamics of Lakes*, New York, New York: Elsevier Scientific Publishing Company, 1979.

Grandin, Temple, *Thinking in Pictures*, New York, N.Y.: Doubleday, 1995.

Johnson, Glen R., *Tracking Dog: Theory & Methods*, Rome, New York: Arner Publications, Inc., 1975.

Killam, Edward W., *The Detection of Human Remains*, Springfield, Illinois: Charles C. Thomas, 1990.

Kirk, Robert W., D.V.M., and Bistner, Stephen I., D.V.M., *Handbook of Veterinary Procedures & Emergency Treatment*, Philadelphia, Pennsylvania: Harcourt Brace Jovanovich, Inc., 1985.

Koehler, William R., *The Koehler Method of Training Tracking Dogs*, New York, New York: Howell Book, 1984.

Lithgow, Scott, *Training and Working Dogs: For Quiet Confident Control of Stock*, St. Lucia, Queensland: University of Queensland Press, 1989.

Mackenzie, Stephen A., *Decoys and Aggression*, Calgary, Aberta: Detselig Enterprises, Ltd., 1996.

Maclean, Norman, *Young Men and Fire*, Chicago, Illinois: University of Chicago Press, 1992.

Maluenda, Pedro Ducar, *Perros Policia: Adiestramiento y cuidados*, Zaragoza, Espana: Acribia, S.A., 1986.

Marnell, Tim, Editor, *Drug Identification Bible*, Denver, Colorado: Kay Publishing, 1993.

Martens, R., Christina, R., Harvey, J., Sharkey, B., *Coaching Young Athletes*, Champaign, Illinois: Human Kinetics Publishers, Inc., 1981.

Mech, L. David, *The Wolf: The Ecology and Behavior of an Endangered Species*, Minneapolis, Minnesota: University of Minnesota Press, 1986.

Miller, Malcolm E., D.V.M., M.S., Ph.D., *Anatomy of the Dog*, Philadelphia, Pennsylvania: W.B. Saunders Co., 1964.

Nader, Ralph, and Smith, Wesley J., *Collision Course*, Blue Ridge Summit, Pennsylvania: McGraw-Hill, Inc., 1994.

Neumann, H.H., *Foreign Travel and Immunization Guide*, Medical Economic Books, 1981.

Ogle, Jr., Robert R., *Crime Scene Investigation and Physical Evidence Manual*, Vallejo, California: Robert R. Ogle, Jr., 1992.

Pryor, Karen, *Don't Shoot the Dog!*, New York, New York: Simon & Schuster, 1985.

Remsberg, Charles, *The Tactical Edge: Surviving High-Risk Patrol*, Northbrook, Illinois: Calibre Press, Inc., 1986.

Robin, Marc R., and Dessery, Bradford L., *The Medical Guide for Third World Travelers*, San Diego, California: KW Publications, 1992.

Roof, L., Kiernan, T., *Oh My Aching Back*, New York, N.Y.: New American Library, 1975

Sakmar, T.P., Gardner, P., Peterson, G.M., *Health Guide for International Travelers: How to Travel and Stay Well*, Lincolnwood, Illinois: Passport Books, 1986.

Setnicka, Tim J., *Wilderness Search and Rescue*, Boston, Massachusetts: Apalachian Mountain Club, 1980.

Strickland, Winifred G., *Expert Obedience Training for Dogs*, New York, New York: Macmillan Publishing Co., Inc., 1987.

Strickland, Winifred G., and Moses, James A., *The German Shepherd Today*, New York, New York: Macmillan Publishing Co., Inc., 1988.

Swanson, Charles R.: Neil C. Chamelin; Leonard Territo, *Criminal Investigation*, 5th ed. New York, New York: McGraw-Hill, Inc., 1992.

Todd, David Keith, *Ground Water Hydrology*, New York, New York: John Wiley & Sons, Inc., 1980.

Western Schools, *Managing Stress*, San Diego, California, 1989.

Willis, Malcolm B., Ph.D., *The German Shepherd Dog*, New York, New York: Howell Book House, 1991.

MAGAZINE ARTICLES, PROFESSIONAL PAPERS, AND VIDEO PRODUCTIONS

Anderson, Dennis, "Surviving Edged Weapons," *Calibre Press Video Production*, Northbrook, Illinois, 1991.

Anderson, Dennis, Remsberg, Charles, Shatner, William, "Ultimate Survivors: Winning Against Incredible Odds," *Calibre Press Video Production*, Northbrook, Illinois, 1992.

Beauchamp, Gary K.; Yamazaki, Kunio, and Boyse, Edward A., "The Chemosensory Recognition of Genetic Individuality," *Scientific American*, pp. 86+, July, 1985.

Bownds, John; Ebersole, Michael; Lovelock, David, and O'Connor, Daniel, "Reexamining the Search Management Function," *Response*, pp. 10+, Summer, 1992.

Bryson, Sandy, Christensen, Sara L., Hart, Lynette A., and Zasloff, Ruth, "Police K-9 Team Study: The Friendly Force," University of California, Davis, 1992.

Cupp, David, and Johnson, Lanny, "Avalanche! Winter's White Death: 'I'm OK, I'm Alive!'," *National Geographic*, pp. 280+, September, 1982.

Department of the Treasury, *U.S. Customs Detector Dog Program*, Washington, D.C.: U.S. Customs Service, 1978.

DiPietro, A. Louis, J. D., "Voluntary Encounters on Fourth Amendment Seizures? Crossing the Line," *FBI Law Enforcement Bulletin*, pp. 28+, January, 1992.

Franklin-Barbajosa, Cassandra, "DNA Profiling: The New Science of Identity," *National Geographic*, pp. 112+, May, 1992.

Gibbons, Boyd, and Psihoyos, Louie, "The Intimate Sense of Smell," *National Geographic*, pp. 324+,September, 1986.

Graham, Judy, Editor, "Disaster in the Sky: SARDA Responds," *SAR Dog Alert*, p. 1+, February, 1989.

Graham, Judy, Editor, "Search Dogs from Many Nations Join Armenian Earthquake Mission," *SAR Dog Alert*, p.1+, February, 1989.

Hill, Kenneth, "Analyzing Lost Person Scenarios," *Response*, pp. 23+, Winter, 1992.

Hyslop, Polly, "If He Barks, Freeze," *Anchorage Daily News*, pp. 1+, August, 1990.

Jennings, Sgt. James, "Going for the Gram," *The California Narcotic Officer*, pp. 22+, May, 1992.

Lenehan, Michael, "Four Ways to Walk a Dog," *The Atlantic Monthly*, pp. 35+, April, 1986.

National Park Service, "Helicopter Rappel, Shorthaul and Insertion Operations Plan," Grand Teton National Park, Wyoming: U.S. Department of the Interior, 1989.

Nugent, Hugh, Connors, Edward F., McEwen, J. Thomas, and Mayo, Lou, "Restrictive Policies for High-Speed Police Pursuits," National Institute of Justice, U.S. Department of Justice, Washington, D.C., 1991.

O'Connor, Vincent, "Four-legged Force," *Corrections Today*, pp. 50+, July, 1990.

Rathbun, David, EMT-P, "Tactical Use of Helicopters: A Multi-Mission Approach," *Response*, pp 19+, Winter, 1990.

Salvesen, L., Wilkerson, J., "Psychological Responses to Wilderness Accidents," *Wilderness Medicine*, pp. 4+, January, 1989.

Schlosser, Eric, "The Bomb Squad," *The Atlantic Monthly*, pp. 23+, January, 1994.

Sessions, Jean, D.V.M., "Managing Stress in Dog Teams on Searches," *Response*, pp. 12+, Fall, 1991.

Smalley, Ann, "When the Movement Is the Message," *The Humane Society News*, pp. 5+, Fall, 1987.

Smith, Dorothy, "Ontario Canine Unit Is Cost Effective," *Law and Order*, pp. 49+, April, 1991.

Ward, Jeff, "SWAT's Best Friend," *Police*, pp. 50+, July, 1989.

INDEX

K
knock and talk 278

L
laminar flow 122, 300,340
latent scent 223
low-head dam 365
LSD 254

M
marijuana 254
masking scent 242, 267
master protection 96
methamphetamine 254
micro-climates 223
mine search 152
minimum resolvable temperature difference
   (MRTD) 176
National Animal Poison Control Center
   (NAPCC) 57
National Water Search Report 364
negative alert 256
nonaggressive behavior 224

O
odor suppressant 263
outside area search 325

P
parcel search 205
passive alert 257
pattern 230
permissive search 278, 285
person search 324
pinpoint 266
point last seen (PLS) 155
policy 43
positive alert 256
Postal Inspection Service (PIS) 308
praise 258, 430
prepping evidence 245

pre-scent 221
pressure principles 368
pretext 280
prey drive 52
probability of area (POA) 337
proof 258, 311

R
rank 53
reindication 403

S
sound temperament 53
spontaneous alert 282, 320
standing waves 365
stimuli 53
strainer 366
sui generis (unique) 242
surface area 325, 364
surface hoar 406, 411
surveillance 149, 158

T
tactile 55
task force concept 216
technical search team 371
temperature gradient 406
thermal currents 122
thermoclines 367
thermodynamics 122
tidal waters 367
timing 258, 291
total jeopardy 423
totality of circumstances 59, 294, 318
trafficking 319
trail 55
transceiver search 408
turbid 373
turbulence 122

U
United Nations Disaster Relief Organization
   (UNDRO) 436
United States Agency for International Devel-
   opment (USAID) 436
use of force 33, 39, 83, 84

V
vaporization (scent) 56, 122, 300, 325, 341,
   422, 427
ventilation 422
verbal control 92
vessels 306
video camera 10
visibility 175, 188
visitor vehicle search 202
visual contact 92
voice command 85
vorticity 122

W
walling off 295
warrant 253
water search 227
weapons 417
wet drowning 369

Z
zone of influence 175

About the Author

Police Dog Tactics is Sandy Bryson's fifth book, her third about canines in law enforcement. A police and rescue dog handler and trainer since 1974, Bryson instructs police dog teams for law enforcement agencies. Founder of the first rescue dog unit in California, she coauthored the UC Davis study, "The Role of Canines in Police Work." She is a reserve deputy for El Dorado County Sheriff's Department and Alpine County Sheriff's Department, California. Current dog is Hawkeye, a one-year-old German shepherd.